TORTS AND PERSONAL INJURY LAW

FIFTH EDITION

CENGAGE Learning

Options.
Over 300 products in every area of the law: textbooks, digital resources, online courses, and more – helping you succeed in class and on the job.

Support.
We offer unparalleled, practical support: robust instructor and student supplements to ensure the best learning experience, custom publishing to meet your unique needs, and other benefits such as our Student Achievement Award. And our sales representatives are always ready to provide you with dependable service.

Feedback.
As always, we want to hear from you! Your feedback is our best resource for improving the quality of our products. Contact your sales representative or write us at the address below if you have any comments about our materials or if you have a product proposal.

Accounting and Financials for the Law Office • Administrative Law • Alternative Dispute Resolution • Bankruptcy Business Organizations/Corporations • Careers and Employment • Civil Litigation and Procedure • CP Exam Preparation • Computer Applications in the Law Office • Constitutional Law • Contract Law • Criminal Law and Procedure • Document Preparation • Elder Law • Employment Law • Environmental Law • Ethics • Evidence Law • Family Law • Health Care Law • Immigration Law • Intellectual Property • Internships Interviewing and Investigation • Introduction to Law • Introduction to Paralegalism • Juvenile Law • Law Office Management • Law Office Procedures • Legal Research, Writing, and Analysis • Legal Terminology • Legal Transcription • Media and Entertainment Law • Medical Malpractice Law Product Liability • Real Estate Law • Reference Materials • Social Security • Torts and Personal Injury Law • Wills, Trusts, and Estate Administration • Workers' Compensation Law

---

CENGAGE Learning
5 Maxwell Drive
Clifton Park, New York 12065-2919

For additional information, find us online at:
www.cengage.com

TORTS AND PERSONAL INJURY LAW

FIFTH EDITION

Cathy J. Okrent

CENGAGE
Learning·

Australia • Brazil • Japan • Korea • Mexico • Singapore • Spain • United Kingdom • United States

CENGAGE
Learning

Torts and Personal Injury Law, Fifth Edition
Cathy J. Okrent

Vice President and General Manager—Skills and Planning: Dawn Gerrain

Senior Product Manager: Shelley Esposito

Senior Director, Development—Skills and Planning: Marah Bellegarde

Senior Product Development Manager: Larry Main

Content Developers: Mary Clyne, Melissa Riveglia

Product Assistant: Diane Chrysler

Marketing Manager: Scott Chrysler

Market Development Manager: Jonathan Sheenan

Senior Production Director: Wendy Troeger

Production Manager: Mark Bernard

Senior Content Project Manager: Betty L. Dickson

Art Director: Heather Marshall, PMG

Media Developer: Deborah Bordeaux

Cover image(s): ©Taurus/Shutterstock #104722601 Gavel on the desktop

©Christian Mueller/Shutterstock #101120680 city traffic with a cyclist and cars in motion blur

©lantapix/Shutterstock #37797451 Man bangs a nail into a wooden wall

©Martin Haas/Shutterstock #84776038 "caution wet floor"

©Andre Blais/Shutterstock #95363269 Businessman man in suit taking drugs from pill bottle
Cover Designer: Riezebos Holzbaur/ Brieanna Hattey

For product information and technology assistance, contact us at
Cengage Learning Customer & Sales Support, 1-800-354-9706

For permission to use material from this text or product, submit all requests online at **www.cengage.com/permissions**. Further permissions questions can be e-mailed to **permissionrequest@cengage.com**

Library of Congress Control Number: 2013939025

ISBN-13: 978-1-1336-9185-3

Cengage Learning
200 First Stamford Place, 4th Floor
Stamford, CT 06902
USA

Cengage Learning is a leading provider of customized learning solutions with office locations around the globe, including Singapore, the United Kingdom, Australia, Mexico, Brazil, and Japan. Locate your local office at: **www.cengage.com/global**

Cengage Learning products are represented in Canada by Nelson Education, Ltd.

To learn more about Cengage Learning, visit **www.cengage.com**

Purchase any of our products at your local college store or at our preferred online store **www.cengagebrain.com**

NOTICE TO THE READER
Publisher does not warrant or guarantee any of the products described herein or perform any independent analysis in connection with any of the product information contained herein. Publisher does not assume, and expressly disclaims, any obligation to obtain and include information other than that provided to it by the manufacturer. The reader is expressly warned to consider and adopt all safety precautions that might be indicated by the activities described herein and to avoid all potential hazards. By following the instructions contained herein, the reader willingly assumes all risks in connection with such instructions. The reader is notified that this text is an educational tool, not a practice book. Since the law is in constant change, no rule or statement of law in this book should be relied upon for any service to any client. The reader should always refer to standard legal sources for the current rule or law. If legal advice or other expert assistance is required, the services of the appropriate professional should be sought. The publisher makes no representations or warranties of any kind, including but not limited to, the warranties of fitness for particular purpose or merchantability, nor are any such representations implied with respect to the material set forth herein, and the publisher takes no responsibility with respect to such material. The publisher shall not be liable for any special, consequential, or exemplary damages resulting, in whole or part, from the readers' use of, or reliance upon, this material.

Printed in the United States of America
1 2 3 4 5 6 7 16 15 14 13

Dedication

This book is dedicated to my dad, Charles I. Okrent, who inspired me to be an attorney just like him, always helping others with a logical plan to solve their problems.

Cathy J. Okrent

Brief Contents

Contents

Chapter 3
Proving Breach of Duty, Medical and Legal Malpractice   60

Chapter 4
Special Negligence Actions   89

Chapter 5
Defense to Negligence   123

Chapter 6
Intentional Torts: Injuries to Persons   145

Chapter 7
Intentional Torts: More Injuries to Persons   176

Chapter 8
Intentional Torts: Injuries to Property   219

Chapter 9
Defenses to Intentional Torts

Chapter 10
Strict, or Absolute, Liability   294

Chapter 11
Products Liability   322

Chapter 12
Special Tort Actions   359

Chapter 13
Tort Immunities   395

Appendices

Preface

■ WHAT IS NEW IN THE FIFTH EDITION?

Introducing the third decade of a best-selling textbook, *Torts and Personal Injury Law*, is a milestone. In its latest reinvention, this is still the most informative text for explaining torts to students in a direct, uncomplicated manner and with an informal writing style. Students like the clarity of material, the organization of each chapter, the number of illustrations for each point, and the plethora of recent cases. Students enjoy the hypotheticals used to make torts memorable and love the chapter feature entitled "The Biggest Mistakes Paralegals Make and How to Avoid Them." Mistakes range from inappropriate insider trading to interviewing blunders and a dozen more unfortunate situations that actually happened! So what else is new in the fifth edition?

Expanded Coverage

▶ A new chapter covers negligence and its elements in greater depth, bringing the total number of chapters to 14

▶ An expanded discussion of the court structure and system

▶ More in-depth coverage of alternative dispute resolution (ADR)

▶ Comparison of *Restatement (Second) of Torts* with *Restatement (Third) of Torts*

▶ Extensive material addressing medical malpractice actions

▶ A new, detailed section dedicated to tort reform, tort trends, and the impact these have for tort victims, the legal profession, and the health care field

▶ Increased coverage of workers' compensation and ethical issues

Updated Topics

▶ Cyber torts, including cyber-bullying and cyber-stalking

▶ Tortious liability for criminal conduct

▶ Tortious interference with contracts and civil liability

▶ Tortious abuse of social media

▶ Wrongful birth and wrongful life causes of actions

▶ Genetic engineering and the unauthorized use of genetic material

▶ No-fault automobile insurance policies

Updated Features

▶ The vital role insurance coverage plays in bringing tort actions is demonstrated throughout the text.

▶ More practical and hands-on activities are available online.

▶ Additional legal references and websites are included for further legal research.

▶ More annotated cases are included—75 in total.

New Cases

More than two-thirds of the cases in this edition are new, ranging from a case where church leaders were "just plumb ugly" to congregants, to a landmark $168 million sexual harassment verdict, to tortious interference with an expected inheritance, as well as cases covering the following, among others: a law firm that hired an attorney with the same last name as the attorney who was let go to give the impression the attorney was still there, a funeral services company that lost a son's cremains, a knock-off product whose name varies from that of another product by one letter, and a disgruntled client who goes on a shooting rampage at a law office.

The logical organization of each of the 14 chapters remains as follows: chapter outline, introduction, definitions in a running glossary on each page where a term is first introduced, hypotheticals, chapter summary, key terms, problems, review questions, and helpful websites and activities.

▋ OVERVIEW

This text provides an overview of tort law for the personal injury paralegal. Chapter 1 discusses tort law generally and historically; it also provides an overview of a civil case and alternative dispute resolution (ADR). Chapter 2 introduces the elements of negligence. Chapter 3 continues the discussion of negligence with proving breach of duty, burden of proof and rejoinder, res ipsa loquitor, violation of a statute, medical and legal malpractice, and tort reform. Chapter 4 discusses special negligence actions, including premises liability, vicarious liability, and negligent infliction of emotional distress. Chapter 5 focuses on the defenses to negligence actions. Chapters 6 and 7 consider intentional torts and injuries to persons. Chapter 8 is devoted to intentional torts and injuries to property. Chapter 9 addresses defenses to intentional torts. Chapter 10 covers strict, or absolute, liability. Chapter 11 illustrates product liability cases. Chapter 12 features special tort actions. Chapter 13 discusses tort immunities, tort trends, and tort reform. Chapter 14 focuses on tort investigation.

▌ CHAPTER FEATURES

Of course, favorite elements have all been retained. Chapters begin with an outlined introduction. Chapters end with a summary, review questions, additional problems, and a list of key terms that were used throughout the chapter, in addition to chapter-specific Internet resources. Many recent cases have been added.

The running glossary features numerous definitions from *Legal Terminology with Flashcards,* © 2012, Cengage Learning, to help students learn or refresh their knowledge regarding these terms.

The text combines theoretical and practical applications. Accompanying each tort topic are hypothetical examples to illustrate how the abstract rules pertain to real life. Illustrative cases are included to portray the actual application of legal principles in appellate court opinions, legal encyclopedia summaries, and the *Restatement (Second) of Torts* and the *Restatement (Third) of Torts.*

All cases included are for educational purposes, as examples of court reasoning in relation to chapter topics. The cases have been heavily edited, and most citations omitted, so as to include as many cases in the text as possible. The reader should always refer to original sources and verify that there have been no recent changes in the law in a particular jurisdiction. Sample letters, forms, and reports are included for illustrative purposes. The people named in the exhibits and hypotheticals are all fictional; any resemblance to known people is purely coincidental.

▌ SUPPLEMENTS FOR TEACHING AND LEARNING
Student Companion Website

The Student Companion Website contains supplementary cases, additional tutorials on ethics and understanding appellate court decisions, PowerPoint® presentations, and additional study materials.

To access these free materials, please visit www.cengagebrain.com and search using this book's ISBN (9781133691853).

Spend Less Time Planning and More Time Teaching

With Delmar Cengage Learning's Instructor Resources to Accompany *Torts and Personal Injury Law,* preparing for class and evaluating students have never been easier!

INSTRUCTOR
RESOURCES

This invaluable instructor CD-ROM allows you anywhere, anytime access to all of your resources:

▶ The **Instructor's Manual** has been expanded to incorporate all changes in the text and to provide comprehensive teaching support. It includes chapter summaries, chapter outlines, lecture hints, problems, and projects.

▶ The **Computerized Testbank** makes generating tests and quizzes a snap. With many questions and different styles to choose from, you can create customized assessments for your students with the click of a button. Add your own unique questions and print rationales for easy class preparation.

▶ Customizable **PowerPoint® presentations** focus on key points for each chapter. PowerPoint® is a registered trademark of the Microsoft Corporation.

Instructor's Companion Website

The Instructor's Companion Website includes all of the instructor resources just described. The complete Instructor's Manual, the Computerized Testbank in Mac and PC formats, and the PowerPoint® presentations are available for download.

To access the Instructor's Companion Website, please go to login.cengage. com, then use your single sign-on (SSO) login to access the materials.

Supplements At-A-Glance

SUPPLEMENT	WHAT IT IS	WHAT'S IN IT
Student Companion Website	Resources for students accessible via single sign-on (SSO) login	• supplementary cases • ethics chapter • understanding appellate court decisions • PowerPoint® presentations • additional study materials
Instructor Resources CD-ROM	Resources for the instructor, available on CD-ROM	• Instructor's Manual with chapter outlines, lecture hints, answers to text questions, and test bank and answer key • Computerized Testbank, with many questions and styles to choose from to create customized assessments for your students • PowerPoint® presentations
Online Instructor's Companion Site Website	Resources for the instructor accessible via Cengage SSO login	• Instructor's Manual with chapter outlines, lecture hints, answers to text questions, and testbank and answer key • Computerized Testbank in ExamView, with many questions and styles to choose from to create customized assessments for your students • PowerPoint® presentations

Please note that the Internet resources are of a time-sensitive nature and URL addresses may often change or be deleted.

Acknowledgments

Torts and Personal Injury Law could not have been produced without the dedication of many people. I thank my editors at Delmar (in particular, Shelley Esposito, Melissa Riveglia, and Diane Chrysler), as well as the American Law Institute and the *National Law Journal* for allowing the use of reprinted portions of their materials. Special thanks to Mary Clyne for her editorial expertise in working with me on this edition. It is much appreciated.

Special thanks to S4Carlisle Publishing Services and Escaline Charlette Aarthi Aloysius and Betty L. Dickson, for managing the production of this book in a timely, thorough, and professional manner. I truly appreciate your assistance.

Additionally, I would like to acknowledge the invaluable contributions of the following reviewers for their helpful suggestions and attention to detail:

Regina Dowling
University of Hartford
Hartford, CT

Constance Herinkova
South College
Knoxville, TN

Kenneth O'Neil Salyer
Brown Mackie College
Louisville, KY

Linda Hibbs
Community College of Philadelphia
Havertown, PA

Scott Silvis
Griffin Technical College
Griffin, GA

Yvonne Hughes
University of Phoenix
Phoenix, AZ
Central Texas Career College
Killeen, TX

Randi Ray
Des Moines Area Community College
Des Moines, IA

Robert Mongue
University of Mississippi
University, MS

Thank you one and all.

ABOUT THE AUTHOR

Nobody is better suited to writing a textbook on the subject of torts than Cathy J. Okrent. Over 35 years ago she had her first torts course as a first-year law student in Massachusetts, and since then her legal career has evolved in several areas of civil litigation, especially tort law. First she embarked on defense work for a large Manhattan insurance company before accepting a position with the Nassau (New York) County of Social Services. At the former, she was a defense attorney in accident cases. At the latter, her people skills complimented her legal acumen in the service of the Commissioner's Office, working with the indigent and adjudicated incompetent residents of the county.

In the next phase of her career, Cathy demonstrated savvy trial technique in torts and medical malpractice cases in Albany, New York. After years of success as a plaintiff's attorney, both at trial and in negotiations, she became counsel at the New York State Workers' Compensation Appeals Board. As the last resort for any worker with such an appeal, Cathy defended the Board's decisions.

After the birth of her two daughters, Cathy began instructing paralegal students as a college professor. Subsequently, she began writing paralegal textbooks as follows:

Torts and Personal Injury
Legal Terminology
Legal Terminology for Court Reporting
Okrent's *Torts* consistently appears on lists of best sellers in the legal profession.

After moving to California, Cathy became a corporate legal consultant and pioneered commercial standards for implementing the Family and Medical Leave Act (FMLA). She lives in Ventura County with her family.

Table of Cases

Chapter 1

Introduction to Torts

and Legal Analysis

THE BIGGEST MISTAKES PARALEGALS MAKE AND HOW TO AVOID THEM

A Damaged Career

Angela was an up-and-coming paralegal in the world of corporate law and intellectual property. On her LinkedIn profile, she described herself as "extremely driven, hardworking, and committed to take pride in each and every aspect of work and life." She had over five years of experience in Security and Exchange Commission (SEC) reporting, stock management, and corporate business. An alumnus of Metropolitan State College in Denver, Angela graduated magna cum laude. Among her many college activities and awards, she was captain of her basketball team, member of the All Academic Team, on the dean's list all four years, and received the All-American Scholar Collegiate Award. Imagine everyone's surprise when a 2012 *Wall Street Journal* headline screamed: "Ex-Paralegal, Father Settle Insider Trading Suit."

(continues)

The SEC alleged that Angela, while working at a Montana semiconductor company, gained confidential information that the company was being acquired by another corporation. According to the SEC, Angela and her father improperly traded on the information to earn $67,000 before the public announcement that Angela's employer was being acquired. Marc Fagel, director of the SEC's office in San Francisco, said, "Angela . . . exploited her access to confidential merger and acquisition information to illicitly enrich herself and her family." Angela and her father were fined $175,000 to settle a lawsuit filed by the SEC against them.

Lesson Learned: Although Angela settled the case with the SEC without admitting or denying wrongdoing, her judgment is forever in question and her once-promising career irrevocably damaged.

▌ INTRODUCTION

This chapter covers the definition of a tort, the three broad categories of torts, the history of tort law, the public policy objectives behind tort law, and the analytical processes used both to understand appellate court opinions and to solve hypothetical problems.

This chapter includes:

- ▶ The definition of torts
- ▶ An initial description of negligence
- ▶ The elements of strict (absolute) liability
- ▶ The historical roots of tort law
- ▶ The public policy objectives of tort law, including compensating injured parties, holding wrongdoers liable, and allocating losses
- ▶ The development of an analytical framework to solve hypothetical problems by applying legal principles to the facts
- ▶ The application of an analytical formula (IRAC) that allows any tort law problem or question to be continuously narrowed to reveal the answer
- ▶ An overview of a civil case
- ▶ A discussion of alternative dispute resolution

tort | A civil (as opposed to a criminal) wrong, other than a breach of contract. For an act to be a tort, there must be: a legal duty owed by one person to another, a breach (breaking) of that duty, and harm done as a direct result of the action.

tortfeasor | A person who commits a tort.

▌ TORTS DEFINED

A **tort** is a wrongful injury to a person or his or her property. For example, when you hurt a person or damage a person's property, these are considered torts. The person inflicting the harm is called the **tortfeasor** (*feasor* meaning "doer"). The word *tort* is French, taken from the Latin *torquere* (meaning "to twist"), and characterizes behavior that warps or bends society's rules about avoiding causing harm to others. The French phrase *de son tort demesne* (meaning "in his own wrong") was used to describe grievous misconduct between individuals and to assign blame to the responsible party.

Sources of Tort Law

Tort law is derived from both **common law** and statutory law. Common law develops from the decisions following court trials. Legislatures often enact statutes to supplement, modify, or supersede common law tort principles. Courts may turn the tables on the legislature by issuing new common law rulings interpreting the meaning of statutes. In this way the law matures, with both courts and legislatures adjusting the law to meet the changing needs of society. A whole new body of law is developing to address torts arising from the use of the Internet, such as cyberbullying and the downloading of music without permission or payment.

common law | Either all case law or the case law that is made by judges in the absence of relevant statutes.

Broad Categories of Tort Law

Tort law considers the rights and remedies available to persons injured through other people's carelessness or intentional misconduct. Tort law also holds persons in certain circumstances responsible for other people's injuries, regardless of blame. Torts are commonly subdivided into three broad categories: negligence, intentional torts, and strict (or absolute) liability (Table 1-1).

Negligence. **Negligence** is the failure of an ordinary, reasonable, and prudent person to exercise due care in a given set of circumstances. Negligence does not require an *intent* to commit a wrongful action. The wrongful action itself is sufficient to constitute negligence. What makes misconduct negligent is that the behavior was not reasonably careful and someone was injured as a result of this unreasonable carelessness—for example, failing to watch the road ahead when driving a car.

negligence | The failure to exercise a reasonable amount of care in a situation that causes harm to someone or something.

In a negligence case, one must always ask whether the following exist: duty, breach, causation, and damages. These elements are explained in greater detail in the chapters that follow.

Negligence	Failure to exercise ordinary care. Intent is not necessary. Someone is injured as a result of unreasonable care. (Most car accidents are examples of this.)
Intentional Torts	Deliberately intend to hurt someone or his or her property. (Assault and battery are examples.)
Strict Liability	Regardless of intent, negligence, or fault, if someone is injured by the product or activity, there is automatic or absolute liability. (Products liabiltity is one example of this.)

TABLE 1-1
Broad categories of tort law

intentional torts | An injury *designed* to injure a person or that person's property.

Intentional Torts. **Intentional torts** are actions expressly designed with the purpose of injuring or the intent to injure another person or that person's property, and not in the criminal sense. Intentional torts, as the name indicates, require the tortfeasor to intend to commit the wrongful act.

The tortfeasor intends a particular harm to result from the misconduct, or acts with intent that harm will occur. There are several different types of intentional torts: intentional, reckless, and negligent. Examples of specific intentional torts are assault and battery, both of which are discussed in detail in later chapters. These are in contrast to injuries caused by negligence. Intent is shown when a tortfeasor acts with a desire to bring about harmful consequences and is substantially certain that such consequences will occur. Although the elements may vary somewhat for each particular intentional tort, as a general rule, for an intentional tort case, one must look for three aspects: an act, the intent to cause harm, and actual harm, or damages.

strict (absolute) liability | The legal responsibility for damage or injury, even if you are not at fault or negligent.

Strict (Absolute) Liability. **Strict (absolute) liability** is the tortfeasor's responsibility for injuring another, regardless of intent, negligence, or fault. Even if a person took all the precautions possible to avoid injury, if an injury occurs, there is automatic liability. All that needs to be proved is that a tort occurred, and that the defendant was responsible. Strict liability is different from intentional torts in that intent to commit a strict-liability tort is irrelevant. Strict liability usually applies to activities that have a high probability of endangering the public, such as using fireworks. Strict liability is distinguishable from negligence, because the tortfeasor is responsible under strict liability regardless of how careful he or she might have been, and even if he or she did not intend harm to occur. The most important type of strict liability is products liability. Under products liability, the manufacturer or other seller of an unreasonably dangerous or defective product is held liable for injuries the product causes. For example, both the car manufacturer and car dealer would be held liable for injuries resulting from a defective car.

These concepts are presented here only to establish basic terminology. Subsequent chapters explore each of these topics in greater detail, and delve deeper into the elements of each.

The Unique Elements of Each Tort. Each type of tort contains its own unique elements, which are needed to bring a lawsuit. Although the elements of each are unique, tort analysis in general is the same.

The elements of negligence are different from strict liability's components, and those of intentional torts. The key to understanding tort law is to identify the type of broad tort category involved in the case. Ask whether the issue contains intentional torts, and, if so, which particular one(s)—negligence or strict liability. Then look to the definition and rules that separate the particular tort in question from other torts in the broad category. For instance, if two people get into a fight and each one purposely hits the other, it must be determined which of the intentional torts definitions most closely fits what occurred. Did an assault or battery occur, or did both intentional torts occur? Next, apply the appropriate rules of law to the specific facts of the case.

Like all forms of law, tort law has undergone a long and interesting period of growth and development. The next section briefly examines the history of tort law.

HISTORY OF TORT LAW

Tort law, like all American law, traces its origins to English and Western European history. After the Norman conquest of England in 1066, William the Conqueror brought Norman law (which was heavily influenced by Roman law) to intermingle with Anglo-Saxon and Celtic legal traditions. The result was the common law, which at the time consisted of the underlying legal principles and social attitudes gleaned from generations of judicial decisions by local tribunals. Even today, the bulk of tort law has been derived from our common law heritage of court decisions.

The King's Writs

During the Middle Ages, much of this common law was passed on orally. As a result, common law often varied widely among localities. To unify these divergent ideas, the king established formal procedures *(king's writs)* by which Crown subjects could petition the king's courts for redress. There were originally only two types of actions permitted to be brought for torts: (1) the **writ for trespass** and (2) the **writ for trespass on the case**. The first action was for serious breaches of the peace, and the second action for minor breaches of the peace. No other actions were permitted.

writ for trespass | A tort action for a serious breach of the king's peace.

writ for trespass on the case | A tort action for a minor breach of the king's peace that was not direct or forceful.

Evolution of Modern Tort Law

During the eighteenth and nineteenth centuries, English tort law began to shift from the old writ system to torts involving intent and fault, known today as intentional torts and negligence. This evolution was copied in the United States. Gradually, the common law grew to include the modern torts discussed throughout this text. Today's tort law is a combination of English and American common law, plus statutory law.

What does tort law seek to accomplish? Next, we examine the social and economic purposes that influence, and are influenced by, tort law.

▌ PUBLIC POLICY OBJECTIVES IN TORT LAW

Like every aspect of our legal system, there are several purposes underlying tort principles. These include (1) protecting persons and property from unjust injury by providing legally enforceable rights; (2) compensating victims by holding accountable those persons responsible for causing such harms; (3) encouraging minimum standards of social conduct among society's members; (4) deterring violations of those standards of conduct; and (5) allocating losses among different participants in the social arena.

Protecting Persons and Property: Accountability

Like the king's writs, modern tort law strives to prevent unjustified harm to innocent victims. Tort law enables private citizens to use the legal system to resolve disputes in which one party claims that the other has acted improperly, resulting in harm.

Compensating the Victim

The system compels the tortfeasor to compensate the injured party for his or her losses. This *accountability* (or *culpability*) factor is crucial to our legal sense of fair play and equity. People should be held responsible for their actions, especially when they wreak havoc on others. Redress should be available for innocent victims of carelessness, recklessness, or intentional injury.

Minimum Standards of Social Conduct: Deterrence

To function meaningfully in American society, citizens must understand society's norms and values. One extremely important norm encourages the public to behave in such a manner as to avoid hurting others or their belongings. Tort law is largely composed of *minimum standards of conduct.* Persons functioning below such thresholds are defined as tortfeasors; individuals acting at or above such criteria are acceptable to the community. However, the intent is not to ensure conformity; rather, the ideal is to inspire people to respect the dignity and integrity each individual possesses.

Deterring Violations of Those Standards

Persons should not infringe heedlessly upon others' activities unless society is willing to accept such interference with its members' lives. Tort law discourages abuses by establishing a clear system of legal rights and remedies enforceable in court proceedings. <u>We know that we can go to court when someone strikes us, invades our privacy, creates a nuisance, or acts negligently toward us</u>. Likewise, we know that we might be hauled into court if we do these things to others. By establishing minimum standards of conduct, tort law sets the rules for living—those "rules of thumb" by which we try to get along with other people.

Allocating Losses among Different Individuals or Groups

It is easy to grasp the idea that an individual tortfeasor should compensate the victim for the tortfeasor's wrongdoing. However, in modern society there are often many different participants in virtually any activity, making it less clear who should be labeled as tortfeasor or victim. For example, at the time of the American Revolution, most Americans were fairly self-sufficient and dealt directly with other individuals for goods or services. If a colonist bought a broken plow, or a poorly shod horse from the local blacksmith, he or she knew whom to hold responsible. However, as the United States became more industrialized, commercial transactions ceased to be one-on-one interactions. Today, people buy canned fruit from a local grocery that bought it from a wholesaler that bought it from a manufacturer that bought it from a grower. If the fruit is spoiled, perhaps the purchaser's spouse or child, rather than the purchaser, will suffer the injury. The lines of culpability become less clear as the producer of the defective item becomes more removed from the ultimate user, and might even have its factory in another country.

Tort law has evolved *products liability* to determine who is in the best position to bear the costs of defective products—the innocent user or the sellers and manufacturers. It is an economic decision that courts and legislatures have made by stating that industry can best afford the costs of injuries caused by dangerously made goods. In other words, the burden of shouldering the economic loss is placed upon commercial business instead of the individual suffering the harm.

Likewise, workers' compensation statutes have been enacted by state law to address whether the employee or employer will bear the cost of workplace accidents. In most instances, it is the employer and not the employee who bears this cost, regardless of fault. With automobile accidents, state insurance laws, called no-fault statutes, have been enacted setting out in which instances an insurance company will be responsible for a collision, regardless of fault. Insurance companies are sometimes referred to as "deep pockets," as they are thought to have the most money when an injured person looks for someone to sue for his or her injuries.

Thus, tort law can be used to assign the expenses associated with misfortune, even when fault is hazy at best. More commonly, though, a single tortfeasor can be identified and saddled with the financial obligation.

■ ANALYZING HYPOTHETICAL PROBLEMS

This book poses many hypothetical fact problems (hypotheticals) to help develop analytical talents. Perhaps the most popular analytical framework is discussed here.

Analytical Framework for Hypotheticals: IRAC

The analytical framework for hypotheticals sequentially investigates four general elements of a problem: the issue, rules of law, application of the rules to the facts, and conclusions (IRAC). With this approach, legal principles are applied to specific factual scenarios. When analyzing a hypothetical, first decide which *issues* are presented. To accomplish this, one must identify the general area of law involved in the problem. For instance, if John takes José's bicycle without permission, then John has committed some type of tort. This identifies the broad area of law (torts).

Next, the different parts of the general legal area must be explored to see which specific tort applies. The particular tort John appears to have engaged in is called conversion. So the issue would be whether or not John converted José's property. This question can be answered by referring to the appropriate *rule of law*. To generalize, the rule of law for conversion defines it as the wrongful deprivation of another's property without consent.

This rule must now be *applied* to the facts. John took José's property without permission. This means John wrongfully deprived José of the use and enjoyment of his property. This constitutes conversion.

The *conclusion* would be that José may successfully sue John to recover possession of the bicycle, plus damages, because these legal remedies are appropriate for conversion (as Chapter 8 explains).

This analytical formula is a useful tool in applying abstract legal principles to different factual situations.

Factual Distinctions Result in Different Conclusions

A rule of law may be applied to various factual situations to reach different results. This is exactly what appellate courts do when deciding cases dealing with similar legal issues. It is also what attorneys and paralegals do when applying rules of law to the particular facts of a client's case. In the following hypothetical, if the puddle of water was there for just two minutes, instead of two hours, Raj's lawsuit would probably not be successful. A single variation in a factual situation can change the legal outcome.

HYPOTHETICAL

Raj visited the Gym Dandy Fitness Center to use its weight and steam rooms. As he walked from the locker room into the weight room, he slipped on a puddle of water on the floor and fell. The puddle was caused by leaking water pipes along the wall leading to the steam room. Raj broke his left arm as a result of the fall. Mary Perrington, another patron, mentioned that she had seen the puddle when she first arrived at the center approximately two hours before Raj's accident.

LEGAL ANALYSIS IN ACTION

Issue: Would Raj's negligence lawsuit against Gym Dandy Fitness Center succeed?

Rule: Applying the rules of law established in other negligence cases, Raj (the plaintiff) must prove that Gym Dandy (the defendant) either created the hazardous condition or had actual or constructive notice of the danger.

Application: The puddle was caused by Gym Dandy's leaking water pipes, so Gym Dandy created the danger that hurt Raj. Further, Mary testified that the puddle had been visible on the floor for two hours. That was sufficient time for Gym Dandy's employees to observe and correct the problem. Thus, Gym Dandy had constructive notice of the puddle and the danger it posed to customers.

Conclusion: Gym Dandy was negligent in creating the puddle that caused Raj to fall and become injured. Accordingly, Raj's negligence lawsuit against Gym Dandy should be successful.

▮ SOLVING TORT PROBLEMS

Another approach to tort problem solving is moving from broad subject areas to specific types of torts. This method identifies the exact issues, rules of law, and conclusions in a problem by helping the reader to narrow the analytical focus.

Tort Analysis: From General to Specific

Tort analysis should go from the general to the specific, as depicted in Exhibit 1-1. For example, how can one tell if infliction of emotional distress has occurred unless one is aware that some type of tort law was involved in the problem? An experienced paralegal may appear to readily know the answer. In reality, that paralegal has streamlined the analytical process, but still has moved from the general to the specific. The paralegal recognized a general negligence problem and then narrowed it to the specific defense—assumption of risk—necessary to excuse the negligent conduct.

Hypothetical

The following hypothetical should more clearly illustrate tort analysis.

HYPOTHETICAL

Jerry lives next to a vacant lot owned by Steven. Jerry dumps his grass clippings onto Steven's lot after mowing his lawn. Eventually, these grass clippings begin to smell and attract rats. Steven never gave Jerry permission to dump grass (or anything else) on Steven's lot. What legal rights does Steven have, if any?

Jerry's actions appear to fall within the intentional torts category, as Jerry is deliberately discarding his grass clippings on Steven's lot.

LEGAL ANALYSIS IN ACTION

Issue: Did Jerry trespass against Steven by dumping grass on Steven's lot without permission?

Rule: The elements of trespass are, generally, unlawful interference with another person's use of his or her property.

Application: Jerry's actions (1) were unlawful, in that he did not have Steven's permission to dump grass onto Steven's lot, and (2) interfered with Steven's use of his property, because Steven could not use his lot freely without having to contend with the grass and vermin.

Conclusion: Jerry is liable to Steven for the intentional tort of trespass.

EXHIBIT 1-1

Sequence of tort analysis from general to specific

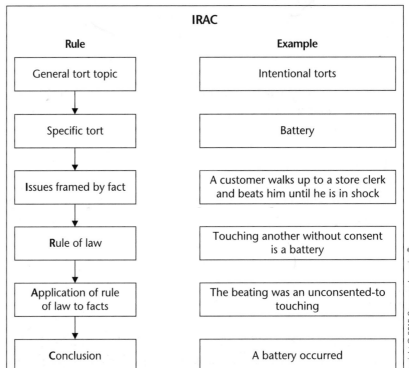

IRAC	
Rule	**Example**
General tort topic	Intentional torts
Specific tort	Battery
Issues framed by fact	A customer walks up to a store clerk and beats him until he is in shock
Rule of law	Touching another without consent is a battery
Application of rule of law to facts	The beating was an unconsented-to touching
Conclusion	A battery occurred

Copyright © 2015 Cengage Learning®.

▌ OVERVIEW OF A CIVIL CASE

Several basic steps occur in civil cases. However, it is important to note that at any point in the litigation process a plaintiff may decide to drop his or her lawsuit or settle with the defendant out of court. In some instances a plaintiff may not even need to institute a lawsuit to recover damages. Sometimes a simple telephone call or letter from a law office can promote the necessary exchange, thus settling the claim. However, a civil case generally proceeds in the following manner:

- ▶ Complaint
- ▶ Answer
- ▶ Discovery
- ▶ Pretrial procedures
- ▶ Trial
- ▶ Post-trial procedures

Complaint

After being injured or harmed in some manner, a plaintiff might seek out legal representation. The attorney will have the client sign a *retainer*, a written agreement authorizing the attorney to represent him or her. The paralegal and/or attorney will conduct an interview of the client. As the interview progresses, the facts must be compared with the particular elements needed for the specific type of action alleged. Even though the facts might seem similar to those of a prior case, each case will have slightly different details that could change the results of the case. Accordingly, it is important to get *all* the facts.

One method of obtaining all the applicable facts is to conduct an investigation. During an investigation, the attorney and/or the paralegal might visit the scene of the occurrence, take photographs, gather evidence, and interview witnesses. It is important to be as thorough as possible while the facts are all fresh for the witnesses, and the scene of the accident or item causing the injury has not be changed or lost.

Either the paralegal or the attorney will then draft a written **complaint** based upon the information gathered and provided. The exact procedural steps as to when the complaint must be filed with the court vary by jurisdiction, as do the precise form and content of the complaint and the time limits and rules for the **service of process**. Accordingly, it is very important to consult local court rules.

Answer

The defendant's response (**answer**) to the complaint must be filed with the court and served upon the opposing party. The defendant's response must either admit to or deny the allegations and, if denying, must explain the reason for the denial. The defendant might also assert affirmative defenses, which if true might relieve the defendant of liability. One example of an affirmative defense is to claim that

complaint | The first pleading filed in a civil lawsuit. It includes a statement of the wrong or harm done to the plaintiff by the defendant.

service of process | The delivery (or its legal equivalent, such as publication in a newspaper in some cases) of a legal paper by an authorized person.

answer | The first pleading by the defendant in a lawsuit. This pleading responds to the charges and demands of the plaintiff's complaint.

the statute of limitations, or the time for filing a suit, has elapsed. This is also the opportunity for a defendant to bring counterclaims against the plaintiff.

Discovery

discovery | The formal and informal exchange of information between two sides in a lawsuit. Two types of discovery are interrogatories and depositions.

Discovery—the exchange of information and narrowing of the issues in dispute in a case—can be either a simple process or a long and drawn-out one that takes years and involves millions of documents. The nature of discovery depends on the type of claim involved. If a case is clear cut and there are witness statements and photographs of the scene, it is possible that not much discovery will be needed. In a complex case involving, for example, exposure to toxic chemicals, the discovery of information can go on for years and involve electronic searches of millions of documents This is just one of the tasks during discovery that might be assigned to paralegals.

Paralegals are typically involved in preparing discovery requests or gathering information to respond to discovery requests. This might involve the request for documents, setting up a time to question witnesses and parties in a case, or summarizing the contents of documents received in response to a request. Discovery is the point in the case at which a paralegal's communication skills come into play. Clients can become frustrated or confused, for example, by not understanding why a court date has not been scheduled immediately after the complaint was filed. The paralegal will need to explain the discovery required for the particular case and the anticipated time frame. It may be that the defendant has asked for additional time to respond to requests, thus delaying the progress of a case.

Pretrial Procedures

pretrial procedures | Any procedure that immediately precedes trial, for example, the settlement conference.

Depending on the kind of case and your local jurisdiction, various **pretrial procedures** might be scheduled. At any time from the informal telephone call to the defendant or his or her representative to the very trial itself, either party can bring motions before the court. One of the parties might seek to have the case dismissed through a motion. Alternatively, one of the parties might seek relief from oppressive discovery demands, or wish to compel the other party to reply to demands. Before trial, a party might seek an order preventing the other party from introducing prejudicial evidence to the jury.

Generally, there is a pretrial conference after the initial summons and complaint are served. During the conference, the judge will set up a schedule to complete discovery, and encourage the parties to settle the case before trial. In some instances, a court date is set, and the parties must commence final preparation for trial. Increasingly, the parties are required, by the judge or by local rules, to select a means other than trial to attempt to settle their dispute. This is called *alternative dispute resolution* and is addressed later in the chapter. Then, only if the parties are still unsuccessful in resolving a dispute will a court date be scheduled.

Trial

The **trial** is your client's "day in court." This is the client's chance to be heard and explain his or her side of an incident. Few cases actually go to trial; most are settled at some point in the litigation proceedings. Because of the time and expense usually required to wait for and actually go to trial, other methods have been sought by attorneys to streamline or avoid this process.

trial | The process of deciding a case (giving evidence, making arguments, deciding by a judge and jury, etc.).

Release-Settlement Agreement. If the case should settle, the client will need to sign a settlement agreement, outlining the terms of the settlement. In addition, the parties will need to file a stipulation discontinuing action with the court. This document is to advise that a case has been settled, and that there is no need for a trial.

Post-Trial Procedures

Post-trial procedures are those that occur after a trial, such as an appeal or the steps necessary to collect on an award. These can be quite expensive and timely, as there are additional attorney fees and court costs, to name a few.

post-trial procedures | The procedures that occur after a trial, such as an appeal or the steps taken to collect on an award.

▌ CASE RESOLUTION

Not all lawsuits go to trial; in fact, as noted, most cases are informally settled by the parties out of court. A very tiny percentage of cases is actually tried before a judge or jury, approximately 5%. When you are initially analyzing a case, you should consider whether the particular case can be resolved early on through **alternative dispute resolution**.

alternative dispute resolution | Method to resolve a legal problem without a court decision.

Alternative Dispute Resolution (ADR)

Alternative dispute resolution is a method to resolve a legal problem without a court decision. This avenue of case resolution is becoming increasingly popular as parties wish to avoid costly public court proceedings. Alternative dispute resolution is also a means of avoiding lengthy waits for a case to reach trial—in some jurisdictions the wait can be as long as three to five years. Many plaintiffs, particularly businesses, would prefer to have a lawsuit resolved privately and quickly, rather than waiting years for closure. Less time is lost from work for ADR than the weeks that employees might spend to attend a trial. ADR also avoids the possibility of negative publicity, and is usually much less stressful on the parties. One negative to alternative dispute resolution is that the parties might lose some of their legal protections, such as their right to have a judge or jury hear the case, and for an appellate court to review the decision. Additionally, if the parties are unsuccessful with alternative dispute resolution, they will have expended additional costs for a mediator or arbitrator, and then still have the costs of trial.

There are various ways to resolve a legal dispute without the formality of a trial—for example, arbitration, mediation, minitrial, rent-a-judge, and a summary jury trial.

Arbitration

arbitration | Resolution of a dispute by a person whose decision is binding. This person is called an *arbitrator*. Submission of the dispute for decision is often the result of an agreement (an *arbitration clause*) in a contract.

Arbitration is the resolution of a dispute by a person other than a judge. This person's decision is binding and not a matter of public record. The person deciding the case is called the *arbitrator*. Sometimes parties agree through a written contract that, in the event of a potential dispute, they will resort to arbitration. Most doctors are now requiring patients to sign arbitration agreements before they will provide medical services. Some companies, such as credit card services, routinely include an arbitration clause in their contracts. Arbitration was frequently used in the past for labor and construction disputes.

Mediation

mediation | Outside help in settling a dispute. The person who does this is called a *mediator*. This is different from arbitration in that a mediator can only persuade people into a settlement.

In **mediation**, the parties use outside help in settling a dispute. Mediation differs from arbitration in that the mediator can only persuade the parties to reach a settlement. The mediator does not dictate an actual decision. Through a mediator's intervention and assistance, the parties reach a mutually agreeable resolution. In this manner, the parties are involved in the process, and all participants might feel victorious. There is not a "winner" and a "loser" per se as would result from a court trial. Mediation is less formal than arbitration, but like arbitration, it is not a matter of public record.

Minitrial

minitrial | Alternate dispute resolution by a panel of executives from two companies engaged in a complex dispute. A neutral moderator helps the two sides reach a settlement.

A **minitrial** is a means of alternative dispute resolution by a panel of executives from two companies engaged in a complex dispute. A neutral moderator helps the two sides sort out factual and legal issues to reach a settlement. This is intended to help the decision makers of the companies to see the merits and weaknesses of their cases and aid in settlement. A minitrial is not as formal as a traditional court trial. Ideally, the parties will maintain their business relationship after the dispute, and continue to conduct business together.

Rent-a-Judge

rent-a-judge | Alternate dispute resolution in which two sides in a dispute choose a person to decide the dispute. The two sides may agree to make the procedure informal or formal.

Rent-a-judge allows the parties to choose a person to decide their dispute, as opposed to having no choice in the judge assigned to the court case. Retired judges often are willing to act in this capacity and preside over these cases. The parties can decide the degree of formality of the procedure and whether the decision will be binding or merely advisory.

Summary Jury Trial

In complex cases, the two sides may present important facts and evidence to a small jury, an action referred to as a **summary jury trial**. Either the parties will agree in advance to be bound by the decision or, based on their interview with the jury, to use the jury's advice to aid in settlement negotiations. The attorneys are not required to follow the strict rules of evidence and procedure that are followed in a court trial.

Parties can save a lot of time and money if they are willing to consider and abide by one of the many forms of alternative dispute resolution. However, it is to be noted that, despite the many advantages, some claimants will insist on their day in court and their right to be heard by a jury. Accordingly, when alternative dispute resolution is elected, it is very important to obtain the client's consent in writing, having him or her acknowledge that this choice has been knowingly and freely made.

summary jury trial | Alternate dispute resolution in which the judge orders the two sides in a complex case to present their cases to a small jury. The parties may agree in advance not to be bound by the verdict.

▌ SUMMARY

Tort law involves the study of wrongful conduct. Torts consist of wrongful injury to another's person or property. The wrongdoer is called the tortfeasor, and tort law provides the injured party with legal rights and remedies that may be enforced in a court of law. Torts may be divided into three general categories: negligence, intentional torts, and strict (absolute) liability. Negligence is the failure to exercise reasonable care to avoid injuring others. Intentional torts consist of misconduct designed to injure another person or that person's property. Strict (absolute) liability holds the tortfeasor liable for injuring another, regardless of intent, negligence, or fault.

Much of tort law comes from ancient English and early American court decisions. In medieval England, there were primarily two torts. Both involved breaches of the king's peace. Today, there are many more tort actions because society is much more complicated than it was during the Middle Ages. Tort law has become correspondingly more sophisticated so as to deal with modern legal problems.

Tort law seeks to accomplish several goals. It serves to protect innocent persons and their property from careless or intentional injury at the hands of tortfeasors. It also attempts to hold tortfeasors responsible for their misconduct. Tort law encourages minimum standards of conduct among the public to avoid injuring others through heedless, reckless, or intentional behavior. It also deters persons from injuring other people and their property by holding tortfeasors liable for such mischief. Tort law allocates losses among different groups or individuals, based upon society's decision (as expressed through its legislatures and courts) as to who is best able to bear such losses.

To apply the rules of law to different hypothetical problems, one method (IRAC) breaks down the factual scenario in terms of the issues, the rules of law that must then be applied to each case's specific facts, and the conclusions regarding the probable outcome of the hypothetical case. When analyzing tort law problems, one decides on the general tort topic area, the specific tort involved, the issues framed by the facts, the rules of law for the particular tort involved, and how to apply those rules of law to the facts. Finally, one draws conclusions regarding the hypothetical or problem.

A civil case generally proceeds in the following manner: complaint, answer, discovery, pretrial procedures, trial, and post-trial procedures. Additionally, at any point during a case, the parties may bring motions seeking a court order to resolve certain issues. Parties often look for alternative means to resolve a dispute. These alternatives to trial are referred to as *alternative dispute resolution*. A few of the means of resolving a case without a trial are the use of arbitration, mediation, a minitrial, rent-a-judge, and summary jury trials.

In this chapter, a brief introduction and overview of torts and personal injury was covered. The next chapter will focus on negligence, one of the three broad categories of torts.

▌KEY TERMS

alternative dispute resolution	mediation	strict (absolute) liability
answer	minitrial	summary jury trial
arbitration	negligence	tort
common law	post-trial procedures	tortfeasor
complaint	pretrial procedures	trial
discovery	rent-a-judge	writ for trespass
intentional tort	service of process	writ for trespass on the case

▌PROBLEMS

Using the definitions of specific torts discussed in this chapter, answer the following hypotheticals using the analytical approaches discussed earlier.

1. Tom Caster is a 12-year-old boy who enjoys climbing trees. The Caster family just moved into a new house. The electrical wires to Tom's house run from an electrical pole through the high branches of an oak tree in his backyard. While the rest of the family was moving into the home, Tom ran to the backyard to climb the tree. As he neared the top, he grabbed the electrical wires with his right hand. The wires were not insulated and Tom was severely burned from the resulting electrical shock. He also broke both his legs when he fell, unconscious, from the tree. Tom's father wishes to know if he might successfully sue the utility company for negligence.

2. Shady Acres is a subdivision being developed by Bartholomew Real Estate Management, Inc. (BREM). While bulldozing the lots and streets, BREM's crews created huge piles of dirt. BREM did not erect any barriers to keep these dirt piles in place. Pamela Jovanco owns a house at the bottom of a hill upon which BREM placed several earth piles. During heavy rains, mud would slide down the hill and cover Pamela's entire yard. Some mud even seeped through her basement windows, damaging her basement carpet and furniture. Pamela wonders if trespass has occurred.

3. Samantha Billingsly stood outside her downtown hotel hailing a cab. The driver screeched to a halt alongside the curb. Samantha opened the rear door of the automobile and began to climb inside. In doing so, she placed her right hand on the roof of the car where the top of the door would close. Suddenly, the cab driver accelerated the automobile, causing the rear door to slam shut onto Samantha's hand. Samantha suffered lacerations and several broken bones in her right

hand and wrist. She also suffered a neck injury as she was thrown against the back seat as the taxi lurched forward. The cab driver later explained that he had accelerated suddenly to avoid being struck by a shuttle bus, which he thought was about to collide with his taxi when he saw it approaching very rapidly in his rearview mirror. Using negligence theory, Samantha would like to sue the cab driver who owns the taxi.

4. Ed Peterson owned a coyote, which he captured while hunting the previous summer in the mountains. The coyote had become quite tame, and at parties, to entertain guests, Ed would routinely allow the animal to eat out of his hand. One day Ed's next-door neighbor, Angela Starlight, a seven-year-old girl, visited Ed's backyard to play with the coyote. Angela's parents had warned her several times to avoid approaching the coyote, although neither they nor Angela had ever seen the animal bite or growl at anyone. When Angela reached out to pet the coyote, it bared its teeth and snapped at her hand, biting and cutting her severely. Angela's parents sued Ed under a theory of absolute liability. Under most states' common law, owners are strictly liable for injuries caused by wild animals kept as pets.

▋ REVIEW QUESTIONS

1. How is a tort best defined? What are the three broad categories of torts? How might you define each variety?

2. What is negligence? How might you distinguish it from intentional torts?

3. What are intentional torts? What are examples of intentional torts?

4. How might you define strict (absolute) liability? What is the most important type of strict liability?

5. Discuss the historical roots of tort law. From what country or countries did torts originate? How have torts changed since their inception?

6. What are the purposes that tort law attempts to accomplish? Do these objectives sometimes conflict? Do they sometimes complement one another?

7. Suggest an analytical formula you might use to answer a hypothetical fact problem. In what order are these steps taken? Why do you think this order is appropriate? Is each step of the technique necessary to reach the next phase?

8. Tort analysis moves from the general to the specific. Why is this best suited to answering tort hypotheticals?

9. Describe the stages of a civil lawsuit.

10. What is the difference between arbitration and mediation?

▋ HELPFUL WEBSITES

This chapter provides an introduction to torts and legal analysis. To learn more about torts, the following sites can be accessed:

General Legal Information

www.fjc.gov

www.law.emory.edu

www.law.cornell.edu

www.findlaw.com

www.law.harvard.edu

www.kentlaw.edu

www.law.indiana.edu

www.camlaw.rutgers.edu

www.lectlaw.com

www.usa.gov

Links to State Courts

www.courts.net

www.lawidea.com

Links to Federal Courts

www.uscourts.gov

www.lawsource.com

www.fjc.gov

Information for Paralegals

www.nala.org

www.paralegals.org

www.paralegalgateway.com

www.paralegal.laws.com

Links to Legal Newspapers

www.netlawlibrary.com

www.law.com

www.americanlawyer.com

STUDENT COMPANION WEBSITE
For additional cases and study materials, please go to www.cengagebrain.com

Chapter 2

Negligence

THE BIGGEST MISTAKES PARALEGALS MAKE AND HOW TO AVOID THEM

Fed Up during and after Lunch

Garnetta was having her usual lunch break at a favorite diner, taking her place at the end of the counter next to a row of booths. After she ordered her food, an attorney Garnetta recognized chose the booth next to her stool. The attorney was accompanied by another person. The attorney was speaking nonstop to the other person (who evidently was a client) or receiving and making cell calls. The issue of his loud conversations was an automobile accident involving the client. While Garnetta tried to read her newspaper, she overheard an hour's worth of details regarding the client's examination before trial from that morning. When Garnetta returned to her office, she was asked to replace another paralegal who became ill that afternoon. When Garnetta entered the conference room, there sat the attorney and his client from the diner.

(continues)

Unbeknownst to her, Garnetta's firm was defending the insurance company. Garnetta excused herself from the examination before trial, leaving the firm scrambling to find another paralegal. An hour passed before another paralegal returned from lunch and took Garnetta's place. Neither Garnetta's firm nor the plaintiff's attorney appreciated the loss of valuable time.

Lesson Learned: This is really a matter of the lawyer violating client confidentiality, and both he and his client should know that there is no expectation of privacy in a public eatery. Although Garnetta should not have had to move her seat, a paralegal with any experience could have turned to the attorney she recognized and said, "It sounds like you are having an important conversation, and I can hear everything you are discussing from my seat." Garnetta's polite message would have given the attorney an opportunity to move or speak more quietly. As a professional, Garnetta's comment may also have served to stop the attorney from behaving in that manner with other clients in the future.

▌ INTRODUCTION

elements | The essential parts or components of something.

The field of negligence is the most complex of the torts. What makes negligence challenging is its conceptual ambiguity. The **elements** of negligence appear to be so broadly defined that it is difficult to discern clear lines for negligent behavior. Negligence is not a mathematical equation. Instead, negligence resembles probability theory, in which specific conduct is more likely than not to be considered negligent under a particular set of circumstances. In this chapter, the following aspects of negligence are discussed:

- ▶ The elements of negligence
- ▶ The tortfeasor's scope of duty and standard of reasonable care
- ▶ Breach of duty, the reasonable person standard, and foreseeability
- ▶ Special duty based upon special relationship
- ▶ Causation and substantial factor analysis
- ▶ Joint and several liability
- ▶ Proximate cause
- ▶ Damages available in negligence actions

▌ NEGLIGENCE

Most people equate negligence with carelessness. The phrase conjures up images of actions that are slovenly, haphazard, heedless, or foolhardy. As a legal concept, negligence is much more precise, but it embodies all of these characteristics.

Negligence Defined: Reasonable Care

negligence | The failure to exercise a reasonable amount of care in a situation that causes harm to someone or something. It can involve doing something carelessly or failing to do something that should have been done.

Negligence may be broadly defined as <u>the failure to exercise reasonable care to avoid injuring others or their property.</u> Reasonable care depends upon the exact circumstances of each case. This is the "shifting sands" aspect of negligence with which legal students—and the legal system—struggle. The key term is *reasonable-ness*. In any tort case in which negligence might exist, ask the threshold question: Did the tortfeasor act unreasonably under the circumstances? This is essentially all that negligence entails.

Acts or Omissions

A tortfeasor can be negligent either by doing or by not doing something. When courts speak of *negligent acts* or *omissions* by the tortfeasor, they mean that the tortfeasor behaved unreasonably either by doing a specific careless activity or by failing to do something that the tortfeasor should have done.

Negligent actions are positive events; something is done. For instance, if Nick lit a fire in high winds that carried sparks onto a neighbor's roof and set the house ablaze, Nick's action (careless burning) would be deemed unreasonable. Negligent omissions are usually phrased negatively; the tortfeasor failed to do a reasonable act. For example, suppose Briana's front porch has a rotten step that she has failed to repair. A salesperson visiting her home falls through the step and breaks a leg. Briana's omission (failure to repair the step) would be considered unreasonable.

Like all areas of law, negligence has developed discernible elements that can be enumerated and outlined more clearly. The next section outlines the four elements of negligence.

▌ ELEMENTS OF NEGLIGENCE

Negligence can be specifically defined as a tortfeasor's failure to exercise reasonable care, thus causing a **foreseeable injury** to another person or that person's property. Negligence includes the following elements:

foreseeable injury | An injury that a reasonably prudent person should have anticipated.

1. Duty of care
2. Breach of the duty by the tortfeasor (unreasonable conduct)
3. Causation of injury to the victim
4. Damages to the victim (actual harm)

Each of these elements is required for negligence to exist, so each element is a threshold question. If "no" answers any single element, negligence does not exist. For example, the first question is: Did the tortfeasor owe a duty of reasonable care to the injured party? If not, then the analysis stops, with the conclusion that no negligence has occurred. If yes, then one must ask: Did the tortfeasor breach the duty of reasonable care? If not, the inquiry is finished, and once again the analyst concludes that there was no negligence. If yes, then one continues querying through the questions of causation and damages. Each element must be satisfied for negligence to exist, and each receives detailed treatment in the following sections.

▌ELEMENT 1: DUTY OF REASONABLE CARE

Negligence analysis begins with determining who is owed a duty of reasonable care.

In tort law, **duty** is the obligation either to do or not to do something. In negligence, the duty of **due (reasonable) care** is the responsibility to act reasonably so as to avoid injuring others. This may also be stated negatively: the duty of reasonable care is the obligation *not* to behave *un*reasonably so as to avoid injuring others.

For example, motor vehicle operators owe a duty of reasonable care to drive carefully and avoid injuring other drivers, their vehicles, or pedestrians.

duty | 1. An obligation to obey a law. 2. A legal obligation to another person, who has a corresponding right.

due (reasonable) care | That degree of care a person of ordinary prudence (the so-called *reasonable person*) would exercise in similar circumstances.

HYPOTHETICAL

Suppose Parker is driving on a four-lane highway and chooses to pass the truck in front of him. He fails to look in the rearview mirror before pulling into the left lane. Unbeknownst to Parker, another vehicle is attempting to pass him, and he pulls directly in front of that driver. This action forces that driver to swerve and collide with a telephone pole. Did Parker violate any duty of reasonable care?

In analyzing this duty hypothetical, the first question is: Did Parker owe the other driver a duty of reasonable care? Parker owed anyone driving or walking upon the street a duty to drive safely. By failing to check his rearview mirror to see if any traffic was approaching from behind in the left lane, Parker breached his duty to the other driver. He acted imprudently by not looking for other traffic before he switched lanes. He failed to see that which was there to be seen.

Scope of Duty

Clearly, one does not owe a duty of reasonable care to everyone else in the universe. **Scope of duty** is a limitation on the persons to whom one owes the duty. First, the scope of the duty must be determined. This focuses on the **foreseeability** of the victim.

For example, while driving on the highway in his city, Parker owes no duty of reasonable care to someone driving in another city hundreds of miles away. Parker's actions (i.e., driving his car) could not possibly have any effect on such a person. Parker's scope of duty does not extend to individuals who cannot directly be affected by his carelessness. Scope of duty is often described in terms of reasonable foreseeability.

scope of duty | In negligence law, defined in terms of those individuals who might foreseeably be injured as a result of the tortfeasor's actions.

foreseeability | The notion that a specific action, under particular circumstances, would produce an anticipated result.

Foreseeable Plaintiffs Theory

Foreseeability limits the scope (extent) of the duty owed to others. One asks the threshold question: Was it reasonably foreseeable that the person injured would be harmed as a consequence of the tortfeasor's actions? If so, the scope of the duty of reasonable care includes the individual hurt. This is sometimes called the **foreseeable plaintiffs theory,** because it was reasonably foreseeable that the **plaintiff** (who is suing the tortfeasor [**defendant**] for negligence) would be damaged because of the tortious conduct. It is the foreseeability of injury or damage that is of concern, not the degree or amount of injury or damage involved.

Unforeseeable Plaintiffs

Persons outside this range of duty are considered **unforeseeable plaintiffs**, because the tortfeasor could not reasonably have anticipated that they would be harmed by the tortfeasor's actions. People driving several streets in front of Parker would not likely be influenced by either Parker or the swerving other driver. They would be beyond Parker's scope of duty, and so he would not be required to exercise reasonable care toward them. However, persons driving close behind Parker and the swerving driver could reasonably be expected to become involved in the accident. These individuals would be within Parker's scope of duty. His failure to use reasonable care (by not looking in the rearview mirror, which caused him to cut off the swerving driver) violated his duty to them as well as to the swerving driver. Table 2-1 outlines scope of duty and the foreseeable plaintiffs theory.

Special Duty Based upon Special Relationship

Most negligence actions are based upon an affirmative duty or act owed to another that is improperly performed. In contrast, if a person fails to act, there generally is no liability in negligence, except under certain limited exceptions.

foreseeable plaintiffs theory | Under this theory, if it were reasonably foreseeable that the injured victim would be harmed as a consequence of the tortfeasor's actions, then the tortfeasor's scope of duty includes the victim.

plaintiff | A person who brings a lawsuit.

defendant | A person against whom an action is brought.

unforeseeable plaintiffs | Persons whose injuries the tortfeasor could not reasonably have anticipated as a result of the tortfeasor's actions.

Scope of Duty	Foreseeable Plaintiffs Theory
The tortfeasor owes a duty of reasonable care to avoid injuring others or their property.	The plaintiff may recover from the defendant only if it was reasonably foreseeable that the defendant's actions would injure the plaintiff.
Duty includes persons for whom it is reasonably foreseeable that injury will occur as a result of the torfeasor's actions.	Persons outside the defendant's scope of duty are considered unforeseeable plaintiffs.

TABLE 2-1
Scope of duty of reasonable care and foreseeable plaintiffs theory

THE CASE OF THE SCALE THAT SHOOK TORT LAW

In this landmark appellate case, heard by the highest court in New York, a man waiting for a train was carrying a package wrapped in newspaper with fireworks inside. The railroad guards were unaware of the contents of the parcel and helped the man board the moving train. As the guards tried to help, the package was dislodged, fell to the tracks, and exploded. This caused the platform to shake, which in turn caused a scale to fall. The scale seriously injured the plaintiff, Helen Palsgraf, who was waiting on the platform. Carefully read the court's reasoning concerning to whom a duty is owed in this situation. Note that the decision was written by Chief Justice Cardozo, who later became a justice of the U.S. Supreme Court. This case gives attorneys direction in interpreting the scope of duty owed to others.

PALSGRAF
v.
LONG ISLAND RAILROAD

Court of Appeals of New York
162 N.E. 99 (N.Y. Ct. App. 1928)
May 29, 1928
Cardozo, C. J.

Plaintiff, Helen Palsgraf was standing on a platform of defendant's railroad after buying a ticket to go to Rockaway Beach. A train stopped at the station, bound for another place. Two men ran forward to catch the train. One of the men reached the platform of the car without mishap, though the train was already moving. The other man, carrying a package, jumped aboard the car, but seemed unsteady as if about to fall. A guard on the car, who had held the door open, reached forward to help him in, and another guard on the platform pushed him from behind. In this act, the package was dislodged, and fell upon the rails. It was a package of small size, about 15 inches long, and was covered by a newspaper. In fact it contained fireworks, but there was nothing in its appearance to give notice of its contents. The fireworks when they fell exploded. The shock of the explosion threw down some scales at the other end of the platform many feet away. The scales struck the plaintiff, causing injuries for which she sues.

The conduct of the defendant's guard, if a wrong in its relation to the holder of the package, was not a wrong in its relation to the plaintiff, standing far away. Relatively to her it was not negligence at all.

Nothing in the situation gave notice that the falling package had in it the potency of peril to persons thus removed. Negligence is not actionable unless it involves the invasion of a legally protected interest, the violation of a right. "Proof of negligence in the air, so to speak, will not do." "Negligence is the absence of care, according to the circumstances." . . . If no hazard was apparent to the eye of ordinary vigilance, an act innocent and harmless, at least to outward seeming, with reference to her, did not take to itself the quality of a tort because it happened to be a wrong, though apparently not one involving the risk of bodily insecurity, with reference to someone else.

One who jostles one's neighbor in a crowd does not invade the rights of others standing at the outer fringe when the unintended contact casts a bomb upon the ground. The wrongdoer as to them is the man who carries the bomb, not the one who explodes it without suspicion of the danger. . . . What the plaintiff must show is "a wrong" to herself; that is, a violation of her own right, and not merely a wrong to someone else, nor conduct "wrongful" because unsocial, but not "a wrong" to anyone. . . . The risk reasonably to be perceived defines the duty to be obeyed, and risk imports relation; it is risk to another or to others within the range of apprehension. This does not mean, of course, that one who launches a destructive force is always relieved of liability, if the force, though known to be destructive, pursues an unexpected path. "It was not necessary that the defendant should have had notice of the particular method in which an accident would occur, if the possibility of an accident was clear to the ordinarily prudent eye." Some acts, such as shooting, are so imminently dangerous to anyone who may come within reach of the missile, however unexpectedly, as to impose a duty of prevision not far from that of an insurer. Even today, and much oftener in earlier stages of the law, one acts sometimes at one's peril. Under this head, it may be, fall certain cases of what is known as transferred intent, an act willfully dangerous to A resulting in injury to B. These cases aside, wrong is defined in terms of the natural or probable, at least when unintentional. The range of reasonable apprehension is at times a question for the court, and at times, if varying inferences are possible, a question for the jury. Here, by concession, there was nothing in the situation to suggest to the most cautious mind that the parcel wrapped in newspaper would spread wreckage through the station. If the guard had thrown it down knowingly and willfully, he would not have threatened the plaintiff's safety, so far as appearances could warn him. His conduct would not have involved, even then, an unreasonable probability of invasion of her bodily security. Liability can be no greater where the act is inadvertent.

One who seeks redress at law does not make out a cause of action by showing without more that there has been damage to his person. If the harm was not willful, he must show that the act as to him had possibilities of danger so many and apparent as to entitle him to be protected against the doing of it though the harm was unintended.

The law of causation, remote or proximate, is thus foreign to the case before us. The question of liability is always anterior to the question of the measure of the consequences that go with liability. If there is no tort to be redressed, there is no occasion to consider what damage might be recovered if there were a finding of a tort. We may assume, without deciding, that negligence, not at large or in the abstract, but in relation to the plaintiff, would entail liability for any and all consequences, however novel or extraordinary. There is room for argument that a distinction is to be drawn according to the diversity of interests invaded

by the act, as where conduct negligent in that it threatens an insignificant invasion of an interest in property results in an unforeseeable invasion of an interest of another order, as, for example, one of bodily security. Perhaps other distinctions may be necessary. We do not go into the question now. The consequences to be followed must first be rooted in a wrong.

The judgment of the Appellate Division for the Plaintiff Palsgraf and that of the Trial Term should be reversed, and the complaint dismissed, with costs in all courts.

Andrews, J. (dissenting). Assisting a passenger to board a train, the defendant's servant negligently knocked a package from his arms. It fell between the platform and the cars. Of its contents the servant knew and could know nothing. A violent explosion followed. The concussion broke some scales standing a considerable distance away. In falling, they injured the plaintiff, an intending passenger.

Upon these facts, may she recover the damages she has suffered in an action brought against the master? The result we shall reach depends upon our theory as to the nature of negligence. Is it a relative concept— the breach of some duty owing to a particular person or to particular persons? Or, where there is an act which unreasonably threatens the safety of others, is the doer liable for all its proximate consequences, even where they result in injury to one who would generally be thought to be outside the radius of danger?

Negligence may be defined roughly as an act or omission which unreasonably does or may affect the rights of others, or which unreasonably fails to protect one's self from the dangers resulting from such acts.

Where there is the unreasonable act, and some right that may be affected there is negligence whether damage does or does not result. That is immaterial.

The proposition is this: Every one owes to the world at large the duty of refraining from those acts that may unreasonably threaten the safety of others. Such an act occurs. Not only is he wronged to whom harm might reasonably be expected to result, but he also who is in fact injured, even if he be outside what would generally be thought the danger zone.

(continues)

But, when injuries do result from our unlawful act, we are liable for the consequences. It does not matter that they are unusual, unexpected, unforeseen, and unforeseeable. But there is one limitation. The damages must be so connected with the negligence that the latter may be said to be the proximate cause of the former.

The proximate cause, involved as it may be with many other causes, must be, at the least, something without which the event would not happen. The court must ask itself whether there was a natural and continuous sequence between cause and effect. Was the one a substantial factor in producing the other?

Was there a direct connection between them, without too many intervening causes?

When a lantern is overturned, the firing of a shed is a fairly direct consequence. Many things contribute to the spread of the conflagration—the force of the wind, the direction and width of streets, the character of intervening structures, other factors. We draw an uncertain and wavering line, but draw it we must as best we can.

The act upon which defendant's liability rests is knocking an apparently harmless package onto the platform. The act was negligent. For its proximate consequences the defendant is liable.

CASE QUESTIONS

1. Was a duty owed to the passenger with the package?
2. Was Helen Palsgraf owed a duty? Explain.
3. How does the dissenting opinion concerning duty differ from the majority opinion?

An example of a failure to act would be when you are walking down the street and see a stranger about to trip and do not try to prevent the accident. In this example, you would have no duty to stop and warn the stranger. Only if the plaintiff and the defendant have a special relationship between them will the defendant's failure to act lead to a cause of action in negligence.

Special Relationships. Just a few of the many special relationships that might create a duty to act are those between an employer and employee, a parent and child, a teacher and student, an innkeeper and guest, a hospital and patient, and a common carrier and passenger (Table 2-2). The law imposes a special relationship between these parties and also a duty to act based upon their relationship. For example, if one student injures another student or is about to hurt another student, their teacher has an obligation to intervene and try to help, even though the teacher was not negligent and did not cause the incident. Likewise, employers may be responsible for workers injured on the job even if the employer did not harm the employee (see Chapters 9 and 13 for more information on workplace injuries). The duty a landowner owes to trespassers and people on the land is discussed in Chapter 8.

Employer/Employee
Parent/Child
Teacher/Student
Innkeeper/Guest
Hospital/Patient
Common Carrier/Passenger

Copyright © 2015 Cengage Learning®.

TABLE 2-2
Special relationships that create a duty to act

There is no obligation to aid or assist others.
Once assistance is started, it must continue.
Some states have laws protecting Good Samaritans from suit.

Copyright © 2015 Cengage Learning®.

TABLE 2-3
Duty rule for good samaritans

Duty Rule for Good Samaritans

There is no duty to come to the assistance of those in need. A **Good Samaritan** is a person who comes to the assistance of another person without being required to act. The **Good Samaritan Doctrine** provides that although a person is not obligated to come to the aid of another, once assistance is attempted, the Good Samaritan has the obligation to do no harm. The rationale for this is that once a person stops to help, others who might have assisted may not stop to help, thinking the injured person is being aided. This doctrine prevents some good-natured people from helping others due to the fear that they will be sued for negligence if the standard of reasonable care is violated. In order to encourage people to help others, some states have enacted laws to protect Good Samaritans from suit. Table 2-3 summarizes the duty rule for Good Samaritans.

good samaritan | A person who comes to the assistance of another person without being required to act.

good samaritan doctrine | Although a person is not obligated to come to the aid of another, once assistance is attempted, the good samaritan has the obligation to do no harm.

Trained versus Untrained Volunteers

A distinction may be drawn between trained and untrained volunteers. Trained people, such as emergency medical technicians (EMTs), who are paid for their services are held to a higher standard; they must exercise reasonable care, and can be sued in negligence for failing to exercise reasonable care. Laws vary as to whether they address the acts of trained paid workers or untrained volunteers. Some examples of state laws are provided in Table 2-4 to show the wide range of different laws.

TABLE 2-4
State laws concerning
volunteers

Alabama	Only trained workers are protected from suit, unless a heart attack is involved.
California	Only people who provide "medical care" are protected. For example, if a person is moved from a scene to protect him because the car might catch fire, and it is not judged as "medical care," the rescuer would be liable.
Minnesota, Vermont	These states have laws that actually *compel* people to help. There is no liability unless there is gross negligence.
Oklahoma	Only untrained workers are protected for controlling bleeding or providing cardiopulmonary resuscitation (CPR).
New York	There is no liability for medical and nonmedical personnel so long as there is no gross negligence and no expectation of compensation. In addition, New York has a new law: If people call for emergency services for drug or alcohol overdoses, no arrests or prosecution will result for personal possession of drugs, paraphernalia, or underage drinking.
Connecticut, New Mexico, Washington	These states of have laws similar to those of New York.

THE CASE OF THE GOOD DEED GONE BAD

The results of this appellate decision from California created fear in the public and potential Good Samaritans, making them think twice before helping others. The determination of the appeal rests on the meaning of just a few words.

Alexandra VAN HORN, Plaintiff and Respondent
v.
Anthony Glen WATSON, Defendant and Appellant
and
Lisa Torti, Defendant and Respondent
v.
Anthony Glen Watson, et al., Defendants and Respondents
Court of Appeal, Second District, Division 3, California

Nos. B188076, B189254
March 21, 2007

The injured plaintiff, Alexandria Van Horn (Plaintiff) now brings this appeal claiming that she is a paraplegic as a result of her friend defendant Lisa Torti (Defendant) pulling her out of a car following a one car accident, rather than from the accident itself. The court below granted defendant summary judgment dismissing her from the case, on the grounds that she acted as a Good Samaritan when aiding her friend, the plaintiff.

The accident happened when defendant Watson, the driver of the car, lost control of his vehicle and crashed into a curb and light post at about 45 miles per hour. The police concluded that it was the speed at which defendant Watson was traveling that had caused the accident.

Plaintiff was in the front passenger seat of defendant Watson's car. When defendant Watson's vehicle crashed, another car which contained plaintiff's friends stopped. The driver and passenger, defendant Torti exited the other vehicle to provide assistance.

Plaintiff sued the driver who caused the accident, defendant Watson, and the Good Samaritan passenger from the other vehicle, defendant Torti. The cause of action against defendant Torti alleged that even though plaintiff was not in need of assistance, and had only sustained injury to her vertebrae, defendant Torti dragged plaintiff out of the vehicle using one arm, pulling plaintiff's arm like a "rag doll," causing permanent damage to her spinal cord. Defendant moved for summary judgment.

Defendant Torti claims she removed plaintiff from the vehicle because she feared the car would catch fire or "blow up." Defendant Torti testified at the deposition that she saw smoke coming from the top of the other vehicle, and also saw liquid coming from the vehicle, these facts were subject to dispute. Defendant Torti alleged that she placed one arm under plaintiff's legs and the other behind plaintiff's back to lift her out of the car.

There is a dispute whether the accident itself caused plaintiff's paraplegia. The trial court, relying exclusively on California's Good Samaritan Law, section 1799.102, concluded that defendant Torti was immune from liability, and granted her motion for summary judgment.

The question presented is whether the trial court correctly applied the law for Good Samaritans, to find that defendant Torti is entitled to summary judgment, or whether it is Civil Code section 1714 which states that people are responsible for their willful and negligent acts, that applies.

Our primary duty when interpreting a statute is to determine and effectuate the Legislature's intent. "When the language of a statute is clear, there is no need for interpretation and we must apply the statute as written." (Lafayette Morehouse, Inc. v. Chronicle Publishing Co. Cal.App.4th at p. 1382, 46 Cal.Rptr.2d 542.)

Good Samaritan Law Section 1799.102 states: "No person who in good faith, and not for compensation, *renders emergency care* at the *scene of an emergency* shall be liable for any civil damages. The scene of an emergency shall not include "emergency departments and other places where medical care is usually offered." The issue is whether section 1799.102 applies to any emergency care rendered at the scene of any emergency, or whether it applies only to emergency medical care rendered at the scene of a medical emergency.

A definitional section defines "emergency" to mean "a situation in which an individual has a need for immediate medical attention." Since section 1799.102 provides immunity for the rendition of "*emergency care at the scene of an emergency*" (italics added), it only applies to emergency medical care rendered at the scene of a medical emergency. Additionally, Health and Safety Code section 1797.5 provides the legislative intent of the act as follows: "It is the intent to promote emergency medical services. People shall be encouraged and trained to assist others at the scene of a medical emergency in cardiopulmonary resuscitation and lifesaving first aid techniques."

We conclude the immunity provided by section 1799.102 applies only to the rendition of emergency medical care at the scene of a medical emergency. Defendant Torti did not provide emergency medical care to plaintiff at the scene of a medical emergency. Even if Torti believed plaintiff had to be immediately removed from the car due to a risk of fire or explosion, this was not a medical risk to plaintiff's health, and was therefore not emergency medical care.

A dispute of facts exists as to whether Torti's removal of plaintiff from the car was negligent, and whether that negligence increased the risk of harm to plaintiff. The judgments in favor of defendant Torti and against plaintiff and Watson are reversed, and the matter is remanded for further proceedings. Costs on appeal to plaintiff and Watson.

(continues)

CASE QUESTIONS

1. What would you have done if placed in the Good Samaritan's position in this case? Explain.
2. Why would defendant Watson join in this appeal? What would Watson gain by it?
3. What do you think was the plaintiff's motive in bringing her original action and this appeal against her friend?

Volunteer Protection Act of 1997 (VPA), Public Law 105-19. In order to protect and encourage volunteers who work for nonprofit organizations, a federal law called the Volunteer Protection Act of 1997 was enacted. This law affords protection to nonprofit organizations when volunteers offer their services without compensation (except for expenses under $500), and exempts them from liability for acts and omissions. An exception to this is acts of willful and reckless misconduct, or gross negligence that causes harm. This federal law pre-empts state laws that are inconsistent with it. In the event that state law provides more generous protection, state law governs.

THE CASE OF DRUNKEN DUTY

In negligence litigation, an injured plaintiff always tries to argue that the defendant's scope of duty extends to the plaintiff, the injured party. Plaintiffs attempt to avoid responsibility for their own injuries by claiming that the defendants breached a duty of care. In the following case, the defendant owner of the bar (Wesco, Inc.), referred to as the "licensee," is accused of furnishing liquor to the minor plaintiff Gregory Colby. Plaintiff Colby argues that his injuries are directly linked to the bar. A careful reading of the liquor law determines how far the defendant's duty extends.

Gregory A. COLBY, Plaintiff-Appellant
v.
Rodney NOAH, Defendant, and Wesco, Inc., Defendant-Appellee
Court of Appeals of Michigan
Docket No. 275154
May 22, 2007

Under the liquor control code of 1998, MCL 436.1101 *et seq.*, also referred to as the dramshop act, it is unlawful for a retail licensee to "directly, individually, or by a clerk, agent, or servant sell, furnish, or give alcoholic liquor to a minor" and to "directly or indirectly,

individually or by a clerk, agent, or servant sell, furnish, or give alcoholic liquor to a person who is visibly intoxicated." MCL 436.1801(2). An individual who is "personally injured by a minor or a visibly intoxicated person by reason of the unlawful selling, giving, or furnishing of alcoholic liquor to the minor or visibly intoxicated person" has a cause of action against the licensee "if the unlawful sale is proven to be a proximate cause of the . . . injury" and the licensee has "caused or contributed to the intoxication of the person or who has caused or contributed to the . . . injury. . . ." MCL 436.1801(3).

The elements of a claim predicated upon an unlawful sale to a visibly intoxicated person are: (1) the plaintiff was injured by the wrongful or tortious conduct of an intoxicated person, (2) the intoxication of that person was the sole or contributing cause of the plaintiff's injuries, and (3) the defendant sold, gave, or furnished to the alleged intoxicated person the alcoholic beverage which caused or contributed to that person's intoxication.

Defendant Rodney Noah purchased a 15-pack of 22-ounce cans of beer from defendant while allegedly visibly intoxicated. He took them home for a party to which plaintiff, a minor, had been invited by another guest. Noah offered the beer to plaintiff, who consumed four full cans and part of a fifth during the next hour to hour and a half. Plaintiff also smoked marijuana. Plaintiff thereafter went outside and dove into Noah's backyard pool and broke his neck.

Plaintiff failed to show that Noah's intoxication proximately caused plaintiff's injuries. To the extent plaintiff seeks to hold defendant liable on an agency theory of liability, his claim must fail. If plaintiff contends that defendant illegally furnished beer to a minor (himself) through Noah as his agent, defendant cannot be held liable because the statute only precludes direct sales to minors. Further, a minor or intoxicated person who becomes intoxicated and injures himself cannot recover damages from the licensee for his own injuries. Thus, where the injured minor seeks to hold the licensee liable for furnishing him alcohol through an intermediary, his claim must fail.

CASE QUESTIONS

1. What was the court's justification for its decision?
2. Suppose defendant Rodney Noah was a minor, and purchased the liquor for himself. If it had been Noah who dived into the pool, would the court's decision have been different?

▌ ELEMENT 2: BREACH OF DUTY

After establishing to whom a duty is owed, the next step is determining if the duty was breached. A **breach of duty** is when a person's actions fall below a certain standard of care. In order to determine this, the standard of reasonable care needs to be defined, to see if the tortfeasor's actions fell below the standard of care.

In tort law, foreseeability is the notion that a specific action, under particular circumstances, would produce an anticipated result. If an injury is foreseeable, then one should take precautions to avoid the behavior that might be expected to cause harm. If a tortfeasor failed to take such precautions, he or she breached the duty of reasonable care. Breach of duty balances the foreseeability of harm against the probability of harm and the magnitude of harm; it is the failure to take reasonable care under the circumstances.

For instance, in the earlier car accident example, Parker did not check his rearview mirror before attempting to pass on a four-lane highway. Is it foreseeable that another vehicle might be passing Parker in the lane he was trying to enter, and that his failure to look behind him could result in a collision? This consequence is clearly foreseeable. Suppose, however, that it is late at night, and that

breach of duty | when a person's actions fall below a standard of care.

the other driver trying to pass Parker did not have headlights on. Thus, Parker could not see the car approaching as he moved into the left lane to pass the truck. In this case, is it reasonably foreseeable that another driver would come up from behind without headlights? No—so the result (the other driver swerving to avoid hitting Parker's car) was not foreseeable under these facts. A slight difference in the circumstances changes the answer.

THE CASE OF THE OBVIOUS HAZARD

Shopkeepers have a duty to warn shoppers of known hidden dangers. The plaintiff in this case stated that the shop owner, Tires Plus, had a duty to make a planting bed safe for walking across. Tires Plus argued it had no duty to make safe something that was never designed for that purpose. This case demonstrates the difference between open and obvious dangers and hidden dangers.

Dandal DAMPIER, Appellant
v.
MORGAN TIRE & AUTO, LLC, etc., Appellee

District Court of Appeal of Florida, Fifth District
No. 5D11–1201
82 So.3d 204
March 16, 2012

Dandal Dampier appeals a final summary judgment entered against him in a trip and fall case. We affirm.

Dampier visited Morgan Tire & Auto, LLC d/b/a Tires Plus ("Tires Plus") on Enterprise Road in Orange City, Florida, to get an oil change and have the tires on his vehicle rotated. While Dampier's vehicle was being serviced, he decided to walk to a McDonald's restaurant down the street. To access a public sidewalk that runs in front of Tires Plus, he walked across a raised landscape planting bed. He successfully negotiated the planting bed on the way to the McDonald's, but on his return, tripped on a stump in the planting bed and fell headlong into the parking lot, resulting in various injuries.

Dampier brought suit against Tires Plus, alleging that the planting bed was part of a "clearly defined walking path," that the company had failed to inspect and maintain in a reasonably safe condition by removing stumps within the walking path, and that it had failed to warn of the dangerous condition created thereby. In its answer, Tires Plus denied that the planting bed was a walking path, denied any negligence, and asserted a number of affirmative defenses.

Tires Plus moved for summary judgment, arguing that it had no duty to warn of the stump in the planting bed because the dangerous condition created thereby was open, obvious and apparent. The company also argued it had no duty to make the planting bed safe for walking, as the bed had not been designed for that purpose.

Depositions submitted by the parties showed that the planting bed is eight or ten feet wide, is bordered by a raised curb, and is mulched and somewhat sparsely filled with bushes. On the far side of the planting bed is a public sidewalk that also runs parallel to the road. The front door of the business opens to the parking lot, but there is no sidewalk linking the front door of the business to the public sidewalk running along the road. Instead, patrons of Tires Plus wishing to access the public sidewalk must walk to one side of the property and out the driveway. The only other alternative is to walk across the parking lot, step over the curb and walk through the mulched planting bed.

This Court reviews de novo the grant of summary judgment in favor of an appellee. *Krol v. City of Orlando*, 778 So.2d 490, 491 (Fla. 5th DCA 2001). "Summary judgment is proper if there is no genuine issue of material fact and if the moving party is entitled to judgment as a matter of law."

Generally, a property owner owes two duties to an invitee: (1) the duty to use reasonable care in maintaining the property in a reasonably safe condition; and (2) the duty to warn of latent or concealed dangers which are or should be known to the owner and which are unknown to the invitee and cannot be discovered through the exercise of due care. *Aaron v. Palatka Mall, L.L.C.*, 908 So.2d 574, 577 (Fla. 5th DCA 2005). The open and obvious nature of a hazard may discharge a landowner's duty to warn, but it does not discharge the landowner's duty to maintain the property in a reasonably safe condition. *See Pittman v. Volusia Cnty.*, 380 So.2d 1192 (Fla. 5th DCA 1980).

Some conditions are so obvious and not inherently dangerous that they can be said, as a matter of law, not to constitute a dangerous condition, and will not give rise to liability due to the failure to maintain the premises in a reasonably safe condition. *See, for example, Schoen v. Gilbert*, 436 So.2d 75 (Fla.1983) (holding difference in floor levels is not inherently dangerous condition, even in dim lighting, so as to constitute failure to use due care for safety of person invited to premises). The rule applied in these circumstances is to absolve the landowner of liability unless the landowner should anticipate or foresee harm from the dangerous condition despite such knowledge or obviousness. *Id.; Etheredge v. Walt Disney World Co.*, 999 So.2d 669, 672 (Fla. 5th DCA 2008); *Aguiar v. Walt Disney World Hospitality*, 920 So.2d 1233, 1234 (Fla. 5th DCA 2006).

Landscaping features are generally found not to constitute a dangerous condition as a matter of law. A number of cases have held that a landowner has no liability for falls which occur when invitees walk on surfaces not designed for walking, such as planting beds. *See City of Melbourne v. Dunn*, 841 So.2d 504 (Fla. 5th DCA 2003)

In *Dunn*, a woman fell when she walked in or along the raised timbers of a large planting bed located near a park exit. She thought the strap of her sandal may have caught on a large nail that had become dislodged from the landscaping timbers. This Court held that the City of Melbourne could not be held liable for her fall because the City had no duty to make the planter safe for walking, as it was not foreseeable that the surface would be used for walking, a function for which it was not designed

The opinion reasoned:

> An owner of land is not required to give an invitee warning of an obvious danger, and is entitled to assume an invitee will perceive something obvious. *Moultrie v. Consolidated Stores International Corp.*, 764 So.2d 637 (Fla. 1st DCA 2000). Some conditions are so open and obvious, so common and innocuous, that they can be held as a matter of law to not constitute a hidden dangerous condition. *Gorin v. City of St. Augustine*, 595 So.2d 1062 (Fla. 5th DCA 1992). In the instant case, the gap between the intersecting planks was a blatant, yawning separation, and Dunn admitted that if she had been looking, she would have seen it. We conclude that anyone walking across this planter "is held to know that this is a hazard to walking." Because Dunn had "ample notice of an open and obvious hazard," she cannot blame the city for her fall.

Furthermore, the city had no duty to make the planter safe for walking, a function for which it was not designed. *Compare, McCain v. Florida Power Corporation*, 593 So.2d 500 (Fla.1992); *Acree v. Hartford South Inc.*, 724 So.2d 183 (Fla. 5th DCA 1999). The city had no reason to suspect that a grown woman would consider the planter an exit path, or use it to perform a sort of tightrope act, instead of proceeding to the parking lot by simply walking around it along the adjacent path.

In this case, Dampier was injured when he walked through a large planting bed to get from a sidewalk outside the premises back to the parking lot of Tires Plus. As in *Dunn*, the planting bed, and the stump within the planting bed, did not constitute a dangerous condition that could give rise to liability on the part of Tires Plus due to the alleged failure to maintain the premises in a reasonably safe condition. Likewise, there was no duty to warn Dampier of the danger of walking in the planting bed, because the planting bed and stump did not constitute a dangerous condition when used as a planting bed and not for walking.
AFFIRMED.

(continues)

CASE QUESTIONS
1. Do you think most people would have behaved as the plaintiff here did? Explain your answer.
2. If Tires Plus knew that the planting bed had become a shortcut, do you think Tires Plus had any duty to make the area safe? Explain your answer.

Standard of Reasonable Care

Reasonable care is a very difficult concept to define in negligence law. It depends upon the particular facts of each problem. Still, tort law has developed an abstract measure of reasonable care—the **reasonable person test (standard)**.

reasonable person test (standard) | A means of determining negligence based on what a reasonable person would have done in the same or similar circumstances.

The Reasonable Person Standard. *The reasonable person* is an imaginary individual who is expected to behave reasonably under a given set of circumstances to avoid harming others. The tortfeasor is alleged to have done something that was unreasonable, or have failed to do something, and that caused the victim's injuries. The tortfeasor's conduct is measured under the reasonable person standard in this fashion: In the same or similar circumstances, would the reasonable person have acted as the tortfeasor behaved? If so, then the tortfeasor did not violate his or her duty of reasonable care. If not, then the tortfeasor breached the duty.

In the previous driving hypothetical involving Parker, would the reasonable person have looked in his or her rearview mirror before entering the left lane to pass a truck on a four-lane highway, when it was reasonably foreseeable that another vehicle might already be occupying that lane while attempting to pass the reasonable person's car? Checking the rearview mirror when changing lanes seems reasonable, and so the reasonable person could be expected to do so under these conditions. Parker did not, however. Therefore, Parker acted unreasonably in this case. He violated his duty of care to the swerving driver because he did not act as the reasonable person would have behaved in the same situation.

The mythical reasonable person may seem too intangible to compare to real-life persons. Nevertheless, American and English courts have relied on the concept in over 200 years of court decisions (although older opinions refer to the *reasonable man*).

Who Decides How the Reasonable Person Would Have Acted.

The trier-of-fact in a negligence lawsuit determines whether the defendant failed to act as the reasonable person would have behaved in a specific case. This is usually a jury, but it could be the judge in a bench trial. In effect, the jurors decide what was reasonable by investigating how they, and others they know, would have behaved. Suddenly, the reasonable person standard becomes clear: it is what the jurors conclude was reasonable under the circumstances. This settles the question of whether the defendant breached the duty of reasonable care to the plaintiff.

At first glance, the reasonable person standard seems arbitrary, as each juror determines the defendant's negligence based upon his or her own personal, gut-level response. However, sociologists would remind us that this is precisely how each individual views the world—through the eyes of his or her own experience. The judicial system safeguards against one capricious definition of reasonableness by offering the option of a jury trial, which forces several persons to agree upon an appropriate measure of due care. Although a judge in a bench trial is the sole trier-of-fact, the judge's legal training is presumed to compensate for any bias in defining reasonableness.

Cost-Benefit Analysis of Behavior.

Although a person might not always be conscious of it, a certain mental process occurs when deciding what to do in a particular situation. Generally, four factors are involved: (1) foreseeability of harm, (2) foreseeability of serious injury, (3) amount of effort needed to prevent the injury, and (4) the social value or benefit of the behavior (Table 2-5). The reasonable person weighs these factors in determining how to behave in any given situation. Generally, if there is a good chance of serious injury, and not much effort is needed to prevent it, the reasonable person would take the necessary steps to prevent the harm. However, where there is a social benefit to society in the behavior, a reasonable person might be more willing to take some risk, even though injury might occur.

For example, consider the situation where students are joking around before a class starts, and one student decides to throw a ball made of crunched-up paper at another student. There is minimal chance of injury, little effort is needed to

1. Foreseeability of harm
2. Foreseeability of serious injury
3. Effort needed to prevent serious harm
4. Benefit to society of the behavior

TABLE 2-5
Factors in breach-of-duty evaluation process

prevent injury, and there is no social value to the act. Most likely, the student might think about throwing the paper ball and continue with the act. However, if the student was thinking about throwing a hard-covered textbook at another student, it is foreseeable that the other student would be injured, it would take some effort not to injure the other student, and there is no social value in this act. Thus, the reasonable person would not throw the textbook.

So, if there is a high chance of serious injury, the reasonable person would make every effort to prevent the harm, unless there is a very large benefit to society with the act. On the other hand, if there is little chance of injury, and it would take a lot of effort to prevent the injury, most likely the reasonable person would not try to prevent the injury. This line of analysis was established in a court decision by Judge Learned Hand in *United States v. Carroll Towing Co.*, 159 F.2d 169 (1947).

Matching Skills and Abilities. The reasonable person is supposed to resemble the defendant as closely as possible in terms of special abilities. This enables the trier-of-fact to assess reasonableness more precisely in a specific case.

Professional Community Standard of Care

professional community standard of care | The standard of reasonable care used in negligence cases involving defendants with special skills and knowledge.

The **professional community standard of care** is the standard of reasonable care used in negligence cases involving defendants with special skills and knowledge and is based on the custom and practice among professionals working in the defendant's community. If the defendant, for example, was a teacher and was alleged to have negligently supervised students, the reasonable person used to evaluate the teacher's actions would possess the same training and knowledge as teachers employed in the defendant's geographical area. So, for instance, in a small town with few resources, where teachers' salaries are lower than in other areas of the country, the established basic training for a teacher might be a bachelor's degree. Teachers might not have access to training in the latest theories of education. In contrast, in a wealthier community, obtaining a master's degree and frequently attending educational conferences might be considered the professional community's standard of care. This measure is determined through expert testimony from members of the defendant's **profession.**

profession | An occupation that requires specialized advanced education, training, and knowledge. The skill involved is mostly intellectual rather than manual.

national standard | A standard applied throughout the nation.

National Standard of Care. The standard for experts is now a **national standard** in most jurisdictions. This means that a pediatrician's actions in one town, for example, are measured against the standard of care pediatricians would apply throughout the country, rather than in a particular area. This standard requires professionals to obtain the same level of knowledge and skill no matter where they have their practice.

Children

The behavior of children is based upon a child of the same age, intelligence, and experience. For example, whereas a 12-year-old would be fully aware that it is dangerous to play with a gun or matches, a 4-year-old might not totally comprehend that playing with these items can cause serious and permanent injury. Depending on the jurisdiction, a child under a certain age (usually 5) is not capable of negligence. Additionally, if a child is engaging in certain "adult" activities, such as driving a car, the child may be held to the standards used for an adult (*Sobczak v. Vorholt*, 640 SE 2d 805—NC: Court of Appeals, 2007).

Emergencies

With cases involving emergencies, a person is held to act as the reasonable person would have acted under the same emergency situation, so long as the person is not the one that caused the emergency. This standard provides a bit of leeway, as a person acting under pressure during an emergency might not act as soundly as someone who has had a chance to think about what should be done.

Disabilities

The defendant's limitations are also important in shaping the reasonable person standard. For instance, if the defendant is physically disabled, then the reasonable person used to evaluate his or her actions would likewise share identical disabilities. One could hardly decide how a blind defendant should have behaved by comparison with a reasonable person who has normal vision. This forces the trier-of-fact to empathize with the defendant's situation to understand more clearly how the defendant acted. In effect, the jury must conceptualize how the reasonable person would have behaved if he or she had the same impairment, such as being in a wheelchair or having a hearing disability. The result of this should be a more accurate definition of reasonableness that best fits the defendant and the circumstances of the case. The result, ideally, is a just and equitable outcome in the litigation.

Mental Illness

Generally, people who are mentally ill or insane are held to the reasonable person standard, an objective standard, even if they cannot appreciate the danger of their actions. This is based on the premise that accidents due to mental illness are considered foreseeable (*Breunig v. American Family Insurance Co.*, Sup. Ct. of Wisc., 45 Wisc.2d 536, 173 N.W.2d 619 [1970]). The public policy considerations for holding the mentally ill liable for their actions are threefold: (1) to illustrate that if two innocent people are hurt, the one who caused the harm should be responsible; (2) to encourage people with close relationships with individuals with mental illness to help control them; and (3) to prevent the filing of false claims of mental illness to escape liability.

Table 2-6 summarizes the reasonable person standard.

TABLE 2-6

Reasonable person
standard

1. Ask: Would the reasonable person have acted as the defendant did, under the same or similar circumstances?
2. Match the skills or abilities of the reasonable person to those of the defendant (e.g., plumber, rodeo rider) if these abilities were involved in the alleged negligent actions (community or national standard).
3. The trier-of-fact decides how the reasonable person would have acted in a particular situation.

Professional Malpractice

A professional's negligent failure to observe the appropriate standard of care in providing services to a client or patient, or misconduct while engaging in the practice of a profession, is considered malpractice. Failure to exercise the degree of care and skill reasonably required of like professionals in similar circumstances, if that failure causes damage or injury, is malpractice. Originally, the precise degree of skill used to judge a professional's actions was the care and skill of other professionals practicing in the same community. Many jurisdictions expanded this to include the same community *or* a similar locality.

Now, many jurisdictions have taken this a step further and hold specialists to a national standard, without regard to their location. Some jurisdictions are applying the national standard to general practitioners as well. Professional malpractice cases have been brought against doctors, lawyers, accountants, travel agents, and even priests, depending on the jurisdiction. Malpractice is covered in greater detail in Chapter 3.

MCDONALD'S COFFEE, A BURNING ISSUE

In Albuquerque, New Mexico, in August 1994, a jury awarded Stella Liebeck $2.7 million in punitive damages and $200,000 in compensatory damages (to be reduced for the plaintiff's being 20 percent at fault) against McDonald's Corporation. Liebeck was riding as a passenger in her grandson's car when she bought a cup of coffee at McDonald's. She tried to hold the cup between her knees when she removed the lid, but the cup tipped over and caused third-degree burns. The ultimate award was reduced substantially below the verdict. In 2011, an HBO documentary entitled *Hot Coffee* by Susan Saladoff was released, purporting to reveal the "truth" about this case.

Stella Liebeck, Plaintiff

v.

McDonald's Restaurants, P.T.S., Inc., Defendant

Bernalillo County, N.M. Dist. Ct
No. D-202 CV-93-02419, 1995 WL 360309
August 18, 1994

This case caused a sensation when the jury award was first reported, and continues to receive attention. Few people were privy to all the facts. Most people were aware that a woman was burnt while drinking coffee from McDonald's, but few could understand why the woman was suing McDonald's if it was she who spilled the coffee. More puzzling was why a jury would award almost $3 million in punitive damages against McDonald's when the plaintiff was either careless enough or foolish enough to be drinking hot coffee in a car. Plaintiff ultimately was awarded $160,000 in compensatory damages, and $460,000 in punitive damages by the trial judge. However the parties settled the matter privately, before their appeal was heard.

The details put a different slant on the case than the media initially revealed. As a company policy, McDonald's sold coffee at between 180 and 190 degrees Fahrenheit. It takes two to seven seconds for coffee at this temperature to cause third-degree burns, which require skin grafts and debridement. The burns can leave a person in pain and disabled for many months or years, and can result in permanent and disfiguring injuries. Liebeck ended up in the hospital for a week and was disabled for more than two years.

During trial, McDonald's acknowledged having been aware of the risk of serious burn injuries from its coffee for over 10 years. In fact, more than 700 people reported being burnt by McDonald's steaming coffee prior to Liebeck's incident. Witnesses who appeared for McDonald's admitted that consumers were unaware of the risk of serious burns from the coffee and that customers were never warned. Most incredible, witnesses for McDonald's stated that the company had no plans to reduce the temperature of the coffee sold, despite the fact that the coffee was "not fit for consumption" when sold because it could cause scalding burns.

CASE QUESTIONS

1. Considering the case from the perspective of McDonald's, are there any possible reasons for selling such hot coffee?
2. Balancing the need of McDonald's to sell hot coffee versus the possible risk of serious injury posed, could there be any reason that McDonald's did not have a plan to reduce the coffee's temperature in the future, despite the prior incidents?

▌ ELEMENT 3: CAUSATION OF INJURY

The third element in proving a negligence case is causation. Even if the defendant breaches his or her duty of care owed to the plaintiff, the defendant will not be legally negligent, nor liable for the plaintiff's injuries, unless the defendant's actions proximately caused the harm. To have causation, both *cause-in-fact* and *proximate cause* must be present.

Cause-in-Fact

Causation is a critical component of negligence. To be liable, the tortfeasor must have caused the victim's injuries. *Causation of injury* relates to the tortfeasor's actions that result in harm to the injured party. Courts frequently refer to this as **cause-in-fact,** meaning that, in negligence litigation, the defendant's misconduct produced the plaintiff's injuries.

cause-in-fact | The cause of injury in negligence cases. If the tortfeasor's actions resulted in the victim's injuries, then the tortfeasor was the cause-in-fact of the victim's harm.

The defendant's acts must be the *actual* and *factual* cause of the plaintiff's injuries. The formula is straightforward: "but for" the tortfeasor's (defendant's) actions, the victim (plaintiff) would not have been harmed. The tortfeasor's behavior is usually the immediate, direct, and dominant cause of the victim's injuries. For example, if Samantha spills a beverage on a stairway and does not clean it up, and Daniel slips on the slick spot and falls down the stairs, Samantha has caused Daniel's injuries. The causation is direct: but for Samantha's failure to clean the drink spill on the stairs, Daniel would not have slipped and fallen.

Consider another illustration. Suppose an automobile mechanic changes the tires on Zach's car but neglects to tighten the lug nuts properly. While the vehicle is moving, the left rear tire comes loose and flies off. The car skids out of control and crashes into a telephone pole, hurting Zach. Again, there is causation: but for the mechanic's failure to tighten the nuts sufficiently, the tire would not have come off and Zach would not have collided with the pole.

Sometimes several forces combine to produce injuries. For example, in the loose tire example, suppose the tire had not come completely off the automobile but was wobbling loosely. However, as Zach was driving, he encountered broken glass on the highway, which punctured his left rear tire. Because of the flat tire and the looseness of all the tires, Zach lost control of the car and crashed. Here, two factors resulted in Zach's injuries: the glass that ruptured his tire and the loose nuts that lessened his control of the vehicle.

Substantial Factor Analysis

Substantial factor analysis states that the tortfeasor is liable for injuries to the victim when the tortfeasor's misconduct was a *substantial factor* in producing the harm. In the preceding tire illustration, the broken glass flattened Zach's tire and made the car difficult to handle. However, had the lug nuts not also been loose, the tires would not have been wobbling. Zach probably would have been able to control the vehicle better and might not have crashed at all. The mechanic's failure to tighten the nuts was a substantial factor in Zach's losing control and colliding with the pole. Thus, the mechanic would be liable, even though the broken glass and punctured tire also influenced the accident.

Substantial factor analysis | A test for indirect causation in negligence cases. The tortfeasor is liable for injuries to the victim when the tortfeasor's conduct was a substantial factor in producing the harm.

A classic substantial factor analysis case is *Summers v. Tice, 33* Cal. 2d 80, 199 P.2d 1 (1948). In this case, the plaintiff was hunting quail with two defendants. When the birds were flushed out, the defendants aimed and fired their shotguns in the plaintiff's direction, striking the plaintiff and causing severe physical injuries. It was unclear which defendant's shot hit the plaintiff, because both defendants used the same gauge of shotgun and size of shot. The California Supreme Court applied the substantial factor test in determining causation and liability. Although it could not be conclusively established which defendant's weapon caused the plaintiff's injuries, either defendant's action was sufficient to produce the resulting harm. Quoting a Mississippi Supreme Court case, Justice Carter stated: "We think that . . . each is liable for the resulting injury . . . , although no one can say definitely who actually shot [the plaintiff]. To hold otherwise would be to exonerate both from liability, although each was negligent, and the injury resulted from such negligence."

Joint and Several Liability

The case of *Summers v. Tice* illustrates a fact pattern in which multiple forces combine to produce harm. When two or more defendants act together to produce the plaintiff's injury, the courts consider them to have *acted in concert*. All defendants are held liable for their combined conduct in such cases. This is called **joint and several liability,** another form of causation, in which multiple tortfeasors are each held individually accountable to the victim for the combined negligent behavior of all the tortfeasors. (The entire *Summers v. Tice* case can be found online in the CourseMate companion to this text: http://www.cengage brain.com.)

For instance, suppose that a construction firm contracts with an engineer, a concrete worker, and a drywall specialist, and all work together to build a parking garage that later collapses. All of the laborers who acted together in the operation are said to have functioned in concert. Their collective conduct produced harm to the people and vehicles in the garage at the time of the collapse. Thus, each individual would be personally liable for the injuries and damages caused. In other words, all of the personnel would be jointly and severally liable.

Multiple tortfeasors may injure a person by acting in sequence, rather than simultaneously as in the medical malpractice example. The sequence of combined events produces the harmful results. For example, assume that a shipping company does not refrigerate a shipment of perishable food. As a result, the items spoil in transit. The shipment arrives at a supermarket, where workers fail to notice the spoiled condition of the products and stock them on the shelves. Jerome's roommate buys some of the goods but does not check them for freshness, despite obvious odors and discoloration. After his roommate cooks dinner, Jerome eats the bad food and becomes seriously ill.

Whom does Jerome sue? The negligent behavior of several tortfeasors combined to produce his injury. First, the shipper failed to refrigerate the food, and it became rotten. Next, the grocery store failed to notice the spoiled

joint and several liability | When two or more persons who jointly commit a tort are held liable, both together and individually.

Codefendants or third party defendants [handwritten marginalia]

TABLE 2-7

Causation-of-injury theories

Cause-in-Fact (But-For Causation)	Substantial Factor Analysis	Joint and Several Liability
But for the defendant's actions, the plaintiff's injury would not have happened.	When multiple defendants combine to injure the plaintiff, a single defendant is liable if his or her actions were a substantial factor in producing the harm.	When multiple defendants act together to injure the plaintiff, all defendants are liable for the harm.

food and stocked it. Then Jerome's roommate failed to notice the spoilage and prepared the food for him to eat. All of these tortfeasors—the shipping company, the supermarket, and Jerome's roommate—contributed to a sequence of events that resulted in his illness. Jerome would not have become sick had any of these tortfeasors identified the threat (spoiled food) and taken reasonable precautions to avoid injuring customers. But for the concerted conduct of these tortfeasors, Jerome would not have been hurt, thus establishing **but-for causation**. Therefore, they are all jointly and severally liable to him for the harm caused.

but-for causation | But for the defendant's acts, the plaintiff's injury would not have happened.

Table 2-7 outlines the causation-of-injury theories.

SHARE AND SHARE ALIKE?

Here, parents who are fully aware of their son's past criminal history and violent conduct toward women feel no obligation or duty to warn his new girlfriend of his conduct. Are they obligated to warn?

Catryn Denise BRIDGES, Plaintiff

v.

Harvey S. PARRISH and Barbara B. Parrish, Defendants

Court of Appeals of North Carolina

No. COA12–181

2012 WL 3568961

August 21, 2012

Plaintiff appeals the order granting defendants Harvey and Barbara Parrish's motion to dismiss. Plaintiff argues that she stated a negligence claim upon which relief could be granted. We affirm the trial court's order granting defendants' motion to dismiss.

Plaintiff made the following allegations in her complaint. Lyle Bernie Parrish ("Bernie"), defendants' son, was 52 years old at the time of the incident that gave rise to plaintiff's cause of action. He lived in a building that was owned, maintained, and controlled by defendants. Bernie has been charged with a wide array of crimes throughout his adult life, including numerous drug and weapon charges. Bernie also exhibited a pattern of violent behavior toward women. Specifically, plaintiff contends Bernie hurt former wives and girlfriends. Defendants were aware of Bernie's criminal history and violent conduct toward women.

Plaintiff and Bernie began a romantic relationship shortly after they met in April 2010. Plaintiff met defendants multiple times, and defendants were aware of plaintiff's relationship with their son. Defendants did not inform plaintiff of their son's past violent behavior.

Plaintiff claims that beginning in the year 2000, defendants took it upon themselves to prevent Bernie from continuing any unlawful conduct by providing him with lodging, financial assistance, guidance, and advice. However, Bernie was charged in 2007 with first degree kidnapping, assault with a deadly weapon with intent to kill or inflict serious injury, and possession of a firearm by a felon. Defendants were aware of these charges and did not reveal them to plaintiff.

Plaintiff ended her relationship with Bernie in early November 2010 after Bernie engaged in "controlling, accusatory, and risky" behavior. Plaintiff contends Barbara assured her that Bernie was not a threat. At that time, neither defendant informed plaintiff of their son's violent history.

In mid-January 2011, plaintiff claims she agreed to see Bernie again "from time to time." On or about March 7, 2011, Bernie called plaintiff and accused her of seeing other men. On March 8, 2011, Bernie drove defendants' red pickup truck to the office building where plaintiff worked. He shot plaintiff in the abdomen with a .38 caliber handgun, which was registered to Harvey, and was possessed and used by both defendants. Plaintiff was seriously injured as a result of the shooting.

Plaintiff asserts three theories by which defendants owed her a legal duty: (1) defendants engaged in an active course of conduct that created a foreseeable risk of harm to plaintiff; (2) defendants negligently failed to secure their firearms from Bernie; and (3) defendants negligently entrusted Bernie with the handgun and truck.

In order for a claim of negligence to survive a motion to dismiss, the plaintiff must allege all of the following elements in the complaint: "(1)[a] legal duty; (2) breach of that duty; (3) actual and proximate causation; and (4) injury." *Mabrey v. Smith,* 144 N.C.App. 119, 122, 548 S.E.2d 183, 186 (2001). A claim of negligence necessarily fails if there is no legal duty owed to the plaintiff by the defendant. If no duty exists, there logically can be neither breach of duty nor liability.

Duty is defined as an "obligation, recognized by the law, requiring the person to conform to a certain standard of conduct, for the protection of others against unreasonable risks." *Prosser and Keeton on The Law of Torts* § 30, at 164–65 (5th ed.1984). Here, plaintiff contends that defendants owed her a legal duty because the harm she suffered was a foreseeable result of actions undertaken by defendants. Specifically plaintiff alleges that defendants owed her a legal duty based on their: (1) active course of conduct; (2) negligent storage of their guns; and (3) negligent entrustment. Therefore, the issue becomes whether, taking plaintiff's allegations as true, she established a legal duty sufficient to plead a negligence claim upon which relief can be granted.

First, plaintiff argues that defendants owed her a duty because they engaged in an active course of conduct that created a risk of harm to plaintiff. Specifically, plaintiff alleges that by providing Bernie with assistance and shelter, downplaying his behavior, and failing to secure their guns, defendants engaged in an active course of conduct that resulted in plaintiff's harm. We disagree.

Generally, the law imposes upon every person who enters upon an active course of conduct the positive duty to exercise ordinary care to protect others from harm, and calls a violation of that duty negligence. The duty of ordinary care is no more than a duty to act reasonably. The duty does not require perfect prescience, but instead extends only to causes of injury that were reasonably foreseeable. Therefore, there is no legal duty to protect against the results of one's conduct that are "only remotely and slightly probable."

Here, plaintiff is not suing Bernie, the person who shot her, but defendants, based on the contention that she would not have been shot if they had not engaged in an active course of conduct by providing assistance to Bernie, "attempt[ing] to downplay [Bernie's] behavior," telling plaintiff he posed no threat, and failing to take steps to secure their firearms. However, there is no allegation in the complaint, treated as true, that establishes "facts supporting any nexus of foreseeability between defendant [s'] [conduct] and plaintiff's subsequent injury."

(continues)

Plaintiff fails to establish how her harm was the reasonably foreseeable result of defendants' conduct of assisting Bernie, downplaying his behavior, or saying that he posed no threat. The complaint does not allege that any of Bernie's violent behavior was "in any way associated," with defendants' conduct in the past. Furthermore, the complaint does not indicate that defendants were "on notice," or in any way aware that their conduct would cause Bernie to act violently. Therefore, we cannot hold that defendants had the duty to guard against such an unforeseeable result of their actions. Because the injury was not foreseeable, we find no duty imposed by defendants' active course of conduct.

Plaintiff next argues that defendants had a duty to secure their firearms from their son. We decline to recognize such a duty based on the facts of this case. Other jurisdictions have recognized a duty to secure firearms under general negligence principles, while persuasive, they are not controlling. Our Courts have not recognized a duty to secure firearms under common law principles.

Finally, plaintiff argues that in the alternative to negligent storage of firearms, defendants' duty is based on negligent entrustment of their handgun and truck to Bernie. We are not persuaded. Almost all negligent entrustment cases in North Carolina involve automobiles, and the cause of action generally arises when "the owner of an automobile 'entrusts its operation to a person whom he knows, or by the exercise of due care should have known, to be an incompetent or reckless driver' who is 'likely to cause injury to others in its use.'" The basis for the defendant's liability is not imputed negligence, but the independent and wrongful breach of duty in entrusting his automobile to one who he knows or should know is likely to cause injury.

Entrustment, for the purposes of establishing a claim under this doctrine, requires consent from the defendant, either express or implied, for the third party to use the instrumentality in question. Although this Court has not had occasion to determine whether a defendant's consent to mere possession of an instrumentality rises to the level of entrustment, we have concluded "where a party did not give another permission *to use* the vehicle in the accident, our Courts do not appear to have applied the doctrine of negligent entrustment in a situation where the vehicle was *operated* without the owner's knowledge or consent."

Here, plaintiff alleges that defendants were aware that Bernie Parrish had possession of their handgun, and . . . failed to take reasonable and/or prudent steps to have said handgun removed from his possession and control. The complaint fails to allege that defendants, expressly or impliedly, entrusted the handgun's "operation" to Bernie at any time. Nor does plaintiff allege that defendants ever gave Bernie "permission to use" the handgun. In fact, plaintiff acknowledges in her brief that "[i]t is not yet known exactly how Bernie obtained the firearm from [d]efendants[.]"

Because plaintiff failed to allege that defendants expressly or impliedly consented to the use of the handgun, their alleged conduct does not rise to the level of "entrustment." Additionally, defendants here could not have reasonably foreseen that Bernie's possession of the gun would cause plaintiff's harm. Therefore, defendants owed no duty under the theory of negligent entrustment of the handgun. Because we conclude plaintiff failed to establish that defendants owed her a duty, the trial court did not err in granting defendants' motion to dismiss. Therefore, we affirm the trial court's order.

CASE QUESTIONS

1. Which of the three theories presented was the plaintiff's strongest argument? Explain.
2. What additional allegations would the plaintiff have needed to state for there to have been a different result in this case?
3. Who would have been the most likely defendant in this civil case? Why do you think this defendant was not included?

Contribution

Contribution is another issue that comes up when multiple defendants are involved in a negligence action. Most jurisdictions permit one tortfeasor to seek contribution from the others. Contribution means that one tortfeasor pays all or part of the liability for a wrong and is then allowed to recover all or part of this amount from the other tortfeasors. Some jurisdictions allow parties to seek contribution only when there was no concert of action, when the wrong was not an intentional one, or when the person seeking contribution was not primarily liable. For example, Marie sues Adam, Bobby, and Cindy and is awarded a judgment for $12,000. Each defendant's share is one-third of $12,000, or $4,000. If Adam pays the entire $12,000 judgment, he can seek contribution of $4,000 from Bobby and $4,000 from Cindy.

contribution | 1. The sharing of payment for a debt (or judgment) among persons who are all liable for the debt. 2. The right of a person who has paid an entire debt (or judgment) to get back a fair share of the payment from another person who is also responsible for the debt.

Indemnity

Sometimes there is an **indemnity** policy of insurance involved in a case, which would change the outcome of a claim. Indemnity insurance specifically provides for reimbursing a party for actual losses or damages sustained. This is in contrast to liability insurance, which provides for payment of a specified sum upon the occurrence of a specific event, regardless of the amount of actual losses or damages.

indemnity | A contract to reimburse another for actual loss suffered.

Courts and Causation

American Jurisprudence 2d, a legal encyclopedia, provides an excellent and accurate summary of causation analysis.

57A AMERICAN JURISPRUDENCE 2D *Negligence* §§ 431, 434, 436, 464, 471, 474-75, 478 (1989)

[§ 431] Cause in fact as an element of proximate cause means that the wrongful act was a substantial factor in bringing about the injury and without which no harm would have been incurred. . . .

[§ 464] In all cases where proximate cause is in issue, the first step is to determine whether the defendant's conduct, in point of fact, was a factor in causing plaintiff's damage. . . . If the inquiry as to cause in fact shows that the defendant's conduct, in point of fact, was not a factor in causing plaintiff's damage, the matter ends there. But if it shows that his conduct was a factor in causing such damage, then the further question is whether his conduct played such a part in causing the damage as makes him the author of such damage and liable therefor in the eyes of the law. . . .

[§ 471] Most jurisdictions have historically followed this so-called "but-for" causation-in-fact test. It has proven to be a fair, easily understood and serviceable test of actual causation in negligence actions. . . . Where the "but for" test is recognized, it is useful for the purpose of determining whether specific conduct actually caused the harmful result in question. It cannot be indiscriminately used as an unqualified measure of the defendant's liability. . . .

[§ 474] The "but-for" test, while it explains the greater number of cases, does not in all instances serve as an adequate test. If two causes concur to bring about an event, and either one of them, operating alone, would have been sufficient to cause the identical result, some other test is needed. . . . The response of many courts to this problem has been to apply the "substantial factor" test, either in addition to or in place of the "but for" test. . . .

[§ 475] The substantial factor test . . . makes the question of proximate or legal cause depend upon the answer to the question, "was defendant's conduct a substantial factor in producing plaintiff's injuries?"

From 57A American Jurisprudence 2D *Negligence*. Reprinted with permission of Thomson Reuters

Causation becomes clearer through an example. The following illustration should lend substance to the analytical formula.

HYPOTHETICAL

Angel runs a beauty salon. Vivica is one of her regular customers. Angel received a shipment of hair-coloring products in unlabeled bottles. Rather than return the shipment, Angel placed the bottles in a storeroom for future use. She applied one bottle to Vivica's hair without care fully checking its contents beforehand. Because of unusually high pH levels in Vivica's hair, the product turned Vivica's hair bright blue. Did Angel cause Vivica's injury?

But for Angel's failure to inspect the bottle's contents prior to treating Vivica's hair, Vivica would not have suffered hair discoloration. Direct causation functions easily and clearly to conclude that Angel caused Vivica's injury.

Suppose instead that Solange, one of Angel's employees, had taken the bottle from the storeroom and applied it to Vivica. Would both Angel and Solange be liable for Vivica's harm and damage? Angel failed to identify the unlabeled bottles before storing them. Solange failed to check the bottle's contents before applying them to Vivica's hair. The unreasonable actions of both Angel and Solange combined to produce the harmful result. Accordingly, Angel and Solange are jointly and severally liable to Vivica.

Suppose instead that the bottles had been mislabeled by the manufacturer. Angel unknowingly stocked the bottles, assuming the labels to be correct. Solange then applied the contents of one bottle to Vivica's hair without observing that the contents were the wrong color and texture (a point that an experienced beautician should reasonably have known). The but-for test does not produce clear results in this case. One cannot say that but for the manufacturer's mislabeling, Vivicia would not have been hurt, because Solange actually misapplied the product to Vivica hair. Neither may one contend that but for Solange's use of the improperly labeled product, Vivica would not have been harmed, because Solange was not responsible for the mislabeling. Substantial factor analysis, however, helps to reach an acceptable answer. Solange's failure to inspect the bottle's contents and determine the error before applying the mixture to Vivica's hair was a substantial factor in producing Vivica's injury. Accordingly, Solange would be liable to Vivica.

Proximate Cause

In order to establish liability for negligence, the tortfeasor must be the legal or proximate cause of injury. However, the tortfeasor is not liable for *all* injuries. When a plaintiff suffers unusual injuries or the tortfeasor has started a chain of events causing injury, at some point the tortfeasor's liability might be cut off and limited to those injuries that were foreseeable.

Foreseeability of Injury

Duty is governed by foreseeability. **Proximate cause**, or *legal cause* as it is sometimes called, exists when the tortfeasor's actions caused a foreseeable injury to the victim. If foreseeability is not present, then no duty is owed. Court opinions often refer to the plaintiff's injuries as the natural and probable consequence of the defendant's misconduct. The key to proximate cause is foreseeable injury. Was the victim's injury the reasonably foreseeable result of what the tortfeasor did? If so, then the tortfeasor's actions proximately caused the plaintiff's harm and a duty is owed. If not, then proximate cause did not exist, and the defendant will not be liable to the plaintiff under negligence theory.

Proximate cause is a subcategory of causation. *Causation* is the chain of events linking the tortfeasor's conduct to the victim's injury. *Proximate cause* is the zone within which the plaintiff's injury was reasonably foreseeable as a consequence of the defendant's behavior. Think of proximate cause as a circle. Actions inside the circle cause foreseeable injuries to victims. Actions outside the circle are beyond the zone of danger. Exhibit 2-1 illustrates this concept.

proximate cause | The "legal cause" of an accident or other injury (which may have several actual causes). The proximate cause of an injury is not necessarily the closest thing in time or space to the injury.

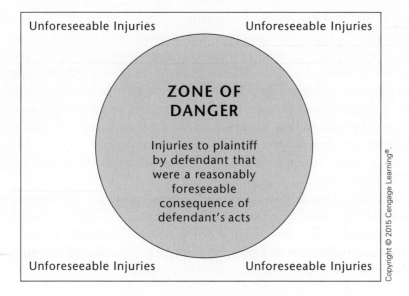

EXHIBIT 2-1
Proximate cause zone of danger

Unforeseeable Injuries   Unforeseeable Injuries

ZONE OF DANGER

Injuries to plaintiff by defendant that were a reasonably foreseeable consequence of defendant's acts

Unforeseeable Injuries   Unforeseeable Injuries

Consider a hypothetical. Patrick is building an additional garage and workshop in his backyard. As he is excavating to install the foundation, he hits an underground natural gas pipeline that services his neighborhood. The pipe ruptures and disrupts gas supplies to the other houses in the area. As a result, those houses with gas heat cannot use their furnaces. It is January, and outside temperatures fall well below freezing at night. With no heat, the water pipes in the neighbors' homes freeze and burst, causing substantial water damage to the structures and furnishings. Did Patrick proximately cause the harm to the neighbors' houses?

It was reasonably foreseeable that an underground utility line might be severed. If this line were carrying a heating source, such as natural gas, it would likewise be reasonably foreseeable that neighboring homes would lose their heat service. Because it was winter, it was also reasonably foreseeable that temperatures could go below freezing and cause water pipes in unheated buildings to freeze and burst. Water damage to structures and furnishings is a natural and inevitable consequence of broken pipes. Clearly, Patrick's actions proximately caused the injury to his neighbors' homes, because the harm was reasonably foreseeable as a result of Patrick's breaking the natural gas pipeline.

Proximate Cause and Scope of Duty Combined

Some legal scholars have included scope of duty as an aspect of proximate cause. This seems logical, as both include the element of foreseeability, but there is a subtle distinction. Scope of duty examines whether it was reasonably foreseeable that the plaintiff would be injured as a result of the defendant's actions. Proximate cause focuses upon whether the injury itself was reasonably foreseeable.

Unforeseeable Harm. It is possible for the tortfeasor to owe a duty of reasonable care to the victim but not proximately cause the injury if the harm was unforeseeable. For instance, suppose that Shannon, who manages a shoe store, gave away free helium balloons to families as a promotional gimmick. One of her customers, Addison, suffered from a rare allergy to helium, but was unaware of this condition. Addison inhaled some helium from the balloon to make himself talk in a high-pitched, funny voice, which is a common side effect of helium inhalation. Instead, Addison went into anaphylactic shock, suffered cardiac arrest, and died. Did Shannon proximately cause Addison's death?

Definitely, Shannon owed a duty of reasonable care to all of her patrons to maintain reasonably safe premises. But Addison's uncommon sensitivity to helium (of which even he was unaware) was not something that Shannon could reasonably have been expected to anticipate. The injury simply was not reasonably foreseeable. The vast majority of the population would not possess this allergy and would suffer no ill effects. Accordingly, Shannon did not proximately cause Addison's injury.

Intervening Causes

An **intervening cause** is something that occurs or goes between the original act of negligence and the injury caused. <u>An intervening cause breaks the chain between a wrongful act or omission and an injury when the act or omission is foreseeable.</u> In these instances, whatever happens to be the intervening cause then becomes the proximate cause of an injury, and is called the **superseding cause** of the negligence. An example of this is when a house is broken into by an angry coworker of the owner, who just wants to scare the family, and the front door lock is damaged in the process. The coworker did not take anything. Later that night, a man seeing the broken lock tries the door, walks in, finds a woman alone in the home, and sexually attacks her. Assuming the irate coworker left a piece of clothes behind and he's identified, although he is responsible for the break-in and any harm caused, he would not be responsible for the later attack, as it was an intervening and superseding cause of harm. The sexual attack was not foreseeable. Also see the case of *Overseas Tankship (UK) Ltd v. Miller Steamship Co Pty* (1966) 2 All E.R. 709, an Australian case about a ship in the Sydney Harbor that is often cited to explain this principle.

> **intervening cause** | Something that goes or occurs between the original act of negligence and the injury caused.

> **superseding cause** | An intervening cause that becomes the proximate cause of an injury.

THE CASE OF THE LOST LIGHTER

A 16-year-old throws a party for his friends at his home while his parents are away. A seemingly common occurrence, students having a party when parents are not around, goes horribly wrong. One friend ends up seriously injured because another friend has lost a cigarette lighter. The 16-year-old thinks he is being really careful—he instructs his friends where to park their cars, he does not let his friends party in the house but only outside, and he does not supply any alcohol. Yet, the injured partygoer claims the 16-year-old host is the cause of his injuries.

Juan OTERO
v.
Tim FAZIO et al.
Superior Court of Massachusetts, Worcester County
No. 200401841
August 22, 2007

This is a civil action brought by the plaintiff to recover damages for personal injuries he suffered while in attendance at a party at the home of defendant Tim Fazio on September 21, 2001. The party occurred while Tim's parents, Kathleen and Michael Fazio, were away and without their knowledge or permission. The plaintiff, a 16-year-old minor at the time who had consumed a quantity of alcohol before arriving at the party, was asleep near a tree that abutted the unpaved driveway of the Fazios' property when he was run over and injured by another person, Jennifer Wright, who also was in attendance at the party.

Tim Fazio let it be known that a party would take place at his parent's home on the evening of September 21, 2001. There were between seven and ten guests present outside the Fazio home. Defendant Tim Fazio did not serve any alcohol to anyone on the night in question, although he was aware that

(continues)

people at the party were drinking alcohol that they brought with them. As guests arrived, he instructed them that no one was allowed inside the home, that vehicles were to be parked on an unpaved driveway adjoining the home, and that guests were to remain outside the home on the Fazios' property. Due to the natural darkness, defendant Tim Fazio also set up some spotlights on a tripod stand to illuminate the backyard. During the party, the plaintiff went over near a tree on the Fazio property to lie down and fell asleep. The injury occurred when Jennifer Wright backed up her motor vehicle in an apparent effort to illuminate an area to find a cigarette lighter lost by her friend and ran over the sleeping plaintiff.

Even if there was negligence on the part of defendant Tim Fazio not to illuminate all areas of the property to which guests had access, the evidence produced by the plaintiff would not support a finding that the defendant's negligence was a causal factor in bringing about the harm suffered by the plaintiff. Massachusetts law provides that a negligent defendant is not liable where "the causal connection between the original wrong of a defendant and the ultimate harm . . . has been broken and . . . something so distinct . . . has thereafter happened as to constitute an intervening efficient, independent and dominant cause." Although causation questions are usually reserved for the fact-finder, this court may properly decide, as a matter of law, that the harm suffered is sufficiently remote from the defendant's negligence that no reasonable jury could find that the injury was a reasonably foreseeable consequence.

The parents, who were not home at the time of the incident, did not give their permission for the party hosted by their son, and had no knowledge of such parties taking place in the past. On such facts, they did not owe a duty of care to the plaintiff.

CASE QUESTIONS

1. Was there any negligence on the part of Tim Fazio?
2. What act broke the causal connection between Tim Fazio's alleged negligence and the ultimate harm that occurred?

HYPOTHETICAL

Colleen operates a laundromat. Geoffrey often washes and dries his clothes there. One day, while Geoffrey was loading his laundry into the washer, the machine unexpectedly began agitating and injured his arms and hands. Did Colleen proximately cause Geoffrey's injuries?

Foreseeability of injury is the starting point of analysis. Was it reasonably foreseeable that the washer Geoffrey used would short-circuit and suddenly begin operating while Geoffrey was loading his clothes? It is not uncommon for electrical mechanical devices to jump to life by themselves unexpectedly. This often occurs when electrical wiring short-circuits after the wires' insulation has frayed. Because people must insert their hands and arms inside the washing machine drum to load clothing, it is reasonably foreseeable that a shorted machine might start itself while a patron's arms are inside. Thus, Geoffrey's injuries were reasonably foreseeable and Colleen proximately caused the harm suffered.

Suppose, however, that Geoffrey's arms and hands were not trapped inside the machine when it suddenly began agitating. Suppose, instead, that the surprise simply frightened Geoffrey, who was unusually susceptible to sudden, loud noises, and he suffered a heart attack as a consequence of the shock. Could Colleen have reasonably anticipated this tragedy? Most courts would reverse the reasonable person standard (applying it to the plaintiff) and say that a reasonable person would not be so easily alarmed (to the point of heart failure) by the sudden start of a washing machine. However, a few courts would employ taking-the-victim analysis and say that even this remote and unexpected injury was foreseeable.

PRACTICAL APPLICATION

Many legal cases, such as the *Routledge* case that follows, involve numerous parties and incidents. Sketching out a complex case with either a picture diagram or a timeline can help keep the facts in perspective. Sometimes designating each party by role, such as passenger, driver, or witness, along with the party's name, serves as a guide that can be referred to while reading a case. For vehicle accidents, the cars can be labeled as car #1, car #2, and so forth to distinguish them.

THE CASE OF THE FALLEN AXLE

This case reads like a law school examination. There are multiple accidents, parties, and issues. Although the facts are very important, the case hinges on a legal principle.

Darrel Routledge, Appellant

v.

Lankford and Hargis, Appellees

Mo. App. S.D., 2012

372 S.W.3d 82, 2012 WL 1453811 (Mo.App. S.D.)

Darrel Routledge ("Appellant") caused a collision to occur on Highway 60 when he attempted a left turn in front of a vehicle driven by John Hoffman. A second accident occurred within minutes when Lankford and Hargis collided. The jury found Appellant eighty percent at fault and Lankford twenty percent at fault. Appellant claims that the negligence of Lankford was, as a matter of law, the intervening cause of the second accident.

(continues)

U.S. Highway 60 is a two-lane highway with shoulders on both sides of the road. The "shoulders" of the roadway near the accident site are very wide. This area of the highway is as straight and flat as a road can be. Ms. Mendenhall, a driver of another vehicle, slowed her vehicle and traveled through the area of the roadway where the collision had just taken place and pulled off on the shoulder in front of the Hoffman vehicle to provide assistance. Ms. Mendenhall observed the second accident take place. . . . Ms. Mendenhall believes that there was debris in the form of a truck axle in [the] roadway which Mr. Lankford's vehicle hit.

Several witnesses managed to drive through the area where the accident occurred. Once Mr. Lankford realized he was coming upon the scene of an accident, he let his foot off the accelerator, but, did not apply his brakes. Mr. Lankford testified he did not cross the centerline. He claims that he scooted to the left to avoid running over any debris and avoid hitting someone if they got out of one of the vehicles. The accidents occurred within a few minutes, at the most, of each other and at dusk.

Appellant's argument rests on the proposition that Lankford's negligence in failing to drive on the right side of the road and failing to keep a careful lookout was the proximate cause of the accident between Lankford and Hargis. In other words, he claims as a matter of law that Lankford's negligence was an independent and superseding cause of the claimed injuries.

Actionable negligence requires a causal connection. The mere fact that injury follows negligence does not necessarily create liability; a plaintiff must show the negligence was the proximate cause of the injury. If the cause operates to produce a particular consequence without the intervention of an independent or superseding cause then proximate cause exists.

The practical test of proximate cause is generally considered to be whether the negligence of the defendant is that cause or act of which the injury was the natural and probable consequence. The test is not whether a reasonably prudent person would have foreseen the particular injury but whether, after the occurrences, the injury appears to be the reasonable and probable consequence of the act or omission by the defendant. The negligence of the defendant need not be the sole cause of the injury, as long as it is one of the efficient causes thereof, without which injury would not have resulted.

When a person negligently makes a left-hand turn onto a busy highway and thereby causes a car to strike him, it is probable that multiple collisions will follow. It is particularly probable that other automobiles will collide with vehicles involved in the initial accident. Clearly, the negligent act of the driver who made a left-hand turn onto the busy highway, was not the sole cause of the injury in the second accident. Rather, it was one of the efficient causes thereof . . . without which the second injury would not have occurred. Since a party is liable if his negligence, combined with the negligence of others, results in injury, the first driver . . . is liable.

Viewed in the light most favorable to Lankford, there was substantial and probative evidence demonstrating that Appellant proximately caused the collision between Lankford and the Hargises. It is clear that the negligence of Appellant was certainly one of the efficient causes of the accident without which injury would not have resulted. Lankford's actions were a foreseeable, natural product of the original negligence. The injuries from the second accident were put in place by Appellant, which "set in motion the chain of circumstances leading to Hargis's injuries."

Lankford's negligence was not an independent, intervening cause of the injuries incurred in the second accident. The comparative fault of the drivers, Appellant and Lankford, was properly submitted to the jury for consideration. The judgment is affirmed.

CASE QUESTIONS

1. How did the appellate court reach its decision in this case?
2. What facts would need to be added or changed concerning the accident scene to change the result of the case?

▌ ELEMENT 4: DAMAGES

The fourth and final element to prove in a negligence case is damages. **Damages** are restitution for the injuries that the plaintiff suffered as a result of the defendant's tortious conduct. As in all torts, damages must be proven for negligence. Courts will not compensate a victim unless some documentable harm has been done.

With certain intentional torts, such as battery, assault, or trespass, no physical harm is required. With a technical trespass, it is sufficient that the tortfeasor engaged in the unauthorized act. Battery can be achieved merely by unconsented-to touching. In negligence law, however, some determinable injury must be proven for the tortfeasor to be held liable to the injured party. Normally, this involves monetary losses as a result of harm to a person or the person's property. For instance, if someone loses muscular control in the legs after an automobile accident caused by a careless driver, then the injured party could demonstrate economic loss as a consequence of the harm. The plaintiff could determine the losses sustained through lost wages, inability to continue an occupation, loss of bodily function, emotional impairment, and related damages.

This vital element of liability is often glossed over by legal scholars and courts. Following such reasoning, damage is often assumed from the fact that the plaintiff sued the defendant for negligence. Of course, it is always a mistake to assume anything in legal study. The plaintiff must prove actual injury to recover in a negligence action. This harm may be physical or emotional or both, but it must exist.

Contrary to popular belief, the largest amounts of damages have been awarded to businesses, rather than individuals bringing lawsuits. The two kinds of cases that most often result in large awards are intellectual property cases and business contract actions.

Compensatory Damages

Compensatory or actual damages are most common in negligence cases. They consist of general and special damages. As the name suggests, **compensatory damages** are designed to compensate the victim for the tortfeasor's negligence. Normally, the plaintiff proves monetary losses, such as out-of-pocket expenses (e.g., medical bills, cost of property repair), lost income, pain and suffering, and loss of property value. The policy behind compensatory damages in tort law is to make the plaintiff whole.

Hedonic Damages.
Damages for the loss of the enjoyment of life, or value of life, are called hedonic damages (*Daubert v. Merrell Dow Pharmaceuticals Inc.*, 113 S.Ct. 2786). Examples of such enjoyment are seeing your children married, enjoying the sunshine, and being able to play with your grandchildren. Some jurisdictions feel that this type of damages is similar to compensation for pain and suffering and do not allow it. The issue of hedonic damages has caused a lot of controversy, as such damages attempt to compensate the victim for something that

damages | Money that a court orders paid to a person who has suffered damage (a loss or harm) by the person who caused the injury.

compensatory damages | Damages awarded for the actual loss suffered by a plaintiff.

is intangible. Not everyone feels that you can place a value on human life, or define enjoyment of life. There is also a concern that the award of this kind of damages will raise the cost of obtaining insurance. There is also a school of thought arguing that some people adapt to their circumstances, and that loss of enjoyment of life is a temporary situation. Most states do not allow a hedonic award in death cases. Just a few states allow hedonic awards for wrongful death actions.

General Damages.

General damages are those compensatory damages that naturally result from the harm caused by the defendant's actions. For example, in a slip-and-fall action, anyone who is injured in this manner might suffer some degree of pain and suffering. Some attorneys multiply the medical bills and lost wages by a number between 1 and 5 that represents the severity of the injuries (with 1 being the least severe and 5 being the most severe). Others attempt to set a figure on what a day of pain is worth multiplied by the projected days of suffering. Others use very complex formulas they have devised that take into consideration a variety of factors, and calculate these figures into the future. There are also computer programs for this purpose.

Special Damages.

Special damages, unlike general damages, are compensatory damages that are specific to a particular plaintiff. In the slip-and-fall example discussed earlier in the chapter, the special damages might include a dry-cleaning bill for a stained suit, lost wages, medical expenses (depending on the severity of the fall), and **loss of consortium**. Depending on the jurisdiction, loss of consortium might also include a parent's loss of love and affection of a child, or a child's loss of his or her parents' love and affection following an incident causing disability or death. One of the higher loss-of-consortium verdicts on record is the case of *Bissell v. Town of Amherst* (Appellate Division, 4th Dept., 2008), in which a wife was ultimately awarded a million dollars following her husband's paralysis and sexual dysfunction. More typical loss-of-consortium awards amount to a very small percent of what the injured spouse is awarded, if anything at all.

Usually special damages must specifically be pleaded and proved. In contrast, general damages need not be pleaded with specificity, as they are presumed by law. Another name used for special damages is *consequential damages*.

loss of consortium | The loss of a spouse's services (i.e., companionship, or ability to have sexual relations).

Economic and Noneconomic Damages.

Compensatory damages are divided into economic and noneconomic losses. Economic losses are the out-of-pocket expenses a plaintiff incurs, such as medical expenses and lost earnings. Conversely, noneconomic losses, such as pain or humiliation, have no particular objective dollar amount that can be placed on them.

Verdict. The trial judge will give the jury instructions in awarding damages in the event a verdict is awarded for the plaintiff. It is often difficult to place an exact dollar figure on pain and suffering. In some states, as a result of recent tort reform, the legislatures have enacted caps on the amount of damages that can be awarded in particular types of cases, such as medical malpractice claims.

Nominal Damages

Nominal damages are not recoverable in actions for ordinary negligence when damages are an element of the cause of action. Nominal damages are awarded in situations in which no actual damages have occurred, or when the amount of injury has not been proven even though a right has been violated in an intentional tort action. The court might then award a dollar to a winning party as a symbolic gesture.

nominal damages | Small or symbolic damages awarded in situations in which no actual damages have occurred, or the amount of injury has not been proven even though a right has been violated in an intentional tort action.

Punitive Damages

Punitive (exemplary) damages, extra money (over and above compensatory damages) given to a plaintiff to punish the defendant and to keep a particularly bad act from happening again, are often awarded for intentional torts such as fraud or intentional infliction of emotional distress but are almost nonexistent in negligence cases, because negligence involves carelessness rather than wanton or intentionally tortious behavior. The punishment component of punitive damages would be excessive in most negligence cases, although exemplary damages are occasionally used in gross negligence cases. **Gross negligence** involves carelessness that exceeds ordinary, reasonable care standards and approaches willful and wanton misconduct. If the negligence is sufficiently excessive, the court might allow punitive damages for the injured party. For instance, if a surgeon was drunk and left a scalpel inside a patient during an operation, this might be considered gross negligence by the medical community. Such misconduct exceeds the degree of reasonable care ordinarily expected of doctors. Physicians simply are expected to avoid harming patients.

punitive (exemplary) damages | Extra money (over and above compensatory damages) given to a plaintiff to punish the defendant and to keep a particularly bad act from happening again.

gross negligence | Recklessly or willfully acting with a deliberate indifference to the effect the action will have on others.

Table 2-8 summarizes the types of damages, and Table 2-9 summarizes proving damages in negligence actions. See Chapter 1 for methods of resolving cases other than by trial.

"Taking the Victim as You Find Him"

Many appellate courts speak of a tortfeasor's **"taking the victim as you find him."** This means that peculiar health conditions are considered to be reasonably foreseeable, as one must always assume that a victim could suffer from an odd affliction, such as in the helium allergy example discussed earlier. Most of these cases, however, involve more deliberate actions (such as striking the head of a person with "a thin skull" or an "eggshell skull" and killing him or her). Such cases involve more intentional torts than negligence (battery, in the eggshell-skull cases),

"taking the victim as you find him" | A theory in negligence cases stating that the victim's injuries were reasonably foreseeable even if the tortfeasor was unaware of the victim's peculiar physical, health, or other preexisting conditions.

TABLE 2-8
Types of damages

Compensatory	Damages awarded for actual loss suffered (e.g., medical bills, property repair, lost income, pain and suffering, and hedonic damages).
General	Compensatory damages that naturally result from the harm. These are expected from this type of harm (e.g., pain and suffering, property repair).
Special or Consequential	Compensatory damages that are specific to a particular plaintiff. (e.g., as a result of a slip and fall, the plaintiff dropped a valuable vase, and also could not work for weeks.)
Nominal	When no actual damages occur; a right has been violated but the amount of injuries has not been proven. (e.g., the court awards $1 symbolically to show that the plaintiff is the victor.)
Punitive or Exemplary	Awarded for intentional torts. Used for wanton or reckless conduct. On occasion used for gross negligence, but not for ordinary negligence.

Copyright © 2015 Cengage Learning®.

TABLE 2-9
Proving damages
in negligence actions

Plaintiff must suffer actual loss as a result of injury.
Loss is usually gauged in monetary terms.
Compensatory damages provide the plaintiff with recovery for losses that resulted from the defendant's actions (out-of-pocket expenses, pain and suffering, lost income, lost property value, loss of bodily function).

Copyright © 2015 Cengage Learning®.

as is typical with the taking-the-victim cases. Still, taking-the-victim analysis surfaces in pure negligence cases as well.

Taking-the-victim cases make almost any physical injury reasonably foreseeable. However, it still must be proved that it was foreseeable that an injury would occur from the defendant's actions.

▌SUMMARY

Negligence is the failure to use reasonable care to avoid injuring others or their property. Reasonable care is dependent upon the particular facts of each case. The key is the reasonableness or unreasonableness of the tortfeasor's actions under the circumstances.

There are four elements of negligence: duty of reasonable care, breach of duty, causation, and damages. The elements are considered sequentially. If any one element is missing, then no negligence occurred.

The duty of reasonable care is the tortfeasor's obligation to act reasonably to avoid injuring others. The tortfeasor does not owe this duty to everyone in the world, however; the injured party must fall within the scope of the tortfeasor's duty. This means that it must have been reasonably foreseeable that the plaintiff would be harmed as a consequence of the defendant's actions. This is called the *reasonable plaintiffs theory*. Only foreseeable plaintiffs (who were actually injured as a result of the defendant's conduct) may recover damages in a negligence lawsuit.

Breach of duty is the second element in proving a negligence case. Reasonable care is defined by the standard of the mythical reasonable person. Would a reasonable person have acted in the same way the defendant did, under the same or similar circumstances? The trier-of-fact decides how the reasonable person would have behaved. The reasonable person standard is adjusted to reflect the defendant's special skills or limitations.

In professional malpractice actions, professionals such as physicians are held to exercise the degree of care and skill reasonably required of like professionals in similar circumstances. Depending on the jurisdiction, the professional will be judged by the skills of professionals in the same community, a similar locality, or (as is the trend) nationally.

The third element in a negligence case is causation. The tortfeasor's actions must cause the victim's injuries. Causation under negligence is usually shown through cause-in-fact. "But for" the defendant's misconduct, the plaintiff would not have been harmed. When multiple tortfeasors are involved in producing the victim's injuries, however, but-for causation does not function well. An alternative causation theory, substantial factor analysis, states that each defendant is liable for the plaintiff's injuries if each defendant was a substantial factor in producing the harm. Joint and several liability holds multiple defendants liable for a plaintiff's injuries when those defendants combine to create the harm.

Proximate cause is an element of causation. Proximate cause declares the line at which injuries are reasonably foreseeable. Inside the boundary are tortfeasors' actions that could reasonably have been anticipated to produce the victim's harm. Outside the perimeter are injuries that were not reasonably foreseeable as a consequence of the tortfeasor's behavior. This circle is sometimes called the *zone of danger*. Some courts speak of proximate cause in terms of foreseeability and scope of duty. Other courts state that tortfeasors take their victims as they find them, which means that the particular injury the plaintiff suffered (usually due to some peculiar physical condition) is always considered foreseeable. Although a person failing to act to stop a harm from happening to another is often not held liable for the inaction, under certain specific relationships, such as employer/employee or teacher/student, a person might have an obligation or special duty to act and may be held liable if he or she does not.

Damages are the fourth and last element that must be proven in every negligence case. The plaintiff must prove that he or she suffered some actual loss as a result of the defendant's actions, whether physical injury, emotional injury, lost wages, or harm to property. This loss is normally quantified in monetary terms as compensatory damages.

In the next chapter, we focus on methods for proving breach of duty in negligence cases. Also covered are the basics concerning legal and medical malpractice claims.

▌KEY TERMS

breach of duty	compensatory damages	defendant
but-for causation	contribution	due (reasonable) care
cause-in-fact	damages	duty

elements	joint and several liability	proximate cause
foreseeability	loss of consortium	punitive (exemplary) damages
foreseeable injury	national standard	reasonable person test (standard)
foreseeable plaintiffs theory	negligence	scope of duty
Good Samaritan	nominal damages	substantial factor analysis
Good Samaritan Doctrine	plaintiff	superseding cause
gross negligence	profession	taking the victim as you
indemnity	professional community standard	find him
intervening cause	of care	unforeseeable plaintiffs

▌PROBLEMS

In the following hypotheticals, determine if negligence exists and if the tortfeasor will be liable to the injured party. Identify the plaintiff(s) and the defendant(s).

1. Carl operates a tanning salon. Meg is one of his customers. The salon uses tanning beds that are equipped with ultraviolet lights above and below the customer. These lights are automatically regulated to control radiation exposure. Meg visited the salon and, while lying upon one of the tanning beds, fell asleep. The automatic regulator became stuck at maximum intensity. Meg was severely burned by the radiation.

2. Dan operates a backhoe for a construction company. Houge hired the company to excavate a swimming pool in his backyard. Dan dug the hole using the backhoe. Unbeknownst to Houge, Dan, or the neighbors, the U.S. Army had used the area during World War II as an undercover training facility for minesweepers, and several unexploded land mines remained buried in the ground. Dan hit one with the backhoe shovel, which detonated the explosive. The shovel was blasted away from the machine, flew several feet into the air, and crashed into Houge's new truck. The impact pushed the truck into the street, causing Leyla, a neighbor who was driving a van down the street, to swerve into Houge's front yard, hitting and felling an oak tree (that had been weakened

by termites), which crashed into Mia Farlow's house next door to Houge's home.

3. Brad is a professional painter. He bought exterior latex paint to apply to Matt's barn. The paint store incorrectly labeled the paint as oil-based paint when in fact it was water-based paint. Brad painted the barn without noticing the difference. After several severe summer thunderstorms, the paint wore off.

4. Sam is a chemical dependency counselor. One of her clients, Trevor, has been addicted to alcohol and tobacco for years. He has suffered severe liver damage. Sam recommended hypnotherapy as a possible cure. Hypnosis is frequently used to treat chemical addiction, and Sam is a state-certified hypnotherapist. After hypnotizing Trevor, she discovered through regression that he had experienced a traumatic event involving alcohol at age seven. She felt certain that this memory was the key to his current addiction. When Sam attempted to bring Trevor out of his hypnotized state, however, she discovered, much to her dismay, that he had fixated and would not return to consciousness. As a result, Trevor remained regressed at seven years of age. Psychiatrists indicate that this condition occurs in only 1 in every 10,000 hypnosis cases.

5. Dwanita plays guitar and sings in a rock-and-roll band at a local tavern, The Whiskey Slick. One of her songs, "Death to Phone Solicitors," contains

certain explicit and graphically descriptive details. Josie, a bartender at the Slick, suffers from paranoid delusions. She found Dwanita's lyrics overwhelmingly absorbing, and she took them literally.

After hearing Dwanita's "Death" song at work one night, Josie returned to her apartment, loaded her revolver, drove downtown to a local telephone solicitation business, entered, and shot six operators.

▌ REVIEW QUESTIONS

1. Provide a broad definition of negligence. What key factors are involved in analyzing negligence problems?

2. List the elements of negligence. How do they fit together? How do you apply each part to a particular problem?

3. What is duty? How does it relate to reasonable care? How do you define the scope of duty?

4. What role does foreseeability play in scope of duty? What is the foreseeable plaintiffs theory? What is reasonable care?

5. Who is the reasonable person, and why is he or she important in negligence analysis? Who defines this standard and how? How does the standard vary in different cases?

6. Define *causation*. What is cause-in-fact? But-for causation?

7. What is substantial factor analysis, and when is it used? How does it differ from joint and several liability? How is it similar?

8. Define *proximate cause*. What role does foreseeability play? What is the zone of danger? How is scope of duty involved? What is taking the victim as you find him, and how is it applied?

9. How are damages determined in negligence cases? What are consequential damages?

10. What effect does the special relationship between a teacher and a student have on a student's claim of negligence?

11. What is the purpose of loss of consortium? Who can bring this action?

▌ HELPFUL WEBSITES

This chapter deals with the field of negligence. To learn more about negligence, the following sites can be accessed:

General Legal Information

www.doi.nebraska.gov
www.findlaw.com

www.law.emory.edu
www.hg.org
www.dri.org
www.law.com
www.martindale.com
www.law.georgetown.edu

STUDENT COMPANION WEBSITE
For additional cases and study materials, please go to www.cengagebrain.com

Chapter 3

Proving Breach of Duty, Medical and Legal Malpractice

THE BIGGEST MISTAKES PARALEGALS MAKE AND HOW TO AVOID THEM

If You Receive This Email in Error . . .

When paralegals at the firm where Ashleigh works send an email with the firm's address, recipients receive this standard disclaimer at the end: "This message contains privileged, confidential and/or proprietary information and if it is received in error, do not use, distribute, copy or disclose to another person. You should destroy this message and notify the sender by reply email." The disclaimer is always attached to emails sent to opposing counsel, judges, and clients.

Ashleigh is always quick with a prank or practical joke and loves to "punk" others. One morning, she placed a pleading on the new law clerk's desk, where she had changed the due date for the responsive pleading to a day that had already passed. Ashleigh waited to see the clerk's alarm before shouting, "Got you!"

(continues)

The clerk was not amused, but being new, he said nothing about the prank to anyone.

The next month, on April Fool's Day, Ashleigh decided to place the following addition to the firm's standard disclaimer on all her emails: "If this message is received by anyone other than the intended recipient, that person must delete and destroy the message immediately. Failure to do so will result in the unintended recipient's immediate extradition to Guantanamo Bay, where they will join people who illegally removed mattress tags." The firm's compliance department was not amused and asked for Ashleigh's immediate dismissal. Ashleigh defended herself by asserting that nobody reads disclaimers.

Lesson Learned: Although some believe that disclaimers are unenforceable, Ashleigh's firm believes they serve a purpose, alerting recipients that they do not have a right to take advantage of privileged and proprietary information received by accident. No matter that the firm's disclaimer is a warning, like a mattress tag, the disclaimer must appear unedited per the firm's policy for all emails sent by employees.

▌ INTRODUCTION

In the previous chapter, the four basic elements of negligence were discussed. In order to bring a negligence claim, proof of breach of duty must be demonstrated. Proof of breach of duty focuses on the second element of a negligence case. There are a variety of ways to show that a party breached the standard of care required under the circumstances. Medical and legal malpractice actions are special forms of negligence cases that clearly demonstrate the deviation from due care and breach of duty and are often seen by paralegals. Malpractice claims have their own special rules and nuances. In this chapter, the following aspects of negligence are discussed:

- ▶ Proof of breach of duty
- ▶ Burden of proof and rejoinder
- ▶ Res ipsa loquitur
- ▶ Violation of a statute
- ▶ Malpractice
- ▶ Medical malpractice
- ▶ Legal malpractice

▌ PROVING BREACH OF DUTY

Proof is an essential aspect of all litigation. A cynic might suggest that what is true or false is irrelevant; rather, what can be proven during a lawsuit is all that matters. Negligence claims are normally proven through the typical evidentiary processes. These include oral testimony, written transcripts of discovery depositions, documentary evidence, and demonstrative evidence (such as photographs or computer simulations).

Affirmative defenses must be alleged or proven by the defendant. Unless alleged and proven, the law will presume that no defense exists. These defenses are covered in Chapter 9.

▌ BURDEN OF PROOF AND REJOINDER

The plaintiff has the **burden of proof** and must prove that the defendant was negligent. This forces the plaintiff to prove by a **preponderance of the evidence** that all negligence elements existed (duty, breach, causation, and damages). The evidence must establish that the defendant's actions were negligent and caused the plaintiff's injuries. Burden of proof is sometimes referred to as the *burden of production.*

Once the plaintiff has made a **prima facie case** (meaning that proof has been established by or beyond a preponderance), the burden shifts to the defendant, who must then counter the plaintiff's evidence with proof of his or her own. This is sometimes called the defendant's **burden of rejoinder,** burden of persuasion, or **rebuttal**. The defendant must refute the plaintiff's case against him or her. Table 3-1 summarizes the burdens of proof and rejoinder.

In some cases, however, the burden of proof is different. What if the plaintiff cannot prove the defendant's negligence? Consider an example. Suppose a patient was unconscious during an operation. Suppose the surgical nurse failed to remove all the sponges from the patient, and later the patient contracted peritonitis during an appendectomy. How could the plaintiff prove that the defendants (nurse, surgeon, and hospital) were negligent in leaving the sponge inside the plaintiff? What witnesses could the plaintiff call to testify, other than the surgical team? The plaintiff was unconscious and unaware of the entire procedure. How could the plaintiff meet the burden of proof in such circumstances? Such unusual cases require a special burden of proof, which is called *res ipsa loquitur*. The case

burden of proof | The party bringing an action has the obligation to go forward with proof of the burden of proof. The defendant's burden of proof to refute the plaintiff's evidence in a lawsuit.

preponderance of the evidence | The greater weight of the evidence. This is a standard of proof generally used in civil lawsuits. It is not as high of a standard as *clear and convincing evidence* or *beyond a reasonable doubt.*

prima facie case | A case that will be won unless the other side comes forward with evidence to disprove it.

burden of rejoinder | The defendant's burden of proof to refute the plaintiff's evidence in a lawsuit.

rebuttal | Evidence that disproves what the other party has offered.

TABLE 3-1
Burden of proof and rejoinder (rebuttal) and res ipsa loquitur

BURDEN OF PROOF AND REJOINDER (REBUTTAL)	RES IPSA LOQUITUR
Plaintiff must generally prove the defendant's negligence beyond a preponderance of the evidence.	"The thing speaks for itself." This doctrine shifts the burden of proof to the defendant, who must disprove the presumed negligence.
	Elements: (1) the defendant has exclusive control over acts or objects that injured the plaintiff; (2) the plaintiff's injury must be one that ordinarily does not occur without negligence; and (3) the defendant is in the best position to prove that he or she was not negligent.

of *Ybarra v. Spangard,* 25 Cal.2d 486, 154 P.2d 687 (Cal.1944), is often cited as an example of res ipsa loquitur; in this case the patient woke up following surgery with injuries that were not present prior to surgery.

RES IPSA LOQUITUR

Res ipsa loquitur is a Latin term meaning "the thing [*res*] speaks [*loquitur*] for itself [*ipsa*]." It is used in negligence cases in which the plaintiff is in a disadvantaged position for proving the defendant's negligence because the evidence is unavailable to the plaintiff, but is or should be available to the defendant. Under the doctrine of res ipsa loquitur, the defendant's negligence is presumed as a result of his or her actions. This shifts the burden of proof to the defendant. In other words, the defendant must disprove his or her negligence from the outset of litigation. The plaintiff's burden of proof is converted into the defendant's burden of rejoinder.

res ipsa loquitur | (Latin) "The thing speaks for itself." A rebuttable presumption (a conclusion that can be changed if contrary evidence is introduced) that a person is negligent.

Elements of Res Ipsa Loquitur

The plaintiff must prove only certain essential facts, such as what injury occurred, what the defendant was doing, and how the defendant's action (or inaction) related to the plaintiff's harm. To use res ipsa loquitur, whatever occurred must not ordinarily occur without someone acting negligently. One of the earliest cases involving res ipsa is the case of *Byrne v. Boadle* (Court of Exchequer, 1863. 2 H. & C. 722, 159 Eng.Rep. 299). In this case, plaintiff Byrne walks past Boadle's shop, a barrel of flour falls out of a window, and Byrne's head is injured. Byrne had no way to really prove what happened. He just knew he did not do anything to cause the accident. The court stated that the mere fact that an accident occurred is evidence of negligence. Normally, barrels of flour do not fall out of windows, unless someone performed some act negligently and caused the fall.

Court opinions often quote the following elements of res ipsa loquitur:

1. The defendant (or his or her employee[s]) must have been in exclusive control of the object or action that produced the plaintiff's injury.
2. The plaintiff's injury must be of a type that ordinarily would not have happened unless negligence were involved.
3. The defendant must be in a better position to prove his or her lack of negligence than the plaintiff is to prove the defendant's negligence.

Certain courts and legal scholars add a fourth element, which states that the plaintiff cannot have contributed to his or her own injuries. This, however, simply states contributory and comparative negligence, which are two similar defenses to negligence.

Defendant's Exclusive Control. For res ipsa loquitur to apply, the events that led to the plaintiff's injury must have been under the defendant's exclusive control. This includes the defendant's employees. For example, suppose the plaintiff was walking through the defendant's warehouse. Suppose the defendant's employees had stacked many crates of merchandise, and the stacks rose 30 feet high. If a top crate fell upon and injured the plaintiff, but nobody except the plaintiff was present in that part of the building, who could the plaintiff point the finger toward as having been negligent? Using res ipsa loquitur, the plaintiff would shift the burden of proof to the defendant (warehouse owner) to show that the crates had been safely stowed. Because the crates were under the defendant's exclusive control, and one crate fell and hurt the plaintiff, the first element of res ipsa loquitur would be satisfied.

Presumption of Negligence. Res ipsa loquitur insists that the plaintiff's injury be one that normally would not have happened unless negligence were involved. Consider the preceding illustration. Crates usually do not fall over in warehouses unless they are improperly stacked. Negligence may be presumed in this case because the box fell. This would not normally occur if ordinary, reasonable care were used to store the crates. Because the box did fall on the plaintiff, then the defendant must not have exercised reasonable care in stacking the crates. At least the court will make this presumption and allow the defendant to refute it by proving that reasonable care was used when storing the boxes. See also the Chapter 4 discussion of negligence per se, as this is another method of proving breach of duty.

THE CASE OF THE FALLING MERCHANDISE

When all else fails and you cannot explain what happened, it is time to do some further investigation of a negligence case. Mistakenly believing that you can just say, "Res ipsa loquitur" to magically prove your case is not a solution.

Quiano LACY, et al.,
Plaintiffs-Appellants
v.
WAL-MART STORES, INC.,
Defendant-Appellee
Court of Appeals of Ohio, Seventh District,
Belmont County
2012 WL 1307075 (Ohio App. 7 Dist.)
March 27, 2012

Lacy filed a complaint against Wal-Mart alleging that while shopping in the electronics department, he was struck in the head and neck by negligently secured and positioned merchandise located six to eight feet off the ground. He asserted that Wal-Mart negligently failed to exercise its duty of reasonable care to inspect and maintain its merchandise in a reasonably safe condition, and that he sustained injuries as a direct and proximate result of this negligence. Lacy

(continues)

also set forth loss of consortium claims for his wife, Satina Lacy, and his son, Quamari Lacy.

During Lacy's deposition, he testified that he was bent down to look at a printer-scanner when he heard a sound like something breaking loose. He looked up, and a monitor fell and hit him in the head. The shelf broke loose, causing the monitor to fall. However, when asked if he knew if the shelf itself broke so that it was no longer usable or it came undone from the poles in the back that held it up, Lacy responded that he did not look. He then said that all he knew was that he heard a sound, he looked up, and the monitor came down. He also said, that he had not previously noticed anything that would lead him to believe there was a dangerous condition. He also did not know if Wal-Mart knew of any danger. Lacy confirmed that he did not know why the monitor fell. He stated that his wife and child were not tall enough to touch the monitor. As far as he was aware, nobody bumped the shelf prior to the box falling.

Wal-Mart filed a motion for summary judgment, arguing that there was no evidence of an unreasonably dangerous condition. Lacy responded, asserting that the doctrine of res ipsa loquitur applied; because there was evidence that the premises were not in a reasonably safe condition, and that Wal-Mart had knowledge or notice of the condition. In support, Lacy attached the deposition of Wal-Mart assistant manager Joshua Amos, who was familiar with the incident.

Amos explained that every associate at Wal-Mart is trained to do safety inspections of the store and if they see anything wrong while working, they are supposed to fix it. He testified if the shelves were empty, a person could not stick their hand through the shelf to the next aisle because there is pegboard that separates every aisle. Amos did not recall if there was any merchandise on the floor. Amos did not recall that the shelf was broken. He said, when shelving breaks in the store, it is replaced, and he was not aware of any shelf being replaced that day. Amos further testified that he watched the surveillance video of the incident: "What I saw in the video was Mr. Lacy knelt down in front of a shelf. It appears an object starts to fall and his wife, or whoever it is at the time, stops that object from falling and he stands up and looks around, and that is all I seen of the video." Amos confirmed that the merchandise fell from the top shelf, and he agreed that it did not look as if Lacy caused it to fall.

On August 30, 2011, the trial court found that insufficient evidence existed in the record to support an inference that Wal-Mart, by its action or failure to act, proximately caused the monitor to fall on Lacy. The trial court noted that Lacy testified that he had no idea how the monitor fell, no evidence was submitted to show what caused the incident to occur; although there was testimony about a video of the incident, the video was not submitted into evidence, nor were pictures of the scene of the accident. The trial court also found that the evidence was insufficient to establish that Wal-Mart had actual or constructive knowledge of an unreasonably dangerous condition prior to the incident and failed to take action to prevent it.

The evidence demonstrates that the monitor fell from the shelf, the question remains as to the exact reason it fell. And rather than submitting additional evidence to satisfy its burden under Civ.R. 56(E), Lacy chose to argue that res ipsa loquitur applied, which the trial court found did not apply because Lacy did not produce sufficient evidence to establish that Wal-Mart had exclusive control over the monitor that struck him. Further, the court found the evidence was insufficient for it to conclude that the injury occurred under such circumstances that it would not have occurred if Wal-Mart exercised ordinary care. Finally, the trial court refused to consider Lacy's argument regarding the pegboard being missing from the top shelf, because Lacy submitted no supporting evidence.

For Lacy to sustain a claim of negligence he must show: a duty owed by the defendant to the plaintiff, a breach of that duty, injury or damages, and the existence of proximate cause between the breach and the injury or damages. Lacy was on Wal-Mart's premises as a business invitee for a purpose, which is beneficial to the owner. An owner or occupier of a business owes its invitees a duty of ordinary care in maintaining the premises in a "reasonably safe condition" and has the duty to warn its invitees of latent or hidden dangers.

Lacy argues that Amos testified that the pegboard was a safety precaution to prevent customers from knocking down merchandise. Lacy is misconstruing Amos's testimony. Amos's testimony simply relates the presence of the pegboard, not its purpose. Beyond Lacy's unsupported allegation of the absence of pegboard causing the dangerous condition, the record lacks any evidence regarding what caused the incident. Lacy's arguments regarding the unreasonably dangerous condition are merely speculation, which is not sufficient to defeat summary judgment. See *Hansen v. Wal-Mart Stores, Inc.,* 4th Dist. No. 07CA2990, Lacy has presented no evidence beyond speculation, and the fact that the injury occurred, Lacy's argument that Wal-Mart had superior knowledge of the dangerous condition because it created the display is also meritless.

Lacy's evidence was insufficient to establish that an unreasonably dangerous condition existed. Rather, Lacy relies on mere speculation and the fact that he was injured to attempt to establish negligence. Accordingly, the judgment of the trial court is affirmed.

CASE QUESTIONS

1. Why did the plaintiff/appellant's claim of res ipsa loquitur fail?
2. Based on the court's suggestions, what could have been done differently in an effort to prove negligence?

Defendant's Superior Proof Position. Under res ipsa loquitur, the defendant must be in a better position to prove that he or she was not negligent than the plaintiff is to establish the defendant's negligence. In the warehouse example, the plaintiff did not see how the crate fell. None of the defendant's employees were present or nearby when the accident occurred. No witnesses actually saw why the crate fell. But the defendant originally stacked the crates. This makes it easier for the defendant to prove that reasonable care was used in stacking the boxes. The plaintiff is at a disadvantage to prove the defendant's negligence. However, the defendant can more easily show that safeguards were used in stacking the crates (such as ropes tied to support beams and crates, or walls and doors, surrounding the stacked boxes). In this fashion, the defendant could prove that reasonable care was used when stacking the crates and therefore no negligence occurred. Res ipsa loquitur cases often involve medical malpractice, particularly surgery. However, the doctrine is not restricted to such negligence cases, as the following hypothetical illustrates.

▌ VIOLATION OF A STATUTE

Sometimes there will be an allegation in a negligence claim that the defendant also violated a particular statute. For example, there might be a local ordinance requiring all outdoor swimming pools to be fenced. A couple in the area affected by the statute had a pool party for their child and their neighbors. The homeowners had taken down the fence when they bought the house and had not yet

HYPOTHETICAL

Eugene supervises a road-repair crew employed by Pavement Plus, Inc. The county contracts road construction and renovation to Pavement Plus. Eugene's crew was filling potholes on Elm Avenue one spring day. One of Eugene's employees, Walter, improperly mixed the asphalt so that it would not harden adequately. This bad asphalt was used to fill the Elm Avenue holes. Rutherford, who lives on Elm Avenue, drove over the patched potholes a few days later. The asphalt collapsed and the front right tire of Rutherford's automobile wedged in a hole, bending the front axle. Rutherford discovered that Pavement Plus had repaired the street, but had kept no record of the asphalt mixtures used.

Could Rutherford use res ipsa loquitur to shift the burden of proof? Evaluate the elements under these facts. Pavement Plus's foreman, Eugene, and an employee were under exclusive control of the weak asphalt used to fix the street. Asphalt does not normally collapse under vehicular weight unless it is improperly prepared or applied. The defendant is in the best position to prove that the mixture was suitable, as its employees prepared and applied the asphalt. Thus, res ipsa loquitur applies in this case, and the plaintiff need only prove what happened (i.e., his car was damaged when it fell through an asphalt-filled hole that the defendant repaired). The defendant must now establish that its employees used reasonable care in preparing and applying the asphalt. Besides, this problem also illustrates the value of retaining written records (in this case, of asphalt mixture) to document reasonable care.

decided what kind of fence they would replace it with. One of the children dove into the pool, struck the bottom, and was severely injured. The question then arises as to what effect the possible violation of the statute might have upon the negligence action. In analyzing the case, you must look to see if the statute was in fact violated, and if so, whether this caused the accident or played a significant role in the accident. It is also important to see if the person injured was the kind of person the statute was designed to protect and whether the statute covers the kind of harm suffered by the plaintiff. In this example, the fact that there was no fence had nothing whatsoever to do with the accident.

However, if the facts had been different and a neighbor's child had wandered into the unfenced backyard, fell into the pool, and drowned, this statute would have a direct bearing on the negligence case. *In most states, the violation of such a statute would be considered negligence per se.* This would mean that the proof of the violation of the statute would be sufficient to show that there was negligence; the defendant would thus be prevented from introducing evidence as to

demurrer | To file a pleading objecting to the sufficiency of the plaintiff's complaint, stating that even if everything the plaintiff alleges is true, it does not state a cause of action, and the case should be dismissed.

motion for summary judgment | When a party brings a motion to the court for a judgment in his or her favor, claiming there is no genuine issue as to a material fact to be decided in a case,

motion to dismiss | When a party brings a motion requesting that a case be terminated.

malpractice | A professional's negligent failure to observe the appropriate standard of care in providing services to a client or patient.

specialist | A professional who limits his or her work to a particular subject or narrow field within his or her broad field of practice.

Medical malpractice | When a medical provider's treatment of a patient falls below the standard of care and causes injury or death.

the degree of care or reasonableness used. This subject is also covered in Chapter 4 under "Negligence Per Se."

Defendant's Response to Plaintiff's Claim of Negligence

A defendant has a variety of ways to respond to a plaintiff's allegations of negligence in a lawsuit. For instance, after the pleadings are served, a defendant can use a **demurrer**, file a **motion for summary judgment,** or file a **motion to dismiss**. The reason the defendant would file these is to show that one or more of the four elements needed for a negligence case are missing. In this manner, a defendant can bring a halt to costly and time-consuming litigation, if successful, without the need for trial. Most likely, the key to a case will involve duty and causation. Without these, any case quickly falls apart.

▌ MALPRACTICE

There are many different kinds of professional malpractice. A professional's negligent failure to observe the appropriate standard of care in providing services to a client or patient is **malpractice.** There are as many types of malpractice actions as there are professions. A lawyer, accountant, teacher, physician, priest, or pharmacist, to name a few, can all be sued for malpractice. As mentioned in the prior chapter, the standard of care for professionals is now a national standard for the most part, rather than based on a particular locale. A **specialist** in any city or state would need to possess the degree of skill and competence that the same type of specialist anywhere in the United States would possess, without regard to location.

▌ MEDICAL MALPRACTICE

Medical malpractice occurs when a medical provider's treatment of a patient falls below the standard of care and causes injury or death. The Hippocratic Oath was written by the Greek physician Hippocrates over 2,000 years ago. It established the basic standards of ethics and for practicing medicine. The most well-known part of the oath is the phrase "Never do harm."

Typically, medical malpractice cases involve one or more of the following:

- ▶ Abandonment (failure to attend to a patient)
- ▶ Improper diagnosis, missed diagnosis, or delayed diagnosis
- ▶ Medical instruments, such as sponges, needles, and clamps, or other foreign objects left in patient after surgery
- ▶ Lack of informed consent
- ▶ Errors in prenatal diagnostic and genetic testing
- ▶ Death or disability from labor/delivery/post-delivery
- ▶ Failure of hospital to supervise employees

- Prescription medication errors
- Sexual assault on patient
- Death after induction of anesthesia
- Death or disability from a fall or restraints
- Record-keeping errors
- Failure to maintain proper hygiene standards, often leading to a **hospital-acquired infection** (HAI)
- Surgical errors (performed on a wrong body part, or causing injury)

hospital-acquired infection (HAI) | When a patient enters a hospital without infection and acquires an infection in the hospital; also called a *nosocomial infection*.

Malpractice Insurance

Physicians purchase medical malpractice insurance to cover injuries or deaths that occur as a result of malpractice. In high-risk specialties such as neurosurgery and obstetrics, insurance premiums can run as high as $200,000 per year, greatly driving up the cost of medical services. As a result, there is a shortage of physicians in some regions where the malpractice insurance rates are particularly high. What makes a malpractice case particularly challenging for the legal team is that two types of research are required. Not only must the legal team be apprised of the legal theories pertaining to the claim, but medical research is required as well.

Deciding Whether to Proceed with a Malpractice Case

To prove a medical malpractice case, generally one or more medical expert witnesses will be needed at the time of trial. This major expense prevents attorneys from bringing suit for anything but cases involving very serious and/or permanent injuries. Each physician's time away from practice in preparing for trial and time spent in court testifying can add up to thousands of dollars in expert's fees. In fact, many law firms will not take a medical malpractice case unless there is at least $100,000 in damages. Generally, a physician is initially retained shortly after the attorney meets with the new client. All the medical records are reviewed, and the medical practitioner is asked whether anything appears to have been done improperly.

Then the attorney must evaluate the file—based on the client interview, the medical records and opinion, and the amount of medical bills, lost wages, and anticipated future medical bills and lost wages—and decide whether or not to proceed with the case.

Expert Witnesses Are Needed. A physician in the same specialty as the physician being sued will be needed as an expert to testify at trial and explain why the physician fell below the standard of care. The expert is questioned at length during trial about his or her credentials, any books or papers he or she may have written on the subject at issue, what happened in the case at trial, and what he or she would have done in a similar situation. In a small town, or rural area, it may be difficult to find an expert willing to testify against a physician in the same field. In these instances, an expert from another locale may be called in to testify. Some jurors will be leery of an "outsider" who comes to town to testify against a local physician, particularly when the physician is well known, or has a good reputation.

Eyewitnesses. Just like in other negligence actions, eyewitnesses to the occurrence may be called in to testify. Various medical staff may have been present when the alleged malpractice occurred. Also, other medical providers who had some part in the medical treatment, such as nurses, surgical aides, and x-ray, lab, or ultrasound technicians may be called in to testify concerning their involvement in the alleged malpractice, what they observed during the incident, and/or the condition of the patient before or after the alleged malpractice.

PRACTICAL APPLICATION

As a practical note, it is important to remember that the mere fact that there is an injury, or the occurrence of a bad outcome, as a result of medical treatment does not necessarily mean that there has been malpractice.

Elements of Medical Malpractice

To establish a medical malpractice case, the basic four elements of a negligence claim must be proved. First, a duty must be owed. To demonstrate this, it must be shown that there was a physician/patient relationship. Next, there must be a breach of duty, which is proved by showing that the physician affirmatively did something or neglected to do something and fell below the standard of care owed to the patient. Then, the element of causation is needed to show that it was the physician's acts or omissions that actually caused the harm the plaintiff suffered. Last, there must be damages—some sort of physical or mental injury must have resulted from the medical treatment.

Hospital Responsibility. Hospitals are often responsible for the negligent medical treatment provided to patients at their facilities, as a result of their own negligence and those of their employees. A hospital might be negligent in not checking a physician's credentials, for example, or failing to adequately staff a floor with nurses during a certain shift. Hospitals are liable for the negligence of physicians, nurses, and other staff they employ. This is considered vicarious liability under the theory of respondeat superior. However, not all staff members are employed as employees by a particular hospital or medical care center. In fact, many of the physicians are independent contractors.

Hospital Nonresponsibility.

A hospital is not responsible for an **independent contractor's** medical malpractice. An independent contractor agrees to work for a hospital in his or her own manner, controlling the way in which the work is done. For example, if the physician working at a particular hospital controls her own hours, vacation days, the fees she sets, and the manner in which she treats her patients, she is most likely an independent contractor.

independent contractor |
An individual who works for a business or other entity, in his or her own manner, controlling the way in which the work is done; not an employee of the business or entity.

Exceptions to Hospital Nonresponsibility.

Usually, a hospital informs patients of a physician's employment status through intake forms and documents. If the patient is informed that a particular physician is an independent contractor prior to treatment, the hospital would not be responsible for any negligent acts of that physician in the course of treatment. However, there are two main exceptions to this rule: (1) when a hospital continues to use the services of an independent contractor whose services are known to be negligent, and (2) in an emergency room setting when a patient is not aware and/or not advised of a particular treating physician's status due to the immediacy of the treatment needs.

THE CASE OF THE DELAYED DISCOVERY

In addition to medical malpractice actions having special jurisdictional rules and procedures, the statutes of limitations governing these actions vary. Oftentimes, there is a maximum time allotted for bringing an action, as well as another time period set for discovery of malpractice, which must be carefully interpreted.

Winn, Appellant
v.
Sunrise Hosp. & Medical Center
et al., Respondents
The Supreme Court, State of Nevada
No. 54251
277 P.3d 458, 128 Nev. Adv. Op. 23
May 31, 2012

On December 14, 2006, 13-year-old Sedona Winn underwent heart surgery at respondent Sunrise Hospital and Medical Center. Respondent Michael Ciccolo, M.D., was the physician who performed the surgery, and respondents Robert Twells, CCP, and Lee Steffen, CCP, were the perfusionists who acted as the pump team to maintain Sedona's blood flow during surgery (collectively, the physicians). On the day after her surgery, Sedona's father, Robert Winn, was informed that she had suffered an "extensive brain injury" during the surgery. This has led to permanent neurological impairment. The physicians were unable to provide an explanation for how this arose during a minor surgery.

In mid-January, Winn's counsel sent a letter requesting that Sunrise produce "all patient records" relating to Sedona's surgery. Three days later, Winn's attorney sent Sunrise a second records request, this time for records pertinent to filing a claim for Social Security Disability benefits. On February 14, 2007, in connection with the Social Security-related request, Sunrise provided Winn's attorney with a copy of 184 pages of records, which included Dr. Ciccolo's December 14, 2006, postoperative report. According to an affidavit Winn's medical expert would later produce, Dr. Ciccolo's report indicated that a "notable volume of air" was present in Sedona's left ventricle at "inappropriate times during the procedure."

Sunrise did not provide any additional records until December 2007. The records provided were a "nearly complete" set. Not until February 12, 2008, did Sunrise provide a complete set of records, including a post-surgery MRI and CT scan. Winn's attorney then procured an expert affidavit in which a medical expert opined that Sunrise and the physicians had negligently caused Sedona's injuries. Winn's expert relied primarily on Dr. Ciccolo's postoperative report received from Sunrise on February 14, 2007. Winn filed suit against Sunrise and the physicians on February 3, 2009.

Nevada's statute of limitations for medical malpractice actions provides that such actions be filed within three years of the injury date, and within one year of the injury's discovery. Both deadlines are tolled however, when the health care provider has concealed information upon which the action is based. Respondents moved to dismiss because more than one year had elapsed between the time when Winn "discovered" Sedona's injury, December 15, 2006, and the time when he filed suit. The district court granted respondents' motions. All parties to this appeal agree that Sedona's injury occurred no later than December 15, 2006, the day after her surgery, when she was rendered comatose.

The parties disagree as to when Winn "discovered" Sedona's injury for purposes of triggering the one-year discovery period. There is also a dispute about the term "concealed" concerning Sunrise's piecemeal production of records, and Winn's resulting delay in filing suit. Lastly, Winn and the physicians disagree as to whether Sunrise's alleged concealment can toll the one-year discovery period on claims against the physicians, who played no role in the alleged concealment.

Although the evidence in this case does irrefutably demonstrate the accrual date for the one-year discovery period, this date was two months later than the date identified by the district court. We conclude that this difference in timing, combined with our analysis below, may render Winn's claim against Sunrise timely if tolling principles apply.

We next conclude that a plaintiff must satisfy a two-prong test to establish that the discovery limitation period should be tolled for concealment. Because factual issues remain as to whether Sunrise intentionally withheld information that was "material," and would have hindered a reasonably diligent plaintiff from timely filing suit, we vacate the district court's summary judgment in favor of Sunrise and remand so that Winn has the opportunity to make these showings.

We further conclude, however, that one defendant's concealment cannot serve as a basis for tolling limitation periods as to defendants who played no role in the concealment. This combined with the date when the one-year discovery period accrued, renders Winn's claims against the physicians time-barred.

The statute's discovery date may be determined only when the evidence demonstrates that a plaintiff has been put on inquiry notice. Winn filed suit against all respondents on February 3, 2009. Absent any tolling of the one-year discovery period, Winn would have had to discover Sedona's injury no earlier than February 3, 2008.

The district court concluded that Winn discovered Sedona's injury on December 15, 2006, the day following her surgery. We disagree. The record is unclear as to what respondents specifically conveyed to Winn in the wake of Sedona's surgery. It is unlikely that a prudent person would begin investigating whether a cause of action exists on the same day as being advised that a child's surgery had gone wrong.

The evidence does demonstrate that Winn discovered Sedona's injury no later than February 14, 2007—the date when he received the initial 182 pages of medical records. At this point, Winn had not only hired an attorney to pursue a medical malpractice action, but he also had access to Dr. Ciccolo's postoperative report that referenced air being present in Sedona's heart at inappropriate times during the surgery. By this an ordinarily prudent person would investigate further whether Sedona's injury may have been caused by someone's negligence.

The plaintiff must show that this information would have hindered a reasonably diligent plaintiff from timely filing suit. In order to establish that the

(continues)

one-year discovery period should be tolled it must be shown that Sunrise intentionally withheld information, and that it would have hindered a reasonably diligent plaintiff from procuring an expert affidavit. Factual issues remain as to when Sunrise was presented with an unequivocal request for medical records, and whether Sunrise intentionally withheld the requested records.

As to whether such withholding would have hindered a reasonably diligent plaintiff from procuring an expert affidavit, Sunrise indicates that once Winn procured his expert affidavit, the expert relied largely upon Dr. Ciccolo's postoperative report, that was part of records that Sunrise provided in February 2007. Sunrise contends, the delay in providing a complete set of records would not have hindered a diligent plaintiff. We are unable to affirm the district court's summary judgment in favor of Sunrise, and we therefore vacate that order. Winn is to be afforded an opportunity to show that the one-year discovery period should have been tolled as to his claim against Sunrise.

CASE QUESTIONS

1. Which statute of limitations did the appellate court find applied to the physicians? What was the end result of the claim against them?
2. Which statute of limitations did the appellate court find applicable to Sunrise Hospital? How was the claim against the hospital resolved?

Tort Reform

Due to **tort reform**, caps have been placed on the amount of money an injured plaintiff can collect in medical malpractice actions. Individual states have enacted statutes that limit the amount a plaintiff can receive from these lawsuits. Tort reform is addressed in detail later in this chapter.

tort reform | The movement by state legislatures to reduce the amount or kinds of awards that plaintiffs can receive in certain legal actions.

State Licensing. Because physicians and hospitals are licensed by the states, it is the states that have the option of regulating medical malpractice. States maintain their sovereignty over torts, medical care, and medical malpractice claims. Therefore, there is a great variety of limitations on malpractice actions, including statutes of limitations as was demonstrated in the preceding case.

State Legislation. One example of state legislation in this field is that of the state of Massachusetts. In August 2012, Massachusetts enacted legislation requiring physicians who make medical errors while treating patients to disclose their mistakes. Additionally, physicians are now allowed to apologize without facing lawsuits under a new health care law. In the past, attorneys prohibited physicians from discussing medical errors with their patients, greatly angering some patients and leading to suits they may not have brought.

One novel solution was considered by the state of New Hampshire in 2012, but was ultimately vetoed: Health care providers could offer injured patients a cash settlement to avoid a trial. The measure, known as "early offer," was strongly sought by some hospitals. If the injured plaintiff refused the offer and did not receive significantly more from a jury during a trial, he or she would be required to pay the health care provider's legal fees.

Federal Legislation. Efforts to regulate medical malpractice suits have been repeatedly proposed at the federal level, but the argument needs to be made that these regulations require national uniformity, and fall under the commerce clause of the U.S. Constitution. In one instance, for medical devices, the U.S. Supreme Court held in favor of national legislation. The Supreme Court ruled in *Riegel v. Medtronic, Inc.* (2008) that federal regulation of certain medical devices by the Food and Drug Administration (FDA) preempted state tort law.

Some of the proposed federal regulations for medical malpractice actions seek a reduced statute of limitations for claims, a limit on pain-and-suffering damages of $250,000, and the requirement that each party be liable only for its proportionate share of damages. Legislation is also being considered that would allow courts to reduce lawyers' contingency fees, allow testimony at the time of trial that shows the injured plaintiff has insurance coverage for some of the damages, and set limits on punitive damage amounts. In response, some argue that these proposals merely give bad physicians immunity, and lower the overall quality of medical care. Additionally, because it usually does not pay to sue unless at least $100,000 in damages is at stake, and because there is a **cap on damages** of $250,000 for awards in some jurisdictions, in a complex case it would be a lose/lose situation.

cap on damages | A limit on the amount of damages that can be awarded or collected.

Certificate of Merit. In an attempt to reduce the volume of unsuccessful medical malpractice actions using up the courts' resources, many states have started a system that requires each case to be "certified" by a medical physician as having "merit," and that a **certificate of merit** be filed with the court. In effect, this causes a plaintiff to have a medical evaluation of the case early on, so that physicians will not be repeatedly subject to suit each time a patient is not satisfied with his or her recovery or outcome. There needs to be an evaluation showing that some potential for negligence exists to proceed with a case.

certificate of merit | Part of a system in many states that requires each medical malpractice case to be certified by a medical doctor as having "merit"; the certificate of merit must be filed with the court.

Medical Malpractice Panels. Another attempt at reducing the amount of medical malpractice suits is the institution of medical malpractice panels. Again, these vary by state, and are nonexistent in some states. They are also referred to as medical malpractice review panels and medical malpractice screening panels. A **medical malpractice panel** usually consists of a neutral lawyer, physician, and judge who evaluate the case for elements of malpractice. Plaintiffs' attorneys see this as an added hurdle to jump before bringing a malpractice claim. Putting together such a panel can take anywhere from six months to more than a year and thus further delays the case. The panel does not award damages and is not a

medical malpractice panel | A group that usually consists of an independent attorney, judge, and physician selected to evaluate the merits of a medical malpractice claim.

substitute for a trial. The findings of the panel can be introduced at the time of trial, thus making many physicians reluctant to sit on these panels.

The following hypothetical examines another situation in which the standard of care is at issue. Note how scope of duty, foreseeability, and the reasonable person standard are established.

HYPOTHETICAL

Jamal makes an appointment to see his family physician. Jamal's throat has been hurting him for the past week. The physician takes a throat culture. The physician determines that Jamal has strep throat, a condition that requires antibiotics. Jamal's physician calls Jamal with the results and advises that he will call the pharmacy and order medication. Unbeknownst to Jamal, the drug that the physician orders is one in a category of drugs to which Jamal is highly allergic and should never take. The physician failed to check Jamal's chart for known allergies before ordering the prescription. Because the drug has a different name than the drug Jamal previously had a reaction to, Jamal assumes that the drug is a different drug that is safe for him to take. Minutes after taking the prescription, Jamal goes into shock and dies. Did the physician owe Jamal a duty of reasonable care? If so, did the physician breach that duty?

To establish negligence by a physician, it must be shown that the injury complained of was caused by the physician's failing to act as a reasonable family physician would have acted under like circumstances. Failing to check a chart for allergies falls below the standard of care that a family physician of ordinary skill would have used under similar circumstances. The physician did not follow professional practices and failed to comply with the reasonable standard of care owed to Jamal. It was foreseeable that Jamal would be hurt.

THE CASE OF RESTRAINT

Once again, the court is left in the position of telling the plaintiff how the case should have been tried. Imagine the plaintiff's reaction when reading this court decision.

Melissa MARTINO, Appellant

v.

James MILLER, Respondent

Supreme Court, Appellate Division,
Third Department, New York
97 A.D.3d 1009, 949 N.Y.S.2d 225
July 19, 2012

This is an appeal from an order of the Supreme Court entered April 19, 2011 which granted defendant's motion for summary judgment dismissing the complaint.

Defendant, a board-certified plastic surgeon, performed numerous surgeries on plaintiff, including, in late September 2006, a bilateral breast reduction surgery, and, at the same time, liposuction and bra-chioplasty (an arm lift). During the breast reduction surgery, defendant used a technique known as the pedicle technique, which involves preserving a pedicle of pyramid-shaped tissue attached to the nipple areo-lar complex (hereinafter NAC).

Plaintiff was released from the hospital and pre-sented to defendant for follow-up care. On her third follow-up visit, defendant noted that the NAC tissue on plaintiff's right side displayed some superficial skin loss and diminished sensation. The tissue contin-ued to deteriorate and, by the end of November 2006, defendant informed plaintiff that reconstructive sur-gery might be needed to correct the damage done to it. Plaintiff ceased treating with defendant and com-menced this action alleging that he was negligent in the manner in which the surgery was performed, and in the care he provided following the surgery.

As the movant for summary judgment in a medical malpractice action, defendant was required to establish that during his treatment of plaintiff, "'there was no departure from accepted standards of practice or that plaintiff was not injured thereby'" (*Menard v. Feinberg*, 60 A.D.3d 1135, 1136, 875 N.Y.S.2d 309 [2009].

Here, defendant affirmed that there were no com-plications during the surgical procedure he performed on plaintiff and that he comported with appropriate standards of medical care. Defendant stated that he chose the surgical technique—one that he had maintained is commonly employed in breast reduc-tion surgical procedures performed in the United States—because "the viability of the [NAC] is main-tained by preserving a pedicle of pyramid shaped tis-sue attached to the NAC." Defendant explained that, to avoid compromising the viability of tissue during surgery, he periodically examined the NAC on both breasts to ensure that their color was normal and that there was adequate "capillary refill." He stated that, he "removed tissue from the right breast while maintaining the vascular pedicle intact, sparing as much tissue as possible, slowly, meticulously, care-fully excising the tissue around the pedicle to pre-serve a broad base and blood supply to the NAC." He averred that "[t]his technique met or even exceeded all standards of care for a plastic surgeon performing

this procedure" and that "even with this technique, compromise of the NAC is a well known complication of breast reduction surgery and can and does occur in the absence of negligence."

In addition, defendant stated that, prior to the surgery, he consulted with plaintiff's hematologist, who recommended that Heparin be given to plaintiff to prevent any clotting that might occur as a result of the surgery. This affidavit was sufficient to shift the burden to plaintiff to demonstrate that triable questions of fact exist as to whether defendant de-parted from accepted standards of medical practice in the manner in which the surgical procedure was performed—and in the post-surgical care provided plaintiff—and, as a result, plaintiff was injured

Plaintiff submitted the affirmation of Peter Neumann, a board-certified plastic surgeon. Neumann concluded that defendant was negligent because he de-parted from accepted standards of medical practice in the treatment rendered plaintiff, but failed to identify what those accepted practices are and how defendant's treatment of plaintiff deviated from them. Neumann also contended that defendant committed malpractice by performing "blunt force liposuction to the lateral chest wall at the same time as breast reduction," but does not explain why performing such a procedure contemporaneously with the breast reduction surgery constituted a departure from acceptable medical prac-tice or how performing the two procedures during the same surgery caused plaintiff's injury.

Neumann's assertion that defendant failed to "timely diagnose and treat wound abscess" is belied by the record and ignores, defendant's deposition testimony and medical records documenting the postoperative examinations performed on plaintiff by defendant. In particular, this evidence, which is essentially uncontradicted, established that during plaintiff's first two postoperative appointments with defendant, the wound appeared "clean" and only upon the third visit was "some NAC superficial epidermis lysis" with diminished sensation noted. During these examinations, defendant treated plaintiff's wound with topical medication and discussed with her pos-sible approaches to be employed in remedying the

(continues)

tissue damage. Further, defendant recommended that plaintiff wear a looser fitting brassiere to enhance circulation to the area. Finally, while plaintiff argues that defendant's use of an ACE bandage to dress her wound following the surgery constituted a departure from accepted medical standards, Neumann, in his affirmation, does not suggest any other method that should have been employed to dress plaintiff's wounds following the surgery.

As such, the affirmation of plaintiff's expert failed to raise any triable issues of fact as to whether defendant deviated from accepted standards of medical practice in the care he provided plaintiff and, therefore, defendant's motion for summary judgment was properly granted. As a result, we need not reach plaintiff's claims regarding her cross motion.

ORDERED that the order is affirmed, with costs.

CASE QUESTIONS

1. Did the plaintiff meet her burden of proof? Explain your answer.
2. What did the court say was missing from the plaintiff's expert's affirmation?
3. Note that five years elapsed between the surgery and the final resolution of this case. Based on what you have read in this case, do you think the plaintiff would have had a different result had the plaintiff entered into settlement talks after filing the initial pleadings? Explain your answer.

THE CASE OF THE USELESS DRUG

When a physician prescribes a dose of a prescription at the low or high end of the recommended dosage range, what role does the pharmacist play?

Dorothy Brumaghim, et al., Respondents

v.

Rebecca R. Eckel, et al., Respondents

v.

Rite Aid, et al., Appellants

State of New York Supreme Court, Appellate Division, Third Department

94 A.D.3d 1391, 944 N.Y.S.2d 329

April 26, 2012

Plaintiff Dorothy Brumaghim (hereinafter plaintiff) and her husband, derivatively, commenced this action against defendants after plaintiff suffered a stroke. Plaintiffs alleged that plaintiff's physician, defendant Rebecca R. Eckel, improperly prescribed an inadequate dosage of Coumadin, a medication intended to treat her medical condition. They further alleged that the pharmacy at which plaintiff filled her prescription, which was operated by defendants Rite

Aid Corporation and Rite Aid Pharmacy (hereafter referred to as Rite Aid) was negligent in failing to contact plaintiff's physician to inquire about the prescribed dosage. Rite Aid moved to dismiss the complaint pursuant to CPLR 3211(a)(7) for failure to state a cause of action. Supreme Court denied the motion, prompting this appeal by Rite Aid.

"The standard of care which is imposed on a pharmacist is generally described as ordinary care in the conduct of his [or her] business. The rule of ordinary care as applied to the business of a druggist means the highest practicable degree of prudence, thoughtfulness and vigilance commensurate with the dangers involved and the consequences which may attend inattention."

Generally, a pharmacist cannot be held liable for negligence in the absence of an allegation that he or she failed to fill a prescription precisely as directed by the physician or was aware that the customer had a condition that would render the prescription of the drug at issue contraindicated. In addition, liability or culpable conduct on the part of a pharmacy may be found where there was some active negligence on the part of the pharmacist.

Here, plaintiffs do not allege that Rite Aid failed to fill the prescription as written by the physician, and it is undisputed that Coumadin was not contraindicated for plaintiff. Rather, plaintiffs allege that Rite Aid filled "an incorrect and inconsistent prescription medication of a *contra-indicated dosage for plaintiff*" (emphasis added).

Indeed, plaintiffs' claim is not that Rite Aid filled a prescription that was contraindicated on its face—such as if the dosage of the drug prescribed fell below or exceeded the medically acceptable range of dosages that should be provided under any circumstance. Rather, they assert that Rite filled a prescription for a dosage that was inappropriate and inadequate *for her in particular.* Imposing a duty upon a pharmacist to contact the prescribing physician whenever there has been a change in dosage—within medically acceptable ranges—of a particular patient's medication would, in essence, require the pharmacist to question the physician's judgment regarding the appropriateness of each customer's prescription. Sound policy reasons exist for not imposing such a duty.

Here, in support of its motion, Rite Aid submitted documentary evidence establishing that Coumadin is supplied in tablets of different dosages ranging from 1 to 10 mg. It is undisputed that the prescription at issue was for 1 mg dosages of Coumadin. As one court observed, a prescription which is excessive for one patient may be entirely reasonable for the treatment of another. To fulfill the duty which the plaintiff urges us to impose would require the pharmacist to learn the customer's condition and monitor his [or her] drug usage. To accomplish, the pharmacist would have to interject himself [or herself] into the physician/patient relationship and practice medicine without a license."

A physician may often have valid reasons for altering a patient's dosage of a particular medication based on the patient's unique condition. "It is the duty of the prescribing physician to know the characteristics of the drug he [or she] is prescribing, to know how much of the drug he [or she] can give [the] patient, to elicit from the patient what other drugs the patient is taking, to properly prescribe various combinations of drugs, to warn the patient of any dangers associated with taking the drug, to monitor the patient's dependence on the drug, and to tell the patient when and how to take the drug. Further, it is the duty of the patient to notify the physician of the other drugs the patient is taking. Finally, it is the duty of the drug manufacturer to notify the physician of any adverse effects or other precautions that must be taken in administering the drug. Placing these duties to warn on the pharmacist would only serve to compel the pharmacist to second guess every prescription a physician orders in an attempt to escape liability."

We do not suggest that "a pharmacy is no more than a warehouse for drugs and that a pharmacist has no more responsibility than a shipping clerk who must dutifully and unquestioningly obey the written orders of omniscient physicians." However, we do recognize that a pharmacist's professional judgment must defer to the prescribing physician's training, experience, and knowledge of the particular patient's condition. We therefore conclude that, under the circumstances here, Rite Aid had no duty to warn plaintiff or contact the prescribing physician to inquire about the dosage of the drug prescribed. Accordingly, the complaint must be dismissed against Rite Aid.

CASE QUESTIONS

1. Based on the court's ruling, if a physician prescribed a drug that a patient was allergic to, and the druggist filled the prescription as written, what would the court rule in regard to a claim of malpractice against the pharmacy?
2. Did the court's reasoning in this case meet your expectations? Explain your answer.

▌ LEGAL MALPRACTICE

Like medical malpractice, **legal malpractice** occurs when an attorney falls below the standard of care required. Courts look at the standard of reasonably prudent care by an attorney in the same jurisdiction. The Model Rules of Professional Conduct enacted by the American Bar Association (ABA) have been adopted by a majority of the states. Falling below these rules is often cited as possible malpractice, but is not conclusive. Because attorneys are licensed by individual states, attorney behavior is judged by the ethics rules of the particular state where the attorney practices law. The rules were not meant for civil prosecution; their intent is to establish a baseline of how attorneys should conduct themselves. An expert, an attorney practicing in the same jurisdiction as the defendant attorney, is usually needed to establish standard custom and practice and whether an attorney's actions fell below a standard of care and skill.

　　It is not enough to prove that a client did not like an attorney's legal strategy. Actual errors that fell below the standard of care must be shown. Additionally, it must be proved that the injured plaintiff would have prevailed at the time of trial, and the damages awarded would have been collectible. Although some attorneys have professional liability insurance, not all attorneys do; it is not a requirement for the practice of law. Professional liability policies generally do not cover intentional acts, such as fraud or theft.

legal malpractice | When an attorney's behavior falls below the standard of care owed to the client and damages occur.

Statute of Limitations

The statutes of limitations for bringing legal malpractice actions vary from as short as one year to as long as four years depending on the jurisdiction. Some states provide a different amount of time to bring the action based upon the date of discovery of the malpractice. The laws for a particular jurisdiction need to be checked for the precise time period allowed.

Consequences of a Malpractice Action

If successful with a legal malpractice action, a client may receive money damages. On occasion, there may be criminal prosecution against the attorney as well if theft or fraud was committed. In these cases, restitution may be ordered, and the attorney will be required to repay what was taken from the client. Clients have the option of reporting an offending attorney to the state disciplinary board. This can result in sanctions against the attorney, up to and including disbarment. An attorney may be fined, receive public or private **censure**, or be ordered to suspend practice for a period of time.

censure | To publicly or privately criticize or condemn the acts of an attorney.

Examples of Legal Malpractice

Sometimes when a client's case is lost, the first thing the client will do is look to the attorney for money that the client did not receive at the time of trial. Other types of malpractice actions involve misuse of client funds, **commingling** of client funds with attorney funds, or an attorney placing his or her own interests before those of the client. Also involved are cases where an attorney misses a

commingling | The unethical mixing of a client's money with that of an attorney. Client money should always be kept separate.

deadline, forgets about a court appearance, fails to keep up with changes in the law, or fails to perform any of the services promised in the retainer agreement. Some clients might claim, for example, that they were unduly pressured to take a settlement that was not in their best interest. Use of drugs or alcohol can also factor into legal malpractice, such as when an attorney has an addiction that affects the quality of work performed. On occasion, clients will sue attorneys for malpractice when they receive their bills for services rendered and wish to delay payment or believe the bills are too high. In addition, a disgruntled client may bring a counterclaim when sued for unpaid fees.

One of the more recent types of actions brought against attorneys is for **e-discovery malpractice**. This may occur when a law firm fails to supervise an outside vendor, its attorneys, or its staff, and during the course of discovery confidential privileged documents are produced and supplied to the adversary law firm.

e-discovery malpractice | One of the newer claims of malpractice in which a law firm fails to supervise an outside vendor, its attorneys, or its staff, and during the course of discovery confidential privileged documents are produced.

disengagement | When a client no longer wishes to retain his her attorney and ends the attorney/client relationship.

fiduciary relationship | The attorney has a client's trust and confidence, and in return must act in good faith, being honest and loyal.

Refusal of Case and Disengagement

Should a lawyer refuse to take a case or a client wishes to replace the attorney (**disengagement**), it is important that the attorney send a letter advising of the time limit for bringing the action with another attorney.

Judging Attorney Conduct

An attorney/client relationship is a **fiduciary relationship**. This means that that attorney has a client's trust and confidence, and in return must act in good faith, being honest, and loyal. Attorney conduct is governed by a code of ethics and professional standards established by the ABA. These Model Rules of Professional Conduct, mentioned earlier in the chapter, demonstrate how an attorney should conduct oneself, and merely provide guidance for an attorney. The rules specifically state that they are not to be used as the basis for a civil action. Attorneys may be disciplined for not complying with the rules. Because the rules were not enacted by a legislative body, they are not used in the courts as proof of malpractice.

Suing a Colleague

A key point to be remembered about legal malpractice cases is that an attorney who accepts a malpractice case is put in the position of suing a fellow member of the profession. Some attorneys do not feel comfortable in accepting this type of case, particularly in a small town or city where they will run into the defendant on occasion, both in court and possibly socially.

Experts Are Not Always Needed to Prove Legal Malpractice

Unlike medical malpractice cases, an expert is not needed in every legal malpractice situation. Sometimes the malpractice is obvious; it can be proved without an expert. An example of this would be where an attorney keeps a client's property to which he or she is not entitled. Establishing an ethical violation, however, might not always be as straightforward.

THE CASE OF THE DISSOLVING LAW FIRM

What does a law firm do when the main partner, whose name is contained in the law firm's name, is no longer a part of the firm? This case sheds light on professional disciplinary hearings, and also takes you behind the scenes to view the private workings of a law firm in turmoil. An analogy might be made here between the dissolution of a law firm and the dissolution of a marriage.

In the Matter of DISCIPLINARY PROCEEDINGS AGAINST Joseph W. WEIGEL, Attorney at Law Office of Lawyer Regulation, Complainant-Respondent

v.

Joseph W. Weigel, Respondent-Appellant

Supreme Court of Wisconsin

817 N.W.2d 835

June 29, 2012

ATTORNEY disciplinary proceeding. *Attorney publicly reprimanded.*

PER CURIAM.

Attorney Weigel was admitted to practice law in Wisconsin in 1960. He is a personal injury attorney. The background giving rise to this proceeding stems from the contentious dissolution of a Milwaukee law firm. The Office of Lawyer Regulation (OLR) filed a complaint against Attorney Weigel on June 21, 2010. The complaint alleged that Attorney Weigel had: (1) entered into an impermissible noncompetition agreement contrary to former SCR 20:5.6(a); (2) misled clients and the public by continuing to use the firm name "Eisenberg, Weigel, Carlson, Blau & Clemens, S.C." contrary to SCR 20:7.1(a)(1) SCR 20:7.5(a), and SCR 20:8.4(c); and (3) paid impermissible bonuses to a paralegal contrary to SCR 20:5.4(a)(3).

Alvin H. Eisenberg, an experienced lawyer, organized the law firm of Alvin H. Eisenberg, S.C., as a service corporation. In 1990 six attorneys, including Attorney Weigel, acquired shares in the Eisenberg firm. On March 1,

1999, Attorney Weigel became the president of the firm, which was known during the relevant period as Eisenberg, Weigel, Carlson, Blau & Clemens, S.C.

On March 11, 1999, Attorney Weigel, on behalf of the firm, entered into a Stock Redemption Agreement by which the firm redeemed all of Attorney Eisenberg's shares of stock. As a condition of the redemption, the firm agreed to employ Attorney Eisenberg under an Employment Agreement which contained a covenant against competition which specified that Attorney Eisenberg was prohibited from practicing law in the Greater Milwaukee area for a period of six months after he ceased to be employed by the firm.

In January 2005 the Firm, without giving prior notice to Attorney Eisenberg, moved its law office to a new location. A letter was left for Attorney Eisenberg saying there was no office space for him at the new location, that he should go home, and that his paychecks would be sent to him.

Concerning the first count: We accept the referee's findings that the noncompetition clause in the Employment Agreement violated SCR 20:5.6(a).

The second count of the OLR complaint alleged that Attorney Weigel misled clients and the public by continuing to use the firm name "Eisenberg, Weigel, Carlson, Blau & Clemens, S.C," and implied that Attorney Alvin Eisenberg was still associated with the firm. The issue is the firm using the "of counsel" relationship with Donald Eisenberg (an attorney not related to the firm), as a pretext for continuing to use the name "Eisenberg" as the lead name for a law firm founded by Alvin Eisenberg after the termination of Alvin Eisenberg from the firm. This, coupled with advertising that "nothing had changed" was misleading, and violated the rules of professional conduct.

The third count of the complaint involves the payment of bonuses to a paralegal. The paralegal is paid a base hourly wage ($7.00 or $7.50 per hour). In addition, the paralegal receives two forms of bonus: (1) thirty cents per thousand dollars (three-tenths of one percent) of the gross recoveries from personal injury cases she worked on; and (2) a quarterly bonus consisting of $1,500 plus $250 per thousand (25 percent) of the difference between a weekly average (computed quarterly, over 13 weeks) of gross recoveries from personal injury cases she worked on and her weekly goal of $127,500 per week.

Supreme Court rule 20:5.4 is based on the American Bar Association's Model Rule 5.4 which "clearly prohibits fee 'splitting' with paralegals." See ABA Model Guidelines for the Utilization of Paralegal Services (2004). The underlying purpose of the fee-splitting rule is to guard the professional independence of a lawyer. It seeks to avoid the situation where a nonlawyer with a financial stake in the outcome of a case could influence how that case is handled, for instance by pressuring the lawyer either to settle faster or to hold out for more, based on the nonlawyer's financial interest.

It is well settled that a lawyer may compensate a nonlawyer assistant based on the quantity and quality of their work and the value of that work to the law practice. Thus, in addition to regular compensation, paralegals and legal assistants routinely and properly receive discretionary merit-based bonuses or bonuses based on the overall success of the firm. The ethical issues arise when the nonlawyer's compensation is tied too directly to specific clients, cases or work performed by the nonlawyer such that the professional independence of the lawyer is compromised.

Generally, bonuses are deemed permissible where the bonus is not tied to fees generated from a particular case or class of cases from a specific client. The potential ethical concern here stems from the fact that the employee's bonus is based upon net profits of a specific law practice area, rather than upon the net profits of the law firm's entire practice. We find no indication that the paralegal would be interfering with the lawyer's independent judgment. Accordingly, we dismiss the third count of the complaint.

We turn to the appropriate discipline for Attorney Weigel. We conclude that a public reprimand rather than a suspension of practice is sufficient for Attorney Weigel's misconduct. This should not be interpreted as indicating this court is untroubled by his misconduct. Attorney Weigel should be required to pay the full costs of this disciplinary proceeding, which are $17,447.28 as of January 20, 2012.

CASE QUESTIONS

1. Do you think the attorney's discipline was appropriate for his actions? Explain your answer.
2. How can a paralegal protect him- or herself from agreeing to a payment plan that might be considered unethical by the American Bar Association?

Elements in a Legal Malpractice Claim

Just like with medical malpractice, or any other kind of professional malpractice, the four elements of negligence must be shown (Table 3-2). One difference is that instead of establishing a physician/patient relationship, an attorney/client relationship must be proved to establish a duty owed. Another difference is that

A legal malpractice claim has four elements:	**TABLE 3-2**
1. Duty owed—attorney/client relationship	Legal malpractice elements
2. Breach of duty—attorney failed to properly represent the client	
3. Causation—attorney's acts caused harm	
4. Damages—damages are present (the outcome of the case was effected)	

in order to prove damages, it must be proved that the legal case had merit, and that the client would have been awarded damages or would have received more damages had the attorney taken the proper action.

Case within a Case. When reviewing malpractice court decisions, there is often reference to the "**case within the case.**" This refers to the original case for which the malpractice action is being sought. It is also referred to as the *underlying case*. There are two cases: the case within the case, and the malpractice case concerning this case.

case within the case. | The original case for which the malpractice action is being sought; also referred to as the underlying case.

Attorney Judgment Rule. If an attorney does not use the best judgment in a certain situation, that alone does not constitute malpractice. There must be some gross error in judgment. Different attorneys will use different strategies and cannot be faulted for this, so long as they acted in good faith, focusing on the client's best interest.

Loss of Attorney/Client Privilege. Something for the client to ponder is the loss of attorney/client privilege during a malpractice action. It would be very difficult to evaluate a malpractice claim without being privy to the attorney/client communications to see what was said and what was promised.

Multiple Attorneys. When clients replace attorneys during an action it can complicate the case. For example, it makes it more difficult to establish precisely when malpractice occurred and who is the offending party. In the *Snolis v. Clare* case that follows, the injured plaintiff Snolis switched attorneys two times after retaining her initial attorney, further complicating the malpractice claim. Note how the case pivots on a simple fact that was missed during the initial interview process. An attorney, or paralegal, can never be too thorough in getting the details of the case.

THE CASE OF THE CHANGING ATTORNEYS

Some attorneys are reluctant to accept a case if advised that a client has had numerous attorneys, as it would appear that the client will not be satisfied no matter which counsel is retained. In this instance, this generalization by some attorneys proved to be true.

Tara Snolis et al., Respondents-Appellants

v.

**Timothy W. Clare, Defendant,
and William J. Poisson, Esq.,
Individually and as a Partner in Poisson &
Hackett, Esqs., et al.,
Appellants-Respondents**

State of New York, Appellate Division, Second Department

81 AD.3d. 923

February 22, 2011

The plaintiff Tara Snolis was involved in a motor vehicle accident in May 1999 with a car driven by John Biondo. Tara Snolis and the plaintiff Albert Snolis, suing derivatively, subsequently commenced an action to recover damages for personal injuries against Biondo (hereinafter the personal injury action).

In April 2002, the defendants William J. Poisson, and Poisson & Hackett, Esqs. (hereinafter together the defendants), were substituted as the plaintiffs' counsel in the personal injury action. When Biondo was deposed in February 2003, long after the expiration of the statute of limitations, it was learned for the first time that he had leased the car he drove on the day of the accident. In April 2003, the defendants were provided with documentary evidence showing that the vehicle was actually owned by American Suzuki Automotive Credit (hereinafter the owner) at the time of the accident. The defendants did not move for leave to amend the complaint to add the owner as a defendant, and filed a note of issue in September 2003.

In May 2004, the defendants were replaced by different counsel, who immediately moved for leave to amend the complaint to add the new defendants. That motion was denied. The plaintiffs thereafter commenced the instant action to recover damages for

legal malpractice and breach of contract. The plaintiffs moved for summary judgment on their legal malpractice cause of action insofar as asserted against the defendants, and the defendants cross-moved, inter alia, for summary judgment dismissing the complaint insofar as asserted against them. The Supreme Court denied both the motion and the cross motion.

In order to prevail in an action to recover damages for legal malpractice, a plaintiff must establish that the attorney failed to exercise the ordinary reasonable skill and knowledge commonly possessed by a member of the legal profession, and that the breach of this duty proximately caused the plaintiff to sustain actual and ascertainable damages. To establish the element of causation, a plaintiff must show that he or she would have prevailed in the underlying action or would not have incurred any damages but for the attorney's negligence.

The failure to demonstrate proximate cause requires dismissal of a legal malpractice action regardless of whether the attorney was negligent (*see Theresa Striano Revocable Trust v Blancato*, 71 AD3d at 1124).

The plaintiffs failed to demonstrate their prima facie entitlement to judgment as a matter of law because they failed to establish that any negligence on the part of the defendants in failing to move for leave to amend the complaint in the personal injury action to add the owner as a defendant, immediately upon learning of the owner's identity, was the proximate cause of their alleged damages. Accordingly, the Supreme Court properly denied the plaintiffs' motion.

The Supreme Court improvidently exercised its discretion in denying, as untimely, that branch of the defendants' cross motion which was for summary judgment dismissing the complaint insofar as asserted against them. While the defendants' cross motion was made more than 120 days after the note

(continues)

of issue was filed and, therefore, was an untimely cross motion for summary judgment may be considered by the court where, as here, a timely motion for summary judgment was made on nearly identical grounds.

In such circumstances, the issues raised by the untimely cross motion are already properly before the court and, thus, the nearly identical nature of the grounds may provide the requisite good cause to review the merits of the untimely cross motion. Notably, a court, in deciding the timely motion, may search the record and award summary judgment to a nonmoving party.

The defendants demonstrated their prima facie entitlement to judgment as a matter of law dismissing the legal malpractice cause of action insofar as asserted against them by demonstrating that any negligence on their part did not proximately cause the plaintiffs' alleged damages. It is true that the more than one-year delay in moving for leave to amend the complaint in the personal injury action to add the owner as a defendant, which was attributable to the defendants' failure to seek that relief,

prejudiced the owner and, thus, was a sufficient basis for denying the motion for leave to amend the complaint in the personal injury action.

However, the defendants demonstrated that even if they had expeditiously made such a motion in April 2003, immediately upon learning of the owner's identity, the motion could not have been granted. Specifically, they demonstrated that the plaintiffs could not have met their burden in the underlying action of establishing that an amended complaint against the owner related back to the timely complaint against Biondo, since the owner did not have notice of the plaintiffs' personal injury action within the limitations period. In opposition, the plaintiffs failed to raise a triable issue of fact.

Accordingly, that branch of the defendants' cross motion which was for summary judgment dismissing the legal malpractice cause of action insofar as asserted against them should have been granted. In addition, the Supreme Court should have awarded the defendants summary judgment dismissing the plaintiffs' breach of contract cause of action as duplicative of the legal malpractice cause of action.

CASE QUESTIONS

1. Notice that it took almost 12 years from the plaintiffs' initial car accident for resolution of the legal malpractice claim. Had the plaintiffs kept their original attorneys throughout the case, do you think this case would have resulted in a malpractice action? Explain your answer.
2. Why do you think the three law firms all failed to establish the one crucial fact in a timely fashion?
3. Go online and see whether you can locate law firms in your jurisdiction advertising that they handle legal malpractice claims. Do you think an attorney should be uncomfortable in suing a fellow attorney for malpractice? Explain your answer.

▌ SUMMARY

Most often, the plaintiff must prove that the defendant was negligent in causing the plaintiff's injuries. This burden of proof calls for a preponderance of the evidence. Once established, the defendant has the burden of rejoinder, or rebuttal, to counter the plaintiff's prima facie case. In certain cases, however,

the plaintiff is at a disadvantage in proving the defendant's negligence.

Res ipsa loquitur allows the plaintiff to shift the burden of proof to the defendant. Thus, the defendant must disprove the plaintiff's allegations of negligence. Res ipsa loquitur applies in cases in which the defendant exclusively controlled the object or action that hurt the plaintiff, the plaintiff's injury was one that ordinarily would not happen without negligence, and the defendant is in the better position to prove that he or she was not negligent.

A defendant's violation of a statute might have an effect on the outcome of a negligence case. This is especially true when a specific statute was designed to prevent the kind of accident that occurred.

A defendant has a variety of ways to respond to a plaintiff's allegations of negligence in a lawsuit. After the pleadings are served, a defendant can use a demurrer, file a motion for summary judgment, or file a motion to dismiss. The defendant would file these to show that one or more of the four elements needed for a negligence case are missing. In this manner, a defendant can bring a halt to costly and time-consuming litigation.

There are many different kinds of professional malpractice. A professional's negligent failure to observe the appropriate standard of care in providing services to a client or patient is malpractice. Lawyers, accountants, teachers, physicians, priests, and pharmacists can all be sued for malpractice.

The standard of care for professionals is now a national standard for the most part, rather than based on a particular locale. Thus, a specialist in any city or state must possess the degree of skill and competence that a specialist anywhere in the United States would possess, without regard to location.

Medical malpractice occurs when a medical provider's treatment to a patient falls below the standard of care and causes injury or death. Malpractice cases are challenging for the legal team, and both legal and medical research are required.

Medical malpractice cases most often involve the following issues: abandonment; improper, missed, or delayed diagnosis; medical instruments or foreign objects left in patients after surgery; lack of informed consent; errors in prenatal diagnostic and genetic testing; death or disability from labor/delivery/post-delivery;

failure of hospitals to supervise employees; prescription medication errors; sexual assault; death after induction of anesthesia; death or disability from a fall or restraints; and surgical errors.

In an attempt to reduce the volume of unsuccessful medical malpractice actions using up the courts' resources, many states have started a system that requires each case to be certified by a medical physician as having "merit" to proceed.

To prove a medical malpractice case, generally one or more medical expert witnesses will be needed at the time of trial. This major expense prevents attorneys from bringing suit for anything but cases involving very serious and/or permanent injuries. Many law firms will not take a medical malpractice case, unless there is at least $100,000 in damages at stake.

Due to tort reform, caps have been placed on the amount of money an injured plaintiff can collect in medical malpractice actions. Tort reform is the movement by state legislatures to reduce the amount and kinds of awards plaintiffs can receive in certain actions. States have enacted statutes limiting the award amount a plaintiff can receive for these lawsuits.

Legal malpractice occurs when an attorney falls below the standard of care required. Courts look at the standard of reasonably prudent care provided by an attorney in the same jurisdiction.

The Model Rules of Professional Conduct enacted by the ABA have been adopted by a majority of the states. Falling below these rules is often cited as possible malpractice, but is not conclusive. The rules were not meant for civil prosecution. An expert, an attorney practicing in the same jurisdiction as the defendant attorney, is usually needed to establish standard custom and practice, and whether an attorney's actions fell below a standard of care.

In the next chapter, we focus on special negligence actions concerning certain well-defined activities. Some of the most common of these actions involve property ownership, employer/employee activities, and motor vehicle use.

▌ KEY TERMS

burden of proof	e-discovery malpractice	motion for summary judgment
burden of rejoinder	fiduciary relationship	motion to dismiss
cap on damages	hospital-acquired infection	preponderance of the
"case within the case"	(HAI)	evidence
censure	independent contractor	prima facie case
certificate of merit	legal malpractice	rebuttal
commingling	malpractice	res ipsa loquitur
demurrer	medical malpractice	specialist
disengagement	medical malpractice panel	tort reform

▌ PROBLEMS

In the following hypotheticals, determine if negligence exists and if the tortfeasor will be liable to the injured party. Identify the plaintiff(s) and the defendant(s).

1. Mrs. Sanders works as a paralegal for a firm that occupies six floors at the top of the Hunt Center. She works on the 30th floor. She often travels from one floor to another within the firm by way of elevators. On October 10, 2013, Mrs. Sanders took an elevator to the 32nd floor. When she went back to the elevator to return to her office, the elevator went up to the 34th floor instead, and the doors would not open. Mrs. Sanders again pushed the button for the 30th floor. This time, the elevator moved downward, and began to drop intermittently, falling approximately 20 times. Mrs. Sanders used the intercom system to call the lobby clerk, Larry Leven, for help. The clerk immediately called Houston and West, the company that designed and installed the elevator and has a weekly maintenance contract for its care. Mrs. Sanders was trapped for two hours before the elevator descended rapidly to the ground, injuring her during the landing.

2. A gynecologist failed to detect breast cancer in his patient who came in for a yearly physical examination. Three months later, when another physician detects the highly aggressive cancer, it is too late for treatment and the patient is advised that she has missed the chance to be cured of the disease. Her life expectancy is greatly diminished.

3. Thomas Warren was in a car accident in which he was rear-ended by a car driven by a teenager. He believes the damage to his car is minor, and that his headaches from the concussion he suffered during the accident should go away any day and are that not serious. The day before the statute of limitations to bring his action is about to expire, Thomas wakes up and decides he better see a lawyer. Thomas gets the last appointment available with the law firm early that evening. An associate listens to his recitation of the facts, and then tells Thomas he is going to check with one of the partners the next day to see whether the firm will take the case. The next day the associate has a family emergency that takes him out of state, and he does not follow up on the case. One week later, Thomas calls to see how his suit is progressing.

4. A man is admitted to a hospital for a hip transplant. His wife advises during the admission process that her husband falls often, as he has Parkinson's disease and frequently becomes confused. She requests that restraints be used on her

husband during his recovery. The day after surgery, the man was in good spirits and in a stable condition when seen by his physician. The next morning the man was found between the side rails of his bed, and had suffered a fracture of his femur. He did have a vest restraint on. The man's spouse is angered to learn of his injury, and that there was no formal order in the chart for restraints. She feels that her husband was not properly supervised and wants to bring a lawsuit.

▌ REVIEW QUESTIONS

1. How is negligence normally proven?

2. Which parties generally bear the burden of proof, the burden of rejoinder, and the rebuttal in a negligence case?

3. When is negligence presumed? What Latin phrase is used to describe this presumption?

4. What are the elements of the doctrine noted in the proceeding question, and how are they used?

5. What is medical malpractice? If a needle is left in a patient after surgery, can the doctrine of res ipsa loquitur be used to prove the plaintiff's case? Explain your answer.

6. How can the violation of a statute affect the outcome of a negligence case?

7. What factors might be considered by a law firm in deciding whether to accept a medical malpractice case?

8. In a legal malpractice case, what needs to be proven?

9. Are there any differences between legal and medical malpractice actions? If so, describe them.

10. Describe three examples of tort reform in medical malpractice actions.

▌ HELPFUL WEBSITES

This chapter deals with the field of malpractice. To learn more about malpractice, the following sites can be accessed:

General Legal Information

www.paralegal.delmar.cengage.com

www.institutefortorlegalreform.com

www.justice.org

www.atra.org

www.arbd.org

www.legalmalpracticelawreview.com

STUDENT COMPANION WEBSITE
For additional cases and study materials, please go to www.cengagebrain.com

Chapter 4

Special Negligence Actions

THE BIGGEST MISTAKES PARALEGALS MAKE AND HOW TO AVOID THEM

"It's Not What You Say That Counts—It's What You Don't Say"

During her latest paralegal job search, Michaela thought she had mastered all the frequently asked questions: *Why do you want to work here?* She knows this question poses the opportunity to show she has done her homework and knows something about the firm. *What are your strengths?* For this question, Michaela chooses something in her background that directly addresses the firm's mission statement. *What are your weaknesses?* Michaela has a bevy of examples to explain where her relative inexperience was countered by her problem-solving skills. *Name a professional failure, and how did you rise above it?* Michaela cites the knowledge she gained from experiences that confounded her yet offered her great foresight for future dilemmas. Michaela enters the interview process with the knowledge that a firm is looking for paralegals who are team players and have a genuine interest in bringing value to the firm.

(continues)

Michaela knows that her résumé proves all of those prerequisites and is the reason she has received an appointment to interview. But what happens when seemingly simple questions have a hidden agenda? One such question is: *Is there anything else you want to tell us that would influence our decision?*

To this exact question, Michaela revealed that she had a six-month-old baby and a three-year-old, and hoped the job hours were not too long and would not conflict with her babysitter's schedule. Michaela felt the interviewer appreciated her experience and glowing résumé. She left the interview feeling confident that she was the most qualified candidate, and that her candor and honesty were appreciated. Michaela was not offered the position.

Lesson Learned: Michaela gratuitously and prematurely revealed her personal circumstances, when the firm did not specifically ask that question. Personal questions about child-care arrangements and the ages and number of children are not relevant to the job and are illegal for employers to ask. Michaela should have waited until she was offered a position before requesting specific hours of work to accommodate her personal situation.

▌ INTRODUCTION

Negligence theory has evolved special legal concepts that apply, in certain circumstances, to particular types of activities.

Special negligence actions are cases involving certain well-defined activities. Special rules of negligence apply in these instances. The most common special negligence actions involve property ownership, employer/employee activities, and motor vehicle use. Theories of vicarious liability, in which someone is held accountable for the negligence of another person, and negligent infliction of emotional distress add unique and recognizable elements to the study of torts.

The basic negligence formula applies to all special actions discussed in this chapter. Negligence includes the following elements: duty of reasonable care, breach of duty, causation, and damages. Always keep this approach in mind when examining any negligence problem. However, each special action has its own peculiar analytical twists and turns that distinguish it from the other torts. This chapter covers the following:

- ▶ Vicarious liability and respondeat superior
- ▶ Premises liability
- ▶ Distinctions between trespassers, licensees, and invitees
- ▶ Modern trend in evaluation of premises liability based on ordinary negligence
- ▶ Attractive nuisance
- ▶ Negligent infliction of emotional distress
- ▶ Negligence per se

▌VICARIOUS LIABILITY

The previous chapter presented cases in which someone acting on behalf of the defendant actually caused harm to the plaintiff. In most of the cases, these individuals were employees of defendant businesses. This illustrates one aspect of vicarious liability.

Vicarious Liability Defined

Vicarious liability is the liability of one person, called the *principal,* for the tortious conduct of another, subordinate individual, called the *agent,* who was acting on the principal's behalf. In negligence law, principal/agent relationships most often involve employers and employees. The situation is simple. The principal is the employer, who hires the agent (employee) to work on the employer's behalf. So, for example, if an employee of Tom's Auto Shop, Inc. negligently repairs the brakes on a car and the car owner is injured as a result, the employer, Tom's Auto Shop, Inc., is liable for the negligence. Tom's Auto Shop, Inc. is the principal, responsible for its employee, who is the company's agent.

vicarious liability | Legal responsibility for the acts of another person because of some special relationship with that person; for example, the liability of an employer for certain acts of an employee.

Employment Is Not an Essential Element. The principal/agent relationship, however, need not be that of employer and employee. Nineteenth- and early-twentieth-century cases spoke of relationships between *master* and *servant.* This older classification suggested that the servant could work for the master without being paid. Thus, whether the agent is compensated for acting upon the principal's behalf is largely irrelevant to the issue of vicarious liability. Instead, focus upon this inquiry: Was one person acting on behalf of another? If so, a principal/agent relationship is present, and vicarious liability can exist.

Respondeat Superior

The employer is responsible for the negligence (or, for that matter, any torts) that his or her employees commit while working. This doctrine of vicarious liability is called **respondeat superior**, a Latin phrase meaning, "let the master answer."

respondeat superior | (Latin) "Let the master answer." Describes the principle that an employer is responsible for most harm caused by an employee acting within the scope of employment. In such a case, the employer is said to have vicarious liability.

Liability within Scope of Employment. Not every employee activity triggers the respondeat superior doctrine, however. An employer is responsible for an employee's actions that fall within the scope of employment. **Scope of employment** can be described as the range of conduct that the employer expects the employee to perform as part of his or her job. For example, a truck driver is expected to make deliveries and pickups for the employer; these actions fall within the scope of employment. But the driver is not expected to rob a liquor store while driving the company truck; this action falls outside the scope of employment.

scope of employment | The range of actions within which an employee is considered to be doing work for the employer.

Outside the Scope of Employment: Examples.
Employers are not liable for torts committed by employees that fall outside the scope of employment. Thus, in the preceding example, the employer would be responsible if the truck driver negligently crashed into another vehicle while making deliveries. However, the employer would not be accountable for the robbery (which actually involves criminal behavior but illustrates the scope concept).

Suppose the driver used the truck for personal purposes while not working, thereby going against company policy. Assume that the driver then negligently collided with another vehicle. Would the employer be responsible? No—the driver was acting outside the scope of employment by using the truck not for the employer's business, but for unauthorized personal use.

Frolic and Detour Rule

Employers are not vicariously liable for the negligence of their employees when employees go off on their own to handle personal matters, even though they might be performing work otherwise. For instance, suppose that while making deliveries for the employer, the truck driver decided to drive 180 miles to stop by and visit a friend in the next state. The employer probably did not authorize this sidetrack from the employee's assigned duties. Visits to socialize with friends fall outside the employee's scope of employment. Thus, if the driver were negligent while pursuing activities unrelated to employment during ordinary working hours, this would be considered to fall under the **frolic and detour rule**, and the employer would not be vicariously liable. Under the more modern view, an employee whose deviation is slight in terms of distance and time is considered to be acting within the scope of employment. An example of this would be where an employee who was making deliveries detoured one mile away from his route to buy an energy drink.

frolic and detour rule | Conduct of an employee that falls outside of the scope of employment that is purely for the benefit of said employee. An employer is not responsible for the negligence of an employee on a "frolic of his or her own."

Coming and Going Rule

Employers are usually not vicariously liable for the negligence of their employees while the employees are coming to or going from work. This is called the **coming and going rule**. A situation in which an employer would be liable in such circumstances is if the employee were performing work-related activities while on the way to or from the job, such as picking up office supplies at the employer's request.

coming and going rule | Rule used when employees commit torts while coming to or going from work. In respondeat superior cases, this rule helps decide whether an employee's actions fall outside the scope of employment.

Independent Contractors

An **independent contractor** is someone who has entered into a contract with another person to perform a specific task. The independent contractor controls how he or she accomplishes the job. The individual hiring the independent contractor simply agrees to pay him or her for doing the chore. Independent contractors are distinguishable from employees in that the employer does not control how an independent contractor does the job. In contrast, employers do control how their

independent contractor | A person who contracts with an "employer" to do a particular piece of work by his or her own methods and under his or her own control.

employer has no liability

employees perform their tasks. Whereas an employer must deduct social security and withholding taxes from an employee's pay, this is not required of an employer for an independent contractor. (See Internal Revenue Ruling 87-41.) Independent contractors must use their own tools, and they control the way in which a job is performed. A housepainter is an example of an independent contractor.

No Vicarious Liability for Independent Contractors. Persons hiring independent contractors are not vicariously liable for the independent contractors' negligence. The reasoning is that the independent contractor is engaging in his or her own work and should be responsible for his or her own negligence. The hirer is simply buying the independent contractor's finished service, and has nothing to do with how the independent contractor achieves the desired results.

For example, suppose Manuel hires a plumber to install a new shower in his house. Manuel has nothing to do with the actual job; in fact, he only lets the plumber in to go to work. The plumber negligently installs the water lines so that the hot faucet is connected to the cold water line and vice versa. After the shower is completed, Manuel's visiting friend is the first to use it and shockingly discovers the mistake, suffering severe burns. Is Manuel vicariously liable to his friend for the plumber's negligence? No—the plumber was an independent contractor. Manuel had no say in how the plumber completed the job. Manuel merely paid the final price after the plumber did the work. Thus, Manuel cannot be vicariously liable for the plumber's negligence. Instead of suing Manuel, his friend should sue the plumber.

Motor Vehicle Vicarious Liability

Since the first half of the twentieth century, courts have ruled that passengers in automobiles could be held vicariously liable for the driver's negligence. Using this analysis, if the automobile occupants were involved in a joint enterprise, such as a family traveling to a single destination, then the driver's negligence could be **imputed** to the passengers. This outcome may seem unfair, because a passenger has no actual control over how the driver operates the vehicle. Legal commentators have long criticized this type of vicarious liability. The better principle, long employed by the courts, holds the vehicle owner vicariously liable for the negligence of a driver other than the owner. For instance, suppose Britney's younger brother is driving her car negligently. He crashes into a motorcyclist, injuring her. Under vicarious liability, Britney would be accountable for her brother's negligence, because he was carelessly using her vehicle and injured another person as a result.

Many state legislatures have enacted statutes imposing vicarious liability on owners for the negligence of others who drive their vehicles. These are sometimes called *motor vehicle consent statutes*. An example of this is California's Vehicle Code § 17150 *et seq.*

imputed | When someone is blamed for something based merely on his or her relationship with another person.

Table 4-1 outlines vicarious liability. Table 4-2 shows some states where the owner of the car has vicarious liability for the driver.

TABLE 4-1
Vicarious liability summary

Vicarious Liability	Liability of principal for negligent actions of agent serving on principal's behalf. Commonly involves employer/ employee relationships.
Respondeat Superior	"Let the master answer." Doctrine through which employers may be held vicariously liable for employees' negligent actions committed within the scope of employment.
Scope of Employment	Range of conduct that employer expects of employee during performance of assigned employment responsibilities.
Frolic and Detour Rule	Employers are not vicariously liable for employees' negligence when employees deviate from assigned tasks within scope of employment, unless the deviation is minor. Usually this involves employees going off on their own to pursue personal needs.
Coming and Going Rule	Employers are not vicariously liable for employees' negligence while employees are coming to and going from work, unless employer has specifically requested employee to carry out a specific work-related task during such times.
Independent Contractors	Employers are not liable for independent contractors' negligence, because independent contractors act independently and are responsible for their own conduct.
Motor Vehicle Vicarious Liability	Motor vehicle owners may be held vicariously liable for the driver's negligence. Liability may also be established in motor vehicle consent statutes.

Copyright © 2015 Cengage Learning®.

TABLE 4-2
States in which the owner of the car has vicarious liability for the driver

STATE	VICARIOUS LIABILITY OF OWNER FOR DRIVER
Arizona	Yes
California	Yes
Connecticut	Yes
Delaware	Yes
Florida	Yes
Idaho	Yes
Iowa	Yes

State	Vicarious Liability of Owner for Driver
Maine	Yes
Michigan	Yes
Minnesota	Yes
Nevada	Yes
New York	Yes
Oklahoma	Yes
Pennsylvania	Yes
Rhode Island	Yes
Wisconsin	Yes

TABLE 4-2

States in which the owner of car has vicarious liability for the driver

HYPOTHETICALS

Sarah is a physician. Her nurse's aide, Gladys, draws blood from patients as part of her responsibilities on the job. One day, Gladys used a contaminated needle and thus infected a patient when she drew blood for testing. Would Sarah be vicariously liable for Gladys's negligence?

Gladys was performing a specific job assignment on Sarah's behalf. Drawing blood falls within Gladys's scope of employment. Under respondeat superior, Sarah would be accountable for Gladys's negligent act of using a contaminated needle and infecting a patient.

Suppose Gladys worked for a blood bank that routinely did blood draws and tests for area physicians. Under this scenario, Sarah would not have control over how Gladys acted. Gladys's employer is the blood bank, which would be an independent contractor in relation to Sarah. Accordingly, Sarah would not be accountable for Gladys's negligence.

* * *

Fargo is a fast-food restaurant manager. Mitchell is one of his employees. Fargo asked Mitchell to drive across town to a soft-drink supplier and pick up additional carbonated water. While on this errand, Mitchell stopped by the post office to check his mail. As he was leaving the post office parking lot, he failed to look both ways and collided with another vehicle. Would Fargo be vicariously liable for Mitchell's negligent driving?

Although Mitchell was running a business-related errand on Fargo's behalf, stopping by the post office to check personal mail falls outside Mitchell's scope of employment. However, as this is only a slight deviation, frolic and

(continues)

detour would not apply here. Thus, Fargo would be responsible for Mitchell's negligent conduct.

Suppose Fargo had been a passenger in Mitchell's car during this incident. Fargo (as the boss) could have controlled his employee, Mitchell, and instructed him not to stop at the post office. By permitting Mitchell to check his mail, Fargo implicitly consented to Mitchell's detour. This would place the detour within the scope of Mitchell's employment. Assuming that no statutes stated differently, Fargo would be vicariously liable.

▌ PREMISES LIABILITY

occupier | An individual who does not own but who uses real estate; includes tenants (lessees).

Special negligence rules apply to owners and occupiers of land. **Occupiers** are individuals who do not own but who do use real estate; this includes tenants (lessees). For simplicity's sake, we will speak in terms of the owner. The term *occupier* may always be substituted for *owner,* because negligence theories apply to both.

Landowner's Different Duties of Reasonable Care

As negligence law developed in the late nineteenth and early twentieth centuries, American courts devised different standards of reasonable care for landowners or land users. The distinctions depended upon whom the injured party (plaintiff) was, in terms of the victim's purpose for being on the land where the owner's negligence was alleged to have occurred.

Victim's Status on Land Defines Scope of Duty

For example, under old common law, the landowner owed a different duty of reasonable care to the injured party depending upon whether the victim was a trespasser, a licensee, or an invitee. (These terms are explained later in this section.) Thus, the plaintiff's status as a trespasser, licensee, or invitee determined the scope of duty that the owner owed. These distinctions affect the balance of risk of injury to others from the tort in question versus the possible benefits that might be received by the owner. Intentional torts involve intentional acts, and as such carry a high degree of risk and usually a low degree of social benefit. That is, the risk greatly outweighs the benefit. Therefore, the duty not to intentionally injure someone or something is great.

Modern Judicial Trends

For decades, courts and legal scholars have complained that this three-tier analytical approach is arbitrary and unnecessary. After all, ordinary negligence theory appears adequately equipped to establish the landowner's duty of reasonable care. If an owner acted unreasonably in maintaining his or her realty, and as a result a victim was harmed, then the owner should be liable. Regular negligence theory works well to produce a just result, say these critics.

Many courts have in fact abolished the three-tier landowner standards of care. The landmark case was *Rowland v. Christian,* 69 Cal. 2d 108, 443 P. 2d 561, 70 Cal. Rptr. 97 (1968) (superseded by statute, as explained in *Perez v. Southern Pacific Transport Co.,* 218 Cal. App. 3d 462, 267 Cal. Rptr. 100 [1990]), in which the distinctions were eliminated in favor of traditional negligence theory. Many states have followed the California Supreme Court's lead. Still, many courts continue to apply the three-tier system, which is described in the following sections.

Table 4-3 shows the duty of care owed by the landowner to others by state.

Tier 1. Landowner's "Zero Duty" toward Trespassers

Landowners owe no duty of reasonable care toward trespassers. The risk to a trespasser should be essentially nonexistent compared to the benefit of keeping the trespasser away. Owners may not intentionally injure trespassers upon their real estate, but they need not search their realty and safeguard it for trespassers' unauthorized uses (*Katko v. Briney,* 183 N.W.2d 657). Courts favoring this policy reason that a landowner should not be required to exercise ordinary reasonable care to protect a tortfeasor (i.e., trespasser) from harm. Because the trespasser is committing an intentional tort, negligence law insists only that real estate owners avoid intentionally injuring trespassers. Otherwise, the trespasser *assumes the risk* of entering someone else's land without permission.

Special Rule for Trespassing Children: Attractive Nuisance. However, landowners owe a higher duty of reasonable care to trespassing children. This rule affords greater protection to children than to the ordinary trespasser. The reasoning behind this special rule states that children, especially when young, are so inexperienced and naive that they may not fully appreciate dangers lurking

State	Duty Owed
Alaska	Standard of reasonableness
California	Standard of reasonableness
Florida	Depends on status: invitee, licensee, trespasser, child trespasser
New York	Standard of reasonableness
Ohio	Depends on status: invitee, licensee, trespasser, child trespasser
Pennsylvania	Depends on status: invitee, licensee, trespasser, child trespasser, recreational guest
Texas	Depends on status: invitee, licensee, trespasser, infant trespasser, recreational guest

TABLE 4-3
Duty of care owed by landowner to others by state

upon the land. Therefore, owners must exercise ordinary, reasonable care to safeguard their realty for trespassing children who are enticed onto the land to investigate the dangerous condition that injured them. Young children are often attracted, out of curiosity, to investigate dangerous conditions on realty, such as abandoned wells, railroad tracks, swimming pools, or unused machinery. These alluring items are often hazardous, a fact that the trespassing child may not understand. The attraction element has given this special rule its name of the **attractive nuisance doctrine** or, more commonly, **attractive nuisance**.

Currently, a four-part test is employed to hold the landowner liable under the attractive nuisance doctrine:

1. The owner must know or have reason to know of the artificial condition (i.e., not a natural feature of the land) on the premises.
2. The structure, instrumentality, or condition must be alluring to children and endanger them. They cannot know or appreciate the danger.
3. The presence of children must reasonably have been anticipated.
4. The danger posed to the children outweighs the cost of making the condition safe.

If a trespassing child is injured as a result of having been enticed onto the land to investigate some dangerous condition, then the landowner is liable for such harm.

Table 4-4 shows states that follow a form of the attractive nuisance doctrine.

TABLE 4-4
States that follow a form of the attractive nuisance doctrine

State	Attractive nuisance doctrine
California	No—legislates against specific dangers instead (i.e., must fence pools)
Florida	Yes
New York	Yes
Ohio	Yes
Pennsylvania	Yes
Texas	Yes

THE CASE OF THE INVITING POOL

Pool accidents are a tragedy waiting to happen. Adults are keenly aware of the dangers of open pools. Here, even with adult supervision, a drowning could not be prevented. Although an adult might find a cloudy pool unappealing, a child might not recognize that anything is amiss and even find the pool more attractive.

UDDIN, Admr., Appellee,
v.
EMBASSY SUITES HOTEL et al., Appellants

Supreme Court of Ohio
No. 2006-0189
Submitted February 13, 2007
Decided May 2, 2007

A ten-year-old girl, Shayla Uddin, drowned in an indoor pool at a hotel while under adult supervision and while other children played around her. A witness stated that it was not possible to see the bottom of the pool, even though it was no more than five feet deep at its greatest depth. According to that witness, "when a child went underwater . . . you lost sight of them because the water was so murky." Shayla was located by someone feeling along the bottom of the pool for her body.

Shayla and her family were invitees of the hotel, and accordingly the hotel was required to exercise reasonable care for their safety and protection, and to advise them of latent dangers on the premises.

The hotel, however, owed no duty to Shayla and her family regarding dangers on the premises that were open and obvious. The rationale for the open-and-obvious doctrine is that "'the open and obvious nature of the hazard itself serves as a warning. Thus, the owner or occupier may reasonably expect that persons entering the premises will discover those dangers and take appropriate measures to protect themselves.'"

Ohio's appellate courts generally have held that a swimming pool constitutes an open and obvious danger. Our courts also have suggested generally, based on law from other jurisdictions, that the doctrine applies to both adults and minors.

Ohio's appellate courts have been reluctant to apply the open-and-obvious doctrine to children of tender years. ("We decline to determine whether a swimming pool is an open-and-obvious danger to a child under seven years of age.") Nevertheless, the trial court here held, without citation of authority, that the hotel's "indoor swimming pool was an open and obvious danger of which even a child of ten years old . . . should have been aware."

Given the importance of the issue presented here and the unique issues presented by children in Ohio tort law, I believe that this court should answer the question of whether the hotel owed a duty to Shayla, or whether no duty existed because the open-and-obvious doctrine applied to young children like her.

This court should also address whether the increased peril of drowning associated with opaque or murky water in a swimming pool, is sufficiently apparent to a child of tender years to warrant the application of the open-and-obvious-danger doctrine to her. On the facts presented by this case, I would hold that the open-and-obvious doctrine is not applicable to children of tender years.

An adult may instantly recognize that cloudy water increases his or her risk of drowning because the diminished clarity impairs the vision of those supervising, thereby hindering potential rescue efforts. To a ten-year-old child, however, the danger may not be as readily apparent. I agree with the Court of Appeals that the trial court erred by finding that the open-and-obvious doctrine applied to a ten-year-old child on the facts presented here, and in granting summary judgment in favor of the hotel. Accordingly, I would affirm.

CASE QUESTIONS

1. Was it foreseeable that children might be hurt as a result of the pool being poorly maintained?
2. What conditions must be found for the court to hold that an attractive nuisance exists?
3. Would the case have been decided differently if the pool had not been cloudy?

The *Restatement (Second) of Torts*

For decades, the American Law Institute has assembled Restatements of the Law, which summarize the legal principles discussed in common law decisions. These are highly regarded secondary sources of law, and are frequently cited by courts. These include the *Restatement of Torts* and its successors, the *Restatement (Second) of Torts* and the *Restatement (Third) of Torts*.

HYPOTHETICAL

Belle is a student attending the local community college. She occasionally trespasses across Farmer Bob's cattle pasture when she walks from her apartment to campus. One day, while cutting across the land, Belle encountered Bob's prize bull, which was in a particularly agitated frame of mind. The bull charged and knocked Belle to the ground, injuring her. Is Bob liable?

Because Belle was a trespasser, Bob owed her no duty of reasonable care. Accordingly, she took her chances by walking across the pasture without permission. Bob would not be liable for her injuries.

Suppose that Belle was five years old and came upon Bob's farm to play on the swing set. The set is rickety and old. Attractive nuisance theory would hold Bob liable when Belle cuts her hand on a broken, jagged edge of the swing. Belle was enticed onto the realty by the swing set, which, due to her youth, she did not notice was old and in disrepair. Bob failed to exercise reasonable care to protect trespassing children such as Belle from the risk of being cut by a sharp edge on the swing. The threat of being hurt on the swing was unreasonable, as a child of Belle's age could not be expected to realize that the set was too old to be used safely. Young children are likely to be lured onto land to play on playground equipment. The dangerous condition was artificial because Bob installed the swing set on his property and then failed to repair the set or take it down. Any of the attractive nuisance theories discussed previously would hold Bob accountable under these facts.

Suppose, instead, that Belle was a cat burglar who was breaking into Bob's barn late one night. Unbeknownst to Belle, Bob had wired a shotgun to the windows inside the barn; anyone raising the window frame would instantly be shot. Belle tried to enter through the window and was seriously hurt by the gun blast. Would Bob be liable?

Although Bob owes Belle (who was trespassing) no duty of reasonable care, he may not set a lethal trap for would-be burglars. Landowners cannot create an unreasonable danger to injure trespassers. Bob would be liable for Belle's injuries in this factual scenario.

Restatement (Second) of Torts § 339. Many courts now follow § 339 of the *Restatement (Second) of Torts* and hence have discarded the attraction element of the theory. For these courts, it is sufficient that (1) the injury to the trespassing child was reasonably foreseeable; (2) the danger on the land presented an unreasonable risk of harm to trespassing children; (3) the danger on the land was artificial, meaning manmade rather than natural; (4) because of the child's youth, he or she could not appreciate the risks involved or did not discover (and understand) the threat; (5) the threatening condition was located at a place across which children were likely to trespass; and (6) the landowner failed to exercise reasonable care to protect trespassing children from the danger that caused the harm. Under this version of attractive nuisance, the danger did not have to entice the child onto the land. It is adequate that the child encountered and was hurt by a danger that he or she did not fully discern.

Beneath all its trimmings, *Restatement* § 339 is simply negligence theory applied to trespassing children. The basic negligence elements are there, and the reasoning is identical.

Numerous jurisdictions depart from the *Restatement*'s artificial condition element. These courts would include natural dangers, such as streams, quicksand, or rock formations, as risks against which the landowner must take precautions to protect trespassing children.

Tier 2. Landowner's Duty of Reasonable Care toward Licensees

Licensees Defined. **Licensees** are persons who have permission to be upon another's land. They are distinguishable from trespassers in that the landowner has consented to their presence upon his or her realty. This consent may be expressed or implied. Examples of licensees include social guests, such as friends who gather at a person's house to study or neighbors coming over to borrow tools; door-to-door salespersons or charitable solicitors (when the landowner has not prohibited their entry by posting warning signs); and frequent trespassers to whose incursions the landowner implicitly consents (such as when trespassers frequently use shortcuts that the landowner does not discourage through fencing or sign-posting).

Owners owe licensees a duty of reasonable care in using the real estate, because the risk and the benefit are equal. This includes the owner's obligation to correct known dangers (both artificial and natural) on the land. In other words, if the owner knows (or reasonably should know) that a hazardous condition exists on the realty, then he or she must exercise reasonable care in safeguarding licensees from these risks. For example, if an abandoned well has not been covered, and a travelling salesperson visits and falls into the well (which cannot be seen because of overgrown grass), then the landowner has breached his or her duty of

licensee | A person who is on property with permission, but without any enticement by the owner and with no financial advantage to the owner.

reasonable care to the salesperson, assuming that the owner knew (or should have known) that the well was there and could not be detected.

For licensees, the owner is not required to discover and correct unknown threats on the land. For invitees, however, the owner is obligated to do this, as we shall see later.

HYPOTHETICAL

Ben owns an apartment building. Fundraisers for a local charity frequently solicit contributions from his tenants. Ben does not object to this solicitation, although he does not encourage it. Alex is one of the charity's fundraisers. While visiting Ben's apartment complex, Alex broke his leg when he fell through a rotten wooden stairway. Alex could not see the rotting condition from the top of the steps, but the damage was evident if one looked up from below the stairway. Is Ben liable to Alex?

Alex is a licensee, because Ben permitted him to come onto the apartment premises. The key in this case is whether the rotten steps were a known hazard. Perhaps Ben did not know that the steps were rotten. However, Ben reasonably should have known that his apartment steps were dangerous. A building owner is expected to be aware of such easily discoverable risks, as it is easily foreseeable that a stairway user might be hurt if rotten steps collapse. Thus, Ben would be liable for Alex's injuries.

Suppose, instead, that Ben had posted signs clearly warning, "NO SO-LICITORS ALLOWED! ALL TRESPASSERS WILL BE PROSECUTED!" Would he be liable for Alex's injuries? In this version of the facts, Alex would be a trespasser, and so Ben would not owe a duty of reasonable care to Alex. Accordingly, Ben would not be liable for the harm to Alex.

Suppose that Ben had posted such signs but did nothing further to discourage solicitors from coming onto his premises. Suppose that door-to-door salespersons and charitable solicitors, including Alex, regularly visited the apartments with impunity. Under this set of facts, Ben has implicitly consented to the solicitors' presence, including Alex's. Thus, Alex would be a licensee.

Tier 3. Landowner's Highest Duty of Reasonable Care toward Invitees

invitee | A person who is at a place by invitation.

Invitees Defined. Invitees, or *business invitees* as older court opinions call them, are persons invited upon the landowner's premises. Originally, the common law restricted the term to individuals invited onto premises for business purposes, such as customers to a grocery store, clothing store, amusement park, or tavern. Modern cases, however, state that an invitee need not be involved in any business-related purposes when he or she enters another's real estate. It is sufficient that the landowner encourage the invitee to visit.

Usually, invitees are persons coming onto the land for some purpose that the owner wishes to serve. Commonly, this includes any business, but could also include nonprofit organizations, such as churches, soup kitchens, charitable hospitals, or even colleges.

Landowners owe the highest duty of reasonable care to invitees, because the risk of injury is greater and the benefit is more personal than social. Owners must not only repair known dangers on the property but also must discover and correct unknown risks. This is a broader standard, requiring the landowner to take extra efforts to render his or her premises reasonably safe for invitees.

The logic underlying this stiffer standard of care suggests that owners who invite someone onto realty should be expected to exercise greater caution to ensure that the premises are reasonably danger-free. After all, the invitee would not be on the land to begin with had it not been for the owners' invitation.

Invitees and Licensees Distinguished.

Invitee is a subcategory of *licensee,* yet the terms are distinguishable. All licensees have the owner's implied or expressed permission to be on the land, but the landowner does not have to invite or encourage licensees to visit; rather, the owner may just passively tolerate the licensees' presence. With invitees, however, the owner either implies an invitation or expressly invites them onto the real estate. This reflects the owner's active role in getting the invitees onto his or her land. Usually, the owner seeks customers for business; hence, courts often speak of business invitees.

Implicit or Express Invitation.

The landowner's invitation to others to enter the premises may be expressed (e.g., a welcome sign outside a church or a business posting its hours on its door) or implied (e.g., a business leaving its doors open during business hours).

HYPOTHETICAL

Mike operates a shelter for homeless persons. Anyone forced to live on the streets is welcome at the facility. Liz frequently visits the shelter for free meals and a bed for the night. While sleeping one evening, Liz was stabbed by a loose, rusty wire through the mattress upon which she slept. She had to undergo precautionary medical treatment for tetanus. Would Mike be liable for Liz's injury?

Liz was an invitee, because she was homeless and Mike expressly encouraged persons such as her to use his premises. Liz was injured as a result of a hidden danger (the loose wire) that could have been discovered if Mike had inspected the

(continues)

mattresses for wear and tear. Thus, Mike failed to exercise reasonable care to make the shelter reasonably safe for his patrons. As a result, one of his customers, Liz, was harmed, so Mike is liable to her.

* * *

Karla manages a local appliance store. Wade came in one day to look for a new washer and dryer. Karla showed Wade a popular model. Wade wished to see the units operate, but there were no electrical outlets nearby. Karla went to her office to get an extension cord. Meanwhile, Wade wandered through a set of swinging doors labeled "warehouse—employees only," hoping that he might find another salesperson who could locate an extension cord. Instead, he found a fork-loading truck that swerved around a wall and knocked Wade to the ground, severely injuring him. The truck driver did not expect anyone to be in the area. Is Karla liable to Wade?

Wade was an invitee when he visited the store to look for new appliances. However, he ceased to be an invitee when he entered the restricted area (the warehouse) without permission. Because he had been invited into the store originally, most courts would say that Wade became a licensee once he entered the storeroom, as it is reasonably foreseeable that customers might mistakenly trespass into such a limited-access area. Karla owed Wade a duty of reasonable care to discover and correct known dangers on the premises. In this case, the fork truck was not threatening in and of itself, as a rotten stairway or improperly stacked boxes would be. The danger would be considered unknown, as it was not reasonably foreseeable that a patron would be hurt by a truck moving around a restricted-access warehouse. Accordingly, Karla would not be liable for Wade's injury.

Arguably, though, the threat of the fork truck harming a wayward customer *was* foreseeable, because the truck driver reasonably should have anticipated that patrons might enter the warehouse from time to time, looking for salespersons or restrooms. This would make the risk known and, arguably, Karla thus breached her duty of reasonable care when her employee failed to watch for patrons while driving the truck through the warehouse. This reasoning is equally sound and persuasive. This case points out the artificial distinctions in classifying people by the reason they are on the premises. The traditional negligence approach would be much simpler.

Limited Areas of Invitation. Obviously, most landowners do not invite people into every nook and cranny of their property. Certain regions are off-limits. For example, most businesses have storage rooms, manager's offices, or machinery rooms that patrons are specifically discouraged from entering. Virtually any business has door signs warning "private," "authorized personnel only," "keep out," and similar prohibitions. The owner's invitation to invitees does not include such areas. If an individual was injured while visiting an off-limits zone, that person would be considered merely a licensee, or perhaps even a trespasser (depending upon how sternly the warning was phrased—such as "no trespassing—keep out!"), rather than an invitee.

From a plaintiff's standpoint, being included as an invitee spells maximum tort relief, at least in terms of monetary damages. This concludes the description of the three different standards of duty owed by a landowner under the older three-tier system. The next section focuses on the more modern system for landowner cases.

Using Traditional Negligence Theory in Landowner Cases

As noted earlier, many courts have eliminated the trespasser/licensee/invitee approach in favor of regular negligence theory. Instead of forcing the injured party into one of these three categories, many courts simply ask the routine negligence questions: Was the injury reasonably foreseeable? Did the landowner's scope of duty include the victim? Did the owner cause the victim's injury? and so forth. Many courts, however, cling tenaciously to the older three-tier analysis. This demonstrates how entrenched precedent becomes; once a rule of law becomes settled, it is difficult to change precedent. The law changes at a snail's pace. More often than not, this provides valuable stability and predictability in legal problem solving. Nonetheless, it also makes legal principles slow to adapt to the rapid changes of our dynamic society. Table 4-5 summarizes the special negligence analysis for landowners and occupiers.

Duty to Trespasser	Landowner/occupier owes no duty of reasonable care; is required only to avoid intentional (or willful and wanton) injury.
Duty to Licensee	Landowner/occupier owes duty of reasonable care to correct known dangers on premises.
Duty to Invitee	Landowner/occupier owes duty of reasonable care to discover and correct unknown dangers on premises.
Traditional Negligence Theory	Applies regular negligence standards to determine landowner/occupier liability.
Duty to Trespassing Children (Attractive Nuisance Theory)	Landowner/occupier owes duty of reasonable care to protect trespassing children from artificial dangers on premises, when (1) owner knows or has reason to know of the dangerous condition on the premises; (2) the structure, instrumentality, or condition is alluring to children and endangers them; (3) the presence of children can reasonably be anticipated; and (4) the danger posed to the children outweighs the cost of making the condition safe.

TABLE 4-5

Landowners'/occupiers' negligence liability

THE CASE OF THE ICY RECEPTION

At first blush, this case might seem like a plaintiff's attorney's perfect case. There is an extremely sympathetic fact pattern to present to a jury. A shopper is injured during a slip and fall on ice in the parking lot. Although the facts might seem clear cut, the elements of negligence must still be proved, and the relationship of the parties considered.

Mitchell R. GARRITY and Sherry L. Garrity, Plaintiffs

v.

WAL-MART STORES EAST, LIMITED PARTNERSHIP, Defendant

288 F.R.D. 395

W.D. Kentucky,

United States District Court,

Owensboro Division.

December 20, 2012

On February 12, 2010, Plaintiffs Mitchell Garrity and Sherry Garrity took their daughters to Wal-Mart Store # 701 to get their Ford Explorer serviced. Mr. Garrity also planned to exchange some items that he had previously purchased at Wal-Mart. Mr. Garrity parked his vehicle in the oil-express lane on the west side of Wal-Mart near the entrance of the Tire & Lube Express ("TLE") Department. He then walked with his family through the entrance of the TLE Department.

Mr. Garrity registered his vehicle for service. He then asked the Wal-Mart employee who took his service order whether he could return his items through the TLE Department. Both parties agree that the employee informed Mr. Garrity that he could not return the items through the TLE Department. Mr. Garrity exited the TLE Department through the same door that he entered and proceeded toward the front of the store. According to Mr. Garrity, both the TLE parking lot and the area immediately outside the TLE Department were clear of ice and snow.

Mr. Garrity then began walking on the only sidewalk that connects the TLE Department to the front of the store, which sidewalk is adjacent to Wal-Mart's lawn and garden area. Mr. Garrity slipped and fell on black ice, breaking his hip and injuring his lower back. Mr. Garrity testified that the sidewalk on which he slipped "looked like it had been worked on, and it was wet in areas". He further testified that it "looked like somebody had cleared a path," as the snow appeared to have been cleared to the sidewalk's sides. After Mr. Garrity fell, he first discovered the black ice.

Soon after Mr. Garrity fell, he was approached by another Wal-Mart customer. She testified that she did not see the ice when she looked at the sidewalk, but when she went to help Mr. Garrity, she almost slipped and fell. The customer stated that the existence of ice was deceptive, as "it looked like the sidewalk was wet." Also, an EMT who arrived on the scene to treat Mr. Garrity testified that the sidewalk appeared to be only wet and that he almost slipped on ice. Wal-Mart concedes that "no clearing or attempt at clearing was performed on the concrete sidewalk where Mitchell fell."

Wal-Mart argues that it is entitled to summary judgment because it did not have a duty to protect Mr. Garrity from the ice on which he fell. Kentucky law provides that "the owner of a business premises has no duty to protect invitees from injuries caused by 'natural outdoor hazards which are as obvious to an invitee as to an owner of the premises.'" According to Wal-Mart, since Mr. Garrity did not observe the ice until he fell, and since others who came to his aid did not see the ice until they slipped, the ice was as obvious to invitees as it was to Wal-Mart. *See, e.g., Bryan v. O'Charley's Inc.*, 2003 WL 21949182, (Ky.App. Aug. 15, 2003) (recognizing that black ice "would be virtually impossible for anyone to discover" and holding that it is "as obvious to the invitee as to the owner"). By contrast, Plaintiffs suggest that the Kentucky Supreme Court's decision in *Kentucky River Medical Center v. McIntosh*, 319 S.W.3d 385 (Ky.2010) renders summary judgment inappropriate in this case.

Prior to the *McIntosh* decision, Kentucky law was "not generous to business invitees who suffer[ed] an injury as a result of a risk created by an obvious, outdoor natural condition. . . ." The general rule was that "the owner of a business premises [had] no duty to protect invitees from injuries caused by 'natural outdoor hazards which [were] as obvious to an invitee as to an owner of the premises.'"

In *McIntosh,* however, the Kentucky Supreme Court modified the open and obvious doctrine, making it more compatible with Kentucky's comparative fault regime. 319 S.W.3d 385, 389–90 (Ky.2010). The case arose when a paramedic tripped over an unmarked curb located between an ambulance dock and a hospital's emergency room, suffering a fractured hip and sprained wrist. The court adopted the modern trend on premises liability as stated in the Restatement (Second) of Torts § 343A(1) (1965).

A possessor of land is not liable to his invitees for physical harm caused to them by any activity or condition on the land whose danger is known or obvious to them, unless the possessor should anticipate the harm despite such knowledge or obviousness. The court then stated that there are cases where a land possessor "can and should anticipate that the dangerous condition will cause physical harm to the invitee notwithstanding its known or obvious danger."

Wal-Mart claims that *McIntosh* is inapplicable to cases involving natural outdoor hazards. The court disagrees. The Kentucky Court of Appeals has interpreted *McIntosh* to apply to natural outdoor hazard cases. In *Bruner v. Miami Management Co.,* the court of Appeals recognized the defendant's argument that "*McIntosh* should be narrowly applied to its facts, that is, when the danger is manmade, not when the danger is the result of a natural hazard." It then asserted, however, that it did "not read *McIntosh* that narrowly."

Wal-Mart also claims that it is entitled to summary judgment when the facts are considered in light of *McIntosh*. The court must first decide whether the ice that posed the danger to Mr. Garrity was open and obvious.

Plaintiffs argue that a genuine issue of material fact exists as to whether the ice was open and obvious. The court agrees. Kentucky courts have long held that a danger is obvious when "both the condition and the risk are apparent to and would be recognized by a reasonable man in the position of the visitor

exercising ordinary perception, intelligence, and judgment." In this case, the court cannot say as a matter of law that the ice upon which Mr. Garrity slipped was open and obvious. Plaintiffs have presented evidence that there was no precipitation for at least two days prior to Mr. Garrity's fall.

Plaintiffs have also presented testimony that the sidewalk seemed wet and that the ice upon which Mr. Garrity slipped appeared to be water. Plaintiffs have presented testimony that it may have been difficult to distinguish the ice from water because there was a fence next to the sidewalk that created a shadow. Thus, there is a genuine dispute of material fact as to whether the ice was open and obvious.

Even if the ice was open and obvious, summary judgment would still be inappropriate. Rather, you must ask whether the land possessor could reasonably foresee that an invitee would be injured by the danger. If the land possessor can foresee the injury, but nevertheless fails to take reasonable precautions to prevent the injury, he can be held liable. The questions thus become whether Wal-Mart could have foreseen Mr. Garrity's injury and, if so, whether it failed to take reasonable precautions to prevent that injury.

The Kentucky Supreme Court in *McIntosh* detailed three circumstances where injuries are foreseeable—and thus where land possessors owe a duty to invitees despite a condition's obviousness. 319 S.W.3d at 393. First, a land possessor owes a duty when it is foreseeable that an invitee might be distracted from a danger. Second, a land possessor owes a duty when it is foreseeable that an invitee might forget a danger previously discovered. Third, a land possessor owes a duty when it is foreseeable that an invitee might choose to encounter a danger because the advantages of doing so outweigh the apparent risks.

In the present case, the court finds that there is a genuine dispute of material fact as to whether Wal-Mart could foresee Mr. Garrity's injury. Particularly, the court finds that there is a question as to whether an invitee might choose to encounter the ice

(continues)

because the advantages of getting to the front of the store outweigh the apparent risks. The court finds *Schmidt v. Intercontinental Hotels Grp. Res., Inc. & Hotel*, 850 F.Supp.2d 663 (E.D.Ky.2012) persuasive. In that case, the court paid particular attention to the fact that the hotel's attendant instructed Ms. Schmidt on where to walk. The court also highlighted the fact that the hotel had cleared the parking lots and some of the sidewalks—but had not cleared all of the sidewalk where Ms. Schmidt fell. According to the court, "[a] possessor that knows an area is dangerous and yet tells an invitee to encounter the danger . . . surely could foresee that a guest, unfamiliar with the premises, would trust and follow the hotel's entry advice. . . ."

In this case, Plaintiffs presented evidence that Wal-Mart had cleared the parking lots and some of the sidewalks—but had not cleared the sidewalk where Mr. Garrity fell. Moreover, Wal-Mart concedes that no clearing attempt was undertaken on the sidewalk where Mr. Garrity fell. Further, Mr. Garrity testified that a Wal-Mart employee instructed him to exit the TLE Department and walk to the front of the store to make his exchange. Since a reasonable jury could conclude that Wal-Mart knew that the sidewalk had not been cleared and yet told Mr. Garrity to walk to the front of the store, summary judgment is not appropriate.

In this case, the court concludes that summary judgment is not appropriate. While Wal-Mart argues that the sidewalk was not cleared because the lawn and garden area was closed to customers in the winter, the court finds that the evidence in the record could lead a reasonable jury to conclude that Mr. Garrity might choose to encounter the ice because the advantages of getting to the front of the store outweighed the apparent risks. The fact that Mr. Garrity had alternative options of walking on the cleared parking lot or making the returns at another time does not change this fact.

The court also finds that summary judgment is inappropriate because there are two additional genuine disputes of material fact relating to the parties' comparative fault. First, if the jury finds that Wal-Mart owed a duty to Mr. Garrity, there is a genuine dispute of material fact as to Wal-Mart's fault. While Wal-Mart concedes that it did not clear the sidewalk of ice and snow accumulation, it also claims that it was not required to do so, as the lawn and garden area was closed in the winter.

Whether it was reasonable to leave the sidewalk in an un-maintained condition is a question of fact for the jury. In its analysis of this question, the jury may consider the industry standards, Owensboro's adopted codes and ordinances, and Wal-Mart's maintenance policy.

Second, if the jury finds that Wal-Mart owed Mr. Garrity a duty, there is a genuine dispute of material fact as to Mr. Garrity's fault. In its analysis of this question, the jury may consider Mr. Garrity's evidence that: the sidewalk on which he fell is the only sidewalk from the TLE Department to the front of the store; he received instructions from Wal-Mart to return his items to the front of the store; and since the Wal-Mart parking lot had been cleared, he believed that the sidewalks were safe. Moreover, the jury may consider Wal-Mart's evidence that its employee did not instruct Mr. Garrity to walk to the front of the store and that Mr. Garrity had several alternatives, including the options of: waiting until his vehicle was finished and driving to the front of the store; walking on the cleared driveways and parking areas west of the pallets; and making the exchange at another time.

The court notes that Plaintiffs presented evidence that Mr. Garrity was not aware of the ice that injured him before he fell and that a Wal-Mart employee instructed him to walk toward the hazard.

In sum, because genuine disputes of material fact exist, summary judgment is inappropriate. Therefore, Wal-Mart's motion for summary judgment must be **DENIED**.

CASE QUESTIONS
1. Whose argument do you think was more persuasive, the plaintiff's or the defendant's? Explain your answer.
2. Do you think it is fair to hold a defendant responsible for injuries caused by black ice? Explain your answer.

In the section that follows, another special negligence action called *negligent inflic-tion of emotional distress* is addressed.

NEGLIGENT INFLICTION OF EMOTIONAL DISTRESS

Emotional distress consists of mental anguish caused by a tortfeasor. This con-dition includes fright, anxiety, shock, grief, mental suffering, shame, embarrass-ment, and emotional disturbance. The tort exists when the tortfeasor inflicts psychological injury on the victim. **Negligent infliction of emotional distress** consists of: (1) Outrageous conduct by the tortfeasor, which (2) the tortfeasor reasonably should have anticipated would produce (3) significant and reasonably foreseeable emotional injury to the victim; when (4) the tortfeasor breached his or her duty of reasonable care to avoid causing such emotional harm to the victim; and (5) the victim was a reasonably foreseeable plaintiff. When a former enemy telephones you and, to hurt you, tells you that he heard that your parents have died, when they are alive and well, this is just one example of negligent infliction of emotional distress. Stories you hear of the wrong person being buried in a fam-ily grave are also examples of this tort.

Extra Elements in the Common Law

These generalized elements of negligent infliction of emotional distress are syn-thesized from those of many jurisdictions. Different courts apply various special requirements to negligent infliction cases, and it is always wise to check the rules and cases of the particular jurisdiction in which your case lies.

Impact Rule

A minority of courts insist that some physical impact accompany the emotional injury. Thus, the tortfeasor must negligently do something that physically touches the victim if the victim is to recover damages for negligent infliction of emotional distress. This is often called the **impact rule**, and it has been severely criticized in the legal literature and judicial decisions.

The purpose of the impact requirement is to protect against false claims of emotional distress. Because mental anguish is largely invisible, courts at the turn of the century felt that the defendant had to make contact with the plaintiff to justify compensating something that was not always apparent, such as mental harm. Modern courts utilizing the impact rule have seen impact in almost any physical touching. Something as casual as putting one's hand on a classmate's shoulder would be con-sidered sufficient contact to satisfy the impact rule. Hence, it would seem that, as a safeguard against false claims of emotional distress, the physical impact requirement does little or nothing to ensure honesty and sincerity for allegations of mental hurt.

emotional distress | Mental anguish. Nonphysical harm that may be compensated for by damages in some types of lawsuits. Mental anguish may be as limited as the immediate mental feelings during an injury or as broad as prolonged grief, shame, humiliation, despair, and so forth.

negligent infliction of emotional distress | Outrageous conduct by the tortfeasor that the tortfeasor reasonably should have anticipated would produce significant and reasonably foreseeable emotional injury to the victim.

impact rule | The rule (used today in very few states) that damages for emotional distress cannot be had in a negligence lawsuit unless there is some physical contact or impact.

Physical Manifestations Rule

The majority of courts have abandoned the impact rule in favor of the **physical manifestations rule**. This requires that, in addition to mental suffering, the plaintiff must experience physical symptoms as a result of the emotional distress. This rule is also thought to protect against false claims of emotional injury. After all, if a victim experiences some physical malady associated with an emotional harm, such as an ulcer, hives, sleeplessness, weight loss, or bowel dysfunction, then the probability is that the emotional harm is genuine.

Zone of Danger Rule

What happens when the negligent action occurs to someone else, and the plaintiff is a bystander who witnesses a negligent injury to another person? Could the tortfeasor be liable to the bystander for negligent infliction of emotional distress? Consider an example. Suppose parents witnessed their child being struck by a negligent driver. Would the parents have a cause of action against the driver for negligent infliction of emotional distress?

No impact occurred to the parents, although they may suffer physical manifestations as a result of witnessing their child's injury. The proper question, however, may be phrased in ordinary negligence terms: Did the driver owe (and breach) a duty of reasonable care to the parents by injuring their child? Did the driver's actions cause the parents' emotional suffering? Does proximate cause exist? Were the parents injured?

Certainly, the driver could not reasonably anticipate that any bystander would suffer emotional distress as a result of the driver's negligent act of hitting a pedestrian. There must be some way to limit the scope of duty (and, hence, the range of foreseeable plaintiffs). Courts have attempted to establish such limits by creating the **zone of danger rule**. Under this rule, only bystanders who fall within the zone of danger can recover for negligent infliction of emotional distress. In other words, these individuals must have been threatened by the original negligent action (e.g., negligent driving of a vehicle) and have reasonably feared for their own safety, or have certain family relationships, as discussed next.

THE CASE OF THE DISTRESSED BRIDE

In this case, one of a bride's worst nightmares occurs. Her carefully selected dream wedding venue and specified date are given to another bride months before the wedding. Could this have been avoided? The bride approached the situation with great seriousness and made sure that a contract was signed and a deposit given. Slowly this situation unraveled. What is the lesson here for future brides?

Maureen MURPHY
v.
LORD THOMPSON MANOR, INC.

Appellate Court of Connecticut

No. 28106

Decided January 29, 2008

We are born, some marry and we die. In this list of life events, it is only in marriage that we make choices. This appeal arises out of an action by the plaintiff, Maureen Murphy, to recover damages from the defendant, Lord Thompson Manor, Inc. (manor), for its failure to perform a contract for wedding related services and accommodations. Following a trial to the court, the court found the manor liable under theories of breach of contract and negligent infliction of emotional distress and awarded the plaintiff $17,000 in economic and noneconomic damages, plus costs.

The plaintiff considered the manor her ideal wedding site, as it could accommodate a "weekend celebration," consisting of a Friday night rehearsal dinner, a Saturday evening wedding reception and after party, and a Sunday brunch.

On February 21, 2003, the plaintiff and her mother, Sandra Powers, visited the manor and met with its owner and agent, Andrew Silverston. Silverston gave the plaintiff the manor's standard letter of agreement. Plaintiff signed the letter, and Powers submitted $2000 in deposit money on behalf of the plaintiff, thus fulfilling each condition the letter requested for finality. The letter further identified the date of the wedding as September 10, 2005.

In the two years following the signing of the contract, a Shakespearean drama of confusion and lost opportunities ensued that would result in the manor contracting with another wedding party for the September 10, 2005 date and the plaintiff holding her wedding at another location. This outcome was brought about by a series of miscommunications leading to Silverston's mistaken belief that the plaintiff was abandoning her wedding plans.

In February, 2005, Silverston became uncertain about whether the plaintiff's wedding was going

forward. His insecurities were caused by his continued mistaken belief that there was no signed agreement or paid deposit. At the same time, Silverston had an inquiry from another couple who wanted to be married on September 10, 2005. He advised them that he might have a cancellation. On February 8, 2005, Silverston sent the plaintiff an express mail letter, asking her to contact him. The letter, however, contained no notice that the manor was uncertain of her wedding plans.

Silverston believed that his suspicions that the plaintiff's wedding was cancelled were confirmed by the lack of an immediate response from the plaintiff, as it was his experience that brides were anxious by nature and responded promptly to inquiries from their wedding coordinator.

On February 23, 2005, Silverston sent a letter to the plaintiff in which he inaccurately portrayed the February 21, 2003 letter agreement as tentative. Silverston's depiction of the parties' agreement as tentative was in direct contradiction of the agreement's language. He assumed that they were no longer interested in reserving the date of September 10, 2005.

The receipt of Silverston's letter stunned the heretofore unaware plaintiff.

During this period, the plaintiff's anxiety about her wedding plans increased, and feelings of extreme distrust for the manor developed. Because of her uncertainty that the manor would honor its contractual obligations, the plaintiff feverishly attempted to locate a venue that would accommodate her September 10, 2005 wedding date. After calling numerous sites, the plaintiff was able to find one venue. The wedding was a far cry from the weekend celebration the plaintiff originally had planned. The plaintiff testified that these events were the most stressful in her life.

A successful claim of negligent infliction of emotional distress "essentially requires that the fear or distress experienced by the plaintiffs be reasonable in light of the conduct of the defendants."

Here, we agree with the trial court that the actions of the manor's agent, Silverston, "created an unreasonable risk of causing [the plaintiff] emotional distress." The court noted in particular that "the manor gave

(continues)

[the plaintiff] no notice that it had questions about her wedding plans. The first direct notice she received of the manor's concerns was the manor's cancellation letter of February 23, 2005. [Although] the Manor's breach occurred approximately seven months before [the plaintiff's] wedding was to take place, it left her with limited options for alternative venues and the significant task of coordinating the details in light of a different venue and a different wedding day schedule, as well as informing 100 guests of the changes. . . . In addition, the Manor informed [the plaintiff] that it had given her date to another couple on February 16, 2005, when in fact it did not have a contract with the second party until March 6, 2005." The cumulative effect of the conduct described by the court undoubtedly would risk causing any bride emotional distress.

CASE QUESTIONS
1. The claimant was awarded $15,000 for her emotional distress. Do you think this was a fair amount?
2. Explain your answer to question 1.

Family Relationships Rule

Other courts have restricted recovery in negligent infliction cases to bystander plaintiffs who are related to the victim whom they witnessed being injured. This may be called the **family relationships rule**.

family relationships rule | Doctrine used in negligent infliction of emotional distress cases. A bystander may recover damages if he or she witnesses the tortfeasor injuring one or more of the bystander's relatives.

Sensory Perception Rule

Still other courts have insisted that the bystander must perceive the traumatic, negligent event directly through the senses (e.g., seeing the collision; hearing the child's screams; feeling the heat of the car exploding; smelling the burning clothing). This may be labeled the **sensory perception rule**.

sensory perception rule | Doctrine used in negligent infliction of emotional distress cases. A bystander may recover damages if he or she witnesses a tortfeasor injuring another person, so long as the bystander perceives the event directly through his or her own senses.

California Approach

The California courts were first to produce a further evolutionary development in negligent infliction law. In *Dillon v. Legg*, 68 Cal. 2d 728, 441 P.2d 912, 69 Cal. Rptr. 72 (1968), the California Supreme Court dispensed with the zone of danger rule and focused upon pure foreseeability. The straightforward question was, simply: Was the emotional injury reasonably foreseeable, given the tortfeasor's actions? This analysis neatly handled bystanders as well as immediate victims of negligent conduct. The court produced the following guidelines to decide the foreseeability issue, termed the *Dillon* approach:

1. The bystander's closeness to the emotionally disturbing incident *(physical proximity)*
2. The bystander's relationship to the injured party *(family relationships rule)*
3. The bystander's personal perception of the emotionally distressing occurrence *(sensory perception rule)*
4. Physical manifestations arising from the emotional distress

elements for forseeable emotional distress to bystanders/witnesses [handwritten marginalia]

The *Dillon* approach has been both praised and debunked by other courts and legal scholars. It presents another twist in negligent infliction cases, in a continuing attempt to clarify the circumstances in which a plaintiff may hold a defendant liable for this type of negligence tort.

The diversity of negligent infliction of emotional distress formulas used in different jurisdictions makes analysis dependent upon a specific state's version. The following hypothetical considers the varieties discussed in this section.

HYPOTHETICAL

Lamar owns an apartment building. Duane and Tyrel are brothers who share an apartment. One day, while barbecuing on their apartment balcony, Duane stepped upon rotten floorboards, which collapsed. Lamar had known about this dangerous condition for months but had not corrected it. Duane fell through the balcony floor and hung upside down by one leg 30 feet above the ground. Meanwhile, Tyrel, who was waxing his car in the parking lot below, became very upset upon seeing this situation develop. As he ran upstairs to assist his brother, Duane fell and suffered debilitating injuries. Subsequently, Tyrel began having horrible nightmares involving endless falling. He would awaken nightly in cold sweats. He lost weight, had little appetite, and developed a phobia about heights. This phobia made it extremely difficult for Tyrel to continue his occupation as a roofing installer. Lamar's liability to Duane is an issue of landowner liability, which we discussed at the beginning of this chapter. Would Lamar be liable to Tyrel for negligent infliction of emotional distress?

Clearly, Tyrel suffered no physical impact as a result of Lamar's negligence. Tyrel did not come into contact with the rotten balcony when it gave way. In states following the impact rule, Tyrel could not recover damages against Lamar for negligent infliction.

In states following the zone of danger rule, Tyrel was not sufficiently close to the dangerous balcony to be threatened by its condition. He was not even below the point at which Duane fell, which would have placed him at risk. Under the zone of danger test, Tyrel could not recover.

In jurisdictions following California's approach, it was reasonably foreseeable that Tyrel would be emotionally harmed by witnessing Duane's life-threatening situation, which Duane became involved in because of Lamar's negligent maintenance of the balcony. Tyrel is Duane's brother, so the family relationship test is met. Tyrel saw Duane dangling from the balcony and knew that he could fall and be killed. This satisfies the sensory perception rule. Tyrel was standing close to the accident site, and thus met the physical proximity standard. He also displayed physical symptoms resulting from his mental anguish. All of the *Dillon* criteria have been satisfied. Accordingly, Lamar would be liable to Tyrel for negligent infliction of emotional distress under the California theory.

TABLE 4-6

Elements of negligent infliction of emotional distress

General Legal elements for emotional distress (handwritten)

Common Elements (applying standard negligence theory to emotionally distressing conduct)	(1) Outrageous conduct by tortfeasor, when (2) tortfeasor reasonably should have anticipated that behavior would produce (3) significant and reasonably foreseeable injury in plaintiff, (4) tortfeasor breached duty of reasonable care, and (5) victim was foreseeable plaintiff.
Impact Rule	Plaintiff must experience physical impact from defendant's actions to recover for negligent infliction of emotional distress.
Physical Manifestations Rule	No physical impact is required, but plaintiff must experience physical symptoms associated with mental anguish that defendant caused.
Zone of Danger Rule	Bystander witnessing negligent injury to third party must have been immediately threatened by the negligent activity.
Family Relationships Rule	Bystander must be a family relative of the person injured by the tortfeasor's negligent act.
Sensory Perception Rule	Bystander must perceive with his or her senses (sight, hearing, smell, touch, taste) the injury to another person as a result of the tortfeasor's negligent act.

Table 4-6 illustrates the various analytical approaches to negligent infliction of emotional distress.

NEGLIGENCE PER SE

negligence per se | Negligence that cannot be debated due to a law that establishes a duty of care that the defendant has violated, thus causing injury to another.

Negligence per se is negligence that is beyond debate because the law, usually a statute or ordinance, has established a duty or standard of care that the defendant has violated, thus causing injury to the plaintiff. An example of this is where a state vehicle and traffic law prohibits, and makes it a violation, to drive through red traffic signals. If a driver proceeds to drive through a red light at an intersection and strikes another car, the tortfeasor is presumed to have acted negligently.

When a statute defines certain conduct as negligent, and a tortfeasor violates the statute by engaging in that activity, then the tortfeasor is presumed to have been negligent by violating the statute. To meet the burden of proof, an injured plaintiff need only show that the defendant's actions violated the negligence statute. The defendant is then presumed negligent. This shifts the proof burden to the defendant, who must then present effective negligence defenses to avoid liability. A per se negligent defendant might also avoid liability by showing that he or she was not the proximate cause of the plaintiff's injuries. In other words, the defendant would have to prove that his or her violation of the statute did not proximately cause the plaintiff's harm. An example of this would be where the defendant drove through a red light, and then the plaintiff's car hit another car in the intersection due to an oil spill on the road.

Defenses to Negligence Per Se

The negligence defenses of contributory negligence, comparative negligence, and assumption of risk also apply to negligence per se cases.

THE CASE OF THE UNYIELDING DRIVER

Sometimes the liability of drivers in automobile accidents will be clear cut. Here, one driver has the right of way by law, and the other driver questions whether this absolves the other driver from all liability, or whether the negligence of both parties must still be considered.

Jessica L. TONNER, Plaintiff and Appellant,

v.

Holly Ann CIRIAN, Defendant and Appellee

Supreme Court of Montana

No. DA 12–0178

Submitted on Briefs October 3, 2012

Decided December 27, 2012

Jessica L. Tonner (Tonner) appeals an order of the Nineteenth Judicial District Court, Flathead County, granting summary judgment to Holly Ann Cirian (Cirian).

On March 19, 2007, Tonner was driving her Nissan Titan pickup truck east on Balsam Street in Libby, Montana. At the same time, Cirian was driving her Hyundai Elantra north on Washington Avenue, which meets Balsam Street at an uncontrolled intersection. Cirian approached the intersection from Tonner's right, and Tonner was to Cirian's left. As Tonner was driving through the intersection, the front of Cirian's car collided with the rear quarter-panel of the passenger side of Tonner's truck.

The collision damaged both vehicles and injured Tonner. Tonner filed an amended complaint against Cirian on July 25, 2011, alleging that the "collision was the direct and proximate result of the negligence of [Cirian]." Tonner contended in part that Cirian was

negligent because she had failed "to maintain a proper lookout for other vehicles lawfully driving upon said roadway" and because she had failed "to operate her vehicle in a reasonable and prudent manner, under the circumstances then and there existing."

Cirian moved for summary judgment under M.R. Civ. P. 56(c), contending that she was not negligent "as a matter of law" because she "approached the intersection to the right of Tonner," and thus Tonner had an absolute "statutory duty to yield the right-of-way to Cirian" under § 61-8-339, MCA (2007). Tonner opposed Cirian's motion, arguing that "the simple allegation of a right of way violation . . . does not conclude issues of comparative negligence, which are distinctly factual." She contended that "the fact that one driver enjoys the right of way does not absolve the favored driver of his duty to maintain a proper lookout."

Each driver testified in her deposition that she was driving at or under the posted speed limit and was unimpaired. Both admitted, however, that neither saw the other's car prior to entering the intersection. Tonner explained in her affidavit that she slowed and looked down the street to her right before crossing Washington Avenue, but she did not see Cirian's car. Cirian, on the other hand, testified in her deposition that she did not look to her left before entering

(continues)

the intersection. She stated, "I'm pretty sure I was just looking straight, I mean, but at the last minute I saw her, so I was looking straight instead of anywhere else." Cirian later explained that, even if she had looked left, she would have been unable to see Tonner because "bushes and a fence" rendered that side of the intersection "very unvisible" to her. With her affidavit in response to Cirian's motion, Tonner attached photographs of the intersection , purporting to demonstrate that Cirian's view of Balsam Street was not obstructed.

The District Court granted Cirian's motion for summary judgment on February 16, 2012, on the ground that "no genuine issue of material fact exists and that [Cirian] is entitled to judgment as a matter of law." The court faulted Tonner for failing to offer "admissible evidence to support [her] allegations." It refused to consider Tonner's contention that Cirian had received a traffic citation, noting that she had failed to submit an affidavit from the investigating officer and that issuance of a traffic citation was not admissible in the civil case in any event (citing *Hart–Anderson v. Hauck,* 239 Mont. 444, 449, 781 P.2d 1116, 1119 (1989)). The court also noted the lack of evidence that Cirian was speeding. The court concluded that, "[a]s a matter of law," Cirian "was not negligent nor did she proximately cause the accident, as the collision would not have occurred without [Tonner's] violation of the right-of-way statute."

We review a district court's ruling on a motion for summary judgment de novo, applying the same M.R. Civ. P. 56(c) criteria as the district court. The party moving for summary judgment bears the initial burden of "establishing that no genuine issue of material fact exists."

Is Cirian entitled to judgment as a matter of law? The District Court relied on § 61–8–339(1), MCA (2007), in granting summary judgment to Cirian. The statute provides, "[w]hen two or more vehicles enter or approach an intersection from different highways, the driver of the vehicle on the left shall yield the right-of-way to all vehicles approaching from the right that are close enough to constitute an immediate hazard." Montana's right-of-way statutes are "intended to accord vehicles approaching or entering an intersection the status of

favored and disfavored drivers 'to facilitate the orderly movement of automobiles.' " *Yates v. Hedges,* 178 Mont. 488, 496, 585 P.2d 1290, 1295 (1978).

Tonner disputes the District Court's conclusion that, under the plain language of § 61–8–339, MCA (2007), Cirian—the favored driver under the statute—could not be negligent as a matter of law because Tonner had a statutory duty to yield the right-of-way. According to Tonner, "the direction in which the parties approach an uncontrolled intersection is but one factor to consider, even under [§ 61–8–339, MCA (2007)]," and that, even if Cirian had the right-of-way, she still was "subject to legal duties e.g., to drive in a careful and prudent manner, to not speed, and to maintain a proper lookout. . . ." Tonner contends that where "there is active negligence which can be attributed to *both* drivers, and an issue of comparative negligence, summary judgment is inappropriate to resolve those issues.

In similar cases, we have affirmed judgment as a matter of law only when the undisputed facts supported but one conclusion—that the cause of the collision was the disfavored driver's failure to yield to an approaching vehicle that was so close as to be an immediate hazard under the right-of-way statute. *Roe v. Kornder–Owen,* 282 Mont. 287, 292, 937 P.2d 39, 42–43 (1997).

Our decision in *Spinler v. Allen,* 1999 MT 160, 295 Mont. 139, 983 P.2d 348, demonstrates that summary judgment is not appropriate in an intersection collision case when the parties dispute material facts with regard to the disfavored driver's failure to yield the right-of-way. Even in that situation, where it was alleged that a disfavored driver violated the right-of-way statute, we held that whether a favored driver maintained an adequate lookout is a material fact that should be weighed by the finder of fact. Maintaining a proper lookout requires a driver "to look not only straight ahead but laterally ahead as well and to see that which is in plain sight." *Payne v. Sorenson,* 183 Mont. 323, 326, 599 P.2d 362, 364 (1979).

The statute requires vehicles from the left to yield the right-of-way to a vehicle approaching from the right if it is "close enough to constitute an immediate hazard." Section 61–8–339(1), MCA (2007). Similar to the defendant in *Spinler*, Cirian has not presented any evidence regarding the location of her vehicle at the time Tonner entered the intersection that demonstrated that her vehicle posed an immediate hazard to Tonner as Tonner entered the uncontrolled intersection. The only testimony in the record regarding the location of Cirian's vehicle in relation to Tonner's is found in Tonner's affidavit. In that document, Tonner swore that as she approached the intersection, "she looked to both her left and right before entering the intersection" and that, although she was "able to see between a quarter and a half a block to the right," she "observed no cars on the intersecting street." It cannot be determined that Tonner's entry into the uncontrolled intersection constituted negligence as a matter of law such that the issue whether Cirian maintained an adequate lookout was immaterial.

Cirian testified that she was "looking straight ahead instead of anywhere else," and even if she had been looking laterally ahead, she would not have been able to see Tonner's vehicle because her view to the left was obstructed by "bushes and a fence." After Cirian filed her motion for summary judgment, Tonner challenged Cirian's recollection of her ability to see laterally ahead to her left by submitting photographs of the intersection. Those photographs allegedly showed that if Cirian had been looking laterally ahead to her left, she should have been able to see Tonner's vehicle approach the uncontrolled intersection.

Drawing all reasonable inferences in favor of Tonner, we conclude that a jury reasonably could find both parties partially responsible for the collision. Whether Tonner's duty to yield the right-of-way arose under § 61–8–339(1), MCA (2007), and whether Cirian maintained a proper lookout are matters of factual dispute. These disputed facts are material because they raise issues of comparative negligence. We have held that the defense of contributory negligence on a defendant's part is available to a plaintiff who is accused of violating a traffic statute; it falls upon "the factfinder to determine the comparative degree of negligence on the part of plaintiff and defendant." Under such an analysis, "the jury must consider evidence of negligence from violation of a highway traffic statute, which was a proximate cause of the accident, with other evidence of negligence on the part of *both parties*" and the "jury must then weigh or compare the negligence of both parties in reaching its verdict."

Thus, even if Tonner is found to be negligent per se for violating § 61–8–339, MCA (2007), the fact finder still must weigh Tonner's negligence against any potential negligence of Cirian and compare the negligence of both in reaching its verdict.

After viewing the evidence in the light most favorable to Tonner, we hold that Cirian is not entitled to judgment as a matter of law. Notwithstanding the exclusion of evidence regarding the alleged traffic citation, the deposition and affidavit testimony established factual issues concerning the parties' comparative negligence. The District Court erred by concluding that the issue whether Cirian was maintaining a proper lookout was not a genuine issue of material fact.

CASE QUESTIONS
1. What legal principles did the appellate court consider in its decision?
2. If no statute were involved, would the duty owed by the parties have been any different?

Plaintiff within Class of Persons Protected by Statute

Not every statutory violation constitutes negligence per se. To recover under negligence per se theory, the plaintiff must be within the class of persons protected by the statute or ordinance and the statute must be designed to protect the class of

[handwritten margin note: Normally with product safety]

persons from the type of harm that occurred. For example, suppose a restaurant serves insect-infested meat to its customers. This violates several state and local health statutes. Suppose Kent ate at the restaurant and became ill. He would fall within the class of persons protected by the health statutes that require restaurants to serve wholesome food to patrons. The restaurant's violation of the statutes would be considered negligence per se, and Kent would have an excellent cause of action against the establishment.

Absolute Liability Mislabeled as Negligence Per Se

Courts occasionally equate negligence per se with strict, or absolute, liability. However, the two tort theories are distinct. Negligence per se simply presumes negligence because of the tortfeasor's violation of a statute. Negligence is based upon the tortfeasor's failure to exercise reasonable care. Absolute liability holds the tortfeasor accountable, regardless of fault, for doing an abnormally dangerous activity. No degree of care is sufficient to avoid strict liability.

This confusion between absolute liability and negligence per se occurs because of the outcomes in each type of case. If the defendant violates a negligence statute, he or she automatically is presumed negligent. Liability is almost as certain as in strict liability cases. Thus, the two concepts are often equated, although they are substantially different.

Toxic Torts as Negligence Per Se

Statutes sometimes declare that violations of regulations regarding the transportation, disposal, or management of hazardous or toxic substances create a presumption of negligence as a matter of law. These statutory provisions boost plaintiffs' causes of action against tortfeasors who carelessly control abnormally dangerous materials.

Not every statutory violation is negligence per se. All elements must be satisfied for the doctrine to apply. Table 4-7 summarizes the elements of negligence per se, and yhe following hypotheticals further demonstrate this principle.

TABLE 4-7
Elements of negligence per se

[handwritten note: Know these]

Defendant's actions are automatically considered negligent because they violated a negligence statute or ordinance.
Plaintiff must fall within class of persons protected by statute.
Defendant's actions must fall within the area for which the statute was created.
Defendant's statutory violation must proximately cause plaintiff's injuries.
Negligence defenses apply to negligence per se.

HYPOTHETICALS

Wes was driving his automobile at night along the Old River Road. Although it was pitch black, he did not have his headlights on. This violated a local county ordinance and state statute requiring headlight use at all times beginning an hour before sundown and ending an hour after sunrise. Wes collided with Mai Ling, a pedestrian walking along the side of the road. Mai Ling sues Wes for negligence per se. Was he negligent per se?

By driving without headlights, Wes violated an ordinance and statute that required motor vehicles to use lights at night. This was intended to protect other drivers and pedestrians from "invisible" vehicles hitting them in the dark. Mai Ling falls within the classification of persons protected by the statute and ordinance. Therefore, she could successfully sue Wes for negligence per se.

* * *

Consider another hypothetical. Barfly Beer Company sells "Brewster's Choice," a "light" beer low in calories. One of its distributors, the Brothers Emporium, sells the product in town. A state health statute requires any manufacturer or seller of items for human consumption to distribute them in containers free from foreign substances. Brothers collected empty bottles to send back to Barfly to be cleaned and reused. Sometimes, drinkers would put cigarette butts into the bottles. Neither Brothers nor Barfly checked the bottles for foreign substances; they were simply sent back to the Barfly plant, refilled, and redistributed. Ann drank one of the beers from a bottle with a cigarette butt floating in the bottom. As one might imagine, Ann became physically ill as a result. Aside from the clear products liability issue, has Barfly or Brothers been negligent per se?

The health statute was intended to protect consumers like Ann from injuries caused by foreign objects floating inside beverage bottles. Barfly and Brothers each violated the statute. Their negligence may be presumed.

▮ SUMMARY

Vicarious liability is the liability of one person (principal) for the negligent actions of another (agent). Many vicarious-liability situations involve employer/employee relationships. Under the doctrine of respondeat superior, the employer must answer to the injured party for the employee's negligence when the employee has acted within the scope of his or her employment. This normally involves assigned tasks during normal working hours. Special rules apply for employees coming to and going from work, and for employees who frolic and detour from assigned tasks to pursue personal pleasures. A person hiring independent contractors is not vicariously liable for their negligence. Many states have motor vehicle consent statutes holding a vehicle owner liable for another driver's negligence.

In premises liability, owners and occupiers of land owe special duties of reasonable care to individuals who are injured while visiting the premises. Traditionally, courts have defined these duties differently, depending upon the injured party's status on the realty. There are three such distinctions: trespasser, licensee, and invitee. Landowners owe no duty of reasonable care to trespassers; they must simply refrain from intentionally injuring trespassers. Special rules, called attractive nuisance theory, apply to trespassing children. Licensees are persons whom the owners permit to come onto their real estate. To licensees, landowners owe a duty to correct known dangers on the premises. Landowners owe a duty to discover and correct unknown risks on the premises for invitees, who have come onto the premises at the owners' expressed or implied invitation. The owner may limit the places on the land to which such invitation extends. Many courts have abandoned this three-tier analysis in favor of regular negligence theory.

Negligent infliction of emotional distress occurs when the tortfeasor engages in conduct that produces a reasonably foreseeable mental injury in a reasonably foreseeable victim. Many states have different rules to decide negligent infliction cases. A few courts require that the tortfeasor cause some physical impact to the emotionally distressed victim. Many courts hold that

mental anguish is recoverable when accompanied by physical manifestations or symptoms. Others allow bystanders to recover when they witness negligent injuries to other people when the bystanders fall within the zone of danger. Courts that follow California's reasoning base liability upon foreseeability, using physical manifestations, physical proximity, family connection, and whether the bystander witnessed the injury to determine the outcome of negligent infliction litigation.

Negligence per se is any activity that violates a negligence statute. It is considered automatic negligence simply because the defendant's conduct violated the statutory provisions. To recover damages, the plaintiff must fall within the class of persons that the statute was intended to protect. The same defenses apply to negligence per se that apply to ordinary negligence cases. Furthermore, the defendant's statutory violation must have proximately caused the plaintiff's injuries.

The next chapter focuses on tort defenses. These defenses are of particular interest to defense firms, as they may be used to excuse a defendant's negligent behavior.

▍ KEY TERMS

attractive nuisance	imputed	occupier
attractive nuisance doctrine	independent contractor	physical manifestations rule
coming and going rule	invitee	respondeat superior
emotional distress	licensee	scope of employment
family relationships rule	negligence per se	sensory perception rule
frolic and detour rule	negligent infliction of emotional	vicarious liability
impact rule	distress	zone of danger rule

▍ PROBLEMS

In the following hypotheticals, determine which type of special negligence action applies, if any. For the sake of convenience, use the three-tier analysis for landowner/occupier liability.

1. Clint rents an apartment from Whisperwood Property Management, Inc. His next-door neighbor, Leslie, frequently visits to watch basketball

on Clint's big-screen television. Clint had a can of aerosol cleaner in his utility closet. He set the can too close to the gas furnace, and the can slowly became overheated. One evening while watching the game, Leslie dropped and broke a glass. She opened the utility closet to fetch a broom to clean up the mess. Unfortunately, the cleaner can exploded just as she opened the closet door, injuring her severely.

2. Emily owns a pasture outside of town upon which she has her cattle and horses graze. Ted sometimes crosses the pasture as a shortcut to work. All around the property are posted signs stating, in clear red-and-black letters, "NO TRESPASSING! YES, YOU!" One day Emily saw Ted cutting across her land and warned him not to continue doing so in the future. Ted ignored the warning. Weeks later, Ted fell into a mud bog (which he could not see, because it was covered by fallen leaves). He sank to his chest and could not escape. He remained there for three days until a passing postal carrier stumbled upon his predicament. Ted suffered from severe malnutrition and exposure from the incident. As a result, he contracted pneumonia and was hospitalized for two weeks.

3. Davis operates a beauty shop. Kate comes in regularly for perms and haircuts. One of Davis's employees, Flower, absentmindedly left her electric shears on the seat of one of the hair dryers. Davis did not notice the shears when he had Kate sit in that chair to dry her newly permed hair. Unknown to everybody, the shears had an electrical short. When Davis turned on the hair dryer, the shears shorted out and electrocuted Kate, who was unknowingly sitting against the shears.

4. Susan hired Grass Goddess, a lawn care company, to fertilize and water her yard. One of the company's employees, Gupta, incorrectly mixed the fertilizer so that it contained 12 times the necessary amount of potassium. Gupta applied this mixture to Susan's grass. Honey, Susan's neighbor, came to Susan's party that night and played volleyball in the backyard. She frequently fell and rolled on the grass while diving to return the ball over the net. The next day, Honey developed a painful rash all over her body. She usually noticed these symptoms, although less severely, when she ate bananas, which are high in potassium.

5. Jon is a sales executive for a local automobile dealership. He often drives to the manufacturing facility 150 miles from the dealership to check on new orders. Jon's employer reimburses him for gasoline, food, and lodging, and provides Jon with a dealer car to drive. While driving to the manufacturing plant, Jon decided to stop by his cousin's house for dinner. His boss accompanied him on the visit "to get a decent meal for a change." While on the way there, Jon collided with and injured a motorcyclist.

6. Matthew has a five-year-old son with whom he often plays catch in the front yard. Sometimes the wind catches their ball and blows it into the street. Matthew has warned his son never to chase the ball into the road, but one day, when the ball blew into the street, Matthew's son ran after it. A truck driver swerved and struck the boy with the edge of the vehicle's bumper. The child suffered only a few bruises and scrapes. Matthew, however, developed a nervous twitch, ulcers, and an extreme sensitivity to sudden movements. He lost weight and experienced terrible nightmares about the incident.

▋ REVIEW QUESTIONS

1. Define the three classes of plaintiffs to whom landowners and occupiers owe duties of reasonable care.

2. Describe the landowner/occupier's duty of reasonable care to trespassers. Does the rule apply to all trespassers?

3. What is attractive nuisance? To which type of plaintiffs would the doctrine apply? Why is the landowner/occupier's duty of reasonable care different for these plaintiffs?

4. Using common law principles, discuss the landowner/occupier's duty of reasonable care to

licensees. How do licensees differ from trespassers? From invitees?

5. Using common law principles, what duty of reasonable care does the landowner/occupier owe to invitees? Why and how are invitees distinguishable from licensees and trespassers?

6. Explain how you might use traditional negligence theory to determine land owners/occupiers' liability to persons injured on the real estate. Do you find this approach easier than the three-tier analysis discussed in problem 1? Why or why not?

7. Define vicarious liability. What types of relationships are involved in this theory? What is respondeat superior? Explain scope of employment, the coming and going rule, and the frolic and detour rule. Why are these important to your analysis? How does vicarious liability relate to independent contractors? To motor vehicle owners or passengers?

8. Explain negligent infliction of emotional distress. What are its elements? In what types of factual situations would the tort apply? Describe the different analytical approaches to this tort. Define the impact rule, the physical manifestations rule, the zone of danger rule, the family relationships rule, and the sensory perception rule. How have the California courts combined these concepts in negligent infliction cases?

9. What is negligence per se? How does negligence per se differ from negligence?

▍ HELPFUL WEBSITES

This chapter focuses on special negligence actions. To learn more about special negligence actions, the following sites can be accessed:

General Information
www.findlaw.com
www.law.emory.edu
www.lawguru.com

Insurance Information
www.insurancejournal.com

STUDENT COMPANION WEBSITE
For additional cases and study materials, please go to www.cengagebrain.com

Chapter 5

Defenses to Negligence

THE BIGGEST MISTAKES PARALEGALS MAKE AND HOW TO AVOID THEM

Neither a Borrower Nor a Lender Be

The office where we work has a congenial and friendly culture. If someone needs help in a time crunch or with the workload, everyone pitches in to get the job done. Likewise, when one or another of us has personal problems, there is always someone offering assistance or at least a shoulder to cry on.

To say that one paralegal in our office—namely, Lucia—had personal problems would be an under-statement. She was always sweet but burdened with the responsibilities of being a single mom, caring for her elderly parents, and dealing with multiple health issues of her own, so she was frequently stressed. Evidently, she had financial troubles as well. No one really thought much about her being short a couple of bucks when we had lunch out, but she started asking each of us individually for short-term loans—"just until payday," she would

(continues)

say. And, to her credit, she always came through when she got her check.

Then her car broke down and she asked nearly everyone (including a few of the attorneys) in the office to cosign for a new car loan. Surprisingly, she did get a new car and quit the firm about a month later. One day a guy named Tim from our copy center was asking if anyone had Lucia's address or new cell number. It seems he had signed for Lucia's car loan on her assurance that "nothing would happen." Now the bank wanted the payment from him because it could not locate Lucia. Tim was distraught and Lucia was in parts unknown with her new car financed by Tim.

Lesson Learned: Never lend money to coworkers unless you can afford to lose it—period. It is always a gamble—Lucia carelessly placed Tim's finances and credit standing in jeopardy.

How to avoid lending? Tell the would-be borrower you need to check on some things, and you'll get back to him or her. This gives you more time to seriously consider the matter. Ask the borrower if the need is due to poor money management. If the answer is yes, borrowing will not solve the problem. If you choose to ignore the first rule about not lending money, always get the borrower to acknowledge in writing the full amount of the debt and the date you cosigned. Have the document notarized, as this will provide legal standing should the borrower default. In the worst-case scenario, a debt of $10,000 or more may be deducted from your income taxes if you made efforts to sue.

▌ INTRODUCTION

Tort defenses are an important protection for defendants. They provide legal justification for the defendants' actions. Defendants' defenses excuse negligent behavior. In effect, defenses provide defendants with a blame-shifting tool. Negligence defenses examine any plaintiff misconduct that was involved in causing the plaintiff's injuries. Even though the tortfeasor was negligent toward the victim, the tortfeasor's mischief may be forgiven (totally or partially) because of the victim's participation in producing his or her injuries.

This chapter discusses:

- How negligence defenses are used
- Statutes of limitations
- Contributory negligence
- Last clear chance
- Comparative negligence
- Assumption of risk

Also see Chapter 13, where immunity from torts is discussed.

HOW NEGLIGENCE DEFENSES ARE USED

Once the plaintiff has alleged a cause of action for negligence in the complaint, it is assumed that the defendant has no defense unless he or she specifically pleads one (or more) in his or her answer. Always remember these basic analytical rules:

1. *Negligence defenses are used only by the defendant against the plaintiff.* Put more generally, these defenses are responses to negligence allegations. The party alleged to have been negligent can use defenses against the party alleging negligence.
2. *Negligence defenses are applied only in response to the plaintiff's allegations that the defendant acted negligently or with willful and wanton negligence, not to claims of intentional action.*
3. *Once a plaintiff alleges the defendant's negligence, both parties' failure to be careful may be at issue.*
4. *Ask who is alleging negligence and who is alleged to have been negligent.* The alleged tortfeasor, usually the defendant, is the person who may utilize defenses.

How to plan out a negligence defense

STATUTES OF LIMITATIONS

Statutes of limitations are statutes restricting the time within which a plaintiff may file a lawsuit for particular causes of action against a defendant. (In some jurisdictions, these statutes are called *limitations of actions*.) There are also such statutes for negligence actions. Many of these statutes specify that various negligence lawsuits must be filed within two years of the negligent acts giving rise to the plaintiff's claims.

States' statutes of limitations vary in numbers of years and among the different types of negligence. The period for medical malpractice claims, for instance, may be two years in one state and three years in another. Similarly, lawsuits involving premises liability may have one-year statutes of limitations in one state and three-year statutes in another. One should become familiar with the specific statutes of limitations in one's own state for the various types of negligence causes of action.

Note that the statute of limitations is one of the few areas in the practice of law for which there is no remedy if one misses the deadline. Generally, there are provisions throughout the various civil practice acts that allow attorneys to amend, change, and supplement pleadings, and to remedy oversights in their handling of a case. Should a statute of limitations run out, though—no matter what the reason—judges are powerless to help you. Consequently, this is one of the areas in the practice of law in which malpractice claims most frequently arise.

statutes of limitations | Laws that set a maximum amount of time after something happens for it to be taken to court, such as a three-year statute for lawsuits based on a contract, or a six-year statute for a criminal prosecution.

THE CASE OF CONTINUOUS REPRESENTATION

The outcome of this lawsuit rests on the calculation of the applicable statute of limitations. In this case, the running of the statute of limitations for malpractice was found to be tolled or stopped, giving the plaintiff additional time in which to bring his action. Notice the 10-year lapse between the time the plaintiff initially sought legal counsel for his injuries and the time of this appeal.

POLLICINO
v.
ROEMER AND FEATHERSTONHAUGH P.C.

Supreme Court, Appellate Division,
Third Department, New York
260 A.D.2d 52, 699 N.Y.S.2d 238
December 2, 1999

This appeal requires us to decide a question of first impression, namely, whether in a legal malpractice action a law firm's continuous representation of a client should be imputed to a former associate for purposes of tolling the Statute of Limitations against the associate. On the particular facts presented herein, we hold that it should be and reverse the contrary determination of Supreme Court.

On April 11, 1989, plaintiff retained the law firm of defendant Roemer and Featherstonhaugh P.C. (hereinafter the law firm) to represent him in connection with a July 1, 1988 accident wherein he lost sight in his right eye. His injury is alleged to have occurred when a New York City Transit Authority bus ran over a glass bottle, the bottle exploded and a shard of glass struck plaintiff in the eye. In September 1989, the law firm moved for leave to serve a late notice of claim against the Transit Authority. Attached to its moving papers was a proposed notice of claim reflecting the accident date of July 1, 1988. After the motion was granted, however, a notice of claim incorrectly listing the accident date as June 30, 1988 was served. . . .

It was not until December 1, 1992 that the law firm moved on behalf of plaintiff for leave to serve an amended notice of claim to set forth the correct date of plaintiff's accident. . . .

While a cause of action for legal malpractice accrues on the date on which the claimed malpractice occurred, under the rule of continuous representation the Statute of Limitations is tolled while representation on the same matter in which the malpractice is alleged is ongoing. A twofold rationale underlies this rule, which is derived from the "continuous treatment" doctrine earlier crafted in medical malpractice actions. First, having sought professional assistance, the client "has a right to repose confidence in the professional's ability and good faith, and realistically cannot be expected to question and assess the techniques employed or the manner in which the services are rendered. . . ."

Here, it is uncontroverted that without application of the continuous representation rule, plaintiff's suit against defendant is time barred. The gravamen of plaintiff's malpractice claim is the erroneous accident date listed on the notice of claim, which led to dismissal of plaintiff's suit against the Transit Authority in 1994. His cause of action thus accrued when defendant allegedly committed the original error in November 1989 (or when he failed to correct it when a similar error in the summons and complaint was discovered and corrected in December 1989). Supreme Court held that since defendant's professional relationship with plaintiff ended when he left the law firm in September 1990, the rule of continuous representation did not apply. . . . Supreme Court's decision, however, failed to squarely address the question presented: whether the law firm's continuous representation of plaintiff should be imputed to defendant so as to toll the Statute of Limitations against him.

We conclude that under the circumstances of this case, the principles underpinning the continuous representation rule militate in favor of its application to defendant. As a starting point, we observe that without application of this rule, the Statute of Limitations against defendant would have expired *before* plaintiff's action against the Transit Authority was dismissed based on the faulty notice of claim. We also note that beginning in December 1992 and continuing through May 1997, the law firm undertook efforts to rectify the 1989 error which, if successful, would have rendered plaintiff's malpractice claim moot.

Critical to our resolution of the question, however, is the fact that in retaining the law firm to represent him, plaintiff forged his professional relationship with the firm, not with any individual attorney. Defendant, as well as several other associates, worked on plaintiff's case as employees or agents of the law firm, whose representation of plaintiff was continuous and uninterrupted until May 1997. . . . Given the law firm's legal responsibility for the actions of defendant, its employee, commencing an action against defendant would have required plaintiff to sever his relationship with the law firm. Prevention of such a disruption in the professional relationship, together with any ongoing efforts, is a paramount value underlying the doctrine of continuous representation.

. . . "The Statute of Limitations was enacted to afford protection to defendants against defending stale claims after a reasonable period of time had elapsed during which a person of ordinary diligence would bring an action." Largely based on the same principles informing the continuous representation rule and rendering its application appropriate here, we do not believe it can be fairly said that plaintiff lacked diligence or failed to bring his action within a reasonable period of time.

CASE QUESTIONS

1. Explain why the statute of limitations was tolled and what effect this had on the case.
2. How can you explain the 10-year passage of time between when legal counsel was originally retained and this appeal?
3. What lesson concerning the drafting of pleadings can a paralegal learn from this case?

PRACTICAL APPLICATION

To obtain malpractice insurance, attorneys must assure the malpractice insurance carrier that they have a reliable calendaring system. In fact, backup systems for recording important dates and deadlines are often required as well. Frequently, a paralegal is called upon to maintain a diary system and keep members of the firm alerted to approaching deadlines and dates. In addition, some firms automatically have all files pulled for review every three months, six months, and yearly to ensure that the cases are not being neglected.

Table 5-1 shows two typical statutes of limitations for negligence actions. Table 5-2 shows sample statutes of limitations for negligence by state.

TABLE 5-1

Typical statutes of limitations for negligence actions

Two-Year Statute of Limitations	Three-Year Statute of Limitations
16.003. Texas Two-Year Limitations Period: (b) Except as provided by Sections 16.010 and 16.0045, a person must bring suit for trespass for injury to the estate or to the property of another, conversion of personal property, taking or detaining the personal property of another, personal injury, forcible entry and detainer, and forcible detainer not later than two years after the day the cause of action accrues. (b) A person must bring suit not later than two years after the day the cause of action accrues in an action for injury resulting in death. The cause of action accrues on the death of the injured person.	New York Civil Practice Law & Rules § 214 (McKinney): The following actions must be commenced within three years: * * * 5. an action to recover damages for a personal injury except as provided in sections 214-b, 214-c and 215; . . . [providing special rules concerning specific torts and time injury was detected].

TABLE 5-2

Sample statutes of limitations for negligence by state

State	Negligence	Medical Malpractice
Alabama	2 years	2 years
California	2 years	3 years
Florida	4 years	2 years
Massachusetts	3 years	3 years
New York	3 years	2 1/2 years
Texas	2 years	2 years
Washington	3 years	3 years
Wyoming	4 years	2 years

CONTRIBUTORY NEGLIGENCE AND LAST CLEAR CHANCE

With this fundamental approach in mind, it is time to examine contributory negligence, used by a minority of jurisdictions. The majority uses comparative negligence as a primary defense, which is described later in this chapter.

Contributory Negligence Defined

Contributory negligence is the plaintiff's own negligence that contributed to his or her injuries. The elements of contributory negligence include duty, breach, causation, and injury. In some jurisdictions, this doctrine totally bars an injured plaintiff from recovering anything. This is very harsh.

contributory negligence | The plaintiff's own negligence that contributed to his or her injuries. In some jurisdictions this bars any recovery by a plaintiff.

Duty of Care to Oneself.
Suppose that Zelda is driving to school. Suppose that another driver runs a stop sign and the vehicles collide with one another. By failing to stop at the sign, the other driver breached the duty of reasonable care to other vehicle users such as Zelda. The other driver's negligence proximately caused injuries to Zelda and her vehicle. However, because Zelda was looking at herself in the mirror for a second, instead of looking at the road, she contributed to her own injuries.

Common Law Rule.
At common law, contributory negligence barred the plaintiff from recovering any damages from the defendant. Even if the defendant was negligent in causing 99 percent of the plaintiff's harm, and the plaintiff was only 1 percent contributorily negligent, the courts ruled that the plaintiff could collect nothing against the defendant. Very few states still use contributory negligence as a defense. Because of the harshness of the rule, courts have sought ways to avoid it.

Last Clear Chance

When a defendant uses the contributory negligence defense against a plaintiff, the plaintiff has a responsive weapon to defeat this defense. This is called the **last clear chance** doctrine and is a rebuttal to a contributory negligence defense. This rule is not followed in all states and has many variations and names.

    In other words, the defendant cannot escape liability for his or her negligence (by invoking the contributory negligence defense) if the defendant had the last clear chance to avoid the injury.

last clear chance doctrine | Even though the plaintiff was at fault in causing his or her own injuries, the defendant had the last opportunity to avert harm and failed to do so; therefore, the plaintiff can still recover.

    An example of last clear chance would be where a defendant enters a highway and goes in the wrong direction. The plaintiff sees the defendant's car coming at plaintiff in plaintiff's lane of traffic, and instead of trying to switch lanes or honk his horn to avoid the impending collision, the plaintiff does nothing and continues to drive in his lane of traffic. In this example, it was the plaintiff who had the "last clear chance" to avoid the incident. The fact that the defendant was the one who was originally negligent does not affect the plaintiff's obligation to try to avoid the collision.

THE CASE OF THE LAST CLEAR CHANCE

In this case, a hotel had a video monitoring system with 16 video cameras that one might assume would be used to survey the premises. The question arises as to what duty the hotel owes its customers, and whether it had the last clear chance to protect the plaintiff.

The ESTATE OF K. David SHORT by Judith Y. SHORT, Personal Representative, Appellant—Plaintiff,

v.

BROOKVILLE CROSSING 4060 LLC d/b/a Baymont Inns & Suites and MPH Hotels, Inc. d/b/a Baymont Inns & Suites, Appellees—Defendants

Court of Appeals of Indiana
No. 49A02–1112–CT–1128, -- , 972 N.E.2d 897
(Ind.App.)
July 31, 2012

Judith Short, as personal representative of the estate of David Short (the "Estate"), appeals the trial court's grant of summary judgment in favor of ("Baymont"). On the evening of January 3, 2009, at around 10:20 p.m., David Short checked into the Baymont Inn & Suites in Indianapolis, Indiana (the "Hotel") with front desk clerk Laura Sentman. Short did not act peculiar in any way. Between the hours of 11 p.m. and 7 a.m., night auditor Seth Devine was the only Baymont employee on duty. Devine was aware that the temperature that evening was below freezing.

At some point, Short left the Hotel. A video camera documented that at approximately 3:20 a.m., Short was returning to the Hotel when collapsed, hitting his head against a wall before falling to the ground. The camera was part of a system in which a monitor was located in the general manager's office which displayed images from each of 16 video cameras. After falling, Short was visible on the camera and did not move.

At approximately 7 a.m., a Baymont maintenance employee, noticed Short lying outside the north door, and called the front desk. Short was purple and appeared to be dead. The Marion County Health Department pronounced Short dead at 7:38 a.m. from "Complications of acute alcohol intoxication

and atherosclerotic coronary artery disease" and noted that "Environmental Cold Exposure" was a "*Significant Condition [ ] Contributing To Death* But Not Resulting In The Underlying Cause. . . ." The Estate filed a complaint for wrongful death alleging negligence by Baymont which caused Short's death.

Devine was deposed and testified that, during his shift, he does not walk around the building to make routine or periodic inspections of the exterior doors not visible from the front desk and that he is to stay at the main entrance because that is where unregistered guests must enter and it is a danger to have the desk unmonitored during overnight hours. Devine also testified that he will make observations if there is a reason to leave the front desk, such as if a guest requests something, but that "if there's no need for me to be away from the desk, there's no possibility for me to check those doors." Devine testified that he had been told that the purpose of the video monitoring system was to deter potential crime and to record crimes committed to aid police.

This action sounds in negligence and specifically concerns the duty element in a negligence claim. It is well-settled that, an individual does not have a duty to aid or protect another person, even if he knows that person needs assistance. However, there are exceptions to this general rule and among them is a duty which arises from certain special relationships between the parties. First, the Estate argues that "a duty exists in this case by virtue of the hotel—guest relationship." The Estate also argues public policy supports that a duty should be imposed in this situation because the storeowner, who is deriving this economic benefit from the customer, should assume the affirmative duty to help customers.

Baymont argues that it did not have "actual knowledge" of Short's presence at the back door, or his need for assistance until 7:00 a.m. Baymont also argues that "Short's collapse, which is the event that led to his death, was not foreseeable." According to the Restatement (Second) of Torts, the defendant "is not required . . . to give aid to one whom he has no reason to know to be ill." The evidence reveals that Devine was supposed to stay at the main entrance because it was a danger to have the front desk unmonitored during overnight hours, that he examines the exterior of the building when he arrives and leaves during his shift. He will make observations of other parts of the Hotel including the north door if he has an independent reason to be in that part of the building. Thus, routine door checks were not within the scope of Devine's nightly duties such that he should have known of Short's peril.

The evidence also reveals that Devine had been told that the purpose of the video monitoring system was to deter potential crime and to record crimes committed to aid police investigation. The monitor was a nineteen inch screen, displayed 16 images at once, and the image of the main entrance was larger than the others such that it was the only image large enough for Devine to see at that distance as he glanced at it. We conclude that Baymont did not have reason to know of Short's peril and thus the court did not err in granting its motion for summary judgment.

CASE QUESTIONS

1. Under what legal theory was the estate proceeding with the lawsuit? Why do you think this particular legal theory was selected?
2. Did the court's decision meet your expectations? Explain your answer.

Table 5-3 summarizes the different elements of contributory negligence and last clear chance.

Contributory Negligence	Last Clear Chance
Plaintiff's duty of reasonable care to himself or herself.	Although plaintiff was contributorily negligent, defendant had the last reasonable opportunity to avoid harming plaintiff (as a consequence of defendant's negligence).
Plaintiff breaches duty.	Nullifies contributory negligence defense.
Plaintiff acts, or fails to act, which contributes to his or her injuries.	Plaintiff uses last clear chance to respond to defendant's use of contributory negligence defense.
Plaintiff may be prevented from recovering anything.	Defendant may be held liable for incident.

TABLE 5-3
Contributory negligence and last clear chance

▌ COMPARATIVE NEGLIGENCE

The comparative negligence defense has replaced contributory negligence in most states' common law or statutes. Since the 1960s, courts and legislatures increasingly have adopted the defense as an alternative to the rigid, unfair comparative negligence results that contributory negligence often produced when a plaintiff could recover nothing if found even slightly at fault. The defense of comparative negligence enables the defendant's liability to be adjusted according to the extent of the plaintiff's contribution to his or her own injuries. **Comparative negligence** may be defined as a measurement and comparison of the plaintiff's and the defendant's negligence in causing the plaintiff's injuries.

comparative negligence |
A legal rule, used in many states, by which the amount of "fault" on each side of an accident is measured and the side with less fault is given damages according to the difference between the magnitude of each side's fault.

Elements of Comparative Negligence

The comparative negligence defense has three elements:

1. The plaintiff's negligence contributed to his or her own injuries.
2. Calculation of the percentage of the plaintiff's negligence that contributed to his or her injuries.
3. Calculation of the percentage of the defendant's negligence that produced the plaintiff's injuries.

 In some jurisdictions, a fourth element is included: the defendant must have been more negligent than the plaintiff.

Table 5-4 shows states' contributory and comparative negligence policies.

TABLE 5-4

States' contributory and comparative negligence policies

State	Contributory and Comparative Negligence Policies
California	Pure form of comparative negligence. Contributory negligence does not bar recovery even if plaintiff is most responsible for accident.
Florida	Comparative negligence. Any contributory fault by plaintiff lessens the proportionate amount of damages.
New Jersey	Contributory negligence cannot be greater than negligence of defendants. Damages diminished by the percentage of damages attributable to plaintiff.
New York	Comparative negligence. Contributory negligence does not bar recovery. Damages reduced in proportion to culpable conduct.
Pennsylvania	Contributory negligence does not bar recovery provided plaintiff's negligence is not greater than defendant's. Amount of damages is reduced in proportion to plaintiff's fault.
Texas	Proportionate responsibility. Contributory negligence limits a plaintiff's recovery. Plaintiff's negligence cannot be greater than defendant's. Award reduced in proportion to negligence.

The Balancing Act

Comparative negligence balances the degrees of each party's negligence that produced the plaintiff's harm. In effect, the plaintiff's and defendant's negligence are compared to see which was more responsible for causing injury. This comparative negligence balancing is typically measured in percentages of negligence. This is sometimes called **culpability factoring (liability apportionment).**

For instance, consider the stop sign example discussed earlier in this chapter. The defendant ran a stop sign. This is more negligent than a driver momentarily not paying full attention to the road, as the plaintiff's acts would not have produced the accident. It took the greater negligence of the defendant (i.e., failing to stop at the sign) to cause the damage. The defendant was more negligent than the plaintiff in that example. But what percentages of negligence would be assigned to the plaintiff (for contributing to the injuries) and the defendant (for negligently causing the harm)? Well, the defendant was more than half responsible, so the defendant's percentage must be higher than 50 percent. What percentages would be used? Defendant 75 percent, plaintiff 25 percent? 60/40? 90/10?

Readers may find this approach frustrating. What are the correct percentages? There is no exact formula. It depends upon the facts of each case. Whatever percentages are selected, readers and triers-of-fact probably rely on intuition and gut feeling as much as anything.

Who Decides the Percentages. The trier-of-fact decides the percentages in comparative negligence. Thus, the jury (or judge, in a bench trial) must closely examine the facts and assign negligence percentages to the plaintiff and the defendant.

Why Calculate Percentages? Comparative negligence is used to calculate the amount of the defendant's liability to the plaintiff. Assume that the following percentages were selected for the stop sign problem: defendant 75 percent negligent, plaintiff 25 percent negligent. What would be the outcome of the case? The defendant would be liable to the plaintiff for 75 percent of the amount the plaintiff received in damages. If the plaintiff recovered judgment against the defendant, receiving a $100,000 damages award, under this percentage the defendant would be liable for $75,000, with $25,000 having been subtracted out for the plaintiff's comparative negligence.

The advantages of comparative negligence are immediately apparent. Instead of completely barring the plaintiff's recovery (as common law contributory negligence would have done), culpability factoring enables the plaintiff to recover damages for the defendant's share of responsibility in causing the injuries. Liability apportionment also protects the defendant from paying for the plaintiff's

culpability factoring (liability apportionment) | A defense to negligence. When the plaintiff's negligence contributed to his or her injuries, comparative negligence calculates the percentage of the defendant's and the plaintiff's negligence and adjusts the plaintiff's damages according to the numbers.

The jury or the judge

share in harming himself or herself. The result is a just and equitable outcome to the litigation. It allows a plaintiff to bring an action even though he or she is somewhat at fault.

Criticism of Comparative Negligence

Comparative negligence has been criticized for its arbitrary and capricious approach to assigning percentages of negligence. Critics complain that liability apportionment is imprecise and based entirely upon the emotional attitudes of the jury or judge. Think back to the stop sign illustration. If one disapproved of running stop signs more than driver inattention, would one not be more likely to raise the defendant's percentage of liability? Of course, juries are composed of several people, a fact that is intended to balance out such personal biases. Still, disapproval of comparative negligence continues in legal literature and court opinions.

Table 5-5 lists the elements of comparative negligence.

TABLE 5-5

Elements of comparative negligence

Plaintiff was negligent in contributing to his or her own injuries (defendant was also negligent in causing plaintiff's injuries).
Liability apportionment: Calculate each party's percentage of negligence. (How much did plaintiff contribute to his or her own injuries? How much was defendant responsible for plaintiff's harm?).
In some jurisdictions, defendant's percentage of negligence must be greater than plaintiff's percentage of negligence (modified comparative negligence).
In some jurisdictions, there is no minimum percent for defendants (pure comparative negligence).

THE CASE OF THE UN-EASY RIDER

Negligence is contagious. Those around a careless person sometimes find themselves infected by carefree, irresponsible attitudes. As a result, it is occasionally difficult to determine the degree to which each party is at fault.

The old contributory negligence defense made no effort to apportion fault. It simply and arbitrarily torpedoed the plaintiff's action if he or she was the least bit at fault for his or her injuries. Comparative negligence attempts to resolve this unfairness. The following case discusses last clear chance and contributory and comparative negligence.

PENN HARRIS MADISON SCHOOL CORPORATION, Appellant (Defendant below),

v.

Linda HOWARD, Individually and as Next Best Friend of David Howard, A Minor, Appellees (Plaintiffs below)

Supreme Court of Indiana
March 1, 2007

Two decades ago, the Legislature abolished the harsh doctrine of "contributory negligence" by which a man or a woman, injured through the fault of another, was denied any recovery if he or she was even slightly at fault. However, the defense of contributory negligence remains available to government entities like public schools.

David Howard attended Penn High School in the Penn Harris Madison School Corporation ("PHM"). Throughout high school, Howard helped his friend, Jon West, produce theatrical plays and build sets for those plays. West was a music teacher in a PHM elementary school.

During his senior year, Howard, age 17, helped West produce "Peter Pan" at the elementary school. Howard, who had experience rock climbing and rappelling, devised and constructed a pulley mechanism designed to allow the Peter Pan character to "fly" above the audience. Howard himself tested the apparatus several times.

On the night of dress rehearsal, Howard climbed a ladder that West was holding and connected himself to the webbing through a loop on the back of the harness. Howard jumped from the ladder. The apparatus failed and Howard fell to the gym floor, suffering serious injuries to his face, spleen, hands, and wrists.

Howard's mother, individually and as his next friend, sued PHM, alleging its negligence caused Howard's injuries. During the trial on their claims, the plaintiffs requested [that] the trial court give the jury certain instructions. The jury returned a verdict for the plaintiffs and awarded them $200,000 in damages.

At the plaintiffs' request, the trial court instructed the jury that in deciding whether Howard

was guilty of contributory negligence, it must determine whether he had exercised the "reasonable care [that] a person of like age, intelligence, and experience would ordinarily exercise under like or similar circumstances."

The Court of Appeals properly determined that the instruction given by the trial court was not a correct statement of Indiana law. Children over the age of 14, absent special circumstances, are chargeable with exercising the standard of care of an adult.

The standard of care we impose on individuals over the age of 14 is a neutral principle of law, operating irrespective of whether the child is plaintiff (as here), defendant (e.g., a 14-year-old or 16-year-old driver), or even a non party.

Even when a jury is given an incorrect instruction on the law, we will not reverse the judgment unless the party seeking a new trial shows "a reasonable probability that substantial rights of the complaining party have been adversely affected."

We are unable to find that PHM has made such a showing here. The offending instruction asked the jury to determine whether Howard exercised the "reasonable care [that] a person of like age, intelligence, and experience would ordinarily exercise under like or similar circumstances." We find the error in giving the instruction here to have been harmless.

At the plaintiffs' request, the trial court instructed the jury that it could find in favor of Howard, notwithstanding contributory negligence on his part, if the plaintiffs established entitlement to recovery under the "last clear chance" doctrine.

The doctrine of last clear chance, as a general proposition, provides that the contributory negligence of a plaintiff does not prevent recovery by that plaintiff for the negligence and injuries caused by the defendant if the defendant by exercising reasonable care might have avoided injuring the plaintiff.

The Court of Appeals faithfully applied the last clear chance doctrine in this case. It properly noted that Howard had the burden of proving, among other elements, that the defendant "had the last

(continues)

opportunity through the exercise of reasonable care to avoid the injury." It quoted controlling authority that "the defendant . . . must have the last clear chance to avoid the injury to the plaintiff."

We agree with the Court of Appeals that there was no evidence that PHM had the last opportunity to "avert" or prevent Howard's fall.

[T]he undisputed evidence shows that Howard climbed the ladder of his own accord and attempted to hook himself to the pulley before he fell. While West was holding the ladder steady for Howard, there is no evidence that West or any other [PHM] employee assisted Howard in getting himself attached to the pulley. While no one knows for certain what mechanism failed and caused Howard's fall, the evidence clearly shows that Howard had the latest opportunity to avoid it. He had a choice whether to descend from the ladder or to attempt the stunt.

The instruction on last clear chance given by the trial court in this case was an accurate statement of law.

We affirm the judgment of the trial court.

CASE QUESTIONS

1. Which do you consider the more just of the following doctrines: (a) contributory negligence and last clear chance, or (b) comparative negligence? Do you agree with this court's opinion? Explain.
2. Has your state adopted a statute similar to the Pennsylvania statute discussed here?

HYPOTHETICAL

Ikeda Osaka manages and owns a hotel. Frances Borgioni is a guest. The smoke detector in Frances's room has a dead battery and does not function. None of Ikeda's employees has checked the detector recently, despite a management protocol instructing maintenance to check the batteries every month. The customer staying in the room next to Frances's smoked in bed and started a fire. Smoke poured under the door adjoining the two rooms, but the malfunctioning detector did not awaken Frances before the room became filled with smoke. Frances awoke, coughing, and stumbled to the hallway door. He could not get the door open, however, because he had placed his own safety lock on the door, and that lock jammed as he was trying to escape. Frances passed out from smoke inhalation and suffered severe burns. Fortunately, the fire department rescued him.

Frances sued Ikeda for negligently failing to maintain an operative smoke detector in the room. Ikeda responded that Frances had contributed to his own injuries by placing his own lock on the door, so that he could not escape. May Ikeda invoke the defense of comparative negligence?

Was Ikeda negligent in failing to maintain a functioning smoke detector in Frances's room? Analyze the facts and apply the elements of negligence. If one decides that Ikeda was negligent (which is arguably the correct answer), then the comparative negligence defense should next be considered. Apply its elements. Was Frances negligent in contributing to his own injuries? Frances breached his duty of reasonable care to himself by placing a defective lock on the door, which prevented his escape during the fire. But for this act, Frances could have escaped before passing out from the smoke. Frances was negligent in harming himself. Next, decide if Ikeda's negligence exceeded Frances's. Would Frances have been endangered by the smoke at all if the smoke detector had activated? This would have given Frances more time to escape the room before the smoke thickened and rendered him unconscious. Ikeda's negligence exceeded Frances's. Now use liability apportionment. What percentages would be assigned? Ikeda's must be at least 51 percent. 60/40? 70/30? 80/20? There is no single correct answer here. A juror must use his or her best judgment based upon the facts.

ASSUMPTION OF RISK

Assumption of risk is another defense to negligence. **Assumption of risk** means that the plaintiff assumed the risk of doing (or not doing) something that resulted in his or her injuries. Assumption of risk involves (1) the plaintiff's voluntary assumption of a known risk, (2) with a full appreciation of the dangers involved in facing that risk. It is important to note that not all risks are assumed, just those that are reasonable.

assumption of risk |
Knowingly and willingly exposing yourself (or your property) to the possibility of harm.

Voluntary Assumption of Known Risk

For the assumption-of-risk defense to insulate the defendant from negligence liability, the plaintiff must have voluntarily decided to engage in an activity that the plaintiff knew (or reasonably should have known) was dangerous. In other words, the plaintiff must willfully face a known risk.

For instance, suppose Gilda's employer orders her to carry stacked boxes down a long flight of stairs. Her employer specifically instructs her to carry all the boxes in a single trip. To do this, however, Gilda must hold the boxes in front of her, blocking her forward vision. She knows that it is dangerous to descend stairs when she cannot see where she is going. Gilda slips and falls because her right foot misses a step. She sues her employer for negligence. The employer alleges that Gilda assumed the risk. Did she? No—Gilda did not voluntarily assume the dangerous activity. In fact, she was coerced into carrying all the boxes in one trip. She would not have done so but for her employer's command. Thus, Gilda did not voluntarily assume the risk of falling down the stairway.

Suppose that Brian slipped on some liquid somebody had spilled on the stairway. Brian thought the stairs were clean and dry, because he had walked up them just a few minutes earlier. He was unaware of the new danger that had appeared to threaten his safety. Brian did not assume a known risk.

Suppose that Gilda was carrying the boxes into a storeroom instead of down a stairway. The room was pitch black, and she knew that the ceiling lightbulb was burned out. Nevertheless, she carried the boxes into the room in which she could not clearly see. Gilda stumbled over a mop and broom on the floor, and the boxes fell upon and injured her. Again, she sues her employer for negligence in failing to replace the burned-out bulb. Her employer replies that Gilda voluntarily assumed a known risk—she knew the bulb was burned out. Further, she knew that the room was so dark that it would take her eyes several minutes to adjust. Still, she entered the room despite the obvious danger that she could fall over not-visible objects. Gilda assumed the risk in this version of the facts.

What if Jonathan decides to go bungee jumping off the local bridge that spans a river? Lots of people go there for bungee jumping because the bridge is the perfect height and the river is so scenic. Jonathan uses a harness and follows all precautions from the company providing the equipment and instructions for the rides. Instead of jumping forward toward the river, Jonathan gets nervous and jumps swinging toward the bridge, hitting his head and sustaining a concussion. Has Jonathan assumed the risk, or can he bring an action against the company providing the bungee rides? Jonathan knew or should have known that bungee jumping is extremely dangerous. He assumed the risk of injury in this instance.

Full Appreciation of Danger

The plaintiff must fully understand the dangerous nature of the activity that he or she voluntarily undertakes. Suppose that Brett visits a friend's woods. He comes across a cavern and decides to explore it. He has no way of knowing that higher above him, on a nearby hill, a highway construction crew is preparing to detonate dynamite. They explode a powerful charge, which sends a shock wave through the ground and causes part of the cavern walls to collapse, trapping Brett inside the cave. He sues the highway company for negligence in detonating excessively powerful explosives. Run through the negligence formula to determine if the company was negligent toward Brett, closely examining foreseeability of the injury and foreseeable plaintiffs theory. Presuming that the company acted negligently, it responds with the defense of assumption of risk.

Did Brett voluntarily assume a known risk with a full appreciation of the dangers involved? He willfully entered the cave. He knew (or reasonably should have known) that cavern walls sometimes fall in. That risk was known, but he had no way to anticipate the additional danger created by a forceful explosion. He did not fully appreciate this aspect of the risk in entering the cave. Arguably, the dynamite was also an unknown risk to him. Thus, the company's defense would fail.

Proof of Assumption of Risk

There are two categories of assumption of risk. In *express assumption-of-risk* cases, a plaintiff voluntarily assumes a known risk by an express agreement. An example of this would be a plaintiff being given an agreement with a release clause to sign, thus acknowledging a particular danger associated with an activity and agreeing not to hold the other party liable—for example, a boxing match. This express assumption is valid so long as it does not violate **public policy,** such as a situation in which there is unequal bargaining power between the parties, and one of the parties is forced to waive his or her rights.

    In *implied assumption of risk,* a plaintiff accepts a risk knowingly and voluntarily by reason of the plaintiff's knowledge. In implied assumption, although there is no express agreement, the assumption is implied based upon a party's conduct—for example, a plaintiff entering a barricaded structure despite seeing a large no-entry sign at the entrance. Just as with express assumption cases, the implied assumption cannot violate public policy, such as where a contractor fails to take adequate measures to protect the public and installs a defective barricade.

public policy | The law should be applied in a way that promotes the good and welfare of the people.

The Complete Defense

Assumption of risk is a complete defense to negligence in some jurisdictions. Like common law contributory negligence, it totally bars the plaintiff's recovery. If the plaintiff assumed the risk, the defendant cannot be liable for negligence.

    Assumption of the risk is commonly raised in spectator sport situations. There is a known risk that if you attend a baseball game, you might get struck by a ball hit into the stands. Likewise, observers of speed car races, monster trucks, or demolition derbies might get hit by a car or piece of equipment hurled into the air. A spectator assumes these risks with full appreciation of the dangers and thus is barred from bringing suit as a result of any injuries sustained. Conversely, consider a situation in which bleachers collapse at a football stadium. Seats caving in is not a known or foreseeable risk, nor could the dangers be appreciated; thus, in this case, assumption of the risk would not apply and suit would be allowed.

    Assumption of risk is somewhat more difficult to establish than contributory or comparative negligence. The following example demonstrates how the elements must be carefully considered.

THE CASE OF THE RISKY BUSINESS

The doctrine of assumption of the risk is questioned when a child is injured at a birthday party. Consider whether plaintiff's injury could have been avoided, and whether this is a realistic or practical expectation under the circumstances.

Brenna H. Main and Danielle J. Main,
Plaintiffs/Appellants
v.
Gym X–Treme, et al. Defendants/Appellees

Court of Appeals of Ohio
Tenth Appellate District
2012–Ohio–1315., 2012 WL 1059668
March 27, 2012

Plaintiffs-appellants, Brenna H. Main and Danielle J. Main, appeal from the grant of summary judgment in favor of defendant-appellee, Gym X–Treme.

On February 17, 2007, ten-year-old Brenna H. Main attended the birthday party of one of her friends at appellee's gymnastic facility. After most of the children had arrived, one of appellee's employees opened the door of the party room to allow the children to enter the main gymnasium. Approximately 12 children, including Brenna, quickly gathered on the "spring floor" in the gymnasium. Within a few minutes of entering the gymnasium, Brenna jumped on the spring floor, fell, and broke her arm. The spring floor is a very large, thickly padded floor typically used by gymnasts for floor exercises.

Ohio law recognizes three categories of assumption of the risk as defenses to a negligence claim; express, primary, and implied or secondary. Here, the trial court granted summary judgment in favor of appellee based upon the doctrine of primary assumption of the risk. Under this doctrine, a plaintiff who voluntarily engages in a recreational activity or sporting event assumes the inherent risks of that activity and cannot recover for injuries sustained in engaging in the activity unless the defendant acted recklessly or intentionally in causing the injures.

The doctrine applies regardless of whether the activity was engaged in by children or adults, or was unorganized, supervised, or unsupervised. The rationale behind the doctrine is that certain risks are so intrinsic in some activities that the risk of injury is unavoidable. Moreover, by engaging in the activity, the plaintiff has tacitly consented to these inherent risks.

The test for applying the doctrine of primary assumption of the risk to recreational activities and sporting events requires that: (1) the danger is ordinary to the game; (2) it is common knowledge that the danger exists; and (3) the injury occurs as a result of the danger during the course of the game. *Santho v. Boy Scouts of Am.*, 168 Ohio App.3d 27.

Primary assumption of the risk completely negates a negligence claim because the defendant owes no duty to protect the plaintiff against the inherent risks of the activity in which the plaintiff engages. Primary assumption of the risk serves to negate the duty of care owed by the defendant. "Because a successful primary assumption of risk defense means that the duty element of negligence is not established as a matter of law, the defense prevents the plaintiff from even making a prima facie case." *Gallagher v. Cleveland Browns Football Co.*, 659 N.E.2d 1232.

Under the doctrine of primary assumption of the risk, the injured plaintiff's subjective consent to and appreciation for the inherent risks of the recreational activity are immaterial to the analysis. Those entirely ignorant of the risks of the sport, still assume the risk by participating in the sport. The law simply deems certain risks as accepted by plaintiff regardless of actual knowledge or consent. If the activity involves risks that cannot be eliminated, then a finding of primary assumption of the risk is appropriate. The defendant's conduct is relevant only if it rises to reckless or intentional conduct.

Here, the court determined that "play time and gymnastic activities," are recreational activities to which the doctrine of primary assumption of the risk applies. We agree. Playing and/or jumping on a spring floor in a large gymnasium at a birthday party is a recreational activity. <u>The trial court also found that tripping, slipping, and falling are all normal inherent risks with these activities</u>. We agree with the trial court that the doctrine of primary assumption of the risk applies.

Appellants have not alleged or argued that appellee's conduct was reckless or intentional. Appellants contend that the basis for their claim against appellee is negligent supervision and that negligent supervision is an exception to the doctrine of primary assumption of the risk. We expressly rejected this argument and previously expressly held that negligent supervision is not an exception to the doctrine of primary assumption of the risk. Because the doctrine of primary assumption of the risk bars appellants' negligence claim, we agree with the trial court that appellee is entitled to summary judgment. Therefore, we affirm the judgment of the Franklin County Court of Common Pleas.

CASE QUESTIONS

1. Give an example of some conduct that the defendant might have done that would have prevented the doctrine of primary assumption of the risk from being applied.
2. Strategically, why did the plaintiffs' counsel raise the issue of negligent supervision?

HYPOTHETICAL

Julie owns East of Tansmania, a tanning salon. Elizabeth is one of Julie's customers. She has been visiting the salon twice a week for 10 years. She always uses the same tanning bed. Because of faulty equipment, Elizabeth was exposed during each session to five times more ultraviolet radiation than is normally emitted by tanning equipment. Elizabeth was diagnosed with skin cancer. She sues Julie for subjecting her to excessively intense ultraviolet light, which is a powerful carcinogen. Julie was negligent in exposing Elizabeth to such extremely high doses of ultraviolet radiation. Can she offer assumption of risk as a defense?

Did Elizabeth voluntarily assume a known risk with a full appreciation of the dangerous consequences? Clearly, she willfully visited the salon twice weekly for 10 years. She chose to use the same bed each time. She knew (or reasonably should have known) that ultraviolet radiation is carcinogenic. But did she fully understand the danger? Did she realize that the equipment emitted five times more radiation than normal? Could she have known about this aspect of the threat? Not likely. Accordingly, she did not assume the risk, and the defense would not protect Julie from liability.

Suppose a warning were posted above the tanning bed that Elizabeth used, declaring, "DANGER! EMITS EXCESSIVE ULTRAVIOLET LIGHT. USE AT YOUR OWN RISK." Now Elizabeth would have been alerted to the threatening condition. She would have a full appreciation of the dangers involved in using the equipment. Under this version of the facts, Elizabeth would have assumed the risk, and Julie would not be liable for negligence.

Table 5-6 outlines the elements of assumption of risk.

TABLE 5-6
Elements of assumption
of risk

Plaintiff voluntarily assumes a known risk.
Plaintiff fully appreciates the dangers involved in facing the risk.

SUMMARY

Negligence defenses are used only by the defendant against the plaintiff. The defenses are applied only in response to the plaintiff's allegations that the defendant acted negligently. To determine which party uses negligence defenses, one should ask who is alleging negligence and who is alleged to have been negligent.

Contributory negligence is the plaintiff's negligence that contributed to his or her own injuries. The plaintiff was negligent toward himself or herself and caused (in whole or in part) the harm. This defense exonerates the defendant whose negligence harmed the plaintiff. At common law, any amount of contributory negligence by the plaintiff, however small, would bar the plaintiff's recovery against the negligent defendant. Critics have argued that this defense is unreasonably harsh. Last clear chance is the plaintiff's response to the contributory negligence defense. Last clear chance means that although the plaintiff was contributorily negligent, the defendant still had the last opportunity to avoid harming the plaintiff. Last clear chance nullifies the contributory negligence defense.

Comparative negligence is an alternative defense that has largely replaced contributory negligence in both the common law and statutes. Comparative negligence measures and compares the negligence of both the plaintiff and the defendant. This allows the trier-of-fact to adjust the plaintiff's recovery to reflect more

accurately each party's degree of negligence in causing the harm. The calculation is often in percentages of negligence. This is sometimes called culpability factoring or liability apportionment. These percentages are based entirely upon the trier-of-fact's subjective opinion regarding the specific facts of each case. Critics have criticized the defense for this uncertainty.

Assumption of risk is another negligence defense. It states that the plaintiff voluntarily assumed a known risk with full appreciation of the dangers involved. Like contributory negligence, assumption of risk is a complete defense to negligence. In other words, it totally excuses the defendant's negligence and erases the defendant's liability to the plaintiff.

Most state statutes of limitations restrict the time period within which a plaintiff may file a negligence cause of action against a defendant. In most states, these are two-year statutes, meaning that a plaintiff has two years from the date that the negligent act was committed within which to file a lawsuit against the tortfeasor. It is vital to research the specific statutes of limitations for each particular tort.

In the next chapter, intentional torts are introduced. These actions are examples of instances where a party intends to hurt another party. This is in contrast to negligence actions, where intent is not a factor, and harm is caused by negligence or accident.

KEY TERMS

assumption of risk
comparative negligence
contributory negligence

culpability factoring (liability apportionment)
last clear chance doctrine

public policy
statutes of limitations

PROBLEMS

In the following hypotheticals, determine which negligence defense applies, if any.

1. The Tàpàjós Inn, owned by Guillermo Estaben, has a swimming pool with no lifeguards on duty. The pool is surrounded by a high-wire fence, and access to the pool is restricted to guests, who must use their room keys to reach the facility. Signs posted in several places on the fencing read, in bold, black lettering: "NO LIFEGUARD ON DUTY. SWIM AT YOUR OWN RISK! NO DIVING, RUNNING, OR HORSEPLAY. ADULTS MUST SUPERVISE CHILDREN. BE CAREFUL!" Tony Harmon, a 16-year-old, and his family are staying at the Inn. Tony and his 17-year-old girlfriend, Tanya, went swimming in the pool after midnight. There were no signs indicating times when the pool was opened or closed. At 1:45 a.m., hotel maintenance activated the automatic pumps to drain the pool for cleaning. None of the Inn staff checked to see if the pool was being used. While swimming underwater, Tanya got her left foot caught in a pool drain as a result of the powerful suction of the pumps. She would have drowned had Tony not rescued her. She suffered torn tendons in her foot and ankle, and she developed an extreme phobia of water. She experienced nightmares and acute nervousness after the incident. There were no signs indicating that the pool could be drained remotely, nor that the drains were dangerous when the pumps were running.

2. Farabee St. Claire owns an ice-skating rink. Charles and Kelly visited the rink on their 10th wedding anniversary. Charles had not skated since high school (15 years earlier), but Kelly often went skating at the rink. Because of a broken thermostat, ice in one corner of the rink thawed and a small puddle formed. As Charles skated through the water, he slipped and fell to the ice, breaking his right arm. Kelly, who was skating close behind, collided with Charles and also fell to the ice, suffering a concussion. Kelly was a talented skater and could have avoided Charles by leaping over his body, but she did not think to do so in her surprise and confusion.

3. The Happy Hollow Mental Health Hospital houses many emotionally disturbed individuals. One patient, Jasmine, a convicted arsonist, escaped from her maximum-security room. No guards were on duty in that part of the hospital, and an attendant had left Jasmine's door unlocked. As Jasmine wandered out of a wooded area onto a highway, she hitchhiked a ride from Kate, who was driving back to the university at which she worked. Kate noticed that Jasmine was dressed in a hospital gown and blue jeans, but Jasmine explained that she was a medical student at the university and often wore these gowns because they were comfortable. Kate dropped Jasmine off at a bus stop located only a few hundred yards from Kate's home. Jasmine saw Kate stop at the house and then drive away again. Later that day, Kate's house burned down. Police arrested Jasmine for having set the fire.

4. Beth is an accountant. Ruben is one of her clients. Beth completed Ruben's federal and state tax returns for 2009. Beth made a critical addition error, however, and as a result, Ruben underpaid his taxes. Both the Internal Revenue Service and the State Department of Revenue assessed hefty penalties against Ruben for the underpayment. Ruben had signed the returns without reading them, although the instructions on each return clearly advised the taxpayer to read carefully through the returns to verify their accuracy, even if a professional tax preparer had been used.

5. Beau owns a sporting-goods store. Matt came in to buy a new shotgun. One of Beau's employees,

Saul, handed Matt a shotgun that, unbeknownst to Saul or Matt, was loaded. Neither Saul nor Matt checked the gun to see if it was loaded. The trigger, however, had a keyed lock that prevented it from being pulled. Matt asked that the lock be removed so that he could feel the trigger's sensitivity. Saul opened the lock and Matt tested the trigger. The gun discharged, shooting another customer, Clay, in the stomach. Clay saw Matt aim the gun in his general direction. Instead of stepping aside, Clay jokingly shouted, "Hey, do not shoot me, I'm on your side!"

▌REVIEW QUESTIONS

1. How are negligence defenses used? Which party uses them? Against whom are the defenses used? What is the purpose of negligence defenses?

2. Define *contributory negligence*. What are its elements? What is the common law rule regarding this issue? Why was contributory negligence a particularly effective defense? How would it arise today?

3. Explain last clear chance. How is it used? Who uses it against whom? What is its importance to contributory negligence?

4. Why is the contributory negligence defense unfair? What changes have courts and legislatures made to create a more equitable defense? What is this defense called?

5. Define *comparative negligence*. What are its elements? What is culpability factoring? Liability apportionment? Why are percentages used? Who decides these percentages? Is this defense more fair than that of contributory negligence? Why or why not?

6. What is assumption of risk? List its elements. Who uses the defense against whom? Must the risk be voluntarily assumed? What is "full appreciation of danger," and why is it significant? How effective is this defense in avoiding the defendant's liability? What level of risk does a person assume?

7. What are statutes of limitations? What time period is most commonly allowed for negligence causes of action? How can limitations statutes be used as a defense to negligence?

▌HELPFUL WEBSITES

This chapter focuses on defenses to negligence actions. To learn more about defenses to negligence actions, the following sites can be accessed:

General Information

www.uscourts.gov   www.firstgov.gov

www.courts.net   www.findlaw.com

STUDENT COMPANION WEBSITE

For additional cases and study materials, please go to www.cengagebrain.com

Chapter 6

Intentional Torts: Injuries to Persons

THE BIGGEST MISTAKES PARALEGALS MAKE AND HOW TO AVOID THEM

Bully for Him!

Jason was becoming a problem with his arrogant behavior. A technological whiz, his performance with the exhibits in court was without peer—and he knew it. Even opposing counsel marveled at Jason's expertise, as well as some judges. Worse yet, he knew the firm needed him, and he knew that members of the firm knew they needed him. Jason's raises were often and criticism was muted. Others left the firm because Jason was impossible to work with or they were the targets of his acid and foul tongue. One of the attorneys who practices employment law suggested that Jason was creating a hostile work environment and possibly putting the firm at risk of suit with his bullying behavior. Some wondered if that would be the next shoe to drop and whether it was already too late to avoid a suit from a current or past employee.

(continues)

Lesson Learned: A bully does not respond to reason or a mature conversation. Jason cleaned up his act only when his ambitions and fears were addressed. Promotions and pay raises were important to Jason, as well as the kudos he received with his techno-wizardry at trial. Finally, when Jason heard "enough is enough" enough times from on high, he knew his career at the firm was endangered. According to the Workplace Bullying Institute (WPI), many states outlaw bullying fellow employees in the workplace on the basis of race, religion, or sexual orientation. Outlawing "status-blind" harassment for all manner of claims is a growing legal trend across the nation. Why? One poll reveals that half of American workers are victims of bullies or witnesses of others being bullied in the workplace.

INTRODUCTION

Generally, a person has a right to be free of threats and actual contact that injures or offends him or her. Therefore, one has a duty not to intentionally injure, offensively touch, or threaten other people. A person also has a right to be free of conduct that harms his or her property. Likewise, one has a duty not to intentionally harm the property of others. Intentional torts can be against both persons and property.

Negligence cases are far more common than intentional tort cases in the practice of law. However, it is still important to be aware of what constitutes an intentional tort, and to be able to distinguish it from a negligence action. A primary reason that intentional torts are brought far less often is that the tortfeasors who commit intentional acts usually do not have assets to cover the harm they have caused. Additionally, automobile insurance, which covers injuries from automobile accidents, and other types of insurance, such as homeowners' policies, generally do not cover intentional acts. This chapter discusses:

- ▶ Intentional torts in general
- ▶ Assault and battery
- ▶ False imprisonment
- ▶ Sexual harassment
- ▶ Tortious interference with expectations of inheritance
- ▶ Patient dumping
- ▶ Spoliation of evidence

INTENTIONAL TORTS IN GENERAL

intentional tort | An injury *designed* to injure a person or that person's property, as opposed to an injury caused by negligence or resulting from an accident.

Intentional torts consist of conduct that is fashioned to harm another person or his or her property. The mischief is directed with the purpose of inflicting injury. All intentional torts include three elements: act, intent, and injurious behavior.

Intent can be broadly defined as the desire to achieve a particular result. Specifically, the tortfeasor must intend to accomplish the harmful consequences of his or her actions. This does not require malice or ill will; the tortfeasor simply must intend to cause the consequences that give rise to the tort, or the tortfeasor must know with substantial certainty that certain consequences would result from that act. Commonly, though, those consequences include some type of harm. These acts also must actually conclude in the injury that was intended.

For certain peculiar intentional torts, intent, strictly speaking, is not required. For example, for reckless infliction of emotional distress, intent is not essential. The tortfeasor need only know (or reasonably should know) that his or her outlandish or outrageous actions will produce emotional injury. This knowledge element acts as a substitute for intent.

Intentional torts involve intentional acts, and as such carry a high degree of risk of injury, and usually a low degree of social benefit. The risk generally greatly outweighs the benefit received. Therefore, the duty not to intentionally injure someone or something is great.

Intent and Action Together

Intent reflects the tortfeasor's state of mind and must occur simultaneously with the misconduct. For example, assume that David and Steven are carpenters. Steven tosses a piece of wood across a room into a pile, but before it lands the wood strikes David in the throat. Steven would not be liable for battery because although the board struck David, Steven did not intend this to happen. Suppose David thought about throwing the board back at Steven, but did nothing and walked away. David would not be liable for assault because no action accompanied his desire.

Intentional torts present a relatively black-and-white image of the law, in which it is fairly easy to distinguish the "good" person from the "bad." The victim seems truly exploited, and the tortfeasor is clearly responsible and to blame (from a moral or ethical point of view) for having purposefully injured the victim. Our sense of fair play is rewarded when intentional tortfeasors are held accountable for their mischief.

Crimes Versus Torts

It is important to note that a single act can be the basis for both a tort and a criminal action. Both crimes and torts involve wrongs. A *crime* is considered a wrong against the state or society as a whole, in addition to the actual victim. Therefore, the state brings actions against alleged criminals. With tort actions, one person brings suit against another individual or group; the action is brought by a private attorney on behalf of the injured party. Thus, a tort is considered a civil action.

Suppose that a person is walking down the street at night. Another person comes up, aims a gun, and then shoots the pedestrian. In this situation, both

intent | The resolve or purpose to use a particular means to reach a particular result. *Intent* usually explains *how* a person wants to do something and *what* that person wants to get done.

an assault and a battery have occurred. The pedestrian was first put in fear of harm and then actually harmed. As a result of the same act, the attacker may face both criminal and civil prosecution. The state may seek criminal damages against the attacker.

Criminal Actions. Depending on the seriousness of the crime charged, the attacker may face incarceration, a fine, or both as punishment for the act or omission. The punishment is meant to deter others from committing the same crime. A crime is a violation of a state or federal law. The standard of proof in a criminal action is higher than in a civil action. In a criminal action, proof beyond a reasonable doubt is required to find guilt. The decision of the jury must be unanimous. The jury is composed of 12 jurors. Unlike a civil case, only a defendant can appeal a criminal case. Whereas a criminal defendant is always entitled to a trial by jury, there is no such guarantee for all civil matters.

preponderance of the evidence | Just enough evidence is required to tip the scales in favor of one party over another party.

clear and convincing evidence | More than enough evidence to tip the scales, but less evidence than proof beyond a reasonable doubt is required. The evidence must be clear and convincing; it should be substantially more likely true than not true.

Civil Actions. In a civil action, a case must be proved by a **preponderance of the evidence** to find liability, just enough to tip the scales in favor of one person over another. For a few cases, the decision must be made by **clear and convincing evidence**. A civil jury consists of a minimum of 12 jurors. The decision need not be unanimous. In the previous example, where one person deliberately shoots another, the injured party may proceed with a civil action against the attacker, for money damages for injuries caused as a result of the attack. In addition, the government might decide to bring a criminal action. The criminal and civil action are each independent of each other. The results need not be the same.

A Crime and a Tort. One of the most publicized cases of where both a civil and criminal action were brought as a result of the same occurrence concerns former football legend O. J. Simpson. Simpson was charged with the murder of his ex-wife Nicole Brown Simpson and her friend Ronald Goldman. Although Simpson was ultimately acquitted of the criminal charges, a civil jury found him liable for wrongful death of Goldman and battery of his ex-wife. The civil action was brought by the families of the decedents. Table 6-1 compares torts versus crimes. Note that the civil and criminal definitions of acts constituting intentional torts are not necessarily the same.

▌ASSAULT AND BATTERY

The preceding example of the careless carpenters tossing wood depicts two of the most common intentional torts: assault and battery. Of all torts, these are perhaps the most straightforward.

	Tort	Crime
Goal	Compensation	Punishment and deterrence
Burden of Proof	Preponderance of evidence	Beyond reasonable doubt
Victim Harmed	Individual	Society
Rules of Evidence	Civil rules	Criminal rules
Who Brings the Action	Injured party	The state or federal government

TABLE 6-1
Comparison of torts versus crimes

Assault Defined

Assault is the intentional threat, show of force, or movement that reasonably makes a person feel in danger of physical attack or harmful physical contact. There are three basic elements to this tort:

1. The tortfeasor attempts to make unconsented harmful or offensive contact.
2. The victim is apprehensive for his or her physical safety.
3. The threat of contact is imminent.

Actual physical contact is not necessary; in fact, contact converts an assault into a battery. Assault is distinguishable from battery in that no touching is required for assault.

assault | An intentional threat, show of force, or movement that could reasonably make a person feel in danger of physical attack or harmful physical contact.

Imminent Threat of Contact. Assault involves the imminent or immediate threat that unconsented contact is about to occur. The fear arises from the likelihood that someone or something unwanted is about to strike. For instance, Michelle's threat to hit George while talking to him on the telephone does not present an immediate risk, as the task cannot be completed at the time the threat is made. Therefore, no assault has taken place.

Freedom from Apprehension. The rights being protected by recognition of this tort involve each person's right to control what touches his or her person. The tort of assault is also intended to protect individuals from the fear or apprehension that unconsented contact will take place. **Apprehension** means that a person reasonably fears for his or her physical safety in anticipation of being struck by the unconsented harmful or distasteful contact. This apprehension must be reasonable, meaning that the anxiety must be rational given the perceived threat of contact. For example, if a four-year-old warns that she is going to punch her father's head off, her father probably would not be overly

apprehension | Fear or anxiety.

concerned, as it would be unreasonable for an adult to fear a child's threatened battery under such circumstances. Threats at a distance do not present sufficient reason for alarm because it is physically impossible for the threatening party to fulfill the threat. This states the next legal requirement for assault: immediate threat of contact.

THE CASE OF THE UNFRIENDLY SECURITY OFFICERS

This case highlights the intersection of tort law and insurance law. What might look like a slam-dunk case can quickly evaporate, in this case when it is discovered that there is no insurance coverage for an incident.

THE BURLINGTON INSURANCE COMPANY, Plaintiff,

vs.

CHWC, INC. dba CRAZY HORSE RESTAURANT AND NIGHTCLUB; and RUDY MARTINEZ, JR., Defendants. RUDY MARTINEZ, JR., Counterclaimant,

vs.

THE BURLINGTON INSURANCE COMPANY, Counterdefendant

United States District Court for the Central District of California

CASE NO. CV 11-02926 R (FFMx)

2012 U.S. Dist. LEXIS 6530

January 20, 2012

Plaintiff The Burlington Insurance Company ("Burlington") filed a motion for summary judgment against defendant Rudy Martinez, Jr. ("Martinez"). Burlington insured defendant CHWC, Inc. dba Crazy Horse Steak House and Saloon ("Crazy Horse") through a Commercial General Liability Insurance policy, which provides that Burlington "will pay those sums that the insured becomes legally obligated to pay as damages because of 'bodily injury' . . . to which this insurance applies." By **endorsement**, the policy contains an assault or battery **exclusion**, which provides that the policy does not apply to bodily injury "[a]rising out of assault or battery, or out of any act or

omission in connection with the prevention or suppression of an assault or battery."

Mr. Martinez filed a lawsuit against Crazy Horse in state court. The complaint alleged that Crazy Horse is "a restaurant, bar, and nightclub . . . which touts its 'wild and crazy nightlife' on its website." Its "security employees, and other employees, routinely used excessive force handcuffed patrons, beat patrons, and generally physically abused patrons, causing injuries. On the night of January 19, 2008, Martinez was a patron when Crazy Horse's security employees "physically removed him from the dance floor and struck him with closed fists, feet and flashlight(s)" while plaintiff was handcuffed on the floor, injuring plaintiff.

The West Covina Police Department's crime report ("Crime Report") was provided to Burlington with the Martinez complaint. It identifies the crimes committed against Mr. Martinez as "battery" and "battery with serious bodily injury." The report summarized that Martinez "was getting kicked out" of the Crazy Horse "when a fight broke out" and he was struck several times. Martinez resisted removal. At the exit, he continued to resist removal, and backed up toward a vacant stool and fell. Two officers each saw Mr. Martinez get up from his fall and move to attack an officer. An officer grabbed Martinez "in a bear hug style grip and took him to the ground."

Burlington denied a duty to defend Martinez in the state court action. Its denial letter stated that the allegations of the complaint, "clearly stem from 'assault or battery' and acts or omissions in connection with an assault or battery." Thus, it stated that coverage was excluded by the assault or battery exclusion in the insurance policy.

Martinez later filed a first amended complaint against Crazy Horse that was never provided to Burlington. The specific causes of action for assault and battery were dropped. Martinez still alleged that he "was tackled, brutally beaten and injured by the security employees of defendants." Each cause of action was based on Crazy Horse having "improperly hired, trained, and retained security employees who were trained to use unnecessary and excessive force" and that they "became violent on January 19, 2008," and inflicted serious injuries to Martinez. The court found that Crazy Horse was negligent in the hiring, supervision, and training of its security guards, and that they were "negligent in the manner in which they handled Plaintiff that evening."

The interpretation of an insurance policy is an issue of law for the court. Words in an insurance policy are interpreted according to the plain meaning a layman would attach to them. An insurer has a duty to defend its insured if the underlying claim is potentially covered under the policy "But where there is no possibility of coverage, there is no duty to defend." *Fire Ins. Exch. v Abbott*, 204 Cal. App. 3d 1012, 1029, 251 Cal. Rptr. 620 (1988).

The existence of a duty to defend turns on what facts are "known by the insurer at the inception of a third party lawsuit." The determination whether the insurer owes a duty to defend usually is made in the first instance by comparing the allegations of the complaint with the terms of the policy. The assault or battery exclusion in the Burlington policy is broadly written to bar coverage for any assault-or-battery-related claim that might be made against an insured. The court finds this language to be clear, explicit, and unambiguous. Pleading separate claims for separate negligent acts cannot sidestep the exclusion. There was never a possibility of coverage for the complaint Mr. Martinez filed in state court.

The duty to defend is broader than the duty to indemnify. Therefore, "a conclusion that [the insurer] did not have a **duty to defend** will be dispositive of [a] claim that [the insurer] had a **duty to indemnify**." Burlington owed no duty to defend and thus, *a fortiori*, it owed no duty to indemnify. Accordingly, Burlington owes no duty to pay the claim of Mr. Martinez, the judgment creditor.

Because Burlington did not owe a duty to defend or indemnify, it cannot be liable for breach of the implied covenant of good faith and fair dealing. *Manzarek v. St. Paul Fire & Marine Ins. Co.*, 519 F.3d 1025, 1034 (9th Cir. 2008). A **bad faith claim** cannot be maintained unless policy benefits are due under the policy.

IT IS HEREBY ORDERED, ADJUDGED AND DECREED: Judgment is entered in favor of plaintiff The Burlington Insurance Company and against defendant Rudy Martinez, Jr.

CASE QUESTIONS

1. What do you think is more important to a defendant, an insurer's duty to defend or indemnify? Explain your answer.
2. Had the plaintiff alleged negligent hire instead of assault and battery in the original complaint, would the result have been any different here? Explain your answer.

The following hypothetical examples should help to illustrate these elements. Although assault is a fairly straightforward tort, its elements can best be explored hypothetically.

endorsement | A written document added to an insurance policy to make modifications or changes.

exclusion | An item or occurrence specifically not covered by insurance.

duty to defend | Obligation to provide a legal defense.

duty to indemnify | Obligation to pay or reimburse a party for damage or losses sustained.

a fortiori | (Latin) Meaning for the reason that is the stronger argument than another one that has been offered.

bad faith claim | Under insurance law, when an insurance company has an opportunity to settle a matter within the coverage of an insurance policy and refuses to do so without a good reason, a defendant may bring a bad faith claim against the insurance company.

HYPOTHETICALS

Hong and Davis begin arguing in a bar. Hong balls up his fists and pulls his arm backward as if to swing at Davis. Davis ducks in anticipation of a punch. Has Hong committed assault?

Applying the legal elements of assault, as previously discussed—which are (1) the tortfeasor's attempt to make unconsented harmful or offensive contact, which (2) makes the victim apprehensive for his or her physical safety, and (3) the threat of contact is imminent—it is clear that Hong has assaulted Davis. Hong attempted to touch Davis in a harmful or offensive manner when he drew his arm back to swing. Davis did not consent to this action and feared for his safety, as is obvious because he ducked, expecting to be pelted with Hong's fist. The danger of contact was immediate, as Hong could complete his swing and punch within a matter of seconds.

* * *

Consider another example. Nabeel and Brandon are playing basketball in a gymnasium. Brandon yells that Nabeel stepped out of bounds as he dribbled the ball upcourt. Nabeel smiles and fakes a forceful pass to Brandon's head, causing Brandon to flinch in anticipation that the ball will hit him in the face. Has Nabeel committed assault?

Consent is the key to this hypothetical. Nabeel and Brandon had agreed to play basketball together. It is well known that sports activities such as this involve a certain degree of incidental contact to which participants consent. This could involve being struck by the ball as it is deliberately passed from one player to another. Because Brandon implicitly agreed in advance to such types of contact while playing the game, Nabeel did not assault him.

All elements must exist for assault to occur. If any one feature is absent, then there is no assault. For instance, suppose in the first illustration that Davis had not reacted at all to Hong's arm gesture. Perhaps Hong and Davis often indulged in horseplay, such as by pantomiming fistfights, and so Davis assumed that it was just another joking episode. That would remove the apprehension element and thus there would be no assault. Suppose in the second example that Nabeel simply threw the ball down and shouted at Brandon, "Next time you call me a liar, I'll plant this right upside your head!" In that case, the threatened contact would not be imminent, as Nabeel warned only of behavior at some unspecified future time, which might in fact never take place. Accordingly, no assault would have happened.

Battery Defined

Strictly defined, **battery** is the intentional, unconsented touching of another person in an offensive or injurious manner. There are three basic elements to this tort:

1. Nonconsensual physical contact
2. Offensive or harmful contact
3. The tortfeasor's intent to touch another person in an offensive or injurious manner

battery | An intentional, unconsented-to physical contact by one person (or an object controlled by that person) with another person.

Physical Contact Required. Actual touching is necessary for a battery to occur. However, contact need not be made with a person's body. It is sufficient for the tortfeasor to touch the victim's clothing, or an object that the victim is carrying, such as a purse, or an object in which the victim is sitting, such as a chair or automobile. These items are said to become extensions of the person that, if touched, translate into touching the person himself or herself.

Lack of Consent. Battery occurs only if the victim did not consent to the physical contact. Consent can be expressed or implied. Expressed consent is relatively easy to identify. For example, participants in sporting events readily consent to the physical contact routinely associated with the activity. Implied consent arises out of particular situations in which individuals, by being involved, implicitly agree to some types of minor contact. For instance, people walking in crowds impliedly consent to incidental contact as they accidentally bump into passersby. It is reasonable and normal to expect that this will occur in crowded places, and those involved are (or should be) willing to tolerate some minor jostles. Consent is a defense to a battery claim.

Harmful or Offensive Contact. Battery requires touching that is harmful or offensive. Although harmful contact should be relatively simple to perceive, offensive touching may present some surprises. Often, offensive contact may be intended as positive or complimentary, such as a pat on the back or kiss on the cheek from a coworker. The recipient, however, may find these actions distasteful. This addresses the consent issue. People do not usually consent to touching that repulses them.

Whether or not the physical contact is offensive is judged by the **reasonable person standard**. Would a reasonable person have been insulted by the contact, given the same or similar circumstances? Reasonableness is often

reasonable person standard | What a reasonable person would have done in the same or similar circumstances.

based upon the victim's actions in conjunction with the tortfeasor's. For example, if two friends are accustomed to "goofing around" by jokingly touching one another (pats on the back, fake punches, tickling, etc.), then such behavior would not reasonably be offensive. In effect, the participants consented to the activity. In contrast, a male supervisor touching a female employee in a sexually explicit fashion could reasonably be perceived as degrading and offensive. Repeated, unwelcome, sexually offensive behavior or contact might also be construed as sexual harassment. This is covered later in the chapter.

Hazing. Some civil assault and battery actions have been brought as a result of **hazing** incidents at schools, in clubs, and even in the military. Every year, prospective members are seriously injured and even killed as a result of hazing that gets out of control. In order to show their commitment to a particular group, prospective members are forced to undergo degrading, embarrassing, and sometimes painful and dangerous tests and trials in order to join.

hazing | In order to show their commitment, incidents in which students are forced to undergo degrading, embarrassing, and sometimes painful tests and trials before joining a particular group.

Most recently, numerous hazing incidents at colleges involved alcohol poisoning. Some of the participants were seriously injured and others died. As a result, some of the students have been criminally prosecuted for causing bodily injury to other students, and the victims and their families have also brought civil actions against their classmates for assault and battery, as well as wrongful death.

Intent. Like all intentional torts, battery includes an element of intent. The tortfeasor must have intended to make contact with another individual in a harmful or offensive manner. Thus, accidentally bumping into someone in an elevator as it jerked into motion would not be battery, because the contact was unintentional. But pinching that person while leaving the elevator would be battery, as the act was purposefully designed to make offensive contact.

Transferred Intent. Sometimes the tortfeasor tries to strike someone but ends up hitting someone else or intends one wrongful act and another occurs. For instance, if Robert threw a stone at Chad but struck Mark instead, then Robert has committed battery against Mark. Although Robert intended to strike Chad, his intent is said to be carried along by the object he set into motion—the stone—and his intent is thus transferred with the stone onto whomever it reaches—in this case, Mark. Note, too, that Robert has assaulted Chad by throwing the stone and missing, provided that Chad was placed in reasonable apprehension, and so on.

transferred intent | In tort law, the principle that if a person intended to hit another but hits a third person instead, he or she legally intended to hit the third person. This "legal fiction" sometimes allows the third person to sue the hitter for an intentional tort.

Transferred intent is an effective tool for protecting persons from misdirected physical contacts. It holds the tortfeasor accountable for the consequences of his or her actions even though, strictly speaking, he or she did not desire to hit the third person involved.

THE CASE OF THE TEACHER'S ASSAULT PAY

Teachers may joke that in some public schools there is so much violence that the teachers should receive "hazard pay" for their service. In this case, based upon a statutory plan, transferred intent becomes the key factor as to whether an injured teacher's pay will end after one year or continue indefinitely throughout a disability.

John P. STOSHAK
v.
EAST BATON ROUGE PARISH SCHOOL BOARD

Court of Appeal of Louisiana, First Circuit
959 So. 2d 996, 2006-0852
(La. App. 1st Cir. 2/21/07)
February 21, 2007

On August 20, 2004, John Stoshak, a teacher at Istrouma High School in Baton Rouge, was injured when he attempted to break up a fight between two of his students. During the course of the students' fistfight, one of the punches struck Mr. Stoshak in the back of the head, causing him to fall to the ground and lose consciousness.

Louisiana Revised Statute 17:1201(C) provides two different sick leave pay provisions for public school teachers who sustain injuries on the job, depending on the cause of the injury. Louisiana Revised Statutes 17:1201(C)(1)(a), commonly referred to as the "assault pay" provision, states, in pertinent part:

> Any member of the teaching staff of the public schools who is injured or disabled while acting in his official capacity as a result of assault or battery by any student or person shall receive sick leave without reduction in pay and without reduction in accrued sick leave days while disabled as a result of such assault or battery.

Louisiana Revised Statutes 17:1201(C)(1)(b)(i), commonly referred to as the "physical contact" provision, states, in pertinent part:

> Any member of the teaching staff of the public schools who while acting in his official capacity is injured or disabled as a result of physical contact with a student while providing physical assistance to

a student to prevent danger or risk of injury to the student shall receive sick leave for a period up to one calendar year without reduction in pay. . . .

The evidence reveals that on the morning of August 20, 2004, Mr. Stoshak was teaching a group of pre-GED students when a fight erupted in his classroom between 17-year-old Jordan and 18-year-old Orange. Jordan was seated at a computer when Orange entered the classroom and punched him from behind. Jordan chased Orange into the hallway and the two began fighting. Mr. Stoshak attempted to break up the fight. During the course of the fight, a punch thrown by one of the boys hit Mr. Stoshak in the back of his head. Neither boy admitted to hitting Mr. Stoshak. Mr. Stoshak stated that he did not believe either of the boys had punched him deliberately; rather, he got in the way of the fighting boys who, in his words, were "tear[ing] each other up."

Mr. Stoshak contends the student who hit him committed an assault or battery as those terms are defined under Louisiana's criminal and civil law, entitling him to benefits under the "assault pay" provision.

The Board contends that the "physical contact" provision applies in this case because it is undisputed that the student intended to cause harmful physical contact to the other student, but not to Mr. Stoshak.

Under the tort law, a battery has been defined as a "harmful or offensive contact with a person, resulting from an act intended to cause the plaintiff to suffer such a contact."

In defining what type of conduct constitutes a battery, our courts have employed the doctrine of transferred intent. Under this theory, if a person intended to inflict serious bodily injury while trying to

(continues)

hit another person, but missed and accidentally hit someone else instead, such intent is transferred to the actual victim.

The legislature authorized the highest level of benefits to a teacher injured as a result of "assault or battery by any student or person." There is no language in this provision requiring that the teacher be the intended victim of an assault or battery.

Accordingly, we construe the benefits provided for in the "assault pay" provision to apply whenever the teacher is the victim of a battery at the hands of a student. The benefits provided for under the "physical contact" provision apply to injuries a teacher sustains when coming to the aid of a student that result from physical contacts that do not rise to the level of an assault or battery.

Under the doctrine of transferred intent, the student who hit Mr. Stoshak while attempting to hit the other student is deemed to have had the requisite intent to commit a battery on Mr. Stoshak. Therefore, because Mr. Stoshak's injuries resulted from a battery by a student, the Board was obligated to provide him with leave without reduction in pay for the duration of his disability.

CASE QUESTIONS

1. How would the fact pattern of this case have to be changed so that the "physical contact" statute for leave and not the "assault pay" statute would have been applicable to Mr. Stoshak?
2. How was the "transferred intent" provision applicable to the injured plaintiff Stoshak?

HYPOTHETICALS

Erin is a production analyst for a local investment firm. She is one of only three women in the operation. Another analyst, Calvin, regularly flirts with her. Erin responds politely but coolly to these episodes. One day Calvin, while standing behind Erin, takes hold of her upper arms and leans over her shoulder as if to inspect the file she has before her on her desk. Calvin wisecracks about the "nice view," to which Erin responds by grimacing. Has Calvin committed battery against Erin?

The three basic elements of battery have been satisfied. Erin did not consent to Calvin's touching. Her previous encounters with Calvin did not establish a playful relationship in which she might have encouraged such actions; in fact, she expressly discouraged Calvin's flirting. A reasonable person would have found Calvin's behavior offensive. Erin was insulted by the contact, as evidenced by her expression. Calvin intended to touch Erin in a way she found distasteful. Accordingly, Calvin is liable to Erin for battery. If Calvin's behavior continues to be a problem, it might also be actionable as sexual harassment, which is discussed later in this chapter.

* * *

Consider another illustration. Shelley is a clerk at a hotdog stand in a football stadium. Ben, a customer, purchased lunch from another clerk. Shelley thought

Ben was unusually rude, so, as Ben turned to walk away, Shelley threw Ben a plastic catsup bottle, shouting that he had forgotten his condiments. The bottle brushed Ben's jacket sleeve and caused him to spill his beverage onto his pants. The bottle then struck Iris in the head, covering her with catsup. Has Shelley committed battery against Ben and Iris?

Again, the elements unfold clearly. Ben did not consent to being touched. Shelley's intent to make contact transferred to the catsup bottle that struck Ben's clothing, which was an extension of his person. Shelley's contact was harmful because it caused Ben to spill his drink onto himself. Shelley purposefully touched Ben in a fashion that injured him. Furthermore, Shelley's intent to strike Ben was transferred with the bottle, so that in hitting Iris, transferred intent applied. Shelley is liable to both Ben and Iris for battery.

What if Shelley had been merely another spectator at the football game and, instead of throwing anything, had simply jostled Ben, causing the spillage onto both Ben and Iris, as they all were walking down the stairway to their seats? This would be considered incidental contact to which Shelley, Iris, and Ben impliedly consented. Thus, no battery would have happened.

Battery lends itself to a variety of boisterous hypotheticals. Consider the following examples, as well as the elements of assault and battery noted in Table 6-2.

Other intentional torts are less straightforward than assault and battery. False imprisonment poses particular wrinkles and is discussed next in the chapter.

▌ FALSE IMPRISONMENT

False imprisonment occurs when the tortfeasor intentionally confines someone without that person's consent. This might occur during a kidnapping or, more simply, when a person is held against his or her will by another for an unreasonable period of time. Typically this is claimed when an alleged shoplifter is questioned by store security personnel for an inordinate length of time. This tort

false imprisonment | An unlawful restraint or deprivation of a person's liberty, usually by a public official.

Assault	Battery
Attempt to make harmful or offensive contact with another person without consent	Unconsented physical contact
Placing the victim in reasonable apprehension for physical safety	Offensive or harmful contact
Threat of imminent contact	Intent to touch another person in offensive or injurious manner

TABLE 6-2
Elements of assault and battery

is meant to protect each individual's right to control his or her own freedom of movement. Essentially, there are four elements to false imprisonment:

1. Confinement without captive's consent
2. Tortfeasor's intent to confine victim
3. Confinement for an appreciable length of time
4. No reasonable means of escape

Note that in some jurisdictions, knowledge or awareness of the confinement is required.

Confinement

All methods of confinement include (1) a restriction of the victim's freedom of movement, (2) the captive's awareness or fear of the restriction, and (3) the victim's nonconsent to the restriction. The second element prevents the victim from escaping, either because no routes of escape are available or because the victim is afraid to attempt escape for fear of the tortfeasor's reprisals.

There are several ways in which the tortfeasor may confine his or her captive. These include physical barriers and express or implied threats of force. Table 6-3 illustrates the elements of false imprisonment.

Physical Barriers Restricting Movement. Physical barriers are the most common method of falsely imprisoning someone. Placing the captive in a locked room or a moving automobile (while refusing to stop) are common examples. However, the physical barriers need not be so small as a single room or vehicle. A captive may be restricted to the grounds of a series of adjacent buildings. It is even possible for the victim to be penned in by such unexpected blockades as an automobile blocking the victim's access from a driveway to a street. The physical barrier need only restrict the captive's freedom of movement. This essentially traps the victim, either by some actual physical obstruction, such as a locked door, fence, or wall, or by an object that the tortfeasor is using to restrain the captive, such as an automobile blocking the driveway or even the tortfeasor's own body obstructing a doorway. In some jurisdictions, the victim must be aware of the confinement.

TABLE 6-3

Elements of false imprisonment

Confinement without captive's consent
Intent to confine
Confinement for appreciable length of time
No reasonable means of escape

THE CASE OF THE MINOR IMPRISONMENT

A bus driver claims to have been so lost trying to find a school that it took four hours to take his only passenger to school. The outraged parents of the four-year-old special-needs student bring an action claiming false imprisonment, among other things. Was this an extreme case of the bus driver having no sense of direction, or did something more occur?

The SCHOOL BOARD OF MIAMI-DADE COUNTY, FLORIDA, Appellant,

v.

Francisco and Lourdes Trujillo, individually as the natural parents of Christopher Trujillo, a minor, Appellees

Nos. 3D04-77, 3D04-300

906 So. 2d 1109 (Fla. Dist. Ct. App., 3d Dist.)

May 4, 2005

The pertinent facts are as follows: On the first day of school, a Miami-Dade County school bus picked up the Trujillo's four-year-old son, Christopher ("Christopher"), a special needs child. The bus arrived at 8:40 a.m., almost an hour later than his scheduled pick-up time. The bus driver then drove around the area and unsuccessfully attempted to pick up the other students and find Blue Lakes Elementary School.

Eventually, the driver obtained directions and arrived at the elementary school at 12:50 p.m. By this time, Christopher had urinated on himself at least once and appeared to be thirsty and dehydrated. Although Mr. Trujillo immediately took Christopher to a pediatrician, the pediatrician found no signs of abuse or physical injury. After the incident, however,

Christopher began having nightmares, started wetting his bed and appeared to develop a fear of school buses. The Trujillos decided that Christopher would no longer ride the school bus.

The Trujillos sued the School Board alleging negligence, false imprisonment and a violation of Christopher's civil rights. The Trujillos sought damages for Christopher's pain and suffering and for the additional child care and transportation costs they incurred because Christopher no longer rode the school bus.

Here, neither the pediatrician nor the psychologist who examined Christopher found any physical or emotional injuries.

Because Christopher did not suffer a physical injury or impact and his emotional injuries are intangible, the impact rule applies and therefore precludes recovery of damages.

There is no evidence that the School Board or its employees intended to confine Christopher, had knowledge that confinement would result, or that Christopher was prevented from leaving the bus or held against his will. Rather, the evidence shows that the bus driver picked Christopher up and thereafter got lost. This hardly amounts to false imprisonment.

CASE QUESTIONS

1. If the impact rule did not apply, would the court's decision be different?
2. What facts would be needed to show false imprisonment?

Express or Implied Threats of Force.

Sometimes no locked door or wall is necessary to confine a person. Threats of physical or emotional violence can be quite effective, as are threats against the victim's family or property. In this way, confinement is achieved by expressed intimidation. The victim is afraid to escape for fear of physical or emotional injury. For example, when the tortfeasor warns, "If you leave this room, I will break your legs," the captive is likely to remain as instructed. Similarly, the tortfeasor could threaten, "If you leave this house, I will tell Joe that you wrecked his new car." In this situation, the victim is restrained by the threat of emotional injury, if certain information is revealed that would incriminate the captive.

These types of threats need not be explicit, however. Implied threats also work effectively. For instance, if a store manager tells a shoplifting suspect to wait in a room for questioning "so that nobody has to telephone the police," the threat of arrest and criminal prosecution is clearly implied, and the suspect will probably comply out of fear.

Captive's Consent to Confinement. The intentional tort of false imprisonment cannot occur if the victim consents to the captivity. **Consent** includes awareness and acceptance of the confinement. Thus, if a shoplifting suspect agrees to remain in a room pending questioning by store security, this would constitute consent, because the patron knows and accepts the restriction to the room. However, there could be instances where the suspect stays, and has not voluntarily consented.

consent | Voluntary and active agreement.

Intent to Confine. The tortfeasor must intend to confine the victim for false imprisonment to happen. Consider the example of an accidental lock-in at a department store, where a customer is inadvertently locked inside the store after closing hours. There would be no false imprisonment, because the store management had no desire to confine the patron.

Intent may be expressed or implied by conduct. The tortfeasor who states his or her intention to confine another person is easiest to identify. Often, however, intent is indicated by conduct. Again, the shoplifting illustration presents a good example. A shoplifting suspect is stopped by store security and is asked to accompany the guard. Without any word of explanation, the guard takes the suspect to a back room, has the suspect enter, closes the door, and departs. There have been no explicit indications of confinement—the door was not locked—but implicitly it is understood, based on the behavior of the guard, that the suspect is to remain in the room. Accordingly, the intent to restrain may be implied.

Confinement for Appreciable Time Period. Although no definite time period is required, false imprisonment occurs only if the confinement has existed for an appreciable length of time. This depends upon the specific facts of each case. Usually, *appreciable confinement* is defined as unreasonable under the circumstances. That could be a matter of seconds, if someone is restrained in an extremely hazardous situation, such as in a burning building, or it could be a question of an hour or two, such as during a shoplifting investigation.

No Reasonable Means of Escape. False imprisonment cannot happen if the captive has a reasonable avenue of escape. In other words, the confinement must be complete. If the victim could simply walk away from the situation, then no false imprisonment transpired. Reasonable means of escape depends upon the facts of each case, but usually includes any route that a reasonable person would use to flee given the circumstances. For example, if Wes makes improper advances upon Sarah in his automobile, and Sarah has only to open the door to leave, then she has a reasonable avenue of escape, and no false imprisonment has happened. However, if Wes made the same advances on Sarah in a fourth-floor apartment, in which the only exits were one door (which Wes blocked) and the windows, then false imprisonment would have occurred. Sarah could hardly be expected to escape by leaping from a fourth-story window.

Many false imprisonment cases involve shoplifting or alleged shoplifting. The difficulty in these cases stems from the conflicting interests involved: the patron's freedom to move about freely versus the business's right to protect its property from theft. Notice that there are competing tort interests here. The customer seeks protection from false imprisonment, whereas the store owner wishes to prevent conversion and trespass to chattel.

Shopkeeper's Privilege. In many states, there is a common law right called the **shopkeeper's privilege** to stop and detain a suspected shoplifter at the store for a reasonable period of time, so long as the shopkeeper has reason to believe the person detained has actually stolen or attempted to steal property. This gives the shopkeeper the right to stop and question suspected shoplifters before they leave the store. It is important that the shopkeeper's acts be seen as reasonable. Questioning a suspect for a few minutes is acceptable. Hours of interrogation would not qualify for this privilege. A shopkeeper must have a reason to suspect the theft; mere hunch or assumption would not be acceptable.

shopkeeper's privilege | A shopkeeper is allowed to detain a suspected shoplifter on store property for a reasonable period of time, so long as he or she has cause to believe that the person detained in fact committed, or attempted to commit, theft of store property.

THE CASE OF THE OVERZEALOUS STORE SECURITY OFFICER

As noted, many false imprisonment cases involve shoplifting. All too often, store employees, anxious to curb theft of merchandise, become overzealous in their efforts. Suspected shoplifters, on the flimsiest circumstantial evidence, are occasionally subjected to unreasonable searches, confinements, interrogations, and the accompanying stresses and embarrassment. When the evidence against such suspects is extremely speculative, as in the case reprinted here, the result is often tort litigation. The suspect becomes the plaintiff. The store, as the defendant, suddenly finds itself attempting to justify its employees' conduct. In the following case, false imprisonment was successfully claimed.

(continues)

ROGERS
v.
T.J.X. COS.

Supreme Court of North Carolina
329 N.C. 226, 404 S.E.2d 664 (1991)
Martin, Justice

The action arose out of events occurring at the T.J. Maxx department store in Cary, North Carolina, owned by defendant T.J.X. Companies, Inc. Taken in the light most favorable to the plaintiff, as we must for summary judgment purposes, the evidence tends to show the following. Plaintiff entered T.J. Maxx, hereinafter "the store," about 4:30 p.m. shopping for linens. She wore bermuda shorts and a T-shirt and carried a pocketbook, approximately 12 inches by 12 inches. The purse contained two cosmetic bags, a wallet, two pens, a glasses' case, and a ziploc bag containing material and wallpaper samples. Plaintiff went first to the cosmetics area and then to the linens department. After leaving the linens department, she walked around a counter containing dishes and crystal and then left the store without making a purchase. Plaintiff never entered the lingerie department and never examined any items of lingerie.

As plaintiff exited the store, Michael Nourse stopped her, identified himself as a store security officer, and asked her to return to the store because he wished to talk with her about some merchandise. Nourse carried a badge of his own design and an identification card issued by the company; he showed these items to plaintiff. Plaintiff told him that he was making a mistake, but complied with his request and accompanied Nourse to his office at the back of the store. Plaintiff testified that she did not feel that she had a choice about accompanying Nourse because "he was the law of the store," and she had to obey him. On the way to the office, Nourse asked another store employee, Sheri Steffens, to join them and act as a witness.

Once inside the small office, plaintiff immediately dumped the contents of her purse onto the desk. Nourse told plaintiff to take a seat, but she refused, saying that this would not take long because she was a good customer and had not stolen anything.

Nourse responded, "Good customers will steal," and again directed her to have a seat. Telling her he would soon return, he then left the office for five to fifteen minutes. Plaintiff testified that she believed that he might have gone to call the police, and she stepped out of the office to look for them. Seeing no one, she gathered up her belongings, but did not feel free to leave because Nourse had told her he would return. Steffens paged Nourse, who returned momentarily. He said to plaintiff, "Ma'am, all we want is our merchandise. What did you do with it? You were in our lingerie department." Plaintiff denied wrongdoing, again dumped her purse on the desk, and told him that he must have seen her putting the packet of material samples into her purse. As she reached to gather her belongings, Nourse instructed her not to touch anything.

Nourse pulled down a clipboard hanging on the wall and showed her a card which said that the store employees had the right to detain her if they had reason to believe she had been shoplifting. Nourse repeatedly questioned plaintiff about the location of the missing merchandise as she tried to read the card. Plaintiff told him to "shut up" so that she could concentrate. Nourse remarked to Steffens, "Usually the dog that barks the loudest is guilty." Nourse then told plaintiff that he could call the police if she wanted them to settle it; that he could handcuff her to a chair; and that he would call the police and have them put her in jail. Plaintiff continued to deny the allegations and asked if he wanted her to take her clothes off to prove that she had not done anything, even though she was a very modest person. Steffens testified that plaintiff was very upset throughout the incident and that Nourse's attitude and demeanor toward plaintiff was sarcastic.

Nourse instructed plaintiff to sign two forms, one of which was a waiver of Miranda rights. The other form released T.J. Maxx from liability for any claims arising out of the incident. Neither of the papers had been filled out when plaintiff signed. Plaintiff testified that she signed the release form only because she believed that she would not be allowed to leave the store and go home if she did not sign it. Nourse refused to give plaintiff copies of the forms, because it was not company policy. After signing the papers, plaintiff left the store and drove home. She had been in the security office approximately 35 minutes. About one-half hour after plaintiff left the store, Nourse announced to Steffens that he had found the missing merchandise, a beige brassiere.

False imprisonment is the illegal restraint of the person of any one against his or her will. The tort may be committed by words or acts; therefore, actual force is not required. Restraint of the person is essential, whether by threats, express or implied, or by conduct. The Court of Appeals held that plaintiff had established facts sufficient to support her claim for false imprisonment....

Taken in the light most favorable to the plaintiff, the evidence tends to show that (1) defendant Nourse impersonated a police officer by using a badge of his own design; (2) plaintiff was restrained against her will in the store security office for approximately one-half hour; (3) plaintiff was badgered, insulted and pressured to confess by defendant Nourse despite her efforts to prove her innocence; (4) plaintiff was frightened and upset and asked if she could leave; (5) defendant unlawfully detained plaintiff after [a] determination that no offense had been committed; (6) plaintiff was made to give up personal information including her driver's license number, telephone number, and social security number; and (7) plaintiff was forced to sign a release of liability as a condition to her release from Nourse's custody.

We hold that there was sufficient evidence of conduct constituting the false imprisonment, to survive defendants' motion for summary judgment.

CASE QUESTIONS

1. Given the facts in this case, did the plaintiff establish the elements (as discussed in this chapter) for false imprisonment?
2. Read and compare North Carolina's common law regarding false imprisonment with the law of your state. What are the similarities and differences?

HYPOTHETICALS

Consider Sophie's predicament. A cashier thought he spotted Sophie taking some merchandise and placing it in her purse without paying for it. As Sophie walked out the exit, store security grabbed her. She violently protested, but the guards, without explanation, bodily forced her into a small, unlit room in the rear of the store. They then locked the door, and Sophie sat for three hours until the store manager, who had been on a delivery errand, returned to question her. She was, in fact, innocent of any wrongdoing. Was there false imprisonment?

The confinement was without Sophie's consent, as evidenced by Sophie's protests of the guards' physical handling of her. The restraint was obvious because the door was locked. The store security guards intended to confine Sophie by locking her in the room. She was restrained there for three hours, which would probably be considered unreasonable, particularly because the room was small and unlit. She had no reasonable means of escape, again

(continues)

because the only door to the room was locked. Therefore, the store would be liable to Sophie for false imprisonment.

* * *

Consider also the case of Murphy. Murphy drove his automobile into a restricted area of a manufacturing plant. Plant security instructed him to remain parked in his vehicle pending the arrival of the supervisor. Murphy said he had no reason to hang around, as he had done nothing wrong. The security officers then left. There were no barriers preventing Murphy from simply driving off the premises, through an open gate, to the highway. Was there false imprisonment?

The critical element in this hypothetical is the reasonable route of escape. Murphy could easily have slipped away, and the guards made no implied or expressed threats (such as arrest and criminal prosecution if he attempted to leave). Accordingly, no false imprisonment took place.

▍SEXUAL HARASSMENT

sexual harassment | Unwelcome sexual advances, requests for sexual favors, and other verbal or physical conduct of a sexual nature, when this conduct affects an individual's employment, unreasonably interferes with an individual's work performance, or creates an intimidating, hostile, or offensive work environment.

Title VII of the Civil Rights Act of 1964 makes it unlawful for an employer to discriminate against an individual because of that individual's race, color, religion, sex, or national origin, 42 U.S.C. § 2000-2(a)(1). In addition to tort actions, **sexual harassment** claims can be brought under the provisions of Title VII. Complaints can be filed with the federal or state government, and in some instances even the county government. The federal agency that handles discrimination complaints is the U.S. Equal Employment Opportunity Commission (EEOC). At the state and county levels, there are varying names for such agencies. The definition for discrimination and the procedure for bringing a complaint may vary at each agency. It is essential to check the agency's website for applicable laws, procedures, claim forms and other documents.

A sexual harassment claimant must show that there are unwelcome sexual advances, requests for sexual favors, and other verbal or physical conduct of a sexual nature, when this conduct affects an individual's employment, unreasonably interferes with an individual's work performance, or creates an intimidating, hostile, or offensive work environment.

To show hostile work environment, a plaintiff must show that the workplace is permeated with discriminatory intimidation, ridicule, and insult that alter the conditions of the victim's employment, thereby creating an abusive and hostile work environment. Tangible psychiatric injuries need not be proven.

It should not be very difficult to imagine scenarios of emotional damage infliction in the workplace. However, there are many instances in which the behavior is more subtle.

THE CASE OF INCREDIBLE SEXUAL HARASSMENT

Two women detail graphic sexual harassment they allege occurred over the course of their employment. They both speak of vulgar and hurtful remarks made to them on a daily basis. The jury must weigh their testimony against that of the alleged harassers.

Kristina Conti, et al., Appellants

v.

Spitzer Auto World

Amherst, Inc., et al., Appellees

State of Ohio, County of Lorain

Ohio Court of Appeals, Ninth Judicial District

2008 Ohio-1320

March 24, 2008

Conti, Dutton, and Smith (collectively "Employees") each worked for a period of time for a car dealership owned and operated by Appellee Spitzer Auto World Amherst, Inc. Employee benefits were provided to this dealership through Appellee Spitzer Management, Inc. At the time employees worked at the dealership, the general manager was Joe Garrett, and the sales managers were Todd Meek and Tim Dalzell. Further, both Spitzer entities were owned and/or controlled by Alan Spitzer.

Employees alleged that during their employment they were subjected to sexual harassment on a near daily basis. Conti asserted that Meek and Dalzell routinely viewed pornography on work computers and forced her to view the pornography on numerous occasions. Conti also asserted that Meek rubbed up against her from behind and forced her to touch his buttocks on several occasions.

In order to demonstrate a prima facie case of sexual harassment, each plaintiff must produce evidence of the following:

"(1) she was a member of a protected class;
(2) she was subjected to unwelcome sexual harassment in the form of sexual advances, requests for sexual favors or other verbal or physical conduct of a sexual nature;
(3) the harassment complained of was based upon sex;

(4) the charged sexual harassment had the effect of unreasonably interfering with the plaintiff's work performance and creating an intimidating, hostile or offensive working environment that affected the psychological well-being of the plaintiff and
(5) the existence of respondeat superior liability."

In order to determine whether an environment is sufficiently hostile to warrant a finding of sexual harassment this court examines the totality of the circumstances including:

"the frequency of the discriminatory conduct; its severity; whether it is physically threatening or humiliating, or a mere offensive utterance; and whether it unreasonably interferes with an employee's work performance. The effect on the employee's psychological well-being is, of course, relevant to determining whether the plaintiff actually found the environment abusive. But while psychological harm, like any other relevant factor, may be taken into account, no single factor is required." Harris v. Forklift Sys. Inc. (1993), 510 U.S. 17.

We also note that the standards for judging hostility are demanding such that "the ordinary tribulations of the work place, such as, sporadic use of abusive language, gender-related jokes, and occasional teasing" will not constitute a hostile work environment. Faragher v. Boca Raton (1998), 524 U.S. 775.

Moreover, the Sixth Circuit has established the standards by which employees might prove their constructive discharge claims based on sexual harassment. "A finding of constructive discharge in this circuit requires an inquiry into both the objective feelings of the employee and the intent of the employer. . . . This court has . . . held that 'proof of discrimination alone is not a sufficient predicate for a finding of constructive discharge, there must be other aggravating factors.'

(continues)

We have also required some inquiry into the employer's intent and the reasonably foreseeable impact of its conduct on the employee . . . ."

Accordingly, to prevail on their claim of constructive discharge premised on a hostile working environment, Smith and Dutton were required to demonstrate a hostile working environment and "show that a reasonable employer would have foreseen that [they] would resign, given the sexual harassment [they] faced."

Smith testified as follows. She was subjected to harassment by Meek on nearly a daily basis. Meek routinely asked if she was wearing underwear, and what color her underwear were. Once, Smith called in to tell Meek that she would be late for work that day. Meek responded by asking Smith to "scrub it" before coming to work. Smith understood this comment to be sexual in nature. On the final day of her employment, Smith was discussing the fact that her infant child had thrush. According to Smith, Meek then stated that the infant "should not be sucking on my vagina." Smith went immediately to Ruth Sadowsky to report Meek's comment. Sadowsky, a financial manager for Spitzer, had Smith write a report detailing the harassment she described. Smith detailed the "scrub it" incident that had occurred six weeks earlier and Meek's comment that day. Smith did not report any other alleged harassment during her employment.

Dutton testified as follows. During the first week of her employment, when she was 17 years old, Meek asked to see her breasts. Meek also asked whether Dutton and her boyfriend engaged in anal sex and whether Dutton had performed oral sex.

On another occasion, Meek walked past a van in Spitzer's showroom and asked Dutton if she would "get in there with him and give him a lap dance." On still another occasion, Dalzell asked her to spread her legs so that he could see up her skirt.

The jury was presented with two very different views of the workplace at Spitzer. Employees and their witnesses presented an atmosphere rife with crude comments and sexual innuendo. In contrast, Spitzer and its witnesses presented testimony that no inappropriate behavior took place at the dealership. There is little question that the jury was best situated to determine the credibility of these witnesses and determine which atmosphere existed at Spitzer. We find no error in the jury's apparent reliance on the testimony of Spitzer's witnesses. One relevant fact was undisputed. Smith and Dutton testified that the harassment occurred on a daily basis. Both, however, conceded that they had never mentioned this daily harassment to anyone in their lives prior to filing suit against Spitzer. From this admission, the jury was free to find that Smith and Dutton lacked credibility with respect to describing the frequency and severity of the alleged harassment.

Upon our review, the jury had before it competent, credible evidence to find in favor of the defendants on the claims brought by Dutton and Smith. The jury's verdict, therefore, was not against the manifest weight of the evidence.

CASE QUESTIONS

1. What part of the women's testimony was the key to the jury's decision? Explain.
2. Whose testimony did you find more convincing, that of the men or the women? Explain.

CHOPOURIAN ORDER AND JUDGMENT

A new record has been set with a jury awarding a California woman $168 million following a sexual harassment and retaliation claim. Previously, awards of this magnitude were made to groups rather than an individual claimant. The award was later reduced to $82 million. A portion of the landmark judgment and order follows. The judgment covers punitive damages, lost wages, and compensation for mental distress. Not only was the plaintiff supported in her testimony by former coworkers who had endured similar abuse, but her allegations were particularly outrageous.

Ani Chopourian, a physician's assistant, alleged that she was forced to undergo daily bullying, hostile work environment, and sexual harassment while at work assisting cardiac surgeons in the operating room of a hospital. Chopourian also alleged she was denied meal breaks in violation of the wage and hour laws. She made complaints to human resources on numerous occasions, but nothing was done. One week after formally complaining with a certified letter, she was terminated from employment.

Claimant alleged she was deliberately stuck with a needle by one surgeon, patted on the behind by another surgeon as he greeted her each morning and told her he was "horny," and repeatedly called a "stupid chick" by another surgeon. Claimant was also teased about being of Armenian descent, and repeatedly asked whether she had joined Al Qaeda yet.

ORDER AND JUDGMENT
Ani CHOPOURIAN, Plaintiff,
v.
CATHOLIC HEALTHCARE WEST, Defendant
United States District Court, Eastern District, California

On April 10, 2012, the court heard argument on the parties' proposals for entry of judgment. The purpose of this order is limited to entering judgment based on the jury's verdicts. On February 24, 2012, the jury retired to consider plaintiff's claims for two Title VII violations-hostile work environment and retaliation—as well as claims for discharge in violation of public policy, discharge in retaliation for complaints about patient safety, intentional interference with prospective economic advantage, defamation, and failure to provide meal and rest breaks.

The court ORDERS, ADJUDGES, AND DECREES that judgment is entered in favor of plaintiff Ani Chopourian and against defendant Catholic Healthcare West, in the following amounts:

Title VII : $300,000.00
Total economic damages: $3,730,488.00
Noneconomic damages : $22,000,000.00
Punitive Damages: $56,250,000.00
Meal and Rest Period Wages: $32,716.80
30 Day Penalty: $17,280.00

Judgment is entered in favor of plaintiff Ani Chopourian and against defendant Catholic Healthcare West in the total amount of $82,330,484.80.
Dated: April 30, 2012.
UNITED STATES DISTRICT JUDGE

TORTIOUS INTERFERENCE WITH REASONABLE EXPECTATIONS OF INHERITANCE

A newer tort that has been accepted by almost half of the states **tortious interference with reasonable expectations of inheritance**. The *Restatement of Torts* 2d § 774B defines the tort as follows: "One who by fraud, duress or other tortious means intentionally prevents another from receiving from a third person

tortious interference with reasonable expectations of inheritance | Interfering with another person's right to receive an inheritance that the person would have otherwise received.

an inheritance or gift that he would otherwise have received is subject to liability to the other for loss of the inheritance or gift," Beckwith v. Dahl, CAAppDiv 4th, 2012, GO 44479. Generally the following elements are required for tortious interference with expectations of inheritance:

1. A person or entity must have an expectation that he or she will receive an inheritance.
2. A third party must intentionally interfere with this expectation.
3. It is wrongful or tortious behavior to interfere.
4. It is reasonably certain that without the interference, the inheritance would have been received.
5. There must be damages as a result.

Know these [handwritten note in margin]

THE CASE OF THE STEPMOTHER WHO HAD IT ALL

Imagine the disappointment of two daughters when they learn that their stepmother has inherited their dad's entire estate, and that no money was left for them. As you read, decide whether this situation could have been prevented, and if so, by what methods.

Mercedes R. SAEWITZ, et al., Appellants/ Cross–Appellees,

v.

Lynn SAEWITZ, etc., Appellee/ Cross–Appellant

District Court of Appeal of Florida,
Third District
79 So.3d 831
January 4, 2012

This is an appeal by Mercedes R. Saewitz and Brooke A. Saewitz, daughters of Max Saewitz, deceased, from a directed verdict and final judgment of dismissal at the close of the daughters' case-in-chief in a lawsuit filed by them against their stepmother, Lynn Saewitz, for conversion and tortious interference with an expected inheritance. The trial judge dismissed the case for failure of the daughters to meet and satisfy the damage element of their prima facie case. We affirm the decision of the trial court.

The daughters' initial brief on this appeal persuasively chronicles the record evidence presented to the jury of manipulative activity taken by their stepmother during their father's dying days and preceding months to contravene their father's wishes with respect to the disposition of his estate. A plaintiff's initial proof of a prima facie case of both conversion and tortious interference in her case-in-chief requires more than proof of liability. Prima facie proof of damages is required as well.

The substance of the evidence the daughters presented to the jury on the element of damages is found in the testimony of three witnesses: Jack Rosenberg, the decedent's accountant; Ron Goldstein, a friend of the decedent; and Lynn Saewitz. Rosenberg provided general testimony that the value of the assets involved in the litigation was "over a million dollars" or "in the millions [of dollars]." Goldstein similarly testified the value of the allegedly misappropriated assets at "seven figures." Although denying any wrongdoing, Lynn Saewitz similarly indicated the value of the assets in question was in the "millions of dollars." However, none of the testimony was tied to a legally relevant time period. *See R & B Holding Co. v. Christopher Adver. Group, Inc.*, 994 So.2d 329, 331 (Fla. 3d DCA 2008) (holding the measure of damages for conversion is the fair market value of the interests at the time of the conversion); *Restatement (Second) of Torts* § 774B (1979) ("[R]ecovery [can be] only for an inheritance or gift that the other would have received but for the tortious interference of the actor."). This omission alone deprives this testimony of any probative value.

Additionally, this testimony is insufficient to satisfy the "reasonable certainty" threshold necessary to be considered legally probative of the amount or extent of damages suffered by the daughters. "Under the reasonable certainty rule, . . . recovery is denied where the fact of damages and the extent of damages cannot be established with a reasonable degree of certainty. The amount of damages claimed need not be proven with exactitude, but it must not be based upon speculation or guesswork. The proof adduced must be sufficiently definite for a reviewing court to perform its review obligation."

In the case before us, the proof adduced by the daughters in their case-in-chief fails to meet this fundamental requirement. See *Smith*, 538 So.2d at 129 (finding testimony that $15,000 would be a "fair assessment" or "good gauge" of expense of restoration of leased premises recoverable against lessee insufficient to satisfy "reasonable certainty" test for damage award against lessee); *see also Del Monte Fresh Produce Co. v. Net Results, Inc.,* 77 So.3d 667, 673 (Fla. 3d DCA 2011) (finding the plaintiff's assumptions and extrapolation for over ninety percent of its claimed damages pushed its proof of damages into the realm of conjecture and speculation).

The daughters argued below, and renew their argument, that they were prevented from proving their damages by the failure of counsel for the stepmother to engage in discovery in good faith. The daughters specifically point to the fact, that defense counsel failed to inquire of Jack Rosenberg, or his accounting firm for documents relating to the value of the decedent's assets in response to a request for production that included them. As trustee of the Max P. Saewitz Revocable Trust, Lynn Saewitz had the legal obligation to make such an inquiry.

The testimony of Jack Rosenberg indicated his firm had responsive documentation. During the course of the argument on the motion for directed verdict, counsel for the daughters placed reliance on this lapse by defense counsel to ask the trial court to either re-open the case to allow more evidence on the element of damages, or, alternatively, grant a new trial as a sanction against Lynn Saewitz and her counsel for abuse of discovery.

The trial court denied relief. The trial court did not abuse its discretion in so doing. In the first place, counsel for the daughters acquiesced in the production made by defense counsel by not first pursuing a motion to compel the records. A sanction remedy for failure to allow discovery is legally unavailable to a party until the opposing party is first subject to and violates an order to provide such discovery. Counsel for the daughters counter they did not know defense counsel failed to perform its duty or that such documents existed and were in the control of Lynn Saewitz; thus, they did not move to compel. But neither is there any evidence in the record that counsel for the daughters made any effort to confirm compliance. Notably, counsel for the daughters neither subpoenaed the records of the decedent's accounting firm before trial, nor sought to take the deposition of the accounting firm or any of its employees. In short, whatever lapse— legal or ethical—may be laid at the feet of defense counsel, it is true as well that counsel for the daughters was never affirmatively misled by the defense.

Finally, the precise identification of each asset at issue was known to counsel for the daughters well before trial. If a prima facie case of the value of these assets could have been proven through the records or testimony of the decedent's accountants, it follows the assets also could have been valued by experts retained by the daughters. Unless knowingly waived or excused by the daughters themselves, counsel's obligation to the daughters in this case included an independent obligation to be prepared to present a prima facie case on the value of the daughters' damage claim at trial. The actions of defense counsel, even if a violation of a legal or ethical obligation existed, were not the "but for" cause of the daughters' failure to present a prima facie case to the jury. Affirmed.

(continues)

CASE QUESTIONS

1. Why was the testimony that the damage the daughters sustained was "in the millions" not sufficient to meet the damages element for their cause of action?
2. What did the judge think the sisters' attorney should have done in regard to discovery proceedings?

▌ PATIENT DUMPING

patient dumping | Denial of treatment to emergency patients or women in labor, or transferring them to another hospital while in an unstable condition.

Patient dumping, another intentional tort, occurs when a patient is denied treatment or transferred while in an unstable medical condition. This usually occurs when a hospital or other medical facility is trying to save money and limits treatment, or sends a patient to another facility before it is medically sound to do so.

A federal statute addressing patient dumping is the Emergency Medical Treatment and Active Labor Act (EMTALA). The act only covers hospitals that participate in Medicare. The act provides that if a person goes to a hospital with an emergency medical condition and the person requests treatment or an examination, the person must be provided with an appropriate medical screening exam. If this does not occur and the person suffers harm, the person will have a claim against the medical provider or institution.

▌ SPOLIATION OF EVIDENCE

spoliation of evidence | Deliberate withholding, hiding, or destruction of evidence relevant to a legal proceeding. This is a new tort.

In some states, **spoliation of evidence** is now a tort as well as a civil action. It is also a criminal act. Spoliation of evidence is the deliberate withholding, hiding, or destroying of evidence relevant to a legal proceeding. An example of this would be in a products liability case where the injured plaintiff who was in possession of the car that allegedly caused his serious injuries is unable to produce it at the time of trial. In these cases, the court can draw an adverse inference, preclude evidence or testimony, or dismiss a claim at the time of trial. Different states vary as to how they define the tort or whether they choose to acknowledge this tort.

THE CASE OF THE SPOILED EVIDENCE

Multiple legal issues covered in this chapter intersect in this case: assault and battery, false imprisonment, the shopkeeper's defense, and spoliation of evidence. In the end, the court imposes its sense of fair play on the parties.

RHONDA MICHELLE BRITTON, GLENN BRITTON, CHRISTOPHER BRITTON, and DAMIAN BRITTON, Plaintiff,

vs.

WAL-MART STORES EAST, L.P., Defendants

United States District Court for the Northern District of Florida, Tallahassee Division

U.S. Dist. LEXIS 86901

June 8, 2011

Pending in this case is Plaintiffs' motion for sanctions for spoliation of evidence. Plaintiff Rhonda Britton is the mother of Plaintiff's Christopher and Damian Britton, two teenage children. Glenn Britton is her husband. It is alleged that on October 29, 2009, Rhonda Britton and her children shopped at the Wal-mart. While Ms. Britton shopped for groceries, her two sons walked throughout the store. It is alleged that at no point did the children touch any digital cameras. As the Brittons left the store, it is alleged that a Wal-Mart security officer stopped them and profanely accused the children of stealing a digital camera, displaying to them an empty cardboard box as evidence of the theft. It is alleged that he then committed child abuse, assault, battery, and falsely imprisoned Damian Britton, and then falsely imprisoned Ms. Britton and Christopher Britton. Ms. Britton suffered a heart attack caused by the actions of Wal-mart employees.

It is alleged that the store manager admitted to a Florida Highway Patrol trooper that came to the scene, that the surveillance videos did not show Christopher Britton taking any merchandise from the shelves or taking any items into the bathroom. It is alleged that the two Britton children were under video surveillance the entire time they were inside the store, and the store manager was aware of this.

Florida Statute § 812.015(3)(a) provides that a merchant who has probable cause to believe that a retail theft has been committed by a person has authority to take the offender into custody and detain the offender for a reasonable period of time. Subsection (5)(a) of that statute provides a defense from civil liability for false imprisonment or false arrest if there was probable cause.

On April 5, 2011, Plaintiffs filed a motion seeking expedited production of the surveillance videos in the possession of defendant. Defendant opposed production, arguing that this would "eliminate impeachment value." I granted Plaintiffs' motion. The next day the video recordings were made available to Plaintiffs.

Defendant's objection to expedited production was obfuscation of the first order. A video record of surveillance did not even exist at that time that defendant argued that it would be unfair to produce it. The record had been written over by subsequent surveillance. This motion for spoliation of evidence followed.

Defendant claims that former maintenance associate Steven Steele observed Plaintiffs Christopher and Damian Britton in the restroom. He heard a ruffling of merchandise packaging in a toilet stall while Plaintiff Christopher Britton was in the stall for a lengthy period of time. Plaintiff Damian Britton was walking around the restroom outside the stall. When Plaintiff Christopher Britton exited the stall, Mr. Steele found and retrieved an empty package for a digital camera in the trash can within the stall that was not present in the trash can an hour earlier. Mr. Steele exited the restroom, gave the packaging to former asset protection associate Derrick Lott, notified Mr. Lott of his observations, and identified Plaintiffs Christopher and Damian Britton to Mr. Lott.

Mr. Lott watched Plaintiffs Christopher and Damian Britton as they walked from the men's restroom in the back of the store to the store's exit at the front of the store. When Mr. Lott saw Plaintiffs Christopher and Damian Britton exit the building without making any purchase, he asked them if they had dropped something and he showed them the digital camera's empty packaging. Plaintiffs began cursing. When Christopher and Damian Britton met up with their mother, near Plaintiffs' car, Plaintiff Rhonda Britton began cursing at Mr. Lott.

Plaintiffs' Exhibit 5 is a letter dated November 2, 2009, from Steven Andrews Esq. to Michael Taylor, the general manager at the Wal-mart store in

(continues)

question. The letter states that the subject is "Legal Representation and PRESERVATION OF EVIDENCE, regarding incident at Wal-mart, and Britton Family," . . . requesting that you maintain all surveillance video and/or audio tapes recorded, both indoors and outdoors. The original of the letter was delivered to Wal-mart the next day.

James Sims worked at Wal-mart as an asset protection associate. Sims said that he routinely can "pull" a video from a DVR that is 45 days old since the DVRs often hold videos for longer than 30 days. During examination, Sims was shown the November 2, 2009, letter to Taylor. Sims had not seen the letter, but had he seen it, he would have preserved the videos.

Michael Taylor testified that he has been the general manager of Wal-mart, and he was notified of the altercation by cellphone. The next day, he looked at the videos that were available. He did not see anything on the video of the children touching merchandise in the camera section, and he did not see them take merchandise into the restroom.

The indoor video evidence was damaging to Wal-mart's defense of whatever claims might be brought by the Britton family. I find that Mr. Taylor intentionally sat on the November 2, 2009 letter, hoping that video evidence would be overwritten and disappear because it was damaging to Wal-mart.

It is telling that he said: "I felt like we had the video *to support* the incident." He acted to preserve only defensive evidence. He found himself in the uncomfortable position of being unable to continue to sit on it on November 30, 2009. Then, Taylor "noticed" the November 2nd letter, which he had already known about for weeks, and sent it to his home office. He could no longer pretend that he had not received it. The spoliation of the evidence in this case was an intentional act by defendant, through actions of its managers.

"[S]poliation is defined as the destruction of evidence or the significant and meaningful alteration of a document or instrument." Green Leaf Nursery v. E.I. DuPont De Nemours and Co., 341 F.3d 1292, 1308 (11th Cir. 2003). A party moving for sanctions must establish, among other things, that the destroyed evidence was relevant to a claim or defense such that the destruction of that evidence resulted in prejudice. Eli Lilly and Co. v. Air Exp. Intern. USA, Inc., 615 F.3d 1305, 1318 (11th Cir. 2010).

Bad faith has been shown here. Defendant intentionally let the inside video evidence be destroyed over time, knowing that claims were coming and that counsel for Plaintiffs had asked that the surveillance evidence be preserved. Defendant let the evidence be lost because defendant knew that it would not help its defense. Plaintiffs are now severely prejudiced in their litigation of the issue of probable cause. The sanction of entry of judgment in favor of Plaintiffs is arguably warranted since the spoliation was intentional, but I believe it would be too harsh. A better sanction, is to prohibit defendant from presenting a defense of probable cause, or any other justification or mitigation, based upon testimony from Steele, Lott, or any other person.

CASE QUESTIONS

1. Would the store have been better off if it did not have video cameras? Explain your answer.
2. What do you think really happened in this case?

▌SUMMARY

Intentional torts include actions designed to injure another person or his or her property. All intentional torts consist of an act, intent, and injurious conduct. These elements must occur together. Intentional torts harming the individual include assault, battery, false imprisonment, tortious interference with expectations of inheritance, patient dumping, and spoliation of evidence, to name a few.

Assault is the tortfeasor's attempt to inflict harmful or offensive contact upon another person without consent. Assault places the victim in fear of his or her physical safety, even if the anticipated contact would produce only a distasteful reaction. The threat of contact must be imminent. Battery is a completed assault. It is the intentional, unconsented touching of another person in a harmful or offensive manner. Physical contact is required, although it may occur only with the victim's clothing or objects held. Transferred intent means that the contact directed at one person carries over to another individual who was inadvertently struck; battery would thus have occurred to the unintended victim.

False imprisonment is the confinement of someone without his or her consent. Confinement must exist for an appreciable length of time. The victim must have no reasonable means of escape. The tortfeasor must intend to confine the victim and act to accomplish confinement. Confinement may be achieved either by physical barriers or by threat of force that intimidates the victim into remaining in the restricted area. The shopkeeper's privilege allows a shopkeeper to detain a suspected shoplifter on store property for a reasonable period of time, so long as he or she has cause to believe that the person detained in fact committed, or attempted to commit, theft of store property. The key is reasonable time.

Sexual harassment constitutes unwelcome sexual advances, requests for sexual favors, and other verbal or physical conduct of a sexual nature, when this conduct affects an individual's employment, unreasonably interferes with an individual's work performance, or creates an intimidating, hostile, or offensive work environment. The EEOC is the federal agency that handles these kinds of claims. There are also state agencies that handle discrimination claims.

Patient dumping is the denial of treatment to emergency patients or women in labor, or transferring them to another hospital while they are in an unstable condition. This is a new tort that evolved to protect uninsured and poor patients from unequal medical treatment.

Tortious interference with expectations of inheritance is another intentional tort. It occurs when a person interferes with another person's right to receive an inheritance that he or she otherwise would have received. This tort has been accepted in almost half of the states.

Spoliation of evidence, another new intentional tort, involves withholding, hiding, or destroying evidence relevant to a legal proceeding. Some jurisdictions do not feel that this tort is necessary, as there are other similar actions that cover this kind of situation.

The next chapter focuses on additional intentional torts which cause harm to people. Some of these torts are the center of the more sensational headlines in news stories such as invasion of privacy, libel, slander and infliction of emotional distress.

▌ KEY TERMS

apprehension
assault
battery
consent
false imprisonment
intent

intentional tort
patient dumping
reasonable person
    standard
sexual harassment
shopkeeper's privilege

spoliation of evidence
tortious interference with
    reasonable expectations
    of inheritance
transferred intent

▮ PROBLEMS

In the following hypotheticals, identify the intentional tort(s) committed, if any, and support your answers.

1. Alicia was waiting in line outside The Elegant Shop just before the store opened on the day of the shop's annual savings sale. Dozens of customers milled around the entrance in anticipation. Many patrons began to grow impatient. Suddenly, the doors were opened, and Alicia was knocked to the ground by Marie Harrington, another customer. Alicia covered her face with her arms in anticipation of being trampled. In her haste to enter, Marie stepped on Alicia's hand and broke Alicia's ring finger.

2. Malcolm is the manager of The Soft Touch, a ladies clothing store. Paris, a customer, was looking at accessory jewelry next to the full-length mirrors. Malcolm glanced at the mirrors and thought he saw Paris place something in her purse. He thought it might be jewelry, but he did not actually see the object. As Paris began to exit the store, Malcolm asked her politely to stop. She did so, whereupon Malcolm identified himself and requested that she accompany him to the back room for questioning. She refused. Malcolm insisted, threatening to telephone the police if she attempted to leave the store. She then agreed and the two went to a small room at the rear of the store. Inside, Malcolm asked Paris to empty her pockets and purse, which she did. No jewelry was found. He asked her a few questions about the jewelry and what he had seen. She explained that she had put a handkerchief into her purse, and there was in fact a kerchief inside it. Malcolm apologized for any inconvenience and Paris then left. The interview in the room lasted five minutes.

3. Patty Patient arrives via ambulance at Mercy General Hospital's emergency room. Her first words to the triage nurse are, "I do not have insurance—did they bring me to the right place?" Then Patty starts moaning and passes out. The triage nurse Henry is glad he heard Patty's last words and whispers to the emergency medical technician, Pete, who has just wheeled Patty in, "Take her out of here." Off goes Patty to the County Medical Center. En route to that hospital, she dies.

4. Gina Lee loves her new job as office assistant. She cannot believe her good luck: there are so many good-looking guys working in her department. Gina is determined to start dating someone new by the end of the month. When Gina sees her co-worker Brad each morning, she tries to think of something different and provocative to say. Brad seems kind of quiet and it is hard to get a reaction out of him. Gina is not sure if he is just trying to play it cool or what. Gina tells Brad in detail about her exciting nights with her last boyfriend. Brad does not seem to care, but Gina still thinks he is playing it cool. The next morning, Gina decides she needs to be more forward. Gina asks Brad about his sex life and whether he thinks John or Scott in the next cubicle would make good lovers. Again no response from Brad. Gina brushes against Brad's crotch with her hip and walks away.

5. Sean Leroy, the driver of one vehicle, has sued another driver, Ethan Rogers, concerning a motor vehicle accident that seriously injured both drivers. Rogers was unemployed at the time of the crash and desperately needed to sell his vehicle and some other possessions for cash. Rogers took the first offer to buy his car, despite the fact that his attorney had just advised that Rogers needs to make the car available for inspection by Leroy's expert mechanic.

REVIEW QUESTIONS

1. How are negligence claims distinguishable from intentional tort cases?

2. Explain at least four differences between a criminal action and a tort action.

3. Provide an example of when both a criminal case and a civil case might be brought as a result of the very same incident.

4. Define *assault* and *battery*. How are they similar? Distinguishable? Is intent required?

5. Explain the role transferred intent plays in the torts of assault and battery.

6. Define *patient dumping*. Is this a cause of action for incorrect treatment or nonuniform treatment? Explain your answer.

7. Provide one example of sexual harassment. How can sexual harassment be distinguished from innocent flirting? Is a coworker allowed to ask a coworker to go out on a date, or is this considered sexual harassment?

8. Define *spoliation of evidence*. What are some other similar legal actions that could be brought instead of using this new tort?

9. What is the shopkeeper's privilege? Do you think this is used appropriately in most instances, or does it create more problems than it solves? Explain.

10. What elements are needed to bring a claim for tortious interference with reasonable expectations of inheritance? Why do you think it was necessary to create this tort?

11. If a particular state does not have a law against hazing, what intentional tort action(s) will typically be brought by the victims of this type of behavior?

HELPFUL WEBSITES

This chapter deals with intentional torts and injuries to persons. To learn more about personal injury law, the following sites can be accessed:

General Information

www.lawguru.com
www.jurist.org
www.emory.edu
www.hg.org
www.ilrg.com
www.badfaithinsurance.org

Publications

www.law.com
www.lawresearch.com

Medical Information

www.webmd.com
www.healthfinder.gov
www.mayohealth.org
www.health.nih.gov

Expert Witnesses

www.expertpages.com

STUDENT COMPANION WEBSITE
For additional cases and study materials, please go to www.cengagebrain.com

Chapter 7

Intentional Torts: More Injuries to Persons

THE BIGGEST MISTAKES PARALEGALS MAKE AND HOW TO AVOID THEM

The Devil is in the Details

While interviewing a prospective client who was in a serious car accident, Jacqui learned of the injuries suffered. As the paralegal in charge of completing initial forms, Jacqui inquired about the client's medications, doctor visits, and hospitalizations. Jacqui became very upset when she learned of all the injuries and began to cry. Finally, Jacqui asked the client if she thought the devil was responsible. At first, the client believed

Jacqui was referring to the driver who hit her as the "devil." Then Jacqui asked the client if they could pray for her quick recovery right there in Jacqui's office, which they did. While praying, the client noticed the office was decorated with a few religious pictures and icons. After thinking about the office visit later while discussing it with her husband, the client opted not to retain the firm in her personal injury action.

Lesson Learned: No matter your personal beliefs, Jacqui's behavior, as a paralegal, was wrong on many levels. Her personal and religious beliefs should never violate her obligations to her firm and, by extension, to the client. In addition to losing business for her firm, the professional boundaries crossed by Jacqui raise serious ethical concerns.

▌ INTRODUCTION

In the preceding chapter, several intentional torts that injure a person were discussed: assault, battery, false imprisonment, patient dumping, intentional interference with expectations of inheritance, and spoliation of evidence. All require an act, intent, and injurious behavior. The tortfeasor must intend to accomplish the harmful consequences of his or her own action. In this chapter, more intentional injuries to persons are detailed:

- ▶ Infliction of emotional distress
- ▶ Fraud and misrepresentation
- ▶ Malicious prosecution and abuse of process
- ▶ Invasion of privacy
- ▶ Defamation: libel and slander

Some of these torts are the kind you see in the newspapers and online with celebrities headlining the stories.

▌ INFLICTION OF EMOTIONAL DISTRESS

We have all encountered episodes in our lives in which other persons have intentionally caused us emotional upset. Anyone with a sibling can relate to misconduct designed to annoy and distress. In the law of intentional torts, infliction of emotional distress has developed as a separate cause of action to protect injured parties from other people's efforts to cause shock, fright, or other psychological trauma. One owes a duty to others not to intentionally inflict emotional distress. The breach of that duty is called *intentional infliction of emotional distress*.

Emotional distress can be broadly defined as mental anguish caused by a tortfeasor. Synonyms such as *fright, anxiety, shock, grief, mental suffering,* and *emotional disturbance* are commonly used by the courts to describe this tort. The condition can include shame or embarrassment as well.

The critical aspect of infliction of emotional distress is that the victim suffers from mental anguish rather than from some physical injury caused by the tortfeasor. It is the psychological harm that this tort intends to remedy.

Not just any insult or offensive behavior will result in this tort, however. The misdeed must be so outrageous that a reasonable person would suffer severe

emotional distress | Mental anguish. Nonphysical harm that may be compensated for by damages in some types of lawsuits. *Mental anguish* may be as limited as the immediate mental feelings during an injury or as broad as prolonged grief, shame, humiliation, despair, and so forth.

emotional injury as a consequence. This is the key element in all cases involving infliction of emotional distress. <u>Minor annoyances or indignities are part of everyday life, and these are not included in this tort</u>. If it were otherwise, the courts would overflow with lawsuits, based upon the irritations we all encounter from other people almost daily. Obviously, the law cannot reshape the world into the loving, peaceful utopia we might prefer, but it can discourage flagrant actions tailored to cause mental suffering.

In the field of intentional torts, there are two varieties of infliction of emotional distress: intentional and reckless. A third version, negligent infliction, is discussed in Chapter 4.

Intentional Infliction

intentional infliction of emotional distress | An intentional tort that occurs when the tortfeasor's outrageous conduct, which is intended to cause severe emotional anguish in the victim, actually causes the victim such emotional suffering as a result of the tortfeasor's actions.

Intentional infliction of emotional distress consists of three elements:

1. Outrageous conduct by the tortfeasor
2. Conduct intended to cause severe mental anguish in the victim
3. The victim's suffering of severe mental anguish as a consequence of the tortfeasor's behavior

Outrageous Conduct. As noted earlier, the tortfeasor's behavior must be sufficiently outrageous. The common test for outrageous conduct is one of reasonableness. Would a reasonable person suffer substantial emotional distress as a result of the tortfeasor's actions? Were these activities so outlandish as to *shock the conscience* of a reasonable person? Or, put another way, would a person of *ordinary sensibilities* suffer mental pain as a consequence? This generally excludes all but the most extreme types of egregious conduct.

Examples of outrageous conduct abound in legal literature. Tasteless practical jokes often provide fodder for emotional distress litigation. Consider the person who places a dead mouse inside a soda-pop bottle from which someone is drinking and then tells the drinker about the mouse. Or the heartless prankster who tells a parent that his or her child has just been struck and killed by an automobile when, in fact, this never occurred, as the joker knew perfectly well. Or the person who places revealing photographs of a nude sunbather all around the sunbather's place of employment for fellow workers to see. Or the individual who repeatedly telephones another at all hours of the day and night over several weeks. These are clear instances of outrageous conduct that most people would agree are highly offensive and would cause intense emotional dismay to the victims. In addition, the circulation of hurtful comments, videos, and photos on the Internet; the posting of hurtful remarks on Twitter, Facebook, and other social network sites; and the sending of cruel and outrageous instant messages and highly personal photos via cell phone are more recent methods of causing emotional distress to victims.

Intentional Acts. Obviously, intentional infliction cases must include the element of intent. The tortfeasor must purposefully behave so as to create mental anguish in the victim; the tortfeasor desires to cause anguish. This separates intentional infliction from reckless infliction, which does not require that the tortfeasor tailor his or her acts to cause mental suffering, as discussed later in this section.

Actual Emotional Distress. Naturally, the victim must actually suffer emotionally as a result of the tortfeasor's antics. Again, the test for anguish revolves around the way a reasonable person of ordinary sensibilities would react to the tortfeasor's actions. Courts have often complained that determining genuine emotional suffering from faked distress is extremely difficult, because anyone can pretend to be upset by something. However, physical symptoms usually accompany mental distress, such as loss of sleep, weight, appetite, or vigor; illnesses brought on after the mental shock; or other signs of effect, such as tremors, twitches, or sensitivity to loud or sudden noises. It is important to note, though, that modern courts do *not* require physical manifestations in intentional infliction cases. Mental suffering alone, unaccompanied by physical effects, is sufficient, provided that the trier-of-fact is convinced of the authenticity of the distress.

THE CASE OF THE BASHFUL BAD BOY

In this case, a couple's intimate moments are shared with the reader because the defendant failed to disclose his sexual history to his girlfriend. The defendant is accused of intentional and negligent infliction of a sexually transmitted disease, which caused great emotional distress The court found that the defendant breached his duty by failing either to warn of his condition or to abstain from relations.

DEUSCHLE
v.
JOBE

Missouri Court of Appeals, Western District
30 S.W.3d 215
October 31, 2000

Ms. Deuschle contends that Missouri recognizes a cause of action for reckless infection of a sexually transmitted disease. She alleges that her sexual partner, Mr. Jobe, infected her with herpes and genital warts. Ms. Deuschle claims Mr. Jobe knew he was infected with the diseases at the time he had sexual relations with her, and he failed to disclose his condition.

There is no statutory basis for this cause of action. But since 1986, Missouri common law has recognized a cause of action for negligently transmitting herpes.

In our case, the parties are unmarried. However, we find no justification for excluding an unmarried individual from bringing suit against her sexual partner for transmitting herpes under general tort law. . . .

Here, Ms. Deuschle alleged both intentional and negligent transmission of the disease. In Missouri, it has long been established that the elements of a negligence action are "(1) [a] legal duty on the part of the defendant to conform to a certain standard of conduct to protect others against unreasonable risks; (2) a breach of that duty; (3) a proximate cause between the conduct and the resulting injury; and (4) actual damages to the claimant's person or property."

. . . Missouri courts have long recognized the importance of preserving public health and welfare by creating legal duties, which help prevent the spread of dangerous, communicable diseases.

(continues)

In furtherance of this objective, we hold that one has a legal duty to exercise reasonable care by disclosing a contagious venereal disease before entering into sexual relations with another. Several other jurisdictions that recognize this cause of action support this proposition. In an action for negligent transmission of a venereal disease, a person is liable if he knew or should have known that he was infected with a disease and failed to disclose or warn his sexual partner about this unreasonable risk of harm before engaging in a sexual relationship.

In order to establish whether or not this duty has been breached, we must determine if the foreseeability of actual harm exists. The standard for foreseeability is measured by "whether or not a reasonably prudent person would have anticipated danger and provided against it."

When a disease such as herpes is almost exclusively spread through sexual contact, it is foreseeable that one's sexual partner is susceptible to the contagion if the infected partner is aware he has the disease or suffers from symptoms of the disease.

Ms. Deuschle also alleges in the petition that Mr. Jobe's actions were the direct and proximate cause of her medical conditions. As with any incurable sexually transmitted disease, once infected we infer that actual harm exists. Hence, a negligence action has been sufficiently pled by Ms. Deuschle in the petition.

As noted previously, the petition in some respects sounds like an intentional tort claim in alleging that Mr. Jobe knowingly failed to tell her of his disease, and knowing she was likely to become infected, that he intended injury, and that his conduct was outrageous. It is unclear exactly what intentional tort she is attempting to plead. We direct the trial court to allow her to amend the petition to allege a specific intentional tort.

CASE QUESTIONS

1. What is the difference between negligent infliction of a disease and intentional infliction of a disease?
2. Is there an intentional tort in Missouri that would have been applicable to Ms. Deuschle's claim?

THE CASE OF THE HUMILIATED LADY

In this case, the court found itself in the uncomfortable position of judging the behavior of a pastor and church leaders. The court's focus is on whether the plaintiff has alleged "extreme" and "outrageous" conduct to establish the tort of intentional infliction of emotional distress. Judges are very reluctant to find a defendant liable for this tort. Most feel that there are other torts available that are more precise, and better describe a tortfeasor's duty to others.

Ardie LAW
v.
Harold HARRIS et al.,
Court of Appeals of Georgia
H295 Ga. App. 628
January 6, 2009
JOHNSON, Presiding Judge.

Ardie Bell Law sued Sardis Presbyterian Church, its pastor, and one of its deacons for intentional infliction of emotional distress. Law appeals the trial court's grant of summary judgment in favor of the defendants, claiming that the trial court erred in finding that the defendants' alleged conduct was insufficient as a matter of law to support her claim. Finding no error, we affirm.

The record reveals that Law was a long-time member of the church and that she managed the church's food bank, which was located in the church basement. Law claims that Harold Harris, who was the pastor of the church, "was verbally abusive . . ., humiliated her in front of other [c]hurch members, and made direct threats to [her] that he intended to take over the food bank." Law alleges that, during an April 6, 2005 meeting at which Harris was in attendance, church leaders "demanded that [she] return the keys to the [c]hurch, remove all food bank property from the [c]hurch, and cease operations of the food bank." She further claims that when she arrived at the church the next day, George Fields, who was a church deacon, "became confrontational" with her in the presence of others and demanded that she "surrender the [c]hurch keys at once."

A plaintiff asserting a claim for intentional infliction of emotional distress must show that she suffered severe emotional distress as a result of intentional or reckless conduct that is extreme and outrageous. The alleged conduct must be "so outrageous in character, and so extreme in degree, as to go beyond all possible bounds of decency, and to be regarded as atrocious, and utterly intolerable in a civilized community." Whether conduct rises to the requisite level of outrageousness to sustain a claim is a question of law.

While Law asserts that church leaders were rude and "just plumb ugly" to her, the law does not provide a remedy for alleged conduct that is merely rude or insulting. As a result, the trial court properly granted summary judgment on Law's claim for intentional infliction of emotional distress.

Judgment affirmed.

CASE QUESTIONS
1. Why do you think the law does not provide a remedy for conduct that is merely rude or insulting?
2. Do you think that Ms. Law was close to meeting the threshold for alleging atrocious and intolerable conduct? Explain your answer. Why do you think Ms. Law brought this action?

Reckless Infliction

In general, recklessness is often a substitute for intent in tort law. Many cases involving **reckless infliction of emotional distress** include the mishandling of the remains of deceased persons. Consider a common fact pattern: A funeral home cremates the deceased instead of following the family's clear and explicit instructions regarding burial. Even though the funeral home did not intend this error, the conduct could be construed as so reckless as to fall within this tort.

reckless infliction of emotional distress | An intentional tort that occurs when the tortfeasor's outrageous conduct causes the victim to suffer severe mental anguish. Intent to produce the emotional suffering is not necessary. Instead, it is sufficient that the tortfeasor knew, or reasonably should have known, that his or her misbehavior would produce emotional distress. The tortfeasor's conduct is wanton and reckless, with no apparent regard for the victim's suffering.

THE CASE OF THE MIXED CREMAINS

This case illustrates how allegations of a defendant's reckless behavior can be substituted for intentional behavior in a claim of intentional infliction of emotional distress. Sometimes acts are so outrageous that whether they were intended to cause harm or were so reckless that they caused harm, the effect on the injured plaintiff is the same.

(continues)

Rondal AKERS et al.

v.

PRIME SUCCESSION
OF TENNESSEE, INC. et al.

Supreme Court of Tennessee, Knoxville
387 S.W.3d 495
September 21, 2012

Dr. Rondal D. Akers, Jr. and Lucinda Akers sued T. Ray Brent Marsh for the alleged mishandling of their deceased son's body, which had been sent to Mr. Marsh's crematorium for cremation. Following a jury verdict for the Akerses, the trial court entered judgment against Mr. Marsh based on the intentional infliction of emotional distress claim.

Rondal Douglas Akers III (the "Deceased") died at the age of 34 on November 23, 2001, following a brief illness. His parents, Dr. Rondal D. Akers, Jr., and Lucinda Akers, made funeral arrangements with Buckner–Rush Funeral Home in Cleveland, Tennessee. Dr. and Mrs. Akers authorized and arranged for the cremation in accordance with their son's wishes. After their son's funeral service, his body was transported to Tri-State Crematory in Noble, Georgia, for cremation. Later, the Akerses received what was purported to be their son's cremains (the "Cremains").

Subsequently, it was discovered that Mr. Marsh had not been cremating bodies that were sent to Tri-State for cremation, but rather burying or dumping the bodies in various places on the Tri-State property. The Georgia Bureau of Investigation ("GBI") began an investigation in February 2002. The investigation soon turned into a massive search and recovery effort, that lasted roughly three months.

From the Tri-State property, authorities recovered bodies and body parts of over 230 persons, in widely varying stages of decay. Some were buried in shallow graves. Some had been dumped in surface trash pits. Human remains and bodies were found in virtually every building on the property. A body was found in a hearse, another in a van, and a partially mummified corpse of a man in a suit was discovered in a box.

After the Akerses learned about the problems at Tri-State, they took the box containing their son's "cremains" to the GBI and were told that the box contained potting soil and cement. The Akerses suffered under this misconception from 2002 until September 2008 when they learned that the box contained human cremains.

On July 26, 2002, the Akerses sued Mr. Marsh. The complaint alleged several causes of action including "outrageous conduct"; fraud and/or negligent misrepresentation; and "intentional/negligent infliction of emotional distress." The case against Mr. Marsh proceeded to trial before a jury.

During the jury trial, several experts agreed that no scientific test exists to determine whether the Cremains delivered to the Akerses are those of Deceased or of someone else. Dr. William M. Bass, a forensic anthropologist, testified that metal items were mixed with the ashes and small bone fragments of the Cremains. One of the items was a metal stud from blue jeans. Deceased, however, was not wearing blue jeans when he was sent to Tri-State for cremation. Dr. Bass testified that he would have expected teeth to be in the Cremains if the person cremated had teeth because "teeth roots tend to appear, come through in cremations." At the time of his death, Deceased had all of his teeth except one, but no teeth were found in the Cremains. Dr. Bass further testified that the amount of ashes by weight in the Cremains was one-third to one-half what it should have been for a man of Deceased's size, over 300 pounds at the time of his death. Dr. Bass explained that he believed the Cremains were not those of Deceased because the weight of the ashes was "way too low."

The legal argument supporting Mr. Marsh's assertion that the trial court should have granted his motion for a JNOV or for a new trial on the intentional infliction of emotional distress claim is a rather nuanced one. Mr. Marsh argues that in *Doe 1 ex rel. Doe 1 v. Roman Catholic Diocese of Nashville*, 154 S.W.3d 22 (Tenn.2005), this court effectively created two separate causes of action for the infliction of emotional distress—one for intentional infliction and another for reckless infliction. Because the Akerses did not specifically allege a claim for "reckless infliction of emotional distress," Mr. Marsh argues that they should be precluded from recovery based on a theory of reckless infliction because they did not specifically allege reckless infliction of emotional distress. We disagree with this argument.

In *Rogers v. Louisville Land Co.,* 367 S.W.3d 196 (Tenn.2012), we reviewed the tort of intentional infliction of emotional distress and reaffirmed that the "elements of an intentional infliction of emotional distress claim are that the defendant's conduct was (1) *intentional or reckless,* (2) so outrageous that it is not tolerated by civilized society, and (3) resulted in serious mental injury to the plaintiff."

We have observed numerous times that intentional infliction of emotional distress can be proven by a showing of either reckless or intentional behavior. This approach is consistent with the Restatement (Second) of Torts and the Restatement (Third) of Torts: Liability for Physical and Emotional Harm § 45 (Tentative Draft No. 5, 2007). Courts uniformly hold that reckless conduct, not just intentional conduct, can support a claim for intentional infliction of emotional disturbance.

The Akerses are not precluded from recovery because they did not specifically allege reckless infliction of emotional distress in their complaint. Because a claim for intentional infliction of emotional distress can be proven by a showing that a defendant acted recklessly, and the Akerses asserted a claim for intentional infliction of emotional distress, the trial court did not err in allowing the claim to go to the jury and entering judgment on the jury verdict.

We find there is sufficient material evidence of Mr. Marsh's reckless conduct to support the jury verdict imposing liability for intentional infliction of emotional distress. The proof demonstrates that Mr. Marsh routinely treated bodies sent to him for cremation in a disrespectful and inappropriate manner, dumping or improperly burying them instead of cremating them. When he did cremate them, it was done in an improper manner. We affirm the jury verdict for intentional infliction of emotional distress.

CASE QUESTIONS

1. Why do you think Mr. Marsh acted so recklessly with regard to cremations?
2. Part of the Akers' distress was as a result of the Georgia Bureau of Investigation's (GBI) wrongly advising them that the box that was thought to be their son's cremains was potting soil and cement. Which do you think caused more distress, the acts of Mr. Marsh or those of the GBI? Explain your answer.

Another type of fact situation that illustrates reckless infliction of emotional distress involves the unanticipated effect of a practical joke. Consider the pranksters who vandalized someone's automobile by smearing it with manure, knowing that the vehicle owner took enormous pride in the car's appearance. The jokers knew that the owner had a weak heart, but were only expecting to shake up the owner. When the owner saw his prize automobile, he collapsed from a heart attack. This illustrates wanton misconduct. Although the pranksters did not intend the victim to suffer heart failure as a consequence of their deed, the tortfeasors' behavior revealed utter disregard for the health and well-being of the victim, and accordingly they would be liable for reckless infliction of emotional distress.

Claims of reckless infliction of emotional distress are sometimes made regarding unwanted, insulting, and demeaning sexual advances from a supervisor or coworker at a place of employment. These claims are also known as sexual harassment suits and are addressed in Chapter 6.

HYPOTHETICALS

Fantasia's situation could offer an example of intentional infliction of emotional distress. She owed money on a charge account at a local appliance store. Unfortunately, she missed several payments because of financial difficulties. Susan, the store sales manager, began repeatedly telephoning Fantasia at work and late in the evenings at home, demanding that Fantasia pay the balance due. The calls continued over several weeks. Fantasia's supervisor became angry that Fantasia was wasting company time taking these phone calls. The calls at night woke Fantasia several times and agitated her enough to keep her awake. As a result, Fantasia's job performance slumped. Fantasia lost weight and became irritable because of lack of sleep. Has Susan intentionally inflicted emotional distress upon Fantasia?

Susan's actions were designed to upset Fantasia greatly to coerce Fantasia to pay the overdue debt. Susan acted in an outrageous manner—reasonable persons would find repeated telephone calls late at night and on the job to be highly offensive. Fantasia suffered substantial mental anguish (with physical manifestations) as a result of Susan's conduct. Accordingly, Susan would be liable to Fantasia for intentional infliction of emotional distress. (In addition, Susan most likely violated several provisions of the Fair Debt Collections Practices Act in her fanatical attempts to collect on the debt.)

* * *

Consider another illustration. Gupta and Colin are accountants with the same firm. Gupta planted a fake letter of termination on Colin's desk, in which the office manager accused Colin of misappropriation of client funds. Upon reading the letter, Colin became distraught, shaking and sweating violently and feeling nauseous. Colin burst into the manager's office to deny the allegations, at which time Gupta disclosed his gag. Has Gupta inflicted emotional distress upon Colin?

All of the necessary elements are present in this hypothetical, including intent to cause mental anguish. Gupta should tally his own personal accounts, because he will be liable to Colin for intentional infliction of emotional distress.

Table 7-1 summarizes the elements of both types of infliction of emotional distress.

Intentional Infliction	Reckless Infliction
Outrageous conduct	Outrageous conduct
Conduct intended to cause severe mental anguish	Conduct known (or reasonably should be known) to cause severe mental anguish; recklessness is a substitute for intent
Victim suffers severe mental anguish as result	Victim suffers severe mental anguish as result
Example: Deliberately playing a joke on someone, such as telling him or her that a family member died.	**Example:** Carelessly burying the wrong corpse in a cemetery plot.

TABLE 7-1

Elements of infliction of emotional distress

FRAUD AND MISREPRESENTATION

Fraud, or **deceit**, as some states call it, occurs when a tortfeasor makes false statements to entice the victim to give up something of value to the tortfeasor. Fraudulent **misrepresentation** exists when the tortfeasor knowingly makes false statements or purposefully behaves in such a way as to deceive the victim. The two torts are quite similar. Both involve false statements or actions. Both include deception as the tortfeasor's objective. Yet fraud features the element of underhanded economic gain: the victim surrenders something valuable to the tortfeasor as a result of the false comments. As a practical matter, however, a tortfeasor who commits fraud also commits misrepresentation, although they technically are not the same tort. Still, many courts view them as synonymous. Note that when a salesperson uses puffery (exaggerates), this is not considered a misrepresentation.

Definitions and Distinctions

Fraud. For fraud to be proved, the following must exist:

1. The defrauder must intend to deceive by making a false representation of material fact.
2. The defrauder must know that the statements made are false.
3. The purpose of the false statements must be to entice the victim into giving the tortfeasor something of value.
4. The innocent party must justifiably rely on the misrepresentation.
5. The innocent party must be injured.

Misrepresentation. For misrepresentation to be proved, the first two elements of fraud must occur. Some courts, however, also add the other elements to

fraud (deceit) | Any kind of trickery used to cheat another of money or property.

misrepresentation | A false statement that may be of three types:

1. *Innocent misrepresentation* is a false statement that is not known to be false.
2. *Negligent misrepresentation* is a false statement made when the one making the statement should have known better.
3. *Fraudulent misrepresentation* is a false statement known to be false and meant to be misleading.

TABLE 7-2
Elements of fraud
and misrepresentation

Fraud	Misrepresentation
False statements intended to deceive	False statements intended to deceive
Knowledge of falsity of statements	Knowledge of falsity of statements
Plaintiff relies on the statement	Plaintiff relies on the statement
Statements designed to entice victim into surrendering something of value	
Innocent party is injured	Innocent party is injured

misrepresentation, making it identical to fraud. In such jurisdictions, the two concepts are thus redundant. Table 7-2 outlines the elements of fraud and misrepresentation.

False Statements Intended to Deceive

material | Significant or important.

A tortfeasor commits fraud or misrepresentation by making **material** false statements designed to delude the victim. For example, if Aaron tells Stephanie that he can repair her broken dishwasher for $100, when Aaron knows that he lacks the requisite skill and knowledge to do so, then Aaron has made false statements intended to mislead Stephanie into paying him the money for work he cannot perform.

Knowledge of Falsity of Information

The tortfeasor must have known or should have known that the information given to the victim is false for fraud or misrepresentation to happen. For instance, if Henry sells Michelle a new computer with a defective floppy disk drive of which Henry is totally unaware, then Henry has not engaged in either fraud or misrepresentation, because he did not know about the product defect when he made the sale.

Tortfeasor's Profit from Deception

For fraud, the defrauder must make false statements tailored to encourage the victim to surrender something of value to the tortfeasor. In the preceding dishwasher-repair example, Aaron duped Stephanie in order to receive her money. This constitutes fraud.

Justifiable Reliance

The injured party must justifiably rely on the false statement. This means the party must know about the statement. The false statement must be a substantial factor in the plaintiff's decision, or reason for an action taken based upon the statement. However, the false statement need not be the sole factor in the decision or action.

Innocent Party's Injury

Like all torts, the innocent party must prove actual injury as a consequence of the false statements or misrepresentation.

THE CASE OF CONTINUING ABUSE

Fraud and misrepresentation are usually thought of in the context of a business setting, where one person tells a falsehood in order to obtain money or property from another. This case provides a whole new meaning to fraud and misrepresentation—here, silence, or an omission (such as the failure to warn), is considered a misrepresentation to sustain the cause of action.

Tom DOE, Plaintiff,

v.

PRESIDING BISHOP OF THE CHURCH OF JESUS CHRIST OF LATTER–DAY SAINTS; Boy Scouts of America; Defendants, et al.

2012 WL 3782454

United States District Court, D. Idaho

August 31, 2012

Plaintiff Tom Doe joined Troop 101 in 1964 at the age of 11. Plaintiff's Troop was sponsored by the LDS Church. He alleges that he was repeatedly sexually abused by his Scoutmaster and Quorum Advisor Larron Arnold. Because of the abuse, Doe has suffered physical and emotional damages. His physician diagnosed him with posttraumatic stress disorder, and Doe also alleges, he suffers from sexual dysfunction.

Doe claims that both organizations knew about the danger of abuse. But instead of disclosing this to Doe, they promoted scouting as a safe, and fun organization for boys. According to Doe, they also represented that Arnold was a trusted youth leader, despite knowing that he had previously molested another boy. Larron Arnold became Scoutmaster of Troop 101 in 1964, the same year Doe joined. As Scoutmaster and Quorum Advisor, Arnold led spiritual, educational, and Boy Scout-related activities for the youth of the Nampa 2nd Ward and Boy Scout Troop.

Arnold led the Troop on overnight camping trips. In addition, Doe accompanied Arnold, alone, on several day trips. During at least five of these trips Arnold sexually abused Doe. According to Doe, his experience mirrors examples of other Scout experiences set forth in the Ineligible Volunteer Files maintained by the Scouts: "Scouts entrusting themselves to a Scout leader's guidance, only to be sexually abused by the Scout leader."

Doe claims that the Boy Scouts of America "has always had a known problem with adult volunteers abusing Scouts." In the early 1900s, the Boy Scouts of America began keeping "Ineligible Volunteer Files" on individuals banned from volunteering in scouting. The "Perversion" category contains the most files and comprises any type of sexual misconduct, including child abuse. Before Doe became a Scout, the Boy Scouts of America had compiled "thousands of incidents of child abuse" within scouting involving its adult volunteers.

Doe claims that both the Boy Scouts and the church defendants had specific notice that Arnold was a child molester. Richard White, a member of the Nampa 2nd Ward, testified that he told Bishop Leon Hales that his son had been molested by Arnold, his Scoutmaster. Bishop Hales purportedly responded that he would "take care of it." And a week later, Bishop Hale told White that he "had taken care of it."

The church defendants contend that Doe based his fraud claims "on the allegation of a *generalized danger of sexual abuse within scouting*"—not on specific fraudulent representations regarding the danger Arnold posed. Because the church defendants had general notice of Doe's constructive fraud theory and because they also had notice of White's statements, the court will consider the church's alleged knowledge regarding Arnold.

(continues)

"An action in constructive fraud exists when there has been a breach of a duty arising from a relationship of trust and confidence, as in a fiduciary duty." *Gray v. TriWay Const. Services, Inc.*, 147 Idaho 378, 210 P.3d 63, 71 (Idaho 2009). To prove constructive fraud, a party must prove the existence of a confidential relationship. When a confidential relationship is found to exist, the one in whom confidence was reposed may be held to a higher standard of disclosure and fairness than in an arm's-length relationship. ". . . (W)here, as here, there was a duty to speak because of a confidential relationship, a failure to do so is a specie of fraud for which equity may afford relief." The church defendants' attempt to confine constructive fraud claims to business situations is contrary to general common-law principles.

"One who by a fraudulent misrepresentation or nondisclosure of a fact that it is his duty to disclose causes physical harm to the person ... of another who justifiably relies upon the misrepresentation, is subject to liability to the other." Restatement (Second) of Torts § 557A (1977). Courts in other jurisdictions have allowed an action for fraud outside a business or contractual setting. In *B.N. v. K.K.*, 312 Md. 135, 538 A. 2d 1175 (Md.1988), the court allowed a claim for wrongful transmission of genital herpes to be stated in terms of fraud even though the fraud did not occur in a business setting. The court found that the defendant implicitly represented he was in good health by concealing the fact he had genital herpes.

A fiduciary relationship is more likely to arise between a child and a church than between an adult and a church. Many courts appear to follow a parishioner-plus rule. These cases hold, that a fiduciary relationship does not arise between the church and all parishioners generally. Instead, a parishioner plaintiff must submit facts demonstrating that his relationship with the church differed from other general parishioners' relationship with the church. *See, e.g., Doe v. Holy See (State of Vatican City)*, 17 A.D. 793, 795 (N.Y.App.Div.2005).

Four key facts operate in Doe's favor: (1) he was a minor child (2) he was an active participant in church-sponsored activities; (3) he was encouraged by the church to participate in scouting; and (4) the church allegedly knew of the specific danger that Arnold posed. Also, the church taught Doe to respect and trust his church and Scout youth leaders. Additionally, the church's alleged knowledge of Arnold's dangerousness is a factor triggering a duty to disclose simply by virtue of the information disparity.

Based on these facts, a jury could find that the church occupied a superior position of influence and authority over Doe, who in turn reposed trust and confidence in the church. This is enough for Doe to survive summary judgment on the confidential relationship issue. Doe may recover damages for mental anguish that are traceable to the church defendants' alleged failure to disclose a known danger.

The Scout defendants deny that they had a duty to disclose the risk of sexual abuse by adult male volunteers. The scope of any duty to disclose would naturally be limited by the extent of the Scout defendants' knowledge regarding the risks of sexual abuse in scouting. A jury could conclude that any notice Bishop Hales received could be imputed to the Boy Scouts of America.

In conclusion, the court will deny both the church and the Scout defendants' motions for partial summary judgment on Doe's fraud claims. The court does not know whether the claims will bear out at trial, but Doe has presented enough evidence to present the issue of fraud to a jury.

CASE QUESTIONS

1. Can an omission, rather than a misstatement, be the basis for a fraud claim? Explain your answer.
2. Does the fact that the Boy Scouts of America had set up an "Ineligible Volunteer File" in the early 1900s, with a "Perversion" category, help or hurt its defense in this case? Explain your answer.

Classic illustrations of fraud or misrepresentation often utilize used-car-sales situations, which have become the brunt of many jokes. Still, the examples profile the elements quite well, as in the following hypothetical.

HYPOTHETICALS

Ask Mayfield, for instance, who purchased an automobile from Honest Eddy's Used Car Palace, his opinions about fraud and misrepresentation. Honest Eddy himself assured Mayfield that the chosen vehicle had been driven only 5,000 miles by a driving instructor from Ontario, that the brakes had just been replaced, and that the engine had been re-tuned. Honest Eddy knew that none of this was true and merely wanted to make the sale at all costs. Mayfield bought the car and drove away. Much to Mayfield's horror and embarrassment, within a week the automobile began to emit huge plumes of blue smoke from its exhaust. It also shook violently upon acceleration and made grinding noises. Has Honest Eddy committed fraud and misrepresentation against Mayfield?

The elements piece together: Honest Eddy knew that the automobile was defective, but lied about its condition to induce Mayfield to buy it. Mayfield surrendered to Honest Eddy something of value (namely, money—the car's purchase price). Because there was deception, misrepresentation exists. Honest Eddy is liable to Mayfield for fraud and misrepresentation.

* * *

Richard supplies another good illustration. He purchased a home from Quality Construction Company (QCC). QCC's sales director assured Richard that the house had been treated for termites when, in fact, it had not. QCC had paid an exterminator to inspect the house, and the exterminator's report advised of the need for termite treatment. After living in the house for a few months, Richard discovered a serious termite infestation. Did QCC engage in fraud or misrepresentation?

The critical elements here are intent and knowledge. Did QCC's sales director know that no termite treatment had been done? QCC had received the exterminator's report recommending treatment. Thus, the sales director should have known that treatment was necessary and should have known that QCC had not performed this task. Thus, knowledge may be *imputed* under the circumstances. Intent, however, is more difficult to ascertain. Did the sales director purposefully mislead Richard? Because the director should have known that no treatment had been applied, his contrary statement to Richard demonstrated his desire to deceive Richard. This equals intentional deception. Thus, misrepresentation can be proven. Also, because QCC's objective was to entice Richard to buy the house, the third element of fraud exists.

▌ MALICIOUS PROSECUTION AND ABUSE OF PROCESS

Usually the common law distinguishes malicious prosecution from abuse of process in this way: Malicious prosecution occurs in criminal prosecutions, whereas abuse of process happens in civil litigation. They are similar intentional torts.

Malicious Prosecution

malicious prosecution | A tort committed by bringing charges against someone in order to harm that person and with no legal justification for doing it.

Malicious prosecution arises when a private citizen files with the prosecutor a groundless criminal complaint against another person (who is named as the defendant in the subsequent criminal proceeding). This tort is comprised of the following elements:

1. Groundless criminal prosecution against the accused without probable cause
2. The complainant's malice in filing the spurious charges
3. The accused's acquittal from, or dismissal of, the criminal charges
4. Injury to the accused as a result of the prosecution

complainant | 1. A person who makes an official complaint. 2. A person who starts a lawsuit.

probable cause | A reasonable belief that the accused is guilty of the alleged crime.

Groundless Criminal Prosecution. The individual registering a criminal complaint with the police or prosecutor is sometimes called the **complainant**. The complainant's actions are considered bogus if he or she pursued criminal charges without probable cause that the accused was guilty of the crime. **Probable cause** is routinely defined as the reasonable belief that the accused is guilty of the alleged crime. This belief need exist only at the time the criminal charges are initiated for probable cause to exist. However, if it later becomes obvious through investigation that the accused did not commit the alleged crime, then the complainant's insistence on the government's continuing prosecution would be malicious prosecution.

malice | 1. Ill will. 2. Intentionally harming someone. 3. In defamation law, with knowledge of falsity or with reckless disregard for whether or not something is false.

Malice. Malice in filing spurious criminal charges may be inferred from the circumstances surrounding the case. If the complainant knew (or reasonably should have known) that the accused did not commit the alleged crime, then malice is implied. Also, if the complainant is using the criminal prosecution to obtain some improper objective, such as intimidating the accused into settling a disputed civil claim or to extort money from the accused, then this likewise implies malice.

Accused's Acquittal from, or Dismissal of, the Criminal Charges. To recover successfully for malicious prosecution, the accused must have been acquitted of the groundless criminal charges initiated by the complainant, or the prosecution must have been otherwise disposed of in the accused's favor (dismissal of charges, for instance).

Injury to the Accused. Like all torts, the accused must prove actual injury as a consequence of the wrongful prosecution. This is most often accomplished by showing damage to the accused's reputation in the community or financial standing, mental anguish, or legal expenses associated with defending the criminal charges.

Abuse of Process

Abuse of process is the civil equivalent of malicious prosecution. It occurs when the tortfeasor misuses a legal proceeding against another person to achieve an unlawful objective. The elements of abuse of process are as follows:

1. Misuse of a legal proceeding, or threat of such misuse
2. Misuse to achieve unlawful objectives
3. Injury to the victim as a result of the misuse

abuse of process | Using the legal system unfairly; for example, prosecuting a person for writing a "bad check" simply to pressure him or her to pay.

Misuse of Legal Proceedings to Achieve Unlawful Goals. The

tortfeasor must intentionally misuse (or threaten to misuse) a legal proceeding against another person to accomplish an objective to which the process abuser is not legally entitled. In this situation, the tortfeasor normally threatens frivolous civil litigation in an attempt to frighten the victim into paying a disputed claim. For example, the process abuser might file a groundless lawsuit against an innocent defendant in an attempt to "scare up some quick money." This occasionally occurs in personal injury litigation when fault is difficult to assign and prove; the personal injury plaintiff abuses process by suing a convenient (but innocent) defendant (who usually has assets or insurance but seems unlikely to defend a frivolous lawsuit). An example of this type of common scam is when the same man sued multiple restaurants, claiming that a waiter had spilled food or beverages on his new suit, permanently staining it. Many restaurants willingly paid for the cost of a new suit, rather than spending the time and money to defend such a frivolous lawsuit.

Litigation is not the only legal process that may be misapplied, however. Creditors filing improper mechanic's liens against debtors to collect on disputed debts, or a wife accusing her spouse of sexually abusing their children to gain an advantage in a custody hearing, when there are no grounds for the claim and she knows the claim is false, would also be guilty of abuse of process.

The pivotal aspect of abuse of process is the tortfeasor's misuse of a legal proceeding to gain some indirect benefit to which he or she is not legally entitled. The tortfeasor has an ulterior motive for manipulating the legal proceeding. The following hypotheticals illustrate how legal process may be exploited in this way.

When tortfeasors engage in malicious prosecution and abuse of process, their victims are often left feeling powerless as a result of the experience. The victims

TABLE 7-3

Elements of malicious prosecution and abuse of process

MALICIOUS PROSECUTION	ABUSE OF PROCESS
Groundless criminal prosecution	Misuse of legal proceeding (or threat of misuse)
Complainant's malice	Misuse to achieve unlawful objectives
Accused's acquittal or dismissal of charges	
Accused's injury	Injury to victim

may develop a cynical bitterness toward the apparent ease with which the legal system was manipulated against them. But tort law strives to restore the balance (and the victims' faith in the system) by affording remedies against these intentional torts.

Table 7-3 specifies the elements of malicious prosecution and abuse of process.

The following examples demonstrate how the legal system reacts when misused in this manner.

HYPOTHETICALS

Andrew was offended when a bookstore that sold provocative literature opened in his neighborhood. He registered with the prosecutor a criminal complaint for pornography against the bookstore in the hope that it would shut down or move away. Nothing that the bookstore sold violated the city's pornography ordinance, as the prosecutor informed Andrew. Nonetheless, Andrew exerted pressure on the prosecutor (through a contact in the mayor's office) to proceed, and subsequently the court dismissed the charges upon the bookstore's attorney's motion. The bookstore lost substantial business as a result of adverse publicity in the newspapers surrounding the case. Has Andrew maliciously prosecuted?

Andrew's criminal complaint against the bookstore was frivolous, because its merchandise did not violate any criminal ordinance. The prosecutor had told Andrew that the bookstore was not acting illegally, so Andrew lacked probable cause to believe in the bookstore's guilt. Andrew's malice could be inferred, because he knew of the bookstore's innocence but insisted on pressing the criminal prosecution to coerce the bookstore into closing or moving. The bookstore successfully had the criminal charges dismissed. It also suffered financial injury as a result of Andrew's actions. Accordingly, Andrew is liable to the bookstore for malicious prosecution.

* * *

Jennifer's Shipping Company delivered a shipment of desks to Northern Office Supply Corporation. One of Northern's employees, Tony, damaged several desks while moving them into storage with a fork-loader truck. The desks were undamaged previously. Northern's president, Carrie, filed suit against Jennifer's, claiming that the desks had been damaged in shipment by Jennifer's employees. Has Northern abused process against Jennifer's?

Carrie knew that Jennifer's was not responsible for the marred desks, as she had observed Tony carelessly operate the fork loader and damage the desks. Thus, Northern's lawsuit against Jennifer's was groundless. Filing frivolous litigation constitutes misuse of legal process. It may be deduced that Carrie's purpose in filing Northern's lawsuit was to intimidate Jennifer's into settling the case out of court through its insurance carrier. Jennifer's injury exists in that it must defend against this baseless legal action, incurring attorneys' fees, litigation expenses, and lost time for employees required to testify. The lawsuit could also damage Jennifer's reputation if the business community became aware of the action, which could easily occur, as lawsuits are a matter of public record. Northern will therefore be liable to Jennifer's for abuse of process.

THE CASE OF THE GROUNDLESS ACTION

A good attorney must analyze a case from all perspectives. What happens when an attorney is overzealous in an effort to elicit a settlement offer, and pursues a claim that he or she knows is baseless? With that in mind, should an insurance policy for professional malpractice cover such an action?

John SHIDDELL, et al., Appellant,
v.
The BAR PLAN MUTUAL, et al., Respondent
Missouri Court of Appeals, Western District
2012 WL 3079101
July 31, 2012

The Shiddells own Anchor Insurance Company. One of their customers, Alpha Omega Express, Inc., asked to add Airborne Express, Inc., a company for which it performed contract work, to Alpha Omega's business automobile policy with Cameron Mutual. Shiddell conveyed that request to the insurance company, and issued certificates of insurance.

On April 4, 2002, David Dodson filed suit against Alpha Omega and Airborne Express claiming that

one of their drivers had negligently caused an automobile accident that had left him paralyzed. Cameron Mutual hired Dysart Taylor to examine whether there was a way to avoid coverage for the accident. Kent Bevan, the attorney working on the case, determined that there was coverage.

Without any knowledge of any facts to support the claim, in an effort to get Appellant's E & O insurance carrier to contribute to pay a portion of Dodson's claim, Bevan filed suit against Appellants, on behalf of Cameron Mutual, alleging that they had forged the document adding Airborne Express as an insured to the policy after the Dodson accident. After litigating the case for two years, long after Bevan was made aware that the claim was baseless, when the E & O carrier refused an offer

(continues)

of mediation, Bevan dismissed the action against Appellants.

After the case was dismissed, Appellants filed a malicious prosecution action against Dysart Taylor and Bevan.

Dysart Taylor and Bevan sought coverage under a legal malpractice insurance policy they had with The Bar Plan. The Bar Plan offered to defend the case under a reservation of rights but noted that the policy excluded coverage for malicious and intentionally wrongful acts.

When Dysart Taylor and Bevan demanded that The Bar Plan assume their defense unconditionally, The Bar Plan declined, and Dysart Taylor and Bevan assumed their own defense. Shortly thereafter, Dysart Taylor and Bevan entered into a settlement agreement with Appellants. Dysart Taylor agreed to confess liability and stipulate damages of $4,500,000.00 in exchange for the dismissal of Bevan from the case and an agreement by Appellants to limit execution of the judgment to proceeds that could be obtained from Dysart Taylor's malpractice insurance policy with The Bar Plan.

The trial court approved the settlement agreement and entered judgment in favor of Appellants and against Dysart Taylor. The judgment stated: The court finds that an ordinarily careful lawyer would not have believed the facts alleged against the plaintiffs or that the underlying judicial proceeding against the plaintiffs was valid. The court further finds that the conduct of Dysart Taylor was motivated by legal malice. In other words, Dysart Taylor initiated and continued civil proceedings against the plaintiffs primarily for a purpose other than that of securing the proper adjudication of the claims on which they were based. The court then awarded the plaintiffs a total of $4,500,000.00 on that claim.

After that judgment became final, Appellants filed their petition against The Bar Plan seeking equitable garnishment of the policy limits of Dysart Taylor's legal malpractice policy. The Bar Plan filed its motion for summary judgment, contending that the judgment against Dysart Taylor was not covered under the policy. In response, Appellants argued that the term "malicious" was ambiguous and, interpreted in the manner most favorable to Appellants, would not preclude coverage of the judgment against Dysart Taylor because the judgment was based upon a finding of legal malice and not actual malice. The trial court entered summary judgment in favor of The Bar Plan. The trial court noted:

> In this case, the parties do not dispute that "legal malice" is the appropriate element applicable to lawyers and law firms, and recognized in Missouri for lawyers being sued for malicious prosecution.

The trial court further found:

> By consenting to a judgment for malicious prosecution, an intentional tort, Dysart's conduct is also a deliberately wrongful act. The underlying judgment states that "Dysart . . . *initiated* . . . civil proceedings against plaintiffs *primarily for a purpose* other than that of securing the proper adjudication of the claims on which they are based." Purposeful conduct is intentional conduct which is deliberate conduct.

Appellants contend that the circuit court erred in entering summary judgment because the terms "malicious" and "deliberately wrongful" contained in Dysart Taylor's insurance policy were ambiguous and could be interpreted to afford coverage.

In cases against non-attorneys, a showing of malice in law is all that is required to support a malicious prosecution claim. "The test to establish malice on the part of an attorney depends on whether the attorney acted upon a statement of facts provided by the client, or whether the attorney obtained the information acted upon." Where the attorney acts solely upon facts related by the client, malice is shown by demonstrating that (1) the attorney knew that there was no probable cause for the prosecution and (2) the attorney knew that the client was acting solely through improper motives. Where an attorney acts after his or her own investigation, however, malice is proven by demonstrating that (1) the attorney knew that there was no probable cause for the prosecution of the action and (2) the attorney's primary purpose for initiating or continuing the proceedings was something other than securing a proper adjudication of the claim.

Appellants rely upon a rule of construction in an attempt to create ambiguity where there is none. The "deliberately wrongful acts" exclusion is unambiguous. No ordinary person of reasonable intelligence would interpret the term "deliberately" to mean "criminally." The "deliberately wrongful act" exclusion simply cannot be read to be limited to only criminal acts as asserted by Appellants. This is undoubtedly a "deliberately wrongful act" under the plain and ordinary meaning of those terms. Thus, as a matter of law, Appellants' claim of malicious prosecution was clearly excluded under the policy language. Dysart Taylor cannot be deemed to be an "innocent insured" under the language of the policy. The judgment is affirmed.

CASE QUESTIONS

1. What would have been a better course of action for Bevan, rather than to make a false claim?
2. Why did the appellate court disagree with the appellants' argument that the law firm's actions should be covered by malpractice insurance?

INVASION OF PRIVACY

Invasion of privacy is largely a twentieth-century concept. In 1888, Judge Cooley of the Michigan Supreme Court, in his famous torts treatise, analyzed a series of nineteenth-century court decisions on defamation, trespass upon a personal property right (such as lectures or publications), and breach of confidence under implied contract law. Cooley surmised that a broader right was being protected and defined the legal interest in the famous phrase "the right to be let alone" (Cooley, *Torts* 29 [2d ed. 1888]). In 1890, a famous *Harvard Law Review* article co-authored by Louis Brandeis (who later became a U.S. Supreme Court justice) substantially expanded Cooley's theory, coining the phrase "right to privacy" (Warren & Brandeis, "The Right to Privacy," 4 *Harv. L. Rev.* 193 [1890]). American courts and legislatures throughout the twentieth century have incorporated this tort into their common law and statutes. It may be fairly said that this cause of action arose primarily because of this law-review article.

Simply put, **invasion of privacy** exists when someone publicly exploits another person's private affairs in an unreasonably intrusive manner. In tort law, there are four separate types of invasion of privacy:

invasion of privacy | A violation of the right to be left alone.

1. Appropriation
2. Unreasonable intrusion
3. Public disclosure of private facts
4. False light in the public eye

Appropriation

Appropriation occurs when the tortfeasor uses a person's name or likeness without permission to gain some benefit. For example, if an advertising company used

appropriation | Taking something wrongfully.

a person's photograph to sell a product without that person's consent, then the firm would be liable to the person for invasion of privacy by appropriation. Most cases involving this variety of invasion of privacy consist of the unauthorized use of photographs, artist's sketches, or quotations associated with names to sell someone else's goods or services. An example of this is when celebrity Kim Kardashian complained that the clothing company Old Navy was using a Kim Kardashian look-alike model, Melissa Molinaro, to imply that Kardashian was associated with the company. The lawsuit was settled in August 2012 for an undisclosed sum.

THE CASE OF THE INTERNET AFFAIR

Many an argument is made to publish seemingly personal and embarrassing facts based on "the public's right to know." This must be balanced against and individual's right to privacy.

John Patrick LOWE, Bankruptcy Trustee, Plaintiff,

v.

HEARST COMMUNICATIONS, INC. and Hearst Newspapers Partnership, L.P., Defendants

United States District Court, W.D. Texas, San Antonio Division

414 F.Supp.2d 669

February 6, 2006

Plaintiff, John Patrick Lowe, Bankruptcy Trustee for the Estates of Mary and Ted Roberts, brought this suit seeking damages for public disclosure of private facts and intentional infliction of emotional distress. The disclosure of private facts occurred with the publication on June 13, 2004 in the "San Antonio Express-News," a daily newspaper of general circulation, of an article headlined, "Sex, lawyers, secrets at heart of sealed legal case" ("the article"). The article was written by Maro Robbins and Joseph S. Stroud. The article describes how Ted Roberts and his wife Mary bilked several of Mary's lovers out of tens of thousands of dollars. According to the article, Mary ran a personal ad on the internet seeking "erotic and intellectual" relationships with men. Ted would prepare draft petitions and settlement agreements and present them to Mary's lovers, naming them as potential defendants and threatening them with legal

action that would publically expose their affairs with Mary. As many as five men ultimately entered into settlement agreements with Ted to avoid litigation. Ted collected from $75,000 to $155,000 from the men, according to the article.

Hearst intervened in a state court lawsuit involving the Robertses and a former associate of their law firm. In an appeal in that suit, the Texas Fourth Court of Appeals issued an opinion on August 29, 2003 holding valid a trial court order sealing from public view a set of documents referred to as the "202 Documents." The 202 Documents are described by the Court of Appeals as:

A group of documents which includes not only proposed pleadings but also related factual documents such as e-mails. The pleadings are a set of proposed petitions prepared by Ted Roberts, naming himself as plaintiff and his wife Mary as a defendant along with other third parties. Among the related documents are draft settlement agreements for the proposed defendants.

On June 11, 2004, Mary Roberts received a call on her cell phone from Robbins and Stroud who identified themselves as Express-News reporters and told Roberts they were writing an article regarding Ted Roberts, the 202 Documents, and related matters. Ted Roberts delivered a letter to the Express-News that day warning against contravening the sealing order and noting the privacy issues involved. Also on June 11, the Robertses sought emergency relief from the Fourth Court of Appeals, which granted the relief and issued its mandate relating to its August 29, 2003 opinion. The mandate was delivered to the Express-News on June 11. The article was published two days later. At some point thereafter, the Robertses declared bankruptcy. The bankruptcy trustee is pursuing this action on behalf of the Robertses' bankruptcy estates.

Plaintiff contends that the article included information contained in the 202 Documents and thus violated the sealing order and mandate. An individual has the right to be free from the public disclosure of embarrassing private facts about the individual. *Industrial Found. of the South v. Texas Indus. Accident Bd.*, 540 S.W.2d 668, 682 (Tex.1976). To establish the tort of invasion of privacy based upon the public disclosure of private facts, the plaintiff must demonstrate that (1) publicity was given to matters concerning his private life, (2) the publication of which would be highly offensive to a reasonable person of ordinary sensibilities, and (3) the matter publicized was not of legitimate public concern. *Star-Telegram, Inc. v. Doe*, 915 S.W.2d 471, 473-74 (Tex.1995); *Industrial Found. of the South*, 540 S.W.2d at 682.

Plaintiff argues that the court must remain narrowly focused on whether he has properly pleaded a cause of action for invasion of privacy based on the Express-News' publication of facts contained in the sealed 202 Documents. Hearst counters that plaintiff cannot legally establish a privacy claim because the Robertses had no expectation of privacy and because the article reported on a matter of legitimate public concern.

Hearst first argues that the Robertses lacked any legally cognizable expectation of privacy in the facts published because they had already distributed the draft petitions, settlement agreements, and e-mails contained in the 202 documents to their potential legal adversaries. Plaintiff asserts that this argument is an assertion of a defense, not a pleading defect. Plaintiff also argues that, in any event, the "publication"

did not extend beyond the Robertses and Mary's paramours—they were not circulated publicly.

The tort requires circulation of the private facts to more than a small, closed circle of people. "'Publicity' requires communication to more than a small group of persons; the matter must be communicated to the public at large, such that the matter becomes one of public knowledge." *Industrial Found. of the South*, 540 S.W.2d at 683-84 (citing RESTATEMENT (SECOND) OF TORTS § 652D, comment a). The mere fact that the Robertses disclosed these documents to a handful of individuals who had every incentive not to disclose them publicly does not destroy the Robertses' expectation of privacy as a matter of law.

The third element that plaintiff would have to prove to establish invasion of privacy by public disclosure of private facts is that the matter publicized was not of legitimate public concern. *Star-Telegram, Inc.*, 915 S.W.2d at 473-74. Whether a matter is of public concern is a question of law for the court. *Cinel v. Connick*, 15 F.3d 1338, 1346 (5th Cir.1994). The inquiries regarding legitimate public concern are the same under the First Amendment and the law of Texas. *Ross v. Midwest Communications, Inc.*, 870 F.2d 271, 273 (5th Cir.1989).

Reports of the investigation of crimes or matters pertaining to criminal activity have almost without exception been held to be newsworthy or matters of legitimate public interest as a matter of law. Without question, the facts depicted in the article are matters of legitimate public concern. The article described an alleged blackmail scheme by lawyers who were willing to bend if not break the law to procure money from Mary's unsuspecting paramours. The public is legitimately interested in and entitled to know that two local lawyers, who hold themselves out as pursuers of justice and skilled and vigorous advocates on behalf of their clients, are using the processes of the law in such a legally and morally questionable manner. The article also presented insights into the operation of the legal system and a debate involving the ethics and legality of the Robertses' scheme.

(continues)

In the presence of the publication of matters of legitimate public concern, the courts must refrain from invading the discretion of editors. *See, e.g., Cinel, 15 F.3d at 1346* ("we are not prepared to make editorial decisions for the media regarding information directly related to matters of public concern"); *Ross,* 870 F.2d at 275 ("judges, acting with the benefit of hindsight, must resist the temptation to edit journalists aggressively"). Because, as a matter of law, plaintiff cannot establish an essential element of his invasion of privacy cause of action, that cause of action must be dismissed. It is therefore unnecessary to reach the issue of whether Hearst obtained the information for the article in violation of the Court of Appeals' order.

Hearst also argues that plaintiff cannot maintain an intentional infliction of emotional distress action. Intentional infliction of emotional distress is a "gap-filler" tort, allowing recovery in the rare instances in which a defendant intentionally inflicts severe emotional distress in an unusual manner so the victim has no other recognized theory of redress. *Hoffmann-La Roche, Inc. v. Zeltwanger,* 144 S.W.3d 438,

447 (Tex.2004). "Where the gravamen of a plaintiff's complaint is really another tort, intentional infliction of emotional distress should not be available." Properly limited, the tort is not available when the actor "'intends to invade some other legally protected interest,' even if emotional distress results." Because plaintiff's action is grounded on an invasion of privacy which itself provides damages for emotional distress, *Billings v. Atkinson,* 489 S.W.2d 858, 861 (Tex.1973), a simultaneous action for intentional infliction of emotional distress is unavailable.

Even if a cause of action for intentional infliction of emotional distress were available in conjunction with a privacy action involving the same facts, Hearst argues that as a matter of law its conduct was not extreme or outrageous. A review of Texas case law confirms that position. Publication of truthful, albeit embarrassing, information has again and again been determined not to constitute extreme and outrageous conduct. For the reasons set forth above, Hearst's motion to dismiss plaintiff's intentional infliction of emotional distress claim will be granted.

CASE QUESTIONS

1. Do you agree with the court that the public had a right to know about a blackmail scheme by lawyers? Explain your answer.
2. Why would not the court grant the claim for intentional infliction of emotional distress?

Unreasonable Intrusion

unreasonable intrusion | One type of the intentional tort of invasion of privacy. Occurs when the tortfeasor engages in an excessive and highly offensive invasion upon another person's seclusion or solitude.

Unreasonable intrusion involves an excessive and highly offensive assault upon one's seclusion or solitude. Several illustrations should clarify this concept. If store security personnel demand that a suspected shoplifter disrobe, or if they rifle through the suspect's personal belongings in an illegal search, this would be considered unreasonable intrusion. Intentional eavesdropping upon a private conversation is another example. Recall the Fantasia/Susan hypothetical discussed in connection with infliction of emotional distress. Susan's incessant telephone calls in attempt to collect money owed by Fantasia would also constitute unreasonable intrusion. Searching another's mail to discover private information or obtaining unauthorized access to someone's bank account or tax records are yet other instances. Courts have also found that illegal, compulsory blood tests are an unreasonable intrusion. Simple trespassing onto an individual's land to snoop would also constitute this type of invasion of privacy.

Public Disclosure of Private Facts

When a tortfeasor communicates purely private information about a person to the public without permission, and a reasonable person would find this disclosure extremely objectionable, then invasion of privacy by **public disclosure of private facts** has taken place. Truth is *not* a defense against this tort, because it is the unauthorized and offensive public revelation of private facts that is being protected against.

The most common example of such disclosure involves communications by the mass media. For example, if a newspaper article mentions an ordinary citizen by name and discusses in detail his or her drug dependency problems, and the person did not consent, then public disclosure of private facts has occurred. Public figures, however, generally do not succeed in lawsuits against the media when such disclosures are made without malice.

public disclosure of private facts | One type of the intentional tort of invasion of privacy. Occurs when the tortfeasor communicates about a person to the public without permission, and a reasonable person would find this disclosure extremely objectionable.

THE CASE OF THE VIEWING ROOM COVERED BY THE UMBRELLA

In some cases, the statement "truth is stranger than fiction" really rings true. As a paralegal, you will be privy to numerous stories—some of which, if you heard them outside the law office, would cause you to burst out laughing in disbelief. As a professional, you must learn to maintain your composure no matter what the client reveals to you, or how absurd it sounds. In this example, you get to see a case from an insurance company's perspective.

LINEBERRY

v.

STATE FARM FIRE & CASUALTY CO.

885 F. Supp. 1095 (M.D. Tenn. 1995)
United States District Court, Middle District of Tennessee
April 4, 1995
Echols, District Judge

Plaintiffs, Dewey Lineberry and Bill Robinson, seek a declaratory judgment requiring State Farm Fire & Casualty Co. ["State Farm"] to defend and indemnify them against actions in state court pursuant to personal liability policies of insurance.

Plaintiffs are currently defending four separate actions brought in the Circuit Court of Wilson County,

Tennessee by four women. The allegations of all four suits are essentially the same. Lineberry apparently had sexual relationships with the four women over the period of time stated in the lawsuits. In the course of building himself a new office building, Lineberry enlisted the help of Robinson to construct a "secret" viewing room adjoining the recreation room and the restroom of Lineberry's personal office. Two-way mirrors were constructed into the walls of the recreation room and restroom so that anyone in the viewing room could look through the mirrors and observe occupants of the recreation room and restroom without the occupant's knowledge. The occupants of the recreation room and restroom could see only their own reflections in the mirrors. Lineberry and Robinson set up a video camera in the viewing room so that

(continues)

the persons and activities in the recreation room and restroom could secretly be filmed through the two-way mirrors.

On occasions Lineberry brought the unsuspecting females to his office where Robinson, who was hiding in the viewing room, secretly videotaped their sexual activities. Lineberry contends this scheme was approved or suggested by his attorney as a way to preserve proof of his sexual activities in the event one of his unsuspecting female guests falsely accused him of some impropriety. He maintains that this extraordinary precaution was taken only for his own protection, and that he had no intention of disclosing the video tapes of his sexual escapades to any other person. At some later time, Lineberry and his attorney had a dispute. Subsequently, Lineberry's attorney notified the Wilson County District Attorney of Lineberry's clandestine videotaping activities. After a search warrant was obtained, Lineberry's office was searched, and the tapes were seized by local law enforcement officials. The women depicted in the videotapes were then asked to come to the Sheriff's Department, identify themselves on the videotapes, and explain their actions. All four women deny they were aware they had been filmed.

Each of the four women filed a separate lawsuit in the Circuit Court of Wilson County. The suits charge Lineberry and Robinson with outrageous conduct, intentional infliction of emotional distress, fraud or constructive fraud, misrepresentation, appropriation, and invasion of their rights to privacy. Each of the women seek recovery for humiliation, mental distress, and emotional pain and suffering, which resulted from the actions of Lineberry and Robinson.

Both Lineberry and Robinson possess personal liability umbrella insurance policies with State Farm. They contend that pursuant to the provisions of those policies, State Farm must defend and indemnify them against the claims for invasion of privacy in the four lawsuits filed in Wilson County, Tennessee. The policies also contain a provision which excludes coverage for intentional acts or acts which are expected.

Plaintiffs contend that State Farm, having specifically insured them against losses caused by the invasion of the right to privacy, must both defend them against the claims presented in the four lawsuits and indemnify them for any damages awarded to the four women. State Farm contends it is not required to defend or indemnify against these claims because the losses were not the result of an "accident" and the claims fall within the policy's exclusion for intentional or expected acts.

Plaintiffs counter Defendant's arguments by pointing to the language in the policy which defines "personal injury" by specifically listing a number of intentional torts, including invasion of the right of privacy. In other words, the losses insured against are those resulting in personal injury, which under the policy's definition includes certain types of intentional torts. An intentional tort is a civil wrong or injury, which occurs as a result of the intentional act of another person. For example, one cannot commit an act of assault and battery accidentally.

Defendant alleges that the insurance policy provisions are not contradictory and the coverage is not illusory, because an invasion of the right to privacy is not necessarily an intentional tort. If that were correct, the policy would not necessarily be ambiguous, as the policy would cover injuries resulting from unintentional invasions of the right of privacy and would exclude those which are intentional.

> In the instant case, the **umbrella policy** expressly covered injuries resulting from invasion of the right of privacy, an inherently intentional tort, but excluded injuries which were intended or expected. Therefore, the court finds the coverage is illusory, and the policy is ambiguous and must be interpreted against the insurer and in favor of the insured. Accordingly, State Farm must idemnify Plaintiffs for injuries arising from Plaintiffs' alleged invasion of rights to privacy.

The court will now turn to State Farm's duty to defend. . . . The obligation to defend arises whenever the complaint against the insured alleges a claim upon any ground for which there might be a recovery within the terms of a policy. The purpose of such duty is for the insured to obtain protection against the expense of defending suits, whether meritorious or groundless, *within the area and scope of liability covered by the policy.*

Because this court has found that the claims for injuries resulting from the alleged invasion of the right to privacy fall within the coverage of the policies, State Farm has a duty to defend against that portion of the complaints against Lineberry and Robinson.

For the foregoing reasons, Lineberry's Motion for Summary Judgment is GRANTED, Plaintiff Robinson's Motion for Summary Judgment is GRANTED, and Defendant State Farm's Motion for Summary Judgment is DENIED.

CASE QUESTIONS

1. Why did the court find that the defendant insurance company had an obligation to defend the plaintiffs?
2. Do you think that insurance was designed to cover the deliberate and intentional acts of those who are insured? Explain.

False Light in the Public Eye

Invasion of privacy by placing a person in a **false light in the public eye** happens if the tortfeasor publicly attributes to that individual false opinions, statements, or actions. For instance, if a magazine uses someone's photograph and name without permission and in an embarrassing fashion, this would place the victim in a false light publicly. One fact pattern repeated in many court cases concerns a plaintiff's photograph and name appearing in a newspaper adjacent to a negative story appearing on the same page, when the story and photograph appear in such a way as to suggest a connection between the two. Another example would be the advertisement mentioned previously involving Old Navy and Kim Kardashian regarding appropriation.

umbrella policy | An additional insurance policy that is purchased to extend the liability limits beyond what is covered under an insured's basic policy of insurance.

false light in the public eye | One type of the intentional tort of invasion of privacy. Occurs when the tortfeasor publicly attributes to another individual false opinions, statements, or actions.

THE CASE OF THE NOT-SO-BAD LIGHT

This case raises many interesting points. Madonna's bodyguard, James Albright, claims, among other things, that he has been defamed, that his privacy has been invaded, and that he has been shown in a false light because a photograph of an "outspoken homosexual" was incorrectly labeled as being him. Albright asks the court to recognize a new tort that other states recognize that is not recognized in Massachusetts, the tort of false light. However, Albright must overcome a major hurdle: he must first prove defamation (that a false statement about him was made and published), and then additionally he must show that it would have been highly offensive to the reasonable person. Unlike in the case of defamation, the statement need not harm his reputation, but must only show

(continues)

him in a false light. Sometimes these two standards can be quite similar. This is why some courts refuse to recognize the tort of false light. They feel that defamation covers most situations. Defamation is discussed in the next section.

**AMRAK PRODUCTIONS, INC.;
JAMES ALBRIGHT,
Plaintiffs, Appellants, v.
ANDREW MORTON; MICHAEL O'MARA;
MICHAEL O'MARA BOOKS LIMITED et al.,
Defendants, Appellees,
NEWS GROUP NEWSPAPERS, LTD.,
Defendants
APPEAL FROM THE UNITED STATES
DISTRICT COURT FOR THE DISTRICT
OF MASSACHUSETTS**
United States Court of Appeals for the First Circuit
No. 04-1449
June 3, 2005

Amrak employed Albright—who has been involved in the personal and professional security business for over 10 years—as a professional bodyguard. From January to July 1992, Albright served as Madonna's bodyguard, during which time he became romantically involved with the artist and remained so until 1994.

In December 2000, Albright entered into a contract with O'Mara Books to sell information about Madonna for an upcoming biography. The book, entitled *Madonna*, was written by author Andrew Morton and published by O'Mara Books in the United Kingdom and by St. Martin's Press in the United States in 2001. Chapter 11 of the book details Albright's relationship with Madonna.

The book also contains 48 pages of photographs, including one in which Madonna is accompanied by two men. The man to the left is wearing black pants, a black and white shirt, a black leather jacket, tinted sunglasses, a string necklace, and an earring. The caption states:

Madonna attends ex-lover Prince's concert with her secret lover and one-time bodyguard Jimmy Albright (left). Albright, who bears an uncanny resemblance to Carlos León, the father of Madonna's

daughter, enjoyed a stormy three-year relationship with the star. They planned to marry, and had even chosen names for their children.

This photograph allegedly defamed Albright because the man pictured was, in fact, José Guitierez, an "outspoken homosexual" who "often dressed as a woman," and engaged in what appellants describe as "homosexual, sexually graphic, lewd, lascivious, offensive, and possibly illegal" conduct. Guitierez was employed as one of Madonna's dancers.

On November 12, 2001, *People* magazine, a publication of Time Inc., published the same photograph along with the erroneous caption. News of the World, a publication of News Group Newspapers, Ltd., published the same on March 17, 2002.

Appellants subsequently sued for defamation, invasion of privacy, negligence, negligent, and intentional infliction of emotional distress, along with violations of state statutory prohibitions on unfair trade practices, and unauthorized commercial use of a name or likeness.

The district court granted appellees' motion to dismiss on all counts. First, the court held that no reasonable view of the photograph and text would suggest that Albright is homosexual, and thus the publication cannot be construed as defamatory. Alternatively, the court held that imputing homosexuality cannot be considered defamatory per se in Massachusetts, particularly given the rationales in the U.S. Supreme Court's decision in Lawrence v. Texas (invalidating state statute criminalizing same-sex sexual conduct), as well as the decision in Goodridge v. Dep't of Pub. Health (invalidating limitations to civil marriage for same-sex couples under state equal protection principles). Given appellants' failure to state a defamation claim, the court dismissed the derivative claims of commercial use, false light invasion of privacy, emotional distress, negligence, and unfair trade practices.

To prevail in a defamation claim, plaintiffs must establish that "defendant[s] w[ere] at fault for the publication of a false statement regarding the plaintiff, capable of damaging the plaintiff's reputation in the community, which either caused economic loss or is actionable without proof of economic loss." This threshold question, "whether a communication is reasonably susceptible of a defamatory meaning, is a question of law for the court."

A communication is susceptible to defamatory meaning if it "would tend to hold the plaintiff up to scorn, hatred, ridicule or contempt, in the minds of any considerable and respectable segment in the community." The communication "must be interpreted reasonably," leading a "reasonable reader" to conclude that it conveyed a defamatory meaning. Context matters in assessing such claims: The Massachusetts Supreme Judicial Court, for example, has required that allegedly defamatory photographs or headlines be interpreted in light of the entire context of the publication.

The miscaptioned photograph in the instant case is not reasonably susceptible of a defamatory meaning. Nothing in Guitierez's appearance, particularly given the accompanying caption stressing Albright's heterosexuality (e.g., Madonna's "secret lover"), gives any indication that Albright is homosexual. To draw such an inference, the reader—who would have to view homosexuals with "scorn, hatred, ridicule or contempt"—must follow Madonna and her cohort closely enough to recognize Guitierez as a gay man, but not closely enough to know Guitierez's name or what Albright looks like. Few, if any, readers would fall into this "considerable and respectable segment in the community."

The context of the text accompanying the photograph further deflates any argument that the photo conveys a defamatory meaning. When we "consider all the words used" in the accompanying text, including phrases such as Albright's "long-time girlfriend," his "hot and heavy" affair with Madonna, their sexual encounters, and Albright's "fling" with a "girl at a club"—we find that no reasonable reader could conclude that Albright is homosexual. This conclusion is supported by the caption, which states that Albright was Madonna's "secret lover," that they "enjoyed a stormy three-year relationship," and that they planned to marry. Similarly, the caption for the People Weekly photograph states that Albright felt "overwhelming love" for Madonna.

Given appellants' failure to satisfy the threshold question of defamatory meaning, we affirm the court's dismissal of the defamation claim.

We have considered appellants' derivative claims—commercial use, negligent and intentional infliction of emotional distress—and find them all without merit. We likewise reject appellants' urging that the false light invasion of privacy claim should be recognized in Massachusetts, particularly given the state court's repeated refusal to do so.

CASE QUESTIONS

1. Do you think Albright has been harmed? Explain.
2. What would harm Albright more, the photo in the book or the publicity surrounding this suit? Explain.

Perhaps no other intentional tort excites the public indignation more than invasion of privacy. Almost everyone desires a sanctuary from the daily intrusions that dominate our urbanized, highly technological, and mobile society. However, the popular conception of the right to privacy does not always afford legal remedies. The following hypotheticals illustrate how the tort elements must first be satisfied.

T. J. rents a house from Eric. After T. J. had lived there for six months, Eric notified T. J. to move out of the house within 10 days, because Eric needed the house for his bedridden mother. T. J. refused, pointing out that the lease ran for a full year and that it could not be terminated by either party without 30 days' advance notice. After 10 days, Eric moved into the house with his mother and her two grandchildren. T. J. refused to leave the house, and everyone lived in a state of considerable tension for two weeks before T. J. could not stand it any longer and left. Did Eric invade T. J.'s privacy by unreasonable intrusion?

Eric's actions interfered with T. J.'s solitude in an excessive and highly offensive manner. T. J. had complied with the lease agreement and had a legal right to occupy the premises. Eric's invasion with his invalid mother and two grandchildren substantially disrupted T. J.'s domestic tranquility. The stress among the house occupants became so extreme that T. J. was at last compelled to abandon his residence. Accordingly, Eric would be liable to T. J. for invasion of privacy by unreasonable intrusion.

* * *

Aaron was aghast when he opened the day's newspaper to see an advertisement with his picture, in which he was holding a can of Bartell's Beenie-Weenies. Under the photograph was the caption, "Bartell's Makes the Best Beenie-Weenies!" Aaron could not recall ever buying this brand and made no such endorsement to anyone associated with the product. He did not give his permission to use the photograph. Has Bartell's invaded Aaron's privacy by appropriation?

Bartell's used Aaron's likeness in its photograph without his consent. Bartell's hoped to profit from increased sales as a result of this "customer's" endorsement. Bartell's would thus be liable to Aaron for invasion of privacy by appropriation.

Furthermore, Bartell's publicly attributed a spurious opinion to Aaron in its photograph caption. This would place Aaron in a false light in the public eye. Thus, Bartell's would also be liable to Aaron for this type of invasion of privacy.

defamation | Transmission to others of false statements that harm the reputation, business, or property rights of a person. Spoken defamation is *slander* and written defamation is *libel.*

libel | Written defamation. Publicly communicated false written statements that injure a person's reputation, business, or property rights.

slander | Oral defamation. The speaking of false words that injure another person's reputation, business, or property rights.

Table 7-4 summarizes the elements of the four types of invasion of privacy.

▌ DEFAMATION: LIBEL AND SLANDER

Defamation consists of two varieties: libel and slander. **Libel** is a written false and disparaging statement about an individual that the tortfeasor communicates to a third party. **Slander** is an oral false and disparaging statement about a person that

APPROPRIATION	UNREASONABLE INTRUSION	PUBLIC DISCLOSURE OF PRIVATE FACTS	FALSE LIGHT IN THE PUBLIC EYE
Unconsented use of person's name or likeness for profit	Excessive and highly offensive invasion of one's seclusion or solitude	Public communication of private information about person without permission	Publicly attributing false opinions, statements, or actions to a person
		Reasonable person finds disclosure extremely objectionable	

TABLE 7-4
Elements of invasion of privacy

the tortfeasor communicates to a third party. Courts often refer to this communication element as **publication.** Publication of the defamatory information must injure the victim's reputation in the community. The elements can be outlined as follows:

publication | Making public; communicating defamatory information to a person other than the person defamed.

1. Written (libel) or oral (slander) statement
2. False and defamatory statement about a person
3. Tortfeasor's communication of the statement to a third party
4. Harm to the victim's reputation in the community

Although the first element is obvious, the others require some elaboration.

Nature of the Statement

For libel, the statement must generally be written in some fashion. This does not necessarily mean writing, such as handwriting, or printed words, such as those appearing on this page. There are many forms of written expression, including such unusual methods as billboards, skywriting with smoke or banners pulled by an airplane, or placing objects such as stones into the shapes of letters. The critical element of writing is whether the information is communicated visually through means of an alphabet. Libel can also appear in the form of films, records, DVDs, and downloadable computer files.

For slander, the statement must be orally delivered, but it does not have to be words. Gestures, particularly obscene ones, also qualify, provided that the meaning of the gestures is sufficiently clear to onlookers to be defamatory.

THE CASE OF THE FAMILY FEUD VIA INTERNET

This case brings to light a whole new avenue for defamation: defamation via Internet. Five years after a contentious divorce, the partners are fighting again in a whole new domain. A sheriff's former wife has set up websites and posted a good deal of information from the divorce file on the Net for all to read. Allegations against her husband include alleged physical abuse and harassment against the wife. The sheriff, on learning of this public display of private matters, sought an injunction to stop the "slanderous" conduct against him, which he claimed is an invasion of privacy.

Thomas C. Evans, Plaintiff and Respondent,

v.

Linda A. Evans, Defendant and Appellant

Superior Court of San Diego County on Appeal

No. GIC 881162

No. D051144 (Cal. App. Ct., 4th Dist., Div. One)

May 12, 2008

Thomas is a law enforcement officer with the San Diego County Sheriff's Department. He and Linda were married in 1985, and separated in 1998. In 2002, the court entered a judgment dissolving the marriage. During the next five years, the parties had substantial ongoing conflict over custody, child support and other issues.

In March 2007, Thomas filed a complaint against Linda, alleging harassment, slander and defamation, various common law torts, breach of privacy claims, and breach of contract. The gist of the allegations was that Linda has engaged in a series of acts intended to harass Thomas and cause him severe emotional stress and injury to his reputation and career.

Shortly after, Thomas moved for a temporary restraining order and preliminary injunction.

Thomas said that in April 2005, Linda filed a complaint with the Sheriff's Department, alleging "a number of departmental and state law violations," including "child abuse, lying, falsifying departmental reports, [and] abuse of position . . . ." After a criminal and internal investigation, these allegations were found to be unsubstantiated and/or unfounded. Twenty months later, in December 2006, Thomas "was informed by [his] superiors . . . that the District Attorney and Sheriff had both received letters about [Thomas] that were very defaming in nature."

Thomas did not say who wrote these letters, but in a supplemental declaration, Thomas said information about these letters would be "fleshed out through discovery" in the action. Thomas also stated that in March 2007, Linda filed another "harassing request" to the Sheriff's Department.

Thomas said he "believe[d]" these prior communications with the Sheriff's Department were "a major factor" in his "inability to [be] promote[d] within the Department." Thomas also asserted that the "embarrassment" resulting from Linda's conduct caused him to decide to "seek a less prominent job within the Department."

With respect to the Internet postings, Thomas stated that: "In December 2006, I was informed that there were internet websites posted by [Linda and her mother Preddy] with numerous defaming comments and statements about me as a sworn law enforcement officer, and the lawyers, judges, and counselors involved in our family court case." Thomas also said he "discovered in December 2006 and January 2007 that [Preddy] had apparently inappropriately gained access to both my family court medical records and financial records, and had published information from them on the internet."

Thomas also submitted copies of Web site pages in which it appeared that Linda posted statements accusing Thomas of physical abuse against her and her son, and statements suggesting that several San Diego Superior Court judges were biased and/or "incompetent." Thomas also stated "[a]s recently as February 19, 2007, a Google search of my name on thepetitionsite.com generated a blurb posted by [Linda] stating the following: 'Our eldest son was returned to my "Primary Care" after his father, San Diego County

Sheriff's Sergeant, Thomas C. Evans, struck him with a belt repeatedly . . . .' This statement is entirely false."

Five days later, on April 18, the court issued the preliminary injunction challenged in this appeal. The preliminary injunction stated: "1. [Linda and Preddy] are enjoined from publishing false and defamatory statements and/or confidential personal information about [Thomas] on the internet; and] 2. [Linda and Preddy] are enjoined from contacting [Thomas's] employer via e-mail or otherwise regarding [Thomas]. Since [Thomas] is employed by the San Diego Sheriff's Department, this injunction should not be construed to prohibit defendants from calling 911 to report criminal conduct."

An order prohibiting a party from making or publishing false statements is a classic type of an unconstitutional prior restraint. "While [a party] may be held responsible for abusing his right to speak freely in a subsequent tort action, he has the initial right to speak freely without censorship."

The California Supreme Court recently recognized this fundamental principle, but held the rule does not apply to an order issued after a trial prohibiting the defendant from *repeating specific statements found at trial to be defamatory.*

The California Supreme Court held that although other aspects of the injunction were overbroad, the defendant's "right to free speech would not be infringed by a properly limited injunction prohibiting defendant from repeating statements about plaintiff that were determined at trial to be defamatory."

To establish a valid prior restraint under the federal Constitution, a proponent has a heavy burden to show the countervailing interest is compelling, the prior restraint is necessary and would be effective in promoting this interest, and less extreme measures are unavailable.

Even if an injunction does not impermissibly constitute a prior restraint, the injunction must be sufficiently precise to provide "a person of ordinary intelligence fair notice that his contemplated conduct is forbidden." An injunction is unconstitutionally vague if it does not clearly define the persons protected and the conduct prohibited.

The court's preliminary injunction prohibiting Linda from publishing any "false and defamatory" statements on the Internet is constitutionally invalid. Because there has been no trial and no determination on the merits that any statement made by Linda was defamatory, the court cannot prohibit her from making statements characterized only as "false and defamatory."

This portion of the order is also invalid as unconstitutionally vague and overbroad. The injunction broadly prohibited Linda from publishing any defamatory comments about Thomas. This sweeping prohibition fails to adequately delineate which of Linda's future comments might violate the injunction and lead to contempt of court.

In addition to enjoining "false and defamatory statements," the court also enjoined Linda from "publishing . . . confidential personal information about [Thomas] on the internet."

A prohibition against disclosing confidential information constitutes a prior restraint. However, because it also potentially concerns the countervailing right of privacy protected under the California Constitution, a prohibition may be proper under certain compelling or "extraordinary" circumstances.

In determining whether such circumstances exist, courts generally apply a balancing test, weighing the competing privacy and free speech constitutional rights. Relevant factors include whether the person is a public or private figure, the scope of the prior restraint, the nature of the private information, whether the information is of legitimate public concern, the extent of the potential harm if the information is disclosed, and the strength of the private and governmental interest in preventing publication of the information.

We cannot determine whether the court properly applied the balancing test in this case because the order is ambiguous as to the meaning of "confidential personal information." The order does not contain a definition

(continues)

of "confidential personal information" and it is not reasonably possible to determine the scope of this prohibition from any other source. Without a definition, the injunction is not sufficiently clear to determine whether Thomas's privacy rights to the information substantially outweigh Linda's free speech rights.

In his appellate briefs, Thomas seeks to justify this portion of the order by suggesting that Linda will place (or has placed) his telephone number, address, and Social Security number on the Internet. He argues the disclosure of the information will put his safety and well-being in jeopardy, particularly because of his job as a deputy sheriff. We agree.

However, in the proceedings below, Thomas did not specifically request an order preventing his identifying information from being placed on the Internet. Instead, Thomas focused primarily on his concern that Linda and/or her mother had placed, or planned to place, information about the divorce proceedings on the Internet, including information that had been contained in the family court file. However, the mere fact that information is contained in court files or concerns divorce proceedings does not necessarily mean it is confidential and cannot be disclosed.

An order enjoining the disclosure must be narrowly tailored to protect only these specific interests and should not unnecessarily interfere with a person's free speech rights.

Accordingly, we conclude the order preventing Linda from placing any "confidential personal information" about Thomas on the Internet is vague, overbroad, and not narrowly tailored. On remand, the court should reevaluate Thomas's request. After determining the information that Thomas seeks to be kept private, the court should engage in a balancing test to determine whether there is a compelling reason that such information be kept private.

The record did not support the conclusion that Thomas would prevail on his causes of action challenging Linda's complaints to the Sheriff's Department. A citizen's report to law enforcement personnel seeking investigation of alleged wrongful activities is absolutely privileged. "An absolute privilege exists to protect citizens from the threat of litigation for communications to government agencies whose function it is to investigate and remedy wrongdoing.'"

Additionally, there are less intrusive means to limit Linda's filing false complaints with the Sheriff's Department. Government agencies can establish reasonable requirements before an individual may be permitted to file a complaint. If the Sheriff's Department believes the complaints are unwarranted, it has the authority to take administrative action.

Based on the record before us, the court's order enjoining Linda from contacting the Sheriff's Department about Thomas absent an emergency was overbroad and was not justified by the evidentiary record.

The preliminary injunction order is reversed. The matter is remanded for the court to reconsider the order with the views expressed in this opinion.

CASE QUESTIONS

1. What did Thomas need to do to succeed with his injunction request?
2. When the court advises Thomas to wait for actual defamation to occur before seeking relief on this ground, does this meet your expectations? Explain.

Publication

The tortfeasor must communicate the false and derogatory statement to a third party. This means that statements made by the tortfeasor directly to the victim are defamatory only if seen or heard by another or others.

Publication takes place through any means by which the false information is disseminated. This includes anything spoken, either in person or over amplification (megaphone or loudspeaker at a ballpark, for instance), radio, television, or telephone; videos on YouTube; and anything written, including letters, telegrams, scribbled messages, billboards, or printed and published works (such as a letter to the editor in the local newspaper, for instance).

Harm to Reputation in the Community

A statement is considered *defamatory* if it causes the fourth element—namely, injury to the victim's reputation in the community. For purposes of libel and slander, **community** is narrowly defined as a significant number of persons acquainted or familiar with the victim. Although some courts have held that "a community of one" is sufficient under certain circumstances, most courts maintain that larger numbers are required. Nevertheless, certain expressions, such as "a handful," "a closely associated group," and "associates in the neighborhood or workplace," suggest small numbers in most instances.

Many courts define the victim's injury in more emotional terms. For example, it has commonly been held that statements are libelous or slanderous if they ridicule, humiliate, or subject the victim to contempt or hatred from among his or her peers.

community |

1. Neighborhood, locality, or other grouping of persons. A vague term that can include very large or very small areas.

2. A group with common interests that are shared.

Public Figures

Public figures, such as movie and television celebrities or public officers and employees who exercise substantial governmental power, are treated differently than private individuals. These people are used to being under the public eye and have greater access to the media to refute untrue charges than the ordinary person. Accordingly, not as much protection is afforded to public figures. To be successful in claiming defamation, a public figure must show that a statement was made with actual malice. Because this is very hard to prove, few public figures bring lawsuits to challenge statements made about them, even when they know the assertions to be totally false.

Slander Per Se

Per se is a term indicating that something is automatic or presumed. Some words in and of themselves are defamatory; therefore, injury and damage need not be proven when slander per se is shown. For example, words that imply criminal conduct, words that are harmful to one's business, and words implying that one has a loathsome and communicable disease are all presumed to damage one's reputation, so the victim need not prove damages to be successful in a slander per se claim.

Truth and Privilege as Absolute Defenses

Truth is considered an absolute defense in defamation cases. If the information the tortfeasor communicates is true, then no libel or slander occurred. To successfully use this defense, the tortfeasor must prove the veracity of the statement.

What is true is often a matter of opinion. It always depends upon the nature of the derogatory comments. For example, to call a person born out of wedlock a "bastard" is technically accurate, but in today's society the term is rarely used as defined in the dictionary. Similarly, to refer to a sexually promiscuous individual as a "whore" or a "John" could be deemed factual by reasonable persons, particularly those who are morally opposed to the conduct described. Courts have struggled with the elasticity of truth, and various formulas for pinpointing truth have been inserted in court opinions. The most common court opinion states that literal truth in every detail is unnecessary. If the statement is substantially true, so that a reasonable person would decide that the accusations were justified given the facts, then truth will operate as a defense to defamation actions.

Privilege is also considered an absolute defense in defamation cases. Statements made by attorneys and judges during trials are privileged and cannot be the grounds for a defamation charge. Likewise, legislators are immune from liability for false statements made during debate, even if the lawmakers deliberately make the untrue statements. Members of Congress have an absolute privilege while speaking on the floor of Congress. Privilege allows all these persons to do their best jobs without fear of repercussions should a statement they make later prove to be untrue.

Defamation is another intentional tort, like assault and battery, that virtually everyone has experienced, either as victim or tortfeasor (or both). One need only recall a recent imprudent remark to mentally invoke accusations of slander or libel. Nevertheless, the factual elements determine whether defamation has occurred, as the following illustrations show. Table 7-5 lists the elements of the two types of defamation, libel and slander.

TABLE 7-5

Elements of libel and slander

Libel	Slander
Written statement	Oral statement
False and defamatory statement	False and defamatory statement
Publication to third party	Publication to third party
Injury to victim's reputation in the community	Injury to victim's reputation in the community

THE CASE OF THE LIVING DEAD

Imagine one's horror at opening the daily newspaper and, while glancing quickly at the obituaries, spotting oneself listed as recently deceased! Although this may be a shocking revelation, it is the type of mistake that newspapers easily and promptly correct. As the following case illustrates, an erroneous obituary does not always constitute defamation.

DECKER
v.
PRINCETON PACKET, INC.

Supreme Court of New Jersey
116 N.J. 418, 561 A.2d 1122 (1989)
August 8, 1989
Handler, J.

This case involves a tort action brought against a newspaper seeking damages for defamation and emotional distress attributable to the publication of a false obituary. The court is called on to address whether an obituary that reports a death, this being the only false statement, can possibly have a defamatory interpretation . . . . The trial court and Appellate Division held that defamation and emotional-harm claims were without merit as a matter of law. Plaintiffs appeal these rulings arguing that defendant's publication of a false obituary without verifying its accuracy caused damage to reputation and emotional harm that should be compensated under our tort law.

On February 15, 1985, the defendant, a newspaper, The Princeton Packet, Inc. ("The Packet"), which publishes on Tuesday and Friday of each week, reported the following obituary for Marcy Goldberg Decker, the plaintiff:

> Marcy Goldberg Decker of Princeton died suddenly on Feb. 11. She was 31.
>
> Ms. Goldberg was the fiance of Robert J. Feldman of Princeton.
>
> She was a lifelong resident of Princeton and is survived by a son, Jackson T.; her mother, Charlotte Goldberg of Trenton; and a brother, Ronald Goldberg of California.
>
> Funeral arrangements were incomplete at press time.

This obituary is incorrect because Marcy Decker was not dead.

All other information in the obituary—her age, residence, and family relationships—was accurate . . . . Plaintiff notified defendant by a telephone call two days after the publication that she was in fact alive. The Packet printed the following retraction on February 19, 1985:

> The Packet erroneously reported in Friday's edition that Marcy Decker of Princeton died on Feb. 11. The obituary was false. The Packet regrets the error and any inconvenience this may have caused Ms. Decker or her family.

Plaintiffs deposed three employees of defendant to establish their claims that The Packet was unaware of who had submitted the obituary, [and] that it took no steps to determine the validity of the notice . . . .

A defamatory statement is one that is false and is "'injurious to the reputation of another' or exposes another person to 'hatred, contempt or ridicule' or subjects another person to 'a loss of the good will and confidence' in which he or she is held by others." Thus, if the statement of Marcy Decker's death in the false obituary could be interpreted by a reasonable person to expose the plaintiff to "hatred, contempt, ridicule or disgrace or subject . . . [her] to loss of the good will and confidence of the community," then her action for defamation could proceed to trial.

The principle generally endorsed by most authority throughout the country is that an obituary in which the only false statement concerns the death of the individual, published without malicious intent, is not defamatory *per se*. These cases suggest that publication of a notice of death is usually not defamatory because it does not injure one's reputation. As one court explained, "one is [not] demeaned or belittled by the report of his or her death."

The general rule, however, does have an exception where the false obituary contains additional false information that may be defamatory.

(continues)

This court finds that the general rule and its limited exception should govern this case and other similar cases. Here, the only false aspect of the obituary was the death of plaintiff Marcy Decker. Therefore, under the general rule, the obituary is not defamatory *per se* because the reported death of an individual when viewed from the perspective of a reasonable person of ordinary intelligence and experience does not impugn reputation. As the trial court observed, the publication of the death notice did not impute to the plaintiff any wrong and did not hold her up to ridicule. Death is a natural state and demeans no one.

. . . Moreover, the chance of an obituary being incorrect appears slight, and the newspaper can promptly publish a correction, which occurred in this case. Thus, the plaintiffs did have an adequate remedy to correct any false statement and the published correction should have prevented the false obituary from causing any continuing effects.

. . . Therefore, we hold that where a newspaper mistakenly prints an obituary for a person who is still alive and then retracts its mistake, there is no defamation *per se*, since announcing the death of someone is not by itself injurious to one's reputation.

Accordingly, the judgment below is affirmed.

CASE QUESTIONS

1. Do you believe that the facts in *Decker* satisfy an action for intentional or reckless infliction of emotional distress? For invasion of privacy? Explain.
2. If the plaintiff could discover who planted the false obituary at the newspaper's offices, could she recover for any intentional torts discussed in this chapter against this unknown person? Why or why not?

HYPOTHETICALS

Randy owns an automobile painting service. One of his customers, Jewel, was dissatisfied with Randy's paint job on her automobile; several spots that had not been polished stood out against the rest of the finish. Rather than complain directly to Randy, Jewel called in to a live local radio station and said that Randy was a "con artist" and that he had swindled many other people with sloppy work. Has Jewel slandered Randy?

Jewel communicated information about Randy to third persons, and so publication occurred. The information was false, as Jewel's dissatisfaction with a single paint job hardly documented Randy's dishonesty. The critical issue is whether Jewel's statements were defamatory. It is likely that Jewel's accusations about Randy's honesty and integrity will substantially injure Randy's business reputation in the community. This is particularly true because the allegations suggest criminal conduct by an innocent person. Thus, Jewel has slandered Randy and is liable to him for damages.

* * *

Consider the hypothetical of Britney. She enjoyed writing letters to the editor, and her missives regularly appeared in the newspaper. One day

Britney turned to the editorial page and read the following response to one of her letters:

DEAR EDITOR

In response to Britney Gold's letter in last week's edition, I must say that this woman is mentally ill and needs psychiatric treatment. She suffers from delusions and cannot be trusted. How can she make those ridiculous statements about the city's snow removal policy? I happen to work for the city street department, and I know that we regularly clear side streets after handling the main streets. It usually only takes a few extra days to get to the side streets, not weeks as she said. Why does not she take her medicine and get a grip?

JACKSON WINDERSON

Has Jackson libeled Britney? Jackson's written communication was published—literally—by appearing in the newspaper. Many people would have been exposed to the letter. Britney's reputation in the community undoubtedly will suffer from Jackson's accusations that she is "mentally ill." Although it may be true that Britney was uninformed about the city's snow removal policy, truth as to these matters is irrelevant—the defamatory remarks pertained to Britney's mental capacity. Jackson would be liable to Britney for libel.

THE CASE OF THE "WOODCHIPPER MURDERER"

In this case, a man's wife—a stewardess—disappeared. A news broadcaster suggested that the pilot-husband had murdered his wife like another pilot had in a similar case. Is mere inference enough, or must defamation be proved by explicit words?

BROWN
v.
HEARST CORP.

United States Court of Appeals, First Circuit
54 F.3d 21 (1st Cir. 1995)
May 11, 1995
Boudin, Circuit Judge

In March 1987, Regina Brown, the then-wife of appellant Willis Brown and mother of three children, disappeared. At the time Regina was employed as a flight attendant, and Willis as a pilot, for American Airlines; the couple had lived together in Newtown, Connecticut, but had been separated for four months and were living apart. The police investigated the disappearance and found Regina's car abandoned in New York but no trace of her. The investigation remains open. It is not known whether Regina is alive or dead.

Later in the same year the Browns were divorced in a Connecticut state court, the contested proceedings being completed in Regina's absence. The state court trial was prolonged and a detailed opinion was written by the trial judge pertaining to custody and support.

The trial was widely reported in the press, and publicity continued even after the decree. This was due partly to further litigation and the continuing police investigation, but also to a freakish coincidence. About six months before Regina's disappearance, another woman who lived in Newtown, a Pan Am flight attendant married to an Eastern pilot, had

(continues)

disappeared. Fragments of her bone were found in a nearby river, and her pilot husband was convicted in the so-called woodchipper murder.

In November 1990, appellee Hearst Corporation d/b/a WCVB-TV Channel 5 in Boston ("Channel 5") broadcasted from Massachusetts a segment entitled "The Other Pilot's Wife" as a part of the station's regular "newsmagazine" program. It was prepared by Mary Richardson, a journalist with the station, who conducted a substantial amount of research and a number of interviews in preparing the broadcast.

The broadcast opens with the leitmotif—"Tonight the bizarre story of a small New England town where one stewardess is dead, another is missing"—and then offers a brief reprise of the 1986 murder of the Pan Am flight attendant. Next, turning to the Browns, the broadcast describes and depicts an apparent storybook marriage going sour, the divorce petition, and Regina's disappearance. "In the days following Regina's disappearance," says Richardson, "Willis showed no interest in what had happened to her."

There is other incriminating information about Willis recounted in the program, and the police are described as having suspected Willis and as believing still that "Mr. Brown knows more about the disappearance of his wife than he is letting on." No evidence even remotely exculpatory of Willis is described. On the other hand, Mary Richardson, the "voice over" throughout the program, never asserts that Willis is guilty or even says that she thinks he is guilty. Formally, the program describes the disappearance as a mystery or, at worst, a possible murder still unsolved.

In February 1993, Willis brought the present action against Channel 5 in state court in Texas. The case was removed to federal court and thereafter transferred to the federal district court in Massachusetts. As subsequently amended, Willis' complaint charged defamation, invasion of privacy under Mass. Gen.L. ch. 214 § 1B, "false light" invasion of privacy, and intentional infliction of emotional distress.

After discovery, Channel 5 moved for summary judgment. In a detailed opinion dated July 21, 1994, the district court granted the motion. As to the defamation claim, the court relied in different respects on lack of falsity, the limited protection available for

statements of opinion, the "fair report" privilege, and lack of fault. The privacy and intentional infliction claims were dismissed on grounds described below. Willis has now appealed, asserting that all of his claims should have been submitted to a jury.

On appeal from a grant of summary judgment, we review the decision de novo, drawing inferences in favor of the party opposing the motion. . . .

Channel 5 does not appear to dispute that the broadcast charges Willis with murder or at least that a jury would be entitled to find this to be the import of the program. The broadcast never flatly expresses that accusation. Indeed, it says that the murder is unsolved and makes clear that the police have nothing much in the way of direct evidence against Willis. But defamation can occur by innuendo as well as by explicit assertion, and the suggestion here is a fairly strong one.

The broadcast makes clear that the police suspect Willis, and Regina's parents are filmed making even stronger statements of suspicion. Material from the divorce trial is used to establish or buttress doubts about Willis' character and history. The suggestion of murder runs through the program like a gold thread. The broadcast opens with the dramatic footage relating to the woodchipper murder and closes with Richardson's rhetorical question, could "someone" get away with murder?

A common defense to a charge of defamation is "truth." The Supreme Court tells us that in a suit like this one against the media the burden is upon the defamed plaintiff to show that the statements are not true. Neither side addresses this issue. Perhaps each assumes that to carry his burden of proof, Willis could testify at trial that he did not murder his wife and a jury might believe him. In all events, we take the case as one in which a jury might find that murder had been charged and that the charge was false.

Channel 5's primary response is that "[m]uch of the [b]roadcast, and the entirety of its allegedly defamatory sting, is in essence a 'fair report' of the Brown's divorce trial in Connecticut" and thus falls under the Massachusetts privilege allowed for media coverage of an official proceeding. Such a privilege certainly exists in Massachusetts, and there is little doubt that much of the material in the broadcast is drawn from, and attributed to, the divorce proceeding.

For present purposes, we will assume that the privilege extends to non-contemporaneous reports and that the program—so far as it related to the divorce proceeding and the information developed there—conveyed a fair and accurate report of the proceeding. But only a portion of the broadcast purported to be drawn from the proceeding. And, while that portion may be privileged, we are skeptical of Channel 5's claim that the entire "sting" of the broadcast is privileged material.

Where the evidence is thus enlarged and the charge cast in a more lurid light, it is not clear to us that the fair report privilege automatically shields the larger whole.

The problem for Willis, we think, is that the Supreme Court has instructed that a state libel-suit plaintiff must demonstrate fault on the part of the media; and this requirement applies even where the plaintiff is not a public official or public figure. In such cases, Massachusetts has imposed a requirement that the newspaper or broadcaster be shown to be negligent or worse. Thus, even if a false charge of murder has been made, it remains to see whether Willis provided evidence of negligence to justify submitting the case to a jury. . . .

So far as the murder goes, Willis points to nothing to suggest that Channel 5 was negligent in its mustering of the available evidence. Some might think the broadcast gaudy journalism; certainly the interpolation of the woodchipper murder is largely gratuitous. . . .

Willis' brief says tersely that the police admitted that they had no evidence against him; and he reasons that it was thus "negligent disregard for the truth" for Channel 5 to "insinuate" that "[he] murdered his wife and disposed of her body in the same fashion as did [the woodchipper murderer]." . . .

A different problem is presented by Willis' suggestion that the broadcast charged him with disposing of his wife's body "in the same fashion" as the woodchipper murder. Patently, the broadcast did not so charge; no reasonable juror could draw such an inference. Willis offers no argument to support such an inference, and it is not surprising that elsewhere in his brief he retreats to a more cautious assertion: that the juxtaposition "conveys the message that Brown also murdered his wife and disposed of her body *in some insidious fashion*" (emphasis added).

Even if all of these doubts are resolved in Willis' favor, we think this narrow remaining claim is too thin to survive summary judgment. About the most one can get from the woodchipper episode is the suggestion that, if Willis killed his wife, he also took steps to assure that her body would not be found.

A writing or program is normally viewed as a whole; and that requirement has special force here because the woodchipper episode was assertedly about someone else, and its connection to Willis depended upon the rest of the program. We conclude as a matter of law that the broadcast, taken as a whole, cannot reasonably be taken to charge that Willis brutally disposed of his wife's body.

Willis' non-libel claims do not require much discussion. On appeal, Willis has narrowed his privacy claim to the contention that the program places him in a false light by leaving the viewer with "a false impression," that is, that Brown killed Regina and disposed of her body in the same fashion as did the woodchipper murderer. The district court thought it sufficient that Massachusetts has never adopted the false light theory of privacy invasion.

Lastly, Willis charged Channel 5 with intentional infliction of emotional distress. This is a recognized tort under Massachusetts law requiring intended or foreseeable infliction of such distress, "extreme and outrageous conduct," and causation of distress so severe that no reasonable person could be expected to endure it. The district court said that Channel 5's conduct was not negligent and therefore could hardly be "extreme and outrageous."

In all events, many of the legitimate news stories that appear in the media involve foreseeable distress for the subject of the story, probably severe distress in some cases. Regina's disappearance and the divorce trial were news stories, and so was her continued absence and the failure of the police to solve the case. Willis provides no basis to think that generally accurate coverage in such a case is even remotely close to conduct "beyond all possible bounds of decency" and "utterly intolerable in a civilized community."

Affirmed.

(continues)

CASE QUESTIONS

1. Which of the parties is described as having a privilege?
2. What was the effect of the privilege?

SUMMARY

Intentional torts include actions designed to injure another person or his or her property. All intentional torts must contain an act, intent, and injurious conduct. These elements must occur together. Intentional torts harming the individual include infliction of emotional distress, fraud, misrepresentation, malicious prosecution, abuse of process, invasion of privacy, and defamation.

Intentional infliction of emotional distress involves outrageous conduct designed to cause severe mental anguish in the victim. The victim must actually suffer emotional turmoil as a result of the tortfeasor's actions. Reckless infliction of emotional distress includes outrageous conduct that the tortfeasor knew, or reasonably should have known, would produce significant emotional injury to the victim. The conduct is considered outrageous if it shocks the conscience of a reasonable person with normal emotional sensibilities. Therefore, intent is not necessary.

Fraud consists of false statements made to entice the victim to surrender something of value to the defrauder. Misrepresentation includes false statements or behavior designed to deceive the victim. In many jurisdictions, the two intentional torts are considered virtually identical and interchangeable. The tortfeasor must know that the statements made are false and intend to deceive the victim.

Malicious prosecution happens when a private citizen files a groundless criminal complaint with the prosecutor against an innocent person who is named as the defendant in a criminal prosecution action. To sue the complainant, the innocent defendant must be either acquitted or otherwise victorious in the criminal lawsuit.

The complainant must have filed the frivolous criminal charges out of malice for the innocent defendant, and malice may be implied from the circumstances surrounding the case. The innocent defendant must be injured as a consequence of the baseless prosecution. Abuse of process is the misuse (or threat of misuse) of a legal proceeding against another to obtain an unlawful objective. The victim must be harmed by the frivolous legal action. It is the civil equivalent of malicious prosecution.

Invasion of privacy consists of four independent varieties: appropriation, unreasonable intrusion, public disclosure of private facts, and false light in the public eye. Appropriation is the use of a person's name or likeness, without consent, for profit in some way. Unreasonable intrusion involves excessive and highly offensive interference with an individual's seclusion or solitude. Public disclosure of private facts happens when a tortfeasor publicly communicates purely private information about another person and such a disclosure would offend a reasonable person. False light in the public eye occurs when a tortfeasor publicly attributes to another false statements, opinions, or actions.

Defamation includes libel and slander. Libel is written communication of false and disparaging statements about an individual to third parties. Slander involves oral communication that does the same thing. Communication to third persons is called publication. The misinformation disseminated must injure the victim by harming his or her reputation in the community. Community can be narrowly defined as a small number of persons who know the victim. Even one third party is sufficient in some cases for publication to exist. Truth is an absolute defense in defamation actions. Public figures must prove actual malice to succeed in a defamation claim.

This chapter completes the study of intentional torts to people. The next chapter addresses intentional torts to property such as trespass and toxic torts.

▮ KEY TERMS

abuse of process
appropriation
community
complainant
defamation
emotional distress
false light in the public eye
fraud (deceit)

intentional infliction
  of emotional distress
invasion of privacy
libel
malice
malicious prosecution
material
misrepresentation

probable cause
public disclosure of private facts
publication
reckless infliction of emotional
  distress
slander
umbrella policy
unreasonable intrusion

▮ PROBLEMS

In the following hypotheticals, identify the intentional tort(s) committed, if any, and support your answers.

1. Eugene Bagley III was an aspiring literature student at the state university. He had submitted several short stories and poems to *Rhapsody*, a college literary magazine. Steve lived in Eugene's dormitory and had a reputation for playing pranks on fellow dorm residents. Steve wrote a fake letter of rejection on *Rhapsody* letterhead, which a friend had taken from the magazine's office supplies. The letter was a scathing indictment of Eugene's work as plagiarism and amateurish. The letter threatened to notify the English department and academic dean about the alleged plagiarism. Steve signed the editor of the magazine's name. When Eugene received the letter, he became physically ill and had to visit the university hospital for medication to sleep and concentrate.

2. Mike was a salesperson at a local hardware store. Samuel was a customer looking to buy exterior paint for his storage shed. When Samuel told Mike he needed paint that could be used on metal siding, Mike indicated a wood paint. Samuel inquired about this, but Mike said that it was not just for wood but for any surface. In fact,

the paint would not adhere to any surface other than wood. Mike had worked in the store for only a few days and knew nothing about any of the paint supplies. Samuel bought the paint and applied it. Within two weeks, the paint peeled off.

3. Maria is an honors student at a small college. She is worried that another student, Alex, will take her place as number one in the class and apply for the same scholarship she desperately needs to continue her schooling. Maria calls Alex and pretends that she is a nurse calling from the emergency room of Alex's hometown local hospital. Maria tells Alex that his mother was in an accident and was gravely injured, and that he needs to come there right away. Alex is distraught and returns home immediately. He is so upset he totally forgets about the scholarship deadline and fails to apply.

4. Celeste and David are involved in a bitter custody dispute over their children. After losing the marital home, Celeste decides she is not going to let her husband get one more thing from her. Celeste calls the police after carefully coaching her children and complains that her children have been repeatedly sexually abused by David. David is

immediately arrested at work. Celeste is granted temporary custody over the children. David is later cleared of the false charges of sexual abuse.

5. Newspaper sales have been declining for weeks for the *Gazette Herald*. The owner of the paper knows that people are curious and would like to know more about the personal lives of the residents in town. A reporter is sent to attend meetings of Alcoholics Anonymous and plastic surgeon Dr. John Glassgow's seminars on facial rejuvenation. A new feature is included in the paper, "What You Don't Know about Your Neighbors." A list of those attending Alcoholics Anonymous and those attending the doctor's seminars who are considering plastic surgery is published. As expected, sales of the newspaper increase immediately.

▌ REVIEW QUESTIONS

1. Define *fraud* and *misrepresentation*. How are they similar? Distinguishable? Is intent required? What objectives must the tortfeasor have in giving false information?

2. Describe malicious prosecution and abuse of process. Can you determine why they are separate intentional torts? What makes criminal prosecution groundless? What is malice? Must the victim win in criminal litigation? What injury is required? For abuse of process, how can legal proceedings be misused? For what purposes?

3. What are the four varieties of invasion of privacy in tort law? How is each defined? Do you see any similarities between invasion of privacy and any other intentional torts?

4. What are the two aspects of defamation? How are they comparable? What is publication? What makes a statement false and defamatory? What is the role of truth in defamation?

5. In the field of intentional torts, what is the intentional infliction of emotional distress? What is mental anguish? What constitutes outrageous conduct? When is intent necessary?

▌ HELPFUL WEBSITES

This chapter deals with intentional torts and injuries to persons. To learn more about personal injury law, the following sites can be accessed:

General Information

www.personalinjury.com
www.lawnewsnetwork.com

Publications

www.lawtechnews.com
www.nocall.org
www.nylj.com

Medical Information

www.nlm.nih.gov
www.webmd.com

STUDENT COMPANION WEBSITE
For additional cases and study materials, please go to www.cengagebrain.com

Chapter 8

Intentional Torts: Injuries to Property

THE BIGGEST MISTAKES PARALEGALS MAKE AND HOW TO AVOID THEM

"You're Only Human"

Juan was not much of a joiner. Sure, he had been in a few clubs at school and was a soccer player too, but he thought of himself as more of a loner now. As a paralegal, he came to the office each day, did his work well, and then went home. He was curious about the postings in the employee break room for pickup basketball games against the district attorney's office, and he regularly received emails about after-hours

drinks at a bar in the building where he worked. Sometimes he would be invited to other after-work events by coworkers, but he always turned them down.

Never showing up for anything created the impression that he was antisocial and had no life other than work. Sensing that he was the cause of rumors about his personal life, one day he asked to join the others at the bar after work. Imagine his surprise

(continues)

at how much "shop talk" was exchanged on those stools in the bar, in a more relaxed setting than that in the office. Even the attorneys felt free to exchange information that Juan would never have heard nesting in his cube at the office. Juan realized he had been very foolish for thinking the work day ended when he went home each night.

Lesson Learned: Constantly turning down invitations to after-hours activities with coworkers can cause problems. In addition to avoiding fueling the rumor mill, it is always better to show up once in a while to learn something about your officemates in a relaxed environment. Socializing encourages communication, trust, and cooperation among coworkers. Hob-knobbing with executives can lead to career advancement. On both levels, it demonstrates being a team player, as well as empathy through the sharing of personal information. In short, it shows that you are a real person—human like everyone else.

▌ INTRODUCTION

The previous two chapters (Chapters 6 and 7) examined intentional torts involving injuries to persons (a person's duty to others). This chapter deals with injury to the rights of a property owner or possessor.

This chapter includes:

▶ Intentional torts dealing with injuries to property rights
▶ Trespass to land
▶ Toxic torts
▶ Trespass to chattel
▶ Conversion
▶ Slander of title
▶ Commercial disparagement
▶ Defamation by computer

▌ TRESPASS TO LAND

Trespass is an ancient concept in tort law. In medieval English law, torts originated from trespass and trespass on the case. Under modern U.S. law, trespass is recognized in two varieties: trespass to land and trespass to chattel.

Elements of Trespass to Land

trespass | A wrongful entry onto another person's property.

Trespass to land occurs when a tortfeasor enters upon a landowner's real estate without consent. The tortfeasor trespasses when he or she intentionally acts in such a way as to violate the landowner's exclusive right to use the land. The elements of trespass to land are threefold:

1. Unauthorized entry upon another person's real estate
2. Tortfeasor's intent to enter without consent
3. Tortfeasor's actions interfering with the landowner's exclusive right to use the land (possession)

Entry Defined

The tortfeasor must enter upon a landowner's real estate without permission. **Entry** occurs when the tortfeasor acts so as to interfere with the landowner's exclusive right to use the property. For example, taking a shortcut and walking across someone's front lawn constitutes entry, because the tortfeasor entered the land. Also, entry happens if a person throws trash in a neighbor's backyard, because the trash depositor placed an unwanted substance (trash) on the land. Both of these examples include the interference element. The owner of the front lawn cannot utilize his or her property exclusively if someone is walking across it. The neighbor's use of his or her backyard is severely hampered by the accumulation of another's trash. The tortfeasor's conduct in either case has disrupted the landowner's exclusive use of the real estate. This is the foundation of trespass to land.

entry | The act of entering (as upon real property).

No Actual Harm Required

It is important to note that under trespass law, the unauthorized entry need not cause any damage to the real estate. It is sufficient that the transgression occurred. Trespass law presumes that injury has happened simply because the tortfeasor has interfered with the landowner's use of the realty. Thus, simply walking across someone's front lawn without permission is trespass to land, although no actual harm arises from the conduct. These types of trespasses to land are often called *technical trespasses*. Courts generally award only nominal damages. In technical trespass cases, courts usually award a minimal sum, such as $1 in nominal damages, because no actual injury resulted from the trespass. The judgment award is ceremonial or symbolic of the technical invasion of the landowner's property rights.

As a practical matter, few lawsuits involve technical trespasses. It is simply too expensive to litigate a trespass action when no injury has resulted. Litigants frequently speak of suing "as a matter of principle," but plaintiffs rarely are willing to spend the time and money required for such an action.

Unauthorized Entry

The entry must be without consent. This essentially translates as a permission element. For instance, if a farmer allows a person to cross his fields to reach a lake in which to fish, then that person has not committed trespass—the entry was authorized. Similarly, homeowners may invite visitors onto their premises by extending an implied welcome, such as clearing sidewalks of snow up to a house door or placing doorbells outside the doors. This suggests that people may come upon the property to speak with the landowner. Consequently, door-to-door salespersons would not necessarily be trespassing if they had reason to believe that the homeowner welcomed their presence. However, if the yard were fenced in, with a "no soliciting" sign displayed, then the salespersons would know that they did not have permission to enter the property.

Sometimes persons have a lawful right to enter upon another's land. For example, if the landowner gives an easement to a utility company to install cell towers on his or her property, then the utility company has the legal right to enter the premises to install and maintain the towers. Accordingly, no trespass to land could happen. Also, a process server, such as the county sheriff, generally has the legal right to enter the defendant's land to deliver a plaintiff's complaint and summons. No trespass to land would occur in such an instance.

One's lawful right to be upon another's premises may be withdrawn, however. Consider the example of the patron of a store. Customers are invited to come upon the premises to spend money. Suppose one such individual becomes disruptive, annoying other shoppers and employees. The store manager could demand that the agitator leave immediately. At this point, the customer becomes a trespasser, because remaining means that he or she is present upon another's land without consent. Although the customer was originally invited into the store as a patron, once he or she is ordered to leave, trespass occurs.

Intentional Interference

The tortfeasor must have intended to enter the landowner's real estate without consent. Thus, if Twila is forced to cross a neighbor's front yard to escape a pursuing wild animal, she has not committed trespass to land. Twila did not intend to cross her neighbor's property without permission; rather, she was essentially forced across by the chasing animal. However, if she deliberately strolls across her neighbor's yard, the entry was intentional.

Possession: Landowner's Exclusive Right to Use

exclusive right | A right granted to no one else.

exclusive right of possession | A landowner's right to use his or her property without interference from other persons.

To constitute trespass to land, the tortfeasor's unauthorized entry must interfere with the land owner's **exclusive right** to use his or her realty. This is sometimes called the **exclusive right of possession,** which entitles the landowner to use the property without anyone else's interference. Recall the illustrations from the discussion of entry: the neighbor could not use his or her land exclusively if someone else's trash was being dumped on it. Nor could someone use his or her front lawn exclusively if another person walked across it.

This exclusivity requirement may at first appear overly harsh. One might well ask what wrong has been done just by crossing someone's land. Trespass intends to protect one's real estate in much the same way as assault and battery are intended to protect one's person. The objective is protection from undesired interferences. In this respect, trespass seeks merely to protect one's realty from other people encroaching upon it, just as assault and battery are meant to deter unwanted physical contact.

Trespass above and below Land: Is the Sky the Limit?

Trespass above and below Land: Is the Sky the Limit? Trespass to land may occur not only upon the surface of the realty, but also above and below it. In property law, a Latin phrase summarizes the extent of one's ownership of land: *cujus est solum ejus est usque ad coelum* ("he who has the soil owns upward unto heaven and downward to perdition"). Thus, it is possible for trespass to occur in the air above one's land. For instance, if a utility company erects wires across one's land without consent, this would constitute trespass to land, because the landowner owns the air above the soil. This could present insurmountable difficulties for aircraft. Fortunately, modern common law implies an exception for aircraft to fly over private property.

Similarly, one owns the resources under the earth. Although this enters into the complex area of oil, gas, and mineral law (within which special legal theories have evolved), it may be said generally that one owns the mineral resources beneath one's real estate. Accordingly, if someone mines under a person's land without permission, trespass to land has occurred. Cave exploration cases provide an interesting aspect of this theory. In a famous Indiana court case, *Marengo Cave Co. v. Ross,* 212 Ind. 624, 10 N.E.2d 917 (1937), the Supreme Court of Indiana stated that it was a trespass for the cave company to charge admission for tourists to explore caves below the surface of another landowner's property.

The sanctity of land is an ancient aspect of the human psyche. For millennia, people have used physical force and, as civilization progressed, force of law to protect against invasions. Today, trespass to land remains an active intentional tort, as the following hypotheticals demonstrate.

HYPOTHETICALS

Burrough Excavating Company was digging a basement for a new home. Burrough's backhoe operator dumped the dirt on a vacant lot next to the construction site. This lot was owned by Liza, who never gave Burrough permission to use her lot. Has Burrough committed trespass to land against Liza?

The elements line up nicely: Liza did not consent to Burrough's dirt dumping, and so Burrough engaged in unauthorized entry upon another's realty. Burrough obviously intended this entry, as the backhoe operator dumped the dirt on Liza's lot. This dumping interfered with Liza's exclusive use of her property, because she will now have to contend with the dirt pile if she wishes to use her lot. Therefore, Burrough has committed trespass to land against Liza.

* * *

Consider another hypothetical. Bryan owns a house next to Elizabeth. Elizabeth planted several oak trees on her property with branches that hang over a fence

(continues)

separating her property from Bryan's. Bryan thought the trees were unsightly and trimmed the limbs that hung over onto his yard. He did not ask Elizabeth for permission to remove the limbs. Has a trespass occurred?

First, who has trespassed? By allowing her tree branches to cross over onto Bryan's property, Elizabeth committed unauthorized entry onto another's land without consent. Her trees interfered with Bryan's exclusive right of possession, because the branches obstructed Bryan's use of this part of his property. Recall, too, that Bryan owns to the top of the sky under the *ad coelum* doctrine discussed earlier. Anything encroaching upon his airspace constitutes entry. Intent may be implied, as Elizabeth knew the trees crossed the fence but did nothing to remove the overhanging limbs. Thus, Elizabeth has trespassed upon Bryan's land.

Somewhat more problematic is the inverse inquiry: Did Bryan trespass against Elizabeth by pruning the trees? Because the trees grew on Elizabeth's property, Bryan's trimming (without permission) encroached upon Elizabeth's use of her trees. But does this constitute unauthorized entry onto another's land? The branches hung over onto Bryan's property, so he did not actually enter upon Elizabeth's land to cut the limbs. He was simply "defending" his property from the encroaching branches. Accordingly, Bryan did not commit trespass to land against Elizabeth.

Recent trespass actions have involved one of the most complex and dynamic developing areas of tort law—namely, toxic tort litigation. The next section discusses this type of trespass.

▌ TOXIC TORT ACTIONS

A significant percentage of modern tort litigation is devoted to actions involving toxic chemicals, nuclear waste, pollution, hazardous waste disposal and transportation, and other environmentally sensitive issues. These are sometimes referred to as **toxic tort actions.** These lawsuits cover causes of action involving the following: trespass to land, negligence, absolute liability for ultrahazardous substances, products liability, and nuisance. This chapter focuses on the trespass-to-land aspects of toxic tort litigation.

Nature of the Problem

For much of this century, toxic waste disposal was considered simple. Manufacturers or chemical processors applied a centuries-old approach: "out of sight, out of mind." Hazardous waste was simply buried, dumped into waterways, or burned. Much toxic waste found its way into public and private landfills, rivers,

toxic tort actions | Actions involving toxic chemicals, pollution, hazardous waste disposal and transportation, and other environmentally sensitive issues. Many tort theories, including trespass to land, negligence, absolute liability for ultrahazardous substances, products liability, and nuisance, apply.

and smoke-belching incinerators. This did not eliminate the noxious nature of the waste products; it simply shifted the problem to another location. As the years passed, barrels buried at the underground sites rusted and leaked, sending lethal seepage through the soil, contaminating underground water supplies, and injuring people who drank contaminated well water. Toxic burial leakage also percolated from underground through springs, exposing innocent bystanders to carcinogenic or otherwise lethal substances in surface waters. Rivers and streams simply carried the sludge to haunt downstream landowners, who came into contact with the poisons through irrigation or otherwise working with the polluted waters. Residents near the incineration plants suffered a variety of lung ailments from poisonous air pollutants. Just some of the common causes of injury in toxic tort actions are mold contamination, benzene, PCBs, formaldehyde, pesticides, silica, toxins in air and water, and asbestos.

Traditionally, all of these intrusions fell neatly within the intentional tort of trespass to land. Nuisance provided neighboring landowners another cause of action with which to litigate against the industrial toxic polluters. Absolute liability also applied under the ultrahazardous substances theory. Negligence lent further legal aid to plaintiffs seeking relief against injuries from the unwanted and toxic invaders.

THE CASE OF THE POLLUTING PLUME

This is a case of "buyer beware." The owners of real property find themselves in the middle of a huge lawsuit with the California Department of Toxic Substances Control. Dry cleaning chemicals from the prior businesses located on the property leached into the groundwater and contaminated it. Who should bear the cost of cleanup?

CALIFORNIA DEPARTMENT OF TOXIC SUBSTANCES CONTROL, Plaintiff,

v.

PAYLESS CLEANERS; College Cleaners; Heidinger Cleaners; Norge Village Cleaners; Defendants, et al.,

United States District Court, E.D. California

368 F. Supp. 2d 1069

March 4, 2005

This action arises out of a two-mile wide perchloro-ethylene ("PCE") "plume" located south of the central business district of Chico, California. On October 31, 2002, the California Department of Toxic Substances Control ("DTSC") filed a cost recovery action against various individuals and companies alleging rights under the Comprehensive Environmental Response, Compensation, and Liability Act (CERCLA), 42 U.S.C. §§ 9601 *et seq.* and state law based claims. The DTSC named several dry cleaning businesses as well as the property owners of the sites where those businesses operated upon its belief that the PCE emanated from those businesses. Among the defendants are the Peters. The DTSC seeks to recover its costs in investigating and remediating the contaminated groundwater.

The Peters are the owners of property in the City of Chico from which hazardous substances, including PCE, were allegedly released when a dry cleaner business operated on the property. The Peters bring suit against Maytag as Norge Corporation's ("Norge")

(continues)

successor-in-interest, which, according to the Peters, manufactured and provided the dry cleaning equipment and PCE used on their property.

The Peters allege that, prior to their ownership, third party defendant CAVA, Inc. ("CAVA") constructed, owned, and operated Norge Village Cleaner ("Dry Cleaner") on the property at issue. Pursuant to a franchise agreement, CAVA purchased and used dry cleaning machines and solvents for their dry cleaning operation from Norge, who designed and manufactured the machines and solvents. The dry cleaning machines were designed to use, process and discharge solvents containing PCE. Norge also decided and controlled the layout of the Dry Cleaner, including where the machines were installed and the location of floor drains for disposal of waste water.

According to the Peters, Norge installed the machines to use, process, and dispose of wastewater laden with PCE through a floor piping connected with the City of Chico's sewer system.

Maytag contends that the Peters fail to allege sufficient facts to support a claim for liability under CERCLA.

CERCLA allocates the rights and responsibilities of those involved in hazardous waste remediation. In creating CERCLA Congress provided a right of recovery for potentially responsible parties ("PRPs") who have incurred hazardous waste cleanup costs by expressly allowing a contribution action against other PRPs. Thus, a PRP who is found to be jointly and severally liable for response costs can sue to recover those expenses paid in excess of its own liability by spreading the costs to other PRPs. The Peters bring suit against Maytag for contribution in their capacity as a PRP to the DTSC.

To establish a prima facie case against Maytag, the Peters must show that: (1) PCE is a hazardous substance; (2) there has been a release of PCE at the Peters' facility; (3) the release or threatened release caused the Plaintiffs to incur response costs; and (4) defendants are within one of four classes of persons subject to CERCLA's liability provisions. Maytag challenges only the last of these elements, asserting that it does not fall within any of the four classes as required to be held liable.

The Peters allege that Maytag "designed, manufactured, and actually installed the dry cleaning machines that produced PCE at the Dry Cleaner and/or CAVA."

Maytag's transaction can be described only as the sale of a useful good which, through its normal use, created a waste byproduct.

Although the machines were designed to discharge waste water through a hose, the Peters could have connected that hose to and collected the waste in a tank or disposed of the waste through other means. In sum, these facts do not by themselves establish Maytag's actual authority and control over the disposal of the PCE, rather, that control remained with the Peters.

The Peters allege that Maytag physically installed the dry cleaning machines, including "physically connecting the machines' discharge piping" to the building drain, which was itself connected to the sewer system. This fact, along with the facts concerning Maytag's role as the franchisor, establishes that it had the authority to and did actually control the disposal of the waste water laden with PCE.

If Maytag chose the locations of the floor drains and then inspected to ensure that the waste water was disposed into the sewer system, then the Peters did not exercise independent decisionmaking regarding the disposal, but rather, at the very least, shared this control with Maytag. Although these facts alone seem sufficient to subject Maytag to liability, the Peters present even more compelling allegations that establish Maytag's control over the PCE disposal.

Accordingly, the Peters can seek contribution from Maytag.

CASE QUESTIONS

1. What is the purpose of CERCLA?
2. Has the purpose of CERCLA been met by this case?

Toxic Trespass

Trespass to land occurs when toxic substances enter upon another's property. The trespass elements remain the same:

1. Unauthorized entry upon another person's real estate
2. Tortfeasor's intent to enter without consent
3. Tortfeasor's actions interfering with the landowner's exclusive right to use the land (possession)

In the case of toxic substances, the unauthorized entry is seepage or accumulation of the hazardous material on the victim's land. Few owners consent to having toxins placed over, upon, or under their realty. Most people want such materials to be taken as far away from them as possible.

The tortfeasor's intent to enter without permission may be implied from the disposal method used. For instance, toxic waste buried in metal barrels will, over time, rust through and seep into the underground soil, unless the material is contained in an isolated fashion, such as an underground concrete crypt. If the tortfeasor failed to take sufficient precautions to prevent subterranean seepage, then the intent to trespass may be implied. Another example of implied intent is dumping toxic fluids into waterways. The tortfeasor desired the river or stream to carry the dangerous substances downstream, which would plainly deposit the toxins on the shores of other people's property.

The tortfeasor's interference with the plaintiff's exclusive possession of his or her land is equally clear. The toxic residues are a highly offensive and potent invasion, making some real estate uninhabitable. A more significant illustration of trespass would be difficult to imagine.

When landowners' underground water supplies are contaminated with buried toxic waste seepage, trespass to land occurs. A quick review of the elements shows that they are readily satisfied. Many cases in the court reports tell sad tales of families irreparably harmed through long-term consumption of chemically contaminated well water, poisoned as a result of improper underground waste disposal.

THE CASE OF THE NUISANCE LAKE

The owner of property near an artificial lake brought this action for nuisance and trespass against both the owner of the lake and the operator of a textile mill. The plaintiff claims that the mill discharged wastewater, which polluted the lake. The plaintiff further alleges that the owners of the lake allowed this to occur, thereby harming the plaintiff's neighboring property. Even though the plaintiff's expert testified concerning the contaminants in the lake, the court was not willing to make the inference that the plaintiff's land was actually contaminated.

(continues)

RUSSELL CORPORATION
v.
SULLIVAN et al., AVONDALE MILLS, INC.
Supreme Court of Alabama
2001 WL 29264
January 12, 2001

Russell and Avondale Mills operate textile plants in Alexander City. As part of their operations, they discharge directly into the Sugar Creek Plant large volumes of wastewater containing dyes used in processing textiles. After the wastewater is treated at the Sugar Creek Plant, it is discharged into Sugar Creek at a rate of five to six million gallons a day. This output flows through Sugar Creek, runs into Elkahatchee Creek, and, eventually, into Lake Martin. The plaintiffs are all residents of the Raintree subdivision located on Lake Martin. [APCo owns Lake Martin, a manmade lake APCo uses to generate power.]

The wastewater from Russell and Avondale constitutes 70% to 80% of the water treated daily at the Sugar Creek Plant. This wastewater contains dyes, salts, acid surfactants, and heavy metals, making the water difficult to treat. At least one type of dye treated at the Sugar Creek Plant, azo dye, has been shown to have carcinogenic properties. The plaintiffs presented evidence indicating that the dyes, which are resistant to fading, are also difficult to remove from the wastewater during treatment. As a result of problems in removing color from the treated water, the City of Alexander City installed a chlorination/dechlorination facility at the Sugar Creek Plant.

The Sugar Creek Plant uses an activated-sludge process to treat the wastewater. In that process, the waste is combined with oxygen and bacteria; it then forms a sludge that is removed from the water. The remaining water is decontaminated and is then discharged into Sugar Creek.

Testimony at trial indicated that the plaintiffs noticed the [floating sediment] flocs floating in the lake water near their property. At times, they claim, the water was so stained by the dyes that it would color T-shirts. No evidence was presented to indicate that the dyes or any of the components released by Russell and Avondale in their wastewater were actually found on any of the plaintiffs' properties. The plaintiffs relied on the testimony that waves and high waters could wash the materials ashore. The plaintiffs testified that because the water in Lake Martin is contaminated, their property is not as valuable as it could have been.

The plaintiffs' action against APCo rests on the theory that APCo has a duty to keep Lake Martin clean, and that it breached that duty by allowing Russell and Avondale to discharge contaminants into Lake Martin.

Trespass requires an intentional act by the defendant. In order for one to be liable to another for trespass, the person must intentionally enter upon land in the possession of another or the person must intentionally cause some "substance" or "thing" to enter upon another's land.

The plaintiffs argue that APCo committed trespass by allowing Russell and Avondale to discharge contaminants into Lake Martin and then by allowing those contaminants to remain on the bottom of the lake. In this case, there is no agency relationship between APCo, on the one hand, and Russell and Avondale, on the other. No evidence was presented to indicate that APCo directed Russell and Avondale to discharge their waste in any manner or to indicate that APCo aided or participated in the discharge. Therefore, there was no intentional act by APCo to support a claim of trespass.

APCo operates Lake Martin pursuant to a license issued by the Federal Energy Regulatory Commission ("FERC"). During the trial, the plaintiffs, over APCo's objection, placed that license in evidence.

> "In the construction, maintenance, or operation of the project, *the Licensee shall be responsible for, and shall take reasonable measures to prevent,* soil erosion on lands adjacent to streams or other waters, stream sedimentation, and *any form of water or air pollution. . . .*"

Where a plant discharges effluent into a stream that ultimately runs into a reservoir created by a dam, the owner of the reservoir cannot be liable for maintaining a nuisance, absent evidence indicating that it authorized or participated in the deposit of pollutants or that it had control over the deposits. The only prong of this test that arguably might apply to APCo is the "control-over-the-deposits" prong. However, as previously noted, that control cannot be grounded upon the FERC license charging APCo with a duty to take reasonable measures to prevent water pollution. The record is devoid of any other basis for concluding that APCo had any control over the activities of Russell and Avondale.

We therefore reverse the trial court's judgment as to APCo and render judgment for APCo on both the trespass claim and the nuisance claim.

In this case, whether water actually splashed onto the plaintiffs' property is sharply contested. In summary, several conclusions urged by the plaintiffs are unsupported by evidence. The ultimate conclusion that any chemicals were deposited onto the plaintiffs' properties is, at best, speculative.

The lack of scientific evidence indicating the presence of any chemicals causing "actual substantial damage" to the plaintiffs' properties or to support any of Dr. Gould's opinions is fatal to the plaintiffs' trespass claims.

"A 'nuisance' is anything that works hurt, inconvenience or damage to another. The fact that the act done may otherwise be lawful does not keep it from being a nuisance. The inconvenience complained of must not be fanciful or such as would affect only one of fastidious taste, but it should be such as would affect an ordinary reasonable man." Therefore, although Russell and Avondale argue that their actions were in accordance with state and federal regulations and that they were permissible under various permits, the plaintiffs may still maintain an action against Russell and Avondale if they can prove the elements of nuisance.

In Alabama, a nuisance can be either private or public. "A public nuisance is one which damages all persons who come within the sphere of its operation, though it may vary in its effects on individuals. A private nuisance is one limited in its injurious effects to one or a few individuals."

The distinction between a private and a public nuisance is an important one. "A private nuisance gives a right of action to the person injured" while "a public nuisance gives no right of action to any individual, but must be abated by a process instituted in the name of the state." In order to support an individual's cause of action for a public nuisance, the nuisance must cause a "special damage" that is different in "kind and degree from [the damage] suffered by the public in general." Therefore, if the nuisance allegedly created by the discharge of wastewater into Sugar Creek, and ultimately into Lake Martin, is a public one, the plaintiffs in this case must show that the discharge has caused them special damage, i.e., damage that is different than that suffered by others.

The plaintiffs in the present case, however, have presented no evidence indicating such special damage. The plaintiffs alleged that Russell's and Avondale's actions resulted in the loss of the use and enjoyment of Lake Martin.

The plaintiffs claim that the nuisance they suffered was a private nuisance.

Russell and Avondale correctly argue that the nuisance, if any, is a public nuisance, because, they say, the alleged nuisance is in the water of Lake Martin, a public waterway whose bed is owned solely by APCo. The discharge of contaminants into a public body of water constitutes a public nuisance. Russell and Avondale argue that the plaintiffs never proved that the alleged nuisance prevented them from using or enjoying their "own" property. While the plaintiffs offered evidence that they were unable to use and enjoy the lake, the use and enjoyment of a public area is a public right. Any nuisance caused by the discharge of contaminated wastewater into Lake Martin is a public, not a private, nuisance.

Because the plaintiffs expressly waived any claim to recovery under a public-nuisance theory, thereby avoiding the necessity of proving that they suffered special damage not suffered by members of the general public, it is unnecessary to address whether the record contains substantial evidence of such damage.

The trial court erred in denying Russell, Avondale, and APCo's motion for a judgment as a matter of law. Therefore, its judgment is reversed and a judgment is rendered in favor of Russell, Avondale, and APCo.

(continues)

CASE QUESTIONS

1. Explain the difference between a public and a private nuisance.
2. Why was no trespass found in this case?

Importance of Environmental Statutes

Aside from the torts of trespass, nuisance, absolute liability, and negligence, there are a variety of federal, state, and local statutes regulating environmental toxins. In addition, there are international environmental agreements. One important federal statute is the Toxic Substances Control Act. This act regulates the manufacture, distribution, processing, use, and disposal of hazardous materials. Detailed record keeping regarding the hazardous materials must be maintained, 15 U.S.C. § 2601 *et seq.* (1992). The Hazardous Materials Transportation Act establishes strict requirements for transporters of hazardous waste. Detailed record keeping is required to ensure compliance with the act, 49 U.S.C. §§ 1801–1812 (1992). Another federal statute, the Comprehensive Environmental Response, Compensation and Liability Act (CERCLA), addresses any "imminently hazardous chemical substance or mixture" and allows the federal Environmental Protection Agency (EPA) to file civil lawsuits when the use of such a material will pose imminent risk to health or the environment and the EPA has not issued a final rule to protect against such risk. There are countless other laws to protect the environment.

Trespass to land is one type of trespass action; trespass to chattel is the other.

■ TRESPASS TO CHATTEL

trespass to chattel | Occurs when the tortfeasor intentionally deprives or interferes with the chattel owner's possession or exclusive use of personal property. The tortfeasor's possession or interference must be unauthorized, which means that the owner cannot have consented.

chattel | Item of personal property. Any property other than land.

A tortfeasor commits **trespass to chattel** when he or she possesses someone's personal property without consent. **Chattel** is personal property, as opposed to real property, which is land. Chattel is any property, other than land, that is movable and that can be seen and touched. Animals are included in this definition. An automobile, a textbook, a pet dog or cat, and a desk are examples of chattels. Trespass to chattel has elements similar to those of trespass to land:

1. Unauthorized possession of, or interference with the use of, another individual's personal property
2. Intent to deprive (or interfere with) the owner's possession or exclusive use of his or her chattel

Unauthorized Possession of Another's Chattel

Suppose Nadene takes a neighbor's textbook during class. Unless Nadene obtained the neighbor's consent before seizing the text, Nadene has engaged in unauthorized possession of another's personal property. The book's owner did not give Nadene permission to possess the chattel. When a tortfeasor takes possession of another's personal property without consent, this is sometimes described as the act of **dispossession.**

Consent may be implied under certain circumstances. For instance, if Alfred gives his car keys to a friend, the implication is that the friend may use Alfred's motor vehicle. Similarly, hotel guests may presume that the management intended them to use the electricity, water, soap, and tissues supplied to the rooms. However, if a patron takes the hotel's pillows, sheets, and towels, this would be unauthorized possession, as staying in a hotel does not implicitly entitle guests to keep such items.

dispossession | Wrongfully taking away a person's property by force, trick, or misuse of the law.

Unauthorized Interference with Use

It is possible to trespass to chattel without actually taking possession of the personal property from its rightful owner. Interference with the chattel owner's use of the property is sufficient. For instance, if a tortfeasor purposely fed Reggie's prize hogs a contaminated food, so that the hogs became ill and lost weight, then the tortfeasor engaged in unconsented interference with Reggie's use of the animals. If Cherrie's landlord shuts off the electricity to her apartment without permission, then this would also constitute unauthorized interference with the use of her personal property (provided, of course, that Cherrie had paid her electric bill).

THE CASE OF THE PERSONAL-PROPERTY PET

Frequently, legal decisions must define exactly how property is characterized under the law. In this case, man's best friend is defined as personal property, nothing more. A dog's owner has sued the treating veterinarian, and seeks emotional damages as a result of alleged malpractice.

KOESTER

v.

VCA ANIMAL HOSPITAL

Court of Appeals of Michigan
244 Mich. App. 173, 624 N.W.2d 209
December 26, 2000

Plaintiff left his dog at defendant VCA's kennel for a weekend. Plaintiff left explicit instructions not to use a collar on the dog because of a salivary gland problem for which VCA had previously treated the pet. Upon returning for the dog, plaintiff noticed that the dog's neck area was swollen. Within a few days, when the dog continued to exhibit swelling in the neck area, plaintiff returned to defendant VCA.

Defendant Field, a veterinarian, treated the dog by draining its enlarged gland and bandaging its neck and head. When plaintiff returned to pick up his dog after the procedure, he noticed that the dog appeared to have trouble breathing and asked defendant Field whether the bandages were too tight. Field responded that the dog would be fine once it calmed down. Later that same day, plaintiff left the dog alone for 10 to 15 minutes to run an errand. When plaintiff returned home, he discovered the dog laying motionless on the floor, having apparently choked to death. An autopsy determined that the dog suffocated to death because the bandages were wrapped too tightly.

Plaintiff brought the instant negligence action pleading damages that included plaintiff's pain and

(continues)

suffering, extreme fright, shock, mortification, and the loss of the society and companionship of his dog. Defendants moved for summary disposition pursuant to MCR 2.116(C)(8), for failure to state a claim upon which relief could be granted, arguing that plaintiff was not entitled to the damages pleaded as a matter of law. The trial court agreed, holding that emotional damages for the loss of a dog did not exist.

On appeal, plaintiff alleges that the trial court erred in summarily disposing of his negligence claim. Plaintiff primarily argues that companion animals should not be considered merely personal property. In support of his argument, plaintiff offers the alleged practice of other jurisdictions which have acknowledged the value of companion animals by awarding damages for emotional distress associated with the loss of a pet. Although we recognize that domesticated pets have value and sentimentality associated with them which may not compare with that of other personal property, we cannot agree with plaintiff. In this matter, plaintiff pleaded damages of emotional distress and loss of society and companionship of his dog. Pets have long been considered personal property in Michigan jurisprudence (see *Ten Hopen v. Walker*, 96 Mich 236, 239; 55 NW 657 (1893)). Consequently, the issue before this court is whether plaintiff can properly plead and recover for emotional injuries he allegedly suffered as a consequence of his property being damaged by defendants' negligence. There is no Michigan precedent which permits the recovery of damages for emotional injuries allegedly suffered as a consequence of property damage. Plaintiff requests that we allow such recovery when a pet is the property that is damaged, arguing that pets have evolved in our modern society to a status which is not consistent with their characterization as a "chattel." Although this court is very sympathetic to plaintiff's position, we defer to the Legislature to create such a remedy.

There are several factors that must be considered before expanding or creating tort liability including, but not limited to, legislative and judicial policies. In this case, there is no statutory, judicial, or other persuasive authority that compels or permits this court to take the drastic action proposed by plaintiff. Case law on this issue from sister states is not consistent, persuasive, or sufficient precedent. We refuse to create a remedy where there is no legal structure in which to give it support.

We decline to allow the recovery of emotional distress damages arising from negligence committed against plaintiff's pet; therefore, plaintiff's complaint failed to plead legally cognizable damages and was properly dismissed by the trial court.

Affirmed.

CASE QUESTIONS

1. Why could not the dog owner recover for emotional distress?
2. Do you think tort liability should be expanded to cover emotional injuries for damages to property? Explain your answer.

Intent to Deprive or Interfere

To commit trespass to chattel, the tortfeasor must intend to interfere with or deprive the chattel owner of possession or the exclusive use of his or her personal property. Intent may be expressed, as it was when Nadene took her neighbor's book. It may also be implied under the circumstances. For example, assume that Cherrie's landlord changed the locks on her apartment door in order to lock her

TRESPASS TO LAND	TRESPASS TO CHATTEL
Unauthorized entry upon another person's real estate	Unauthorized possession of another individual's personal property *or* unauthorized interference with another's use of his or her chattel
Intent to enter without consent (no harm to land required)	Intent to dispossess or interfere with owner's use of his or her personal property
Interference with landowner's exclusive right to use land (possession)	Similar to conversion, which also requires tortfeasor to put dispossessed chattel to his or her own use

TABLE 8-1

Elements of trespass to land and trespass to chattel

out, although she had paid her rent and had done nothing to violate her rental agreement. This would imply the landlord's intent to deprive Cherrie of possession of her personal property inside the apartment. Her use of the chattels would definitely be hindered.

Similarly, lack of intent may be implied. For example, assume Bud found his neighbor's cow grazing along a public highway and took the animal to his barn for safekeeping until he could telephone the neighbor. Although Bud took possession of the cow without his neighbor's consent, Bud did not intend to interfere with the neighbor's use of the cow. Nor did he wish to deprive his neighbor of possession. Bud simply wished to protect the animal from harm. This is emphasized by his efforts to contact his neighbor to come claim the cow. Thus, Bud lacked intent to trespass to chattel.

Table 8-1 summarizes the elements of trespass to land and trespass to chattel.

▌CONVERSION

In the early history of tort law, trespass to chattel was frequently subject to litigation, often in cases involving domestic livestock. Court opinions from the nineteenth century abound. More recent cases, however, have tended to focus upon conversion, which is a similar but separate tort regarding chattel.

History

Conversion occurs when a tortfeasor, without consent, deprives an owner of possession of the owner's chattel and puts or *converts* the property to the tortfeasor's own use. It is essentially a broader version of trespass to chattel, but both torts developed separately.

Conversion evolved from the common law action of *trover*, which appeared in England during the fifteenth century as a specific type of trespass action. In

conversion | Any act that deprives an owner of property without that owner's permission and without just cause.

trover lawsuits, the court determined that the plaintiff, the chattel owner, had a legal right to possess the personal property (namely, because of ownership), and that the defendant, the tortfeasor, had taken possession of the chattel for his or her own use. Gradually, this element (taking for one's own use) was described in the English court opinions as "converting the property for one's own use." Thus, the term *conversion* began to replace *trover,* and the modern tort of conversion emerged.

Elements of Conversion

Under modern tort law, conversion consists of three elements:

1. Depriving the owner of possession of the chattel
2. Intent to deprive possession and convert the property to one's own use
3. The owner's nonconsent to the tortfeasor's possession and use of the chattel

Depriving of Possession

Under conversion, the tortfeasor must actually deprive the owner of possession of personal property. The common law usually employs the phrase "exercising dominion and control over the chattel that is inconsistent with the owner's right to exclusive use." This means that the tortfeasor controls another's personal property so as to prevent the owner from using it. For example, suppose Nadene took her neighbor's textbook and refused to return it. Nadene's "dominion and control" over the book prevents the neighbor from using his or her chattel.

Extent of Deprivation.
Normally, conversion is differentiated from trespass to chattel based upon the scope of the deprivation. With trespass to chattel, many courts have held that the deprivation need only be minor or temporary. With conversion, several courts have ruled that the deprivation must be so extensive as to suggest a desire to deprive the owner of possession permanently. There is considerable disagreement among different jurisdictions as to this issue, however. Most courts maintain that conversion has occurred simply because the tortfeasor deprived the owner of dominion and control over the chattel, regardless of length of time or permanent intent.

Methods of Depriving.
Deprivation of possession may occur in a variety of ways. *Physical possession* of the chattel is most common, although deprivation may happen through *damage or destruction* of the personal property. For instance, if someone plows under Kathy's garden to plant grass seed, this amounts to deprivation of possession, because Kathy can no longer use her vegetables. Similarly, if someone opens a window during a thunderstorm, and rain floods Sig's stereo, the injury has deprived Sig of the use of his chattel.

Deprivation may also take place simply through use. Some forms of personal property cannot be picked up and carried away. For instance, electricity, free-flowing liquids, and other intangible items are commonly defined as chattels under state laws called commercial codes. One possesses such things by using them. If Morgan, Colleen's neighbor, plugs his garage heater into her electric outlet without permission, and Colleen's electric bill suddenly soars, Morgan has deprived Colleen of dominion and control over her electricity. This translates as deprivation of possession.

Intent to Deprive and Convert to Own Use.

First of all, conversion requires that the tortfeasor must intend to deprive the owner of possession of his or her chattel. This is comparable to trespass to chattel. However, unlike trespass to chattel, conversion also requires that the tortfeasor convert the personal property to his or her own use. For example, assume Joey and Lisa are acquaintances at school. Then suppose that Joey found Lisa's earrings on a bench at the mall and knew they belonged to Lisa. Joey might keep the earrings until he saw Lisa at school later in the week, rather than seeking Lisa out immediately to return the earrings. Because Joey did not intend to use the earrings himself, he is not guilty of conversion. However, if Joey wore the earrings to the school dance, he would have converted them to his own use.

It is important to note that the tortfeasor does not have to injure the chattel to convert it. Conversion occurs simply because the owner has been deprived of the use of the personal property without having given permission. Injury occurs to the owner's right to exclusively use the chattel.

Lack of Consent.

Naturally, the owner cannot have granted permission to someone to use or possess the chattel. If Victoria allows a classmate to borrow her text overnight to study, then the classmate has not converted the book. Consent may be expressed, as in the book-borrowing situation, or it may be implied. For example, suppose that when Bob leaves his automobile at a mechanic's for an oil replacement the mechanic also repairs a broken valve and pipe. The mechanic did not convert Bob's property, because Bob impliedly gave the mechanic permission to possess the vehicle for repair purposes. Of course, Bob did not authorize the additional work, but that is a breach-of-contract question. However, if the mechanic went joy-riding in Bob's car after changing the oil, this would be conversion, because Bob did not implicitly consent to that use of his car.

Even though the chattel owner may have consented to a tortfeasor's possession, this permission may be revoked. This could result in a conversion. For example, Bob complains that he did not authorize the additional work done on his automobile, but he is willing to pay for the oil change, which he did request. The mechanic insists that Bob also pay for the unauthorized repairs and refuses

Ponzi scheme | Scam wherein investors are promised high payoffs for their investments. However, their money is not really invested, it is merely paid off with the money from the next investors.

to return Bob's car until he pays the extra amount. Because Bob did not agree to these additional charges, he insists that his vehicle be returned immediately. Thus, Bob has revoked the permission he originally gave the mechanic to possess the chattel. If the mechanic does not comply with Bob's demand, the mechanic will be liable for conversion.

THE CASE OF A PONZI SCHEME GONE BAD

Bernard L. Madoff's **Ponzi scheme** bilked many prominent investors out of their life savings. Madoff was criminally prosecuted for his actions and was sentenced to 150 years in prison. In addition, numerous civil suits followed in an effort to recoup some of the investors' lost money. Madoff and his investment company were forced into bankruptcy. The trustee in bankruptcy, whose job is to recover assets for creditors, has brought this action against several of the Madoff family members, claiming that any monies they received as a result of the Ponzi scheme should be returned to the creditors. This case addresses the torts of both trespass to chattel and conversion of chattel.

In re BERNARD L. MADOFF INVESTMENT SECURITIES LLC, Debtor
Irving H. Picard, as Trustee for the Liquidation of Bernard L. Madoff Investment Securities LLC, Plaintiff,
v.
Peter B. Madoff, Mark D. Madoff, Andrew H. Madoff, and Shana D. Madoff, Defendants
United States Bankruptcy Court, S.D. New York
458 B.R. 87
September 22, 2011

The instant complaint differs from all others connected to the Madoff Ponzi scheme in one significant respect: its named Defendants are Madoff's brother, two sons, and niece. As set forth in the complaint, the Defendants held senior management positions at Bernard L. Madoff Investment Securities, (BLMIS), which, the Bankruptcy Trustee asserts was "operated as if it was the family piggy bank," with the Defendants living in multi-million dollar homes and relying on BLMIS funds to pay for vacations, travel, and other personal expenses—all while failing to fulfill their responsibilities as high ranking employees of the business.

This failure was unsurprising given their close familial relationship with Madoff and proximity to BLMIS, both of which undergird the claim at the heart of the Trustee's Complaint: that if anyone was in a position to prevent Madoff's scheme, it was the Defendants, who, instead, stood by profiting mightily while allowing it to persist. The Defendants nevertheless steadfastly contend their involvement with BLMIS was entirely legitimate, and they, above all others, were betrayed by their family's patriarch.

The Trustee accordingly seeks to avoid and recover transfers made to the Defendants in the collective amount of over $198 million under various sections of the Bankruptcy Code (the "Code") and New York Debtor and Creditor Law (the "NYDCL"). In addition, the Trustee seeks tort damages for BLMIS by bringing claims under New York common law for breach of fiduciary duty, negligence, conversion, unjust enrichment, constructive trust, and accounting (the "Common Law Claims"). The complaint, however, contains some correctable pleading deficiencies, and will need to be amended in part in order to stand as a matter of law.

As a matter of law, the "Ponzi scheme presumption" establishes the debtors' fraudulent intent. There is a presumption of actual intent to defraud because "transfers made in the course of a Ponzi scheme could have been made for no purpose other than to hinder, delay or defraud creditors." This court finds most, but not all, of the allegations corresponding to the Constructive Fraudulent Transfers provide sufficient information to sustain the Trustee's **avoidance claims**. BLMIS did not receive "reasonably equivalent value" for any of the transfers alleged to be fraudulent.

Section 720 of New York's Business Corporation law expressly authorizes a corporation or bankruptcy trustee to sue the corporation's officers and directors for breach of fiduciary duty, including misappropriation or diversion of assets. . . . It follows, therefore, that the Trustee has standing to assert the Common Law Claims, to the extent these Claims belong to the BLMIS estate.

The Defendants in the instant proceeding are alleged to be fiduciaries and insiders of BLMIS. General partners, sole shareholders, and sole decision makers are "insiders" or fiduciaries. The complaint alleges that the Defendants were senior officers, directors, and compliance managers of BLMIS.

The Trustee has sufficiently alleged Count Eighteen of the complaint, which states that in order "to compensate BLMIS for the amount of monies the [Defendants] diverted from BLMIS for their own benefit, it is necessary for the [Defendants] to provide an accounting of any transfer of funds, assets or property received from BLMIS." Under New York law, an accounting is a cause of action that seeks "an adjustment of the accounts of the parties and a rendering of a judgment for the balance ascertained to be due."

Here, the Defendants allegedly misappropriated BLMIS's funds for improper personal uses such as funding personal business ventures and homes. The Defendants also allegedly failed to perform legal compliance and supervisory responsibilities they were legally obligated to perform at BLMIS, but nevertheless received astronomical compensation from the same. These and other similar facts alleged in the complaint, sufficiently establish that the Defendants ended up with BLMIS's funds that they should not possess, and more to point, in possessing them, the Defendants unjustly enriched themselves at the expense of BLMIS.

Under New York law, "[c]onversion is an unauthorized assumption and exercise of the right of ownership over [property] belonging to another to the exclusion of the owner's rights." *Traffix v. Herold*, 269 F.Supp.2d 223, 228 (S.D.N.Y.2003). Specifically, a conversion action requires that the plaintiff has legal ownership or an immediate superior right of possession to the property he seeks to recover and that the defendant exercised an unauthorized dominion over that property "to the alteration of its condition or to the exclusion of the plaintiff's rights." *Ancile Inv. Co. Ltd. v. Archer Daniels Midland Co.*, 784 F.Supp.2d 296, 311 (S.D.N.Y.2011). When money, rather than a chattel, is the property at issue, it "must be specifically identifiable." *Interior by Mussa, Ltd. v. Town of Huntington*, 174 Misc.2d 308, 664 N.Y.S.2d 970, 972 (N.Y.App.Div.1997). In fact, "if the allegedly converted money is incapable of being described or identified in the same manner as a specific chattel . . . it is not the proper subject of a conversion."

Because the complaint does not seek a specific amount of money converted from a particular account, but rather "an award of compensatory damages in an amount to be determined at trial" it fails to state a claim for conversion under New York law. The complaint asserts vague, unsubstantiated allegations that "BLMIS had a possessory right and interest to its assets, including its customers' investment funds," and "[t]he Family Defendants converted the investment funds of BLMIS customers when they received money originating from other BLMIS customer accounts in the form of loans, payments, and other transfers. These actions deprived BLMIS and its creditors of the use of this money."

Such allegations "merely refer to unspecified monies and assets" and give "no indication of an identifiable fund or otherwise segregated amount, nor . . . any description of the alleged transfer or transfers from which the court could infer a specifically identified fund of money." *Global View Ltd. Venture*

(continues)

Capital v. Great Central Basin Exploration, L.L.C., 288 F.Supp.2d 473, 480 (S.D.N.Y.2003). These allegations are inadequate to sustain the Trustee's conversion claim against the Defendants. Thus, Count Fourteen of the complaint is dismissed with leave to amend within forty five days.

CASE QUESTIONS

1. The Madoff Ponzi scheme went on for over 20 years, and several major investment funds were severely hurt by the scheme. Why do you suppose the scheme was able to go on for so long without discovery?
2. Do you think it is possible that members of the Madoff family who were involved in the business had no idea about the Ponzi scheme? Explain your answer.
3. Why is money sometimes not appropriate as chattel for a conversion-of-chattel claim?

Conversion as a Crime

Many state statutes define conversion as a criminal offense. Some statutes use the term *theft* instead of *conversion.* Simultaneously, conversion is considered an intentional tort under the common law. This means that the chattel owner may sue in a civil action under the tort theory of conversion and may also contact the county prosecutor (or other local law enforcement authority) to file a criminal complaint for conversion. These separate legal actions are commonly pursued simultaneously in most jurisdictions.

In 2007, Hall of Fame football sports legend O. J. Simpson was arrested in Las Vegas, Nevada, and charged with the crimes of armed robbery and kidnapping. He was found guilty of robbing two sports memorabilia dealers at gunpoint and was sentenced to 33 years' imprisonment.

Simpson entered a hotel room at the Palace Station casino-hotel in Las Vegas, with a group of men, and took sports memorabilia including plaques, photos, and game balls. Simpson acknowledged taking the items, but said they had been stolen from him. The entire criminal case revolved around ownership of Simpson's sports memorabilia and whether Simpson had the required intent to take the property of another. Simpson testified that he was simply retrieving his own property.

Conversion, like trespass to chattel, is a mobile tort, as it is easy in most instances to grab and carry away someone else's personal property. If the personal property can be carried away, it may be converted. Hence, there is a nearly infinite variety of fact situations involving conversion. Both torts enrage the victims. While reading the following hypothetical examples, imagine that your own chattels have been converted; your emotional response may make clear why so many such cases are brought.

Table 8-2 outlines the elements of conversion.

Depriving owner of possession of his or her personal property (dispossession)
Intent to dispossess and convert chattel to tortfeasor's own use
Chattel owner did not consent to tortfeasor's possession and use of personal property

TABLE 8-2

Elements of conversion

HYPOTHETICALS

Nichole is painting her wooden fence in her backyard. Her neighbor, Jason, needs some paint for his garage door. He notices that Nichole has more than enough paint to finish the fence, and so Jason "borrows" two gallons to paint his door. Has Jason converted Nichole's paint?

Jason deprived Nichole of possession of the paint. Jason clearly intended to deprive her of possession and convert the paint to his own use, as he applied the paint to his garage door. Nichole did not consent to Jason's use of the paint. Jason has committed conversion.

* * *

Consider Sherry, who works at an advertising agency. One of her duties is to telephone clients to discuss accounts. Frequently, however, Sherry makes long-distance calls to relatives to discuss family matters. The company has strict regulations prohibiting the use of company phones for personal calls. Has Sherry engaged in conversion?

Deprivation of possession becomes a perplexing query in this hypothetical. Did Sherry deprive her employer of possession of the telephone? The actual property right being taken here is the use (and cost) of the telephone for placing long-distance calls. Most courts would agree that this satisfies the deprivation requirement. Sherry intended to use the company's phones for personal use. The company expressly forbade such activities, and so consent was lacking. Accordingly, Sherry has converted her employer's rights in the telephone system.

▎ SLANDER OF TITLE, COMMERCIAL DISPARAGEMENT, AND DEFAMATION BY COMPUTER

The intentional torts of slander of title, commercial disparagement, and defamation by computer involve defamed property interests. The trio has a common ancestry. All arose from the intentional tort of defamation, which concerns personal challenges as to the truth of statements.

slander of title | Occurs when a tortfeasor makes false statements about an individual's ownership of property.

Slander of Title

Slander of title results when a tortfeasor makes false statements about an individual's ownership of property. The false statements are not designed to defame the owner personally; rather, the purpose of the negative criticism is to injure the owner's ability to use the property. Slander of title contains three basic elements:

1. False statements regarding a person's ownership of property
2. Intent to hinder or damage the owner's use of the property
3. Communication (publication) of the falsehoods to third parties

False Statements Regarding Ownership.

A tortfeasor commits slander of title by making false statements about a person's ownership of property. This usually occurs when the tortfeasor falsely calls into question the title to another's property. Normally, cases involving this tort include real estate and the filing of false liens. Often, businesses that provide services to customers will file liens against the customers' real estate if payment is not received for the services. The lien attaches to the title of the land so that the property cannot be leased or sold without the lien. Suppose a business threatens to file a lien against a customer who does not owe the business any money. If the lienholder wrongfully files a lien, then the lien has defamed the integrity of the landowner's title. The improper lien falsely suggests to the world that the landowner has not properly paid his or her debts to the lienholder. Anyone thinking of buying or leasing the property will think twice, because lien property may be sold under certain circumstances to satisfy the debt. Few buyers or tenants would want to become entangled with property that is encumbered by a lien. Thus, a falsely filed lien could injure the landowner's ability to use the property, even though in actuality the lienholder has no legal right to file the lien against the landowner. This improper lien filing constitutes making false statements about someone's ownership of property.

Intent to Hinder or Damage Owner's Use of Property.

By making the false statements about ownership, the tortfeasor must intend to hamper or injure the owner's use of his or her property. This is visibly demonstrated in the preceding lien example. The lienholder filed the lien to prevent the landowner from selling or using his or her realty without first paying the debt supposedly owed to the lienholder. But, in fact, no money was due, so the lien was falsely filed.

Communication (Publication) to Third Parties.

The false statements about another's property ownership must be transmitted to third parties in slander-of-title actions. The slander in the preceding lien example is communicated to the public when the lien is recorded at the county recorder's office. It then becomes a matter of public record that anyone can access.

THE CASE OF THE MULTIMILLION-DOLLAR HOME

Imagine the outrage of being the owner of a multimillion-dollar home and having a lien placed on your property because a contractor failed to pay a subcontractor for construction work in the building of the home. In this case, the homeowners immediately brought a slander-of-title action to clear the title to their property.

Vivek SAHGAL and Namita Sahgal, Appellants,

v.

DMA ELECTRIC, INC., Appellee,

v.

UMB Bank, N.A., Counterclaim/Defendant

Court of Appeals of Kansas

270 P3d 1230

March 2, 2012

Plaintiffs Vivek and Namita Sahgal hired Patrick Scanlon as the general contractor to build a multi-million dollar home for them in southern Johnson County in 2009. Scanlon hired Defendant DMA Electric, Inc. as a subcontractor to do electrical work on the job. DMA had no agreement directly with the Sahgals. The company worked on the home site. A substantial dispute arose between the Sahgals and Scanlon. They fired him in late October 2009 and confirmed their decision removing him as the general contractor in an e-mail to him on November 6, 2009. DMA did not find out about Scanlon's termination until December 7, 2009.

On November 27, DMA supervisor Vernon Brown went to the home site ostensibly to map out a plan for the installation of additional wiring and electrical systems. DMA's records indicate he spent 80 minutes on site. But Brown installed nothing during the visit and did not improve or alter the property.

With Scanlon's departure, DMA was also off the job. The company sought to be paid $5,261.89 for work it had done. But the Sahgals refused to authorize payment to DMA; they disputed the necessity and quality of at least some of the company's work. On February 12, 2010, DMA's lawyer sent a written demand for payment to the Sahgals' lawyer. On February 23, DMA filed a mechanic's lien in the district court in the amount due for its

work. The Sahgals fired back by filing suit against DMA to have the lien adjudicated and cancelled, and for common-law slander of title. DMA then counterclaimed to enforce the mechanic's lien and for attorney fees.

Just as the trial was set to begin, DMA obtained payment from Scanlon for about 80 percent of what it was owed, so it dismissed the mechanic's lien. The parties went to trial on October 13, 2010. The district court found against the Sahgals on their slander of title claim. It ruled that although DMA's lien was legally insufficient, DMA did not act with the requisite malice to support the claim. The Sahgals appealed the adverse judgment on their slander of title claim.

To prove slander of title—an intentional tort—a party must show "a false and malicious statement . . . made in disparagement of [his or her] title to real or personal property, causing him [or her] injury," *LaBarge v. City of Concordia,* 23 Kan.App.2d 8, 16, 927 P.2d 487 (1996), *rev. denied* 261 Kan. 1085 (1997). This court has recognized the sort of malice supporting a slander of title claim reflects "a state of mind characterized by an intent to do a harmful act without reasonable justification or excuse." *Saddlewood Downs v. Holland Corp., Inc.,* 33 Kan.App.2d 185, 196, 99 P.3d 640 (2004). The existence of malice supporting a slander of title action represents a factual finding. 33 Kan.App.2d at 196. A mechanic's lien encumbers real property and adversely affects the title. Filing a patently insufficient mechanic's lien with the requisite malicious intent would give rise to a slander of title action. But the mere filing of a mechanic's lien later adjudicated to be defective does not prove slander of title.

The district court found DMA's lien invalid because it was not timely filed. Under K.S.A. 60–1103(a)(1), a subcontractor must file a mechanic's lien within

(continues)

3 months of last performing work at or supplying materials used on the construction site. DMA's lien was timely only if Brown's visit to the site on November 27 amounted to lienable work. The district court found it was not the sort of activity covered under the mechanic's lien statutes. The point is not directly before us, but it certainly could be argued either way.

While the district court found DMA's lien untimely and, therefore, unenforceable, the company had a colorable argument that Brown's November 27 appearance on the construction site amounted to covered work. In turn, DMA had reasonable grounds to support the filing of the mechanic's lien. Reasonable grounds would negate malice.

Giving full play to the district court's assessment of the witnesses at, we are in no position to dispute its factual finding that the Sahgals failed to show DMA acted with malice in filing the mechanic's lien. Malice is an essential element of the slander of title claim, and its absence is fatal. We find no error in the district court's decision to enter judgment against the Sahgals on their slander of title action.

CASE QUESTIONS

1. Did the appellate court find there was sufficient intent to sustain a slander-of-title claim? Explain your answer.
2. Do you think there was a way this whole misunderstanding could have been avoided? Explain your answer.

Commercial Disparagement

commercial disparagement | An intentional tort that occurs when a tortfeasor communicates false statements to third parties about a person's goods, services, or business enterprise. The tortfeasor must intend to harm the victim's ability to use goods, furnish services, or conduct business.

Another type of slander focuses directly upon the chattel itself: commercial disparagement. **Commercial disparagement** may be defined as false statements communicated (published) to third parties about a person's goods, services, or business enterprise. The intentional tort of commercial disparagement includes three varieties: disparagement of goods, disparagement of services, and disparagement of business. Like slander of title, *disparagement of goods* impedes the chattel owner's ability to use his or her personal property. *Disparagement of services* interferes with a service provider's ability to engage in provision of services. *Disparagement of business* occurs when the tortfeasor impugns the integrity of another's business venture. Commercial disparagement can be divided into three elements:

1. False statements about an individual's goods, services, or business
2. Intent to injure the victim's ability to use goods, furnish services, or conduct business
3. Communication (publication) to third parties

False Statements about Goods, Services, or Business. The tortfeasor must express false statements about another's personal property, services, or business reputation (sometimes called *goodwill*). For example, if someone carries a sign in front of a grocery store declaring, "This store sells spoiled fruit!," when in fact the store carries fresh and high-quality fruit, then the sign carrier has made disparaging remarks about the quality of the grocery's food products. This hurts the integrity of both the goods themselves and the store's reputation. Similarly, if someone tells his or her friends that a particular dentist uses inferior materials to fill cavities when, in reality, the dentist uses professionally acceptable materials, then the dentist's services and reputation have been wrongfully impaired.

Intent to Harm Victim's Ability to Use Goods, Supply Services, or Conduct Business.
Disparagement of goods requires that the tortfeasor intend to injure the victim's capability to use chattels, provide services, or engage in business. Normally, cases involving goods relate to sales. In the preceding illustrations, the sign carrier obviously desired to discourage other shoppers from buying fruit at that particular grocery, and the person criticizing the dentist wished to stop friends from seeking the dentist's services. The clear underlying objective in both examples is to hamper the ability of these enterprises to conduct business.

Communication (Publication) to Third Parties.
Like slander of title, commercial disparagement requires that the false statements be communicated to third parties. In the previous examples, the sign carrier transmitted the false complaints to anyone reading the sign, and the friends of the disgruntled patient heard the falsehoods about the dentist. Like the intentional torts of slander and libel (defamation) discussed in Chapter 7, publication may occur through oral or written means. The preceding examples illustrate both media.

THE CASE OF DISPARAGEMENT

This case examines whether a similar product (a knock-off product), whose name differs by only one letter from the name of another product, disparages the original product because it is of different quality. Can confusion among buyers caused by a knock-off constitute the disparagement of a product? Once again, the question of the existence of insurance coverage plays a pivotal role in a tort action.

HARTFORD CASUALTY INSURANCE COMPANY,
Plaintiff and Respondent,
v.
SWIFT DISTRIBUTION, INC. et al.,
Defendants and Appellants
Court of Appeal, Second District, Division 3, California
2012 WL 5306248
October 29, 2012

Gary-Michael Dahl (Dahl), who manufactured and sold the "Multi-Cart," sued Swift Distribution, Inc., d/b/a Ultimate Support Systems, Inc., for misleading advertising arising from Ultimate's sale of its product, the "Ulti-Cart." Dahl owned a patent to a "convertible transport cart," which he had sold as the "Multi-Cart" collapsible cart since 1997. The cart can be manipulated into eight configurations, and is used to move music, sound, and video equipment.

(continues)

Dahl alleged that Ultimate impermissibly manufactured, marketed, and sold the "Ulti-Cart," which infringed patents and trademarks for Dahl's Multi-Cart. The complaint attached advertisements for the Ulti-Cart, which do not name the Multi-Cart, Dahl, or any other products other than the Ulti-Cart.

Hartford issued a liability insurance policy to Swift Distribution, Inc. d/b/a Ultimate Support Systems. The Hartford policy's insuring agreement stated: "We will pay those sums that the insured becomes legally obligated to pay as damages because of . . . 'personal and advertising injury' to which this insurance applies." Ultimate made three demands upon Hartford to defend it the *Dahl* action under the Hartford insurance policy. Hartford denied coverage. Ultimate claims on appeal that the *Dahl* action alleged facts that constituted the potentially covered offense of disparagement.

The *Dahl* complaint alleged that Ultimate engaged in this advertising with intent to mislead the public to believe that Ultimate's products were the same as Dahl's or were authorized by or related to Dahl. The *Dahl* complaint alleged that Ultimate's advertising falsely made it appear that Ultimate designed, or was authorized to manufacture and sell, Ultimate's infringing products (the "Ulti-Cart," whose name and design was nearly identical to Dahl's "Multi-Cart"), and that Ultimate owned or had manufacturing rights to the patent and trademark-protected Multi-Cart.

In a cause of action for untrue and/or misleading advertising, the *Dahl* complaint alleged that Ultimate violated Business and Professions Code sections 17500 and 17505 by falsely claiming to be the manufacturer, wholesaler, or importer, or to own or control the intellectual property, factory, or other source of supply, of the Multi-Cart and Dahl's mark. This cause of action alleged that these violations caused Dahl's potential clients to contact Ultimate to buy its infringing product.

Dahl's application for a temporary restraining order alleged: (1) that Ultimate marketed a knock-off of Dahl's "Multi-Cart," and by dropping the "M" from "Multi-Cart," adopted a nearly identical name for its cart that created a likelihood of confusion with Dahl's "Multi-Cart" trademark; (2) that Ultimate's use of a near-identical mark was detrimental to Dahl's trade reputation and goodwill; (3) that if not enjoined by the court, Ultimate's use of the confusingly similar "Ulti-Cart" mark would cause confusion in the public and loss of sales and customers to Dahl; (4) that the infringing "Ulti-Cart" mark would be used to Dahl's detriment since he would have no control over the nature and quality of Ultimate's carts; (5) that any fault with those goods would adversely affect Dahl's future sales and would tarnish his name and reputation; (6) that industry and the consuming public recognized the "Multi-Cart" mark as associated with Dahl and as having a reputation for high quality and the patented design Dahl invented; and (7) that Ultimate's use of the "Ulti-Cart" mark and name would cause confusion or mistake, or would deceive the public as to the source of Ultimate's goods and services.

The Hartford Policy provides coverage for product disparagement, which is "an injurious falsehood directed at the organization or products, goods, or services of another. Disparagement, or injurious falsehood, may consist of publication of matter derogatory to plaintiff's title to his property, its quality, or his business." Tortious product disparagement involves publication to third parties of a false statement that injures the plaintiff by derogating the quality of goods or services. (*Total Call Internat., Inc. v. Peerless Ins. Co.* (2010) 181 Cal.App.4th 161, 169, 104 Cal.Rptr.3d 319.)

The injurious falsehood must specifically refer to the derogated property, business, goods, product, or services either by express mention or reference by reasonable implication. Dahl's complaint, application for a temporary restraining order, do not allege that Ultimate's advertisements specifically referred to Dahl by express mention.

Even if the use of "Ulti-Cart" could reasonably imply a reference to "Multi-Cart," however, Ultimate's advertisement contained no disparagement of "Multi-Cart." As stated, disparagement involves "an injurious falsehood directed at the organization or products, goods, or services of another. . . ." The injurious falsehood or disparagement may consist of matter derogatory to the plaintiff's title to his property, its quality, or to his business in general. Advertisements for the "Ulti-Cart" did not include any of these derogations. Ultimate's advertisements referred only to its own product, the Ulti-Cart. Because Dahl did not allege that Ultimate's publication disparaged Dahl's organization, products, goods, or services, Dahl was precluded from recovery on a disparagement theory. (*Nichols v. Great American Ins. Companies* (1985) 169 Cal.App.3d 766, 774, 215 Cal.Rptr. 416.) Thus Dahl alleged no claim for injurious false statement or disparagement that was potentially within the scope of the Hartford policy coverage for advertising injury.

CASE QUESTIONS

1. What did the court say that Dahl needed to allege in his complaint to succeed with a disparagement action?
2. Was there insurance coverage applicable to Dahl's claim? Explain your answer.

Defamation by Computer

Defamation by computer is a relatively recent intentional tort. Because of the proliferation of computerized databases that can store virtually any information about anyone, the likelihood of mistakes has increased. Further, as access to computerized material expands, the dissemination of inaccurate information can become enormously damaging to the victim.

Computerized Credit Reporting. Customers who are the subjects of credit reports are protected by the stringent guidelines of the Fair Credit Reporting Act (FCRA), 15 U.S.C. § 1681 *et seq.* Defamation by computer most frequently involves cases concerning erroneous credit information entered into a readily accessible computer database. A credit company reports to a national credit reporting agency that a particular individual has become delinquent in account payments. This bad credit rating can have alarmingly negative effects upon the person being reported. If the information reported is false, the injury is especially annoying, as future credit may hang in the balance of good credit reports.

    Defamation by computer can be defined as the inclusion of false information about a consumer's credit rating in a computer record-keeping system that harms the consumer's ability to secure credit. The tort includes four elements:

> **defamation by computer** | An intentional tort that occurs when the tortfeasor includes false information about a person's credit or credit rating in a computer database. This false information must be communicated to third parties, and must injure the victim's ability to obtain credit.

1. False information about a person's credit rating
2. Entering such erroneous data into a computerized record-keeping system
3. Communication (publication) of the incorrect information to third parties
4. Injuring the victim's ability to obtain credit as a result of the false computerized data

A CASE OF INFRINGEMENT

The company that holds the copyright for an adult entertainment video brings an action against both the individual who copied, downloaded, and redistributed the video, and the company that provided the Internet forum for this activity. Does an Internet provider have an obligation to police this kind of activity?

AF HOLDINGS, LLC, Plaintiff,
v.
John DOE and John Botson, Defendants

United States District Court, N.D. California,
San Jose Division
2012 WL 4747170
October 3, 2012

AF Holdings filed this action on April 24, 2012 against Botson and one "John Doe" defendant. The cause of action arises out of the alleged piracy and copyright infringement of one of AF Holdings' copyrighted adult entertainment videos ("the Video"). In its First Amended Complaint, filed June 14, 2012, AF Holdings alleges that the "Doe" defendant unlawfully downloaded, republished, and distributed copies of the Video using an online peer-to-peer sharing tool known as BitTorrent. AF Holdings also alleges that Defendant Botson was the holder of the Internet Protocol ("IP") address used for the allegedly unlawful infringement activity at the time of the alleged infringement.

AF Holdings brings three claims against the unknown "Doe" defendant: direct copyright infringement in the form of unlawful reproduction, copyright infringement in the form of unlawful distribution, and contributory infringement. AF Holdings' sole claim against Defendant Botson is that of the tort of negligence: that Botson breached an alleged duty to secure his Internet connection by failing to prevent its use for an illegal purpose, namely, Defendant Doe's downloading, republishing, and distributing the Video in violation of Plaintiff's copyright.

AF Holdings' negligence claim essentially rests on a theory that Botson had a duty to secure his Internet connection to protect against unlawful acts of third parties. AF Holdings contends that Botson breached that duty when he failed to secure his Internet connection

after he was on "actual or constructive notice of the use of his Internet connection for an unlawful activity."

Section 301 of the Copyright Act provides that all rights in works of authorship that are fixed in a tangible medium of expression and come within the subject matter of copyright are governed exclusively by this title. Botson argues that because AF Holdings' negligence claim seeks to protect rights that are identical to rights exclusively protected by the Copyright Act, the claim is preempted.

The Video, the subject of AF Holdings' claim against Botson, falls within the Copyright Act not only because it has been copyrighted by AF Holdings, but more simply by virtue of the fact that it is a motion picture. See 17 U.S.C. § 102(a) ("Copyright protection subsists, in accordance with this title, in original works of authorship fixed in a tangible medium . . . [which] include the following categories: . . . (6) motion pictures and other audiovisual works. . . .")

Second, in order to determine whether the negligence claim seeks to protect equivalent rights as guaranteed by the Copyright Act, the Ninth Circuit has adopted the "extra element test": if the state law claim contains an extra element beyond a cause of action predicated on the Copyright Act (e.g., unlawful reproduction, distribution, display, etc.), then the claim is not preempted.

Here, AF Holdings' negligence claim alleges that Botson's actions (or inaction) played a role in the unlawful reproduction and distribution of the Video in violation of the Copyright Act. Simply characterizing a copyright infringement claim as a tort does not add the extra element so as to change the nature of the cause of action. Because AF Holdings' negligence claim does not contain an element beyond a copyright infringement cause of action and that claim seeks to protect AF Holdings' copyrighted interest in the Video, the second prong of the preemption element has been met. Having found that both elements of the two-step Copyright

Act preemption analysis to be satisfied, the court thus finds that AF Holdings' negligence cause of action against Botson is preempted.

The Communications Decency Act (CDA) provides, "No provider or user of an interactive computer service shall be treated as the publisher or speaker of any information provided by another information content provider." 47 U.S.C. § 230(c)(1). The CDA goes onto provide, "No cause of action may be brought and no liability may be imposed under any State or local law that is inconsistent with this section." Botson contends that because AF Holdings' claim would hold him accountable as it would a publisher or speaker of the information in question (i.e. the Video), the claim is barred by CDA.

Immunity under the CDA requests that "(1) the defendant be a provider or user of an interactive computer service; (2) the cause of action treat the defendant as a publisher or speaker of information; and (3) the information at issue be provided by another information content provider." *Gentry v. eBay, Inc.*, 99 Cal.App.4th 816, 830, 121 Cal.Rptr.2d 703 (2002).

First, AF Holdings has alleged that Defendant Botson is the provider of a computer service or Internet connection used to pirate the Video. After all, this alleged fact underlies AF Holdings' entire negligence cause of action-that Botson was negligent in allowing the "Doe" defendant to use his IP address and Internet connection to unlawfully distribute and reproduce the Video. Thus, the first element is met.

Second, through its negligence claim, AF Holdings is seeking to treat Botson as an infringer of AF Holdings' copyright or participant in the objectionable activity. This is apparent in the allegation that Botson himself is liable for harm caused by the "Doe" defendant's copyright infringement of the Video. Courts have held that this prong of the CDA immunity test has been met where plaintiffs seek to hold defendants liable for various torts based merely on the fact that the defendant provided the online forum or Internet connection in which the tortious conduct occurred.

In this case, similarly, AF Holdings does not purport to bring a claim of direct copyright infringement

against Botson. However, the negligence cause of action would have the effect of treating Botson as the publisher of damaging content based on Botson's alleged role as the provider of the conduit for the objectionable material. Therefore, this prong of the CDA immunity analysis has been met. *See Kathleen R.*, 87 Cal.App.4th at 697–98, 104 Cal.Rptr.2d 772.

Third, it is undisputed that the information at issue-the pirated Video-was provided by another content provider, namely the "Doe" defendant; AF Holdings alleges that it was this "Doe" defendant, not Botson, who was the party that unlawfully reproduced and distributed the Video over Botson's Internet connection. Therefore, the third element for CDA immunity has been met. *See Delfino*, 145 Cal.App.4th at 807, 52 Cal.Rptr.3d 376.

For these reasons, Defendant Botson has met the qualifications for immunity under § 230 of the CDA.

AF Holdings argues that neither the Copyright Act nor the CDA are applicable because Botson has committed the tort of negligence. The court rejects this argument, and for the reasons set forth above, has found that either one of the Copyright Act or the CDA would sufficiently dispose of this claim. Even addressing the merits of negligence claim, the court nevertheless finds that AF Holdings has failed to state a claim upon which relief can be granted. Botson argues that the negligence claim must be dismissed because AF Holdings has failed to allege facts showing that he had a duty to AF Holdings to protect against infringement.

The existence of a duty is a question of law to be decided by the court. *Bily v. Arthur Young & Co.*, 3 Cal.4th 370, 397, 11 Cal.Rptr.2d 51, 834 P.2d 745 (1992). Here, AF Holdings contends that Botson had a duty to take certain affirmative steps to secure his Internet connection to ensure that no conduct amounting to infringement of AF Holdings' copyrights would occur. As such, the negligence claim does not allege misfeasance, but rather nonfeasance: that Botson failed to undertake an action to prevent damage rather than engaging in activities which created the risk of damage.

(continues)

In *Weitrum v. RKO General, Inc.*, the California Supreme Court explained what effect the distinction between misfeasance and nonfeasance would have on the determination of the defendant's legal duty:

> Misfeasance exists when the defendant is responsible for making the plaintiff's position worse, i.e., defendant has created a risk. Conversely, nonfeasance is found when the defendant has failed to aid plaintiff through beneficial intervention. . . . [L]iability for nonfeasance is largely limited to those circumstances in which some special relationship can be established. If, on the other hand, the act complained of is one of misfeasance, the question of duty is governed by the standards of ordinary care. . . .

A defendant has no duty in situations of nonfeasance unless there exists a special relationship that would give rise to such a duty. *AF Holdings, LLC v. Hatfield*, No. 12–CV–2049–PJH.

AF Holdings has not alleged any special relationship basis for imposing on Botson a legal duty to take affirmative steps to prevent the infringing activity that allegedly occurred over Botson's Internet connection. AF Holdings has also not alleged that Botson engaged in misfeasance which created the risk that AF Holdings' copyright would be violated. Therefore, AF Holdings' negligence claim is based on the unsupported notion that Botson is liable for failing to take affirmative steps to protect AF Holdings' copyright. Because there is no special relationship underlying this claim of duty, the allegation of nonfeasance cannot support a claim of negligence.

For the reasons discussed above, the AF Holdings' negligence cause of action against Botson is DISMISSED.

CASE QUESTIONS

1. Which competing laws was the court considering in this case?
2. Why did the court review negligence principles in reaching its decision?
3. Do you think an Internet provider should be held responsible for the policing activity of those using its services? Explain your answer.

Creation of a New Tort

Legal commentators occasionally spur the development of tort law through their law-review articles and treatises. Perhaps the best example is law professor William L. Prosser's writings, which have had significant and immeasurable influence on the courts for decades. Prosser's tort handbook is the bible for legal students and remains the best available dissertation on the subject.

Other commentators have entered onto the tort scene with exciting new ideas that have spurred courts and legislatures to change the course of the law. A legal article from G. Stevens and H. Hoffman, printed in *Rutgers Journal of Computers & the Law*, blazed the trail for establishment of the intentional tort of defamation by computer.

DEFAMATION

Under common law, a prima facie case for defamation is established if the plaintiff successfully pleads that he was identified in a defamatory matter through a "publication" of the charge by the defendant. The message need only be communicated to one person other than the defamed to be actionable, and any means through which a third party receives it can be considered a publication. While an oral statement may be classified as slander and a written statement as libel, a defamatory message designed for visual perception will be considered libelous.

HYPOTHETICALS

Heather moved from her apartment in the city of Shelbydale to a house in the town of Wellington. Heather had a charge account with The Prime Account, a national credit card company. Heather wrote to all of her credit card companies to report her address change. The Prime Account failed to change Heather's address in its computer billing system and continued to send its monthly invoices to Heather's Shelbydale address. After 90 days, The Prime Account reported Heather's account as delinquent to a national credit rating service. The service indicated Heather's delinquency in its computerized records, which were included in various credit reports to banks. When Heather applied at the Wellington State Bank for a mortgage loan, the bank refused her request, based upon the bad credit information. Is The Prime Account liable to Heather for defamation by computer?

The Prime Account reported that Heather's account was delinquent, and this was accurate. However, the delinquency was due to Heather's failure to receive her monthly statements. The mailing mistake was The Prime Account's fault. However, this error does not negate the truth of Heather's delinquency. The information reported in the computerized credit systems was correct, and thus defamation by computer has not occurred.

* * *

Sylvia owns a bowling alley. Zach is a professional bowler who frequents one of Sylvia's competitors but occasionally bowls at Sylvia's establishment. Zach's scores were repeatedly lower at Sylvia's than at any other bowling alley in town. One day, after a particularly frustrating series, Zach lay down to "sight" the levelness of the alleys. To his eyes, the lanes looked uneven. Zach telephoned the American Bowling Federation (ABF) to report that Sylvia's alleys did not comply with ABF standards. If such a criticism were true, the ABF could revoke its certification of Sylvia's facility. This could result in lost business if bowling leagues relocated to other alleys. In fact, the alleys complied with ABF standards. Has Zach disparaged Sylvia's business enterprise?

(continues)

Zach's comments about Sylvia's alleys were false. The defamed article was the quality of Sylvia's bowling alleys, which would include the integrity of the business itself. Zach communicated these falsehoods to a third party by telephoning the ABF. Zach's intent may be implied by his conduct. What purpose could he have furthered by telephoning the ABF? The reasonable response would be that he hoped that the ABF would remove its certification from Sylvia's and thus discourage patronage. This translates as intent to injure another's ability to conduct business. The damage to Sylvia's goodwill would be substantial if the ABF revoked its certification. Therefore, Zach has committed commercial disparagement.

Table 8-3 illustrates the requirements for slander of title and commercial disparagement , and defamation by computer.

TABLE 8-3
Elements of slander of title and commercial disparagement, and defamation by computer

SLANDER OF TITLE	COMMERCIAL DISPARAGEMENT	DEFAMATION BY COMPUTER
False statements regarding person's property ownership	False statements about person's goods, services, or business	False information about a person's credit rating
Intent to impede or injure owner's use of property	Intent to harm victim's ability to use goods, furnish services, or conduct business	Inputting false information into computerized database
Communication (publication) of falsehoods to third parties	Communication (publication) of falsehoods to third parties	Communication (publication) of falsehoods to third parties
Usually involves the filing of spurious liens against real estate	Includes disparagement of goods, disparagement of services, and disparagement of business	Injury to victim's ability to secure credit, as a result of erroneous credit data

THE CASE OF THE INTENTIONAL CYBERSQUATTER

In the ever-expanding law of computer torts, this court explores the rights associated with the owner of a domain name. In a practice known as **cybersquatting**, an individual registers or uses the domain name of another in order to benefit from that trademark. Frequently, the cybersquatter then offers to sell the domain name to the owner of the trademark for an inflated price. In this case, a cybersquatter with a confusingly similar domain name intends to profit from the goodwill associated with the owner of the domain name joecartoon.com.

SHIELDS
v.
ZUCCARINI

United States Court of Appeals, Third Circuit
2001 WL 671607 (3d Cir. [Pa.])
June 15, 2001

John Zuccarini appeals from the district court's grant of summary judgment and award of statutory damages and attorneys' fees in favor of Joseph Shields under the new Anticybersquatting Consumer Protection Act ("ACPA" or "Act"). In this case of first impression in this court interpreting the ACPA, we must decide whether the district court erred in determining that registering domain names that are intentional misspellings of distinctive or famous names constitutes unlawful conduct under the Act.

Shields, a graphic artist from Alto, Michigan, creates, exhibits and markets cartoons under the names "Joe Cartoon" and "The Joe Cartoon Co." His creations include the popular "Frog Blender," "Micro-Gerbil" and "Live and Let Dive" animations. Shields licenses his cartoons to others for display on T-shirts, coffee mugs and other items, many of which are sold at gift stores across the country. He has marketed his cartoons under the "Joe Cartoon" label for the past fifteen years.

On June 12, 1997, Shields registered the domain name joecartoon.com, and he has operated it as a web site ever since. Visitors to the site can download his animations and purchase Joe Cartoon merchandise. Since April 1998, when it won "shock site of the day" from Macromedia, Joe Cartoon's web traffic has increased exponentially, now averaging over 700,000 visits per month.

In November 1999, Zuccarini, an Andalusia, Pennsylvania "wholesaler" of Internet domain names, registered five world wide web variations on Shields's site: joescartoon.com, joecarton.com, joescartons.com, joescartoons.com and cartoonjoe.com. Zuccarini's sites featured advertisements for other sites and for credit card companies. Visitors were trapped or "mousetrapped" in the sites, which, in the jargon of the computer world, means that they were unable to exit without clicking on a succession of advertisements.

In December 1999, Shields sent "cease and desist" letters to Zuccarini regarding the infringing domain names. Zuccarini did not respond to the letters. Immediately after Shields filed this suit, Zuccarini changed the five sites to "political protest" pages and posted the following message on them:

> This is a page of POLITICAL PROTEST
>
> —Against the web site joecartoon.com—
>
> joecartoon.com is a web site that depicts the mutilation and killing of animals in a shockwave based cartoon format—many children are inticed [sic] to the web site, not knowing what is really there and then encouraged to join in the mutilation and killing through the use of the shockwave cartoon presented o them.

On November 29, 1999, the ACPA became law, making it illegal for a person to register or to use with the "bad faith" intent to profit from an Internet domain name that is "identical or confusingly similar" to the distinctive or famous trademark or Internet domain name of another person or company (see 15 U.S.C. § 1125(d) (Supp. 2000)). The Act was intended to prevent "cybersquatting," an expression that has come to mean the bad faith, abusive registration and use of the distinctive trademarks of others as Internet domain names, with the intent to profit from the goodwill associated with those trademarks.

To succeed on his ACPA claim, Shields was required to prove that (1) "Joe Cartoon" is a distinctive or famous mark entitled to protection; (2) Zuccarini's domain names are "identical or confusingly similar to" Shields's mark; and (3) Zuccarini registered the domain names with the bad faith intent to profit from them.

Under § 1125(d)(1)(A)(ii)(I) and (II), the district court first had to determine if "Joe Cartoon" is a "distinctive" or "famous" mark and, therefore, is entitled to protection under the Act.

Shields runs the only "Joe Cartoon" operation in the nation and has done so for the past fifteen years.

(continues)

This suggests both the inherent and acquired distinctiveness of the "Joe Cartoon" name. In addition to using the "Joe Cartoon" name for 15 years, Shields has used the domain name joecartoon.com as a web site since June 1997 to display his animations and sell products featuring his drawings.

Joe Cartoon T-shirts have been sold across the country since at least the early 1990s, and its products appear on the web site of at least one nationally known retail chain, Spencer Gifts. Shields's cartoons and merchandise are marketed on the Internet, in gift shops and at tourist venues. The Joe Cartoon mark has won a huge following because of the work of Shields. In light of the above, we conclude that "Joe Cartoon" is distinctive, and, with 700,000 hits a month, the web site "joecartoon.com" qualifies as being famous. Therefore, the trademark and domain name are protected under the ACPA.

Under the Act, the next inquiry is whether Zuccarini's domain names are "identical or confusingly similar" to Shields's mark. The domain names—joescartoon.com, joecarton.com, joescartons.com, joescartoons.com and cartoonjoe.com—closely resemble "joecartoon.com," with a few additional or deleted letters, or, in the last domain name, by rearranging the order of the words. To divert Internet traffic to his sites, Zuccarini admits that he registers domain names, including the five at issue here, because they are likely misspellings of famous marks or personal names. The strong similarity between these domain names and joecartoon.com persuades us that they are "confusingly similar."

The statute covers the registration of domain names that are "identical" to distinctive or famous marks, but it also covers domain names that are "confusingly similar" to distinctive or famous marks.

[C]ybersquatters often register well-known marks to prey on consumer confusion by misusing the domain name to divert customers from the mark owner's site to the cybersquatter's own site, many of which are pornography sites that derive advertising revenue based on the number of visits, or "hits," the site receives. . . .

We conclude that Zuccarini's conduct here is a classic example of a specific practice the ACPA was designed to prohibit. The district court properly found that the domain names he registered were "confusingly similar."

CASE QUESTIONS

1. What is the definition of *cybersquatting*?
2. For what purpose did Zuccarini deliberately use a domain name confusingly similar to "joecartoon.com"?

▌ SUMMARY

Trespass to land occurs when a tortfeasor enters upon another's real estate without permission. The tortfeasor must intend to invade the premises without consent. Also, the tortfeasor's entry must interfere with the landowner's exclusive right to use the land, which is called possession.

Toxic tort actions involve toxic chemicals, pollution, hazardous waste disposal and transportation, and other environmentally sensitive issues. This litigation applies many tort theories, including trespass to land, negligence, absolute liability for ultrahazardous substances, products liability, and nuisance. The same formula for trespass to land applies in cases involving toxic substances that invade an innocent landowner's property through underwater seepage or surface or air contamination.

Trespass to chattel occurs when the tortfeasor possesses or interferes with the use of another's personal property without permission. The tortfeasor must intend to dispossess the owner of his or her chattel, or to interfere with the owner's exclusive use of the chattel.

Conversion deprives a chattel owner of possession of personal property, which the tortfeasor converts to his or her own use. The tortfeasor must intend to dispossess the owner of the chattel and then use it without consent. Conversion occurs whenever the tortfeasor deprives the owner of dominion and control over the personal property. In many jurisdictions, statutes define conversion as a crime, in addition to being a common law intentional tort.

Slander of title occurs when false statements are made about an individual's ownership of property. The tortfeasor's intentions are to handicap or harm the owner's use of the property. Commercial disparagement includes disparagement of goods, of services, and of businesses. Commercial disparagement involves false statements about a person's goods, services, or business intended to injure the victim's ability to use the property, supply the services, or conduct business. Defamation by computer concerns false information about a person's credit rating that is entered into a computer database. Communication, or publication, of the false information to third parties is required of all three of these intentional torts.

In the next chapter defenses to intentional torts are discussed. Similar to defenses to negligence actions which were previously covered, these defenses also may excuse a defedant's actions.

▌ KEY TERMS

avoidance claims	defamation by computer	Ponzi scheme
chattel	dispossession	Slander of title
commercial disparagement	entry	toxic tort actions
conversion	exclusive right	trespass
cybersquatting	exclusive right of possession	trespass to chattel

▌ PROBLEMS

In the following hypotheticals, identify the intentional tort(s) committed, if any, and support your answers.

1. Pestro Chemical Corporation manufactures *Dredroxiphine,* a poison used in insect sprays. A railway line delivers tanker cars full of the chemical to be unloaded into the plant. On breezy days, the fumes from the unloading stations drift across the highway onto Elmer Parsley's farm. The odors are pungent and are especially irritating to the sinuses. When Elmer and his family work outside on windy days, they are constantly besieged by the poison's smells. Their eyes water excessively, their noses run, and they are gripped by sneezing fits. Other farmers in the area have complained of similar symptoms. Visits to the family physician have revealed that Elmer has absorbed minute amounts of the chemical in his lungs and through his skin. Medical studies link exposure to the chemical with several forms of cancer. Elmer has farmed on his property since 1999. Pestro constructed its plant in 2001.

2. Ben left the Pick-Em-Up saloon after an evening of heavy drinking. Intoxicated, he stumbled across the street to the Tao, a Chinese restaurant, and ordered a hamburger. The waitress, an exchange student at the local high school, did not understand English well, and because Ben's speech was slurred, she misunderstood him. When she returned with an oriental dish, Ben jumped from his chair and shouted loudly, "I did

not order this stinking slop! Get it outta my face!" Several customers stared at Ben as he yelled at the waitress, "I'll get the health department to shut this dump down, before somebody else gets poisoned!" The manager ran out from the kitchen and demanded that Ben leave the premises immediately. Ben refused to leave.

3. Alexa operates a day-care center for children. Jay, a nine-year-old, attended the center after school while his parents worked. Alexa discovered Jay's parents were delinquent in paying their fees by three months. One day Jay brought in his father's tablet for show-and-tell. Alexa asked Jay if he would like her to keep the computer locked up for safekeeping. Jay agreed. At the end of the day, Jay asked Alexa to return the computer, but she refused, stating that she would keep the computer until Jay's parents paid their bill.

4. Theresa rented an apartment from Whisperwood Apartments. Under the lease, she was responsible for paying for electricity and gas heat. When she moved into the apartment, she noticed that the electricity and gas were already on; the apartment owners paid for the utilities while apartments were vacant. She did not contact the utility companies to have the accounts transferred into her name, and she did not notify the apartment manager about the situation. Theresa lived in the apartment for three months before the error was discovered. She never paid any money for utilities, although utility bills for the apartment totaled $250 for this time period.

5. Steve is a mason. He installed a concrete patio at the home of Jose and Elena Garcia. Elena stopped by Steve's house one day and paid his wife (in cash) for the work. Elena did not get a receipt. Steve's wife, however, never told Steve about the money. Steve sent several invoices to the Garcias, but they ignored them. Thinking the bill remained unpaid, Steve filed a mechanic's lien against the Garcias' real estate. Once the Garcias discovered the lien, they angrily telephoned Steve and explained about the cash payment. Steve's wife admitted to receiving the money, so Steve considered the matter settled. However, Steve did not release the lien at the county recorder's office.

6. Ryan owed his dentist for an oral surgery bill. Ryan faithfully made monthly payments to the dentist. The dentist's accountant reported to a local credit rating service that Ryan had defaulted on the bill. The service included this information in its computerized credit files. Ryan applied for a credit card at a local department store, but was denied as a result of the bad credit rating. The department store was a client of the credit rating service and received monthly credit rating summaries.

▌ REVIEW QUESTIONS

1. What are the intentional torts that involve injuries to property rights? How are these distinguishable from intentional torts in which the harm is focused on persons?

2. Define *trespass to land* and *trespass to chattel.* How do the two intentional torts differ? How are they similar? What is entry? What is exclusive use? What is possession? Can trespass occur above or below land? What role does consent play in trespass? Is harm to the property required? Must the trespass be intentional? Why or why not? Must trespass to chattel involve dispossession?

3. What are toxic torts? What causes of action are available for injured persons? What federal statutes exist to regulate hazardous or toxic substances? What are the provisions of these statutes?

4. What is conversion? How is it different from trespass to chattel? How is it similar? To what extent must the chattel owner be deprived of possession? How might such deprivation occur? Must the tortfeasor do more than simply dispossess the chattel owner? What are dominion and control, and why are they important? What are the roles of intent and consent in conversion? Can conversion also be a crime? Why?

5. Explain slander of title. How might false statements be made about one's ownership of property?

6. List the different types of commercial disparagement. What are the elements of this category of intentional tort? What intent is involved? Why is communication important?

7. What is defamation by computer? Under what circumstances is this intentional tort most likely to arise? Why is communication significant?

Provide an example of this intentional tort. What intent is involved? What is publication, and why is it a necessary element?

▌ HELPFUL WEBSITES

This chapter deals with intentional torts to property. To learn more about intentional torts to property, the following sites can be accessed:

Governmental Agencies

www.statelocal.gov

www.findlaw.com

www.epa.gov (U.S. Environmental Protection Agency)

www.eli.org (Environmental Law Institute)

www.Earthjustice.org (Earth Justice)

www.nrdc.org (Natural Resources Defense Council)

www.americanbar.org (Environment, Energy and Resources Section)

www.vermontlaw.edu (Vermont Law School)

Legal Discussion Groups

www.paralegalgateway.com

Attorneys

www.martindale.com

www.lawoffice.com

State Law and Codes

www.law.washington.edu

www.law.cornell.edu

STUDENT COMPANION WEBSITE
For additional cases and study materials, please go to www.cengagebrain.com

Chapter 9

Defenses to Intentional Torts

THE BIGGEST MISTAKES PARALEGALS MAKE AND HOW TO AVOID THEM

Don't Be Mad at Me Because I Am Mad at You

Carlos was promoted to manager of all the paralegals in the firm. Before he could enjoy his new success, he found that a certain group was always stressing him out. It was very difficult to hold some of the paralegals accountable, especially when they acted like victims just before he was preparing to call them out for failing to complete work.

Carlos realized that the same paralegals who were making excuses caused him to exercise restraint when he really wanted to shout, "Just do it!" Carlos, who had always excelled as a paralegal, felt like a failure as the manager and feared he might be asked to resign from this position.

Lesson Learned: People who consistently fail to do a good job often manipulate the situation by playing the victim card before they can be blamed. Carlos felt this injustice, leaving him powerless and frustrated in his position. His intent to be the "nice guy" with his colleagues and friends conflicted with his duties as a manager. He needed to find a middle ground. Carlos

would need to keep track of when paralegals were not doing their work as requested, as well as the dates where they offered excuses for incomplete tasks. This is a measurable action for any effective manager to take.

Finally Carlos must state to them, "Offer a solution to your problem that is fair and reasonable to you and me, and especially to the firm." In this manner, everyone can continue to work successfully as a team. Sometimes, the solution is as simple as an employee needing more training but being too embarrassed to ask.

▌ INTRODUCTION

Sometimes intentional torts are legally justified; thus, the person engaging in the intentional tort is not liable to the victim. These are collectively called **defenses** to intentional torts. For instance, conduct that normally would constitute an intentional tort, such as battery, could be excused under the theory of self-defense. Defenses are commonly used by the defendant in a civil lawsuit to exonerate the defendant from liability to the plaintiff.

A legal defense arises only when one party responds to another party's allegations in a lawsuit. Usually, the defendant answers the plaintiff's complaint with defenses. However, if the defendant counterclaimed against the plaintiff, it would be the plaintiff who replied with defenses. If third parties were involved in the litigation through cross-complaints, these third parties would answer with defenses. This presumes, of course, that defenses are available with which to respond.

This chapter focuses on *justification of intentional tortious conduct through defenses*. The following questions may be helpful:

▶ May the tortfeasor use a defense to excuse his or her misconduct?

▶ Which defenses apply to which intentional torts?

Intentional torts involve intentional acts. Thus, they carry a high degree of risk of injury to others, and usually there is a low degree of social benefit from the act involved. The risk of injury outweighs the benefits received from the act. Therefore, the duty not to intentionally injure someone or something is great.

defense | 1. The sum of the facts, law, and arguments presented by the side against whom legal action is brought.

2. Any counterargument or counterforce. A defense can relieve a defendant of the liability of a tort.

There are several types of legal defenses to intentional torts. This chapter describes:

- Consent (defense to all intentional torts)
- Self-defense (defense against assault, battery, or false imprisonment)
- Defense of persons or property (defense against assault, battery, or false imprisonment)
- Rightful repossession (defense against trespass to land, trespass to chattel, conversion, assault, and battery)
- Mistake (defense to most intentional torts)
- Privilege (broad category of defense against intentional torts)
- Necessity (defense to various intentional torts)
- Public officer's immunity for legal process enforcement, and law enforcement and private citizen's defense for a warrantless arrest
- Statutes of limitations (defense to all intentional torts)
- Workers' compensation (defense used in workplace incident)

Because intentional torts are rarely covered by insurance, intentional torts, and their defenses are far less common in legal practice than negligence actions.

▌CONSENT

consent | Voluntary and active agreement.

Consent is a broad defense applicable to every intentional tort. **Consent** occurs when the victim of an intentional tort voluntarily agrees to the tortfeasor's actions, provided that the victim understands (or reasonably should understand) the consequences of the tortfeasor's deeds. This knowledge factor is sometimes called **informed consent.**

informed consent | A person's agreement to allow something to happen (such as surgery) that is based on a full disclosure or full knowledge of the facts needed to make the decision intelligently.

The consent defense contains the following elements (1) voluntary acceptance of an intentionally tortious act (2) with full knowledge or understanding of the consequences. Actually, consent is not a legal defense at all. As shown in the previous two chapters, it is a deliberately missing element of intentional torts. If consent existed, then the intentional tort could not have occurred. The ancient common law applied the Latin maxim *volenti non fit injuria,* which translates as, "No wrong may occur to one who is willing." As a practical matter, courts over the centuries have treated consent as a defense to intentional torts.

Informed Consent: Voluntary Acceptance

Consent will be a successful defense to an intentional tort action only if the victim willingly and knowingly agreed to the tortfeasor's conduct. Accordingly, a victim who is coerced into tolerating an intentional tort cannot consent to it, because the victim was compelled to undergo the tort. Further, the victim must comprehend the implications of the tortfeasor's actions to consent to them.

For instance, suppose Randy agrees to wrestle Warren. Assume that both Randy and Warren understand the repercussions of wrestling, including possible inadvertent injury. Randy and Warren will have mutually consented to battery, and so neither could sue the other for this intentional tort if harm did happen.

Part of the voluntary, or **volition**, factor of consent is the victim's mental capacity to agree. Some persons simply lack sufficient mental abilities to understand the consequences of a tortfeasor's actions. Severely retarded or mentally incapacitated individuals, for example, might not grasp the implications of a tortfeasor's misbehavior. Intoxicated individuals may also have insufficient mental faculties to comprehend the results of an intentional tort. Children, particularly when very young, may lack cognitive development adequate to grasp the ramifications of intentional torts. For such persons, consent could become virtually impossible.

volition | When something is done voluntarily, by a person's own free will.

Implied Consent

Consent may be expressed, either orally or in writing, or it may be implied by conduct or circumstances. For instance, public officials or famous persons are assumed to consent to adverse publicity merely by placing themselves in the public limelight. Consent to publicity is therefore implied, and public officials or celebrities cannot recover for libel or slander, unless **malice** is proven.

The most common example of implied consent involves emergency medical treatment. If a patient is unconscious and is taken to a hospital emergency room, the medical personnel may presume that the patient consents to treatment, at least to the extent of the emergency condition. Thus, if someone is found unconscious on the pavement, suffering from gastrointestinal bleeding, and an ambulance takes her to the hospital, the patient is presumed to agree to treatment of the emergency condition, in this case the bleeding, which is often life-threatening. Later, if the patient regains consciousness and protests against the treatment (perhaps upon religious grounds), the patient cannot sue for battery for the unauthorized emergency care. However, once conscious and clear-minded, the patient could insist that there be no further treatment. Failure to stop treatment would then constitute battery. Suppose, instead, that the medical personnel treated beyond the emergency condition, such as removing a portion of diseased skin while treating the intestinal bleeding. Implied consent does not apply to nonemergency treatment, and thus battery would have occurred.

malice | When a person makes a statement he or she knows is false, or with reckless disregard for its truth or falsity.

THE CASE OF THE VOLUNTARY STUNT

Students join a variety of afterschool activities ranging from band to football. At many schools, attending afterschool football games, with cheerleaders rooting for the home team, is a popular event. Can cheerleaders assume that the routines they are taught and expected to perform are safe? When students sign up for sports, they are consenting to the inherent risks of the game. Where do you draw the line as to which injuries can be expected as part of being a cheerleader? Here, a cheerleader is injured and brings up the issue of inadequate supervision to bolster her case.

(continues)

KRISTINA D. (Anonymous), etc., et al., Respondents

v.

NESAQUAKE MIDDLE SCHOOL, Defendant, Smithtown Central School District, et al., Appellants

Supreme Court, Appellate Division,
Second Department, New York
98 A.D.3d 600
August 15, 2012

The infant plaintiff, an experienced middle school cheerleader, allegedly was injured during cheerleading practice when she fell during the performance of a "shoulder stand," a stunt she had performed many times in the past. The plaintiffs commenced this action, alleging, among other things, that the defendants Smithtown Central School District and cheerleading coach Alyssa Papesca (hereinafter the appellants) were negligent in, among other things, failing to supervise the cheerleaders properly in performing the stunt. The appellants moved for summary judgment dismissing the complaint insofar as asserted against them. The Supreme Court denied the motion.

"[B]y engaging in a sport or recreational activity, a participant consents to those commonly appreciated risks which are inherent in and arise out of the nature of the sport generally and flow from such participation" (*Morgan v. State of New York*, 90 N.Y.2d 471,

484, 662 N.Y.S.2d 421, 685 N.E.2d 202; *see Trupia v. Lake George Cent. School Dist.*, 14 N.Y.3d 392, 395, 901 N.Y.S.2d 127, 927 N.E.2d 547). Even where the risk of injury is assumed, however, a school must exercise ordinary reasonable care to protect student athletes voluntarily involved in extracurricular sports from "unassumed, concealed, or unreasonably increased risks" (*Benitez v. New York City Bd. of Educ.*, 73 N.Y.2d 650, 654, 543 N.Y.S.2d 29, 541 N.E.2d 29).

Here, the appellants established, prima facie, that the infant plaintiff voluntarily engaged in the activity of cheerleading, including the performance of stunts, and that, as an experienced cheerleader, she knew the risks inherent in the activity (*see Testa v. East Meadow Union Free School Dist.*, 92 A.D.3d 940, 941, 938 N.Y.S.2d 903; *Lomonico v. Massapequa Pub. Schools*, 84 A.D.3d 1033, 1034, 923 N.Y.S.2d 631; *DiGiose v. Bellmore–Merrick Cent. High School Dist.*, 50 A.D.3d 623, 624, 855 N.Y.S.2d 199). The appellants also made a prima facie showing that the infant plaintiff was adequately supervised (*see Testa v. East Meadow Union Free School Distr.*, 92 A.D.3d at 941, 938 N.Y.S.2d 903). In opposition, the plaintiffs' speculative and conclusory statements and allegations failed to raise a triable issue of fact (*see Alvarez v. Prospect Hosp.*, 68 N.Y.2d 320, 324, 508 N.Y.S.2d 923, 501 N.E.2d 572). Accordingly, the appellants' motion for summary judgment dismissing the complaint insofar as asserted against them should have been granted.

CASE QUESTIONS

1. Provide an example of an unassumed risk that a cheerleader might encounter.
2. Had the plaintiff been able to show that there was inadequate supervision, would this have changed the result of this case? Explain your answer.

Consent is sometimes characterized as the "you asked for it" defense. However, as the following hypothetical demonstrates, there can be doubt as to what the "it" was to which the victim consented.

HYPOTHETICAL

Colleen attended a company banquet in her honor as "sales director of the year." The dinner was a "roast" at which coworkers made humorous remarks about the guest of honor. Several of these comments were loaded with sarcasm and a few were in questionable taste. However, none of the comments was taken seriously by the audience, which understood that it was all in good fun. Under other circumstances, however, some members of the audience might have been offended. Colleen, however, took offense at the more colorful character references. Could she sue her coemployees for slander?

Colleen voluntarily agreed to attend the banquet with a complete understanding that coworkers would use the forum to tease and joke about her. She should have known that some of her fellow employees would push the limits of propriety with a few harsh remarks. Because the audience was not offended (given the "roast" atmosphere), and because Colleen knowingly accepted the potentially slanderous conduct, consent would be a defense to Colleen's slander claim.

Consent is clearly the most pervasive defense to intentional torts. The components of consent are listed in Table 9-1.

TABLE 9-1
Elements of consent

Voluntary acceptance of an intentionally tortious act
Full knowledge or understanding of the consequences

Copyright © 2015 Cengage Learning®.

▌ SELF-DEFENSE

Of the legal defenses, self-defense is probably the most familiar to the average person. It is most commonly applied to the intentional torts of assault and battery, but it may also be used in cases involving false imprisonment. **Self-defense** is the exercise of reasonable force to repel an attack upon one's person or to avoid confinement. The nature of the action is simple: the victim of an assault or battery may use that degree of force necessary to prevent bodily injury (or offensive contact) from the attacker. Similarly, the victim of false imprisonment may use the force needed to prevent or escape confinement.

Consider this likely scenario. Jake is angry at Zach and throws a punch at Zach's face. Zach responds by blocking Jake's fist, grabbing his wrist, and twisting

self-defense | Physical force used against a person who is threatening physical force or using physical force. This is a right if your own family, property, or body is in danger, but sometimes only if the danger was not provoked. Also, deadly force may (usually) only be used against deadly force.

his arm behind his back until he agrees to calm down. This illustrates assault and self-defense: by throwing the punch, Jake placed Zach in reasonable apprehension of an unconsented contact that endangered his physical safety. Under self-defense, Zach was entitled to use whatever force was necessary to repel the attack.

The issue of self-defense would arise only if Jake (as plaintiff) sued Zach (as defendant) for battery. Jake would allege that Zach committed battery by grabbing his wrist and twisting his arm. Zach would reply with the legal defense of self-defense, which justified his actions. Remember that the defendant uses legal defenses to avoid liability to the plaintiff. In our hypothetical, Zach's self-defense argument would defeat Jake's complaint for battery. Bear in mind that Zach would have his own cause of action against Jake for assault, and Jake would not be able to use self-defense as a defense because he initiated the attack upon Zach.

The elements of self-defense are (1) use of reasonable force (2) to counter an attacking or offensive force that is (3) necessary to prevent bodily injury, offensive contact, or confinement.

Reasonable Force

reasonable force | Force that is reasonable, limited to that which is necessary to dispel the attacking force for self-defense.

The neutralizing force a person uses in self-defense is limited. The force cannot be greater than what is reasonably necessary to dispel the attacking force. This is called **reasonable force.** In the preceding example, Zach applied only as much force as needed to prevent Jake from striking Zach. Had Zach broken Jake's arm in retaliation, this would clearly have been excessive force, because breaking Jake's arm was unnecessary to stop the assault. Thus, Zach could not use self-defense as a legal justification. Instead, Zach would have become the aggressor and have engaged in battery against Jake. Common law maintains that the victim of an assault or battery may not turn aggressive once the assailant is incapacitated. Thus, if Jake collapsed after Zach twisted his arm, Zach could not kick Jake into unconsciousness and then claim self-defense.

What constitutes reasonable force varies depending upon the circumstances of each case. If Jake attacked Zach with an axe, then deadly force would be involved. Zach would therefore be warranted in responding with deadly force to repulse the onslaught. If Jake threw rocks at Zach, his force would threaten severe bodily harm. Thus, Zach could react with similarly powerful force, such as knocking Jake down with a pole.

Deadly Self-defense The reasonableness issue is difficult to reduce to clearly defined, black-and-white terms. Much depends upon the options available to the victim, and the particular jurisdiction of the parties. Many courts hold that in the face of deadly force, if a victim might reasonably escape from the attack, then this choice must first be selected before deadly force may be used in self-defense. Several courts apply the same rule to situations involving threats of serious bodily injury. However, the majority of jurisdictions maintain that a person is not required to flee his or her home if threatened by an intruder.

This is sometimes called the **castle doctrine,** in which a dweller is considered "king" or "queen" and may use any amount of force, including deadly force, to resist an intruder, such as a burglar. This varies greatly by state law.

Countering an Attacking or Offensive Force

The party exercising self-defense must be opposing an attacking or offensive force. Jake's fist in our previous example is obviously an attacking force. But suppose Jake spit at Zach. This would be an example of an offensive force, as it is contact by which Zach would probably be offended.

Force Necessary to Prevent Injury, Offensive Contact, or Confinement

The force used in self-defense must be necessary to prevent bodily injury or offensive contact, or to avoid confinement. **Necessary force** is that which is reasonably perceived as required to rebuff an attack or confinement. When Zach grabbed Jake's wrist and twisted his arm, Zach felt this action was required to prevent Jake from continuing his assault. The question again becomes one of reasonableness: Did Zach respond with reasonable force necessary to allay Jake's attack? Or was Zach's force unnecessary (and thus excessive) given Jake's actions? Suppose Jake had only tapped Zach on the shoulder with his finger. Zach's wrist-and-arm twist in response would then be considered unreasonable, unneeded, and extreme. Thus, Zach could not avail himself of a self-defense argument against Jake's battery claim.

Say that Jake was attempting to lock Zach in a room against Zach's will. In self-defense, Zach could reply with as much force as required to avoid being confined. This means that Zach could use that degree of force necessary to escape Jake.

Self-defense is perhaps the easiest legal justification to illustrate. Almost any child who has engaged in a playground shoving match can explain the fundamental concept. However, the legal elements require a more discerning eye, as shown in the following example.

HYPOTHETICAL

Jake Nesmith sat alone at a table in a local bar. He was waiting to meet a friend from work when two men standing nearby got into a shoving match. One of the men, John, pushed the other man, Bruce, into Jake. Jake shoved Bruce back into John, knocking them both to the floor.

John committed battery against Bruce by pushing him. Under the doctrine of transferred intent, when Bruce bumped into Jake, John transferred his battery onto Jake. By pushing Bruce away, Jake used reasonable force to repel an attacking force to prevent injury to himself. Accordingly, Jake could claim self-defense against John.

(continues)

---

castle doctrine | The principle that you can use any force necessary to protect your own home or its inhabitants from attack. Also called *dwelling defense doctrine.*

necessary force | That degree of force reasonably perceived as required to repel an attack or resist confinement. It is an aspect of self-defense.

> There remains a puzzling question, however. Could Jake claim self-defense against Bruce, or did Jake commit battery against Bruce? Bruce was essentially the instrumentality that John put into motion to strike Jake, albeit accidentally. Bruce did not intend to contact Jake. Therefore, Bruce did not commit battery or assault against Jake.
>
> Jake could still claim self-defense against Bruce, however. Jake responded to protect himself against injury from both participants in the shoving match. Thus, self-defense would apply. Further, because Bruce was a voluntary participant in the struggle with John, Bruce consented to physical contact associated with a shoving match. This would include inadvertently bumping into an innocent bystander like Jake. Accordingly, Jake did not commit battery against Bruce, because Bruce impliedly consented to the incidental contact involved, which would include Jake's return shove.

Assault and battery may be justifiable in the defense of others or of property, as discussed in Chapter 6. The elements of self-defense are summarized in Table 9-2.

TABLE 9-2
Elements of self-defense

Use of reasonable force
Countering an attacking or offensive force
Actions necessary to prevent bodily injury, offensive contact, or confinement

Copyright © 2015 Cengage Learning®.

▌ DEFENSE OF PERSONS OR PROPERTY

As a legal justification for assault or battery, defense of other persons or defense of injury to property is similar to self-defense. A person who would otherwise have committed assault or battery may be excused if the action was taken to protect another individual or property from harm. This would include freeing someone subject to false imprisonment.

Defense of Persons: Elements

Defense of persons as a legal justification for assault or battery has the following elements (1) use of reasonable force (2) to defend or protect a third party from injury (3) when the third party is threatened by an attacking force. For example, if Marie were about to throw a vase at Lesley , Simon could use reasonable force to subdue Marie before she could complete the throw. Simon would not have committed battery, because he grabbed Marie to prevent her from harming Lesley. Simon would be entitled to the legal defense of defense of another person to avoid liability for battery.

defense of persons |
A defense to the intentional torts of assault, battery, and false imprisonment. Its elements include the use of reasonable force to defend or protect a third party from injury when the third party is threatened by an attacking force.

The same principles used in self-defense to define reasonable force also apply to defense of persons. Thus, Simon could not use excessive force to repel Marie's attack against Marjorie. For instance, if Simon struck Marie sharply in the head with a two-by-four, this would be unnecessarily brutal force to subdue the vase attack.

Also, like self-defense, the repelling force must be used to counter an attacking force. If Lesley telephoned Simon to complain that Marie had just thrown a vase at her, Simon could not run over and strike Marie and then claim defense of another as an excuse. The defender steps into the shoes of the third person, and only gets the defense if the third person was in the right. Hence, Simon would have the same rights as Lesley.

Defense of Property: Elements

Conduct that otherwise might be assault or battery may be vindicated if the action is taken to defend property from damage or dispossession. A property owner has the right to possess and safeguard his or her property from others. The elements of **defense of property** are (1) use of reasonable force (2) to protect property from damage or dispossession (3) when another person, the *invader,* attempts to injure or wrongfully take possession of the property.

The reasonable force contemplated here is essentially identical to that discussed in regard to self-defense. Many courts, however, restrict the defensive force to the least amount necessary to protect the property from harm or dispossession. This is a narrower definition of *reasonableness,* suggesting that human well-being is more important than the safety of property. Under this theory, most courts would not allow deadly force or extreme force likely to cause serious bodily injury to be used to defend property under any circumstances.

The property owner or possessor uses reasonable force to drive back an attacking force that is attempting to harm or possess the property. For example, if Frederick is in the process of committing conversion or trespass to chattel, then Helen, who owns the personal property in danger, may use reasonable force to dispel Frederick's efforts at dispossession.

The use of reasonable force to expel a trespasser to land is called **ejectment.** Defense-of-real-property cases frequently involve landowners who have placed dangerous traps for trespassers. The trespassers are often seeking to steal personal property and usually violate various criminal statutes involving theft or burglary. Nevertheless, landowners may not set up deadly traps to inflict serious bodily injuries upon such criminals. Spring-loaded guns have been the most common traps litigated. For example, a landowner places a shotgun inside a barn or building that is triggered by a trip-wire placed across a window or doorway. The thief steps upon the wire while trying to enter and is shot. Courts universally condemn this use of deadly force to defend property.

It should be relatively easy to imagine situations in which reasonable force is used to defend another person from attack. Defense of property, however, may be more difficult to conjure.

defense of property | A defense to the intentional torts of assault and battery. Its elements include the use of reasonable force to protect property from damage or dispossession when another person, called the invader, attempts to injure or wrongfully take possession of the property.

ejectment | The name for an old type of lawsuit to get back land taken away wrongfully.

THE CASE OF THE UNHAPPY MARRIAGE

After a night of drinking and socializing, what starts out as a good idea turns deadly. It is 1:00 a.m., and a man sees trucks in his driveway and people on his front and back porches. He can only presume they are up to no good. The often heard phrase, "the more the merrier," proves to not always be true. This case combines the issues of repossession of property and self-defense.

JOSEPH BURTON, et al., Plaintiffs
and
Appellants
v.
GARY SANNER, Defendant
and
Appellant

Court of Appeal of California, Fourth Appellate District, Division One
207 Cal. App. 4th 12
June 21, 2012

This negligence action, for personal injury and wrongful death, arises from shootings by Gary Sanner during an intrusion at his home. The principal question on appeal is whether the trial court prejudicially abused its discretion by admitting the opinions of plaintiffs' expert, on the reasonableness of Sanner's conduct.

Sanner and Jennifer Sanchez married in 2001. Sanchez and her son Shayne moved out of the house in October 2007, and in April 2008 she filed for dissolution of the marriage. On August 8, 2008, Sanchez placed several calls to Sanner about retrieving the title to Shayne's truck, which was at Sanner's house. That afternoon and into the evening, Sanchez and her boyfriend, Joseph Burton, drank beer together.

Sanchez phoned Sanner between 11:00 and 11:30 p.m. Sanner drank at least six beers that evening and he had gone to bed. The phone call awakened him, but he did not answer. Sanchez left a message that she planned to go to his home to retrieve belongings. Sanchez and Burton decided to go to Sanner's home. They again called Sanner about 1:00 a.m. on August 9, and he did not answer. He could see the call came from Burton's cell phone.

Burton's daughter, Jessica Burton (Jessica), and son J. E. were visiting Burton and Sanchez. Sanchez's daughter Shayne, was also visiting. Burton and Sanchez decided the children should help retrieve her belongings. They drove to Sanner's in two trucks. Both trucks backed into and parked in Sanner's driveway at approximately 2:00 a.m. It was a dark night, and there were no streetlights, nor were lights on inside or outside Sanner's house.

Sanner was awakened by the sound of an engine. He saw two trucks backing into his driveway. Sanner thought one of the trucks belonged to Burton and the other belonged to a male friend of Sanchez. Sanner dialed 911 as he loaded his shotgun. He told the 911 operator, "There's two trucks in my yard, and there are three men, and they intend to do me harm. I need help immediately." He also told the operator, "I have a loaded shotgun, and I'm not letting them harm me." "One of them is my estranged wife's boyfriend, and she thinks I've got something of hers that she wants." "They're all intoxicated."

Sanner could see five silhouettes on the front porch. Sanchez claimed that a motion light over the door activated, and she knocked on the door and loudly announced herself. Sanner heard knocking and he told the 911 operator he thought he heard Sanchez's voice. When Sanner did not answer the door, Shayne and J. E went to the back porch. Sanner fired his shotgun mortally wounding J. E. Sanchez heard the gunshot and said, "Gary, no; Gary, stop." Sanner heard yelling. He saw two silhouettes on the front porch. He fired a second shot that hit Sanchez and seriously injured her.

Sanchez and Burton sued Sanner for personal injury and wrongful death, respectively. An expert testified at trial, that in his opinion Sanner's conduct was unreasonable. The jury found Sanner negligent, and that the negligence was a substantial factor in causing plaintiffs' harm. Sanner contends the court erred by instructing the jury on self-defense, and admitting Scott Reitz's expert testimony.

Scott Reitz is a retired police officer who has trained more than 100,000 police officers and military troops in "marksmanship and technique in handling weapons," and in "deadly force." Reitz testified that in his opinion, Sanner's conduct "was not a reasonable response." Reitz faulted Sanner for not exhausting all alternatives to the use of force. Reitz claimed Sanner should have answered the phone call Sanchez made at 1:00 a.m. Reitz testified Sanner could have "simply responded and instructed them not to come over." Reitz also said Sanner should have yelled to make his presence in the house known, warned the intruders he was on the phone with a 911 operator, ordered them off of his property, or fired a warning shot.

"Defendant claims that he is not responsible for plaintiffs' harm because he was acting in self-defense. To succeed, defendant must prove both of the following: (1) That defendant reasonably believed that plaintiffs were going to harm him, and, (2) That defendant used only the amount of force that was reasonably necessary to protect him." The court also gave the following instruction: "The use of deadly force against an alleged intruder is not justified by the law unless the intruder was reasonably believed to have threatened death or serious bodily injury to the defendant."

Whether defendant, as a reasonable man, was justified in believing under all of the circumstances that he was threatened with imminent danger as to justify the use of a deadly weapon in self-defense was a question of fact for the jury. Reitz's testimony inappropriately drew legal conclusions concerning the objective reasonableness of Sanner's conduct. When an expert's opinion amounts to nothing more than an expression of his or her belief on how a case should be decided, it does not aid the jurors, it supplants them

We conclude the admission of Reitz's testimony was prejudicial. The jury was left with the impression that if it found the intruders intended no harm to Sanner, his conduct was unreasonable per se. Further, throughout his testimony, Reitz indicated Sanner should be held to the same standards as police officers. The judgment is reversed. Sanner is entitled to costs.

CASE QUESTIONS

1. Why do you think the decision makes a point of describing the drinking habits of the parties?
2. What standard should be applied to judge Mr. Sanner's behavior? Explain your answer.

HYPOTHETICAL

Consider the case of Isaac, who discovered two teens throwing bricks and stones at his house windows. Isaac crept up behind the duo and leapt from behind some bushes. The delinquents were taken by surprise, and Isaac knocked one to the ground and kicked him in the stomach and tackled the other. Although both teens suffered minor abrasions and bruises, neither was injured severely. The two teens claim that Isaac has committed battery against them. Does Isaac have a defense?

(continues)

Isaac used force against the rowdies to prevent damage to his property. The teens were attempting to damage Isaac's house. The primary question is whether Isaac used reasonable force to prevent the property damage. Because neither of the two teenagers suffered severe harm as a result of Isaac's actions, the force should be deemed reasonable to neutralize the teens. Accordingly, Isaac could successfully apply defense of property against the allegation of battery.

TABLE 9-3
Elements of defense of persons or property

DEFENSE OF PERSONS	DEFENSE OF PROPERTY
Use of reasonable force	Use of reasonable force
To defend or protect a third party from harm	To protect property from damage or dispossession
Third person is threatened by attacking force	Someone attempts to harm or wrongfully possess property

Copyright © 2015 Cengage Learning®.

The elements of defense of persons or property are listed in Table 9-3.

Defense of property is often used in situations in which sellers repossess property from defaulting buyers.

RIGHTFUL REPOSSESSION

An owner of personal property generally has the right to repossess, by force if necessary, a chattel that has been wrongfully taken or withheld. This is the defense of **rightful repossession.** The defense is generally applied to allegations of trespass to land, assault, battery, and sometimes conversion and trespass to chattel. However, the amount of force that may be used is extremely limited. Generally, the elements of rightful repossession include the following (1) use of reasonable force (2) in prompt repossession (3) to retake possession of personal property (4) of which the owner has been wrongfully dispossessed (or to which the owner is denied possession). For this defense, reasonable force is defined along the same lines as defense of property.

rightful repossession |
A defense to trespass to land, trespass to chattel, conversion, assault, and battery. It includes the use of reasonable force to retake possession of personal property of which the owner has been wrongfully disposed, or denied possession.

Retaking Possession of Personal Property

Reasonable Force. The chattel owner seeks to repossess personal property to which he or she is entitled. This is the crux of the defense. If someone has wrongfully dispossessed an owner of his or her chattel, then the owner is entitled to enter upon the dispossessor's land to recover the chattel. This provides a defense to trespass to land. Reasonable force may be applied to recover possession of the personal property.

To illustrate, suppose Raymond took Carl's motorcycle without asking permission and drove the cycle back to his own garage. Carl would be entitled to enter Raymond's garage to recover the cycle. If Raymond attempted to prevent Carl from entering, Carl could use reasonable force to overpower Raymond and recover the cycle. Carl would not be liable for either trespass to land or battery, because he would have the defense of rightful repossession.

Prompt Repossession Efforts

Older common law cases held that a chattel owner's efforts to repossess personal property must occur soon after the chattel had been wrongfully taken away. However, just how promptly this had to occur was not clearly defined. Many nineteenth-century opinions ruled that hot pursuit was necessary. Hot pursuit is usually defined for purposes of criminal law, but its meaning is the same for this tort defense. **Hot (fresh) pursuit,** in this context, may be described as a rapid chase as soon as possible after the owner has discovered that his or her chattel is missing. This presumes, of course, that the personal property owner knows who took the chattel.

hot (fresh) pursuit | The right of a person who has had property taken to use reasonable force to get it back after a chase that takes place immediately after it was taken.

Wrongful Denial of Possession

The chattel owner need not be dispossessed of the personal property for this defense to apply. Consider the example of someone who originally took possession of the chattel with the owner's consent, but later wrongfully refuses to return it. If the owner then attempted to retake possession and was accused of trespass to land, assault, or battery, the owner could apply rightful repossession as a defense.

Most cases involving denial of possession deal with bailments, in which the owner has delivered possession of the chattel to someone else for a specific purpose, with the explicit understanding that the chattel is to be returned at a certain time or upon demand. When an automobile is taken to a mechanic for repair, for instance, there is a bailment. The mechanic would have lawful possession of the vehicle, because the owner left it for repairs. Suppose, however, that the mechanic made unauthorized repairs and sought to charge the owner. If the owner demanded return of the car and the mechanic refused, then this refusal would constitute wrongful denial of possession. The owner could use reasonable force to enter the mechanic's premises to retake the chattel. The owner would not be liable to the mechanic for trespass to land because of the rightful repossession defense.

Note that this result would be different if there had been a dispute over authorized repairs. Most state statutes provide mechanics with possessory liens, which empower repair persons to keep possession of vehicles until repair charges have been paid. However, some statutes provide that the amounts due must be undisputed.

Wrongful Dispossession

For the defense of rightful repossession to apply, the owner's chattel must have been unlawfully dispossessed, or its return have been unlawfully denied. This means that the dispossessor or retainer must not have a legal right to possess (or deny return of) the chattel.

In the preceding bailment example, the mechanic did not possess the automobile unlawfully because the owner had left it for repairs. However, when the mechanic performed unauthorized work and sought payment, and the owner demanded the car's return, then the mechanic wrongfully possessed the vehicle—specifically, the repair person committed trespass to chattel and possibly conversion. Thus, the owner would be entitled to repossess with reasonable force and could use that defense against the mechanic's lawsuit for trespass to land, assault, or battery.

Rightful repossession seems a noble defense, albeit more difficult to conceptualize than self-defense or defense of others and property. One might express the emotional essence of the doctrine as, "It's mine and I'm taking it back now!" The defense appeals to a sense of entitlement. As you read the following hypothetical, with whom do your sympathies lie?

THE CASE FOR REPOSSESSION

Next to buying a home, buying a car is one of the most important purchases a person makes in a lifetime. After falling behind in their payments, a couple is faced with the possibility of their car being taken away from them. Until this happens to a person, little thought is given as to the procedures, if any, a repossession company must follow. The issue of repossession is addressed in this portion of the case. Later in the chapter, a second issue from this case is covered, that of the possible immunity from suit of police officers.

**Nicholaus JOHNSON
and Jennifer Johnson, Plaintiffs,
v.
UNIVERSAL ACCEPTANCE CORPORATION
(MN); Minnesota Repossessors, Inc, the City
of Hibbing, et al.,**
United States District Court, D. Minnesota
2011 WL 3625077
August 17, 2011

This case arises out of the repossession of a vehicle owned by plaintiffs Nicholaus Johnson and Jennifer Johnson ("the Johnsons"). They have sued the companies involved in the repossession, and the police officers for assisting in the repossession. On or about March 21, 2009, the Johnsons acquired a 1999 Ford Expedition. Their purchase was financed by defendant Universal Acceptance Corporation ("UAC"), which acquired a security interest in the vehicle. Within months of purchasing the Expedition, they fell behind on their payments. By December 2009, however, Mr. Johnson

believed they "had worked it out" with UAC and established a verbal agreement with a UAC supervisor.

On January 18, 2010, Thomas and Patrick Lesemann of Minnesota Repossessors, Inc. approached Hibbing Police Officer James Townley while he was parked in his patrol car monitoring traffic. The Lesemanns showed Townley a repossession request from UAC and asked him to standby, while they repossessed the Johnson's car. Townley advised the Lesemanns that "this is a civil matter and I really don't care to get involved" but he agreed to sit in his vehicle and standby to keep the peace. Johnson emerged from his home "really angry and yelling." Townley asked Mr. Johnson to calm down. Mr. Johnson stated: "If you weren't here, these [repossession] guys would be on the ground."

A tow truck arrived and began backing up to the vehicle, which was parked on the street. Mr. Johnson stood between the tow truck and the Expedition. Mr. Johnson was yelling. Officer Nelson arrived in response to Officer Townley's call for police assistance. Officer Nelson advised Ms. Johnson that they were on a public street, along with the vehicle, and that he had no authority to stop the repossession. Mr. Johnson then entered the car while it was hitched, claiming the repossession agents could not take the vehicle while he was sitting inside of it.

Officer Nelson warned Mr. Johnson to calm down or risk arrest for disorderly conduct. According to Mr. Nelson, Mr. Johnson stated, "I am going to get in the truck and I'm going to run those fuckers over." Ultimately, Mr. Johnson gave the repossession agents the keys to the vehicle "because he didn't want them towing and damaging the vehicle." The agents drove the Expedition away. Approximately one week after the repossession, the vehicle was returned to the Johnsons undamaged. The Johnsons' damages resulting from their need to obtain a rental vehicle in the interim period are approximately $400.

The Johnsons filed suit against the repossession agents and companies involved in the repossession. Under Minnesota law, a secured creditor may engage in self-help efforts to repossess collateral upon default as long as such efforts do not result in a breach of the peace. Minn.Stat. § 336.9–609(b)(2). Courts apply a two-part test to "determine whether a breach of the peace has occurred during a repossession of collateral: (1) whether there was entry by the creditor upon debtor's premises, and (2) whether the debtor or one acting in his behalf consented to the entry and repossession." *James v. Ford Motor Credit Co.*, 842 F.Supp. 1202, 1208 (D.Minn .1994). The court in *James* concluded that the limitations on self-help repossession apply only "to those attempts at self-help repossession where the creditor enters the debtor's private residence or business property in the face of the revocation of consent to repossession." Creditors are entitled to self-help repossession on a public street despite debtors' protests. "As a repossession moves farther from the debtor's residence, the argument for a breach of the peace becomes more tenuous." Here,

while the Johnsons made their objection to the repossession abundantly clear, the repossession agents were repossessing the vehicle from a public street, not from the Johnsons' private property.

It is unnecessary for the court to determine whether the agents' repossession was lawful to dispose of the instant motion, however. Given the Johnsons' failure to cite any precedent for the proposition that a repossession in a public street over the debtors' protests violates Minnesota law, the police officers cannot be liable for facilitating the repossession simply because they did not compel the repossession agents to leave. As officer Townley stated in his deposition, "my only job there is to make sure that things go civilly and that the laws aren't broken and nobody gets hurt. I don't have the right to tell the Johnsons to give the vehicle back to the repossession people, and I don't have the repossession people, the right to tell them to leave."

The Johnsons have not cited caselaw in which a vehicle repossession accomplished on a public street was deemed violative of Minnesota law. As discussed above, the officers' threats to arrest Mr. Johnson occurred after the repossession was complete and were appropriate responses to his behavior. The officers needed to diffuse the situation, which necessarily resulted in one of the parties possessing the property when the public peace was restored. No reasonable officer standing in the shoes of Nelson or Townley could have believed their conduct was unlawful in light of clearly established law.

The Johnsons have cited no evidence to suggest that the officers' actions were willful or malicious; they have not responded to the City of Hibbing defendants' arguments regarding their state law claims at all. The court concludes that the officers are entitled to official immunity from the Johnsons' state law claims, as is the City of Hibbing.

The City of Hibbing defendants' Motion for Summary Judgment is GRANTED.

CASE QUESTIONS

1. What distinction does the court make between a car being parked on a driveway versus the public street?
2. Was there a breach of peace? Explain your answer.

HYPOTHETICAL

Ann was buying an automobile from Bryce. Ann wrote a check to Bryce for the final payment and this check bounced (i.e., the bank did not pay it because there were insufficient funds in Ann's account). Bryce angrily went over to Ann's house and drove away in the car. As soon as Ann discovered the check problem, she telephoned Bryce's apartment and left a message on his answering machine that she would be over directly to pay cash.

The first issue is whether Bryce had the right to repossess the automobile once Ann's check bounced. This would depend upon the terms of their agreement, or if the agreement did not address the problem, then upon creditors' rights statutes. For the sake of example, assume that no statutes address the question and that the parties' contract was silent as well. Although it is true that Ann breached her contract by bouncing her payment check to Bryce, she also swiftly corrected the error. Most courts would hold that Bryce could not use self-help remedies such as repossession without first contacting Ann to see if she could make good on the check. By repossessing the car without first talking with Ann, and because Ann has paid nearly the entire purchase price (and thus has a substantial equity, meaning property interest, in the vehicle), Bryce has committed trespass to chattel. Thus, Ann has been wrongfully dispossessed of her chattel. She could then enter Bryce's real estate to recover her automobile without being liable to Bryce for trespass to land. Ann would be entitled to the defense of rightful repossession.

It should also be noted that Bryce would not be able to claim rightful repossession as a defense to trespass to chattel. Because Bryce did not first communicate with Ann regarding the bad check and alternative means of payment, most courts would say that Bryce could not defend his retaking of the car on the grounds of rightful repossession. However, if Bryce had telephoned Ann about the check, and she had replied that she could not or would not make the final payment, then Bryce would be legally entitled to repossess the vehicle. Under this set of circumstances, Bryce could use rightful repossession as a defense to trespass to chattel.

A synopsis of rightful repossession appears in Table 9-4.

TABLE 9-4

Elements of rightful repossession

Use of reasonable force
Prompt repossession
To repossess personal property
Owner has been wrongfully dispossessed of the chattel or has been improperly denied possession

MISTAKE

Sometimes people act based upon inaccurate information or incorrect interpretations of events. The actor intended the result of his or her conduct but behaved under false beliefs. Often, had a person known the truth, he or she would have behaved differently. Tort law recognizes this tendency toward error, in which everyone has engaged at one time or another. The defense of mistake provides individuals with an escape route from intentional tort liability. As a legal defense, **mistake** is the good-faith belief, based upon incorrect information, that one is justified in committing an intentional tort under the circumstances. The elements may be detailed as follows: (1) good-faith conviction that one's actions are justified (2) with the belief based upon faulty information; and (3) the conduct would otherwise be considered tortious but for the erroneous belief.

mistake | An unintentional error or act.

The *Restatement (Second) of Torts*

The *Restatement (Second) of Torts* is a well-respected, often-cited summary of tort law that was created by the American Law Institute in 1952. It is a secondary source of the law. Although it is not considered binding authority, it is viewed as highly persuasive in presenting the current state of tort law, and tort trends. Judges and attorneys alike rely on this reference tool, which states principles in common law decisions that are repeated over and over. The American Law Institute has created three series of Restatements, addressing a variety of legal subjects. Torts are addressed in both the Second and Third series. The Third series focuses on products liability, physical and emotional harm, and apportionment. In the *Restatement (Second)*'s chapter 45, justifications and excuses to tort liability are discussed. The following is an excerpt applicable to the mistake defense.

restatement (second) of torts | One volume of a respected series of books that summarizes tort law; created by the American Law Institute in 1952.

> *Restatement (Second) of Torts* § 890
> **Comments a & f**
> **American Law Institute (1979)**
>
> In some cases the law creates a privilege . . . . [A] privilege is given although it adversely affects the legally protected interests of another. This is ordinarily true when the actor is protected although mistaken (see Comment *f*), as when one acts in self-defense against another whom he reasonably but erroneously believes to be an aggressor . . . .
>
>   *f. Mistake* . . . .
>
>   When the privilege is conditional, a person is sometimes protected by his reasonable belief in the existence of facts that would give rise to a privilege, even though the facts do not exist. Thus one is not liable for using reasonable force in the protection of himself or another against what he reasonably believes to be an aggression of another . . . ; a policeman is not liable for mistakenly arresting one whom he

believes to have committed a felony . . . and a private person is similarly protected if a felony has been committed . . . ; a parent or teacher is not liable for mistakenly but reasonably disciplining a student.

The elements of mistake are summarized in Table 9-5.

TABLE 9-5
Elements of mistake

Good-faith conviction that actor's conduct is justified
Belief based upon erroneous information
Behavior would be tortious except for incorrect belief

HYPOTHETICAL

Diedra was shopping at a local convenience store. The manager thought she saw Diedra put a pack of chewing gum into her purse. When Diedra left the store without stopping at the cashier, the manager asked her to step back inside the store to see the contents of her purse. The manager explained that she thought she had seen Diedra take merchandise without paying. Diedra emptied her purse, but no store items were included. If Diedra claimed that the manager had committed false imprisonment, defamation, or infliction of emotional distress, could the manager use mistake as a defense?

Assume that the manager's acts arguably constituted any one of these intentional torts. Nevertheless, courts would readily rule that, under these circumstances, the manager was justified in detaining Diedra for questioning. So long as the interrogation was conducted reasonably (such as in private for a short time period), then the courts would consider the manager's behavior to be acceptable. The manager had a good-faith belief that Diedra had shoplifted (although, in fact, she had not). The manager acted based upon this erroneous conviction, expecting that her conduct would be legally excused under the circumstances.

PRIVILEGE

privilege | As a defense against an intentional tort, *privilege* is a legal justification to engage in otherwise tortious conduct in order to accomplish a compelling social goal.

As an intentional torts defense, **privilege** is a legal justification to engage in otherwise tortious conduct in order to accomplish a compelling social goal. This defense is based upon the right of a person to do what most people are not permitted to do. It is a right conferred on a person by society. For example, as a landowner, one may eject a person from one's own property, but other people may not do this. Only the landowner is thus privileged.

Privilege is most commonly a defense to trespass to land, trespass to chattel, conversion, assault, battery, and false imprisonment, although it may be applied against other intentional torts as well. Privilege includes the following considerations:

1. Do the actor's motives for engaging in an intentional tort outweigh the injury to the victim or his or her property?

2. Was the actor justified in committing the intentional tort to accomplish his or her socially desirable purposes, or could a less damaging action have been taken instead?

This formula shows how courts balance values between the socially acceptable motives of the tortfeasor (actor) and the tort victim's compensation for injury. Privilege presumes that the intentional tort is legally justified because of the higher purposes to be achieved.

Motives and Socially Desirable Goals

Motive describes the goal that a participant wishes to accomplish by taking a particular action. Motive may be discovered by probing the mental state of the actor. This mind-reading occurs in many areas of law. For example, in criminal law, *mens rea* loosely translates from the Latin as "evil thoughts" and suggests a psychological component to criminal conduct. In tort law, motive is synonymous with **intent,** which is broadly defined as the desire to attain a certain result. For purposes of the privilege defense, motive must be socially advantageous to a point that excuses intentional harm to another person or his or her property. The example of trespassing to save a drowning child's life sharply illustrates the clearly superior social objective that would give rise to the defense against the landowner's trespass-to-land lawsuit.

motive | The reason why a person does something.

intent | The resolve or purpose to use a particular means to reach a particular result. Intent usually explains how a person wants to do something and what that person wants to get done, whereas motive usually explains why.

Less Injurious Alternatives

With privilege defenses, courts frequently ask whether the tortfeasor's objectives could have been reached through behavior that would have been less harmful to the victim. Suppose Sinbad discovers an automobile on fire next to a natural gas storage facility. Given the likelihood that the burning car will ignite the gas tanks, which would explode along with a sizeable portion of the surrounding neighborhood, Sinbad sprays the flaming vehicle with water, irreparably damaging the engine. The car owner would complain against Sinbad's conversion or trespass to chattel. Sinbad would defend by arguing privilege. The court would query: Could Sinbad have saved the storage facility (and surrounding area) through a less damaging act?

The answer to this question depends upon the extent of the fire. If only a small portion of the automobile had been burning, such as something in the trunk, Sinbad could have isolated the danger by concentrating water only into the trunk compartment. If the interior had also been ablaze, Sinbad would be forced to expose more car to the water to put out the fire. Still, he might have spared the engine compartment. However, if the inferno had engulfed the entire vehicle, he would have no choice other than to inundate it with water.

Similarity between Privilege and Other Defenses

Several distinct intentional tort defenses, such as rightful repossession, self-defense, or defense of others or property, are simply particular types of privilege. Each has a social benefit component that justifies otherwise tortious misconduct. Necessity is another form of privilege that has also become a separate defense in its own right. The same is true of public officers' immunity for legal process enforcement, warrantless arrest, and reasonable discipline. These defenses to intentional torts are discussed in the remaining sections of this chapter.

The *Restatement (Second)* Position

The *Restatement (Second) of Torts* § 890 focuses on privileges, noting that the term is broadly defined to include many of the specific defenses discussed throughout this chapter. The illustrations in the Comments section are particularly helpful in understanding the scope of privilege.

Restatement (Second) of Torts § 890 & Comments
American Law Institute (1979)

§ 890. Privileges

One who otherwise would be liable for a tort is not liable if he acts in pursuance of and within the limits of a privilege of his own or of a privilege of another that was properly delegated to him.

Comment

a. As stated in § 10, the word "privilege" is used throughout this Restatement to denote the fact that conduct that under ordinary circumstances would subject the actor to liability, under particular circumstances does not subject him to the liability.

* * *

In some cases the law creates a privilege . . . as when the owner of land is given a privilege to eject a trespasser upon his land or to enter the land of another to abate a private nuisance, or when a citizen is given the privilege of arresting a felon . . . .

c. Purpose of privilege—Conditional privileges created by rule of law. Most of the privileges that are not based on consent are conditioned upon their being performed for the purpose of protecting the interest for which the privilege was given. This is illustrated in cases in which force is used against another; in self-defense or in defense of a third person . . .; in the defense of the possession of land . . .; in the recapture of land or chattels . . . ; in an arrest by a private person or a peace officer . . .; in the prevention of crime . . . ; in the disciplining of children . . . .

d. *Purpose of privilege—Absolute privileges.* In certain cases in which the interests of the public are overwhelming, the purpose of the actor is immaterial. Thus for some or all statements, complete immunity from civil liability exists as to defamatory statements made during the course of judicial proceedings . . . , as well as to statements by legislators and certain administrative officers while acting in the performance of their functions.

HYPOTHETICAL

Anastasia owns a grocery in town. One of her customers notified her that several cans of Buddy Boy's Baked Beans were bulging, which is a symptom of contamination. Anastasia opened these cans and discovered that the food had spoiled. She placed an advertisement in the local newspaper warning her customers to return any can of Buddy Boy's, whether bulging or not, because of spoilage. In fact, only four cans of the product were defective. Buddy Boy's manufacturer, E. I. Wilcott & Company, sued Anastasia for disparagement of goods. Anastasia claimed privilege, arguing that her motive was to protect the public from food poisoning. Would the defense carry the day?

Truth is an absolute defense in any type of defamation action, including commercial disparagement. In our hypothetical, however, the truth was exaggerated. Only a few cans were tainted. Nonetheless, there was no way of determining this without recalling as many cans as possible from Anastasia's customers. A court would rule that Anastasia was justified in advertising the warning to her customers, and so Anastasia would not be liable to E. I. Wilcott & Company for disparagement of goods.

The elements of privilege are shown in Table 9-6.

Actor's motives in committing intentional tort outweigh injury to victim or property
Actor was justified in engaging in intentional tort to accomplish socially desirable goals
No less-damaging alternative action could have been taken
Exception: Absolute privilege of judges, legislators, etc. These actors' motives are immaterial.

TABLE 9-6

Elements of privilege

An example of privilege is where force can be used for self-defense.

NECESSITY

Necessity is another variety of privilege that excuses otherwise tortious misconduct. Under this defense, the tortfeasor is justified in engaging in an intentional tort to prevent more serious injury from an external force. **Necessity** contains four elements: (1) committing an intentional tort (2) to avert more serious injury (3) caused by a force other than the tortfeasor (4) and the tortfeasor's actions were reasonably necessary to avoid the greater harm. This defense is based on the theory that the benefit—prevention of a greater harm—outweighs the risk of the intentional injury (competing harms).

necessity | Often refers to a situation that requires an action that would otherwise be illegal or expose a person to tort liability.

Thwarting a More Substantial Harm

In a necessity situation, the tortfeasor is usually faced with having to choose between the lesser of two evils. On the one hand, the tortfeasor must inflict injury upon a victim or the victim's property. On the other hand, the tortfeasor could do nothing and watch a greater chaos occur. For example, suppose Antonio is aboard a ship that suddenly begins to sink. There are several passengers aboard, including Antonio, as well as valuable cargo. If the cargo were thrown overboard, the boat could stay afloat long enough for help to arrive. So Antonio elects to toss the cargo and save the passengers' lives. The cargo owner could sue Antonio for trespass to chattel, but the defense of necessity would insulate Antonio from liability. Although Antonio committed an intentional tort, he sought only to prevent greater harm caused by a force beyond his control (namely, the ship's sinking).

External Forces

For necessity to operate as a defense to an intentional tort, the more significant danger being avoided must originate from a source other than the tortfeasor. For instance, in the previous illustration, the boat began to sink through no fault of Antonio's. However, suppose he had caused an explosion in the engine room by improper fuel mixing, and thus blew a hole in the hull of the craft. Because Antonio created the greater hazard, he could not claim necessity in throwing the cargo overboard. Had it not been for his misconduct in the engine room, the extreme peril would never have happened. The necessity defense cannot protect a tortfeasor who creates the catastrophic condition and then must engage in an intentional tort to resolve the crisis.

Reasonably Necessary Action

As is generally true with privilege, necessity requires that the tortfeasor's conduct be reasonably necessary to prevent the more substantial danger. Thus, the tortfeasor must use only that degree of force required to avert the greater risk. Using the sinking ship example, suppose that the leak in the ship's hull occurred not because of Antonio's misbehavior but because of faulty sealing techniques. If Antonio could plug the leak rather than abandon ship, it would not be necessary for him to toss the cargo to save the passengers.

Fires further illustrate this aspect of reasonably required action; many necessity cases involve burning buildings. Several nineteenth-century court opinions discussed "row" structures, which were many individual buildings attached in long rows down a street. If one were to catch fire, it was likely that the entire block would burn to the ground. To avoid this calamity, the flaming building was often destroyed. There simply was no less-damaging alternative when the building was fully ablaze. If the building owner sued for trespass to land, the courts routinely applied the necessity defense to protect the tortfeasor from liability to the building owner.

The *Restatement (Second)* Position

The *Restatement (Second)* addresses necessity as a defense in emergency situations in which the tortfeasor is compelled to immediate action by a crisis. In such cases, the defense operates to protect the defendant from liability. Note how the *Restatement*'s elements are distinguishable from those previously discussed in the text.

Restatement (Second) of Torts §§ 890, 892D & Comments
American Law Institute (1979)

[§ 890, Comment a.] [The emergency defense exists] when the protection of the public is of overriding importance, as when one is privileged to destroy buildings to avert a public disaster . . . .

§ 892D. Emergency Action Without Consent

Conduct that injures another does not make the actor liable to the other, even though the other has not consented to it[,] if

(a) an emergency makes it necessary or apparently necessary, in order to prevent harm to the other, to act before there is opportunity to obtain consent from the other or one empowered to consent for him, and

(b) the actor has no reason to believe that the other, if he had the opportunity to consent, would decline.

Comment

a. The rule stated in this Section covers a group of exceptional situations in which the actor is privileged to proceed without the consent of another and without any manifested or apparent consent, on the assumption that if the other had the opportunity to decide he would certainly consent. This privilege must necessarily be a limited one and can arise only in situations of emergency, when there is no time to consult the other or one empowered to consent for him, or [if] for reasons such as the unconsciousness of the other his consent cannot be obtained. The mere possibility that the other might consent if he were able to do so is not enough; and the conduct must be so clearly and manifestly to the other's advantage that there is no reason to believe that the consent would not be given. If the actor knows or has reason to know, because of past refusals or other circumstances, that the consent would not be given, he is not privileged to act . . . .

Necessity can be a puzzling defense. Its elements compel courts to balance competing interests, employing somewhat more value judgment than usual. The following hypothetical illustrates this aspect. A short review of the elements of necessity is provided in Table 9-7.

TABLE 9-7
Elements of necessity

Committing intentional tort
Purpose to avert more harmful injury
Harm threatened by force other than tortfeasor
Tortfeasor's actions were reasonably necessary to prevent danger of greater harm

Copyright © 2015 Cengage Learning®.

HYPOTHETICAL

Kenny owns an exotic pet store, in which he sells, among other wild animals, several species of snakes. One day a customer accidentally knocked a cage containing a python onto the floor, causing the door to spring open. The snake slithered out into the aisles searching for food. An infant was strapped in an automobile safety seat that her mother used as a carrier while shopping. The youngster's mother was several feet away looking at some unusual fish. The snake approached the infant and clearly intended to consume the child. Quickly, another patron, Jeff, impaled the python with a hunting knife (which was on display on a nearby shelf). Kenny sued Jeff for trespass to chattel. Could necessity excuse Jeff's actions?

Reasonably necessary action is the critical element in this hypothetical. Jeff's actions were reasonably necessary. He would not be liable for trespass to chattel.

▌ PUBLIC OFFICER'S IMMUNITY FOR LEGAL PROCESS ENFORCEMENT

Public officials often engage in activity that normally would be considered intentionally tortious. However, because such persons are authorized by law to engage in such conduct, they are protected from liability. This is referred to as **immunity**. Several types of governmental action fall within this protected class. The most common include (1) process serving, (2) execution sales, (3) attachment or replevin, (4) arrest by warrant, (5) prosecutors acting in official capacity, and (6) judges acting in official capacity.

immunity | When persons are authorized by law to engage in certain conduct, and they are protected from liability.

Service of Process

Process, process serving, or **service of process** are the methods by which a defendant in a lawsuit is notified that a plaintiff has filed suit against the defendant. The cases of actual physical delivery give rise to litigation. The defendant might sue the sheriff for trespass to land when the sheriff arrived on the defendant's real estate to deliver the summons. However, the sheriff has the power to enter another person's land to serve process. The landowner's lawsuit against the sheriff would fail.

Execution Sales

When a plaintiff wins judgment against the defendant in a civil action, the defendant usually has a certain period of time to pay the judgment. If the defendant fails to pay, the plaintiff may return to court requesting the court to order the defendant's property sold to satisfy the judgment. These forced sales are often referred to as **execution sales** or **sheriff's sales,** because the sheriff is frequently the public official responsible for seizing and selling the defendant's property. The defendant might sue the sheriff for trespass to land, trespass to chattel, and conversion after the sheriff comes and gets the defendant's property. However, the sheriff is legally protected.

Attachment or Replevin

Attachment is a court-ordered remedy in a lawsuit. When a plaintiff is entitled to a remedy against the defendant in a lawsuit, and the defendant is likely to dispose of his or her property to avoid losing it in a subsequent action, the plaintiff may ask the court to attach the property. The court then orders a law enforcement officer, such as the sheriff, to seize the defendant's property. The defendant might sue the sheriff for conversion or trespass to chattel. However, the sheriff is authorized by statute or common law to take the defendant's property.

Replevin is another court-ordered remedy. A plaintiff sues a defendant who wrongfully possesses the plaintiff's chattel and refuses to return it. The plaintiff asks the court for replevin, which means that the court would order the defendant to return the personal property to the plaintiff. If the defendant refuses, the court could instruct the sheriff to seize the chattel.

Arrest by Warrant

Police officers often arrest suspected criminals under a warrant for arrest. Suppose the suspect was innocent of any crimes. Could the suspect sue the police department for false imprisonment and infliction of emotional distress for having been arrested? If the law enforcement personnel were acting pursuant to an arrest warrant properly ordered by a judge, and if they acted in good faith, then they would not be liable for any intentional torts.

process | A court's ordering a defendant to show up in court or risk losing a lawsuit; a summons.

process serving | The method by which a defendant in a lawsuit is notified that the plaintiff has filed suit against the defendant. Also called service of process.

service of process | The delivery (or its legal equivalent, such as publication in a newspaper in some cases) of a legal paper by an authorized person.

execution sale | A forced public sale held by a sheriff or other public official of property seized to pay a judgment.

sheriff's sale | A sale (of property) held by a sheriff to pay a court judgment against the owner of the property.

attachment | Formally seizing property (or a person) in order to bring it under control of the court. This is usually done by getting a court order to have a law enforcement officer take control of the property.

replevin | A legal action to get back property wrongfully held by another person.

Prosecutors and Judges

prosecutor | A public official who represents the government's case against a person accused of a crime.

judge | The person who runs a courtroom, decides all legal questions, and sometimes decides entire cases by also deciding factual questions.

Prosecutors and **judges** acting in the scope of their positions are privileged and immune from liability for their actions. If this were not so, no one would accept such a position. It is inherent in these positions to occasionally intentionally injure someone mentally, emotionally, and by reputation. Liability for their mistakes would have a chilling effect on their performance. That is, they would be too afraid of making a mistake and thus would act against social benefit. Therefore, public policy has always been to allow these persons immunity from liability in the honest performance of their positions.

There are exceptions to the privilege and immunity doctrines. For example, 42 U.S.C. § 1983 permits liability of public officers (usually other than prosecutors and judges) if the performance of their duties involves activities that deprive persons of their civil rights. Such an action is called a civil rights action or a 1983 action (*1983* is the section number of the law permitting this action, not the year it was passed). If a police officer arrests someone without a warrant and without probable cause, it is a violation of civil rights and the officer may be liable.

THE CASE OF REPOSSESSION (PART II)

Select portions of the case of *Johnson v. Universal Acceptance Corp. et al.* were reprinted earlier in this chapter. The issue of repossession of chattel was addressed. Reread the case as a refresher for the facts pertaining to the acts of the police officers. The court has also addressed a second issue, that of police and state liability, and the immunity defense. These issues were discussed in the previous section, and addressed by the court in the following portion of the case.

Nicholaus JOHNSON and Jennifer Johnson, Plaintiffs,

v.

UNIVERSAL ACCEPTANCE CORPORATION (MN); Minnesota Repossessors, Inc .; John Doe repossessor 1; John Doe repossessor 2; John Doe repossessor 3; Officer James Townley; Officer Ryan Nelson; Officer Eric Hietala; Officer Jeremiah Nutzhorn; and The City of Hibbing, Defendants

United States District Court, D. Minnesota

2011 WL 3625077

August 17, 2011

This case arises out of the repossession of a vehicle owned by plaintiffs the Johnsons. They have sued not only the companies involved in the repossession, but also several police officers who performed a civil standby during the repossession, as well as the officers' employer, the City of Hibbing itself ("the City" and, collectively with the officers, "the Hibbing defendants").

The Johnsons assert that the officers' alleged intervention on behalf of and assistance to the repossessors constituted a deprivation of due process and illegal seizure in violation of the Fourteenth and Fourth Amendments. The Hibbing defendants claim that the officers involved in the incident are entitled to qualified immunity and official immunity for their conduct.

The Hibbing defendants argue that responding police officers Townley, Nelson, and Hietala are entitled to summary judgment on the ground of qualified immunity. "Qualified immunity shields government officials from suit unless their conduct violated a clearly established constitutional or statutory right of which a reasonable person would have known." *Yowell v. Combs*, 89 F.3d 542,

544 (8th Cir.1996). In considering an assertion of qualified immunity, the court considers two questions:

> (1) whether there was a deprivation of a constitutional right; and, if so, (2) whether a reasonable official would understand his conduct was unlawful in the situation he confronted. *Vaughn v. Greene Cnty., Ark.,* 438 F.3d 845, 850 (8th Cir.2006).

The Fourth Amendment protects individuals from "unreasonable searches and seizures . . . ." U.S. Const. amend. IV. Through the Fourteenth Amendment, the Fourth Amendment is applicable to action by state actors. *See* Mapp v. Ohio, 367 U.S. 643, 655 (1961). The Fourteenth Amendment also provides that a state may not "deprive any person of life, liberty, or property, without due process of law." U.S. Const. amend. XIV. "A seizure [for purposes of the Fourth Amendment] occurs when 'there is some meaningful interference with an individual's possessory interests' in the property seized."

Neither the Fourth nor Fourteenth Amendment protects against the conduct of private persons such as the repossession agents in this case. *Moore v. Carpenter,* 404 F.3d 1043, 1046 (8th Cir.2005). Rather, "states are held responsible for private conduct only when the state has exercised coercion or significantly encouraged the conduct, not when the state has merely acquiesced in a private party's initiatives." Accordingly, when a police officer is involved in a private party's repossession of property, there is no state action if the officer merely keeps the peace, but there is state action if the officer affirmatively intervenes to aid the repossessor enough that the repossession would not have occurred without the officer's help.

The court concludes that the officers' behavior with regard to the repossession did not rise to the level of state action. The Johnsons argue that the officers "intimidated Mr. Johnson into not exercising his right to resist the repossession by threatening to arrest him when he became too aggressive, while ignoring his clear objections" and "recognizing the repossessors' repossession order over the Johnsons' insistence that they were current under their agreement with the bank." The record is to the contrary. Townley agreed to perform a civil standby, and requested backup only after Mr. Johnson threatened: "If you weren't here, these guys would be on the ground."

When Ms. Johnson began yelling at one of the repossession agents, Officer Hietala simply separated the two. Both Hietala and Nelson believed they had probable cause to arrest Mr. Johnson based on his conduct, but allowed him to vent his frustrations as long as he did not engage in any physical violence. These actions defeat a finding of coercion or affirmative intervention; rather, they reflect reasonable efforts at keeping the peace.

Given the Johnsons' failure to cite any precedent for the proposition that a repossession in a public street over the debtors' protests violates Minnesota law, the police officers cannot be liable for facilitating the repossession simply because they did not compel the repossession agents to leave. As Officer Townley stated in his deposition; My only job there is to make sure that things go civilly and that the laws are not broken and nobody gets hurt. I do not have the right to tell the Johnsons to give the vehicle back to the repossession people, and I do not have the right to tell the repossession people to leave.

The court concludes that the officers were appropriately neutral in attempting to keep the peace, and that their conduct did not rise to the level of state action. Without state action, there can be no violation of the Fourteenth Amendment. In the absence of any constitutional violation, the officers are entitled to qualified immunity.

Even assuming that the repossession was accomplished under color of state law, the officers are nonetheless entitled to qualified immunity if their actions did not violate "clearly established statutory or constitutional rights of which a reasonable officer would have known." *Harlow v. Fitzgerald,* 457 U.S. 800, 818 (1982). The officers' threats to arrest Mr. Johnson occurred after the repossession was complete and were appropriate responses to his behavior. No reasonable officer standing in the shoes of Nelson, Townley, or Hietala could have believed their conduct was unlawful in light of clearly established law.

A municipality may be held liable for the actions of its agents if its custom or policy caused or was the moving force behind a deprivation of a federal right.

(continues)

Since the court concludes the officers did not violate the Johnsons' rights, this claim fails. When the claim is regarding inadequate training, a plaintiff must establish that such training failures reflect "a 'deliberate' or 'conscious' choice by a municipality." *City of Canton, Ohio v. Harris,* 489 U.S. 378, 389 (1989). The Johnsons have cited no such evidence. Accordingly, the court grants summary judgment to the City.

Based on the foregoing, and the records, files, and proceedings herein, IT IS HEREBY ORDERED that the Hibbing defendants' Motion for Summary Judgment is GRANTED.

CASE QUESTIONS

1. What would be an example of a state action by a police officer?
2. Under what circumstances would a police officer be entitled to qualified immunity?
3. Provide an example of when qualified immunity would not apply to the actions of a police officer.

HYPOTHETICAL

Emily sued Rupa. The sheriff delivered a copy of the summons and Emily's complaint to Rupa's house. Rupa did not appear at trial, and Emily won a default judgment against Rupa. After 30 days, Rupa had failed to pay the judgment. Emily filed a writ of execution with the court, which ordered the sheriff to seize Rupa's property. The sheriff again returned to Rupa's house to collect the chattels that could be sold at an execution sale. The proceeds from the sale went to satisfy Emily's judgment. Rupa sued the sheriff for trespass to land, trespass to chattel, and conversion. The sheriff applied the defense of legal process enforcement.

This hypothetical is probably the easiest to answer of any in the text. The sheriff was acting under court order to enforce legal processes, and so the defense would succeed. Rupa's lawsuit would be promptly dismissed.

The elements of the legal-process-enforcement defense are listed in Table 9-8.

TABLE 9-8

Types of legal-process-enforcement defenses and elements of warrantless-arrest defenses

LEGAL PROCESS ENFORCEMENT	WARRANTLESS ARREST
Process serving	Law enforcement officers' power to arrest if a felony is committed or if they reasonably believe a felony occurred (witness a felony or breach of peace)
Execution sales	Citizen's arrest (felonies or breaches of peace)
Attachment or replevin	
Arrest by warrant	

▐ WARRANTLESS ARREST BY LAW ENFORCEMENT OFFICIALS OR CITIZENS

Police officers, and sometimes even ordinary citizens, engage in *warrantless arrests*. Could they be liable for false imprisonment, battery, assault, trespass to land, and infliction of emotional distress?

Statutes and common law authorize law enforcement personnel to arrest criminal suspects, even without court-issued warrants, under certain circumstances. For example, when a police officer witnesses a felony, he or she may arrest the suspect immediately. This proper enforcement of a legal process would be a defense against the suspect's intentional tort lawsuit.

Private citizens, too, may take suspected criminals into custody under the theory of *citizen's arrest*. Under the common law, a private citizen may take a suspect into custody if the citizen has witnessed the suspect commit a felony or breach of the peace. This would include situations in which the citizen reasonably thinks that the suspect has committed a felony. Historically, this defense was often used to protect store owners who detained suspected shoplifters from liability for false imprisonment actions.

Normally, modern warrantless arrest does not involve private-citizen participation to the extent the pre-twentieth-century cases did. However, private police, such as company security, are often involved in today's cases.

The warrantless-arrest defense, together with the defense of legal process enforcement, are both summarized in Table 9-8.

HYPOTHETICAL

Carter is a security officer on the night shift at a local factory. He noticed someone suspicious lurking in the shadows near a restricted-access building containing company records and other valuables. He turned his flashlight on the suspect, whom he did not recognize. He demanded identification and the reason the stranger was present on factory grounds. The stranger said nothing and attempted to flee. Carter tackled the individual, forcibly returned him to the security office, and telephoned the police. The stranger turned out to be an employee of a competitor to Carter's employer. The stranger sued Carter for battery, false imprisonment, and infliction of emotional distress. Would Carter be entitled to a defense under the citizen's arrest theory?

Carter witnessed a simple trespass to land, which is not a felony under either statutory or common law. The stranger had merely trespassed onto the factory's property. Further, the stranger had not breached the peace. However, Carter reasonably believed that the suspect was about to engage in a felony (namely, burglary or theft). In his experience as a security guard, Carter had seen many felons behave just as the stranger had acted. Thus, Carter's reasonable belief that the suspect was about to commit a felony was sufficient to justify his behavior. Carter would not be liable to the stranger for any of the intentional torts.

▌ STATUTES OF LIMITATIONS

Statutes of limitations are statutes restricting the time within which a plaintiff may file his or her lawsuit for particular causes of action against a defendant. All states have statutes of limitations for almost all tort actions, including intentional torts. (Sometimes they are called *limitation of actions.*) The most common tort statutes of limitations are two years. This means that the plaintiff has two years from the date that an intentional tort occurred to file his or her lawsuit against the defendant. If the plaintiff fails to file within this statutory time period, then his or her cause of action against the defendant is barred forever.

Although two years is a common statute of limitations period for many torts, the exact time period varies among states and different types of torts. One should always research the specific statute of limitations for each cause of action, whether in tort or in other areas of law. This is a vital piece of information for both the plaintiff and the defendant. If the statute of limitations has expired, the defendant may respond with this defense and have the plaintiff's case dismissed or otherwise disposed of (usually by summary judgment). The plaintiff's attorney must be aware of the statute of limitations and file the lawsuit in a timely manner, or risk a malpractice suit.

▌ WORKERS' COMPENSATION

Another defense to an intentional tort action might be that the action is prevented by a state's workers' compensation statute. These statutes cover workers who are injured, are killed, or become ill as a result of incidents occurring during the course and scope of their employment. Workers' compensation statutes bar tort actions against the employer and are considered a worker's sole remedy for on-the-job injuries and death, regardless of fault, in most states. Workers' compensation is also addressed in Chapter 13 in relation to tort immunities.

Workers' compensation is insurance that provides cash benefits and/or medical care for workers who are injured on the job or who become ill or die as a result of their job. Employers pay for this insurance. This is a form of strict liability, a no-fault system by state. In workers' compensation cases, no one party is found to be at fault. However, an employee's injury must "arise out of" and occur in the "course of employment." This means that an injury that occurs at work and is related to work will be covered. In contrast, if an employee is on the way to or from work and injuries are sustained, they will generally not be covered.

The amount a worker collects is not based upon, nor is it affected by, whether an employer is at fault. Unlike a traditional negligence claim, the employee does not have to worry that his or her claim will be defeated by the employer's assertion of defenses such as the employee's contributory negligence, assumption of the risk, or that the injury was actually caused by a fellow employee rather than the employer.

It is important to note that although workers' compensation statutes all but eliminate suits between injured employees and employers, an employee still retains the right to bring an action against a third party who may have also caused or contributed to the injuries. Workers' compensation only bars suits against the employer, not outside third parties. Accordingly, an employee might bring a workers' compensation claim and still sue a private entity such as a janitorial service that left a floor dangerously slippery with wax, or a manufacturer that produced a defective product that was used at work.

However, if an employee intentionally tries to injure himself or herself, or is injured as a result of drug or alcohol intoxication, then the employee cannot collect benefits. Workers' compensation statutes specify which type of employers and which employees are covered by the acts. Not all employees or all forms of employment are covered by workers' compensation.

Employees must report workplace injuries to the employer and fill out a claim form in order to apply for benefits. Generally, there is a waiting period before the employee can collect benefits. An employer cannot fire an employee solely because the employee has filed for benefits.

The injured employee's medical provider determines the extent of disability, if any. Cash benefits are based upon and determined according to disability classifications ranging from temporary partial disability to permanent total disability. In the event of the death of an employee as a result of a workplace injury, the surviving spouse and family may be entitled to a cash benefit. In the event an employee can no longer return to his or her previous type of work, vocational rehabilitation is offered to train the employee for a new career.

THE CASE OF COMPENSATION

As a paralegal, you will run into a lot of different fact patterns when dealing with workers' compensation claims. The important thing to remember is that all compensation cases must still go through the same legal analysis. Were the injuries sustained "arising out of and in the course of employment"? This case presents an additional analysis because some of the injuries alleged are psychiatric injuries.

Michael Rash, Petitioner,

v.

WORKERS' COMPENSATION APPEALS BOARD, Stanislaus County Sheriff's Department, et al., Respondents

Court of Appeal, Fifth District, California

No. F051520

(WCAB No. STK 197752)

May 25, 2007

A sheriff's deputy asks whether the injuries he sustained while returning from a college horseshoeing course to prepare his privately owned horse for mounted duty arose out of and in the course of his employment.

Michael Rash worked as a deputy with the County Sheriff's Department (Department). As a member of the Department's horse-mounted unit, Rash was required to privately own, care for, train, and

(continues)

transport a horse certified for mounted duty to be available for service 24 hours a day, seven days a week.

Lieutenant James Silva is a commander in the Department. He adopted a constant shoeing requirement so that horses approved for mounted duty would be ready at a moment's notice. To replace horseshoes, farriers either travel to the horse or ask the owner to bring the horse to the farrier.

Lieutenant Silva and his wife signed up for a horseshoeing class at Merced College. Due to insufficient enrollment, Lieutenant Silva asked Rash to join the class and advanced his $150 to $160 tuition, which Rash later reimbursed. On about half of the course days, Lieutenant Silva and Rash carpooled.

Department Sergeant Giles New called Rash on Monday, and they agreed Rash would cover a shift of another mounted deputy at the Rodeo the following Saturday and Sunday. Later that afternoon, Rash examined his horse, Indian, and discovered its right rear shoe was missing. Rash decided to shoe Indian at the horseshoeing class.

Rash loaded the horses in his privately owned truck and trailer at the end of Wednesday's class and on the way home went to lunch in Merced approximately one mile from the college. Following lunch, Rash was driving along Route J-59 when another vehicle struck him head-on. As a result of the accident, Rash filed a claim for workers' compensation benefits alleging injury to "multiple body parts," including both legs.

The Department concluded that Rash's injuries were not employment related and denied his claim for workers' compensation benefits. Following hearings in March and May 2006, a workers' compensation administrative law judge (WCJ) agreed with the Department.

An employer is liable for workers' compensation benefits only where an employee sustains an injury "arising out of and in the course of the employment . . . ."

This two-pronged requirement is the cornerstone of the workers' compensation system.

An injury arises out of employment when there is a causal link between the injury and the job. In other words, the injury must have been sustained while performing a particular act reasonably contemplated by the employment; accordingly, the nature of the act, the nature of the employment, the custom and usage of a particular employment, the terms of the contract of employment.

In determining whether an injury arises out of and in the course of employment, the judicially created "going and coming" rule generally precludes workers' compensation recovery for injuries sustained during a local commute en route to a fixed place of business at fixed hours. The rule is based on the notion that an employee usually does not render services for the benefit of the employer while traveling to and from work. Exceptions to the going-and-coming rule exist, however, "'where the trip involves an incidental benefit to the employer, not common to commute trips by ordinary members of the work force.'" As a result, "[w]hen an employee engages in a special activity that is within the course of employment, an injury suffered during the activity or while traveling to and from the place of such activity also arises out of the employment." This type of activity is also known as a "special mission," where "'[s]pecial' means extraordinary in relation to routine duties, not outside the scope of the employment."

An employee performs services arising out of and in the course of employment "when he engages in conduct reasonably directed toward the fulfillment of his employer's requirements, performed for the benefit and advantage of the employer." The burden of proving that an injury arose out of and in the course of employment falls on the employee and generally presents a question of fact.

Agreeing with the WCAB's determination that his injury *arose out of* his employment, Rash asks this court also to consider whether his injury also occurred *in the course of* his employment. The WCJ found that the injury did not occur in the course of employment because Rash created his own "special mission that his employer did not request." It appears, however, that the WCAB failed to consider whether Rash's activity—taking Indian to Merced College to be shod for an impending work-related event—was necessary or impliedly permitted under the terms of his employment as a mounted deputy. There is no indication that taking Indian to be shod at Merced College several days before an assignment exceeded the scope of duties contemplated by Rash's employment as a mounted officer.

Rash's conduct on April 6, 2006, of taking Indian to be shod at the class in the most convenient and inexpensive manner in preparation for duty was both a subjectively and objectively reasonable expectancy of his employment as a mounted deputy and was therefore compensable.

CASE QUESTIONS

1. Did Rash's injuries from the automobile accident arise out of and in the course of his employment? Explain.
2. Did the "special mission" doctrine apply here? Explain.

▌ SUMMARY

Consent may be a defense to all intentional torts. Consent occurs when a victim of an intentional tort voluntarily agrees to endure the tortious actions. Voluntary agreement involves the victim understanding the consequences of the tortfeasor's conduct. This is called informed consent. Consent may be expressed or implied based upon the behavior of the parties.

Self-defense is the exercise of reasonable force to repel an attack upon one's person or to avoid confinement. Self-defense counters an offensive force that threatens bodily injury, repugnant contact, or sequestration. The amount of force a person may use in self-defense is limited to that amount necessary to repel the attacking force. Any greater resistance is excessive and the defense would be ineffective. The defense is used against allegations of assault, battery, or false imprisonment.

Defense of persons or property is another legal justification for assault or battery. Defense of persons involves the use of reasonable force to defend or protect a third party from injury when the third person is threatened by an attacking force. Here, reasonable force is defined identically as for self-defense. Defense of property allows reasonable force to protect property from damage or dispossession when an invader attempts to injure or wrongfully take custody of the property. Reasonable force to protect property is usually defined as less force than would ordinarily be allowed to protect persons. Courts generally do not permit deadly force to be used to protect property, although one may apply deadly force in defense of one's home against intruders, under the castle doctrine.

Rightful repossession empowers a chattel owner to enter upon another's real estate to legally repossess personal property that has been wrongfully taken or withheld. The chattel owner would not be liable for trespass to land, trespass to chattel, or conversion, because he or she was justified in retaking control of the property. The defense also may protect against claims of assault or battery. Reasonable force may be used to repossess the chattel. Reasonable force is defined along the same lines as for defense of property. The efforts to regain possession must occur promptly after the property is first taken from the owner, or from the time the possessor wrongfully refuses to return the property to the owner. For the defense to succeed, the chattel owner must have been wrongfully dispossessed, or return of the property must have been improperly refused.

As a defense to intentional torts, mistake is a good-faith belief, based upon incorrect information, that a person is justified in committing an intentional tort under the circumstances. This belief must be reasonable, and reasonableness is determined on a case-by-case basis. This belief must be based on erroneous details which, if they had been true, would have excused the intentional torts committed.

Privilege is sometimes considered a broad category embracing all the other defenses discussed in this chapter. To use the defense, one must ask if the actor's motives for engaging in the intentional tort outweigh the injury to the victim or property. Further, one must ask if the actor was justified in committing the intentional tort to achieve socially desirable goals (which outweigh the injury factor). Could these goals have been accomplished without inflicting the harm to the victim?

The necessity defense allows a tortfeasor to commit an intentional tort to prevent more serious injury from an external force. The tortfeasor's actions must be reasonably necessary to avert the more substantial danger. Necessity is basically a choice between the lesser of two evils. The tortfeasor cannot cause the greater threat of harm if the necessity defense is to insulate him or her from liability.

Public officials are immune from intentional tort liability for the proper enforcement of legal processes, such as service of process, execution sales, attachment, replevin, or arrest by warrant. Both statutes and common law protect governmental employees involved in these activities, as legal process enforcement is necessary to implement the judicial system. Normally, law enforcement officers, such as sheriffs, participate in these processes.

Law enforcement officials are authorized by statutes and common law to make warrantless arrests, usually when a felony is committed in their presence or is suspected of having been committed. Under the defense of citizen's arrest, private persons may restrain suspected felons without liability for assault, battery, false imprisonment, infliction of emotional distress, trespass to land, or other intentional torts.

Most state statutes of limitations restrict the time period within which a plaintiff may file his or her intentional tort causes of action against a defendant. In most states, these are two-year statutes, meaning that a plaintiff has two years from the date that the intentional tort was committed within which to file his or her lawsuit against the tortfeasor. It is vital to research specific statutes of limitations for each particular tort.

State workers' compensation statutes bar tort actions against workers' employers, regardless of fault.

The following chapter deals with strict or absolute liability, including products liability actions. There is a major difference between negligence and intentional torts compared to strict liability. Fault is unnecessary to prove liability in strict liability actions.

▌ KEY TERMS

attachment	informed consent	process serving
castle doctrine	intent	prosecutor
consent	judge	reasonable force
defense	malice	replevin
defense of persons	mistake	*Restatement (Second) of Torts*
defense of property	motive	rightful repossession
ejectment	necessary force	self-defense
execution sale	necessity	service of process
hot (fresh) pursuit	privilege	sheriff's sale
immunity	process	volition

PROBLEMS

In the following hypotheticals, identify the intentional torts and available defenses involved, if any, and support your answers.

1. Kim drives a delivery truck for The Dough Boy, a local bakery. One day, while making a delivery, Kim saw an automobile parked along the side of the street begin to move. There was no one inside the car, and it appeared to have slipped out of gear. The car rolled with increasing speed down a hill toward a crowded sidewalk along which several businesses were having outdoor sales. None of the shoppers saw the runaway vehicle approaching. Kim rammed her truck into the rear right side of the car, causing it to spin sideways. This stopped it from rolling into the pedestrians. The auto owner sued Kim for damaging the car, and the owner of The Dough Boy also sued Kim for injuring the delivery truck.

2. Todd, a student at the city college, visited the school bookstore to purchase some notebooks. Outside the bookstore were a series of locking boxes within which students placed their backpacks, briefcases, or other belongings that the bookstore forbade customers to bring into the store. Todd placed his backpack into one of the lockers and entered the bookstore. However, he forgot to take the key from the box. Luke, another student, opened the box and thought the backpack was his, as he owned a pack almost identical to Todd's. Luke had placed his own pack in one of the boxes but had also forgotten to take the key. Later, Todd discovered the pack missing, and a bookstore cashier described Luke as the culprit. Luke had not examined the pack closely but had thrown it into his car trunk and forgotten about it. Todd sued Luke.

3. Leroy frequented a pub called Bottom's Up! Late one Saturday night, an intoxicated man began shouting obscenities at a woman sitting at the table next to Leroy's. The woman ignored the man and continued to drink her beer. The man approached the lady, looking ominous. Leroy stood and asked the fellow over to the bar for a drink. The man grumbled that Leroy should mind his own business. The man reached out and grabbed the woman's wrist, and Leroy neatly twisted the man's other arm behind his back while restraining him with a neck hold. The man protested vehemently, but Leroy did not let go. Leroy placed the man firmly into a chair and told him not to move or else Leroy would have to punch him. The woman told Leroy that the man was her husband and asked him to leave them both alone. Leroy left the bar. The man sued Leroy.

4. Peter Delaney works as an assistant manager at a local clothing store. One evening, while emptying trash outside the back of the store, Peter saw someone toying with a lock on the back door of another store. He could not see who the person was. Peter telephoned the police from inside his store and returned to the alley. He yelled out to the mysterious person not to move, because he was armed, and the police were coming. In fact, Peter did not possess any weapons, but bluffed to scare the culprit. The suspicious character turned out to be a new employee at the neighboring store who was trying to determine which key opened the rear door lock. Peter did not know this individual. The person sued Peter.

5. Alyssa was purchasing some merchandise on layaway at a local department store. She had made her final payment and had requested that the items be delivered to her house. After a few days, she telephoned the store manager to complain that the goods had not been delivered. The manager explained that she would first have to pay the entire purchase price before delivery would be possible. Alyssa protested that she had, in fact,

paid in full. She went to the store and showed the layaway clerk her payment receipts. The clerk refused to produce the merchandise. Alyssa walked behind the counter, went up the stairs to the layaway storage area, and retrieved her items. The clerk notified store security, who took Alyssa into custody and locked her in an empty storeroom next to the restrooms. The room was unlit and not heated. The police arrived after an hour to question Alyssa, and after a few minutes she was released. Alyssa sued the store and the store counterclaimed against Alyssa.

▌ REVIEW QUESTIONS

1. What are defenses? How are they applied against intentional torts? In what type of situation would a defense most likely be raised?

2. Describe consent. Is the defense widely applicable to intentional torts? What is informed consent? Implied consent?

3. Explain self-defense. Against which intentional torts might this defense be used? What is reasonable force? How is it defined? How is it similar to necessary force?

4. Discuss defense of persons or property. How is it similar to self-defense? Different? How is defense of persons different from defense of property? Similar? How is reasonable force defined for this defense?

5. What is rightful repossession? What type of property is involved? Against which intentional torts might this defense be applied? How is reasonable force defined? What is the role of wrongful dispossession or denial of possession? Must the property owner's efforts to repossess be taken within a certain time frame? What is this called?

6. Explain mistake. What is the role of the good-faith conviction? Why must the information believed be inaccurate? How broad is the defense?

7. Does privilege include all defenses to intentional torts? Why? Against which intentional torts would the defense be utilized? What are its characteristics? What is the role of motive? Of socially acceptable goals? Of less injurious alternatives?

8. What are the elements of necessity? How is it used as an intentional tort defense? What is the significance of external forces? Why must the action be reasonably necessary?

9. Discuss the various types of immunity for public officials for legal process enforcement. What intentional torts might apply to these cases? How does the defense operate in each such instance?

10. What is warrantless arrest? Citizen's arrest? How are these protected from intentional tort liability?

11. What are statutes of limitations? What is the time period most commonly used for tort causes of action? How can statutes of limitations be used as a defense to intentional torts?

12. What kinds of activities that result in injury at work would not be covered under workers' compensation?

▌ HELPFUL WEBSITES

This chapter focuses on defenses to intentional torts. To learn more about defenses to intentional torts, the following sites can be accessed:

General Information

www.uscourts.gov
www.vls.law.vill.edu
www.atra.org

www.law.indiana.edu
www.dri.org

Workers' Compensation

www.dol.com
www.aba.org

STUDENT COMPANION WEBSITE
For additional cases and study materials, please go to www.cengagebrain.com

Chapter 10

Strict, or Absolute, Liability

CHAPTER OUTLINE

- The Biggest Mistakes Paralegals Make and How to Avoid Them
- Introduction
- An Overview of Strict Liability

- Animal Owners' Liability
- Abnormally Dangerous Activities
- Scope of Liability: Proximate Cause
- Mass Torts and Class Actions

THE BIGGEST MISTAKES PARALEGALS MAKE AND HOW TO AVOID THEM

Drink, Drank, Drunk

Jase, a litigation paralegal, raced up to the senior partner and commandeered the sound system after the partner finished his annual address at our holiday party and dinner. The partner had just warmly thanked the staff for their efforts in making all the firm's goals for the year and wished everyone a happy holiday season. So it was doubly shocking to hear Jase slur into the microphone, "The official results of the sexiest man in the office contest are about to be revealed!" Evidently Jase, in between multiple

visits to the open bar, had polled the employees to determine the "lucky winner." To say that the "winner" was mortified (along with everyone else) is stating it mildly.

Lesson Learned: Just because drinks are free at an office event, that does not mean you have to drink—especially if you cannot remember who you are with and what you are saying. If inhibitions are slipping away at an office party and

294

you feel like saying something inappropriate, the better idea is to go home.

On the other hand, if you are a nondrinker at a holiday party, try not to create an uncomfortable environment for alcohol imbibers. There is no need to point out that you are a member of AA or maintain a holier-than-thou attitude while nursing your virgin piña colada.

INTRODUCTION

Intentional torts and negligence account for the bulk of tort actions. However, there remain several important torts to study. The remainder primarily consists of strict, or absolute, liability. Products liability is one form of strict liability. The terms *strict liability* and *absolute liability* are interchangeable. Strict liability differs from intentional torts and negligence in that fault is unnecessary to establish liability. From the defendant's standpoint, absolute liability can be a serious trouble.

This chapter discusses the following:

▶ An overview of strict liability
▶ Animal owners' liability
▶ Abnormally dangerous activities
▶ Proximate cause
▶ Mass torts and class actions

AN OVERVIEW OF STRICT LIABILITY

Under intentional torts and negligence, tortfeasors are held accountable for their wrongful actions. Fault is an essential part of the reasoning. What was the defendant's misconduct that hurt the plaintiff? Was it intentional, willful, and wanton, or was it negligent action? Placing the blame is second nature in negligence or intentional torts analysis.

Fault Is Irrelevant

Absolute (strict) liability holds the tortfeasor responsible for his or her behavior regardless of fault. In other words, the tortfeasor could have used every possible degree of care to protect against injuring the victim, but this would not prevent liability. Fault is irrelevant to absolute liability. The tortfeasor would be strictly liable just because he or she did something specific that hurt the plaintiff.

absolute (strict) liability |
The legal responsibility for damage or injury, even if you are not at fault or negligent.

Limitations to Absolute Liability

One's sense of fair play may rebel against strict liability. One might think that it is unfair to hold a defendant accountable even if he or she did not intentionally or negligently misbehave. This fault concept extends throughout every area of law. This is why absolute liability is restricted to certain types of activities, such as abnormally dangerous tasks and defectively manufactured products, where the risk involved substantially outweighs the benefit to others.

Public Policy Objectives behind Strict Liability

Under strict liability, society has decided that the person engaged in certain activities should bear the risk of liability to individuals innocently injured as a consequence of the dangerous or defective item or action. Liability is created by the courts and legislatures to protect consumers. It is society's decision that persons owning wild animals, using fire or explosives, or manufacturing defective products are in the best economic position to pay for plaintiffs' injuries arising from these activities. Additionally, injured plaintiffs would generally be at a disadvantage if required to prove negligence in these cases. There is no such requirement in strict liability actions.

Insurance Analogy

Absolute liability resembles insurance. Defendants are insuring, or guaranteeing, the safety of plaintiffs who come into contact with what tort law calls **abnormally dangerous (ultrahazardous) instrumentalities.** These activities or objects are dangerous by their very nature. Even if all precautions are taken, an injury might still occur.

Historical Development

Ancient English common law held the owners of animals, slaves, or objects absolutely liable when any of these caused the death of another person. For instance, suppose a boat broke its mooring and floated downstream, colliding with and drowning a swimmer. In medieval England, the boat would be considered a *deodand,* because it killed someone. The term originated from the Latin *Deo dandum,* which translates as "a thing to be given to God." The ecclesiastical courts insisted that the offending, sinful property be seized and placed into God's service. Deodands had to be forfeited to the church or the crown, or sometimes to the injured party's surviving family, to be used in pious pursuits. It was seen as a charitable redemption: the owner would pay for his or her sinful chattel by giving it up. It did not matter that the chattel killed accidentally. This was probably one of the earliest forms of strict liability. As times change, so can "ultrahazardous" instrumentalities. For example, when first invented, airplanes were ultrahazardous, but are now considered a very safe form of transportation.

▌ ANIMAL OWNERS' LIABILITY

Modern absolute liability first arose in the common law involving private ownership of wild animals and the use of fire or explosives. This section discusses owners' liability for injuries inflicted by their wild animals.

abnormally dangerous (ultrahazardous) instrumentalities |
Activities or objects that are, by their very nature, extremely hazardous to persons or property. These are relevant to strict (absolute) liability cases.

Wild Animals Defined

The ancient common law cases use the Latin term ***ferae naturae,*** meaning "wild nature," to refer to wild animals. These are animals that have naturally wild dispositions, as opposed to tame animals, which are called ***domitae naturae,*** meaning "domesticated nature." Examples of *ferae naturae* include deer, bison, elk, bear, monkeys, snakes, bees, stream or ocean fish, coyotes, foxes, wild birds, lions, tigers, gophers, raccoons, opossums, and prairie dogs.

Ownership of Wildlife

Under ancient English common law, the king owned all wildlife in the realm. This is why trespassers were often hanged or beheaded for taking the king's property during medieval times. As English law evolved, an average person could claim ownership of a wild animal—the trick was to catch the beast. Once someone had control over a wild animal, it was considered to be his or her property until it escaped to its natural, free state. The common law cases call this ownership the exercise of **dominion** and **control** over the wild animal. American common law holds that the state (or the federal government), under its police power, owns wildlife in trust for the benefit of all citizens. This is why one must obtain state or federal hunting or fishing licenses to take wildlife.

For example, suppose Kathleen has an apiary—in other words, she is a beekeeper. The bees are wildlife, *ferae naturae*. However, if Kathleen catches and places them in her apiary hives, they may stay and produce honey for her. Now Kathleen owns the bees. As long as she exercises dominion and control over the insects, they are hers. But once the bees fly away, they are *ferae naturae* again, and Kathleen does not own them (that is, unless she catches them again).

Importance of Wildlife Ownership

Wildlife ownership is important for purposes of absolute liability. If a wild animal injures someone, the victim cannot sue the beast (or, at the very least, cannot easily collect judgment). Instead, the plaintiff looks to the animal's owner for compensation. Owners are strictly liable for the injuries their wildlife inflict. It does not matter that the owner exercised every precaution to safeguard others from being hurt by the wild animals. If the beast attacks and hurts someone, the owner must compensate the victim for the injuries.

Monkeys kept as pets have been a frequent subject of strict liability actions. Some owners have had them for years, dress them in clothes, and claim they have never had a problem. Then, a visitor is severely mauled or even killed by the animal for no apparent reason. Because the common law presumes that wild animals are dangerous by nature, strict liability applies to any injuries they cause.

Suppose Ken's pet bear mauls a visitor to Ken's home. The victim will sue Ken under strict liability. One might argue that premises liability, using negligence

ferae naturae | (Latin) "Of wild nature." Naturally wild animals.

domitae naturae | (Latin) "Domesticated nature." Tame, domestic animals.

dominion | Legal ownership plus full actual control over something.

control | The power or authority to direct or oversee.

theory, should apply instead, because Ken owns the land and the chattels that harmed the plaintiff, but this argument would lose. Because bears are wildlife, Ken is absolutely liable for his pet's mischief.

PRACTICAL APPLICATION

Check to find out if your local jurisdiction has an applicable leash law. Many municipalities have local laws requiring pet owners to keep their pets fenced in or on a leash. Should a victim be injured by a stray dog, you should inquire about local leash laws.

Comparison with Domesticated Animals

Domitae naturae are animals that the law presumes to be harmless. Examples of domestic animals include dogs, cats, pet birds, or livestock such as pigs, horses, cows, and sheep. When a domesticated animal hurts someone, the common law states that the owner is liable if he or she was negligent in handling the animal. Liability would also arise if an owner intentionally used domestic animals to hurt someone. For example, suppose an attack dog's owner ordered the animal to attack a victim. This is a form of battery, as the animal would be considered an extension of the tortfeasor's body.

Vicious Propensity Rule

Owners may be held absolutely liable for injuries caused by their domestic animals if the animals exhibit vicious tendencies. When a dog growls or snarls, when a bull paws the ground and snorts, and when a cat arches its back and hisses, these are all demonstrations of vicious propensities. When a domestic animal routinely displays these characteristics to the point that it gets a reputation for viciousness, it is said to have *vicious propensities*. An owner of such an animal will be held strictly liable for any injuries the beast inflicts, under the so-called **vicious propensity rule.**

vicious propensity rule |
Doctrine in absolute liability cases involving domestic animals. Normally owners are not strictly liable for injuries caused by their domestic animals. However, if the animals display vicious propensities and hurt someone or someone's property, then the owner is absolutely liable.

Defenses in Cases Involving Animal Owners' Absolute Liability

Normally, negligence or intentional tort defenses are ineffective against strict liability. However, certain exceptions have arisen in the common law for particular types of absolute liability, such as cases involving animals. The following defenses can protect an animal owner from strict liability:

1. Assumption of risk
2. Contributory and comparative negligence
3. Consent
4. Self-defense and defense of others

Assumption of Risk. If the individual injured by a wild animal (or domestic animal with vicious propensity) voluntarily assumed a known risk, with full appreciation of the dangers involved, then the owner is not strictly liable for the inflicted injuries. Courts justify this defense on equitable grounds. It would be unfair to hold owners absolutely liable for harm their animals caused if the victims chose to subject themselves to the danger.

Contributory and Comparative Negligence. Courts often rule that the plaintiff's contributory or comparative negligence in an animal attack will prevent the owner's absolute liability. Some courts state that a plaintiff's contributory negligence bars strict liability altogether. This means that the plaintiff would have to prove that the defendant (owner) was negligent in keeping the animal that attacked and hurt the plaintiff. Other courts simply ignore absolute liability theory and reshape the case in a negligence mold, in which the plaintiff's and defendant's respective degrees of negligence are compared.

Consent. An injured plaintiff might have consented to exposure to a dangerous animal. Consent is usually based upon a person's employment responsibilities while working around animals. For example, suppose Gordon works for a police-dog training facility, where he serves as an attack victim. He knows from observation and experience that the dogs are dangerous. Even if Gordon was not wearing his protective padding, and he was bitten by one of the dogs, he has implicitly consented to this danger as part of his job. Basically, this is assumption of risk couched in consent terms. The same reasoning would apply for keepers, trainers, or feeders of wild animals for zoos or circuses.

Self-Defense and Defense of Others. When a wild or vicious domestic animal attacks a victim, but the owner used the animal as a means of self-defense or defense of other persons, then the owner would not be strictly liable for the inflicted injuries. For instance, suppose someone attacks Arthur while he is out walking his dog, which has a vicious reputation around the neighborhood. To repel the danger, Arthur commands his dog to attack. His assailant is knocked to the ground, chewed up a bit, and scared away. Arthur would not be absolutely liable for the injuries caused by his dog. The same scenario would arise if Arthur saw someone attacking a member of his family or a friend and he used the dog to protect that person. However, remember the limitations to these defenses: one may not become the aggressor and still use them to escape liability. Hence, if Arthur's dog had chased the fleeing attacker down the street, Arthur could not use these defenses to avoid liability.

Dog-Bite Statutes

Most jurisdictions have statutes that have changed the common law owner liability (and the available defenses) in dog-bite cases. These statutes can substantially affect a dog owner's liability and defenses. A few states even impose strict liability for dogs with no known vicious propensities.

Dog-bite hypotheticals present interesting applications of absolute liability. In the following example, consider the vicious propensity rule and its effects on the canine owner's liability.

THE CASE OF THE KNOWLEDGEABLE LANDLORD

Thousands of dog-bite cases are reported each year, with the more sensational injury-causing cases making headlines. Here, the landlord as well as the owners of a dog are being sued for injuries sustained by a couple and their dog. The outcome of the case focuses on notice.

Johanna A. GORDON, et al.,

v.

Joey WINSTON, et al.,

Superior Court of Connecticut,
Judicial District of Hartford
No. CV0650040955
November 28, 2006

This case arises from an incident which allegedly occurred on March 19, 2006. The plaintiffs allege that they were both injured when a dog owned by defendants Winston and Williams attacked their leashed dog while they were on their own property.

Defendant Peter Sztaba owns the apartment building where the codefendants lived with their dog. This building is located in close proximity to the plaintiffs' residence. Plaintiffs have sued defendant Sztaba in four counts. The Third and Fourth Counts allege that Mr. Sztaba is liable to them under *Conn. Gen.Stat.* § 22-357. In the Fifth and Sixth Counts, plaintiffs allege that the attack was caused by Mr. Sztaba's negligence, because he had prior notice "of the vicious propensities of the dog, and said dog being allowed to roam at large despite numerous complaints from neighbors as well as a previous event in which said dog killed a dog belonging to a neighbor." Plaintiffs allege that Mr. Sztaba was negligent in that he allowed the defendant tenants to

keep the dog despite a lease provision prohibiting dogs, and by failing to warn neighbors of the dog's propensities.

Defendant Sztaba has moved to strike all four counts against him. The motion to strike is granted as to the Third and Fourth Counts. A landlord is not a "keeper" of a dog "merely because a tenant owns a dog and keeps the dog on the premises." The Third and Fourth Counts contain no allegations that Mr. Sztaba exercised sufficient control over the dog to make him a "keeper" within the meaning of § 22-357.

In *Stokes v. Lyddy,* our Appellate Court affirmed summary judgment in favor of a landlord who was sued by a nontenant bitten by a tenant's dog, with the incident occurring away from the leased premises.

Here, plaintiffs have alleged that prior to said incident, the defendant, Peter S. Sztaba, was made aware of the vicious propensities of said pit bull terrier dog, and said dog being allowed to roam at large despite numerous complaints by neighbors, as well as a previous event in which said dog killed a dog belonging to a neighbor.

If plaintiffs can establish, through the discovery process, that Mr. Sztaba had actual or constructive notice of the dog's prior misconduct, then it is entirely conceivable that this case would survive a summary judgment motion. The motion to strike the Fifth and Sixth Counts is therefore denied.

CASE QUESTIONS

1. Why do you suppose the plaintiffs are trying to bring an action against the landlord in addition to the owner of the dog?
2. Why would the landlord's notice of the dog's propensities change the outcome of a court decision?

HYPOTHETICAL

Toby Jones owns a towing service. He uses Doberman pinscher dogs to guard the parking lot in which he keeps towed vehicles. The area is surrounded by large, barbed-wire fences with "no trespassing" signs attached every few feet. The guard dogs would bark, snarl, bite, and lunge at anyone who came near the fencing. Early one morning, Chet Paisley stopped by to claim an automobile that had been towed for illegal parking. After paying the storage fees, Chet walked back to the holding area. Toby had forgotten to chain the dogs from the night before, and they were running loose in the parking lot. When they saw Chet, they attacked and severely injured him.

The common law presumes that dogs are harmless, domestic creatures. However, there is considerable evidence that Toby's Dobermans displayed vicious propensities. Accordingly, the harmlessness presumption falls aside, and the dogs are viewed as potentially dangerous, like wild animals. Under absolute liability, Toby would be responsible for Chet's injuries. Toby's negligence and intent are irrelevant here. It only matters that the dogs were abnormally dangerous instrumentalities, because of their vicious propensities. Once strict liability applies, the result is easy: the animal owner must compensate the victim for his or her injuries.

Would the result have been different if Toby had posted signs stating, "WARNING! DANGEROUS ATTACK DOGS! DO NOT ENTER WITHOUT AUTHORIZED PERSONNEL TO ACCOMPANY YOU"? If Chet had seen such signs but entered regardless, he would have assumed the risk. Chet would have voluntarily assumed a known risk (the dangerous dogs) with full appreciation of the threat involved (being bitten or mauled). Chet would also have been contributorily negligent in entering the enclosed parking lot without Toby or another employee accompanying him.

Table 10-1 summarizes animal owners' absolute liability and the available defenses.

TABLE 10-1

Animal owners' absolute liability and defenses

WILDLIFE (*FERAE NATURAE*)	DOMESTIC ANIMALS (*DOMITAE NATURAE*)	DEFENSES
Owner strictly liable for injuries caused by wild animals	Owner absolutely liable for injuries caused by domestic animals *only* if such animals display vicious propensities, or liability is imposed by statute or local ordinance	1. Assumption of risk 2. Contributory and comparative negligence 3. Consent 4. Self-defense and defense of others

ABNORMALLY DANGEROUS ACTIVITIES

Abnormally dangerous activities are inherently perilous because of the actions and the devices involved. Common examples include the use of explosives, flammable substances, noxious gases, poisons, hazardous wastes (the so-called **toxic tort actions**), and (in some jurisdictions) electricity, natural gas, and water supplied through unprotected utility lines. Many early-twentieth-century cases refer to *ultrahazardous activities*. This is the term used by the original *Restatement of Torts* § 520 (the *First Restatement*). Although some courts split hairs distinguishing ultrahazardous from abnormally dangerous, the expressions are essentially interchangeable.

toxic tort actions | Actions involving toxic chemicals, pollution, hazardous waste disposal and transportation, and other environmentally sensitive issues. Many tort theories, including trespass to land, negligence, absolute liability for ultrahazardous substances, products liability, and nuisance, apply.

The *Restatement (Second)* Rule

The *Restatement (Second) of Torts* § 520 declares that persons engaged in abnormally dangerous activities shall be strictly liable for injuries caused by their actions. The *Restatement* lists several criteria for absolute liability:

1. The abnormally dangerous activity created a high risk of substantial injury to an individual or his or her property.
2. This risk could not be removed through the use of reasonable care.
3. The activity is not commonly undertaken (the common usage principle).
4. The activity was inappropriately undertaken in the place in which the victim was harmed.
5. The hazards that the activity creates outweigh the benefits that the activity brings to the community.

High Risk of Substantial Injury. To be abnormally dangerous, the defendant's activity must create a great threat of seriously injuring the plaintiff or the plaintiff's property. For instance, consider a highway construction company that uses dynamite to excavate rock and earth. Dynamite is a dangerous stuff. It presents an enormous risk of injuring others nearby if it is not used properly. The threat of harm is significant, as people could be killed or their property destroyed if the dynamite is not used correctly.

Reasonable Care.

If the tortfeasor could have eliminated the risk of harm through the use of reasonable care, then the activity is not abnormally dangerous, and absolute liability does not apply. For example, a utility company could exercise reasonable care and protect citizens from the great threat posed by electricity or natural gas simply by using insulated wires or double-sealed underground pipelines. Reasonable care could easily eliminate the risks of electrocution or explosion. If the utility company actually used these (or other) reasonable precautions, then the activity (supplying electricity or natural gas) would not be ultrahazardous, even if a victim nonetheless was injured.

Note the hidden implication in this element, though. Failure to use reasonable care to safeguard others from the risks involved in the activity could make it abnormally dangerous. For instance, suppose a utility company ran electricity through uninsulated wires. Many courts have held that this would make the activity ultrahazardous, so the utility company would be strictly liable for injuries. However, not all courts interpret the *Second Restatement*'s reasonable care standard in this way.

Common Usage Principle.

Abnormally dangerous activities and substances are those not commonly undertaken or used in everyday life. This is sometimes called the **common usage (use) principle.** For instance, consider explosives, toxic chemicals, and poisonous gases. How often does the average person use them? Does anyone in the reader's neighborhood? What about the manufacturing plant across town? In other words, it could be said that the vast majority of the public does not use such substances. These, then, would be examples of abnormally dangerous substances, because they are not commonly used.

What about flammable substances? Many courts have included these as ultrahazardous items. But virtually everyone uses gasoline every day. Would gasoline not fall within common usage? Whether gasoline is abnormally dangerous depending upon how it is being used. Suppose SludgeCo Oil Company operates a gasoline refinery, with several massive fuel tanks storing hundreds of thousands of gallons. Few people in a community have such facilities in their backyards. Gasoline may be commonly used, but not in the way this storage facility uses it. The gas one keeps in his or her garage for the lawn mower would not be ultrahazardous; however, the huge storage tanks would be abnormally dangerous.

common usage (use) principle | Doctrine in strict liability cases that defines abnormally dangerous activities and substances as those not commonly undertaken or used in everyday life.

Inappropriate Use in Certain Places. To be ultrahazardous, the activity or substance must have been inappropriately performed or used in the place in which the victim was harmed. For example, suppose a chemical manufacturer opened a plant adjacent to a housing subdivision that uses well water. Suppose that the plant dumped toxic chemicals into holding ponds on its premises. Harmful chemicals could seep into the ground and contaminate the water supplies of nearby residents. Perhaps several of these homeowners became ill as a consequence. The activity (using toxic chemical retention ponds) is abnormally dangerous because it created a serious risk of substantial harm, was not of common usage, and was inappropriately undertaken at the location in which the plaintiffs were harmed (adjacent to residences).

Hazards Outweigh Benefits: Balancing Test. Courts often apply a balancing test to decide if an activity is abnormally dangerous. Such an analysis compares the dangers created by the activity with the benefits that the community derives from the activity. This is similar to the benefits analysis used in many nuisance cases.

For example, suppose a local builder is building a new road to improve access between hospitals and an isolated rural town. The construction crew uses dynamite to clear the area for the road. A nearby homeowner suffers structural damage to her house as a result of the blasting and sues the builder under strict liability theory. Courts following the *Second Restatement* would balance the benefits derived against the risks involved. The road would improve the community's access to hospital facilities. The dangers created by dynamite use, which in this case involved structural damage, are probably outweighed by these benefits.

Many courts have applied the *Second Restatement*'s approach. Several jurisdictions, however, have rejected the rule, either in whole or in part. Still, the *Second Restatement* provides a comprehensive, general formula for analyzing abnormally dangerous activities and absolute liability.

Defenses

Many state legislatures have enacted statutes protecting certain abnormally dangerous activities from strict liability. These statutes usually shield public utilities distributing electricity and natural gas, private contractors performing construction (particularly highway) work for the government, and municipal zoos or parks that maintain wild animals. Under these statutes, the protected entities cannot be held absolutely liable for injuries caused by wild animals or ultrahazardous activities. Instead, plaintiffs must prove that the protected defendants were negligent or committed intentional torts, unless the defendants have purchased liability insurance to cover injuries under these circumstances.

THE CASE OF THE QUESTIONABLE ULTRAHAZARDOUS ACTIVITY

A building is leaning and about to collapse. Demolition work is done on the building and it crashes into another business. On the surface, it seems that very hazardous work is being conducted. But, legally, is this considered an ultrahazardous activity?

Gary P. SILVA
v.
ASSOCIATED BUILDING WRECKERS, INC.

Appeals Court of Massachusetts
82 Mass.App.Ct. 1106
July 10, 2012

Pursuant to a contract with the city of Holyoke (city), the defendant began the demolition of an abandoned, leaning building that was adjacent to a garage housing an automotive repair business owned and operated by the plaintiff. During the demolition, the building collapsed onto the plaintiff's garage. Plaintiff, the owner of the adjacent garage, brought actions for negligence, breach of contract, trespass, nuisance, strict liability, and violation of c. 93A, alleging that failure to pay for damage was an unfair or deceptive business practice. The plaintiff sued the defendant for damages to real and personal property, personal injuries, and lost income.

At the close of the plaintiff's case, the judge found for the defendant, by way of a directed verdict, on the nuisance, strict liability, and c. 93A claims. At the conclusion of the trial, the judge awarded the plaintiff $366,607.36 on his breach of contract claim (as a third-party beneficiary of the contract between the city and the defendant), including damages for building repair, removal and demolition costs, and a nominal award of $10,000 for personal property damage. He ruled in favor of the defendant, on plaintiff's negligence theory, the personal injury claims and the trespass claim.

The plaintiff brought this appeal. The plaintiff argues that the judge erred both procedurally and substantively in allowing the defendant's motion for a directed verdict on the plaintiff's strict liability claim. His claim that he was entitled to a judgment on the strict liability count as matter of law because the defendant's activity was "abnormally dangerous" is without merit. While strict liability is applicable to blasting cases, this is not such a case—here, the defendant undertook to demolish the top floors of the building by hand. Therefore, whether the activity in question is an abnormally dangerous or ultrahazardous activity for which the defendant is to be held strictly liable is to be decided in light of attending circumstances on the facts of each case and with the consideration of the following factors:

"(a) the existence of a high degree of risk of some harm to the person, land or chattels of others; (b) likelihood that the harm that results from [the activity] will be great; (c) inability to eliminate the risk by the exercise of reasonable care; (d) extent to which the activity is not a matter of common usage; (e) inappropriateness of the activity to the place where it is carried on; and (f) extent to which its value to the community is outweighed by its dangerous attributes." Restatement (Second) of Torts § 520 (1977). See *Clark–Aiken Co. v. Cromwell–Wright Co.,* 367 Mass. 70, 89 (1975).

It is the last two factors that persuade us that the judge properly held the defendant's activity not to be abnormally dangerous. The judge found that the building was in an active state of collapse, was leaning precariously towards the plaintiff's property, and constituted an imminent hazard. It could not be said that the activity was inappropriate for the place where it was carried on—in fact, the only place where the dismantling of this building could be conducted was at the site where it was standing. Moreover, the value of removal of this building, which presented a great risk to the community, could not be underestimated. Therefore, the judgment of the trial court is affirmed.

(continues)

CASE QUESTIONS

1. What additional kinds of facts would be needed for a court to find an ultrahazardous activity?
2. Suppose the defendant wreckers had blasted the leaning building. Would the court's decision have been any different?

Public Policy Objectives behind Statutory Immunity

Legislatures often justify immunity statutes on the grounds that government (and the private companies that often work under governmental contracts) must be protected from the harshness of strict liability if certain essential activities are to be performed. How, the argument goes, can governments build roads, operate zoos or parks, supply utilities, or enable private industry to satisfy energy demands if these activities carry the burden of strict liability whenever someone inadvertently gets hurt? This reasoning is similar to the benefits balancing act that courts often apply under the *Second Restatement* approach. Because legislatures enact statutes, and the public can change the legislature (through voting) and thus change the statutes, citizens who disagree with the immunity laws can elect new legislators to modify these provisions.

Cases involving toxic substances often revolve around absolute liability theory, applying the abnormally dangerous activity analysis. Of all the causes of action usually associated with toxic torts (including trespass to land, negligence, nuisance, and strict liability), absolute liability offers the best common law avenue for plaintiffs to recover.

THE CASE OF CHEMICALS IN THE AIRA

A woman works with dangerous chemicals at a factory that produces sensors, and products for illumination and signage. The woman has no idea that her workplace may be the cause of her injuries, and the two-year time period for bringing an action passes. Years later, her attorney relies on the discovery principle that tolls the statute of limitations until a plaintiff is "reasonably on notice" as to the cause of his or her injuries.

Roger DANIELS and Tammy Lynn Wallace, Plaintiffs,

v.

OPTEK TECHNOLOGY, INC., John Doe I, John Doe II, John Doe III, XYZ Corporation I, XYZ Corporation II, and XYZ Corporation III, Defendants

Superior Court of Delaware, New Castle County

2012 WL 2026384

May 8, 2012

Defendant argues it is entitled to summary judgment because Plaintiffs' personal injury claims are time-barred, and Plaintiffs have failed to establish any basis to toll the two-year statute of limitations. Plaintiffs concede that a two-year statute of limitations applies to their claims, but argue that this case "falls squarely within the discovery exception for accrual of birth defect/toxic tort cases set forth in *Brown v. E.I. duPont de Nemours & Co., Inc.,*" and thus the statute was tolled until plaintiffs were "reasonably on notice" of the cause of the injury. Plaintiffs further argue that, separate and apart from the discovery exception, Plaintiffs' claims are timely as a result of defendant's fraudulent concealment. Finally, Plaintiffs assert that their claims are tolled by the state law limitations preemption provision of the federal Comprehensive Environmental Response Compensation and Liability Act ("CERCLA").

Plaintiff Tammy Wallace is the mother of Plaintiff Roger Daniels. Roger was born on December 31, 1985 with numerous severe birth defects, including ventricular septal defect, nystagmus and congenital scoliosis. Optek owned and operated an electronic components manufacturing facility in McKinney, Texas, where Ms. Wallace, then 19 years old, began working in approximately March 1983. Prior to working at Optek, Ms. Wallace had no prior experience working in a manufacturing setting or working with chemicals.

Ms. Wallace worked as a "lead" operator in the "symbolization" area of the Optek facility, where ink stamping machines were used to label component parts, such as LEDs. About six to eight workers were located in the symbolization area, which contained two or more stamping machines. Ms. Wallace and the other workers used large quantities of solvent-based inks and stand-alone solvents in their work. Isopropyl alcohol, acetone, and a solvent product called "Markem," among other chemicals, were used extensively throughout the symbolization area. At this stage of the proceedings, Plaintiffs do not yet know the full range of chemicals to which Ms. Wallace was exposed at Optek.

Among other things, Ms. Wallace's job involved dispensing tubes of ink and applying the inks to the stamping machines. To do this, Ms. Wallace squeezed ink directly to her finger and applied it to the machine. Optek provided Ms. Wallace with a finger "cot," which Plaintiffs claim did not prevent the ink from smearing on her hand. Ms. Wallace also cleaned the stamping machines and the individual components by wiping them down with cloths soaked with Markem, acetone, and other solvents. She also cleaned electronic components by placing them in a vat filled with isopropyl alcohol. Retrieving the components required her to insert her unprotected arms and hands directly into the vat of alcohol and lifting out the parts. She filled the vat with isopropyl alcohol by manually pouring the chemical from the gallon jug containers.

According to Plaintiffs, Ms. Wallace was subjected to inhalational exposure as well as dermal exposure to these chemicals. Plaintiffs allege that the small room where she worked had no effective ventilation, and she was exposed to the constant presence of chemical vapors. Plaintiffs further allege that chemical spills occurred often, generating even higher concentrations of airborne chemicals, which sometimes resulted in evacuations of the workers from the area. According to Plaintiffs, not only did chemical spills occur inside the workplace, but on at least two occasions, chemical spills that occurred outside the building produced fumes which infiltrated the work area and sickened the workers. Plaintiffs claim that when they were instructed to go outside, the workers were sickened even further by these fumes.

Plaintiffs allege that Optek failed to provide gloves or any other protective equipment to Ms. Wallace, and as a result, Ms. Wallace received "very heavy chemical exposures" through both dermal contact and inhalation. Plaintiffs further allege that because Optek failed to provide work clothing, changing rooms or laundry services, Ms. Wallace was forced to wear her chemical-laden clothing home where it continued to release toxins into the environment through handling and laundering.

When Ms. Wallace became pregnant with her son, she claims she asked her supervisor at Optek, Brian Stringer, whether it was safe to continue working with and around the chemicals during her pregnancy. According to Plaintiffs, Mr. Stringer assured Mrs. Wallace that the chemicals would have no effect whatsoever on her health or the health of her developing child. Relying on those assurances, Ms. Wallace continued to work in the symbolization area during her pregnancy.

Approximately six or seven months into her pregnancy, Ms. Wallace's doctor informed her that she had toxemia. Because her Optek supervisor and her physician assured her that there was no connection between her work and her toxemia, Ms. Wallace

(continues)

continued to work in the symbolization area at Optek up until she was ordered by her doctor to cease work altogether and to go on bed rest. She did not return to Optek until after Roger was born.

Plaintiffs claim that although Optek required Ms. Wallace to work with and around dangerous chemicals, it never provided safety training with respect to those chemicals, and further, the meager personal protective equipment Optek provided was "woefully inadequate." Ms. Wallace was unaware of the reproductively toxic properties of the chemicals at Optek and was unable to protect herself and her child from these harmful exposures.

Plaintiffs allege that as a consequence of the chemical exposure, Roger was born with a number of severe birth defects. He was diagnosed with ventricular septal defect and nystagmus at birth and later, as he was beginning to walk, he was diagnosed with congenital scoliosis, tipped hips and turned-in feet. At approximately age seven, he was diagnosed with severe depression and bipolar disorder. All of Roger's doctors advised Ms. Wallace that the cause of his injuries was not known. Plaintiffs allege that none of Roger's physicians ever told Mrs. Wallace that there was a potential causal relationship between her chemical exposure at Optek and her son's birth defects.

Plaintiffs allege that up until the time they retained counsel after learning of an attorney advertisement, they never saw or heard any reports of "semiconductor" litigation or any other litigation involving exposure to industrial chemicals and birth defects. As Plaintiffs point out, this case does not involve a "signature disease," such as mesothelioma, whose unique cause, exposure to asbestos, is widely known and can be readily discovered on the Internet or at the public library. Nor does this case involve the ingestion of a pharmaceutical drug, which carries the risk of a known adverse health outcome published directly to physicians and the users of the drug. Rather, this case involves a "complex cause and effect relationship involving multiple chemicals and chemical mixtures, multiple routes of exposures, and a unique array of adverse health outcomes specific to this particular plaintiff."

The "time of discovery" exception, sometimes referred to as the "inherently unknowable injury" doctrine provides that "when an inherently unknowable injury . . . has been suffered by one blamelessly ignorant of the act or omission and injury complained of, and the harmful effect thereof develops gradually over a period of time, the injury is 'sustained' . . . when the harmful effect first manifests itself and becomes physically ascertainable." In such a case, the statute of limitations is tolled until the plaintiff discovers, or in the exercise of reasonable diligence should have discovered, his injury.

In this case, although Roger's physical injuries were apparent at birth and in early childhood, Plaintiffs did not know the cause of his injuries. Optek argues that medical journals and articles published by USA Today and the New York Times should have put Plaintiffs on inquiry notice. However, Plaintiffs claim they did not know of the link between Roger's injuries and Ms. Wallace's chemical exposure because Roger's doctors, upon whom they reasonably and understandably relied, told them that they did not know the cause. The statute of limitations did not begin to run on Plaintiffs' claims until they were on notice of a potential claim against Optek.

Viewing the facts in the light most favorable to Plaintiffs, the court finds that the time of discovery exception applies to toll the statute of limitations in this case. Thus, Plaintiffs' claims are not time-barred, and Optek's Motion for Summary Judgment is therefore **DENIED.**

CASE QUESTIONS

1. Is the tolling of the statute of limitations fair to defendants? Explain your answer.
2. Do you believe the plaintiff's claim that she never heard of a problem with the chemicals until she saw an attorney advertisement? Explain your answer.

THE CASE OF THE LAW FIRM UNDER FIRE

Imagine a client so disgruntled that he goes on a shooting rampage at the law firm. Rather than bringing a lawsuit against the shooter, the maker of the weapons is sued based on strict liability.

Marilyn MERRILL, et al., Plaintiffs and Appellants,

v.

NAVEGAR, INC., Defendant and Respondent

Supreme Court of California

26 Cal.4th 465

No. S083466

August 6, 2001

On July 1, 1993, Gian Luigi Ferri killed eight people and wounded six—and then killed himself—during a shooting rampage at 101 California Street, a high-rise office building in San Francisco. Survivors and representatives of some of Ferri's victims (plaintiffs) sued defendant Navegar, Inc. (Navegar), which made two of the three weapons Ferri used.

Navegar is a gun manufacturer located in Miami, Florida. Doing business as Intratec, it manufactured the TEC–9, a semiautomatic assault pistol. In 1992, Navegar renamed the firearm the TEC–DC9 but did not alter its design or materials. We will refer to them interchangeably as TEC–9's, TEC–DC9's, or TEC–9/DC9's.

Navegar advertised the TEC–9/DC9 in a number of gun-related magazines and annuals. A typical advertisement claimed that in light of the design features—including "32 rounds of firepower," —the weapon "stands out among high capacity 9mm assault-type pistols," and "deliver[s] more gutsy performance and reliability than **ANY** other gun on the market."

In early 1993, Ferri, bought a TEC–9 from the Pawn & Gun Shop in Henderson, Nevada. Ferri seemed interested in a "high capacity type" gun that "holds a lot of rounds." Later, he returned the weapon, stating that he wanted a new gun.

On April 25, 1993, Ferri bought a new TEC–DC9 from Super Pawn, a gun store in Las Vegas. Ferri told the salesperson he wanted a gun for informal target shooting, or "plinking." The salesperson showed Ferri only the TEC–DC9 and a gun manufactured by Glock. Although Ferri did not ask for a TEC–DC9 by name he did not appear interested in any other guns. Ferri nevertheless chose the TEC–DC9.

Ferri purchased another TEC–DC9 on May 8, 1993, at a Las Vegas gun show from a Utah dealer. The TEC–DC9 Ferri was the only handgun the Utah dealer displayed at the show, and the dealer's price ($210) was the lowest at the show for a TEC–DC9.

On July 1, 1993, Ferri entered 101 California Street carrying the TEC–9/DC9's and a .45–caliber Norinco Model 1911A1 pistol in a large briefcase and another bag. He had added to the TEC–DC9's Hell Fire brand trigger systems that made the weapons fire in rapid bursts, and he was equipped with hundreds of rounds of ammunition. He went to the office of a law firm he held a grudge against, and started shooting. He killed eight people and wounded six on three different floors, and then killed himself.

Plaintiffs' asserted a cause of action against Navegar for negligence. Plaintiffs alleged that Navegar knew or should have known that: (1) the TEC–9/DC9 is a "small concealable military assault weapon" and (2) it has "no legitimate sporting or self-defense purpose and is well adapted to assault on large numbers of people." Plaintiffs alleged, Navegar "acted negligently by manufacturing, marketing, and making available for sale to the general public" the TEC–9/DC9.

The complaint also asserted causes of action against Navegar for negligence per se and strict liability for an abnormally dangerous activity. Plaintiffs alleged that Navegar was strictly liable because "making the [TEC–9/DC9] available for sale to the public" was "an abnormally dangerous activity." As

(continues)

to negligence per se, plaintiffs alleged that Navegar violated the Roberti–Roos Assault Weapons Control Act of 1989 (AWCA) by advertising the TEC–9/DC9 in California and that this advertising "was the direct and legal cause in bringing about plaintiffs' injuries" because it "was a substantial factor in causing Ferri to acquire" the Navegar weapons he used.

Navegar moved for summary judgment. It argued it owed plaintiffs no duty not to advertise the TEC–9/DC9 and that plaintiffs had no evidence Ferri saw or was affected by a Navegar advertisement. The trial court granted Navegar's motion since Navegar had "*legally* manufactured and sold" the TEC–9/DC9's Ferri used. The trial court then held that California common law did not impose on Navegar a duty "not to manufacture or sell assault weapons." The court explained that courts have refused to impose a duty upon manufacturers of firearms not to sell their products merely because of the potential misuse of the product by a third party.

As to negligence per se, the court found that plaintiffs' evidence failed to create a triable factual issue as to whether the advertisements influenced Ferri to purchase TEC–9/DC9's or to undertake his attack at 101 California Street. The court explained that "the links that plaintiffs seek to establish between advertisements and carnage amount to little more than guesswork." Finally, as to strict liability for an ultrahazardous activity, the court held that as a matter of law, the manufacture and distribution of a firearm, even an assault weapon, is not inherently dangerous.

Plaintiffs appealed the trial court's decision as to the common law negligence and ultrahazardous activity claims. The Court of Appeal unanimously affirmed as to ultrahazardous activity but, by a divided vote, reversed as to negligence.

We granted Navegar's petition for review on the negligence claim. Plaintiffs did not ask us to consider the Court of Appeal's holding regarding their ultrahazardous activity claim. Therefore, the only question before us is whether plaintiffs may proceed on their common law negligence claim. From the circumstantial evidence a jury could not reasonably infer that the information about the TEC-9/DC9 that influenced Ferri to select the product was derived from Navegar's advertisements or catalogs. The record fails to raise a triable issue of fact as to causation. Summary judgment was properly granted to Navegar.

CASE QUESTIONS

1. Why do you think courts have routinely held that the manufacture and distribution of a firearm, even an assault weapon, is not inherently dangerous?
2. Could the plaintiffs have possibly brought an action against any other person or entity? Explain your answer.

HYPOTHETICAL

Suppose local businesses operated a fourth of July fireworks celebration, which involved shooting the fireworks into the air high above town. Suppose excessive explosives were used in the fireworks. When they were detonated, flaming debris fell onto nearby houses, causing many fires. Could the homeowners succeed in a strict liability lawsuit against the companies responsible for the fireworks display?

Were the fireworks abnormally dangerous activities? Apply the Second Restatement's criteria for absolute liability. Fireworks exploding in mid-air create a tremendous risk that flaming debris could fall onto buildings' roofs, and subsequently set fires. The threat and the harm are substantial. Could reasonable care have avoided the risk? Fireworks that explode in the air are going to fall somewhere, perhaps in flaming pieces. No degree of reasonable care could prevent the danger of resulting fires. Aerial fireworks of the types described in this example are not commonly used by the public. The fireworks were inappropriately used in the area in which the fires occurred, because the power used was excessive and the fireworks detonated above the houses, subjecting them to the severe fire risk. The threat of harm outweighs the benefits to the community, as fireworks displays are conducted only once or twice per year and the benefits are purely aesthetic and momentary. The fireworks promoters will be strictly liable to the homeowners. (This conclusion assumes, of course, that there are no state statutes or local ordinances granting the fireworks promoters immunity from absolute liability.)

Table 10-2 summarizes absolute liability for abnormally dangerous activities, along with available defenses. All absolute liability cases, as discussed in this chapter, must satisfy the requirements of proximate cause, discussed next.

DEFINITIONS AND EXAMPLES	DEFENSES
Abnormally dangerous = ultrahazardous	Statutory immunities for certain types of ultrahazardous activities
These activities are, by their very nature, perilous	Most often include governmental activities involving uses of explosives, chemicals, or energy service
Examples: use of explosives, flammable substances, noxious gases, or poisons	Immunities reflect public policy objectives to balance necessary public services against individual right to compensation for injury
Some courts include unprotected use of utilities (electricity, natural gas, water)	

TABLE 10-2
Absolute liability for abnormally dangerous activities and available defenses

SCOPE OF LIABILITY: PROXIMATE CAUSE

Proximate cause in absolute liability cases is defined similarly to proximate cause in negligence cases. Animals or abnormally dangerous activities must proximately cause the victim's injuries if the tortfeasor is to be held strictly liable. For absolute liability purposes, **proximate cause** has the following elements:

1. The plaintiff's injuries must have been a reasonably foreseeable consequence of the defendant's actions.
2. The victim must have been a foreseeable plaintiff (meaning that it must have been reasonably foreseeable that the plaintiff would be injured as a result of the defendant's activities).

These elements are defined the same as in negligence theory.

proximate cause | The "legal cause" of an accident or other injury (which may have several actual causes). The *proximate cause* of an injury is not necessarily the closest thing in time or space to the injury.

No Duty of Reasonable Care

Negligence is irrelevant to strict liability; therefore, the duty of reasonable care, as used in negligence, is also irrelevant.

In the hypotheticals discussed throughout this chapter, apply the proximate cause standard to each example. Did the tortfeasor's actions proximately cause the victim's injuries? Various answers are possible. As with negligence, proximate cause in absolute liability cases can be a puzzle.

MASS TORTS AND CLASS ACTIONS

A **mass tort** occurs when many people are injured as a result of a single-tortious act. As the world becomes more densely populated, the chances for mass injury to people resulting from a single incident, product, or exposure greatly increases.

mass tort | When large groups of people are injured as a result of a single-tortious act. A mass tort typically involves thousands of claimants, years of litigation, and millions of dollars in attorneys' fees and costs. Generally, a smaller number of defendants is involved.

A mass tort combines many legal cases into a single trial. Each plaintiff of a mass tort is treated like an individual with his or her own individual lawsuit, rather than as a member of a group. In mass torts, many cases that are similar are argued together, saving time and money. Some examples of mass torts that have recently been brought involve the following products: Accutane, asbestos, Bextra/Celebrex, Ciba Geigy, Depo-Provera, HRT, Fosamax, Gadolinium, HRT, Levaquin, Mahwah Toxic Dump Site, NuvaRing, Ortho Evra, pelvic mesh, Risperdal/Seroquel/Zyprexa, Vioxx, YAZ/Yasmin/Ocella, Zometa/Aredia. These cases generally involve a large number of claims regarding a single product, with common facts and legal issues.

The tragic events of September 11, 2001, when planes crashed into the World Trade Center in New York, are examples of a mass tort. More than 100,000 people in New York were affected by this attack through loss of life, injury, property, or lost jobs. Countless others were displaced from their apartments and offices.

IF YOU RECEIVED PRERECORDED CALL(S) OR CALL(S) TO YOUR CELL PHONE USING AUTOMATED DIALING EQUIPMENT WHICH ADVERTISED ADT'S GOODS OR SERVICES, YOU MAY BENEFIT FROM A PROPOSED CLASS ACTION SETTLEMENT

A proposed Settlement has been reached in a class action case regarding telemarketing calls promoting the goods and services of ADT Security Services, Inc. (now known as The ADT Corporation or ADT, LLC) (collectively "ADT" or "ADT Security Services, Inc."). The name of the case is *Desai. et al., v. ADT Security Services, Inc.*. Case No. 1:11 -cv-1925, pending in the United States District Court for the Northern District of Illinois.

What is the lawsuit about?

The lawsuit alleges that certain ADT Authorized Dealers or lead generators, seeking to sell ADT's products and services, made telemarketing calls, either by (1) delivering a pre-recorded message or (2) to cell phones using automated dialing equipment, that violate the federal Telephone Consumer Protection Act (TCPA), 47 U.S.C. §227. ADT and ADT's Authorized Dealers contest the claims. Further, ADT denies that it authorized the calls or is responsible for the acts of those who made them.

What are the terms of the proposed Settlement?

The total amount of the Settlement Fund is $15,000,000.00. To make a claim, you must complete and send in a claim form or submit it online at RobocallSettlement.com certifying that you received a prerecorded call or a call to your cell phone using automated dialing equipment that promoted ADT's goods or services. If the Court approves the Settlement, every Class Member who submits a timely and valid claim form will be entitled to an equal payment from the Settlement Fund. The amount of your payment will depend on how many Class Members return valid claim forms. Each household is entitled to make only one claim regardless of the number of telephone calls received. This advertisement contains only a summary of the Settlement terms. You can receive additional details regarding the proposed Settlement, including a copy of the Settlement Agreement, by visiting RobocallSettlement.com or calling 1 -800-513-1506.

What are my rights?

- **You can make a claim** to get money from the Settlement Fund. All claim forms must be postmarked or submitted online no later than **June 10, 2013.**

- **If you do not want to be a member of the Class,** you **must** send a letter and ask to be excluded. Your request must be postmarked no later than **May 13, 2013,** to Robocall Settlement Administrator, c/o A.B. Data, Ltd., EXCLUSIONS, PO Box 170527, Milwaukee, WI53217. If you do not exclude yourself, you agree never to sue ADT or its Authorized Dealers in the future for the claims covered by this Settlement.

- **You can tell the Court if you do not like this proposed Settlement** or some part of it if you do not exclude yourself. To object, you must file an objection with the Court no later than **May 13, 2013.** You may also hire your own lawyer, at your own cost, to speak for you.

A detailed Notice of Class Action Lawsuit and Proposed Settlement and the claim form are available at RobocallSettlement.com or by writing the Settlement Administrator at the address below. The detailed Notice explains how to exclude yourself or comment on the case. It also explains what rights you are giving up if you stay in the Class.

EXHIBIT 10-1 *(continues)*

Will the Court Approve the proposed Settlement?

The Court will hold a Final Approval Hearing on **June 21, 2013 at 1:30 p.m.** to consider whether the proposed Settlement is fair, reasonable, and adequate, the motion for attorneys' fees and expenses and the motion for compensation awards to the Class Representatives. If comments or objections have been received, the Court will consider them at that time.

For more information and a claim form, visit RobocallSettlement.com. write to Robocall Settlement Administrator, c/o A.B. Data, Ltd., PO Box 170600, Milwaukee, WI 53217, or call 1-800-513-1506.

EXHIBIT 10-1   Legal notice for a proposed class-action settlement

Recent cases brought against the tobacco companies, manufacturers of silicone breast implants, and securities companies are just a few other examples of large numbers of people injured as a result of the same incident, accident, product, exposure, or misrepresentation. Very few law firms could handle the enormous time and money constraints posed by mass-tort claims. Accordingly, some firms have joined together to act in representing those injured by mass torts.

Class Action

class action | A lawsuit brought for yourself and other persons in the same situation. To bring a class action, you must convince the court that there are too many persons in the class (group) to make them all individually a part of a lawsuit and that your interests are the same as theirs, so that you can adequately represent their needs.

A mass tort is distinguishable from a **class action**. A class action encompasses a smaller group of plaintiffs who have been harmed. In a class action, a lawsuit is brought by an individual for himself or herself and other persons in the same situation. To bring a class action, you must convince the court that there are too many persons in the class (group) to make them all individually a part of the lawsuit and that your interests are the same as theirs so that you can adequately represent their needs (e.g., wage and hour claim against an employer). There have been several recent class actions against fast-food restaurants claiming they are the cause of obesity and conditions such as diabetes, high blood pressure, and heart disease. One such case was brought in the District of Columbia by a physician (See page 317.). Exhibit 10-1 shows a legal notice for a proposed class-action settlement.

THE CASE OF THE MASS TOXIC TORT

This case involves a mass-toxic-tort litigation concerning a colorless liquid chemical, benzene. It was used at multiple manufacturing plants and work sites by multiple defendants without issue for many years. Benzene is obtained from coal tar and is used as a solvent for resins and fats; it is also used in the manufacture of dyes. It is very difficult to allege at what point in time which chemical made with benzene caused a plaintiff's particular illness. Here, two different plaintiffs involved in this case have repeatedly attempted to amend their pleadings to give better notice to the defendants.

The court weighs the competing interests of the plaintiffs who are trying to bring their claims for injuries versus the defendants who seek to properly defend themselves.

IN RE BENZENE LITIGATION. Roy Hamill and
Joyce Hamill, his wife.
Kay Heddinger, Individually and as Surviving Spouse of Harold Heddinger, Deceased.

Superior Court of Delaware, New Castle County
C.A. Nos. 05C-09-020-JRS (BEN),
06C-05-295-JRS (BEN)
Submitted: October 26, 2006
Decided: February 26, 2007

Several defendants in this mass tort litigation have filed motions to dismiss complaints on the grounds that plaintiffs have failed to plead sufficient facts relating to their long term occupational exposure to benzene to meet Delaware's pleading requirements and to state a cause of action. The motions ask the court to measure the adequacy of the complaints.

Mr. and Mrs. Hamill filed their original complaint on September 1, 2005, alleging injuries resulting from Mr. Hamill's occupational exposure to products containing benzene. The defendants were divided into two categories: product defendants and premises defendants. The product defendants included those who allegedly manufactured or distributed the benzene-containing products to which Mr. Hamill was exposed. The premises defendants included those who owned or operated the properties where Mr. Hamill alleged his exposure occurred.

Between November 3, 2005 and December 30, 2005, multiple defendants moved to dismiss the first Hamill complaint for failure to state a claim upon which relief may be granted and for failure to plead fraud and negligence with particularity.

After announcing the standard it would apply to the motions, the court dismissed the first amended Hamill complaint because it did not adequately identify the benzene-containing products to which Mr. Hamill allegedly was exposed or the locations where the exposure allegedly occurred. The dismissal was entered without prejudice and with leave to amend.

In reaching its decision on the first motions to dismiss, the court attempted to balance the defendants' need for sufficient notice of the facts supporting the plaintiffs' claims against the potential prejudice the plaintiffs might suffer if required to plead too many details.

On August 31, 2006, Mr. and Mrs. Hamill filed their Fifth Complaint.

The Fifth Hamill Complaint is 47 pages long, 34 of which are devoted to pleading facts. The facts appear to be divided into three parts: the first addresses Mr. Hamill's employment experience and generally describes his alleged exposure to benzene at six identified work sites. In the second section, Mr. Hamill describes in more detail the premises where he alleges he was exposed to benzene. The third section identifies the products to which Mr. Hamill alleges he was exposed during his work history.

Six of the 23 named defendants moved to dismiss the Fifth Hamill Complaint. All six are premises defendants.

On May 26, 2006, more than a month after the court ruled on the first motions to dismiss and set the standard governing the degree of particularity required in her complaint, Kay Heddinger filed her original complaint.

On September 13, 2006, apparently in response to several motions to dismiss her initial complaint, Mrs. Heddinger filed her First Amended Complaint ("the Second Heddinger Complaint") in which she dropped the misrepresentation claims against all defendants.

The Second Heddinger Complaint is 28 pages long with 11 pages devoted to pleading facts.

Four product defendants and the lone premises defendant have moved to dismiss the Second Heddinger Complaint (hereinafter collectively "the Heddinger defendants").

Among the unique difficulties presented in toxic tort litigation is the well-recognized phenomenon whereby plaintiffs who were unwittingly exposed to the hazardous substance years before any

(continues)

injury is manifested are unable, years later, to identify the product(s) and/or the manufacturer(s) of the product(s) to which they were exposed.

There are several compelling reasons to require a plaintiff meaningfully to identify the product or premises at issue and the time and place of exposure. First, in toxic tort cases, plaintiffs typically name multiple defendants. These defendants are entitled at the pleading stage to isolate the wrong they are alleged to have committed. Second, product defendants must be able to ascertain whether other entities—for example, component part manufacturers, designers, distributors—should be brought into the litigation as third-party defendants. This can only occur after the defendants are advised of the specific product(s) at issue, and the time frame of the alleged exposure. Finally, defendants must be able to evaluate the condition and composition of the products and/or premises at issue at the time of alleged exposure and compare these conditions to those that have existed at other relevant time frames in order to determine if others may be liable for subsequent alterations.

The court attempted to strike a balance between the competing interests when it issued its oral ruling on April 3, 2006. Toxic tort plaintiffs usually cannot identify the products by brand name or the premises by address, nor should they be expected to do so. But, by virtue of the fact that they cannot provide the kind of product or premises identification typically provided in a products or premises liability action, plaintiffs must attempt to draw a picture for these defendants by pleading factual circumstances that may not otherwise be required.

By necessity, this effort will require the plaintiffs to plead more facts to make the point that they could make more succinctly if they possessed a specific product name or a specific property location.

With respect to claims against product defendants, when a plaintiff is unable specifically to identify the product at issue, it is reasonable to expect the plaintiff to identify a class of products within which the allegedly defective product fits. In the benzene litigation, the allegedly defective products all seem to take a liquid form of one sort or another. Vague descriptions such as "liquid," "fluid," "solvent," "fuel," without more, do not provide fair notice of the product at

issue. These descriptions, however, when coupled with a meaningful explanation of the location and manner in which the product was used, will begin to draw a picture from which the defendants can ascertain which of their products are involved in the litigation. Plaintiffs' prefiling due diligence must narrow the time frame to no more than a span of years, not decades. Defendants should not bear the burden of pouring through their inventory of products over many years, with little guidance from the plaintiffs, in order to track down potentially relevant products, particularly given that the benzene litigation is in its relative infancy with little institutional history to narrow the products potentially at issue.

To summarize, a plaintiff may identify the premises at issue by: (1) describing its location with the degree of precision dictated by the circumstances of the claim; (2) the type of facility located on the premises and a description of the toxic substances used there; and (3) the activity on the premises that gave rise to the exposure.

When read in a light most favorable to the plaintiffs, the pleading alleges that Mr. Hamill was injured by exposure to benzene while working on the moving defendants' oil fields in Southwestern Kansas, the Panhandle of Oklahoma, and Eastern Colorado. Mr. Hamill has described the nature of his work on these oil fields and the types of benzene-containing products to which he was exposed. He has also identified each of his employers and has stated the time frames in which these employers provided services on the defendants' premises. A search of company records for references to Mr. Hamill's various employers and the locations where these firms provided services to the defendants will likely further narrow the scope of potential sites.

The court has determined that the Fifth Hamill Complaint complies with Superior Court Civil Rules in that it sufficiently identifies the premises at issue and further identifies factual bases upon which claims of premises liability can rest. The motions to dismiss the Fifth Hamill Complaint are DENIED.

The Second Heddinger Complaint adequately pleads claims against some defendants, but not against others.

CASE QUESTIONS

1. In toxic tort cases, usually the plaintiff cannot name the offending product by brand name. Why does this occur?
2. Why is the time frame of a toxic tort considered so significant? Explain.

THE CASE OF THE FATTY CHICKEN

A class action was brought on behalf of all consumers of Kentucky Fried Chicken in the District of Columbia who had consumed the food at any time during the three-year period prior to filing the lawsuit. Dr. Hoyte, who brought this lawsuit, claims that he and others should have been warned about the dangers of eating this kind of fast food. After the suit was commenced, defendant KFC had the claim moved to federal court under the Class Action Fairness Act, because the total amount of money damages sought was more than $5 million.

Arthur HOYTE, M.D.
v.
YUM! BRANDS, INC. d/b/a/ KFC
United States District Court, District of Columbia
06-1127
489 F. Supp.2d 24
May 2, 2007

Dr. Hoyte seeks money for himself and any District of Columbia consumer in the amount up to $74,000 per person for injuries sustained as a result of KFC's use of dangerous trans fats to prepare food for consumers. The suit is for all people who purchased food at KFC in D.C. which was prepared containing trans fats. The class is so numerous that joinder of the parties in impracticable; thousands of people are involved. Dr. Hoyte's claims are typical of the class. He and others have been injured by the wrongful conduct. All KFC's in D.C. used partially hydrogenated oil, which is very high in trans fats. Trans fats have been classified as more harmful to the public than saturated fats.

A pot pie at KFC contained 14 grams of trans fat. The large popcorn chicken contained 7 grams of trans fats. Dr. Hoyte claims he should have been warned that even KFC's "best food," the Tender Roast and Honey BBQ chicken, contained trans fats. Dr. Hoyte alleged that the food was not fit for consumption, that this violated the implied warranty of merchantability, and that KFC was negligent in its misrepresentation. Since the suit, KFC switched its cooking style in 5,500 of its restaurants. KFC also announced plans to discontinue the use of all trans fats in its other restaurants.

Aware that the FDA had cautioned against the consumption of trans fat, plaintiff was trying to avoid products containing such fat. When he purchased food at the KFC, he was unaware that some of it was prepared with trans fat. KFC did not display any warning of the presence of trans fat in its food. KFC advertises on its website and in its restaurants that it sells the "best food," and that KFC products are part of a nutritionally healthy lifestyle. The advertisements do not reveal the use of trans fats.

Plaintiff next alleges that KFC violated the D.C. Consumer Protection Procedures Act, by "[f]ailing to state the material fact of the type of oils they were using for preparing food products, with the intent or effect of deceiving or misleading D.C. Consumers."

(continues)

The suggestion by plaintiff is that, by its silence, KFC misled plaintiffs into believing that its products did not contain harmful trans fat. This is a questionable premise at best, but again, one that need not be tested in this suit. A more fundamental problem is fatal to the claims-the absence of any allegation of injury. Dr. Hoyte does not "allege that the food he ordered was in any way unpalatable or that he suffered any immediate ill effects after he ate his order." He claims no emotional harm, pain or suffering. He does mention "economic injuries," but he does not specify what "economic injury" he has suffered, and none is evident from the facts presented, even under the most charitable reading of the complaint. Absent a claim of any injury, Dr. Hoyte has no standing to present his DCCPPA claim.

Plaintiff also alleges that defendant breached its duty of care to Dr. Hoyte and D.C. consumers by negligently making material misrepresentations about the quality of KFC food. The complaint includes two specific allegations of negligent misrepresentation: (1) a statement that KFC served the "best food" and (2) a statement described by plaintiff in which KFC allegedly informed consumers that KFC food could be consumed as a part of healthy lifestyle. Plaintiff claims that these statements were made in KFC stores and on the KFC website, though the statements are only described rather than quoted in plaintiff's complaint. Plaintiff asserts that, since

KFC knew when these statements were made that several of its food products were prepared with trans fat, it made the statements "at the expense of the public's health and safety . . . with evil motive, intent to injure, ill will," etc. As a direct and proximate result of these statements, plaintiff maintains, Hoyte and others were exposed to unhealthy trans fats and "have suffered or will suffer adverse health effects" therefrom.

KFC's claims that its restaurants serve the "best food" is a nonmeasurable, "bald statement of superiority" that is nonactionable puffery. *See, e.g., Am. Italian Pasta Co. v. New World Pasta Co., 371 F.3d 387, 391 (8th Cir.2004).* Plaintiff has no response to defendant's string citation of cases holding that a merchant's boasts about his product being "the best" or of the "highest quality" is not actionable.

The statement that KFC food could be part of a healthy lifestyle is also nonactionable, for a simple reason: the statement, as characterized by plaintiff himself, does not necessarily suggest that trans fats are healthy. There is nothing in the statement referring specifically to the KFC items prepared with trans fats, and nothing suggesting how frequently one should eat KFC in order to incorporate it into a healthy lifestyle. No conceivable reading of this language could trigger liability for negligent misrepresentation. An appropriate order accompanies this memorandum.

CASE QUESTIONS

1. Did your thoughts about the plaintiff's claim change as you continued to read this case? Explain your answer.
2. Do you think the plaintiff brought this lawsuit for financial gain, or to bring publicity to the type of food sold at some fast-food chains? Explain your answer.
3. New York City has now banned the use of artificial trans fats in restaurant food, as well as the sale of large-size sugary soft drinks. Los Angeles County, California, has banned the opening of any new fast-food chains in certain areas where there is a high percentage of obese residents, and no alternative food sources. Do you think human behavior can be altered through these food bans? Is there a better way to influence consumer behavior? Explain your answer.

▌ SUMMARY

Fault is irrelevant to strict liability. If the tortfeasor is found to be absolutely liable, his or her negligence or intent does not affect the liability. This may seem harsh and unfair, because a tortfeasor might exercise every degree of care to avoid injuring others and still be held responsible under absolute liability. Strict liability is limited to cases involving abnormally dangerous instrumentalities, such as wild animals, vicious domestic animals, ultrahazardous activities, and products liability. Through its courts and legislatures, the public has established absolute liability as an insurance measure to protect innocent victims from harm caused by particularly perilous pursuits.

The common law calls wild animals *ferae naturae* ("wild nature") and domestic animals *domitae naturae* ("domesticated nature"). At common law, wild animals are presumed to be naturally dangerous, whereas domestic animals are assumed to be harmless and docile creatures. Wild animals may be owned by individuals who capture and restrain the beasts. This is called exercising dominion and control. Owners are absolutely liable for injuries their wild animals inflict. However, owners are strictly liable for injuries caused by their domestic animals only if these animals exhibited vicious propensities. The defenses of assumption of risk, contributory and comparative negligence, consent, and self-defense or defense of others apply to animal liability cases.

Abnormally dangerous, or ultrahazardous, activities are inherently perilous. Use of explosives, flammable substances, noxious gases, poisons, hazardous wastes, and sometimes electricity, natural gas, or water utilities are examples. The *Restatement (Second) of Torts* § 520 states that persons engaged in abnormally dangerous activities are strictly liable for injuries caused by these activities. The activity must create a high risk of substantial harm, a risk that could not have been eliminated through the exercise of reasonable care; the activity or substance must not be commonly undertaken or used; the activity must have been inappropriately used in the place in which the injury happened; and the activity's hazards must outweigh the activity's benefits to the community. As a defense to strict liability, many legislatures have enacted statutes protecting certain activities from absolute liability. Some toxic torts have injured so many people that mass-tort actions or class actions were needed for legal recourse.

Absolute liability in cases involving animals and abnormally dangerous activity is limited by proximate cause. For strict liability to apply, the defendant's actions must have proximately caused the plaintiff's injuries. This means that the plaintiff's injuries must have been reasonably foreseeable as a consequence of the defendant's conduct, and it must have been foreseeable that the plaintiff could be injured as a result of the defendant's actions. This is called the foreseeable plaintiffs theory. There is no duty of reasonable care in strict liability cases, because the duty involves negligence theory, which is irrelevant to absolute liability.

In the next chapter the elements of products liability actions are discussed. These actions generally involve defective products, as well as products that do not live up to their advertisements.

▌ KEY TERMS

abnormally dangerous
  (ultrahazardous)
  instrumentalities
absolute (strict) liability
class action

common usage (use) principle
control
dominion
domitae naturae
ferae naturae

mass tort
proximate cause
toxic tort actions
vicious propensity rule

PROBLEMS

In the following hypotheticals, determine if absolute liability applies and if the tortfeasor will be strictly liable to the injured party. Are any defenses relevant? If so, how would they be applied?

1. Heather works at the municipal zoo. She cleans the cages of and feeds the various species of monkey on exhibition. One day, Heather received a telephone call from "Spider," the exhibits supervisor, who instructed her to report to the exotic bird building to substitute for another employee who was ill. Heather had never worked with these birds before and was unfamiliar with their habits, although she received feeding and watering instructions from Spider. As she was cleaning one of the walk-in cages, a toucan landed on the back of her neck, scratching and biting at her ears. The scratches required stitches. There were no municipal ordinances discussing the zoo or its operation, apart from the enabling act that established the zoo and its supervision by the city's department of parks and recreation.

2. Willie owns a bulldog, which he kept chained in his backyard. The dog often barked and growled at anyone passing by the house on the sidewalk. One morning, Lisa, an employee of the electric company, visited Willie's house to read the meter, which was located in the backyard. Lisa had read Willie's meter before and knew about the dog. She peeked around the house but could not see the dog. She assumed it was inside the house, because the chain was lying on the ground. As she walked over to the meter, the dog leaped from the bushes, knocked Lisa down, and chewed on her arms and hands. Lisa was hospitalized as a result of these injuries.

3. Olaf owns a gas station. While a tanker truck was filling his underground fuel tanks, Olaf was using a welding torch inside his garage area to repair a customer's car. He inadvertently knocked over the torch, still lit, which fell into a puddle of gasoline from the tanker. The puddle ignited and burned across the ground to the tanker pipe connected to the underground tanks. Both the tanker truck and the fuel in the underground tanks then ignited and exploded. Several patrons were severely injured and their vehicles damaged.

4. The Belladonna Pharmaceutical Company manufactures medicines. It uses certain chemical solutions that turn bad and must be destroyed. These solutions are kept in steel barrels in the firm's back lot, awaiting pickup from a local waste-disposal company. Brad works for the trash company. He had never collected trash from Belladonna before, as he normally rode the residential trash routes. Brad's supervisor failed to instruct him to take a special sealed tank truck to get Belladonna's chemicals. Instead, Brad drove an open-top trash truck used to haul dry garbage. Brad tossed the barrels into the truck, and several of them ruptured and leaked. As Brad drove down the highway to the dump, chemical sludge spilled out the back of the truck onto an automobile driven by Madison. Madison stopped and touched the sludge caked across the front of his car. It made his hands burn. Frightened, Madison drove to a local hospital emergency room. His skin had absorbed much of the chemical waste, and he became severely ill and had to be hospitalized for several weeks.

REVIEW QUESTIONS

1. How is strict, or absolute, liability different from negligence and intentional torts? What role does fault play in absolute liability? What are the limitations to strict liability? What are the public policy objectives behind absolute liability? How is strict liability like insurance?

2. How does the common law define wild animals? Domestic animals? What does the common law presume about each type of animal? How can wildlife be owned? Why is this important to the question of liability? When does strict liability apply to injuries inflicted by wild animals? By domestic animals? What is the vicious propensity rule? What defenses apply to cases involving animal owners' absolute liability?

3. What are abnormally dangerous activities? Ultra-hazardous activities? How does the *Restatement* *(Second) of Torts* define each term? What elements are required for absolute liability to apply? What is the function of reasonable care? What is the common usage principle? What balancing test do courts apply in cases involving abnormally dangerous activities?

4. How is proximate cause defined in strict liability cases? Why is it important?

5. What is a mass tort?

6. How is a class action different from a mass tort?

▌ HELPFUL WEBSITES

This chapter focuses on strict and absolute liability. To learn more about strict or absolute liability, the following sites can be accessed:

General Information

www.rand.org
www.toxlaw.com
www.osha.gov
www.thefederation.org
www.access.gpo.gov

Wild Animals

www.bornfreeusa.org
www.animallaw.info

Mass Torts

www.lawprofessors.typepad.com
www.judiciary.state.nj.us/mass-tort
www.wlf.org

Class Actions

www.topclassactions.com
Insert Online Student Companion logo and text from design

STUDENT COMPANION WEBSITE
For additional cases and study materials, please go to www.cengagebrain.com

Chapter 11

Products Liability

THE BIGGEST MISTAKES PARALEGALS MAKE AND HOW TO AVOID THEM

When Gambling Stops Being about Entertainment

Every office has one, and litigation paralegal Aiden was ours: the sports pool operator. Energetic and with a personality that lit up the room, Aiden began each "pool year" right after paying off winners for Super Bowl Sunday. "It's time to pick for Final Four," Aiden announced to all, collecting the cash with everyone's selections. The way Aiden ran the pool, winners would transfer their winnings from "Final Four" to the pool for the World Series. Then those winners rolled their winnings to the pool for the Super Bowl. Aiden maintained it was more fun to have a big payout at the end of the "pool year" so winners throughout the year never had to add more money to the pool. "It keeps interest high," he said, and nobody complained because Aiden made all the effort and he made work fun.

After the December holiday season, Aiden seemed stressed out and often depressed, and complained of sleeplessness. His work suffered when he missed important deadlines, and he was placed on a performance improvement plan. Someone said he had a personal relationship that ended badly. Then Aiden announced the unthinkable: He was cancelling his annual Super Bowl party and going on vacation. But Aiden was not going on vacation. He was getting counseling after a suicide attempt. After gambling with borrowed money from the office pool, Aiden sought to recover his losses through more gambling. It did not work.

Lesson Learned: Problem gambling is symptomatic of a larger, underlying issue, just like any addiction. It is not just about the gambler and his or her finances—it touches everyone who has any relationship with the gambler. Aiden exhibited all the behaviors of a problem gambler, including gambling with our money! Assistance and answers for those with a gambling addiction are available by telephoning the HelpLine of the National Council on Problem Gambling.

INTRODUCTION

Products liability is any form of liability arising out of the use of a defective product. A plaintiff can bring three different causes of action depending on the facts: strict tort liability, negligence, or breach of warranty. This chapter focuses on the cause of action for strict liability in tort. Generally, under products liability, the manufacturer or seller of a product is absolutely liable for any injuries caused by a defect in the product. Products liability occupies a prominent position in torts study, as it is involved in a sizeable portion of tort litigation. It is probably the most significant development in tort law since the courts accepted negligence theory as a separate tort.

product(s) liability | The responsibility of manufacturers (and sometimes sellers) of goods to pay for harm to purchasers (and sometimes other users and even bystanders) caused by a defective product.

This chapter includes

- Products liability theory and history
- The parties in products liability cases
- The elements of products liability
- The *Restatement (Second) of Torts*, § 402A
- The *Restatement (Third) of Torts*, §2(b)
- The defenses to products liability
- Comparison of products liability with contract law warranties
- The *Uniform Commercial Code*

PRODUCTS LIABILITY THEORY AND HISTORY

Products liability was established as a distinct tort theory in the landmark case of *Greenman v. Yuba Power Products, Inc.,* 59 Cal. 2d 57, 377 P.2d 897, 27 Cal. Rptr. 697 (1962). In this case, the California Supreme Court completed more than 100 years of legal evolution that culminated in strict products liability.

Public Policy Objectives behind Products Liability

Products liability is society's decision, through its courts and legislatures, that businesses manufacturing and selling defective products are in the best economic position to bear the expenses incurred when a faulty product injures an innocent user. A defective product usually involves shoddy workmanship or poor-quality materials. The theory may be simply put: Why should the unfortunate victim shoulder the burdens (medical costs, permanent injuries, etc.) produced by a defectively made product? Instead, should not the manufacturer or seller of that product be liable for the resulting harms? Does that not seem reasonable and ethical? If one has ever been hurt by a defective product, one might answer affirmatively. A manufacturer or seller, however, might feel differently.

Historical Development of Products Liability

In the early nineteenth century, English and American common law held that persons injured by defective products had to sue under contract law rather than tort law. These courts felt that the appropriate cause of action was breach of contract or, more precisely, breach of warranty. A **warranty** is a guarantee that a product or service meets certain quality standards. If a product fails to meet such standards, as is the case when a product is defective, then the warranty has been breached.

Under early-nineteenth-century English and American common law, only persons who had made contracts with the manufacturer or seller of a defective product could recover damages for breach of warranty or breach of contract. This contractual relationship is called **privity of contract.** Privity exists when parties are directly engaged in an agreement between them. If Joseph enters into a contract with Harris, in which Joseph agrees to sell Harris a product for a certain price, then there is privity of contract between them. The landmark case that announced the privity rule was *Winterbottom v. Wright*, 10 Meeson & Welsby 109, 152 Eng. Rep. 402 (1842). In this case, the plaintiff drove a horse-drawn coach for the postmaster general. This coach was manufactured especially for the postmaster general by the defendant. The plaintiff was maimed when the vehicle's axle broke and threw him from the carriage seat. The plaintiff sued the defendant for failing to properly maintain the coach under a service contract. The court held that the plaintiff was not a party to either the service agreement or the manufacturing agreement. Thus, the plaintiff lacked privity of contract and therefore could not recover for the injuries caused by the defectively assembled coach. The only party that could sue under such circumstances would be the postmaster general, with whom the defendant contracted to make the carriage. But in this case the postmaster general was not harmed. The injured plaintiff was left without compensation.

warranty |

1. Any promise (or a presumed promise, called an *implied warranty*) that certain facts are true.

2. In consumer law, any obligations imposed by law on a seller that benefit a buyer; for example, the warranty that goods are **merchantable** and the warranty that goods sold as fit for a particular purpose are fit for that purpose.

merchantable | Goods that are fit for their usual or customary purpose.

privity of contract | A legal relationship that exists between parties to a contract. In some cases privity must exist in order for an individual to make a claim against another.

Almost immediately, American courts began to carve out exceptions to the privity-of-contract rule. In *Thomas v. Winchester*, 6 N.Y. 397 (1852), the New York Court of Appeals ruled that a mislabeled medicine (which actually contained poison) was inherently dangerous, and accordingly the injured party did not need to have privity of contract with the manufacturer or seller to recover damages. In this case, the plaintiff's husband had purchased a bottle, labeled "dandelion extract," that in actuality contained belladonna, a deadly poison. The defendant manufacturer who mislabeled the product sold it to a druggist, who resold it to a physician, who prescribed it to the plaintiff. There was no privity of contract between the plaintiff and the defendant. Nonetheless, the court permitted the plaintiff to recover damages for injuries caused when she took the poison from the mislabeled bottle. The court reasoned that poisons are imminently danger-ous by their very nature. Accordingly, remote users of a mislabeled drug could be seriously injured. Thus, privity of contract is unnecessary if the defective product (such as a mislabeled poison) is imminently dangerous. Later courts characterized this as the **imminent danger exception** to the privity-of-contract rule.

Throughout the nineteenth century, the New York Court of Appeals, and many courts following its lead, expanded the imminent danger rule to include spoiled food, explosives, improperly assembled scaffolding, an exploding coffee urn, and defectively made automobile wheels. Many courts found liability in con-tract warranty law, but this still required privity of contract. The landmark case in this century, which is often said to have sparked modern products liability law, is *MacPherson v. Buick Motor Co.*, 217 N.Y. 382, 111 N.E. 1050 (1916). Writing for the majority, Justice Cardozo declared that privity of contract was obsolete. If a product, because of its defective manufacture, became unreasonably dangerous, then the manufacturer or seller would be liable for injuries caused by the defective product. Cardozo applied negligence theory to determine whether the defective product was unreasonably dangerous. The manufacturer had to be negligent in making the faulty product.

MacPherson ushered in a cascade of court opinions following and expand-ing its precedent. In *Escola v. Coca Cola Bottling Co.*, 24 Cal. 2d 453, 150 P.2d 436 (1944), Justice Traynor of the California Supreme Court, in his concurring opinion, opined that negligence was no longer necessary for defective product manufacturers to be liable. Instead, he proposed strict liability. It took 18 years be-fore the California Supreme Court adopted this view in *Greenman v. Yuba Power Products*. Many other state courts quickly joined the new common law theory.

The American Law Institute (ALI), which consists of a group of legal scholars, followed the decision in *Greenman* when publishing its famous *Restatement (Second) of Torts* § 402A. Virtually every American jurisdiction has adopted the ***Restatement (Second) of Torts***, in some form or another, as the definitive rule for strict products liability. The Restatements are a series of legal

imminent danger exception | A nineteenth- and early-twentieth-century exception to the privity-of-contract require-ment in defective product cases.

Restatement (Second) of Torts | A legal treatise adopted by all jurisdictions detailing the current state of tort law and trends. It is considered a highly respected secondary source of law published by the American Law Institute (ALI).

treatises covering a variety of subjects that reflect the current state of the law and legal trends. They are considered a highly respected secondary source of law. The *Restatement (Second) of Torts* was revised in 1998, and there is now a ***Restatement (Third) of Torts*** focusing on products liability. Some jurisdictions prefer to follow the earlier edition that they have relied on for over 30 years. Both of the *Restatements* are discussed in greater detail later in the chapter.

Types of Warranties

Three different kinds of possible warranties are involved under strict products liability. To recover under these warranties, a plaintiff need not show that a defendant was negligent or acted intentionally to cause harm. The plaintiff must show a breach of one of the following warranties:

1. Express warranty,
2. Implied warranty of merchantability, or
3. Implied warranty of fitness for a particular purpose.

Express Warranty. **Express warranties** are very common. They are a statement that a particular promise or set of facts is true. When a seller or manufacturer makes such a promise to the buyer, the buyer is relieved of the responsibility to verify such information. If the facts are not as represented, the purchaser will have a claim for any loss as a result. Examples of express warranties vary from statements in a catalogue or brochure, such as "this car is guaranteed for five years or 50,000 miles" to a label on a shirt that states, "never needs ironing." Express warranties address the quality, fitness, and character of goods. A seller's opinion, such as "you'll love this car," or sales puffery, such as "this is the finest camera you'll see," are not considered express warranties. There is no expectation that the buyer will purchase a product based on these statements.

Warranties are also covered under the **Uniform Commercial Code,** which is discussed later in the chapter.

Implied Warranty of Merchantability. Unlike an express warranty in which a specific statement is made, an implied warranty arises by virtue of the law. When a product is sold, the law imposes an **implied warranty of merchantability.** This means that the goods sold will be fit for their ordinary purpose. If you purchase a vegetable peeler, there is an implied promise that you will be able to peel most vegetables with the peeler without too much effort. If you purchase a chair, there is an implied promise that the furniture will support you when you sit down. When you buy food, there is an implied warranty that it is fit for consumption. If you come down with food poisoning after eating canned tuna, then the implied warranty that the food is fit for human consumption has been broken. Likewise, if there is

Restatement (Third) of Torts | A revision of section 402A of the *Restatement (Second) of Torts* that focuses on products liability. Not all jurisdictions follow this edition.

express warranty | A statement that a particular promise or set of facts is true.

Uniform Commercial Code | A set of uniform model statutes concerning commercial transactions.

implied warranty of merchantability | A promise implied but not expressed by law, that goods sold will be fit for their ordinary purpose.

glass in a food product, or other foreign objects, the implied warranty of merchantability has beenv breached. Additionally, products must be properly contained, packaged, and labeled. A product labeled "sunscreen lotion" that does not protect you from the sun's harmful rays would be considered in breach of the implied warranty of merchantability.

Implied Warranty of Fitness for a Particular Purpose.

Least common is the **implied warranty of fitness for a particular purpose**. This warranty generally involves an interaction between the buyer and seller. A purchaser goes into a hardware store and says, "I'm looking for a product that will cover up water stains on my ceiling tiles." The seller's employee or representative then recommends a water-sealing paint product for the buyer's particular needs. The law imposes an implied warranty of fitness for a particular purpose. If the product does not work as needed, then the buyer can return the product. In such a case, the buyer relied on the expertise of the seller and bought a product based upon his or her recommendation.

Exhibit 11-1 summarizes the different types of warranties.

implied warranty of fitness for a particular purpose | When a buyer relies on a seller's expertise in recommending a particular product, there is an implied promise that the product will work as described by the seller.

EXHIBIT 11-1
Warranties

Warranty	Explanation	Example	Breach
1. Express warranty	The manufacturer or seller makes a statement as to quality of goods.	The writing on the bottom of a plate states: "This plate is dishwasher and microwave safe."	If the plate cracks from the heat of the dishwasher, the warranty is breached.
2. Implied warranty of merchantability	The law implies that goods will be fit for the particular purpose for which they are sold.	A cell phone must conduct sound sufficiently clearly so that the user can hear the other party speaking.	A bunch of static noises prevent the user from hearing a party speaking.
3. Implied warranty of fitness for a particular purpose	The law implies a warranty when a seller recommends a particular product to meet a customer's needs.	A customer requests glue that will hold two pieces of wood together without the use of nails.	Two pieces of wood are glued to each other, but the glue does not hold and the pieces separate.

▊ PARTIES

Three classes of parties are involved in products liability cases: the product manufacturer, the seller, and the ultimate user.

THE CASE OF THE HOT CAR

Two cousins go out drinking. The cousin who is driving hears some noise from his van on the way home. Then the car stalls, and he tries to restart the van several times. The driver is severely injured when a rear seat explodes into fire. The court reviews consumer expectations.

Krzysztof SOBCZAK, Plaintiff-Appellant,
v.
GENERAL MOTORS CORPORATION,
Defendant-Appellee

Appellate Court of Illinois, First District, Third Division
No. 1-05-2154
May 23, 2007

At about 9 P.M., on August 28, 1999, Sobczak drove his father's Chevrolet Astro van (YF7 configured, M/L model) to pick up his cousin Arthur. Sobczak and Arthur went to two nightclubs over the course of several hours. Sobczak consumed at least five beers.

After dropping off Arthur, Sobczak noticed that the van was sluggish and was making noises. The car stalled and Sobczak tried to start the car by putting the transmission into neutral and turning the key. The car started but the motor sounded like it was "jumping up and down." Sobczak put his foot on the brake pedal and put the van in gear, but the motor died. This occurred about 10 times in 10 minutes. Sobczak started the van once more but smelled something coming from the back. He climbed over the seat and went to the back bench seat. He started to check around when the seat exploded into flames. His shirt and hair caught on fire. The next thing Sobczak could recall was waking up in the hospital one month after the accident.

John Orisini, the head of the fire and arson investigative unit for the Cook County sheriff's police, testified the fire started near the rear tire on the passenger side. He drew this conclusion based on the fact that the metal in that area was exposed and whitening occurred. There was also evidence of heavy burning in the area of the kickup and the rear wheel. The carpet padding in front of the two rear seats was completely burned away. Orisini concluded that the fire started underneath the van either in or near the muffler and the heat had conducted up through the flooring and traveled inside the van.

At trial, Sobczak pursued his claims for negligence and strict products liability based on design defect that GM had defectively designed the van's heat shields, muffler and fuel management system; and negligently designed the van's heat shields.

A plaintiff may establish a strict liability claim based on a design defect in one of two ways: the consumer-expectation test or the risk-utility test. The consumer-expectation test provides that a product is "unreasonably dangerous" when it is "dangerous to an extent beyond that which would be contemplated by the ordinary consumer who purchases it, with the ordinary knowledge common to the community as to its characteristics." *Restatement (Second) of Torts* § 402A, Comment *i*, at 352 (1965).Under the risk-utility test, a plaintiff must demonstrate that a design defect exists by presenting evidence that the risk of danger inherent in the design of the product outweighs the benefits of the design. In other words, "the utility of the design must therefore be weighed against the risk of harm created" and "if the likelihood and gravity of the harm outweigh the benefits and utilities of the product, the product is unreasonably dangerous."

As previously stated, a plaintiff may prevail under the consumer-expectation test if he or she can demonstrate that the product failed to perform as an ordinary consumer would expect when used in an intended or reasonably foreseeable manner.

The purpose of the heat shielding system is to disburse and deflect any heat created from the operation of the vehicle away from the vehicle.

Clearly, an ordinary consumer purchasing an M/L van would give little or no thought to the heat shielding system selected by GM, but would expect that little or no heat would be transferred from underneath their YF7 configured M/L van into the vehicle compartment.

It is reasonably foreseeable that if the M/L van stalled, an ordinary consumer would make numerous attempts to restart the van without much thought as to whether the heat shielding system would withstand the high temperatures that may be created by revving the engine. Specifically, an ordinary consumer would expect his M/L van either to start or not to start, but would not expect the interior of the van to ignite.

Verdict for Sobczak.

CASE QUESTIONS

1. Did this van meet consumer expectations? Explain.
2. Do you think General Motors Corporation was aware of this defect? Explain.

Manufacturers and Sellers

The **product manufacturer** makes the defective product that gives rise to the entire products liability lawsuit. The **seller** includes anyone who is in the business of selling goods, such as the one that is faulty. This includes the manufacturer as well as wholesalers and retailers. **Wholesalers** are businesses that buy and sell goods to **retailers,** which in turn sell the products to customers, usually individual persons.

The Ultimate User

When we buy a product, we are **purchasers.** In products liability law, however, the party injured by flawed merchandise need not be the original buyer. Instead, a member of the purchaser's family, or a friend of the buyer, could recover damages if hurt by a defective product. The key is whether it is reasonably foreseeable that the user would have utilized the product. This individual is called the **ultimate user,** because that person eventually used the product that caused an injury.

In products liability litigation, the ultimate user becomes the plaintiff who sues various defendants: the retailer, the wholesaler(s), and the manufacturer. The plaintiff uses a shotgun approach to products liability—namely, sue all the sellers. This may seem excessive, but the plaintiff has a logical explanation. The plaintiff

product manufacturer | The maker of a product that, if defective, gives rise to product liability.

seller | One who sells property, either its own or through contract with the actual owner.

wholesaler | One who sells goods wholesale, rather than retail.

retailer | One who makes retail sales of goods.

purchaser | One who acquires property through the purchase of said property.

ultimate user | In products liability law, a person who is injured by a defective product. It must have been reasonably foreseeable that the injured party would use the defective product.

EXHIBIT 11-2 Product Distribution Chain

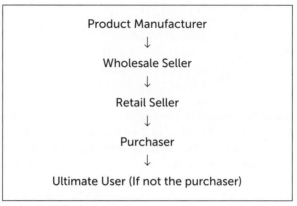

Product Manufacturer
↓
Wholesale Seller
↓
Retail Seller
↓
Purchaser
↓
Ultimate User (If not the purchaser)

deep pocket | The one person (or organization), among many possible defendants, best able to pay a judgment; the one a plaintiff is most likely to sue.

sues all the sellers along the product distribution chain to ensure that one of them (probably the manufacturer) will have sufficient monies to pay a judgment. In tort law, this is called "going for the **deep pocket.**" In other words, the plaintiff tries to sue defendants that have money and could satisfy a damages award. Exhibit 11-2 shows the product distribution chain between manufacturers, sellers, purchasers, and ultimate users. The deficient product passes through many hands before reaching its unfortunate victim.

Now that we have met the parties to products liability actions, it is time to investigate the elements of products liability.

▌ ELEMENTS

Products liability is defined as strict, or absolute, liability for the seller or manufacturer of a defectively made product that injures a user of the item.

No Privity-of-Contract Requirement

Privity of contract is not required in products liability. The ultimate user need not have purchased the merchandise directly from the seller or manufacturer, although some states require that a sale of the product must have occurred somewhere between the manufacturer and the ultimate user. However, it need not be a direct transaction between the two.

Negligence Is Irrelevant

Remember that the seller or manufacturer's negligence is irrelevant to strict liability. It does not matter how much care the seller or manufacturer used in making or maintaining the product. Every possible precaution could have been utilized, but that simply makes no difference. If the product was defective, and a user was harmed as a result, absolute liability applies—period.

A Typical Products Liability Formula

There are five elements of products liability, as defined by most state courts or statutes:

1. The defect must render the product unreasonably dangerous to use.
2. The seller or manufacturer must be in the business of selling products such as the flawed one(s).
3. The product cannot have been substantially changed between the time it left the seller or manufacturer's hands and the time it reached the ultimate user.
4. The defect must have proximately caused the ultimate user's injuries.
5. The ultimate user must have used the product properly, that is, in the way that the product was designed to be used.

In some jurisdictions, several additional elements are required:

6. The ultimate user must have been foreseeable (foreseeable plaintiffs theory).
7. The seller or manufacturer must have been responsible for the condition in which the product was maintained.
8. In a few states, a sale of the product must have occurred. This could be a sale between the manufacturer and a wholesaler, or a wholesaler to a retailer, or a retailer to a customer. Basically, someone at some point had to buy the defective item.

The *Restatement (Second) of Torts* Rule

Section 402A of the *Restatement (Second) of Torts* contains fewer elements than those just discussed. It states:

1. One who sells any product in a defective condition unreasonably dangerous to the user or consumer or to his property is subject to liability for physical harm thereby caused to the ultimate user or consumer, or to his property, if
    (a) the seller is engaged in the business of selling such a product, and
    (b) it is expected to and does reach the user or consumer without substantial change in the condition in which it is sold.
2. The rule stated in Subsection (1) applies though
    (a) the seller has exercised all possible care in the preparation and sale of this product, and
    (b) the user or consumer has not bought the product from or entered into any contractual relation with the seller.

THE CASE OF THE PREMATURE VIEWING

A casket breaks apart and a body flies out in full view of the family. Who are the injured parties and what kind of claim can they bring? Is this a strict products claim, or does the claim really pertain to the wrongful mishandling of a corpse?

S. Randall SWEENEY; George Allen Sweeney; Suzanne Sweeney, Individually; and Suzanne Sweeney, as Guardian for Lorin Neal Sweeney, Appellants

v.

AURORA CASKET COMPANY, INC. and Victoriaville Caskets Limited, Appellees

Court of Appeals of Kentucky

No. 2005-CA-001569-MR

February 9, 2007

OPINION

HENRY, Senior Judge.

This appeal is taken from the Hancock Circuit Court's entry of a directed verdict and judgment as to a number of claims brought by the appellants in connection with an unfortunate incident relating to the burial of their father. Upon review, we affirm.

The facts of the case are as follows: Sherroll Sweeney died in August 2001. Soon after his death, his son, Randall Sweeney, made funeral arrangements with Taylor-Raymond-Spear Funeral Home for Spear to conduct Sherroll's funeral, which was to be held on August 31, 2001. Part of this process included selling Randall a casket for his father's burial. The casket Randall chose was one that Spear had purchased from Aurora Casket Company. Aurora, in turn, had purchased the casket from its manufacturer, Victoriaville Caskets Limited.

Following Sherroll's funeral service, he was to be interred at Lewisport Cemetery after a planned gravesite service. After the funeral procession arrived at the gravesite, J. David Spear, owner of the funeral home, assembled the pallbearers, and they began to remove Sherroll's casket from the funeral coach. When the casket was approximately three-fourths of the way out of the coach, Spear heard a loud pop and a heavy weight—the edge of the casket bottom—hit his foot. Apparently the bottom of the casket where Sherroll's head had been resting had become detached from the rest of the casket, resulting in his head and half of his body spilling forth in clear view of the Sweeney family. Sherroll's body was subsequently returned to the funeral home, where it was placed in another casket before being returned to the gravesite for continuation of the service and burial.

On August 22, 2002, Sherroll's widow, Joan Sweeney, filed a complaint in the Hancock Circuit Court against the appellees and Spear. A week after Joan filed her original complaint, Sherroll's adult children-Randall Sweeney, George Allen Sweeney, Suzanne Sweeney, and Lorin Neal Sweeney (through a guardian)—filed their own complaint in the Hancock Circuit Court against the same parties.

Joan's claims were eventually settled, and she is not a party to this appeal. Spear is also not a party, as the trial court granted the funeral home's unopposed summary judgment motion in an order entered on April 2, 2004. The remaining claims of the Sweeney children against Aurora and Victoriaville proceeded to trial on March 23 and 24, 2005. At the conclusion of the Sweeneys' proof at trial, the trial court directed verdicts in favor of Aurora and Victoriaville as to the negligence, strict liability, and implied warranty claims. The court allowed the remaining outrageous conduct claim to go the jury; however, the jury found in favor of Aurora and Victoriaville. This appeal followed.

On appeal, the Sweeneys challenge the trial court's directed verdict in favor of Aurora and Victoriaville as to their negligence, strict liability, and implied warranty claims. The jury verdict as to the outrageous conduct claim is not part of this appeal.

We first address the Sweeneys' contention that they were entitled to recover damages against Aurora and Victoriaville for mental and emotional anguish under both negligence and strict liability theories due to a manufacturing defect in their father's casket.

As both Aurora and Victoriaville point out, Kentucky courts have consistently held that "damages may not be recovered for shock or mental anguish unaccompanied by physical contact or injury." It is undisputed that the Sweeneys had no physical contact relating to the incident in question and accordingly suffered no resulting physical injuries. Instead, they were simply bystanders to the event. Consequently, a general claim of damages for mental anguish is unavailable to them.

In possible recognition of this fact, the Sweeneys correctly point out that a plaintiff may recover damages for mental anguish arising out of the wrongful mishandling of a corpse, and suggest that this cause of action should have been available to them here to allow for such recovery. In reviewing the record, however, we question whether this cause of action was ever properly presented against Aurora or Victoriaville in the Sweeneys' original and amended complaints or at any other point throughout this litigation. Aurora and Victoriaville argue that a wrongful mishandling of a corpse claim was never made against them, and the Sweeneys provide nothing in their brief to refute this position. In any event, such a claim is also unavailable to them here, as a suit for the mishandling of a corpse is only available to the deceased's "next of kin"—in this case, Sherroll's surviving spouse, Joan.

Accordingly, the trial court's entry of a directed verdict against the Sweeneys as to their negligence and strict liability claims against Aurora and Victoriaville was appropriate, and the appellees' remaining arguments in this respect need not be considered.

The Sweeneys also contend that their breach of warranty claim against Aurora should have gone to the jury because the Taylor-Raymond-Spear Funeral Home "was not the true seller of the casket" and only facilitated Aurora's sale of the casket. Consequently, the Sweeneys contend that there was privity of contract between Aurora and themselves, and the claim should have been allowed to proceed to the jury. The Sweeneys provide absolutely no authority in support of this position, so we therefore reject it.

It is undisputed that Randall Sweeney was the only purchaser of the casket in question. None of his siblings had a contract with any of the defendants involved in this case, and they therefore have no viable breach-of-warranty claim against Aurora. As for any such claim that Randall might have, the Sweeneys have provided us with nothing of substance to suggest that such buyer–seller privity exists here between Randall and Aurora. Instead, the record reflects that Spear sold the casket and Randall purchased it. We therefore conclude that the Sweeneys' implied warranty claim against Aurora was rightfully dismissed via directed verdict, and the appellees' remaining contentions in this respect need not be considered.

The judgment of the Hancock Circuit Court is affirmed.

CASE QUESTIONS

1. What was the court's decision?
2. Did any of the plaintiffs' claims survive? Explain.

Subsection (2)(a) of § 402A of the *Restatement (Second) of Torts* indicates that the seller is liable regardless of the degree of care used to safeguard the public from injury by the defective product. Subsection (2)(b) states that privity of contract is unnecessary for strict liability to apply. Table 11-1 illustrates tort recovery, and Table 11-2 lists the elements required.

TABLE 11-1

Tort recovery

NEGLIGENCE	EXPRESS WARRANTY	IMPLIED WARRANTY	STRICT LIABILITY
Personal injuries	Personal injuries	Personal injuries	Personal injuries
Property damage	Property damage	Property damage	Property damage
Economic loss	Pure economic loss	Pure economic loss	Economic loss if there is also personal injury or property damage

TABLE 11-2

Elements required for tort recovery

NEGLIGENCE	EXPRESS WARRANTY	IMPLIED WARRANTY	STRICT LIABILITY
Duty	Statement of fact that is false	Sale of goods by merchant	Seller
Breach	Made with the intent or expectation that the statement will reach plaintiff	The goods are not merchantable	Sells defective product that is unreasonably dangerous to people or property
Causation	The plaintiff relies on the statement	Causation	Causation
Damages	Damages	Damages	Damages

Unreasonably Dangerous Products

The product must be unreasonably dangerous as a result of its defect. Courts look to see if the product has become unreasonably threatening because of its defect. There are four types of unreasonably dangerous defects: (1) fault in product design, (2) error in product manufacture or assembly, (3) improper product maintenance, and (4) manufacturer/seller's failure to warn.

Faulty Product Design. Products can be unreasonably dangerous if they have a defective design. Courts look to see whether the product is inherently dangerous because of a poor design but for which (that is, if such a defect did not exist) the product would have been safe to use. For instance, suppose a manufacturer assembles a toy with small, removable parts that can be swallowed by an infant, and thereby cause serious injury or death. The toy would be inherently dangerous, because the removable-parts design would expose small children to the dangers of choking. This design defect makes the product unreasonably dangerous.

Courts decide faulty design (which make products unreasonably dangerous) in terms of three tests: the consumer contemplation test, the danger/utility test, and the state-of-the-art discoverability test.

Consumer Contemplation Test. In its Comments section, the *Restatement (Second) of Torts* § 402A states that a product is unreasonably dangerous if the consumer ordinarily would not appreciate the threat inherent in its design. The defect becomes unreasonably hazardous because the reasonable person would not be expected to anticipate the danger created by the faulty design. Legal commentators and courts have labeled this the **consumer contemplation test.** This test has been omitted from the *Restatement (Third) of Torts,* and is no longer considered an independent test to determine whether a product is defectively designed.

For example, suppose that Nicholas bought a top-loading washing machine. He had to lean across the control panel to load his clothing inside. In doing so, he might accidentally press the start button with his body. This might start the machine while his hands were inside the washing drum, injuring him.

Under the consumer contemplation test, a reasonable person would have anticipated this situation. Nicholas should have seen where the start button was located. He knew that the machine could begin operating once this button was pushed. He should have contemplated the risk inherent in the product's poor design. The product was not unreasonably dangerous.

Danger/Utility Test. Many courts have formulated another test to determine if a product is unreasonably dangerous by its design: the **danger/utility test.** A product is unreasonably hazardous if the danger created by its design outweighs the benefits derived from its use. Consider the previous washing machine example. Normally, Nicholas derives tremendous benefits from the device—he gets clean clothes. If he is cautious about where he stands, he should be able to avoid the accidental start risk. Using the danger/utility test, the washer is not unreasonably dangerous.

State-of-the-Art Discoverability Test. If manufacturers could have discovered hazards created by defective product designs, using current, state-of-the-art technologies, then failure to do so makes a design-flawed product unreasonably dangerous. For example, suppose an automobile manufacturer installed ordinary glass in the small vent windows in a vehicle's doors. State-of-the-art crash testing would quickly indicate that this glass shatters into sharp fragments during a collision. If the car maker did not discover this defect through modern testing procedures, then it would be strictly liable for any injuries caused by the fragile windows.

consumer contemplation test | If a reasonable person would not have anticipated the danger created by the fault in the product, then the product is unreasonably dangerous.

danger/utility test | A theory in products liability design that makes a product unreasonably dangerous. if the danger created by its design outweighs the benefits derived from its use.

assembly defect | A theory in products liability concerning whether a defective product is unreasonably dangerous. Errors in production, manufacture, or assembly may render a product unreasonably hazardous despite safe design.

maintenance defect |
A theory in products liability concerning whether a defective product is unreasonably dangerous. If a seller fails to maintain a product properly, and the product later causes injury to the ultimate user, then the product was unreasonably dangerous.

Error in Product Manufacture or Assembly. Safely designed products may become unreasonably dangerous as a result of improper assembly or manufacture. For instance, if a lawn-mower manufacturer failed to tighten the bolt holding the blade with sufficient torque, the blade could fly off during use. Suppose this happened to a purchaser, who was severely cut by the blade. The lawn mower, although designed properly, became unreasonably dangerous because it was not suitably assembled. This is sometimes called an **assembly defect.**

Improper Product Maintenance. Sellers occasionally fail to maintain merchandise properly. When a buyer purchases the product, it might not function correctly because of a **maintenance defect.** For example, suppose a lawn and garden shop sells chain saws. The chain on such a saw must be oiled frequently to operate appropriately. Suppose the seller forgot to keep oil in its chain saws. While displaying one model to a customer, the saw froze up and the chain snapped, sailing into the face of the surprised customer. The product was unreasonably dangerous because the seller did not properly maintain it.

The seller was negligent in forgetting to keep oil in the saw. The seller would also be liable under negligence theory, as well as products liability.

Seller or Manufacturer's Failure to Warn. Sometimes products are unreasonably dangerous by their very nature. Lawn mowers, chain saws, poisons, and chemicals can be lethal if not cautiously used. However, purchasers may not always spot the obvious dangers. Accordingly, manufacturers and sellers have an obligation to warn the ultimate user about inherent product dangers. Failure to warn could result in strict liability. For example, the containers of rat poisons and insect sprays warn not to ingest the contents or get them in one's eyes. These are examples of warnings used to avoid absolute liability. If the user is warned, then the user knows the risks. To apply, the warning must be in an obvious and noticeable place.

Business Requirement

Section 402A of the *Restatement (Second) of Torts,* and most common law and statutory versions of products liability, insist that the manufacturer or seller be engaged in the business of selling products such as the defective item(s) that injured the ultimate user. Its purpose is to exclude products liability for people who are not in the business of selling such goods. For example, suppose Laurie sold Micron a vacuum cleaner, which she had bought from a department store. Because of a design defect, it exploded and injured Micron. Products liability is not intended to hold Laurie liable for this mishap, because she neither manufactured nor was in the business of selling such merchandise. Under products liability, Micron would need to sue the department store and manufacturer.

Substantially Unchanged Condition Requirement

For products liability to apply, the product must reach the ultimate user without any substantial changes in its condition from the time it left the manufacturer or seller. This is a crucial requirement. If something happened along the product distribution chain to alter the product (perhaps creating the unreasonably dangerous condition), then it would be unfair to hold manufacturers or sellers accountable for something they did not cause.

For instance, suppose Rachel purchased milk at a nearby grocery. The milk was fresh when she bought it. However, during the drive home, Rachel gets caught in traffic and it takes her more than an hour to arrive home. During this period, the milk spoiled. A visiting relative later drank the milk and suffered food poisoning. The relative wishes to sue the grocery. However, products liability would not apply, because the milk did not reach the ultimate user (Rachel's relative) in a substantially unchanged condition.

In some states, for strict liability to exist, the manufacturer or seller must be responsible for how the defective product was maintained. If the seller was not in any way responsible for how the product was assembled or stored (until it was sold or used), then that seller would have no control over the products it distributes. Products liability attempts to place the blame on the party responsible for the defect, to protect innocent sellers from absolute liability for product defects caused by someone else.

Proximate Cause

Recall the discussion of proximate cause in strict liability cases. That analysis also applies in products liability cases: the defective product must have been the proximate cause of the plaintiff's injury if liability is to attach.

Proper Use Requirement

The ultimate user must use the defective product properly in order for products liability to apply. In other words, the user must use the product for some function for which it was designed or intended to be used. For example, if Cliff wanted to climb onto his roof, he would probably use a ladder. If one of the ladder's rungs broke (because of the manufacturer's failure to use proper glues), and Cliff fell and broke bones, he would be entitled to sue the manufacturer and seller under products liability. However, if he had used stacked vegetable crates to climb upon, and these collapsed, Cliff could not sue under products liability. Vegetable crates are neither designed nor intended for people to climb on. See the next section on defenses, where "foreseeable misuse" of a product is covered. If misuse can be anticipated, in most cases it will be considered proper use.

Restatement (Second) vs. Restatement (Third). One of the more frequently cited portions of the *Restatement (Second) of Torts* is the section on products liability, section 402A. A major difference between this section and that in the newer *Restatement (Third)* is that a strict liability standard is now applied to manufacturing defects of products, and a different test, a risk-utility standard, is limited to design defects.

For design defects, the burden is placed back on the plaintiff in the *Restatement (Third) of Torts.* There is no longer a "consumer expectation test" as an independent means to determine if a product is defective. This was a lower standard in favor of the plaintiff for when a product did not perform as an ordinary consumer would expect it to. It is now just one of the many factors to consider, not the sole criteria. The plaintiff must now show a reasonable alternative design that would have been safer at a reasonable cost. This is considered more of a negligence standard than a strict liability standard.

Consider, for example, a power drill. It would be almost impossible to design a drill that would be safe, inexpensive, and would not injure a careless person. Instead, the liability of a manufacturer is limited to careful users. If manufacturers were held liable for acts of careless users, those who used a product carefully would be shouldering the cost for all users. The reason for this distinction is that with a manufacturing defect, a lawsuit will involve a limited number of products that were not up to standard. With design defects, if a strict liability test was applied, an entire line of products would be affected.

The Restatement (Third) of Torts Rule. In order to determine whether a product has a defect in design, section 2(b) states that:

> A product is defective in design when the foreseeable risks of harm posed by the product could have been reduced or avoided by the adoption of a reasonable alternative design . . . and the omission of the alternate design renders the product not reasonably safe.

THE CASE OF THE NOT-SO-BRIGHT LIGHT

This case demonstrates the risk-versus-utility analysis used in evaluating allegedly dangerous products. The court must decide whether, as a matter of social policy, the risk of loss should be placed on the manufacturer or supplier of a butane lighter that was not childproof.

SMITH
v.
SCRIPTO-TOKAI CORP.

United States District Court, W.D. Pennsylvania

170 F. Supp. 2d 533 (W.D. Pa. 2001)

November 2, 2001

This is a case for damages arising out of a residential fire started by plaintiffs' three-year-old child using a butane utility lighter manufactured by defendants. On June 15, 2000, we granted defendants' motion to dismiss all claims except negligence. As to the negligence claim, we explained that we were bound to follow the Court of Appeals' decision in *Griggs v. BIC Corp.*, 981 F.2d 1429 (3d Cir. 1992), and chastised defendant's counsel for his lack of candor to the tribunal in failing to acknowledge that case.

As set forth in *Griggs,* 981 F.2d at 1434, plaintiff must establish the following elements of a negligence action: (1) defendants had a duty; (2) defendants failed to conform to the standard required; (3) there was a causal connection between defendants' conduct and the resulting injury; and (4) damages. The "duty" element has two components: foreseeability and unreasonableness. Although foreseeability is not part of a strict liability claim, forseeability "is an integral part of a determination that a duty does exist in Pennsylvania negligence law."

In this case, the Aim 'n Flame lighter is a consumer product and there is "abundant empirical data demonstrating that Tokai could have foreseen the risk of an unsupervised child causing injury by using a lighter." Further, the risk is unreasonable because the high social value placed on the safety of people and property threatened by childplay fires, the high gravity and considerable probability of the risk, and the likelihood of a reasonably available alternative (childproofing) outweigh defendants' interest in producing its lighters without childproofing features. Thus, as the Court of Appeals held in *Griggs,* "if a manufacturer of cigarette lighters may reasonably foresee that they will fall into the hands of children, who, albeit unintended users, can ignite them with a probability of serious injury to themselves and others, and if childproofing the lighters is economically feasible, the manufacturer would have a duty to guard against the unreasonable risk of harm by designing the lighter to be childproof." Accordingly, plaintiffs have established the "duty" element of their negligence claim. Plaintiffs have also established that defendants breached that duty. Indeed, defendants do not seriously contend that the Aim 'n Flame lighter at issue here had appropriate safety features.

There are material disputes of fact that prevent causation from being established as a matter of law. Plaintiffs point out that an Aim 'n Flame lighter was recovered from the wreckage of the home, underneath the point of origin of the fire. Defendants, not so subtly, seek to imply that this evidence was planted. If defendants wish to risk alienating the jury by pursuing this line of reasoning, they shall have that opportunity.

Finally, the existence of damages is undisputed. However, a jury will have to determine the amount of such damages. Plaintiffs have established, as a matter of law, that defendants had a duty to manufacture a childproof lighter and breached that duty. The case will proceed to trial on the issues of causation and damages.

A defendant may be liable for negligence if he (1) knows that the chattel is in a dangerous condition; (2) has no reason to believe that those for whose use the chattel is supplied will realize the dangerous condition; and (3) fails to warn those for whose use the chattel is supplied of the dangerous condition. A warning is sufficient if it adequately notifies the intended user of the unobvious dangers inherent in the product.

Pennsylvania adopted the Restatement (Second) of Torts Section 402A as the law of strict products liability. [T]he Pennsylvania Supreme Court announced a threshold question of law for the court to decide: whether, as a matter of social policy, the product's condition justifies placing the risk of loss on the manufacturer or supplier. A risk-utility analysis, using the Dean John Wade factors, is appropriate in performing this threshold social policy inquiry. If the claim survives this threshold determination, "the jury must determine whether, under the facts, the product, at the time it left the defendant's control, lacked any element necessary to make it safe for its intended use or contained any condition that made it unsafe for use."

We conclude that reinstatement of the products liability claim is appropriate. Developments of the law in the Pennsylvania intermediate courts and in the Court of Appeals have clearly indicated that the threshold products liability question should be based on the risk-utility analysis. The Superior Court has applied this analysis in a closely analogous case and we have no reason to believe that the Supreme Court would apply risk-utility factors any differently.

(continues)

CASE QUESTIONS
1. How would you apply a risk-utility analysis in this case?
2. Why would Scripto have produced a lighter that was not childproof?

Table 11-3 lists different kinds of defective products and provides examples.

TABLE 11-3
Different kinds of
defective products

Type	Example
1. Design defect	Product designed improperly. Parts scrape against each other when in motion, and will eventually break off from the machine.
2. Manufacturing defect	Product manufactured with insufficient screws or bolts where required.
3. Improper product maintenance	Product not kept at proper temperature and spoils.
4. Failure to warn by manufacturer or seller	No warning label on box or product insert. A household cleaner contains ammonia and does not warn that it should not be mixed with chlorine products.

Foreseeable Plaintiffs Theory

In some jurisdictions, it must have been reasonably foreseeable that the ultimate user would use the defective product. This is called the zone of danger (or foreseeable plaintiffs) theory in negligence. Some ultimate users are not reasonably foreseeable and no duty is owed to them. For example, it is highly improbable that a one-year-old infant would come into contact with industrial cleaners used in manufacturing processes. Such a person could not be a reasonably foreseeable ultimate user of such a product. However, members of a product purchaser's family, or the buyer's neighbors, could be foreseeable users of defective goods. How many times in one's family has more than one individual used an appliance or tool? Have you ever borrowed products from your neighbors?

Consider Diana, who borrowed a pen from a classmate with which to take notes during the lecture. The pen had a manufacturing defect that made the plastic casing unusually brittle. While she is writing, the pen shatters in Diana's hand, and she is cut by the many tiny fragments. Was Diana a reasonably foreseeable ultimate user? Yes. Classmates often share pens, pencils, notebooks, and many other products during classes. It was reasonably foreseeable that someone might borrow a pen to take notes in class. Diana could sue the pen manufacturer under products liability as a foreseeable plaintiff.

Having analyzed the various elements of products liability, we may now proceed to apply the theory to hypotheticals.

HYPOTHETICALS

Burgess Primer Corporation manufactures paint. Didi bought Burgess's "Supreme Ease" paint at Painter Place, a local retailer that carried Burgess products. Didi selected various colors, which store employees mixed together. While applying the paint indoors, Didi noticed that the paint stung her skin as it splattered from her roller. Apparently, Didi was allergic to certain oils that had been mixed into the paint. When she showered later that day, she noticed that the paint had left her arms and face mottled with burn marks. Many of these became infected. Medical tests indicated that a significant percentage of the population suffered this allergic reaction to the paint mix.

Are Burgess Primer Corporation (as manufacturer) and Painter Place (as seller) strictly liable for an unreasonably dangerous product? Applying the generic formula, first ask if the defect made the product unreasonably dangerous. The fault here is product assembly (i.e., how the paint was mixed). Using the consumer contemplation test, would a reasonable person anticipate that he or she might be allergic to paint oils? This is not an obvious hazard that an ordinary person would detect from a can of paint. Thus, the product's dangerous condition rendered it unreasonably dangerous to the ultimate user, Didi. Under the danger/utility test, the hazard in using the product outweighed the benefits, as many people were allergic to the particular mix.

Both Burgess and Painter Place were engaged in the business of selling paint. The product reached the ultimate user, Didi, in the same condition as it left the retailer. Also, Didi used the paint properly, in a way in which paint is intended to be used. It was reasonably foreseeable that Didi would use the paint she bought at a retail store, so she is a foreseeable plaintiff. Both Burgess and the retailer were responsible for how the paint was maintained. Further, a sale occurred (for those jurisdictions requiring it). So far, even with the extra elements, it seems as though strict liability will favor Didi.

But who was the proximate cause of Didi's injuries? Burgess manufactured the paint base and the various colors. However, the paint did not become unreasonably dangerous until Painter Place's employees mixed it. Therefore, Burgess, as manufacturer, did not proximately cause Didi's injuries. Painter Place was clearly the proximate cause of the harm. Proximate cause is a crucial determination, because it absolves Burgess from strict products liability. Painter Place is absolutely liable for Didi's injuries under products liability theory.

* * *

(continues)

Consider another hypothetical. Fairfield Seed Company sold sweet corn seeds to retail variety stores. Fairfield had erroneously treated the seeds with a toxic insecticide used for field corn seeds. As the corn grew, this chemical was absorbed into the ears of sweet corn. When the gardeners (who had bought the seed from the retailers) ate the corn, they became ill.

Would the retail variety stores and Fairfield be strictly liable for the gardeners' injuries from an unreasonably dangerous product? Apply either the consumer contemplation test or the danger/utility test. The reasonable gardener would not expect sweet corn seeds to be treated with a poison harmful to humans. The risks far outweigh the benefits. Both Fairfield and the retailers were in the business of selling garden seeds. Fairfield improperly prepared the seeds, which would be a manufacturing defect. The dangerous seeds reached the ultimate users in the same condition as when they left the manufacturer. Fairfield was responsible for the condition of the product. Fairfield's insecticide coating proximately caused the gardeners' injuries, because the ultimate users ate the contaminated ears of corn grown from the poisoned seed. The gardeners used the product as it was designed (i.e., to grow corn to eat) and were foreseeable plaintiffs. All the elements of products liability have been met; thus, Fairfield is strictly liable for the gardeners' injuries caused by the poison corn.

What about the retailers' liability, however? There are two critical queries here. First, did the retailers proximately cause the ultimate users' injuries? Second, were the retailers responsible for the condition in which the defective product was maintained?

The retailers did not contaminate the seeds. The seeds came in sealed packages, which the retailers simply stocked on shelves for customers to pick up and purchase. Thus, the retailers did nothing to proximately cause the gardeners' injuries. Furthermore, the retailers had no control over the manufacturing processes that contaminated the seeds. They were not responsible for how the seeds were prepared. The retailers maintained the condition of the seeds just as they were supposed to, namely, by stocking their shelves with sealed packages. Under this analysis, the retailers would not be strictly liable for the harm to the gardeners.

THE CASE OF THE MODIFIED JACK PIN

Once a problem is pointed out to a manufacturer, should it immediately make a repair? Or should a product be left as is, for fear such remedial actions will be considered a harmful admission of fault? This case is decided based on the *Restatement (Third) of Torts* §2 (b).

Stephen Martin SCOTT, Appellant,

v.

DUTTON-LAINSON COMPANY, Appellee

Supreme Court of Iowa

774 N.W.2d 501

October 23, 2009

Plaintiff Stephen Scott, the employee of a boat dealership, was injured when the jack on a boat trailer collapsed and crushed his foot. Scott brought suit against the jack manufacturer, defendant Dutton-Lainson Company, based on "defects in [the jack's] design and manufacturing and the negligence of the Defendant." Scott planned to present evidence that, subsequent to Scott's injury, Dutton-Lainson modified the tooling for the jack pin which allowed it to move into the pin hole further.

Before trial, Dutton-Lainson filed a motion in limine seeking to exclude evidence of subsequent remedial measures pursuant to Iowa Rule of Evidence 5.407. The district court sustained the motion and excluded the evidence. The court submitted the case to the jury on theories of design defect and failure to warn, and the jury returned a verdict finding Dutton-Lainson was not at fault. Scott appealed, arguing the district court erred when it excluded evidence of subsequent remedial measures. The Court of Appeals held the evidence was admissible and reversed the district court. Dutton-Lainson sought further review with this court.

The district court, relying on Iowa Rule of Evidence 5.407, excluded evidence of a change Dutton-Lainson made to its jack pin. Scott proffered testimony from the deposition of James Byron Wink that Ron Haase of Dutton-Lainson told him the jack pin was lengthened as a result of Scott's injury.

Scott claimed an extended pin would allow the user to verify whether the pin was engaged and therefore prevent accidents like the one Scott suffered. The district court refused to admit testimony of the subsequent change because it found the evidence was of a subsequent remedial measure offered to show negligence or culpable conduct.

Iowa Rule of Evidence 5.407 prevents admission of subsequent remedial measures to prove negligence or culpable conduct, but allows its admission in strict liability claims. It states:

When, after an event, measures are taken which, if taken previously, would have made the event less likely to occur, evidence of the subsequent measures is not admissible to prove negligence or culpable conduct in connection with the event. This rule does not require the exclusion of evidence of subsequent measures when offered in connection with a claim based on strict liability in tort or breach of warranty or for another purpose.

Prior to this court's recent decision in *Wright v. Brooke Group Ltd.*, 652 N.W.2d 159 (Iowa 2002), design defect claims could be brought under a theory of either strict liability or negligence. In *Wright*, we adopted the Restatement (Third) of Torts: [hereinafter Third Products Restatement]. *Wright*, 652 N.W.2d at 169. The Third Products Restatement recognizes that "strict liability is appropriate in manufacturing defect cases, but negligence principles are more suitable for other defective product cases." Therefore, *Wright* adopted a standard of risk-utility analysis, which incorporates a consideration of reasonableness, for design defect claims, but chose to "label a claim based on a defective product design as a design defect claim without reference to strict liability or negligence." Because *Wright* rejected the categorical labels of strict liability or negligence in the context of design defects, the parties dispute whether rule 5.407's categorical exception for strict liability claims applies to design defect claims.

We hold that evidence of subsequent remedial measures, which a party seeks to introduce in an action based on a design defect claim, a failure to warn claim, or a breach of warranty claim brought under either theory, is not categorically exempt from exclusion under rule 5.407 because these claims are not strict liability claims. Instead, trial courts must analyze the reason a party seeks to admit such evidence. Evidence of subsequent remedial measures is not admissible to show negligence.

Such evidence is admissible to show "ownership, control, or feasibility of precautionary measures, if controverted, or impeachment."

(continues)

Rule 5.407's carve out for strict liability in tort and breach of warranty claims remains relevant to only one type of product liability claim: a claim based on a manufacturing defect. A product "contains a manufacturing defect when the product departs from its intended design even though all possible care was exercised in the preparation and marketing of the product." Third Products Restatement § 2(a), at 14. This definition is consistent with strict liability because fault is assessed regardless of the exercise of all possible care, *See Wright*, 652 N.W.2d at 168. ("The Products Restatement demonstrates a recognition that strict liability is appropriate in manufacturing defect cases, but negligence principles are more suitable for other defective product cases.") Therefore, evidence of subsequent remedial measures is admissible in manufacturing defect cases brought under a strict liability theory. However, even when the strict liability exception applies, courts are still required to evaluate relevance under Iowa Rule of Evidence 5.402, and prejudice under Iowa Rule of Evidence 5.403.

In 1997, Federal Rule of Evidence 407 was amended to prevent admission of subsequent remedial measures in product liability claims, including strict liability, unless the need for such evidence falls under a specific exception. Fed.R.Evid. 407 (evidence of subsequent remedial measures "is not admissible to prove negligence, culpable conduct, *a defect in a product, a defect in a product's design, or a need for a warning or instruction*" Therefore, Iowa Rule of Evidence 5.407 allows introduction of evidence of subsequent remedial measures in strict liability claims while Federal Rule of Evidence 407 specifically prohibits it.

Scott contends rule 5.407's specific exception for strict liability should be read to apply to design defect claims after *Wright* because *Wright* refused to classify such claims under a theory of either strict liability or negligence. *Wright*, 652 N.W.2d at 169.

We disagree. Scott's design defect and failure to warn claims are not strict liability claims. Although we chose not to label design defect claims as either negligence or strict liability claims, we recognized that "negligence principles are more suitable" for design defect and failure to warn claims. The standards for design defect and failure to warn claims-as

recognized by the Third Products Restatement and *Wright*-require consideration of reasonableness and therefore incorporate negligence principles. Third Products Restatement § 2(b), (c), at 14. Although the drafters of rule 5.407 intended to create a distinction between strict liability claims and negligence, Iowa tort law no longer supports this distinction in the context of design defect and failure to warn claims. Scott seeks to introduce evidence of a subsequent remedial measure to do exactly what the rule forbids: prove negligence or culpable conduct.

The Third Products Restatement section 2, as adopted in *Wright*, requires plaintiffs in design defect cases to demonstrate the existence of a reasonable alternative design. Third Products Restatement § 2(b), at 14 (stating a product "is defective in design when the foreseeable risks of harm posed by the product could have been reduced or avoided *by the adoption of a reasonable alternative design*" [emphasis added]). Some courts have suggested the reasonable alternative design requirement is inconsistent with a rule of evidence excluding subsequent remedial measures.

Plaintiffs have the opportunity to introduce evidence of subsequent remedial measures if the defendant disputes the feasibility of a suggested alternative design. "Use of subsequent remedial measures to prove 'the feasibility of precautionary measures' ... demonstrates the narrow scope of the general rule excluding such proof." As we have recognized, "the public policy supporting the rule is 'that the exclusion of such evidence may be necessary to avoid deterring individuals from making improvements or repairs after an accident."

The plain language of rule 5.407 specifically prevents introduction of subsequent remedial measures to show negligence but exempts claims brought in strict liability. Therefore, evidence of subsequent remedial measures is inadmissible in design defect claims, failure to warn claims, and breach of warranty claims brought under either of those theories, unless the evidence is offered to prove ownership, control, feasibility, or impeachment. Evidence of subsequent remedial measures continues to be admissible in manufacturing defect claims and breach of warranty claims brought under the manufacturing defect standard. The district court properly excluded Scott's proffered evidence.

CASE QUESTIONS
1. Why was Scott's evidence not admissible?
2. How does the court categorize design defect claims?

Table 11-4 summarizes the elements of products liability under the generic, common law formula.

Typical Common Law or Statutory Formula	Additional Elements Needed (in Some States)
1. Defect makes product unreasonably dangerous	Ultimate user must be reasonably foreseeable (foreseeable plaintiffs theory)
2. Manufacturer or seller must be in business of selling products such as the defective one(s)	Manufacturer or seller must be responsible for condition in which defective product was maintained
3. Defective product cannot have been substantially changed from time it left manufacturer or seller until it was used by ultimate user	A sale of the defective product must have occurred
4. Defect must have proximately caused the ultimate user's injuries	
5. Ultimate user must have used the product properly (in the way in which it was designed or intended to be used)	
6.	Some states, by statute or common law, require a sale

TABLE 11-4
Elements of products liability

▮ DEFENSES
There are several defenses to absolute liability. Some of those defenses also apply to products liability.

Contributory or Comparative Negligence is not a Defense
Courts have generally held that contributory negligence is not a defense in products liability cases. This seems logical, because contributory negligence is a defense to negligence, and negligence has no place in strict liability cases.

Ultimate User's Misuse of Product

Saying that contributory or comparative negligence is not a defense is not to say, however, that the plaintiff (the ultimate user) can use a defective product irresponsibly or wantonly. The ultimate user is expected to use the product properly, as it was intended to be used. This is an element of products liability, although some courts consider product misuse to be a defense. If the ultimate user misuses a defective product and is injured as a consequence, his or her products liability claim against the manufacturer or seller will be denied. This defense is effective even though the misused product was defective.

Foreseeable Misuse. Some product uses may be unusual, but are not actually considered misuses. For example, chairs are designed to be sat on. Yet, how often have you used a chair as a stepping stool to reach something stored on a high shelf? Using a chair as a ladder is not a misuse of the product, because it is reasonably foreseeable that one might use a chair for such a purpose. In other words, reasonably foreseeable uses, even though the product may not originally have been intended or designed for such functions, are acceptable uses. A products liability claim would not be barred if the ultimate user used the product in a reasonably foreseeable fashion.

Removal of Safety Devices. Adult smokers commonly remove the "childproof" safety devices on butane lighters, increasing the risk of injury. Employees who are under great pressure to produce a lot while working on an assembly line or in a factory may deliberately dismantle the very safety device that is there to protect them. If the safety device is removed, a machine might run faster than was intended, or it may become easier to get to the interior of the machine when it jams or needs cleaning. For these injured parties, a products liability cause of action will not be available, because the product was misused and altered.

PRACTICAL APPLICATION

Unfortunately, you will frequently see misuse of products by injured parties who will tell you that they removed the guard or safety device from a machine at work.

Assumption of Risk

Assumption of risk, however, is usually accepted as a defense. The ultimate user assumes the risk of being injured by a hazardous product in three ways: (1) by discovering the defect but disregarding it and using the product anyway, (2) by failing to properly maintain the product, and (3) by failing to follow instructions or heed warnings for safe product use.

Ignoring a Discovered Defect.

Recall the basic definition of assumption of risk. **Assumption of risk** is the plaintiff's voluntary assumption of a known risk with a full appreciation of the dangers involved in facing that risk. In products liability cases, the plaintiff is the ultimate user. The ultimate user assumes the risk by discovering a product defect and then ignoring the risks involved and using the product anyway. For example, suppose Steve discovers that his circular saw blade is bent. The warp would cause the blade to rub against the saw's protective sheathing when it rotated. This would create sparks, which could burn him. Steve decides that the risk is worth taking and he uses the saw. Sparks fly into his eyes (because he does not wear protective eyewear). Steve assumed a known risk with a full comprehension of the possible hazardous consequences.

assumption of risk |
Knowingly and willingly exposing yourself (or your property) to the possibility of harm. In most states, a person who assumes a risk of harm cannot win a negligence lawsuit against the person responsible for the harm.

Failure to Properly Maintain Product.

Ultimate users cannot recover in products liability if they failed to properly maintain the product for safe uses. Courts often characterize this as an assumption-of-risk defense. The earlier circular saw example illustrates this type of assumption of risk. Steve did not maintain the saw so that it could be safely used. The blade was bent. Before using it, he should have replaced the damaged blade with a new blade.

Consider another illustration. Suppose Gil failed to put motor oil in his automobile. If he proceeded to drive for hundreds of miles, his motor would undoubtedly burn out. Gil could not recover under products liability from the manufacturer or seller. He assumed the risk of ruining his car by not properly maintaining it.

Failure to Follow Instructions or Heed Warnings.

How often have you used a product without first reading the instructions? Surely everyone has done this. Most of the time the products we use are sufficiently simple that we can use them properly after a quick glance. With a complex product, however, following instructions could prevent injuries. Products liability plaintiffs often argue that defectively designed products are unreasonably dangerous. However, sometimes these plaintiffs did not follow the manufacturer's instructions or disregarded the manufacturer's warnings that specifically point out the dangers inherent in the product design. Both of these actions are types of assumption of risk. Likewise, if a consumer ignores a safety recall notice sent by the dealer or manufacturer of a product, and fails to cooperate and bring the product to be fixed, the consumer assumes the risk of injury as a result.

Assume, in the saw example, that the manufacturer printed on the side of the saw, "WARNING! DO NOT USE IF BLADE IS BENT!" If Steve disregarded this warning and was hurt from the bent saw, he could not recover damages for a defectively designed product. Steve assumed the risk by ignoring the warning.

Suppose that instead of a bent blade, the blade was merely loose. The instructions included directions for blade tightening. If Steve did not read or follow these directions, and he was hurt because the blade flew off while he was using the saw, he could not recover damages under products liability. Steve assumed the risk by failing to follow the instructions to properly maintain the product.

THE CASE OF THE MISUSED MACHINE

An employer shows an employee how to perform a task using a paper rewinding machine. The employee assumes the work must be safe, as the employer is instructing the employee concerning the manner in which the work should be performed. This case demonstrates how legal staff must continually familiarize themselves with the different terminology in addition to researching the law of the case. Sometimes it will be medical terminology, or even the technicalities of aircraft maintenance or construction. For most, this is one of the benefits of working in the legal field, learning about new subjects in addition to the law.

Juan PEREZ, Plaintiff and Appellant,
v.
VAS S.p.A., Defendant and Respondent

Court of Appeal, Second District, Division 4, California
188 Cal.App.4th 658
September 17, 2010

Plaintiff Juan Perez was injured by a paper rewinding machine designed and manufactured by VAS S.p.A. (VAS). He sued VAS, alleging causes of action for strict products liability and negligence. In a nonjury trial, VAS asserted that its design was not defective, and that Perez and his employer engaged in an unforeseeable misuse of the machine, thereby absolving VAS of liability. The trial court agreed and entered judgment for VAS.

In December 2005, Perez was injured while operating a paper rewinding machine for his employer, Pabco Paper. The rewinder was manufactured by VAS, an Italian company, which sold it to Pabco. His right, dominant hand was crushed when it was pulled into a "pinch point," also referred to as a "nip point," created by two cylinders which rotated toward each other on the VAS rewinder.

Perez's asserted that the rewinder was defectively designed because it had an unguarded nip point, and that VAS was negligent per se for designing a rewinder with an unguarded pinch point in violation of title 8, section 4002(a) of the California Code of Regulations.

A paper rewinder is a large industrial machine that cuts a single large roll of paper weighing over 5,000 pounds, into two smaller rolls. The roll of paper is placed on the rewinder machine, and the operator takes the loose end of the paper and feeds it onto a cylinder parallel to the large roll. This "threading" process is similar to putting film in a camera. Once the end of the paper is secured, the operator increases the speed. As the paper unwinds, the machine cuts the paper in half, and rewinds the paper onto a new cylinder.

Before purchasing the VAS machine, Pabco used an old rewinder machine. Perez began operating the old rewinder in mid-2004. He was trained on the use of the old machine by watching its operator for about one week. Both the old machine and the new VAS machine similarly made two smaller rolls out of one larger roll, and the cylinders on both machines rotated the same way. William Fraser, the plant manager for Pabco recommended selecting VAS. The rewinder machine was custom-built for by VAS, not mass produced.

The handbook states that the machine should be operated only by those who were trained, and who had read the instructions. The operator must never cross the safety protections. The operator must never go near moving parts. The system is protected by guards, that avoid the accidental contact between the operator and the machine. Keep always outside the guards and never lean out during the machine running.

Perez's expert, Kenneth Solomon testified on the VAS machine, the threading process was accomplished with the assistance of air showers and belts, which served to feed the paper tail onto the drum without the operator having to reach in close to the nip point. Section 1.9.3 of the operating handbook stated, "During the tail threading it is necessary to pay attention to the NIP points. This is one of the most dangerous operations in running a paper machine."

When the machine was operating in the slower jogging mode used for the threading procedure, the cradle guard and laser fence did not guard the machine. Fraser considered both the threading phase and the operations phase to be safe to perform on the VAS machine.

After completion of the operations phase, the manual indicated that the cut rolls were to be ejected while the machine was running at operating speed. The operator was not to be in the operations area. On both the machines, Perez would cut off any damaged paper at the end of each roll with a utility knife. With the machine stopped, he would then tape the end of the roll to prevent the paper from unwinding. Next, he taped the end of a roll of thin plastic to the paper roll on the far left side, and turned the machine on at jogging speed. As the paper roll rotated, he slowly moved to his right while holding the roll of plastic in front of him, and the rotation of the paper rolls caused the plastic to wrap around the paper rolls. When the paper rolls were fully wrapped, he tore the end of the plastic and stopped the machine. With the machine again moving at jogging speed and standing at the middle of the paper rolls, he used a knife to cut the plastic to separate the two rolls. Finally, he put plastic bands around the plastic-wrapped paper rolls. All of this was done while the rolls were still on the machine.

Perez's expert, Solomon, stated that putting plastic on the finished rolls and then cutting them was part of the usual and customary procedure at Pabco. He agreed that the operating manual did not contain any information regarding wrapping the finished paper in plastic.

On the date of the accident Perez was operating the old machine and the VAS machine at the same time. Before using the VAS machine, he did not receive any training. He watched a coworker use the VAS machine for 15 to 20 minutes. He approached using the VAS machine as he had the old machine. The first time Perez used the VAS machine, he successfully performed the whole procedure. On the second run, when he tried to cut the plastic, the knife became entangled with the plastic, and it pulled his hand down into the nip point.

Cal–OSHA cited Pabco for a "serious" violation, concluding that "[t]he pinch points created between the revolving paper roll and the in-running roller, and between the revolving paper roll and the frame of the machine were not guarded as required by [California Code of Regulations, title 8, section 4002(a)]."

After Perez's accident, Pabco reversed the direction of the rotation of the drums on the VAS machine, which eliminated the nip point involved in Perez's accident. Doing so created a new nip point up higher, at a height of 9 feet and 7 inches, which was out of reach of the operator. Reversing the direction caused the outer wrap to be distorted, detracting from the appearance of the product, but had no other effect. The change in direction of the roll was accomplished in less than one week by a company in Italy that worked for VAS.

A few days after Perez's accident, Pabco stopped wrapping plastic around the paper by using the rotation of the machine. Pabco continued to cut the loose ends of the paper and to tape the loose paper edge to the roll, while the rolls were still on the VAS machine (both activities were performed with the machine stopped). Pabco also continued to wrap the finished rolls in hard plastic bands, while the rolls were still on the VAS machine, with the machine moving at jog

(continues)

speed. Pabco no longer wrapped the finished roll in plastic film on the machine.

Expert Kenneth Solomon stated that Cal-OSHA found that the direction of rotation of the drum was problematic, and the nip point was unguarded, and at the height of where an operator's hand could reach it. Solomon opined that there was a defect in the design of the machine because during the slow jogging speed operation, there was no physical barrier to the nip point. Solomon did not regard the practice of applying plastic to the finished rolls to be a misuse. He opined that the manner in which Perez used the machine could have been predicted, even though he agreed that it was not a contemplated use of the machine.

Paul Saedler, a forensic mechanical engineer, provided expert testimony for the defense. He concluded that there were no defects or malfunctions of the safety equipment which would have caused or contributed to Perez's injury. The machinery was equipped with proper safeguarding and warning signs. He stated that the process of wrapping plastic around a finished spool of paper and cutting it with a utility knife while the rolls were in motion was not a process specified in the operation manual. He noted that the manual stated that when the machine was running the operator must never cross the safety precautions and must never go near moving or rotating parts.

Saedler disagreed that reversing the direction of the rolls made the equipment safer, because the reversal was unnecessary in that the equipment was properly safeguarded. Wrapping the finished roll in plastic and cutting the plastic was inappropriate because the manual did not provide for that. He thought the manufacturer did not foresee the process that Pabco developed of wrapping plastic around the finished rolls and cutting the plastic with a utility knife.

The trial court found that Perez had the burden of proving that the new rewinding machine was used or misused in a way that was reasonably foreseeable to VAS, and concluded that Perez failed to prove the absence of unforeseeable misuse. The evidence substantially showed that Pabco's machine operators, including Perez, simply did not use the machine in the way it was designed and intended to be used by VAS.

The court concluded that the practice engaged in by Perez "constituted unforeseeable misuse by [Perez

and Pabco]. Perez failed to prove absence of unforeseeable misuse in the circumstances resulting in his injury. He did not use the machine 'in a way it was intended to be used,' as well as designed to be used."

A product can be found defective under one of two tests: the consumer expectations test, or the risk-benefit test. As applicable here, under the risk-benefit test, a product is defective in design if the plaintiff proves that the product's design proximately caused injury and the defendant fails to prove that on balance, the benefits of the design outweigh the risk of danger.

The trial court determined that the finishing process was indeed an unforeseeable misuse of the VAS rewinder. On appeal, Perez contends that the judgment in favor of VAS should be reversed because the trial court erred in its belief that Perez had the burden of proving the absence of an unforeseeable misuse. He asserts that instead VAS was required to prove that the finishing process constituted an unforeseeable misuse of the VAS rewinder.

We agree that the trial court misstated the applicable burdens. The plaintiff bears an initial burden showing that the injury was proximately caused by the product's design. This requires evidence that the plaintiff was injured *while using the product in an intended or reasonably foreseeable manner* and that the plaintiff's ability to avoid injury was frustrated by the absence of a safety device, or by the nature of the product's design.

If the plaintiff's burden is met, it shifts to the defendant to prove that the product is not defective, and that the plaintiff's injury resulted from a misuse of the product.

Given Perez's showing, the burden of proof shifted to VAS to prove that its design was not defective, and in particular, to prove that Perez's injury resulted from a misuse of the machine. It is true that the trial court did not use this burden-shifting formula. However "an error in allocating the burden of proof must be prejudicial in order to constitute reversible error." Here, there is no reasonable probability that the result would have been different. The trial court found that the finishing process was an unforeseeable misuse of the VAS rewinder—in substance, a superseding cause of injury. Because substantial evidence supports the trial court's conclusion, we affirm the order.

CASE QUESTIONS

1. Did the court's decision meet your expectations? Explain your answer.
2. What might have been a very simple way to avoid this type of accident?

Defenses are a defective product manufacturer's best friend. Even if every products liability element is satisfied, defenses can spare the seller from the wrath of strict liability, as the following hypotheticals illustrate.

HYPOTHETICALS

Mike owns a tire repair shop. He sells new tires from all the national brands and repairs old tires. Hailey came into the shop one day with a punctured tire. Mike agreed that it could be patched and repaired, but he instructed Hailey to use the tire only as a spare for emergencies. He recommended that she purchase a reconditioned tire for regular use. Hailey insisted that Mike put her patched tire back onto her car. Mike warned that the patch might not hold up over long-term, constant use. Nevertheless, he had the repaired tire re-mounted on her car. Later the following month, while Hailey was driving to work, the patch failed and the tire blew out. Hailey's car ran off the road, collided with a telephone pole, and was injured.

Hailey's products liability claim against Mike would fail. Hailey assumed the risk of using the patched tire contrary to Mike's specific instructions and warnings. She voluntarily assumed a known risk with a full appreciation of the hazards involved. The defense of assumption of risk would protect Mike from strict products liability.

* * *

The Oasis Sprinkler Company manufactures underground lawn sprinkler systems. Oasis offers a do-it-yourself kit for handy customers. Sarah purchased one of these kits. The detailed assembly instructions directed her to attach the sprinkler heads to the underground pipe using a special copper clamp. "Be certain to crimp the clamp with pliers to ensure a snug connection," read the instructions. Sarah did not crimp the clamps, although she did put them in place. Later, while the sprinkler system was in use, one of the sprinkler heads flew into the air under the force of the water pressure. It struck Sarah's daughter, Janice, in the forehead, causing a wound that required several stitches.

(contintues)

Could Janice and Sarah win a products liability lawsuit against Oasis? Not if the assumption-of-risk defense can be successfully applied. Sarah disregarded the manufacturer's specific instructions for assembling the product. However, Oasis failed to warn about the possible dangers that could occur if the clamps were not crimped. So we have a manufacturer's failure-to-warn situation versus a user's failure-to-follow-instructions defense. Which wins? Is the manufacturer's failure to warn sufficient to hold Oasis liable for an unreasonably dangerous product? Or is Sarah's failure to obey instructions a complete defense under assumption of risk?

The key to this problem is whether a reasonable ultimate user (i.e., a reasonable person) would have anticipated that the sprinkler heads might fly off under high water pressure if the clamps were not crimped. Most people know that water carried through pipes is under great pressure, which makes the water a powerful, focused force. A loose connection could easily give way and send a sprinkler head flying in any direction. Reasonable persons know this from everyday experience with garden hoses or plumbing. Sarah should have anticipated this risk; therefore, it is considered a known risk that she voluntarily assumed, despite a full appreciation of the dangers involved. Assumption of risk will overpower the manufacturer's failure to warn of this particular hazard. Accordingly, the defense of assumption of risk will protect Oasis from strict products liability.

* * *

The Comfort King Corporation manufactures recliner chairs. When Nathan visited a friend who owned such a recliner, Nathan noticed that a lightbulb was burned out in his friend's hallway. He used the recliner as a ladder to reach the light fixture. As he stood on the chair, it reclined, sending him sprawling across the hall, where he smashed his head on a closet doorknob. Nathan thought the chair was unreasonably dangerous, so he sued Comfort King under products liability.

Comfort King, however, shrugged off the lawsuit. The product misuse defense was there to protect the company from strict liability. Recliner chairs are not designed or intended to be used as ladders or stoops. After all, recliners *recline*. They cannot be safely stood upon for that reason. Nathan should have reasonably anticipated the danger created by misusing the chair in this fashion. Nathan's misuse of the product is a solid products liability defense for Comfort King.

Table 11-5 lists the defenses to products liability.

Contributory Negligence	Assumption of Risk	Product Misuse by Ultimate User
Not considered a defense in products liability cases	Ultimate user's voluntary assumption of known risk with full appreciation of dangers involved	If ultimate user misuses the product, then he or she cannot recover under products liability
	Occurs when ultimate user ignores a discovered defect and uses the product while knowing of its dangerous condition	Reasonably foreseeable uses are *not* misuses of products
	Occurs when ultimate user fails to properly maintain product	
	Occurs when ultimate user fails to follow instructions or heed warnings for safe product use	

TABLE 11-5
Defenses to products liability

COMPARISON TO CONTRACT LAW WARRANTIES

Express Warranties

Products liability has roots in contract law warranties. A *warranty* is a guarantee that a product seller gives a buyer. The guarantee states that the product will perform to certain standards or will not break down over a period of time. This warranty is part of the contract between the buyer and the seller.

If the product fails to comply with the guarantee, the warranty is *breached.* This **breach of warranty** is also a violation of the parties' agreement that the product shall remain in a particular condition while used.

breach of warranty | The violation of either an express or implied warranty.

Implied Warranties

The Uniform Commercial Code (UCC) is a model (suggested) statute concerning the sale of goods that has been adopted by all states. One of its provisions, § 2-314, concerns implied warranties that all sellers of goods provide with their goods as to the goods being "merchantable," which means that all goods must be of fair or average quality and fit for their ordinary purpose. This warranty protects the buyer against defective goods.

Another provision of the UCC, § 2-315, provides that if the seller knows of a particular purpose for which the buyer is buying, then the goods must be fit for that purpose.

These two provisions have allowed liability for injuries sustained as a result of defects in products. Because the UCC has been adopted by all states, decisions on these points tend to be similar nationwide.

▋ BAD FAITH

A tort is society's method of addressing the injuries that occur to people and property. As evidenced by all the new tort actions in this chapter, the tort field has greatly developed in response to modern problems; legal theories that allow an injured party to prevail can be flexible to fit the times. An example of this is the tort of **bad faith,** which has developed from California legal cases.

bad faith | Dishonesty or other failure to deal fairly with another person.

When an insurance company unreasonably denies a claim or fails to pay it in a timely fashion within the policy limits, this is called the *tort of bad faith,* or *bad faith liability.* Obviously, where liability is not clear-cut or certain, this tort will not apply. Insurance companies are expected to negotiate in good faith on behalf of an insured person and promptly settle claims for which liability is reasonably clear.

An example of bad faith would be when a plaintiff is willing to settle a lawsuit within the defendant's insurance policy limits, the defendant is clearly responsible for the plaintiff's injuries, and the defendant's insurance company refuses to settle the claim or even make a settlement offer. The plaintiff might then proceed to trial, and the jury may end up awarding a verdict greatly in excess of the amount of the defendant's insurance coverage. In this instance, the defendant ends up owing money to the claimant out of pocket, when this did not need to occur. If an insurance company refuses to bargain in good faith when there was available coverage for an incident, this defeats the purpose of insurance and subjects an insured to unnecessary liability.

The tort of bad faith demonstrates how tort law and contract law can intersect. When an insurance company fails to settle a tort case, the company may be liable to its insured on the basis of contract law as set forth in the terms of the insurance policy.

Table 11-6 lists states' statutes of limitations for products liability cases.

TABLE 11-6

State statutes of limitations for products liability cases

STATE	STATUTE OF LIMITATIONS FOR PRODUCTS LIABILITY CASES
California	Action must be brought within two years from time when injury is or should have been discovered
Florida	Action must be brought within two years from time when injury is or should have been discovered
Massachusetts	Action must be brought within three years of date on which injury occurred
New Jersey	Action must be brought within two years of date on which injury occurred
New York	Action must be brought within three years of date on which injury occurred
Ohio	Action must be brought within two years of date on which injury occurred
Pennsylvania	Action must be brought within two years of date on which injury occurred
Texas	Action must be brought within two years of date on which injury occurred

SUMMARY

Products liability became a distinct tort theory in the early 1960s. For more than 100 years, American and English courts combined contract law and negligence to hold manufacturers and sellers liable for injuries caused by defective products. Finally, in 1962, strict liability was applied to such cases. As a matter of public policy, products liability places the risk of harm created by unreasonably dangerous products upon those who make and sell them. The law presumes that the innocent user should not be forced to bear the costs associated with harmful products.

The parties in products liability cases include the manufacturer, other sellers (such as retailers or wholesalers), and the consumers, or ultimate users, of the product. Often the ultimate user is a member of the product buyer's family or a neighbor or friend. By looking at a product's distribution chain, it becomes clear how the product leaves the manufacturer and reaches the ultimate user.

Products liability is strict, or absolute, liability. No privity of contract is required between the manufacturer or seller and the ultimate user. The manufacturer or seller's negligence is irrelevant. The product must contain a defect rendering it unreasonably dangerous to use. This fault may arise in a design defect, by improper product maintenance, or by the manufacturer or seller's failure to warn the buyer of hazards inherent in using the product. The manufacturer or seller must be engaged in the business of selling products like the defective one. The product cannot be substantially changed from the time it left the manufacturer or seller and reached the ultimate user. The defect must proximately cause the ultimate user's injuries. The ultimate user must use the product in the way in which it was designed or intended, or in a way that is foreseeable.

Contributory negligence is not a defense to products liability. Product misuse is a defense, although it is often included as an element in the products liability formula.

If the ultimate user misuses the product, even though the product is defective, the manufacturer and seller will not be strictly liable for the harm. Assumption of risk is another defense to products liability. If the ultimate user ignores a discovered defect and, by using the product, is hurt, the user has assumed the risk, and the manufacturer or seller would not be strictly liable. The same is true if the ultimate user fails to properly maintain a product, follow instructions, or heed warnings for safe use.

Products liability is similar to contract law warranties. First, both involve absolute liability. Second, both involve defective or unreasonably dangerous products. Third, under many warranty statutes and common law, the ultimate user is protected even if he or she was not the original product purchaser.

The tort of bad faith occurs when an insurance company fails to reasonably or timely settle a case that could have been settled within the policy limits.

The next chapter focuses on special tort actions. Nuisances, wrongful death, wrongful birth and wrongful life are some of the actions that are covered.

▌ KEY TERMS

assembly defect
assumption of risk
bad faith
breach of warranty
consumer contemplation test
danger/utility test
deep pocket
express warranty
imminent danger exception

implied warranty of fitness for a
    particular purpose
implied warranty of
    merchantability
maintenance defect
merchantable
privity of contract
product manufacturer
products liability

purchaser
Restatement (Second) of Torts
Restatement (Third) of Torts
retailer
seller
ultimate user
Uniform Commercial Code
warranty
wholesaler

▌ PROBLEMS

In the following hypotheticals, determine if strict liability under products liability applies, and if the tortfeasor will be strictly liable to the injured party. Are any defenses relevant? If so, how would they be applied?

1. WedgeCorp manufactures golf clubs. The clubs have rubberized grips that golfers hold onto to swing them. Chase bought his wife a set of clubs for her birthday. Cindy is an avid golfer and uses the clubs three times a week at the local country club. When WedgeCorp manufactured the clubs, it used an improperly mixed glue that did not tightly bond the grips to the end of the clubs. While Cindy was swinging a five iron, the grip came loose and the club sailed through the air, striking Cindy's golfing partner, Betty, in the forehead.

2. Better Bovine, Inc. (BB) sells dairy cattle to farmers. These livestock are raised on one of BB's pasturing farms outside of town. To control weeds, BB's employees sprayed pasture land with herbicides. The cattle ate this grass and absorbed the chemicals into their systems. These chemicals reduced the cows' milk production. Several farmers who purchased BB cows suffered substantial economic losses when the animals' milk productivity plummeted.

3. Whopper Toys Corporation manufactures "Mr. Killjoy," a combat doll. Mr. Killjoy comes equipped with sharp plastic swords that you can fit into his hands for mock battles. Whopper indicated on its packaging that this toy was not suitable for children under the age of six years. This was the only

warning printed on the package. Franco bought a Mr. Killjoy figure for his four-year-old son, Francisco. While playing with Charlotte, a three-year-old neighbor girl, Francisco had the doll "attack" her. Its sword stabbed Charlotte through her nose, leaving a permanent scar.

4. Omar is an accountant who lives in an apartment next to Joyce. Omar sold his electric stove to Joyce for $200. Omar had never kept the electric heating elements on top of the stove particularly clean. In fact, they were caked with grease and dirt. The first time Joyce turned on the stove, the heating elements caught fire and set Joyce's long hair ablaze.

5. The Steak Out restaurant has a reputation for excellent steaks. One day it received a meat shipment from the Midwestern Meat Packing Company, a national meat distributor. When the shipment left Midwestern, it was shipped in a refrigerated truck. However, en route to The Steak Out, the truck's refrigeration system broke down, but the driver never noticed. The meat spoiled. When The Steak Out's employees unloaded the truck, they did not notice that the meat smelled bad. In fact, the meat did not smell much, if at all. Nevertheless, customers served from this shipment of beef became seriously ill from food poisoning.

6. Vlad bought a large screwdriver, made by the Hand Tool Manufacturing Company, from his local hardware store. Unknown to anyone, the screwdriver had a microscopic crack in its shaft. If excessive pressure were exerted on the screwdriver, it would snap. Vlad used the screwdriver to pry open sealed crates that he received at work. One day, while he was prying open a crate, the screwdriver broke, severely cutting the tendons in Vlad's left hand.

7. Chase works for the U.S. Department of Defense. One day he noticed that his paper-shredding machine made a loud grinding noise during operation. He opened the maintenance door, but could see nothing wrong with the parts inside. Chase continued using the machine, despite the horrible noise. Several coworkers complained to him about it. The grinding occurred because the machine was out of lubricating oil, which, according to the machine's instruction manual, should have been checked at least monthly. No one had checked the oil level since the machine was purchased more than a year ago. While Chase was using the machine, its gears froze up and broke loose the paper-shredding blades. These lodged in Chase's thighs, cutting him deeply.

▌ REVIEW QUESTIONS

1. What are the public policy objectives behind products liability? How are they similar to the public policy objectives mentioned in Chapter 10 for "regular" strict liability?

2. How did modern products liability evolve? What were some of the landmark cases during the nineteenth and early twentieth centuries that led to these developments? What was the imminent danger exception? It was an exception to what rule?

3. How is negligence relevant to products liability? Is privity of contract required? Who are the parties in products liability cases? Who is the ultimate user?

4. Discuss the elements of a typical products liability formula. How are these different from the elements in *Restatement (Second) of Torts* § 402A? How are they similar?

5. How would you define an unreasonably dangerous product? What is faulty product design? Explain the consumer contemplation test, the danger/utility test, and the state-of-the-art discoverability test. Why are these tests important?

6. Explain how errors in product manufacture or assembly make a product unreasonably dangerous for products liability purposes.

7. In products liability, what role does improper product maintenance play? What about the manufacturer or seller's failure to warn of product hazards?

8. Define (a) the business requirement, (b) the substantially unchanged condition requirement, and (c) the proper use requirement. Why are they relevant to products liability? Does proximate cause play any role?

9. Is contributory negligence a defense to products liability? Why or why not? What about product misuse?

10. Explain how assumption of risk operates as a defense to products liability. Identify the three ways in which the ultimate user assumes the risk of using a defective product.

11. How does the tort of bad faith intersect with contract law?

▍HELPFUL WEBSITES

This chapter focuses on products liability. To learn more about products liability, the following sites can be accessed:

General Information
www.law.cornell.edu
www.hg.org

OSHA
www.osha.gov

Toxic Torts
www.toxlaw.com

U.S. Product Safety Commission
www.cpsc.gov

Statutes of Limitations
www.nolo.com
www.findlaw.com

Directory of Experts
www.expertpages.com

Internet Drug Index
www.drugs.com

Medical Information
www.mayoclinic.com
www.webmd.com
www.nih.gov
www.health.gov

STUDENT COMPANION WEBSITE
For additional cases and study materials, please go to www.cengagebrain.com

Chapter 12

Special Tort Actions

THE BIGGEST MISTAKES PARALEGALS MAKE AND HOW TO AVOID THEM

It's All About the Clients!

Emily, one of a dozen paralegals at her office, exerts minimal effort at work, arrives late in the morning and after lunch, makes frequent personal cell calls all day, and freely admits that she could care less about the clients. She never goes above and beyond to assure that the services she provides are of the highest quality for clients. She's in it just for the paycheck. The aforementioned detail is provided by Emily's 11 colleagues, who resent Emily because supervisors are only concerned with the final work product, not anyone's personal dedication to the job. Shouldn't the bosses acknowledge the difference between Emily and her more industrious paralegal colleagues?

(continues)

359

Lesson Learned: Nobody should expect to be treated differently if bosses accurately assess Emily's work as equivalent in quality to that of the other 11 paralegals. Since Emily's behavior will not change; the healthy attitude is to know that satisfying clients' legal needs is its own reward. In addition to the satisfaction and joy of your work, you get paid for it! Pity poor Emily, who endures a job she doesn't savor just for a mere check. Remember that it is all about the clients and the resentments will subside at work.

INTRODUCTION

You have now reached an area of torts that is often overlooked in paralegal education. These forgotten torts are just as important as the major torts of negligence and strict liability.

Special tort actions include nuisance, which involves issues of both tort and property law, and negligence per se, which is often a statutory tort. Tort litigation also often includes wrongful death actions, which are usually associated with negligence claims. Within the past 30 years, a new, related tort, *wrongful life*, has emerged in the appellate courts.

This chapter investigates these special tort actions. Much of our discussion will incorporate negligence and absolute liability theories. Specifically, the following torts and issues are discussed:

- Private nuisances
- "Coming to the nuisance" defense
- Public nuisances
- Nuisances per se
- Nuisance remedies: abatement, injunctions, and damages
- Wrongful death and survival statutes
- Wrongful birth actions
- Wrongful life actions

PRIVATE NUISANCES

nuisance |

1. Anything that annoys or disturbs unreasonably, hurts a person's use of his or her property, or violates the public health, safety, or decency.

2. Use of land that does anything in definition 1.

A **nuisance** is an unreasonable or unlawful use of one's real property that injures another person or interferes with another person's use of his or her real property. Nuisances are defined by common law and by statute. There are two types of nuisances: private and public. Occasionally, the same activity constitutes both a private and a public nuisance. These are sometimes called *mixed nuisances*.

Private Nuisance Defined

A **private nuisance** occurs when someone (1) uses his or her land in such a way as to (2) unreasonably and substantially interfere with (3) another person's use and enjoyment of his or her land. (4) The defendant's activity proximately causes the plaintiff's injuries. The tortfeasor (defendant) is the land user whose activities offend his or her neighbors. The neighboring land user (plaintiff) sues the tortfeasor for engaging in a private nuisance. The second element in commission of a private nuisance, unreasonable and substantial interference, is the most susceptible to interpretation.

private nuisance | A tort that requires a showing of special harm to you or your property and allows the recovery of damages for the harm as well as an injunction.

Unreasonable and Substantially Defined. Whether the tortfeasor's use of real estate is unreasonable and substantially interferes with another's land use is usually defined in terms of offensiveness. The critical question is: How offensive is the tortfeasor's land use? Offensiveness is determined by applying the reasonable person standard. Would a reasonable person with ordinary sensitivities find the tortfeasor's land use unreasonably offensive? If so, then the tortfeasor has unreasonably and substantially interfered with the plaintiff's use and enjoyment of his or her land. Therefore, the tortfeasor has committed a private nuisance.

Community Standard. The reasonable person standard is normally a community standard. In other words, it asks how people living in the community in which the alleged nuisance is taking place would react to the activity. This *reasonable community* reaction supposedly evaluates whether the tortfeasor's land use is unreasonable and a substantial interference with neighboring land uses. The finder of fact, usually a jury, makes this determination.

Use and Enjoyment. *Use and enjoyment* is a term of art in nuisance law. The two are always used together. The term *use* would be sufficient, but *enjoyment* imparts an emotional aspect to nuisance law. The alleged nuisance activity ruins the pleasure neighbors gain through the ways in which they use their real estate. This seems to make the tortfeasor's activities more blameworthy.

Classic Examples

There are many common examples of private nuisances to which to apply the elements just explained. These situations can be classified in broad categories: (1) physical effects on land, (2) health hazards or offending the sensibilities, and (3) unwanted associations with neighboring uses.

Physical Effects on Land. Neighboring land users often complain if a tortfeasor's use of realty creates constant vibrations, pollution of water or soil, destruction of crops, flooding, excessive clutter, or unwanted excavations.

Ground Vibrations. For example, suppose a manufacturing plant next door to Jenny's house operates 24 hours a day. This plant uses heavy machinery that produces powerful vibrations. These vibrations can be felt for hundreds of feet in all directions. The ground actually shakes slightly from the effect. Over several years, this phenomenon has caused Jenny's house foundation to crack. She would argue that these constant vibrations were an unreasonable and substantial interference with her use and enjoyment of her home. In short, the manufacturing plant would be creating a private nuisance.

Pollution of Water or Soil. Consider another example. Suppose a chemical processing plant dumped its wastewater onto vacant land behind its buildings. This wastewater seeped into the soil and polluted underground water supplies. The chemicals also spread across the soil surface onto neighboring lands, making them sterile. These are unreasonable and substantial interferences with the neighboring landowners' use and enjoyment of their realty. The chemical plant has produced a private nuisance.

Crop Destruction. Consider another hypothetical. The Blackout Power Company burns coal to produce electricity. Thick, black smoke belches from its tall smokestacks. As the wind disperses the smoke, coal dust settles on the neighbors' land, upon which grow corn and soybeans. The neighbors' crops grow poorly because of the coal dust on their leaves. Blackout's activity is an unreasonable and substantial interference with the neighboring farmers' use and enjoyment of their land. A private nuisance exists.

Flooding. Flooding can also be a private nuisance. Suppose Deatra lives along a small creek. Several miles downstream, another landowner erects a dam to create a small lake for fishermen. However, the lake extends beyond the downstream user's land and floods Deatra's property, including her home. Although this case could involve issues of *riparian* (water) law, in terms of nuisance law, the downstream landowner has unreasonably and substantially interfered with Deatra's use and enjoyment of her real estate by flooding her out.

Excessive Clutter. Few individuals would ever want to live adjacent to a junkyard or trash dump. Most people find such land uses to be offensive to many senses, one of which is sight. Having to look at junk or trash piled high next door can be aesthetically depressing. Many courts have found such uses to be private nuisances for this reason, although neighbors are more commonly also offended by refuse odors.

Unwanted Excavations. Excavation companies sometimes purchase soil from vacant lot owners to haul away and use in construction projects. These excavations leave deep and, for some people, unsightly holes in the vacant lots. Suppose Andy's house is next to several vacant lots that have been excavated in this fashion. A quick search of the case law reveals that several courts would find this to be a private nuisance.

Health Hazards or Offending the Sensibilities.

People's **sensibilities** are ways in which their physical senses (sight, hearing, smell, taste, and touch) and their emotional senses (what they find disgusting, repulsive, threatening, and so forth) are affected. Private nuisances offend a person's sensibilities. They can also create health hazards.

Noxious Odors. Land uses that produce harmful, obnoxious odors are frequent candidates for being private nuisances, as in the previous trash-dump example. Suppose Nicki lives next to a livestock farm, a chemical processing plant, or a paper mill. These may not create any bad smells at all hours, but sometimes they emit a powerful and dreadful stench. Much nuisance litigation has involved offensive odors produced by activities such as these.

Smoke and Dust. Smoke and dust emissions can produce serious health hazards for neighbors. Consider the earlier Blackout Power Company example. Neighbors who breathe the coal-dust-laden air could suffer severe respiratory injury. If this happened, the courts would probably rule that Blackout was involved in creating a private nuisance.

Excessive Noise and Temperatures. Land uses that produce excessive noise can harm neighbors' health. In nuisance litigation, many plaintiffs have complained of sleep loss, nervousness, and associated physical and emotional symptoms because of a neighbor's excessive noise. Imagine how Eric might be affected if he lived next to a motor-vehicle racetrack that ran late-night races on weeknights.

Factories producing extreme heat might also pose health problems for neighbors. Persons living adjacent to steel mills have sued for nuisance because of the high temperatures produced by the blast furnaces. The heat from these operations can raise air temperatures to uncomfortable levels. When the heat becomes unreasonable, the courts may find private nuisances.

Toxic Tort Nuisances. The disposal and transportation of hazardous wastes or toxic chemicals are frequently grounds for private nuisance actions. Underground or surface water supplies that are contaminated by leaking toxic-chemical dumps, or air that is filled with poisonous dusts (such as uranium dust vented from a

sensibilities | In nuisance law, ways in which people's physical and emotional senses are affected.

nuclear power plant) are excellent examples of private nuisances. Much of the toxic tort litigation brought today involves nuisance actions.

Incessant Telephone Calls. Creditors occasionally use intimidation tactics to coerce customers to pay delinquent accounts. A favorite technique is the late-night telephone call. The creditor might telephone a delinquent customer several times late at night, every day for weeks at a time, or even months, to try to per-suade , or even months, to try the patron to pay the overdue amounts. Customers subjected to such harassment might suffer emotional distress and related physical manifestations depending on the circumstances.

Courts could determine that such activity constitutes a private nuisance. It is an unreasonable interference with the customer's use and enjoyment of the pri-vacy of his or her home life. In fact, plaintiffs besieged with incessant phone calls often sue the culprit under several causes of action—namely, the intentional torts of invasion of privacy or intentional infliction of emotional distress—along with nuisance. Although there is a National Do Not Call Registry to discourage such activities, many companies are exempted from these provisions and can contact people at will. Charities, political organizations, survey companies, and compa-nies that have "an existing relationship with a customer" are all free to make calls to people within certain constraints. (Also see the Fair Debt Collection Practices Act which greatly limits a debt collector's ability to employ abusive practices in collecting a debt.)

Unwanted Associations with Neighboring Uses.

For decades, land-owners have rushed to the courthouse to file private nuisance actions against the owners of houses of ill repute, X-rated movie theaters, adult bookstores, massage parlors, and liquor or gambling establishments. These cases illustrate clearly the personal nature of offensiveness. Some persons simply cannot abide living in the vicinity of these types of activities. They do not wish to be associated with these land uses. These persons typically become plaintiffs in nuisance lawsuits in an attempt to drive out activities that they find repugnant.

In cases such as these, courts often struggle with community standards to decide if the activities are private nuisances. Are the plaintiffs overreacting, or are their objections reasonable? Would reasonable persons agree that having to live adjacent to establishments engaged in these pursuits is an unreasonable and substantial interference with the use and enjoyment of the realty? This is not an easy question to answer, as can be seen by reading some of the hundreds of ap-pellate court opinions discussing the subject. As the following case illustrates, litigants often have differences in what they consider to be appropriate adjacent establishments.

THE CASE OF THE COUNTRY CLUB NUISANCE

The success of a pro se litigant's action against a country club hinges on the applicable statute of limitations. Although living on lands adjoining a country club is often considered desirable, these litigants would beg to differ.

SILVESTER

v.

SPRING VALLEY COUNTRY CLUB

Court of Appeals of South Carolina
344 S.C. 280, 543 S.E.2d 563
February 12, 2001

In 1983, the Silvesters purchased a residence in Spring Valley subdivision. The rear of their lot adjoins a portion of the Club's golf course. Water from the Club's land channels onto the Silvesters' lot, allegedly causing erosion, the deposit of trash, and a potentially hazardous condition due to standing water. . . . The problem manifested itself shortly after the Silvesters occupied the house.

The Silvesters brought this action in April 1996. They alleged for a first cause of action a trespass occurring in 1992 when the Club constructed a french drainage system to collect and concentrate surface water, thereby exacerbating the Silvesters' drainage problem. . . . For their second cause of action, the Silvesters allege [that] the Club's actions constitute a continuing nuisance affecting the enjoyment of their land.

The action was called to trial on June 17, 1998, with the Silvesters proceeding *pro se.* Prior to selecting a jury, the court heard the Club's motion to dismiss. During argument on the motion, Mr. Silvester admitted they realized the severity of the water problem by 1991.

Mrs. Silvester argued the action should not be dismissed based on the statute of limitations because it was an ongoing nuisance. The trial court granted the motion to dismiss based on the statute of limitations. The Silvesters appeal.

The Silvesters pled trespass as the first cause of action in their complaint. However, at the hearing before the trial court, the continuing nuisance claim was the only issue clearly addressed. We therefore find the grant of summary judgment to the Club on the trespass cause of action is not presented to this court as an issue appropriate for appellate review.

The Silvesters contend [that] the trial court erred in granting the Club summary judgment on their continuing nuisance cause of action. We agree.

South Carolina follows the common enemy rule which allows a landowner to treat surface water as a common enemy and dispose of it as he sees fit. However, an exception to this rule prohibits a landowner from using his land in such a manner as to create a nuisance.

The traditional concept of a nuisance requires a landowner to demonstrate that the defendant unreasonably interfered with his ownership or possession of the land. The distinction between trespass and nuisance is that trespass is any intentional invasion of the plaintiff's interest in the exclusive possession of his property, whereas nuisance is a substantial and unreasonable interference with the plaintiff's use and enjoyment of his property.

A nuisance may be classified as permanent or continuing in nature. A continuing nuisance is defined as a nuisance that is intermittent or periodical and is described as one which occurs so often that it is said to be continuing although it is not necessarily constant or unceasing. A permanent nuisance may be expected to continue but is presumed to continue permanently, with no possibility of abatement. As to a permanent nuisance, such as a building or a railroad encroaching on a party's land, the injury is fixed and goes to the whole value of the land.

When the statute of limitations begins to run hinges on whether a nuisance is classified as permanent or continuing. When the nuisance is permanent in nature and only one cause of action may be brought for damages, the applicable statute of limitations bars

(continues)

the action if not brought within the statutory period after the first actionable injury. When the nuisance is continuing and the injury is abatable, the statute of limitations does not run merely from the original intrusion on the property and cannot be a complete bar. Rather, a new statute of limitations begins to run after each separate invasion of the property.

In discussing the limitations period applicable in a continuing nuisance action, our Supreme Court has stated:

> Since every continuance of a nuisance is a new nuisance, authorizing a fresh action, an action may be brought, for the recovery of all damages, resulting from the continuance of a nuisance, within the statutory period of the statute of limitations, for which no previous recovery has been had, even though the original cause of action is barred, unless the nuisance has been so long continued, as to raise the presumption of a grant, or in case of injury to real property, unless the plaintiff's right of entry is barred. . . .

Furthermore, although the statute of limitations may bar a nuisance action for damages, it "is not a defense in an action based upon nuisance for injunctive relief since such statutes do not bar the equitable relief of injunction."

The Silvesters argue [that] water channels from a man-made ditch dug by the Club onto their property. The Club maintains [that] water channeling through a naturally occurring stream passes over a portion of the Silvesters' lot and only "occasionally" overflows their yard. However, Mr. Silvester testified at the hearing "there was an enormous amount of water coming through the property," and Mrs. Silvester stated "our property daily is being damaged." After reviewing the record, we find there exist genuine issues of material fact making summary judgment inappropriate in this case.

The Silvesters alleged a continuing nuisance and requested damages and injunctive relief. The trial court summarily applied the three-year statute of limitations to the continuing nuisance cause of action without considering the possibility of abatement, the Club's alleged negligence, or the Silvesters' request for injunctive relief. Viewing the evidence in the light most favorable to the Silvesters, we agree the trial court erred in applying the statute of limitations to their continuing nuisance claim and accordingly reverse the grant of summary judgment on this issue.

. . . We find no evidence in the record [that] the trial judge's ruling was based on or influenced by any bias against either the Silvesters or *pro se* litigants as a class.

Based on the foregoing, the order on appeal is affirmed as to the dismissal of the trespass cause of action and reversed and remanded as to the nuisance cause of action.

CASE QUESTIONS

1. Do you think this case would have had a different outcome if the Silvesters had not appeared *pro se*? Explain.
2. What effect does classifying a nuisance as permanent or continuing have on the statute of limitations?

"Coming to the Nuisance" Defense

Often, a person will move into a neighborhood in which one of the activities previously described is already situated. In many cases, the manufacturer, trash dump, junkyard, or adult bookstore has been doing business in the same location for years. The plaintiff came to the area after the alleged nuisance was already there. When this happens, and the plaintiff then sues for private nuisance, the defendant may plead the "coming to the nuisance" defense. The **coming to the nuisance defense** involves the plaintiff who owns or uses land at a location in which the alleged nuisance activity was already occurring. If the plaintiff came to the nuisance, then he or she cannot recover against the defendant. The defense is similar to the defense of assumption of risk, in that the plaintiff knew (or reasonably should have known) that the preexisting activity would offend him or her. Consequently, a reasonable person would not have chosen to buy or use land adjacent to a known, present, and distasteful land use. In essence, the plaintiff assumes the risk of obnoxiousness from the nuisance activity by coming to the place while knowing that the nuisance is already there, waiting to offend the plaintiff. Note that, as is discussed later in this chapter, the defense of coming to the nuisance cannot be used against public nuisances.

Private nuisance hypotheticals provide the reader with some of the earthiest factual situations in tort law. Students can easily relate to intrusions upon their senses or values. However, one must guard against identifying too strongly with the offended individual over the business allegedly creating the nuisance. As the following examples illustrate, each party in the nuisance story has its side to tell.

coming to the nuisance defense | A defense to private nuisance lawsuits that may be used successfully when a plaintiff owns or uses land at a location in which the alleged nuisance activity was previously occurring. The plaintiff is said to have "come to the nuisance" and thus cannot recover against the defendant.

THE CASE OF THE INTRUDING COWS

Incompatible land uses often make unhappy neighbors. Unfortunately, it is not always apparent that such incompatibilities will exist until after the activities have cohabited for some time. Then one of the landowners usually is harmed by the other, and a nuisance action enters the picture. As the case here illustrates, a business can create a nuisance through its own actions.

ERIC STICKDORN and LISA STICKDORN,
Appellants-Plaintiffs,
vs.
ELAM B. ZOOK, SARAH F. ZOOK, SAMUEL L.
LANTZ and MATTIE Z. LANTZ,
Appellees-Defendants

Court of Appeals of Indiana
957 N.E.2d 1014; 2011 Ind. App. LEXIS 1921
November 28, 2011

Two neighboring farmers were conducting business near Cambridge City in Wayne County. The defendants built their dairy in 2003 that included a milking parlor about fifteen feet from the plaintiffs' house. When the defendants emptied a manure pit on the farm in early 2004, the stench of rotten eggs and raw

sewage permeated the plaintiffs' home. The plaintiffs became physically ill, and a stream that crossed their property became polluted. The defendants repeatedly and continuously emptied the manure pit at various times over the next several years until April 2005, when they sold their farm. Because the plaintiffs did not file their cause of action for negligence, trespass, and nuisance until 2009, the defendants are entitled to summary judgment with regard to the negligence and personal injury claims. However, the nuisance and trespass actions survive.

The Stickdorns own a 120-acre farm in Wayne County, where they have resided, farmed, and raised cattle since 1994. Prior to 1994, they lived on a smaller farm in Charlottsville, where they farmed and raised livestock since 1989. In light of their farming

(continues)

experiences, the Stickdorns generally tended to be unaffected by fumes and odors that are known to be associated with animals, including dairy operations.

In 2003, the Lantzes constructed a dairy on the property that was adjacent to the Stickdorns' farm.

From 1994 until the dairy was built, the land next to the Stickdorns' property was used primarily to grow row crops that included corn and soy beans. During that time, the Stickdorns did not notice any unusual odors.

The Lantzes commenced their dairy and milking operations on October 14, 2003. Soon thereafter, the Stickdorns detected odors emanating from the Lantzes' property that were, at first, nothing more than typical smells generated by a livestock farm. However, in mid November 2003, the Stickdorns noticed that the odors were increasing and were more pungent than before. They observed that the Lantzes kept the barn curtains open while their animals were confined and assumed that this was probably the source of the increasing odors because of the prevailing wind directions and proximity of the Lantzes' barn to their home.

Eric contacted the Lantzes about the odors and requested them to shut their barn curtains when the winds were blowing from the west. The Lantzes refused to do so. Sometime in February or March 2004, the Lantzes emptied their manure pit for the first time and spread the waste across the frozen, snow-covered ground. The odors from the pit invaded the Stickdorns' home with the smell of rotten eggs and raw sewage. The fumes made both of the Stickdorns dizzy, confused, and nauseous. Eric informed Samuel how sick he and Lisa had become from the odors and gases. Eric also advised Samuel that applying manure to frozen ground could cause the substance to run into the streams that crossed their property. However, the Lantzes took no action.

On March 17, 2004, Samuel emptied the pit and spilled manure onto the snow-covered ground. The spill caused one of the streams that crosses the Stickdorns' property to become murky and foamy with a foul odor. In response to a telephone call that Eric made, a representative from the Indiana Department of Environmental Management (IDEM) tested the stream and found elevated ammonia-nitrogen levels and advised Eric that the water was unfit for his cattle to drink.

The Lantzes continued to empty the manure pit and spread it across their land. Following an investigation, the IDEM representatives determined that the spill increased the ammonia-nitrate levels that "settled to form putrescent or otherwise objectionable deposits, in an amount sufficient to be unsightly or deleterious, that produced color, visible oil sheen, odor, or other conditions in such a degree to create a nuisance."

Randy Jones of IDEM informed the Lantzes that they would have to change their manure handling practices. Samuel did not believe that it was necessary to change their manure handling practices.

The Stickdorns eventually sought refuge at night by sleeping in their truck, the basement of a church and, the home of a friend. In May 2004, they began sleeping in a camper. By the fall of 2004, the Stickdorns moved to an apartment. The Stickdorns returned to the property only to care for their own animals. Eric made repeated requests to Samuel that he cover the manure pit and refrain from emptying the pit or land applying waste when the winds blew from the west. On October 1, 2004, Eric sent a letter to Samuel, stating:

> Commencing on 17 October 2003, the operation of your dairy . . . has been and continues to be, injurious to our health, offensive to our senses, and is an obstruction to the free use of our property interfering with the comfortable enjoyment of our lives. . .

Samuel dismissed the pleas. On April 12, 2005, the Lantzes sold the dairy operation to the Zooks, who continued to store, handle, and dispose of animal waste in the same manner as did the Lantzes. After failed attempts to convince the Zooks to implement various manure management practices to reduce odors and prevent spills, the Stickdorns filed an action against both the Lantzes and the Zooks on November 12, 2009. The complaint was filed six years and one month after the Lantzes had commenced dairy operations at their farm. To date, the Stickdorns are unable to live in their home on the Stickdorn property

Count IV alleged that the Lantzes' conduct constituted a continuing trespass. In sum, the Stickdorns requested compensatory and punitive damages pursuant to Indiana Code section 34-51-3-4, and for injunctive relief to abate the nuisance and trespass.

On February 26, 2010, the Lantzes filed a motion for summary judgment, contending that the Stickdorns' negligence claims were barred under the two-year statute of limitations. They also argued that the allegations of nuisance and trespass were barred by the six-year statute of limitations.

The trial court granted the Lantzes' motion for summary judgment on November 23, 2010, concluding that there were no genuine issues of material fact on the issue of the statute of limitations. The trial court determined that the two-year statute of limitations barred the negligence claims, and the six-year statute barred the nuisance and trespass claims. More particularly, the order granting summary judgment provided in relevant part that

The Stickdorns . . . allege that the [Lantzes] emptied the manure slurry pit for the first time on February 17, 2004 and every 30 . . . days thereafter. The allegation is that the pit is emptied and the manure spread constantly every 30 . . . days, rendering the nuisance to become the permanent variety.

When a statute of limitations defense is asserted, the party moving for summary judgment must first make a "prima facie showing that the action was commenced outside of the statutory period" and, then the "nonmovant has the burden of establishing an issue of material fact material to a theory that avoids the affirmative defense."

The noxious odors and harmful gases that emanate from the manure slurry pit on the Zook property have and continue to cause the Stickdorns to suffer from adverse health symptoms. It is readily apparent that the Stickdorns are seeking damages for personal injury and not damage to their property, insofar as

the negligence counts are concerned. The two-year statute of limitations applies to the negligence and gross negligence counts set forth in the complaint. The Stickdorns' personal injury claims are barred as a matter of law.

The Stickdorns argue that the trial court erroneously determined that their claims for nuisance and trespass were barred because a six-year statute of limitations applies. The Stickdorns contend that their complaint seeks "damages from and abatement of conditions that have and continue to cause harm to their real property and interference with their property rights," appellants' and the trial court erroneously concluded that the injuries were "permanent" in October 2003. The Stickdorns assert that their injuries were the result of the Lantzes' repeated, wrongful conduct through April 2005.

The distinction between an injury caused by a nuisance that is "permanent" or "original," and one that is considered temporary, transient, continuing, or recurring, is critical to determining when the statute of limitations period for a nuisance action begins to run. Keane v. Pachter, 598 N.E.2d 1067, 1072 (Ind. Ct. App. 1992). An intermittent, nonabated nuisance is a new and separate injury that gives rise to a new cause of action. Successive actions may be maintained so long as the nuisance is permitted to continue, in which damages may be recovered for all injury occasioned prior to the commencement of the action and within the statute of limitations, not extending back of a former recovery. Ind. Pipe Line Co. v. Christensen, 188 Ind. 400, 403, 123 N.E. 789, 790 (1919). When the nuisance is a continuing abatable one, an action that is prosecuted to a finality will not bar another action to recover for harm sustained in succeeding years, when it is made to appear that the nuisance has not been abated and its continuance has resulted in further injury. Ind. Pipe Line Co. v. Christensen, 195 Ind. 106, 121, 143 N.E. 596, 600 (1924). Similarly, a continued trespass that causes harm triggers a new limitations period each time it occurs. C & E Corp. v. Ramco Indus., 717 N.E.2d 642, 644 (Ind. Ct. App. 1999).

(continues)

In accordance with the rules announced in the Indiana Pipe Line cases, the nuisance odors and contaminated streams from the Lantzes' repeated manure spills, improper spreading of the waste, and the refusal to put a cover on their manure pit amount to an intermittent, abatable nuisance. Each time that the odors and polluted streams affected the Stickdorns' property, the statute of limitations began anew. The Stickdorns' damages were recurring and continuing and thus, the manure pit became a temporary, continuing nuisance through its use, and not a permanent one from its mere existence

The Lantzes refused to stop or change their waste storage, disposal and management practices that harmed them through April 2005. Thus, the statute of limitations did not preclude the Stickdorns from complaining about the continued instances of nuisance and trespass. See May v. George, 53 Ind. App. 259, 263, 101 N.E. 393, 394 (1913) (holding that if a nuisance continues from day to day and a fresh injury is created each day, there may still be a right of action for the injuries created within the last six years, though the original right of action has been lost).

It was the intermittent, recurring, and continuing spreading of the manure from early 2003 through April 2005 that caused the damages. As a result, we conclude that the trial court erred in granting summary judgment in the Lantzes' favor with regard to the trespass and nuisance claims.

The judgment of the trial court is affirmed in part, reversed in part, and remanded for further proceedings consistent with this opinion.

CASE QUESTIONS

1. Who do you think was more unreasonable, the plaintiffs or the defendants? Explain your answer.
2. Is there a way this case could have been resolved amicably?

HYPOTHETICALS

Sajjad bought a house in a residential subdivision in 2005. His real estate is adjacent to 70 acres of pasture land. In 2010, the pasture was sold to the Waste Away Company, which erected a trash-processing plant and landfill in 2011. This plant began compacting trash for landfill use as well as incinerating trash. Early in 2012 Sajjad began smelling unpleasant odors and smoke from the trash piles and smokestacks. In warm weather, the smell was extremely nasty. Fumes seemed to hover all around the neighborhood. Does Sajjad have a cause of action for private nuisance?

When Sajjad bought his home in 2005, he assumed that he would be living next door to pasture land, which is free from odors and has a clear, natural view. He probably anticipated that wildlife or livestock would graze the realty next door. This rustic expectation was shattered in 2010 when Waste Away transformed the land into a trash-processing facility and landfill.

Using the private nuisance formula, first ask whether Waste Away's use of its real estate unreasonably and substantially interfered with Sajjad's use and enjoyment of his property. Every day, odors and smoke floated across Sajjad's land from the trash facility. The neighborhood became inundated with the foul smell of piled or burning trash. Reasonable persons with ordinary sensibilities (or, as it is sometimes called, sensitivities) would find such odors and smoke to be offensive. Most subdivision residents in Sajjad's community could reasonably be expected to react adversely to the invading stench. Waste Away has created a private nuisance.

* * *

The Sanctified Brethren Church purchased a building site for a new cathedral in July 2013. Across the street, one block away, were several taverns, an X-rated movie theater, and an adult bookstore. Once construction began, members of the church filed suit against the owners of these businesses, claiming private nuisance. Would the church's lawsuit be successful?

No. Assuming that the church could first prove that these businesses constituted a private nuisance, the businesses could avail themselves of the coming to the nuisance defense. The church knew that these businesses were already located in the neighborhood when it purchased its building site. The church voluntarily decided to situate its cathedral within close proximity to activities that church members found offensive. Therefore, the church would fail in its lawsuit.

There are literally thousands of different factual patterns involving private nuisance to be found in the court reporters. This tort can be quite interesting to study, given the variety and peculiarity of the fact scenarios that allegedly produce nuisances. One might wish to research different examples of nuisances online. These are often entertaining as well as enlightening. Every imaginable intrusion into life is found—one reason that nuisance is frequently regarded as a "fun" tort subject in law study. Table 12-1 lists the elements of private nuisance.

▌PUBLIC NUISANCES

In addition to private nuisances, there are also public nuisances. A **public nuisance** is a land use that injures the public at large rather than just a single individual. A public nuisance unreasonably interferes with the public's enjoyment of legal rights common to the public. The elements of public nuisance may be broken down as: (1) The tortfeasor's activity that (2) unreasonably and substantially interferes with (3) the public's use and enjoyment of legal rights common to the public.

public nuisance | Activity by the tortfeasor that unreasonably and substantially interferes with the public's use and enjoyment of legal rights common to the public.

Elements	Examples	Defense
Defendant uses his or her land	Physical effects on land (vibrations, pollution, crop destruction, flooding, junk clutter, or excavations)	Coming to the nuisance
In an activity that unreasonably and substantially interferes	Health hazards and offending the sensibilities (noxious odors, smoke, dust, extreme noise or temperature, incessant telephone calling)	
With the use and enjoyment of another's land		
Defendant's activity must proximately cause plaintiff's injuries	Unwanted associations with neighboring uses (prostitution houses, distributors of explicit sexual material, massage parlors, gambling institutions)	

Copyright © 2015 Cengage Learning®.

Unlike private nuisances, which can adversely affect a single person, a public nuisance must harm the general public. More than one person *must* be affected (or, at least, potentially affected) by the alleged nuisance activity. This does not require a multitude of angry citizens. Residents of a single neighborhood would suffice.

The standard of unreasonable and substantial interference is identical to that used in private nuisances, except that the interference must be to the public rather than a sole plaintiff.

Use and Enjoyment of Common Legal Rights

The use and enjoyment element in public nuisance is significantly different from the one discussed in private nuisances. With public nuisances, the tortfeasor's obnoxious land use interferes with the public's common legal rights, such as the right to peaceably assemble in public places, the right to use public streets and sidewalks without being subjected to offensive activities, or the right to safe and healthy conditions in one's neighborhood.

Governments as Plaintiffs

Although citizens often file public nuisance complaints with their local governmental agencies, it is the government, through its municipal governing bodies (e.g., city council, county commissioners) or its prosecuting attorneys, that sues defendants alleged to be committing public nuisances. This is because the government represents the public at large and must enforce its citizens' legal rights against tort-feasors. At common law, or by statute or, in some states, by state constitutional provision, state and local governments have the authority to protect their citizens from public nuisances. The source of this power is the states' **police powers,** which give governments authority to file lawsuits or enact legislation to protect the public's health, welfare, safety, or morals. These are usually very broad powers that give governments considerable flexibility to forbid certain offensive activities.

police power | The government's right and power to set up and enforce laws to provide for the safety, health, and general welfare of the people.

Types of Public Nuisances

Almost all public nuisances are defined by statute or ordinance. Many such laws focus on land uses *that legislators believe* a majority of the population would find offensive, unhealthy, or immoral. The reader may know from personal experience that this belief may be unfounded or exaggerated. That, of course, depends upon whether one agrees or disagrees with what the government has labeled a public nuisance. Common targets of public nuisance laws include institutions devoted to (1) gambling, (2) prostitution, (3) distribution of sexually explicit materials, (4) sale of alcohol, (5) nudist colonies, or (6) toxic waste management. Other typical public nuisances include (1) allowing certain weeds or poisonous plants to grow on one's land, (2) failing to comply with health code provisions by not keeping one's residence clean and vermin-free, and (3) keeping unrestrained wild or vicious animals on one's property. However, public nuisances may also include many of the same activities discussed in the private nuisances section.

Mixed Nuisances

Often, the same activity can constitute both a private and a public nuisance. These are sometimes called **mixed nuisances.** Apply this rule of thumb in such cases: The greater the number of persons adversely affected by an allegedly offensive land use, the more likely it will be considered a public, as well as a private, nuisance.

mixed nuisance | A nuisance that is both public and private.

Nuisances Per Se

Courts often consider activities violating public nuisance statutes to be **nuisances per se.** *Per se* is Latin meaning "by itself." In tort law, it usually means that some behavior has violated a statute, and therefore the defendant is automatically liable. Sometimes courts, in the common law, decree that certain conduct is per se tortious. Negligence per se is an example. Per se nuisances have also been established by common law court decisions.

nuisance per se | That which is considered a nuisance at all times and no matter the circumstances, regardless of location or surroundings.

A public nuisance per se is an activity that violates the statute and is automatically considered a public nuisance. An example of this would be smoking in public, where such activity is prohibited. The tortfeasor thus loses from the start of litigation, simply by violating the statute. Statutes (and, rarely, common law) may also declare certain private nuisances to be per se nuisances.

"Coming to the Nuisance" Is Not a Defense

Generally, courts do not recognize the coming to the nuisance defense in public nuisance cases. This defense focuses on the individual plaintiff who purchases or uses land next to a preexisting, private nuisance activity. Public nuisances, by definition, affect the public at large, and the very existence or continuation of the public nuisance activity is considered harmful, whether it was preexisting or not.

What constitutes a public nuisance or a nuisance per se is generally a question of common law interpretation and statutory construction. But underlying questions of substance and form are the value judgments implicit in all nuisance per se or public nuisance cases. The following examples present such choices. Despite the temptation to become caught up in "good" versus "bad," one must concentrate on the legal elements and their application to the facts. However, the remedy of ordering an injunction may involve a balancing of interests.

THE CASE OF THE VERY ANNOYING DOGS

Many people think of barking dogs as nuisances, but the law does not automatically define them as such. As the following case suggests, not all types of dog barking are included in public nuisance ordinances.

Barbara PATTERSON

v.

CITY OF RICHMOND

Court of Appeals of Virginia, Richmond

39 Va.App. 706

February 19, 2003

The evidence established that, between February 12, 2000, and July 25, 2000, Patterson, a sixty-six-year-old legally blind woman, had five to eight dogs at any one time at her single-family residence. At trial, Patterson testified she owned five dogs, two of which she used as service animals. She further testified that, as a member of the Central Virginia Doberman Rescue League, she occasionally provided safehousing for other dogs.

John Russell, who lived with his wife and two children three houses away from Patterson on the same side of the street, testified the "continuous" barking of "any number of dogs" at "any hour of the day" bothered his family since the "day [they] moved into the house in August of 1999." Russell, a dog owner himself, further testified the barking of Patterson's dogs, often lasting for "three to four hours" at a time, woke his family up at 6:30 a.m. during the week and on weekends "on a frequent basis" and "disturbed" his family throughout the day. According to Russell, the barking was "a constant annoyance." Russell testified that, had he known his family would be subject to the "constant and continual" barking of Patterson's dogs, he would not have bought a house in that neighborhood.

In October 1999, "fed up with having to call [Patterson] constantly to tell her" her dogs were barking, Russell began to call Animal Control. Russell filed complaints regarding the barking of Patterson's dogs, on February 12, 2000, March 18, 2000, and May 6, 2000.

Copies of Animal Control's dispatch log were admitted into evidence and confirm that Animal Control received complaints from Russell about the barking of Patterson's dogs on February 12, 2000, and March 18, 2000. The log also shows that Russell's wife complained to Animal Control about the barking of Patterson's dogs on April 14, 2000, April 20, 2000, May 31, 2000, June 9, 2000, and July 18, 2000, and that Russell's next-door neighbor complained about Patterson's dogs on April 1, 2000.

Debra Rhoads, Patterson's next-door neighbor, testified the barking of Patterson's dogs, both when they were in Patterson's backyard or when the windows of Patterson's house were open, was "very annoying." It went on, for "extended periods of time" at night and in the morning, including weekends, and was "extremely loud." The barking was so loud and incessant she could not leave her windows open. Even with her windows closed, the barking disturbed her sleep, and her ability to have a conversation in her family room. Rhoads, who herself had a dog, testified that, had she known about the barking of Patterson's dogs before she moved in, she would not have bought her house.

Rhoads recalled calling Animal Control to complain about the barking on the evening of April 19, 2000, when it "appeared [Patterson] was not home" and "the dogs barked incessantly for quite an extended period of time." On the evening of July 25, 2000, Animal Control Officer Donna Miskovic went to Patterson's house to investigate complaints. Miskovic, who had previously responded to complaints about Patterson's dogs and issued notices to Patterson regarding the "excessive and continuous" barking of her dogs, testified that, upon her arrival she heard Patterson's dogs barking in a manner that was "excessive, continuous," and, it being late in the evening and nearly dark, "untimely." Consequently, Miskovic issued a summons to Patterson for violating Richmond City Code § 4-63

The trial court overruled Patterson's motion to strike the city's evidence as being insufficient to prove she violated Richmond City Code § 4-63, and found Patterson guilty as charged. At sentencing, the trial court suspended the imposition of sentence for two years conditioned on Patterson's compliance with conditions including limiting the number of dogs she keeps to her two service dogs and "responsibly managing her dogs' barking."

This appeal followed. Where the sufficiency of the evidence is challenged after conviction, it is our duty to consider it in the light most favorable to the [city] and give it all reasonable inferences fairly deducible therefrom.

Patterson was convicted of violating Richmond City Code § 4-63. That code section provides, in pertinent part, that "[n]o owner shall fail to exercise proper care and control of a dog or cat to prevent it from becoming a public nuisance. [Public nuisance] means, any dog or cat that . . . barks, whines, howls, or makes other annoying noises in an excessive, continuous, or untimely fashion. It shall be unlawful for any person to violate any provision of this chapter, and upon conviction, such person shall be punished for a Class 4 misdemeanor." None of these code sections require that a certain number of people be affected by "annoying" noise for there to be a violation.

On appeal, the Supreme Court initially stated as follows:

> If an ordinance makes criminal that conduct which is a public nuisance, it is a presumptively valid exercise of the locality's police power. On the other hand, if the prohibited conduct is merely a private nuisance, it cannot be made criminal because a municipality has no authority under its police power to punish conduct which is a private nuisance. Thus, this decision turns on whether the forbidden conduct can be classified as a public nuisance or only a private nuisance.

In drawing a distinction between the two types of nuisance, the Supreme Court described a private nuisance as "one which implicates or interferes with a right or interest that is *unique* to an individual, such as an interest in land." Conversely, the Supreme Court noted,

> [i]f the annoyance is one that is common to the public generally, then it is a public nuisance. The test is not the number of persons annoyed, but the possibility of annoyance to the public by the invasion of its rights.

(continues)

Turning to the noise ordinance before it, the Supreme Court held as follows: The right not to be subjected to "unreasonably loud, disturbing and unnecessary noise," as provided in [the city's noise ordinance], is "common to all members of the general public," Restatement (Second) of Torts § 821B comment g (1977), and not particular to individuals in the enjoyment of their property. This ordinance differs from a case which attempted to control door-to-door solicitation and affected only the individual property rights of householders.

We conclude the city was not required to prove that a particular number of people were actually affected for that barking to constitute a public nuisance. The instant noise ordinance requires that dog owners properly control their dogs to prevent them from barking "in an excessive, continuous, or untimely fashion." Plainly, the "right not to be subjected to" such barking is common to the public generally and not unique to "individuals in the enjoyment of their property." *City of Virginia Beach v.* Murphy, 239 Va. at 356, 389 S.E.2d at 464. Hence, the barking of dogs "in an excessive, continuous, or untimely fashion" is a public nuisance.

Both neighbors of Patterson, offered extensive testimony regarding the excessive, continuous, and untimely barking of Patterson's dogs. Furthermore, Officer Miskovic testified that she heard Patterson's dogs barking in an "excessive, continuous, and untimely" fashion on July 25, 2000. We hold, therefore, that the evidence presented at trial was sufficient, as a matter of law, to prove beyond a reasonable doubt that the barking of Patterson's dogs constituted a public nuisance, in violation of Richmond City Code § 4-63. For these reasons, we affirm Patterson's conviction. *Affirmed.*

CASE QUESTIONS

1. If you were one of Patterson's neighbors, do you think you would have done anything differently than Russell and Rhoads?
2. Why do you think if a nuisance occurs in a hotel, guests should complain to the hotel staff rather than the offending parties?

HYPOTHETICALS

Carter has an apiary in his backyard. He lives in a suburban neighborhood. Several hundred honeybees congregate in Carter's hives. The bees produce honey that Carter sells at local groceries. Frequently, children in the area have been stung by honeybees. Parents complained to Carter, but he simply shrugged off each incident, stating that there was no proof that his bees were responsible. However, there were no other honeybee colonies in the neighborhood. A town ordinance prohibits the keeping of wildlife within the city limits. Has Carter committed a public nuisance, a private nuisance, or a nuisance per se?

Carter's use of his land (maintaining an apiary) substantially and unreasonably interfered with his neighbors' use and enjoyment of the public streets and sidewalks in the area, as well as their own realty. Children were often stung by honeybees, and the only large honeybee colony in the neighborhood was Carter's. A trier-of-fact could reasonably infer that Carter's bees were responsible for the attacks. This would be a private nuisance. A local governmental agency could sue Carter for public nuisance. Reasonable persons would find these bee encounters to be offensive and dangerous. The public at large was threatened by Carter's *ferae naturae*. The bees unreasonably and substantially interfered with citizens' use of public streets and sidewalks. Under its police power, the local government would have authority to sue Carter for public nuisance.

Carter also violated the local ordinance prohibiting the keeping of wildlife within the city limits. This constitutes a nuisance per se, giving the town government another cause of action against Carter.

* * *

Dave operates a massage parlor across from the local public high school. Although there is no evidence of prostitution at the establishment, Dave offers nude massages, during which both customers and masseurs disrobe. From across the street, high-school students can see clearly through the windows of Dave's building. Is Dave engaged in a public nuisance?

Dave's use of his land could adversely affect the students. The erotic views could disrupt school activities as children (and adults) cluster around windows to catch the revealing sights. Arguably, this is an unreasonable and substantial interference with a public right—namely, the right to use the public school for educational pursuits. Under its police powers, the municipal government could sue Dave for public nuisance.

Admittedly, cases such as Dave's involve value judgments and presume a threat to the public morals. One may agree or disagree with the alleged public threat produced by a massage parlor across from a school. However, many cases have involved exactly these fact situations, and courts promptly conclude that public nuisances have occurred.

Table 12-2 lists the elements of public nuisances, mixed nuisances, and nuisances per se.

TABLE 12-2

Elements of
Public Nuisances,
Mixed Nuisances,
and Nuisances Per Se

ELEMENTS	EXAMPLES	DEFENSE
Public Nuisance Activity that unreasonably and substantially interferes with public's use and enjoyment of legal rights common to public at large	Prostitution establishments; pornography distributors	Coming to the nuisance is *not* a defense to public nuisances
Plaintiff is governmental agency responsible for protecting public interest harmed by public nuisance activity	Historically, gambling and alcohol establishments were often considered public nuisances, although not normally at the present time	
State and local governments have authority to litigate public nuisances under general police powers to protect public health, safety, morals, and welfare	Allowing noxious weeds to grow on one's land; failing to comply with public health statutes; keeping unrestrained wild animals on one's land	
Mixed Nuisance Mixed nuisances include public and private nuisances		The coming to the nuisance defense is effective against the private nuisance portion of mixed nuisance actions
Nuisances Per Se Nuisances per se are nuisance activities that violate statutes or ordinances		The coming to the nuisance defense is not usually effective against nuisance per se actions

Copyright © 2015 Cengage Learning®.

▌ REMEDIES FOR NUISANCES

remedy | The means by which a right is enforced or satisfaction is gained for a harm done.

damages | Money that a court orders paid to a person who has suffered damage (a loss or harm) by the person who caused the injury.

When one has identified a private or public nuisance, what does one do about it? In other words, what remedies are available to plaintiffs against defendants? **Remedies** are the relief that plaintiffs receive against defendants in lawsuits. The most common remedy in tort actions is *money* **damages,** in which the defendant must pay the plaintiff a sum of money to satisfy the judgment. The trier-of-fact sets the amount owed after a trial has been held.

Other, nonmonetary remedies are also available for torts such as nuisance. These are called equitable remedies. **Equitable remedies** do not involve money damages; instead, the court orders the defendant to do (or, more commonly, *not* to do) something. Generally, equitable remedies are sought to correct a problem. Equitable remedies are only available where money damages are inadequate and will not make a party whole. With equitable actions, there is no right to a trial by jury. In contrast, the right to a jury trial is preserved in the Seventh Amendment of the U.S. Constitution for civil cases "at common law."

Equity is aimed at a defendant—the court considers the defendant's knowledge and state of mind—whereas with court awards, money damages are directed toward the plaintiff for a loss caused by the defendant. When the court orders a defendant to do or not to do something, it is called an **injunction.**

When a court orders a governmental official to perform a nondiscretionary act, this is called a **mandamus** order; see *Cheney v. United States Dist. Court for D.C.* ([03-475] 542 U.S. 367 [2004]). An example of this is where a judge fails to issue a decision following a motion, and a party seeks to force the judge to issue a decision. Another example is where a party seeks the court's assistance in order to force an agency to release public records. The equitable remedy of mandamus was cited in the case of *Marbury v. Madison* (5 US 137 [1803]), In this case, William Marbury asked the Supreme Court to force the Secretary of State, James Madison, to deliver a justice of the peace commission that former President Adams had awarded to Marbury. The court decided it lacked original jurisdiction to order Madison to deliver the commission. The case would need to go to a lower court first. If the case was appealed, it could then go to the Supreme Court. The case of *Marbury v. Madison* is a landmark case concerning the Supreme Court's right of judicial review.

For centuries, money damages were considered inappropriate in nuisance cases, as it did not necessarily stop the annoyance. Courts would apply only equitable remedies. In nuisance law, the most common equitable remedies include (1) abatement and (2) injunction, although now money damages are occasionally permitted in nuisance cases.

Abatement

In nuisance cases, abatement is the most common remedy plaintiffs seek. With **abatement,** the defendant is ordered to cease, or *abate*, the nuisance activity. Abatement is often permanent. The defendant must desist from conducting the nuisance activity after a judgment for abatement is entered. This provides complete relief for the plaintiff, because the nuisance activity will be discontinued. Abatement can create harsh economic consequences for defendants, but the public policy behind abatement is clear: Nuisance tortfeasors have injured someone (or, if the public, many people). As long as the nuisance continues, the plaintiff(s) will continue to be hurt. The only certain solution is to stop the nuisance altogether.

equitable relief (remedy) | A remedy available in equity; generally nonmonetary relief.

injunction | A judge's order to a person to do or to refrain from doing a particular thing.

mandamus | (Latin) "We command." A *writ of mandamus* is a court order that directs a public official or government department to do something.

abatement | Reduction or decrease of an activity, or complete elimination.

Injunctions

Courts enforce abatement through injunctive relief. *Injunctions* are court orders to defendants to cease and desist from engaging in nuisance activities. There are two types of injunctions: (1) temporary injunctions, including temporary restraining orders (TROs); and (2) permanent injunctions.

Temporary Injunctions. Temporary injunctions are often used from the time a plaintiff files suit until the first court hearing. The plaintiff, in his or her complaint, asks the court to issue a **temporary restraining order (TRO),** which forbids the defendant from conducting an alleged nuisance activity until a court hearing can be held to determine if the activity constitutes a nuisance. Under most rules of civil procedure, TROs may be issued for up to 10 days, while the court convenes a hearing to decide if a nuisance has occurred. After the hearing, if the evidence convinces the judge that a nuisance is happening, the court may order further temporary injunctive relief, banning the defendant's nuisance activity until a trial on the merits may be held.

The purpose of temporary injunctions is to protect the plaintiff from further harm if a nuisance is in fact occurring. Plaintiffs often must post bonds to compensate the defendant if the court or jury later decides that the defendant did not engage in a nuisance. This is to protect the defendant from economic losses suffered while the injunctions were in effect and the defendant was not permitted to conduct the nuisance activity (which could mean lost profits or extra expenses). The court must balance the hardship to the defendant against the interference suffered by the plaintiff.

Permanent Injunctions. **Permanent injunctions** are abatement orders instructing the defendant to permanently stop doing the nuisance activity. They are usually issued after a trial on the merits, once the trier-of-fact has concluded that a nuisance exists. If the defendant fails to obey a permanent injunction by continuing the nuisance, the court can punish the defendant by holding him or her in **contempt.** This punishment may involve monetary fines or even imprisonment.

Money Damages

When abatement could impose an unreasonably severe economic burden upon the nuisance tortfeasor, courts have broken with the ancient common law tradition and awarded plaintiffs money damages instead of abatement. This way, the plaintiffs can be compensated for their injuries produced by the nuisance activities, and the defendant can survive (economically) by staying in business, even though the nuisance also continues. Courts using this alternative are usually attempting to balance interests between conflicting land uses.

temporary restraining order (TRO) | A judge's order to a person to not take a certain action during the period prior to a full hearing on the rightness of the action.

permanent injunction | Abatement orders instructing the defendant to permanently stop doing the nuisance activity. Usually issued after a full hearing.

contempt |

1. An act that obstructs a court's work or lessens the dignity of the court.

2. A willful disobeying of a judge's command or official court order.

THE CASE OF THE POLLUTING TOLL BOOTH

Federal and state statutes often provide private citizens and public agencies with authority to litigate against public agencies concerning public or private nuisances. Private citizens may enforce nuisance actions under the Clean Air Act, Clean Water Act, and a variety of other environmental-protection statutes. However, there are certain precise statutory requirements to follow in order to proceed with these actions. This case clearly demonstrates the difficulties a pro se litigant can encounter in handling complex legal matters.

UNITED STATES ENVIRONMENTAL PROTECTION AGENCY
v.
THE PORT AUTHORITY OF NEW YORK AND NEW JERSEY, et al.,
United States District Court, S.D. New York
162 F. Supp. 2d 173 (S.D.N.Y. 2001)
March 30, 2001

Plaintiffs Kevin McKeown ("McKeown") and his organization No More Tolls (collectively "plaintiffs") commenced this *pro se* citizen's suit against defendants, state authorities and officials responsible for operating toll roads, bridges and tunnels in New York, New Jersey, Delaware and Maryland, alleging that they operate and maintain toll booth facilities in violation of the Clean Air Act, ("CAA"), the Clean Water Act ("CWA"), the Resource Conservation and Recovery Act ("RCRA"), Occupational Safety and Health Administration ("OSHA") regulations, Federal Highway Administration regulations, nuisance law, and civil rights law.

Plaintiff No More Tolls is a public interest organization in Washington D.C. It is "dedicated to the protection and enhancement of the environment of the United States. . . . [I]t supports effective enforcement of Federal and State CAA, CWA, RCRA, and other Federal and State laws." Plaintiff McKeown is the Executive Director of No More Tolls.

Defendants are state authorities and their directors who are responsible for the administration of public transportation including the operation of toll booths in New York (the "New York defendants"), New Jersey (the "New Jersey defendants"), Delaware (the "Delaware defendants") and Maryland (the "Maryland defendants").

On November 29, 1999, plaintiffs sent defendants a Notice of Intent to Sue. The Notice of Intent to Sue states that plaintiffs believe defendants are violating the CAA, CWA and RCRA by operating toll booths.

On February 3, 2000, plaintiffs filed this action by order to show cause, requesting a temporary restraining order and a preliminary injunction.

The CAA, CWA and RCRA all permit a citizen to bring a civil action to enforce those statutes on their own behalf. . . . Moreover, McKeown and No More Tolls have not offered any reason why the EPA and Browner are necessary parties. ("The [CAA] citizen suit provision contemplates actions against the Administrator where he fails to perform a nondiscretionary act. Alternatively, the citizen, after giving 60 days notice to the Administrator, can proceed directly against the violator. When the plaintiff elects this later course, the Administrator has the right to intervene in the suit, but he is not required to be a participant in such litigation and his absence does not render the action infirm.")

Accordingly, defendants' motions to strike the EPA and Browner from the amended complaint are granted.

Defendants argue that the complaint should be dismissed for lack of standing because plaintiffs have not alleged an injury in-fact, or alternatively, that any alleged injury is not redressable by this action.

An organization such as No More Tolls may have standing to "seek judicial relief from injury to itself and to vindicate whatever rights and immunities the association itself may enjoy." No More Tolls, however, has not asserted injury to itself.

The only known member of No More Tolls is McKeown. The only personalized injuries alleged in the amended complaint are that McKeown "has sustained damages as a result of the operation of toll

(continues)

booths" and that "[d]efendant[s'] operation of toll booths damage the business, property and health of the [p]laintiff" in violation of antitrust laws. Neither of those allegations is concrete or particularized, nor do they constitute a "distinct and palpable injury."

Further, even if plaintiffs could establish that they have standing to sue, they failed to comply with the mandatory notice requirement with respect to the Maryland and New Jersey defendants.

Accordingly, the New Jersey defendants' motion to dismiss plaintiffs' CAA, CWA and RCRA claims for failure to comply with the mandatory notice provisions pursuant to those statutes is granted.

Even if plaintiffs had complied with the notice requirements, venue is improper as to the Maryland, New Jersey and Delaware defendants. Moreover, plaintiffs have failed to state a claim upon which relief can be granted.

The CAA was implemented to prevent and control air pollution by providing "[f]ederal financial assistance and leadership . . . for the development of cooperative Federal, State, regional, and local programs to prevent and control air pollution."

Plaintiffs claim that defendants have violated the CAA by slowing "vehicular movement which unnecessarily increases toxic tailpipe emissions." However, the complaint does not identify any violations of specific emissions standards, or limitations under the CAA or legally enforceable strategies or commitments that the defendants made under a current SIP.

Plaintiffs also claim that toll booths are major sources of hazardous air pollutants under 42 U.S.C. The CAA defines a "major source" as a "stationary source that emits or has the potential to emit considering controls, in the aggregate 10 tons per year or more of any hazardous air pollutant or 25 tons per year or more of any combination of hazardous air pollutants. . ." (42 U.S.C. § 7412(a)(1)). A stationary source is defined as "any building, structure, facility, or installation which emits or may emit any air pollutant," (42 U.S.C. § 7411(a)(3)).

Plaintiffs do not allege that toll booths emit or have the potential to emit air pollutants. They claim that motor vehicles emit the air pollutants. Motor vehicles, however, are specifically excluded from the definition of stationary source.

Accordingly, defendants' motions to dismiss plaintiffs' CAA claims for failure to state a claim are granted.

Citizen suits under the CWA are permitted only to enforce "an effluent standard or limitation" or "an order issued by the [EPA] Administrator or a State with respect to such a standard or limitation" (33 U.S.C. § 1365(a)). Effluent standards and limitations are administratively established regulations of particular types of dischargers on the amounts of pollutants that may be discharged.

Plaintiffs assert that "[t]oll booth operators violate 'an effluent standard or limitation' under . . . 33 U.S.C. [§] 1365(a)(1)(A) because of illegal and unpermitted discharges of leachate from toll booth locations," that "[d]efendants violate CWA Section 311 by continuing to cause the diminution of water quality of the surface and subterranean waters by release of pollutants into the surface waters and ground waters under and adjacent to toll booth areas."

Plaintiffs' sweeping allegations do not charge defendants with violating any effluent standards or limitations.

Moreover, the "leachate" that plaintiffs claim is released from toll booths, including carbon monoxide, nitrogen oxide, and sulfur, are air emissions and not water pollutants, covered by CWA.

* * *

For all of the above stated reasons, defendants' motions to dismiss plaintiffs' CWA claims are granted.

CASE QUESTIONS

1. What were the fatal flaws in the plaintiffs' claim?
2. Do the precise requirements of the environmental statutes interfere with their intent?

Equitable Remedies	Money Damages
Abatement (permanent prohibition against nuisance activity)	Money damages may be awarded if abatement would put unreasonable economic burdens on the defendant
Temporary injunctions (forbidding nuisance activity during litigation process)	
Permanent injunctions (used for abatement)	

TABLE 12-3
Remedies for Nuisances

Review of Hypotheticals

Review the hypotheticals from the previous sections of this chapter. Consider which remedies are suitable in each case. In class or study groups, discuss whether money damages are an appropriate alternative to abatement. Table 12-3 restates the remedies available in nuisance lawsuits.

SURVIVAL STATUTES AND WRONGFUL DEATH STATUTES

Under common law, when a plaintiff died, his or her tort action also died, and the spouse and children would lose all right to recovery. To avoid this harsh result, all states have passed survival statutes. Also under common law, a defendant could injure a person and still be liable; however, if the defendant died, then there would be no recovery at all. **Survival statutes** allow recovery to families of persons killed by tortious actions. In this way the injured party's claim survives his or her death. If successful, damages are awarded to the decedent's estate. This is contrasted with **wrongful death statutes,** which give the surviving family members of a deceased tort victim a cause of action against the tortfeasor whose negligence or intentional torts resulted in the victim's death.

survival statute | A state law that allows a lawsuit to be brought by a relative for a person who has just died. The lawsuit is based on the cause of action the dead person would have had.

wrongful death statute | Statute that allows a lawsuit to be brought by the dependents of a dead person against the person who caused the death. Damages will be given to compensate the dependents for their loss, if the killing was negligent or willful.

Typical Facts in Wrongful Death Cases

The factual pattern in wrongful death actions may be summarized as follows: (1) a tortfeasor commits a tort against the victim; (2) the victim dies as a result of the tortfeasor's actions; (3) the victim's spouse, children, estate, or person who relied on the deceased person for economic support, or all of them, sue the tortfeasor for wrongfully causing the victim's death.

Plaintiffs in Wrongful Death Actions

Under wrongful death statutes, the surviving family members, usually the victim's spouse or children, become the plaintiffs. However, some statutes allow the victim's parents or siblings to become plaintiffs. The victim's estate may also be permitted to sue the defendant for wrongful death damages under some statutes. Some states have a limit on damages for wrongful death.

Damages

consortium | The rights and duties resulting from marriage. They include companionship, love, affection, assistance, cooperation, and sexual relations.

Wrongful death statutes usually define the types of damages that plaintiffs may recover against defendants. These damages include lost lifetime earnings potential and loss of **consortium.**

PRACTICAL APPLICATION

Be sure to check the precise wording of the wrongful death statute in your jurisdiction. In some states, such as California, the statute of limitations for wrongful death runs from the date of death, not the date of the accident.

Lost Lifetime Earnings Potential. A tort victim's surviving family members may recover damages for the lost income that the victim would likely have earned had he or she not been killed by the tortfeasor. Wrongful death statutes usually define these damages in terms of the decedent's lost earnings potential based upon income at the time of death. This income base is projected over time. The future time period used is normally the victim's life expectancy, which is calculated from insurance actuarial tables. The projected earnings potential is usually adjusted for the victim's projected living expenses, had he or she survived. An economist is usually hired as an expert witness to introduce this evidence at trial.

loss of consortium | The loss of one or more of a spouse's services.

Loss of Consortium. Wrongful death statutes often permit a tort victim's surviving family to recover damages for the lost love and companionship of the decedent. This is similar to pain and suffering damages. However, many statutes do not allow recovery of such damages. Wrongful death statutes (or courts interpreting them) often label this type of damages **loss of consortium.** Many statutes define *consortium* as both economic and intangible benefits lost to a victim's surviving family because of the victim's death. The intangible elements could include lost love, companionship, and even the survivors' mental anguish upon losing a loved one.

Defenses

In wrongful death actions, the tortfeasor may use any defense applicable to the specific tort that produced the victim's injury. For example, suppose the victim had been contributorily or comparatively negligent, or assumed the risk of the defendant's actions that killed the victim. Suppose the tortfeasor killed the victim while acting in self-defense or defense of others. The tortfeasor may escape liability for wrongfully causing the victim's death if any of the suitable tort defenses apply in the case. Defenses are available in a wrongful death action just as if the victim were still alive and, as plaintiff, were suing the defendant.

A CASE OF "DEATH-AFTER-LITIGATION"

For the most part, law is studied subject by subject, one issue at a time. As the following case illustrates, in practice, when a case reaches the courtroom, there might be several different legal subjects with several different issues before the court. In this matter, the court was confronted with issues ranging from class action, negligence, trust and estates, to civil procedure. Here, the personal representative for plaintiff Della Mae Butler seeks to amend the personal injury complaint and substitute parties after the death of the injured plaintiff. The lower court denied this request, requiring that the action be dismissed and a new complaint filed for wrongful death. At stake is the deceased's benefit of class-action status, where issues of liability had already been litigated.

Wesley SMITH, Jr., as Personal Representative of the Estate of Della Mae Butler, Deceased, Appellant,

v.

R.J. REYNOLDS TOBACCO CO.; Philip Morris U.S.A., Inc.; Lorillard Tobacco Co.; Lorillard, Inc.; Liggett Group, et al., Appellees

District Court of Appeal of Florida, Second District
2012 WL 6216756
December 14, 2012

Della Mae Butler was the plaintiff in a personal injury action against several tobacco companies and industry groups. Following her death, the personal representative of Butler's estate filed a motion for substitution of party and for amendment of the complaint to state a wrongful death claim. The circuit court denied the motion and dismissed the case. We reverse.

Butler was pursuing an individual "*Engle* claim" for personal injury caused by smoking-related illness. In *Engle v. Liggett Group, Inc.*, 945 So.2d 1246, 1256 (Fla.2006), the Florida Supreme Court reviewed a class action lawsuit by cigarette smokers and their survivors against tobacco companies and

industry groups. The suit had been prosecuted in phases. Phase I consisted of a year-long trial on issues of liability and punitive damages, in which the jury considered common issues related to the defendants' conduct and to the general health effects of smoking.

The Supreme Court ruled that most of the findings from Phase I, which were in favor of the smokers and adverse to the tobacco companies, would be res judicata in future individual actions by members of the now decertified class. But the court also held that in order to obtain the benefit of the Phase I findings, former class members had to file their individual suits within one year of the mandate in *Engle*. According to the Supreme Court's online docket, the mandate issued on January 1, 2007. www.floridasupremecourt .org (docket search for case no. SC03–1856).

Butler filed suit alleging that she was a Florida member of the *Engle* class entitled to pursue a personal injury action against the *Engle* defendants. Butler alleged that she smoked, and was addicted to, cigarettes by one or more of the defendants and that as a result she suffered smoking-related medical conditions including chronic obstructive pulmonary disease (COPD) and emphysema. In her five-count

(continues)

amended complaint, Butler alleged claims for strict liability, fraud by concealment, conspiracy to commit fraud by concealment, negligence, and punitive damages. Butler's suit was filed on December 5, 2007, within one year of the Supreme Court's mandate in *Engle*. According to a motion for substitution of party for leave to file an amended complaint, Butler died on April 29, 2009. The proposed amended complaint alleged that Butler died from COPD that was caused by smoking. The circuit court denied the motion for substitution and leave to amend and dismissed the action.

Under the Wrongful Death Act, "[w]hen a personal injury to the decedent results in death, no action for the personal injury shall survive, and any such action pending at the time of death shall abate." § 768.20, Fla. Stat. (2008). The relevant Florida Rule of Civil Procedure provides that "[i]f a party dies and the claim is not thereby extinguished, the court may order substitution of the proper parties." Fla. R. Civ. P. 1.260(a)(1). Here, by denying the motion to substitute the personal representative for the deceased plaintiff, the circuit court essentially ruled that *abate* in the Wrongful Death Act equates with *extinguish* in the civil procedure rules. In reaching this conclusion, the court overlooked both the remedial nature of the Wrongful Death Act and the liberal spirit underlying the rules of civil procedure.

When enacting the Wrongful Death Act, the legislature expressly declared its intention that the act was to be interpreted so as to accomplish its remedial purpose: "It is the public policy of the state to shift the losses resulting when wrongful death occurs from the survivors of the decedent to the wrongdoer."

Applying a liberal construction to the word *abate*, we conclude that *stay* is a more appropriate synonym than *extinguish*. A personal injury action will not survive if the injury resulted in the plaintiff's death, as in this case, but a stay will allow time for the substitution of a party and the filing of an amended or supplemental pleading. This is consistent with the direction of rule 1.190(a) that leave to amend "shall be given freely when justice so requires."

Today we expressly hold that substitution and amendment are consistent with the law in Florida. Allowing the substitution of parties and amendment of the complaint will facilitate "the just, speedy, and inexpensive determination" of the action, as directed by rule 1.010. And it will further the stated public policy of the Wrongful Death Act, particularly in this case. Furthermore, we find this interpretation consistent with rule 1.260(a)(1), which allows the court to order substitution "if a party dies and the claim is not thereby extinguished." In this regard, we note that the damages for a plaintiff's pain and suffering may be extinguished by the plaintiff's death. But other elements of damages—like medical expenses—are not extinguished. They remain as elements of damages for the personal representative or survivors to collect. Thus it cannot be said that the claim, in its entirety, is extinguished.

Our decision, however, conflicts with the conclusion reached by the Third District in *Capone v. Philip Morris U.S.A. Inc.*, 56 So.3d 34 (Fla. 3d DCA 2010), which held that the personal injury complaint could not be amended to state a wrongful death claim. *Capone* stated that filing a separate suit is "required" under the Wrongful Death Act, but it says nothing about pleading requirements. We see nothing in this section that *requires* the filing of a new complaint and forecloses the amendment of an existing complaint.

The personal representative argues that requiring the filing of a new action for wrongful death would result in the loss of the *Engle* findings. The tobacco companies respond by saying that they would not defend in this case based on the estate's failure to file suit within the one-year time limit for *Engle* cases. But as the Supreme Court noted, there were approximately 700,000 class members in *Engle*. 945 So.2d at 1258. And according to *Starling*, "the *Engle* Smokers, the original plaintiffs in these actions, were dying at a fairly constant rate." A ruling on this issue will affect a significant number of the *Engle* cases with no guarantee that the tobacco companies in those other cases will waive the timeliness of the wrongful death action.

Furthermore, this issue affects more than just the *Engle* cases. It has been noted that the transition from a personal injury claim to a wrongful death claim is particularly sensitive in medical malpractice cases. The general statute of limitations for a wrongful death claim is two years from the date of death. But the two-year statute of limitations for a medical malpractice action generally runs from the date the malpractice should have been discovered, even if the malpractice is alleged in a wrongful death action. The authors reported that "it appears courts do permit amendments to assert wrongful death and substitute personal representatives for deceased plaintiffs in such cases."

We reverse the order dismissing the case. On remand the circuit court shall permit the substitution of the personal representative for the deceased plaintiff and the amendment of the complaint to state a wrongful death claim. We certify that our decision conflicts with the decisions of the Third District in *Capone v. Philip Morris U.S.A. Inc.*, 56 So.3d 34 (Fla. 3d DCA 2010), *jurisdiction accepted*, 75 So.3d 1243 (Fla.2011), and *Ruble v. Rinker Material Corp.*, 59 So.3d 137 (Fla. 3d DCA 2011), *jurisdiction accepted*, 75 So.3d 1245 (Fla.2011).

Reversed; remanded with directions; conflict certified.

CASE QUESTIONS

1. Why did the appellate court allow the deceased's plaintiff's personal representative to amend the complaint rather than starting a new action?
2. What were the benefits of being part of the "Engle class"?

The following example illustrates how a wrongful death action might arise under a hypothetical statute.

HYPOTHETICAL

Yee Wen owns a cement manufacturing plant. One of her employees, Evan, drives a cement truck. One of Yee Wen's customers is Sally, who was having a swimming pool installed at her home. Evan came to pour cement for the pool. Sally's husband, Abraham, stood beneath the truck inside the excavated pool area. Without first checking to see if anyone was in the way, Evan dumped the entire truckload of cement on top of Abraham, who suffocated and died. Assume that this jurisdiction's wrongful death statute permits family survivors to sue tortfeasors for "negligently, wantonly, or intentionally" causing a victim's death. What is the likely result?

Sally could sue Evan (and, by respondeat superior, Evan's employer, Yee Wen) for causing the wrongful death of her husband, Abraham. Evan was negligent in pouring the cement without first seeing if anyone was inside the dangerous dumping area. Because Abraham died, Sally has a cause of action for wrongful death.

TABLE 12-4

Elements of Wrongful
Death Statutes

Tortfeasor commits tort against victim, causing victim's death
Victim's surviving spouse and children (or victim's estate) may sue tortfeasor to recover damages under wrongful death statute
Most statutes or courts allow damages for victim's lost lifetime earnings potential and for loss of consortium
Same tort defenses apply in wrongful death actions, depending upon the specific tort the tortfeasor committed against deceased victim

Copyright © 2015 Cengage Learning®.

The family survivors' specific legal rights are entirely dependent upon the language of each wrongful death statute. It is important to become familiar with the wrongful death statutes in one's state, if one intends to work with plaintiffs for this special tort action. Table 12-4 summarizes the standard ingredients of wrongful death statutes.

▌ WRONGFUL BIRTH

wrongful birth | The birth of a child having serious defects that results from a doctor's failure to provide proper information (to advise, diagnose, or test properly) to the child's parents.

Wrongful birth actions are lawsuits for the wrongful birth of a child. The plaintiffs are usually the surprised parents, and the defendant is normally the genetic counselor who missed or failed to reveal a genetic problem. Wrongful birth, then, can be considered another form of medical malpractice, which is a type of negligence.

Typical Fact Pattern: Genetic Counseling Gone Awry

The typical situation involving unwanted pregnancy is as follows: A couple visits a physician and relies on the physician's expertise in making the decision to conceive a child or continue with a pregnancy.

The plaintiffs (parents) then sue the physician for the unwanted birth of a child born with birth defects or other congenital problems. The parents would seek to be reimbursed for the added expenses of raising a severely disabled child. This may occur when a doctor assures a couple that an unborn child will not be harmed by a disease the mother contracted during pregnancy, but when born, the child does in fact have substantial birth defects caused by the mother's infection. Another such situation involves a child who is born with genetic defects that a doctor assured the parents were not present or inheritable.

Damages. The parents may sue to recover for emotional distress, the cost of prenatal care and delivery, and expenses associated with the child's impairment.

Table 12-5 lists the elements of wrongful birth.

	TABLE 12-5
Usually a form of medical malpractice in which a physician has negligently counseled parents concerning genetic issues	Elements of Wrongful Birth Actions
May include cases involving children born with birth defects	
Damages include parents' medical expenses for unwanted birth and, in some jurisdictions, the costs of raising the child	

Wrongful Life: The New Tort

A **wrongful life action** is typically an action by or on behalf of an unwanted child who is impaired. The child is seeking damages. In essence, the child is saying that he or she would have been better off not to have been born, rather than to be born with pain or suffering from particular impairments. This new tort has received mixed reviews from appellate courts across the United States. Some jurisdictions reject the tort altogether, others permit it in circumstances involving birth deformities, and still others allow the action even for healthy but unwanted children when sterilization has failed. Wrongful life litigation demonstrates the ingenuity of attorneys and legal scholars searching for new sources of recovery for harmed plaintiffs.

wrongful life | An action brought by a child, claiming that he or she would have been better off not to have been born, rather than to be born with an impairment.

Damages. The child seeks (and sometimes recovers) damages from the responsible physician(s) for the difference in value of an impaired life versus an unimpaired life. Clearly, this is very difficult to calculate and is only allowed in a minority of states.

Wrongful life and birth cases often carry powerful emotional implications, but the temptation to become lost in value judgments must be resisted. Once again, focusing upon the legal elements carries the reader to the appropriate conclusions, as the following example demonstrates.

THE CASE OF THE ABSENCE OF A PHYSICIAN/PATIENT DUTY

A cause of action for wrongful life is brought on behalf of an injured child against his mother's former obstetrician. The obstetrician argues that he owed no duty of care to a child not yet in existence when he failed to properly document that in the mother's first delivery, her first child received trauma from birth. The court refuses to find a cause of action in Florida for wrongful life and decides the case on medical malpractice grounds. (The mother has a separate related action for wrongful birth that is not a part of this action.)

(continues)

Maria TORRES, as parent and natural guardian of Luis Torres, a minor child, Appellant,

v.

SARASOTA COUNTY PUBLIC HOSPITAL BOARD, d/b/a Sarasota Memorial Hospital; Gary W. Easterling, M.D.; Gary W. Easterling, M.D., P.A.; and Sarasota County Health Department, Appellees

District Court of Appeal of Florida, Second District

No. 2D04-1634

April 13, 2007

During delivery, Luis sustained a brachial plexus injury. The complaint alleges that Dr. Sullivan was negligent because he failed to obtain a complete obstetrical history from Mrs. Torres.

Luis's complaint alleges that the hospital is vicariously liable for Dr. Sullivan's negligence and the negligence of the nurse who assisted him in obtaining Mrs. Torres's history.

During her pregnancy with Luis and during an earlier pregnancy, Mrs. Torres received prenatal care from the Department of Health. The allegations of negligence against the department pertain in one way or another to the medical records created and kept by the department during those pregnancies.

A year before Luis was born, Dr. Easterling delivered Luis's sister, Isaura. The complaint alleges that the standard of care applicable to Dr. Easterling required him to document in Mrs. Torres's medical records Isaura's condition at birth and the complications Mrs. Torres experienced during labor and delivery. It also alleges that he was obligated to tell Mrs. Torres that Isaura had suffered an Erb's Palsy because of birth trauma and that Mrs. Torres should provide this information to future health care providers. The complaint alleges that Dr. Easterling failed to do any of these things and that had he done them, Dr. Sullivan or a reasonable obstetrician under the same circumstances would have performed a Caesarean section.

We write only to discuss the question of whether Dr. Easterling owed a duty to Luis.

Dr. Easterling argues that the summary judgment in his favor was proper because he did not owe a duty of care to Luis. Citing *Pate v. Threlkel*, Dr. Easterling contends that Luis was not his patient and "before a physician can be found to owe a legal duty of care to a third party not under the care of that physician, it must be shown that the physician is aware of the existence of the third party." Dr. Easterling contends that he could not have been aware of Luis's existence because Luis did not exist at the time of his alleged negligence. Dr. Easterling also argues that "the concept of legal duty is based upon whether the defendant's actions place the plaintiff within a zone of danger" and that the question of duty "presupposes the actual existence of the plaintiff as a member of society capable of being injured as the result of the defendant's actions."

In medical malpractice actions, as in other negligence actions, a plaintiff must establish a duty owed to the plaintiff by the defendant, a breach of that duty by allowing conduct to fall below the applicable standard of care, and an injury proximately caused by the defendant's breach of duty. We agree that no physician/patient relationship existed between Luis and Dr. Easterling.

The absence of a physician/patient relationship between Luis and Dr. Easterling is not necessarily fatal to his claim, however, because Florida has extended a physician's duty to third parties in limited circumstances. The question of whether a child has a medical malpractice cause of action for injuries allegedly caused by the negligence of a physician when that negligence occurs before the child is conceived appears to be one of first impression in Florida.

Courts have dubbed the type of claim Luis asserts against Dr. Easterling a "preconception tort." *See, e.g., Grover v. Eli Lilly & Co.* Preconception tort actions are generally defined as actions in which the plaintiff is seeking redress for injuries caused by negligent conduct that occurred before the plaintiff's conception. A claim for "wrongful life" is a preconception tort. A "wrongful life" claim is a malpractice action in which the plaintiff child alleges that if the defendant physician had not been negligent in providing medical advice or treatment to the plaintiff's parents, the plaintiff would not have been born. Most courts that have considered the issue have refused to recognize such an action because of the nature of the "right" invaded-the right not to be born—and the nature of the damages.

The normal measure of damages in tort actions is compensatory. Damages are measured by comparing the condition plaintiff would have been in, had the defendants not been negligent, with plaintiff's impaired condition as a result of the negligence. The infant plaintiff would have us measure the difference between his life with defects against the utter void of nonexistence, but it is impossible to make such a determination. This court cannot weigh the value of life with impairments against the nonexistence of life itself. By asserting that he should not have been born, the infant plaintiff makes it logically impossible for a court to measure his alleged damages because of the impossibility of making the comparison required by compensatory remedies.

The claim Luis asserts is not a claim for "wrongful life," and the damages he seeks are those typically sought in a claim for medical malpractice. Instead of adopting a blanket no-duty rule based on the timing of the physician's alleged negligence. We believe it is appropriate to assess the viability of Luis's claim as we would any other medical malpractice claim brought against a physician by someone other than a patient.

In this case, the parties' experts on the standard of care agreed that it required Dr. Easterling to document Isaura's difficult delivery and the injury she sustained as a result. The information is "useful to those who subsequently care for and provide" obstetrical care for the patient. In this case, the standard of care is premised on the possibility that in the future the patient will have another child. Applying the rationale of *Pate* to this case, we conclude that Dr. Easterling's duty extended to Luis.

CASE QUESTIONS
1. If Dr. Easterling had taken a complete obstetrical history from Ms. Torres, would this have changed the outcome of Luis's birth?
2. Did the court consider this a wrongful life claim?

HYPOTHETICAL

Paul and Colleen Jonson visited Dr. Fritz Halpner, M.D., to see if Paul could get a vasectomy. Paul was concerned that he could transmit a genetic disease to his unborn child. Several members of Paul's family had been afflicted with the congenital disease. Dr. Halpner performed the sterilization surgery. Three months later, the Johnsons were advised that Paul's post-operative semen sample was free of sperm. A few months thereafter, Colleen discovered that she was pregnant. Paul's operation had not remained effective. The Jonsons refused abortion on religious grounds. The Jonsons' baby daughter was born with a deformity resulting from the genetic disease transmitted by Paul. The Jonsons sued Dr. Halpner for medical malpractice, specifically alleging wrongful life.

Dr. Halpner's vasectomy operation did not prevent Colleen from becoming pregnant. Worse yet, the Jonson child was afflicted with congenital deformities due to faulty genes carried in Paul's sperm. This child would not have been born in this unfortunate condition but for the doctor's negligence in performing the faulty operation. The Jonsons would appear to have a valid claim against Dr. Halpner for the tort of wrongful life.

▌ SUMMARY

A private nuisance is an unreasonable and substantial interference with another person's use and enjoyment of his or her land. Whether a nuisance activity is unreasonable and substantial depends upon its degree of offensiveness. The reasonable person standard is applied to test offensiveness and is based upon the community standard for persons living in the vicinity of the nuisance activity. Private nuisances often involve physical effects on the land, such as vibrations, pollution, and flooding. Private nuisance may also produce health hazards, such as poison gases, hazardous wastes, smoke, or dust, or effects offending the plaintiffs' sensibilities, such as odors or even incessant telephone calling. Private nuisances also include unwanted associations with neighboring uses, such as prostitution houses or gambling emporiums. "Coming to the nuisance" is the primary defense in private nuisance actions.

Public nuisances are activities that harm the public at large rather than a single individual. These nuisances unreasonably and substantially interfere with the public's use and enjoyment of legal rights common to the public. Governmental agencies litigate against public nuisance tortfeasors to enforce the general public's legal rights. State and local governments have the authority to litigate public nuisances under the police powers of the states. Public nuisances often involve so-called immoral activities, such as gambling, prostitution, distribution of sexually explicit materials, or the sale of alcohol. Others include permitting noxious weeds to grow on one's property, carelessly disposing of toxic substances, or violating public health laws. Often, nuisances may be both private and public. These are called mixed nuisances. Nuisances per se are activities that violate statutes or ordinances. Public nuisances are often per se nuisances. "Coming to the nuisance" is usually not a defense in public nuisance cases.

Equitable remedies are usually awarded in nuisance litigation instead of money damages. Money damages are sometimes given when equitable remedies would be excessively harsh to the defendant. The relief most often granted involves injunctions. In injunctions, the court orders the defendant to act or to cease and desist the nuisance activity. Permanent injunctions forbid the activity forever. Temporary injunctions, such as temporary restraining orders (TROs), merely halt the defendant's nuisance activity until the court can conduct hearings or a trial on the merits. Defendants who disregard injunctions may find themselves in contempt of court, for which they can be fined or imprisoned.

Survival statutes allow an injured party's claim to survive his or her death. The victim's estate pursues this action. Wrongful death statutes provide surviving family members of a deceased tort victim with the right to sue the tortfeasor for wrongfully causing the victim's death. The tortfeasor's wrong may include negligence or intentional torts. Wrongful death damages usually consist of the victim's lost lifetime earnings potential and loss of consortium. Consortium includes the lost love and companionship between the dead victim and his or her family. The tortfeasor may use any defenses applicable for the alleged tort that caused the wrongful death. If the tortfeasor were accused of negligently causing the victim's death, then negligence defenses would apply. If the tortfeasor's intentional tort killed the victim, then intentional tort defenses would apply.

Wrongful birth actions are lawsuits for the wrongful birth of a child. Usually, parents sue a physician for malpractice for negligently counseling them about genetic issues and concerns. Wrongful life cases often involve actions brought by children born with birth defects. The tort has developed within the past quarter-century. Court reactions to the tort have been mixed. Some jurisdictions reject the tort altogether, whereas others embrace it in whole or in part.

The next chapter covers tort immunities. These are defenses that completely shield a defendant from tort liability.

KEY TERMS

abatement	mandamus	remedy
coming to the nuisance defense	mixed nuisance	sensibilities
consortium	nuisance	survival statute
contempt	nuisance per se	temporary restraining order (TRO)
damages	permanent injunction	wrongful birth
equitable remedy	police power	wrongful death statute
injunction	private nuisance	wrongful life
loss of consortium	public nuisance	

PROBLEMS

In the following hypotheticals, identify the relevant cause(s) of action, suitable defense(s) (if any), and appropriate remedies.

1. Pestro Chemical Corporation manufactures *Dredroxiphine*, a poison used in insect sprays. A railway line delivers tanker cars full of the chemical to be unloaded into the plant. On breezy days, the fumes from the unloading stations drift across the highway onto Jorge's farm. The odors are pungent and are especially irritating to the sinuses. When Jorge and his family work outside on windy days, they are constantly besieged by the poison's smell. Their eyes water excessively, their noses run, and they are gripped by sneezing fits. Other farmers in the area have complained of similar symptoms. Visits to the family physician revealed that Jorge has absorbed minute amounts of the chemical in his lungs and through his skin. Medical studies link exposure to the chemical with several forms of cancer. Jorge has farmed on his property since 2004. Pestro constructed its plant in 2012.

2. Wowser's Video Palace rents X-rated videotaped movies. A local ordinance restricts rental of such materials to persons over the age of 18 years. Wowser's employees never check customer identifications, however, and often rent X-rated movies to underage individuals. Citizens Rallying Against Pornography, a local citizen's group, has asked the county prosecutor to take action against Wowser's. The prosecutor has asked you to summarize the appropriate cause(s) of action in a short paragraph.

3. Quintin and Ursella Xenopher were driving along Interstate 928 on the beltway around the city. Terri was driving while intoxicated. Her blood alcohol level was .214, and a state criminal statute provides that .10 is legally drunk. A related state civil statute provides injured parties with a tort cause of action against a tortfeasor who causes injuries while violating criminal statutes. Terri's automobile collided with the Xenopher's vehicle, killing Quintin. Ursella suffered permanent disability in her left leg.

4. Dr. Sarah Davis, M.D., performed a tubal ligation upon Jennifer Colfield to prevent impregnation. Jennifer was a single, 24-year-old woman who had a sexual relationship with her boyfriend, Scott. Six months after her operation, Jennifer discovered that she was pregnant. She could not afford the costs of raising a child, but she did not want to get an abortion. Scott refused to subsidize Jennifer's medical expenses or contribute to the child's upbringing. The local adoption agencies (managed by rigid-thinking administrators) refused to speak with Jennifer because she had a history of narcotic abuse. She did not consult with out-of-town adoption agencies, which would have been happy to assist her in placing the child in a foster home.

▌REVIEW QUESTIONS

1. Define private nuisance. Who are the parties to this litigation? What is unreasonable and substantial interference? How is it determined? What is the role of the community standard? What is use and enjoyment?

2. Name the common types of private nuisance. Can you provide hypotheticals to illustrate each? What is "coming to the nuisance"?

3. What is a public nuisance? How is it distinguishable from a private nuisance? Who is affected by a public nuisance? Who acts as plaintiff? What are some common examples of public nuisance? Does "coming to the nuisance" apply? What are common legal rights? What are mixed nuisances? What is a nuisance per se?

4. What remedies are used in nuisance cases? What about money damages? What is abatement? What are injunctions? Explain the difference between temporary and permanent injunctions. When is a TRO used? What is contempt?

5. What are wrongful death statutes? Who are the plaintiffs in wrongful death litigation? What types of torts can be involved? What damages are awarded? What defenses apply?

6. What is wrongful birth? What are the usual fact situations involving this special tort? What damages may be awarded? What is wrongful life?

▌HELPFUL WEBSITES

This chapter focuses on special tort actions. To learn more about special tort actions, the following sites can be accessed:

General Legal Sites

www.law.vill.edu
www.findlaw.com
www.law.cornell.edu
www.law.indiana.edu

Administrative Office of the United States Courts

www.uscourts.gov

Nuisances

www.nuisancelaw.com
www.law.harvard.edu

Legal Dictionary

www.lectlaw.com

Law Libraries

www.washlaw.edu

STUDENT COMPANION WEBSITE
For additional cases and study materials, please go to www.cengagebrain.com

Chapter 13

Tort Immunities

THE BIGGEST MISTAKES PARALEGALS MAKE AND HOW TO AVOID THEM

Who Gives a Toot?
(Yes, Incredibly, This Really Happened)

Trent was the longest tenured paralegal at the firm and he could do it all. But he was also the oldest and required heart valve surgery. Prior to surgery, a computerized tomography (CT) scan revealed a small mass above one kidney that had to be removed immediately. Flowers and cards were sent by many of us. As soon as Trent was out of recovery, he sent everyone in the office a lengthy nine-paragraph email from his tablet describing his surgery in graphic detail; some of it is reproduced as follows: "This morning I had the problem of getting rid of the air they put in my abdomen. Later I ate a bowl of bean soup and never played a note, not one! My wife asked,

(continues)

'Have you farted yet?' I got rid of some of the gas late in the day after walking a bit, and then also 'passed' some later. Thankfully that saved me from what could have been lethal, more bean soup they served at the evening meal. I wouldn't have stood a chance against that gas!" Suffice it to say that Trent's email continued with colorful details in several more paragraphs.

Lesson Learned: As happy as everyone was to learn of Trent's rapid recovery from what could have been life-threatening surgery, medical or personal information is best kept to a minimum when sending unfiltered emails to an entire office. Especially in cases like Trent's where the attempt at humor may have been pain-killer induced, it is best to leave the tablets alone in the recovery room.

▌ INTRODUCTION

immunity | An exemption from a legally imposed duty, freedom from a duty, or freedom from a penalty.

Up to now, something has been missing from our torts analysis. That something is tort **immunity**—an absolute defense against a plaintiff's tort claims. If the defendant successfully invokes an immunity defense, he or she cannot be held liable for any torts committed. It is the reverse of absolute liability. Tort immunities absolutely protect the defendant from tort liability. There are many types of tort immunity, but the most common include sovereign (governmental) immunity and legal infirmities such as infancy or insanity. Tort immunities are similar to **privileges,** and the terms are often used interchangeably.

privilege |

1. An advantage; a right to preferential treatment.

2. An exemption from a duty others like you must perform.

3. A special advantage, as opposed to a right; an advantage that can be taken away.

This chapter includes a discussion of

- ▶ Sovereign (governmental) immunity
- ▶ Public officials' immunity
- ▶ Young children's immunity
- ▶ Spousal/family immunity
- ▶ Workers' compensation (employers' immunity)
- ▶ Tort trends and tort reform

▌ SOVEREIGN, OR GOVERNMENTAL, IMMUNITY

Sovereign (governmental) immunity has a long and storied history throughout the years of tort law. To understand modern applications of this doctrine, one must trace its roots and development.

History

sovereign (governmental) immunity | The government's freedom from being sued. In many cases, the U.S. government has waived immunity in certain situations by a statute such as the Federal Tort Claims Act.

In the history of tort law, governments have held an enviable position. Until the twentieth century, governments were immune from liability for torts committed by their employees. This immunity was called **sovereign immunity** or, in modern times, **governmental immunity.** It stemmed from the ancient English (and Western European) legal tradition that a king could not be sued by his subjects unless he consented. Official tortfeasors thus enjoyed an enviable immunity from liability unless they agreed to be sued, which consent one would naturally not give if one had committed any torts.

Courts applied the legal maxim "The king can do no wrong." This maxim traces its origins to pre-Roman times when the emperor was considered divine and thus incapable of errors that the law could remedy.

Modern Applications

For centuries, sovereign immunity protected the Crown and all its subordinates. Later, English and American common law spoke of governmental bodies (and their employees) as enjoying sovereign immunity. The term *king* was replaced with *government* in the American system, because our sovereigns are elected officials serving as presidents, governors, mayors, legislators, or (at the state and local level) judges.

Beginning in the early twentieth century, American courts began to whittle away at the governmental immunity doctrine. Many state courts have abolished sovereign immunity as an absolute defense to governmental liability. Legislatures have enacted statutes, such as the Federal Tort Claims Act, that specifically authorize lawsuits against torts committed by governmental employees (for which governmental agencies could be responsible under respondeat superior).

Early-Twentieth-Century Cases.

Many courts found the absolute defense of sovereign immunity to be unreasonably harsh on the plaintiffs. To avoid the full force of the immunity, early in the twentieth century American courts began distinguishing the different types of governmental activities that were or were not exempt from tort liability. The result was two categories: governmental and proprietary. This is sometimes called the *governmental/proprietary distinction*.

Governmental Actions.

When governmental bodies perform certain public protection activities, such as providing fire, police, or ambulance services, they are considered to be undertaking **governmental functions.** Persons performing governmental functions are immune from tort liability, under the early-twentieth-century court decisions. Even if the fire, police, or ambulance departments committed torts against a citizen while performing their duties, the old case law would define these as governmental actions as immune from liability.

governmental function | An action performed for the general public good by a governmental agency, or by a private organization closely tied to the government. These functions are state actions.

Proprietary Actions.

Governmental bodies also perform certain business-like activities (usually associated with the private sector). These are defined as **proprietary actions** and do not carry immunity from tort liability. For example, a municipality may provide utility services to its residents, such as water, sewer, electric, or natural gas, but this activity more closely resembles a private business

proprietary actions | Certain business-like activities performed by governmental bodies that are usually associated with the private sector, and are not given immunity from tort liability.

enterprise than a public, governmental function. If the governmental agency providing such services committed torts, the government would be liable, and the immunity defense would not prevent liability.

Difficulty with the Governmental/Proprietary Distinction

Courts have struggled with the governmental/proprietary distinction for decades. What about cities that provide garbage collection? What about public parks? Are these governmental or proprietary functions? Courts often decide based upon whether a fee is assessed to users of these services. If a fee is charged, then the activity is considered proprietary. If not, then it is governmental. This may be called the **fee standard.**

Similar to the fee standard is the **pecuniary benefit test**. When governments provide services for profit, then the activities are proprietary. If governments offer services for the common public good, without economic benefit to the governmental units themselves, then the activities are governmental.

Modern Steps to Eliminate the Distinction

Within the past 20 years, many state courts have abolished the governmental/proprietary distinction and with it the defense of sovereign immunity. These courts now focus upon whether the governments committed any torts—just as courts would handle any other tort lawsuit. Many state legislatures and Congress have enacted statutes eliminating or restricting sovereign immunity to particular types of services, such as public parks or utilities.

Suits against States

Even though many courts have abolished sovereign immunity and allow tort suits, not all states permit all kinds of tort suits to be brought against them. The individual state can decide just what suits it will or will not allow. In fact, in some states there is a special court just for tort claims against the state. In New York, it is called the Court of Claims, and a notice of claim is required to bring the action. Arizona is another state where a notice of claim is required to bring an action.

Federal Tort Claims Act—Suits against the United States

The Federal Tort Claims Act (FTCA) of August 2, 1946, is a statute enacted by Congress allowing private parties to sue the United States in federal courts for most torts committed by persons acting on behalf of the United States. Suit is allowed for the negligent or wrongful acts or omissions of employees of the U.S. government occurring during the scope of their employment. Liability is limited to those instances in which a private person would be liable to the claimant, according to the laws of the place where the act occurred. Actions must first be presented to the appropriate federal agency where the alleged harm occurred.

---

fee standard | A test courts use in applying the governmental/proprietary distinction. If a governmental agency assesses a fee for an activity, the activity is considered proprietary; if not, it is considered governmental.

pecuniary benefit test | When the government provides services for money, then the activities are considered proprietary, and there is no immunity from tort liability.

The act does not apply and does not permit suit regarding conduct that is uniquely governmental, that is, that cannot be performed by a private individual. The FTCA exempts and does not permit suits for three major kinds of cases, even where a private person could have been liable for such suits under state law (Feres doctrine): (1) failure to perform discretionary functions that involve a degree of judgment or choice; (2) suits by the military for injuries sustained while in the service; and (3) suits for many intentional torts, such as liable, assault, battery, misrepresentation, false imprisonment, false arrest, and abuse of process. Suits for injuries caused by medical malpractice while in the military and suits by victims of atomic testing are also prohibited against the U.S. government under the FTCA.

THE CASE OF THE MISSING EGGS

Media stories surfaced that three internationally known doctors had taken eggs from women without consent and implanted them as embryos in other women. The doctors were ultimately criminally indicted, and there were more than 80 civil lawsuits filed. At least 70 women were involved, and 10 children were born from stolen eggs. As a result, California became the first state to enact legislation making it a crime to steal human eggs.

This case addresses tort issues from almost every chapter in this text. There are allegations of lack of consent (medical malpractice), conversion, intentional and negligent infliction of emotional distress, spoliation of evidence, breach of duty to defend, fraud, issues regarding agency standard for review, California's State Torts Claim Act, scope of employment, and governmental versus private acts.

Here, the court narrowed the case down to a single issue: scope of employment. For this issue, clarification of the relationship of the defendants is needed. The Regents of the University of California is a state agency, which was in charge of the state university that maintained the health center where one of the accused doctors, Dr. Stone, worked and also saw private patients. As is discussed in the next chapter, the proper naming of parties and understanding of their legal status is essential in the investigation of a tort case.

SERGIO C. STONE, Plaintiff and Respondent,
v.
THE REGENTS OF THE UNIVERSITY OF CALIFORNIA, Defendant and Appellant
Court of Appeal of California, Fourth Appellate District
December 16, 1999, decided
77 Cal. App. 4th 736, 92 Cal. Rptr. 2d 94

Stone is a physician, board certified in obstetrics and gynecology. From 1990 to 1995, he was a partner in the Center for Reproductive Health (CRH), along with two other infertility specialists, Ricardo Asch and Jose Balmaceda. The CRH's offices were on the University of California at Irvine (UCI) campus. The university provided the doctors with space, management and administrative services, and support staff, and charged patients an administrative fee to cover the cost of these services. The university also provided professional liability insurance for the faculty of the department of obstetrics and gynecology (which included Stone) "while working within the course and scope of their University employment," which it stated "includes the management of private patients in facilities which have been previously approved by the University . . . ."

In 1995, Susan and Wayne Clay sued Stone (along with Asch, Balmaceda, CRH, UCI, and the Regents).

(continues)

Susan Clay was a former CRH patient. The Clays alleged their eggs, sperm, and embryos were implanted in another woman without their knowledge or consent. The suit was brought after allegations of "egg stealing" and other improprieties at CRH surfaced, and after the Regents had completed two investigations into the charges and were in the midst of others.

In 1994, two UCI employees working at CRH had notified the university they believed improper activities were taking place in both medical and financial matters. The university appointed an outside clinical panel to investigate the medical allegations.

In March 1995, the clinical panel delivered its report. The report sustained two allegations implicating or involving Stone that are germane to this action. The more serious was the finding that egg stealing took place—human eggs were taken from one patient and implanted in another without the consent of the donor. However, among the three doctors, the panel was unable to say who did what. None of the physicians cooperated in the investigation. They refused to provide patient charts, records, or information about procedures for obtaining patient consents, and they declined to allow the panel to interview patients.

In May 1995, the Regents sued Stone, Asch, and Balmaceda to obtain the sought-after documents. Alleging the doctors removed documents from UCI offices to hinder the investigations, and Asch attempted to alter or modify some records, the complaint set out causes of action for conversion (of university records), replevin (of university records), destruction of documents and spoliation of evidence, among other things. The record does not reveal the outcome of this litigation.

At about the same time, the Clays notified Stone they intended to sue for professional negligence. The Clays sued in September 1995, alleging negligence, fraud (based on the representation the eggs/sperm/embryos would only be implanted in Susan Clay), conversion (of the eggs/sperm/embryos), intentional and negligent infliction of emotional distress, battery (taking Susan Clay's eggs for implantation in another without her consent), spoliation of evidence (alteration and destruction of embryo logs, medical records and genetic material), and a conspiracy to take and use the Clays' genetic material in other women for the purpose of increasing CRH's success rate. The complaint did not specify who did what, with the exception that alleged the Regents' failure to adequately supervise. Nor did it allege what Stone's role was in the Clays' treatment.

Stone wrote to the Regents on May 25, 1995 requesting a defense. The Regents replied they would defend Stone in the anticipated Clay suit but reserved the right to "withdraw that defense at any time."

The Regents refused to defend Stone. John F. Lundberg, deputy general counsel, took the position the conduct alleged was outside the scope of employment, and it was intentional and fraudulent. The trial judge ruled the Regents acted arbitrarily in refusing to defend Stone.

The Regents successfully moved for reconsideration.

The Regents' argument is that they did not abuse their discretion in refusing to defend Stone. We agree.

Stone petitioned for a writ of ordinary mandate under Code of Civil Procedure section 1085. Ordinary mandate is used to review an adjudicatory decision when an agency is not required to hold an evidentiary hearing. The scope of review is limited, out of deference to the agency's authority and presumed expertise: "The court may not reweigh the evidence or substitute its judgment for that of the agency. . . . 'A court will uphold the agency action unless the action is arbitrary, capricious, or lacking in evidentiary support.'"

Under Government Code section 995.2(a), the Regents could refuse to provide Stone with a defense if they determined any one of the three excluding situations existed: conduct outside the scope of employment; conduct involving actual fraud, corruption or malice; or a conflict of interest. They had to reach a decision quickly, because section 995.2(b) required the Regents to respond to Stone's written request for a defense within 20 days, and give their reasons if he was turned down.

Section 995.2 is part of the California Tort Claims Act, which provides that in the usual civil case brought against a public employee, a public entity must provide a defense to the employee and pay any claim or judgment against him. Where the public entity refuses to defend, the employee can seek a writ of mandate, as Stone did.

On the record before us, we conclude there was substantial evidence to support the Regents' decision the conduct alleged in the Clays' suit took place, Stone participated, and his actions were outside the scope of employment. By the time Stone asked for a defense, the Regents had before them the clinical panel report that concluded egg stealing took place at CRH. They did not know if Stone participated, but that was because he refused to cooperate in the investigation by not producing requested medical records or patient charts. We think a reasonable inference was that Stone was involved.

At some point in time, the Regents learned Stone had seen Susan Clay only once, to perform an ultrasound examination. Even if we assume the scenario most favorable to Stone, that the Regents knew this when they turned down his defense, the choice was still reasonable. This fact would eliminate the possibility Stone himself took Susan Clay's eggs without her consent, but not the possibility it was done pursuant to an agreement between Stone and his colleagues to engage in such conduct, as alleged in the conspiracy count in the Clays' action.

Stone's position appears to be that his private practice at CRH was within the scope of employment, so he was entitled to a defense against any suit arising out of it. Stone argues he acted within the scope of employment because he paid the university a portion of his fees from seeing private patients, he reported to the dean of the medical school, and he only performed an ultrasound on Susan Clay, which was "reasonably foreseeable for a physician member of the faculty . . . [and] incident to his responsibilities."

But the issue is not whether seeing private patients or performing one ultrasound was within Stone's employment—the question is whether the alleged conspiracy to misappropriate and misuse Clay's eggs was a part of his employment. Stone, understandably, offered no evidence it was.

Scope of employment is a question of fact, but all that can be required of the Regents when asked for a defense is that their decision be within the range of reason. It was. We cannot say as a matter of law it is typical of the risks of a medical school faculty practice that a physician, for 18 years a tenured professor, with a renowned and successful fertility clinic, would be part of a scheme to enrich himself by using a patient's eggs without her consent. Put in terms of the foreseeability test, this is such startling and unusual conduct that we cannot say, as a matter of law, it would be fair to impose these risks on a university. To the extent the conduct may be viewed as an abuse of job-created authority, it was again a reasonable conclusion the motivations were the purely personal ones of financial reward and professional acclaim.

Stone supplied ammunition for the Regents' argument when he refused to turn over CRH patient records because they were "private patient charts, and are not and have never have been the property of the [university]."

Having concluded the Regents did not abuse their discretion in turning down Stone's defense because the conduct alleged was outside the scope of his employment, we need not consider their other arguments.

The judgment is reversed. The Regents are entitled to costs on appeal.

CASE QUESTIONS

1. What was the Regents' reason for not defending Stone?
2. Do you agree with this decision? Explain.

Eight of the couples referred to in the *Stone* case who claimed their eggs were stolen at the fertility clinic brought suit against the Regents in the case of *Unruh-Haxon et al., v. Regents of the University of California et al.,* (162 Cal.App.4th 343 [2008]). The court decided the issue of whether a story appearing in the news should be considered notice to parties and affect the running of the statute of limitations. The court held that "the fact the scandal was publicized is irrelevant unless the plaintiff admits to having knowledge of the publicity."

An exception to the prohibition against intentional tort suits is if the act was committed by federal law enforcement or investigative officials. The government can be held liable for some intentional torts, including false arrest, false imprisonment, abuse of process, and malicious prosecution.

Tort claims must be presented to the appropriate federal agency within two years after the claim accrues, or unless action is begun within six months after the date of mailing of notice of final denial of the claim by the agency where presented. The attorney general is responsible for defending actions under the FTCA.

PRACTICAL APPLICATION

The paralegal must be careful when preparing a tort claim against a state to see if there are any special rules. Your jurisdiction might require special procedures for bringing tort claims against the state. The pleadings might be different and have different or shorter time limits than usual. Because suits against the state were not always allowed, there may not be a provision for jury trial when the state is sued. Be sure to sue the correct party. For example, name the state in the suit if you also name in the suit agency, such as Missouri State Police or Missouri Department of Transportation.

▌ PUBLIC OFFICERS

Somewhat different from sovereign immunity is the individual tort immunity granted to certain public employees engaged in their official capacities. Certain governmental officials are immune from personal liability for any torts committed while they were performing their public duties.

Exceptions

There are exceptions to the privilege and immunity doctrines; for example, 42 U.S.C. § 1983 permits liability of public officers (usually other than prosecutors and judges) if the performance of their duties involves intentional or reckless activities that deprive persons of their civil rights. Such an action is called a civil rights action or a "1983" action; 1983 is the section number of the law permitting this action, not the year it was passed. If a police officer arrests someone without a warrant and without probable cause, the arrest is in violation of the detainee's civil rights and the officer may be liable. If excessive force is used in an arrest, it is a violation of civil rights and the officer may be liable (*Tennessee v. Garner*, 471 U.S. 1[1985]). If any action under color or authority of the government—whether local, state, or federal—violates civil rights, the actor(s) may be liable regardless of immunity. Note that these exceptions do not address negligent acts.

Who Is Protected

Legislators and judges enjoy an absolute immunity from tort liability for acts in their official governmental capacities. In performing legislative or judicial functions, it is possible that these public officials might commit torts against individual citizens. An example of a judge's absolute immunity is when, in the judge's official capacity, the judge renders an opinion in a case, and some of the statements in the decision offend one of the parties. However, judges are not immune from torts committed in their administrative capacity. For example, when hiring someone, a judge cannot violate the hiring laws and discriminate just because he or she is a judge. The common law protects judges and legislators from any liability whatsoever for having committed such torts. Executive branch officials, however, do not receive this blanket immunity, although administrative officers serving judicial or legislative functions do receive absolute immunity. For example, an agency adjudication officer, prosecutor, or county council legislator would be protected completely from tort liability.

Rationale for Immunity

Governmental official immunity is intended to ensure that legislators and judges may pursue their public duties without the chilling effect that fear of tort liability might create. Imagine how cautious legislators or judges would have to be in decision making if, with each sensitive topic, they had to worry about tort liability. These officials might become paralyzed by second-guessing, and the liability spectre could influence their public policy decisions. This rationale for such immunity is often repeated in the common law. To encourage maximum public benefit from the services of the public's judges and legislators, the law must totally protect these officials from tort liability.

THE CASE OF THE DEADLY TASER

In this "§ 1983" action, a claim is made alleging that two townships' failure to train their officers in use of the Taser gun was a "deliberate indifference" and violation of the deceased plaintiff's constitutional rights. The decedent was shocked at least 11 times in less than one minute.

(continues)

Richard LIEBERMAN, Sr. and Richard Lieberman, Jr., as Co-Administrators of the Estate of Kris Lieberman, Plaintiffs,
v.
David MARINO, et al., Defendants

United States District Court, E.D. Pennsylvania
Civil Action No. 06-2745
March 13, 2007

At the time of his death, Decedent, Kris Lieberman, was 32 years old, and living at a residence on his parent's property. On the evening of June 24, 2004, Decedent, after performing various helpful tasks at home, rode his motorcycle to his brother, Richard Lieberman, Jr.'s home. There, Decedent drove his motorcycle around his brother's pool until Richard Lieberman, Sr. joined the brothers. Decedent took a picture of his family with a disposable camera, and rode away on his motorcycle.

At about 8:46 p.m. that evening, the Northampton County 911 Emergency Center received two telephone calls about a man yelling and screaming. Upon his arrival at the scene, Officer Marino radioed the Emergency Center to request medical personnel for a possible mental health issue; Marino observed Decedent pulling up tufts of grass and throwing them in the air, and yelling obscenities. Thereafter, Defendant Sean Stuber arrived at the scene, and took control as the ranking officer.

Marino unholstered his Taser, and the two Bushkill Township police officers entered the field to approach Decedent. Decedent and Stuber recognized each other, and Decedent called to Stuber by his first name. Apparently misidentifying Marino as one of Decedent's old schoolmates, Decedent called out to "Homoki." Marino gave Decedent verbal commands to "calm down," and "relax." Decedent, apparently oblivious to the officers' commands, continued spinning on the ground and screaming.

He ignored further commands from the officers to stay on the ground, and instead charged at Marino. Marino activated his Taser, discharging a jolt of electricity into the upper body of Decedent. Decedent collapsed to the ground, face-first. As Stuber straddled Decedent in an attempt to immobilize and handcuff him, Marino administered a second jolt from his Taser. Stuber directed Marino to administer a third, continuous discharge from the Taser. One of the Taser wires had broken; however, use of the Taser continued, and Stuber ordered Marino to insert a fresh cartridge into the Taser. Records downloaded from the Taser itself indicate the Decedent was shocked at least 11 times within less than one minute.

Plaintiffs assert that Decedent was kept lying prone on his stomach throughout this time with the weight of at least one defendant on his back, even after his hands had been cuffed behind. Defendant Stubar revised his earlier request to slow the arrival of emergency medical personnel, and requested that the EMTs expedite their arrival to the scene. Decedent was transported to Easton Hospital, where he was declared dead.

Count I alleges violations of 42 U.S.C. § 1983. Defendants move to dismiss the claims against the Townships, arguing they are not liable because the alleged constitutional deprivation did not result from an official policy or custom. Plaintiffs contend that such a policy or custom did exist.

Municipal custom or policy can be demonstrated either by reference to express, codified policy or by evidence that a particular practice, although not authorized by law, is so permanent and well-settled that it constitutes law. Further, Plaintiffs must demonstrate causation, as "a municipality can be liable under § 1983 only where its policies are the moving force behind the constitutional violation." Additionally, for liability to attach under a failure-to-train theory, Defendants' failure to train their employees must "reflect a 'deliberate' of 'conscious' choice by [a] municipality" such that one could call it a policy or custom. The focus must be on whether the program is adequate to the tasks the particular employees must perform. Moreover, such liability arises "only where a municipality's failure to train its employees in a relevant respect evidences a 'deliberate indifference' to the rights of its inhabitants."

Plaintiffs clearly accuse Bushkill and Upper Nazareth Townships of failing to train their officers in what Plaintiffs would characterize as the proper use of a Taser, and that this failure to train shows Defendants' deliberate indifference to Decedent's constitutional rights. Plaintiffs seek to hold Defendants liable for "deliberately failing to train all the Defendants in the recognition of, and proper response to, known dangers created by the use of the taser device." Plaintiffs clearly allege that deficient training and operating manuals caused the individual defendants to misuse the Taser and defibrillator in such a way as to deprive Decedent of his constitutional rights, and that the Townships should have known this was the case. Plaintiffs' complaint goes well beyond the requirements of notice pleading, and is sufficient to require Defendants to defend the case. Accordingly, Defendants' motions as to Plaintiffs' § 1983 claims against Bushkill Township and Upper Nazareth Township will be denied.

CASE QUESTIONS

1. Would Taser training have changed the result for the deceased plaintiff? Explain.
2. Would municipal immunity apply here? Explain.

CHILDREN OF TENDER YEARS

Definition

Children of **tender years** are usually defined as young children under the age of seven years. Under traditional common law, any person under the age of 21 (and in the past 25 or so years, under age 18) is classed as a **minor.** However, only very young children normally enjoy the tender-years immunity.

tender years | Minors; usually those under the age of seven.

minor | A person who is under the age of full legal rights and duties.

Absolute Immunity for Intentional Torts

Most states still follow the ancient common law rule that children of tender years are incapable of committing intentional torts; thus, they are immune from intentional tort liability. This immunity is based upon the concept that young children are mentally and emotionally incapable of having the proper intent to commit an intentional tort. Because they are so young, they lack the experience and development to appreciate fully the significance of their actions, which sometimes are tortious in nature.

Immunity from Negligence

Most courts do not grant absolute negligence immunity to young children. Instead, the child tortfeasor's age is merely one factor to be considered in determining the standard of reasonable care that the reasonable child of tender years would have used in a particular case.

▌ SPOUSAL/FAMILY IMMUNITY

Spousal and family immunity defenses protect certain family members from lawsuits.

Spousal Immunity

Originally, common law dictated that spouses were immune from suit by each other. A husband and wife were considered to act as one unit. Additionally, there was a concern that if family members could sue each other, there was more apt to be fraud or collusion. This tort immunity for spouses has now been abolished to some degree by the majority of states. Some states have only abolished the immunity from suit for specific kinds of tort actions.

THE CASE OF PARENTAL CONTROL

When children fight and serious injuries result, who is responsible for their acts? Is it really the child or the parent's fault that the child is uncontrollable? Whom does the law hold responsible?

Michell ROLLINSON, Plaintiff–Appellant,

v.

Janice R. BERESOWSKYJ, Defendant–Appellee

Court of Appeals of Michigan

2012 WL 1605801

Wayne Circuit Court

Docket No. 300820

May 9, 2012

Plaintiff appeals as of right from the trial court's order granting defendant's motion for summary disposition of her claim of negligent parental supervision. We affirm.

This case stems from an unfortunate incident wherein plaintiff was seriously injured after defendant's 17-year-old son, who had a history of assaultive conduct, struck her with a baseball bat in the head. Although many facts are in dispute concerning the events leading up to and surrounding the altercation between plaintiff and defendant's son, there are four undisputed facts. The first is that plaintiff broke a window of defendant's home, which angered defendant's son. Second, it is undisputed that one of defendant's dogs was somehow let out of the home. It is further uncontroverted that plaintiff struck the dog with a club, and that, subsequently, defendant's son grabbed a baseball bat from defendant's home and struck plaintiff in the head with the bat. Plaintiff

suffered several injuries, including several fractures, hemorrhaging, and hearing loss. Due to her injuries, plaintiff lost her employment and was receiving disability income. Plaintiff sought recovery for her injuries from defendant solely under a theory of negligent parental supervision. Defendant moved for summary disposition under MCR 2.116(C)(8) and (C)(10) arguing that plaintiff failed to present a prima facie case of negligent supervision because there was no factual dispute that defendant lacked the ability to control her son's conduct. The trial court agreed and summarily dismissed plaintiff's claim.

"'This Court reviews de novo a trial court's decision on a motion for summary disposition.'" *Comerica Bank v. Cohen,* 291 Mich.App 40, 45; 805 NW2d 544 (2010), "A motion for summary disposition under MCR 2.116(C)(10) tests the factual sufficiency of the complaint." "Summary disposition is appropriate if there is no genuine issue regarding any material fact and the moving party is entitled to judgment as a matter of law."

"[W]here a person is injured by the act of a child which proximately results from negligent parental supervision over the child, the injured party has a valid cause of action against the parents." *Amer States Ins. Co. v. Albin,* 118 Mich.App 201, 208; 324 NW2d 574 (1982). As our Supreme Court has explained 'Aside from the relationship of master and servant, the parent may be liable for harm inflicted by a child under circumstances that constitute negligence on the part of the parent. This, of course, is not a case of responsibility of a parent for the child's tort, but liability for his own wrong.' [*Dortman v. Lester*, 380 Mich. 80, 84; 155 NW2d 846 (1968), quoting 1 Harper and James, Law of Torts, § 8.13, p. 662.]

Furthermore, the law in Michigan is that a parent is under a duty to exercise reasonable care so to control his minor children as to prevent them from intentionally harming others or from so conducting themselves as to create an unreasonable risk of bodily harm to them if the parent knows or has reason to know that he has the ability to control his children and knows or should know of the necessity and opportunity for exercising such control. [*Amer States Ins. Co.*, 118 Mich.App at 206.]

Viewing the evidence in the light most favorable to plaintiff, the nonmoving party, there is no question of material fact that defendant lacked the requisite ability to control her son to prevent him from assaulting plaintiff. It is undisputed that defendant's son, aged 17 and weighing over 300 pounds, was significantly physically larger and heavier than defendant, who suffered from cancer and a heart condition, was unable to work due to her heart disability, and weighed only 100 pounds. It is also undisputed that defendant's son had a propensity for assaultive conduct against defendant Considering the substantial differential in size between defendant and her son and his past assaultive conduct toward her, we agree with the trial court that there is no genuine issue of material fact that defendant lacked the ability to physically control her son so as to prevent him from assaulting plaintiff, regardless of her awareness of his propensity for assaultive conduct.

This is especially so where, as here, the chain of events leading to the assault started suddenly, occurred rapidly, and was clearly unforeseeable, such that defendant could not have known of the necessity to exercise control over her son, or had an opportunity to do so. Neither a lay nor an expert witness testified that defendant's son was engaged in violence before plaintiff arrived at the home. There was also no testimony that defendant's son uttered verbal threats directed at plaintiff before plaintiff left the home. This leaves us with a firm conviction that the nature and extent of his physical response to plaintiff was not reasonably foreseeable.

We disagree with plaintiff's argument that defendant could have taken other nonphysical measures to control her son's conduct to prevent the assault, but neglected to do so. Although we agree that the applicable law does not limit the requisite "control" to the ability of a parent to physically restrain his or her child to prevent potential harm or injury, the altercation in this case was not reasonably foreseeable, and thus defendant could not have known of the necessity and opportunity to exercise control over her son's conduct by taking the precautionary measures cited by plaintiff. Plaintiff argued that defendant could have called 911, but the rapidity of the events renders such a measure immaterial. Plaintiff also argues that defendant could have removed the bat or hidden the key. However, since the son's actions could not have been foreseen, the necessity for such action was also unforeseeable.

The strongest argument against defendant is that she failed to assure that her son was medicated. However, this argument is based on speculation and its factual predicate is disputed. At best, plaintiff and Shelton testified as lay persons they thought the young man was unmedicated while defendant testified that he had been given his medication on the day of the encounter. Under the circumstances of this case, we conclude that summary disposition of plaintiff's claim was proper.

Affirmed.

CASE QUESTIONS

1. Do you agree with the court's decision in this case? Explain your answer.
2. Whom do you think was the more sympathetic party, the plaintiff or the defendant? Do you think this affected the result here?
3. Based on the facts, do you think the plaintiff's injuries were foreseeable? Explain your answer.

Family Immunity (Parent/Child)

At common law, suits between parents and children were also prevented, in the interest of maintaining family harmony and avoiding fraud. In some states this family immunity has now been abolished. This is particularly true where automobile accidents are concerned. Because most car accidents are typically covered by a policy of insurance, it is thought that there is less chance for causing family disharmony, as the suit would no longer be directly against a family member. It is important to note that the family immunity doctrine only covers parent and child, and not suits between brothers and sisters or other relatives.

▌ WORKERS' COMPENSATION (EMPLOYER IMMUNITY)

workers' compensation |
A form of insurance that covers employers for claims by employees who are injured or killed as a result of incidents occurring during the course and scope of their employment.

In most states, workers who are injured or killed as a result of incidents occurring during the course and scope of their employment are covered for their injuries by state **workers' compensation** statutes. As a result of these workers' compensation statutes, employers are immune from most employee suits. Workers' compensation is a form of insurance. Payments are made through an employer's insurance carrier. An employee is covered regardless of the employer's fault. Recovery is limited to the amount set forth in statutory tables. This is generally much less than would be awarded for similar injuries in a common law tort claim. Workers' compensation is considered the employee's sole remedy. Note also that there are some federal workers' compensation statutes, which apply to certain employees of the U.S. government. Workers' compensation is also covered in Chapter 9, as a defense to intentional torts.

Types of Injuries

Some examples of injuries arising out of employment include a slip and fall where an employee injures his or her back, a chemical splash that burns a worker's skin, or a car accident when an employee is making deliveries, resulting in broken bones and a concussion. Some jurisdictions might also include a psychiatric injury caused by witnessing a theft or shooting at work, or other traumatic incident.

Whereas the injuries just described are caused by a single event or accident, a claim might also arise out of repeated exposures at work, such as to chemical vapors, loud noise, or vibrations. An employee might claim damage to his or her lungs from toxic vapors, a hearing loss from loud noise, or carpal tunnel syndrome to the wrists from using a power drill repetitively.

Benefits

Depending on the state, benefits could include medical care paid for by the employer. If an employee is unable to work, he or she might receive lost wages called disability benefits. Usually there is a time limit up until which these are paid. Permanently injured workers also receive disability payments, and in some areas can elect to receive these in a lump sum instead of weekly payments over time. Vocational rehabilitation is offered to those who are unable to return to their old jobs and need retraining for a new career. If an employee dies as a result of injuries or illness, a death benefit is usually paid to the spouse or children who are dependent on the employee. A burial allowance is also paid.

Reporting and Filing Requirements

Workers' compensation is highly regulated in order to avoid false claims and fraud. Employees are required to immediately report on-the-job injuries to their employers. There are strict time limits for filing a claim to collect benefits. After an employee files a claim, the employer is required to fill out the employer's version of what occurred (the employer portion of the claim form) and submit it to the insurance company. The employer has strict time limits for authorizing medical treatment for the injured employee, or advising as to the reason for denial.

Workers' compensation hearings are considered administrative hearings, and are presided over by an administrative law judge. If an employer disputes that injuries happened on the job, or are work-related, a hearing may be necessary. Any attorney's; fees must be awarded by the administrative law judge, and are deducted from a claimant's benefits. Claimants are prohibited from paying their attorneys directly. Appeals are taken to a state's workers' compensation board. Workers' compensation is designed so that the employee may represent him- herself if desired. Alternatively, an attorney or licensed representative may be hired, but this is not required.

Workers' compensation is also discussed in Chapter 9 regarding defenses to intentional torts.

THE CASE OF THE EXCLUSIVE WORKERS' COMPENSATION

Workers' compensation acts are generally considered an employee's exclusive remedy for on-the-job injuries, providing the employer immunity from suit. In this case, an employee alleges both physical and psychiatric injuries in his workers' compensation claim against his employer. Are these the kinds of injuries that workers' compensation statutes were designed to cover?

(continues)

STATE COMPENSATION INSURANCE FUND, Petitioner,

v.

WORKERS' COMPENSATION APPEALS BOARD and RIGOBERTO GARCIA, Respondents.

Court of Appeal of California, Second Appellate District, Division Six

204 Cal. App. 4th 766

No. B235258

March 28, 2012

In May 2010, Cole Ranch employed Garcia as an avocado picker/high tree worker. Approximately two months later, Garcia fell from the top of a 24-foot ladder while picking avocados from a high tree. He suffered a serious and obvious head injury and sought workers' compensation benefits for industrial injury to his teeth, psyche, neck, and back. Cole Ranch's insurer, State Compensation Insurance Fund (SCIF), admitted liability for the industrial physical injury, but denied the psychiatric injury because Garcia had not worked for Cole Ranch for at least six months, as required by section 3208.3, subdivision (d). Labor Code section 3208.3, subdivision (d) generally bars claims of psychiatric injury if the applicant was employed less than six months. This bar does not apply if the psychiatric injury is caused by a "sudden and extraordinary employment condition."

The sole question submitted for trial was whether Garcia's psychiatric injury qualified as a "sudden and extraordinary employment condition" for purposes of avoiding the six-month employment requirement. SCIF did not dispute the fall was sudden. The issue was whether it was extraordinary. Garcia was the only witness at trial.

Garcia began picking fruit at age 17. He picked both avocados and lemons "[i]n the past," but had worked in construction for about 10 years before joining Cole Ranch. Garcia testified that he had never fallen off a ladder before the incident. He stated he and the other Cole Ranch pickers used ladders daily. At the time of his fall, Garcia was standing on top of a 24-foot ladder picking avocados from a 35-foot tree. No one at Cole Ranch ever advised him of the risk of

falling from a ladder and that "as far as he knew," no other Cole Ranch picker had fallen from a ladder. Cole Ranch did not hold any safety meetings or provide him with a safety harness.

The Workers' Compensation Judge (WCJ) ruled that Garcia's testimony established his injury was the result of a sudden and extraordinary employment condition. The WCJ observed the injury was significant and that safety regulations were not followed. SCIF petitioned the Workers' Compensation Appeals Board (WCAB) for reconsideration, contending that Garcia's injury was not the result of an extraordinary employment condition, but rather an ordinary occupational hazard of picking fruit while standing on a ladder. In a split decision, the WCAB denied reconsideration. The majority emphasized SCIF's failure to introduce any evidence that Garcia's injury was not extraordinary.

Although we give great weight to the WCAB's interpretation of a statute, the WCAB's erroneous interpretation or application of law is a basis for annulment of its decision. (Matea v. Workers' Comp. Appeals Bd. (2006) 144 Cal.App.4th 1435.)

All workers' compensation statutes must be construed liberally in favor of the applicant. (§ 3202; Claxton v. Waters (2004) 34 Cal.4th 367, 373 [18 Cal. Rptr. 3d 246, 96 P.3d 496].) Section 3208.3 outlines the specific statutory conditions that must be met before an applicant may recover for a psychiatric injury. This section "was . . . passed in 'response to increased public concern about the high cost of workers' compensation coverage, limited benefits for injured workers, suspected fraud and widespread abuses in the system, and particularly the proliferation of workers' compensation cases with claims of psychiatric injuries." As a result, the Legislature's expressed intent in enacting Labor Code section 3208.3 was to establish a new and higher threshold of compensability for psychiatric injury.

The six-month limitation pertains to all claims for psychiatric injury, not only stress claims. There remains a substantial potential for the fraudulent inflation of a claim by adding alleged psychic injuries; thus, including such claims to meet the six-month standard is by no means unreasonable. Consequently, when an alleged psychiatric injury occurs within the first six months of employment, as it did here, the applicant must demonstrate by a preponderance of the evidence that a sudden and extraordinary employment condition caused the injury. SCIF contends that Garcia failed to meet this burden. We agree.

The sudden and extraordinary employment condition exception encompasses "the type of events that would naturally be expected to cause psychic disturbances even in a diligent and honest employee." This definition excludes accidental injuries and applies only to extremely unusual events, such as gas main explosions or workplace violence. "If the argument were made that an accidental injury constitutes a 'sudden and extraordinary employment condition,' we would reject it. Such an interpretation would mean that psychological injuries resulting from accidents would not be subject to the six-month rule, but such injuries arising from cumulative physical injury would be governed by that limitation; this distinction would make no sense, and we are reluctant to attribute irrational intentions to the Legislature." Depending upon the circumstances, an accidental injury may be uncommon, unusual and totally unexpected.

In Matea, a rack of lumber suddenly fell on a manager-trainee's left leg while he was in a store aisle at The Home Depot. (Matea, supra, 144 Cal.App.4th at pp. 1449–1450.) He claimed psychiatric injury even though he had been employed less than six months. Because the record contained no evidence that such occurrences of falling lumber were regular or routine, the court "assumed . . . that they are uncommon, unusual and totally unexpected events." In the absence of any contrary evidence, the court held that Matea had satisfied his burden.

Garcia contends the same analysis applies here, but we see two critical distinctions. First, Matea's accident occurred in a store aisle, where "'one assumes that such occurrences [of falling lumber] are quite rare, given that those aisles are open to the public.' Shoppers typically are not on the lookout for falling merchandise." Second, the WCJ determined that Matea's injury occurred when the wall shelf holding up the rack of lumber gave way without warning. Presumably, the lumber would have struck anyone who happened to be in the aisle.

Garcia's injury was far different. It did not occur in a public area or in an area shielded from the typical hazards of his occupation. To the contrary, the injury occurred in the avocado grove where Garcia and his coworkers were picking fruit from high trees while standing on tall ladders. A fall under these circumstances cannot be described as an uncommon, unusual and totally unexpected occurrence.

Garcia injured his head when he fell from a 24-foot ladder while picking avocados. No evidence exists that something particularly unusual happened to cause the fall or that he suffered an injury one would not expect from a fall from that height. Garcia had the burden to prove that his psychiatric injury was caused by a sudden and extraordinary employment event. He did not meet that burden. Garcia's observations during his brief employment at Cole Ranch and his prior unspecified fruit-picking experiences do not establish his injury was caused by an event that was uncommon, unusual and totally unexpected. There was no evidence the employer violated any safety regulations. An event does not become presumptively extraordinary because the employer offers no evidence it is regular or routine.

The order denying reconsideration is annulled, and the matter is remanded to the WCAB with instructions to deny Garcia's claim for psychiatric injury.

CASE QUESTIONS

1. Do you think the six-month rule relied on by the appeals court is fair? Explain your answer.
2. Do you think employees are better off with or without workers' compensation? Explain your answer.

▌ TORT TRENDS AND TORT REFORM

Throughout the text, reference has been made to torts as an evolving field of law. Some tort actions have been refined and some additional actions added in many jurisdictions. The legislatures and courts are constantly faced with new issues that have become a part of daily life.

Tort Trends

tort trends | Changes in the tort system that are predictive of the direction that tort actions are headed for the future.

Tort trends are changes in the tort system that are predictive of the direction that tort actions are headed for the future. With the increasing ability to communicate with a large amount of people instantaneously, for example, certain private wrongs come into focus through the media and individual web postings, and the public responds. In addition, attorneys are able to better communicate with large groups of potential plaintiffs through the Internet. These new and creative types of tort actions are spearheaded for the most part by the plaintiffs' bar.

fracking | A method of creating cracks in rocks by fluid under great pressure, to create a means of extracting natural gas and coal from layers of rock.

off-label use of drugs | When a drug that has been tested and approved for use for a particular condition is used for a different purpose than intended by the manufacturer. An example of this is where a drug commonly prescribed for epilepsy has been prescribed by doctors for their patients to use to reduce headaches or lose weight.

genetically modified food | When genes are taken from different organisms and combined to create a different or better item. An example of this is insect-resistant corn.

latent injury | An injury that occurs many years after exposure.

Evolving Issues. With the ever-changing world, some issues reach hot-button status and will likely be the subject of litigation: same-sex marriage; unions and demands for associated benefits; in vitro fertilization issues; pollution actions against car manufacturers, oil refineries, and electric utility companies for causing global warning; veterinary malpractice; allowing emotional distress claims following land contamination; actions for percolate contaminating groundwater; toxic torts; air and water contamination from **fracking**; cyber-squatting, cyber-stalking, and cyber-bullying.

In addition, there has been increased regulation concerning medical devices and the **off-label use of drugs**, **genetically modified food**, and the sexual abuse of children. Also increasing are class actions, mass torts, and massive automobile recalls and resulting suits. Trends are also seen with public nuisance suits being brought against the lead paint industry, the expansion of an employer's liability for secondhand mesothelioma cases brought by the family members of employees, and food-labeling suits, to name a few.

The effects from exposure to asbestos, some drugs, and certain other chemicals and toxic substances could take many years to develop in a person; such instances are referred to as **latent injury** cases. There is also a trend in increased numbers of latent injury lawsuits.

Tort Reform

tort reform | The effort to reduce the amount and kind of tort litigation and excessive damage awards.

Tort reform involves the effort to reduce the amount and kind of tort litigation and excessive damage awards. This effort is primarily spearheaded by the defense bar. Just some of the criticism leveled at the tort system is that litigation takes too much time, is becoming more complex, costs too much, and mostly benefits the plaintiffs' attorneys.

In fact, there were so many suits brought against asbestos companies in the 1990s that many of the companies were forced into bankruptcy. Plaintiffs are seen as too willing to litigate the most frivolous of issues, and juries are seen as awarding unnecessarily high verdicts that do not correspond with the nature of the issues before them.

Medical providers and businesses alike claim that the cost of business is increased as they must conduct themselves in a preventative manner to avoid costly lawsuits. For the slightest fall, or seemingly routine-type complaints, doctors find themselves ordering unnecessary x-rays, MRIs, and tests to avoid medical malpractice claims. This is referred to as **defensive medicine.** Medical practitioners claim the high jury verdicts have greatly increased the sums charged for medical malpractice insurance premiums, increasing the cost of practicing medicine.

defensive medicine | When medical providers order unnecessary x-rays, tests, and so forth to avoid medical malpractice claims.

Businesses are forced to carefully document their transactions with clients and vendors in the event they will be sued down the road. All correspondence and telecommunications are carefully logged in computer systems. Electronic files of documents are created to protect a business with records of purchase orders, change orders, and receipts for goods sold and delivered.

Alternative Dispute Resolution (ADR). As discussed in Chapter 1, alternative dispute resolution is a major change in tort litigation aiding tort reform. Taking cases away from juries and encouraging parties to settle their differences, or have an impartial party decide their issues, has greatly reduced the sums awarded to injured plaintiffs. ADR has also saved time and money by not using limited court resources and by speeding up the time it takes to have a dispute heard. In addition, cases handled through ADR are generally heard in a shorter time period because they are less formal than court trials.

Statute of Limitations. By carving out a shorter time frame in which to sue for certain actions such as medical malpractice claims, the amount of actions brought is reduced.

Caps on Attorney Fees. Some states limit the amount of fees attorneys can collect for certain matters. This controls the costs of litigation. In some cases such as class actions and bankruptcies, attorneys have received more money than their clients.

Limits on E-discovery. Electronic discovery has increasingly become very time consuming and costly for law firms. Some jurisdictions are reviewing their policies in order to set limits on e-discovery time frames and demands.

joint and several liability rule | When defendants act together, each is responsible for the total amount of damages caused, and for their own particular share of damages. In other words, the plaintiff can collect the total judgment from one defendant, or from all the defendants, to satisfy the judgment.

Eliminating Joint and Several Liability. Most of the states that in the past followed the **joint and several liability rule** have abolished or reduced it.

By doing away with this principle, each defendant is no longer responsible for the entire judgment. Each defendant is only liable for his or her proportionate share.

Eliminating the Collateral Source Rule.
The argument for eliminating the **collateral source rule** is that plaintiffs get a windfall or "double recovery" if the defendant pays for damages and the plaintiff also had other sources such as insurance responsible for paying the same amounts. The collateral source rule was thought to prevent the defendant from benefitting if an injured plaintiff happened to have insurance for a particular occurrence.

collateral source rule | The amount of damages a defendant is responsible for should not be reduced by sources (such as insurance) that are available to the plaintiff to cover such damages.

Closely Regulating Lawsuits.
For medical malpractice actions, almost every phase of litigation has special requirements, unlike in other tort suits. Many jurisdictions now require a medical practitioner to submit an affidavit on the plaintiff's behalf, stating that there is reasonable likelihood that the medical practitioner's actions fell below the standard of care. This affidavit is generally required at the start of litigation. Cases must be screened by malpractice panels before going to trial. Limits have also been placed on the amount an injured plaintiff can collect for noneconomic damages, around $250,000 to $500,000 in some states. Caps also have been placed on the amount of punitive damages that can be awarded. Allowing an insurance company to pay an award over time rather than in a lump sum has also been instituted in some jurisdictions as a means of tort reform.

Questioning the Constitutionality of Caps.
Although the general trend in tort reform is to reduce awards, in some states just the opposite is happening. In states such as Illinois, the legislature's capping of noneconomic damages in malpractice claims was found to be unconstitutional. The reasoning here is that regulation of awards violates the separation of powers provision in the U.S. Constitution. The legislature cannot interfere with the courts' power to determine damages.

Contracts.
Attorneys can tightly draw written contracts and try to cover almost every eventuality should a business relationship break down. This can eliminate the need for most suits.

Requiring Consent to Arbitration.
Businesses such as credit card providers and medical providers now require that customers sign a consent to arbitration form. If a customer refuses to sign the form, the business will refuse to deal with the customer. This is viewed as a method to avoid lengthy jury trials.

SUMMARY

Tort immunities are absolute defenses against a plaintiff's tort claims. Sovereign, or governmental, immunity is an ancient common law defense that protected governments from tort liability. The doctrine was based on the presumption that "the king could do no wrong," which, in America, translated to the idea that the government could not be sued without its consent. American courts drastically reduced or eliminated sovereign immunity during the twentieth century. In the early decades of the century, courts avoided the immunity by distinguishing between governmental and proprietary actions in which government agencies were engaged. Many states have abolished sovereign immunity altogether as an absolute defense.

Public officers, such as judges or legislators, are immune from personal liability for any torts committed while they are performing their official duties. This ensures that governmental officials may act independently and freely to perform their civil responsibilities, without fear of constant tort liability for their every public action that might tortiously affect individual citizens in some way.

"Children of tender years" are very young children, often under the age of seven years, although many courts have defined the term as including children to age 12 or even through the teenage years. Children of tender years are immune from intentional tort liability in most jurisdictions. Often, a specific age boundary is used. Many courts state that children under seven years are absolutely immune. Others do not rigidly follow any age barrier. For negligence, most courts apply a reasonable-child-of-tender-years standard to decide whether negligence has occurred. A few states use definite age limits, such as the seven-year-old rule, for negligence cases.

At common law, various family members were immune from suit. Spouses could not sue spouses, and children and parents could not bring actions against each other. These immunities have been abolished in varying degrees depending on jurisdiction.

State workers' compensation statutes prevent suits by injured employees against employers.

Tort trends are changes in the tort system that are predictive of the direction that tort actions are headed for the future. Examples of recent torts trends are mass tort suits and suits involving global warming, fracking, and cyber-stalking and cyber-bullying.

Tort reform involves the effort to reduce the amounts and types of tort litigation, as well as excessive damage awards. This effort is primarily spearheaded by the defense bar. Examples of tort reform include alternative dispute resolution (ADR), reducing the statute of limitations for certain actions, caps on attorneys fees and punitive damage awards, limits on e-discovery, the elimination of joint and several liability and the collateral source rule, closely regulating lawsuits, and the use of contracts and consent-to-arbitrate forms by businesses. The next and final chapter focuses on tort investigation.

KEY TERMS

collateral source rule
defensive medicine
fee standard
fracking
genetically modified food
governmental function
immunity

joint and several liability rule
latent injury
minor
off-label use of drugs
pecuniary benefits test
privilege
proprietary actions

sovereign (governmental)
  immunity
tender years
tort reform
tort trends
workers' compensation

PROBLEMS

In the following hypotheticals, identify the kind of tort committed, and whether any type of immunity exists to protect the defendant from tort liability.

1. Superior Court Judge Emily Doud McKinnley granted summary judgment to the defendant in a negligence lawsuit. The plaintiff had sued the defendant for negligently causing personal injuries. The plaintiff suffered extensive injuries and was unable to work for the remainder of his life. Upon appeal, the state court of appeals reversed Judge McKinnley's summary judgment order. The appellate court admonished the trial judge for refusing to accept certain key evidence that the plaintiff offered at hearing. The appellate court stated that there was no legal basis for granting summary judgment in the case. The trial transcript clearly indicated that the judge had become angry at the plaintiff's counsel's attempts to admit the evidence despite warnings to desist. After the appeal, the plaintiff wished to sue Judge McKinnley for judicial malpractice.

2. Shelby Sarville drives a garbage truck for the City of New Ventura. The city charges its customers a monthly trash-hauling fee, which is based upon the size of the trash container used. Citizens may use the city's service, although many people hire private trash companies instead. One day, while backing up to empty a trash dumpster, Shelby failed to look in his rearview mirrors. A five-year-old girl tried to squeeze between the truck and the dumpster on her bicycle. She mistimed the squeeze, and the truck crushed her against the dumpster, causing severe internal injuries. (Be sure to address the contributory negligence issue in this case.)

3. Daphne is an eight-year-old girl who often plays with her neighborhood friends. While hiking through the woods on Saturday afternoon, two of Daphne's neighbors, Paul (age 7) and Anne (age 10), decided to "ditch" Daphne—that is, the duo would abandon Daphne in the woods and flee the scene. The sun had just gone down, and it was becoming quite dark when Paul and Anne ditched Daphne. Once Daphne realized she was alone in the forest, she became frightened and ran toward home. She twisted her ankle and fell, striking her head against a tree root. She was knocked unconscious. Several hours later, a police search party located her. She suffered a concussion and dehydration.

REVIEW QUESTIONS

1. What are tort immunities? What is their function in tort litigation? Whom do they protect?

2. Define sovereign, or governmental, immunity. What is the historical rationale behind the defense? How have modern U.S. courts applied the doctrine?

3. What is the governmental/proprietary distinction? How it is used? How are governmental actions defined? Proprietary actions? What is the significance of these distinctions?

4. How has the sovereign immunity defense changed during this century?

5. What are public officers' immunities? Whom do they protect? Why are these governmental officials granted immunity?

6. Define *children of tender years*. Who is protected by this defense? How does the immunity differ for intentional torts and negligence?

7. What are the two family immunities?

8. What is the purpose of workers' compensation?

9. What are tort trends? Give three examples of tort trends. What is tort reform and why is it necessary? Give three examples of tort reforms.

▍HELPFUL WEBSITES

This chapter focuses on tort immunity. To learn more about tort immunity, the following sites can be accessed:

Workers' Compensation

www.law.cornell.edu
www.dol.gov
www.washlaw.edu

State Courts

www.courts.net

State Resources

www.findlaw.com
www.statelocal.gov

U.S. Supreme Court

www.supremecourtus.gov

U.S. Government Agencies

www.lib.lsu.edu

U.S. Department of Labor

www.dol.gov

Employment Discrimination Laws

www.eeoc.gov

Tort Trends and Reform

www.toxictortlitigationblog.com
www.rand.corp
nationalcenterforstatecourts.gov
whatistortreform.com
www.atra.com

STUDENT COMPANION WEBSITE
For additional cases and study materials, please go to www.cengagebrain.com

Chapter 14

Tort Investigation

THE BIGGEST MISTAKES PARALEGALS MAKE AND HOW TO AVOID THEM

A Rose by Any Other Name ...

Jack was the paralegal who relished investigations. To maintain confidentiality, he always assigned names invented for subjects of the investigation while the case was pending. Jack's investigations were peppered with notes about "sly dog," "pig sandwich," "potted palm," and the like.

Come to find out, Jack had assigned nicknames for all of us coworkers as well. One day a list surfaced with Jack's code names for his office mates. It was fairly obvious from knowing Jack who was who on the list. "Retread" was a derisive name for a paralegal who returned to our office after moving to a rival firm for one year. "FWC" was given to someone who always flirted with clients. "B.A.," for "battle axe," was assigned to a woman who always argued about everything. Although the nicknames were fairly harmless in Jack's mind, his "name game" incensed the entire office.

Lesson Learned: Name calling is name calling, no matter how harmless it seems to the person who practices it. Jack's use of an alias for the subject of an investigation is professional, whereas employing the same tactic for coworkers is sophomoric as well as unprofessional. Political correctness aside, call colleagues by the names they choose for themselves.

▌ INTRODUCTION

Investigating the facts and circumstances surrounding tortious injury or death offers many challenges. Every tort case presents the following fundamental questions, which journalists use every day in a reporting context: *Who? What? Where? When? Why? How?* In tort cases, the paralegal queries: Who injured the victim (plaintiff)? What injuries happened? How did the victim (plaintiff) get hurt? Where and when did the injuries occur? Why did the victim (plaintiff) incur injuries (that is, did the defendant[s] cause the victim's/plaintiff's injuries)? How did the injuries occur? What were the actions of the defendant?

This chapter examines the procedures paralegals use to investigate tort cases. This chapter includes

▶ Tort investigation

▶ The importance of tort case investigation

▶ Witness interview techniques and questions

▶ Determining and locating defendants

▶ Documenting the scene

▶ Public- and private-sector resources

▶ Additional areas to investigate

▶ Investigating different types of tort cases

▌ TORT INVESTIGATION

Very few paralegals in the United States specialize in personal injury litigation. Many more paralegals work on personal injury cases from time to time, as it is one of the many areas of law routinely handled by general-practice firms.

Some of the many tasks a personal injury paralegal performs are:

▶ Interviewing clients to elicit the particular facts of their cases

▶ Obtaining witness statements

▶ Investigating the accident, condition, or occurrence

- Assisting in the preparation of legal documents, such as the summons, complaint, answer, or reply
- Preparing settlement summaries
- Obtaining medical authorizations and requesting records
- Preparing discovery requests, tracking and monitoring responses to discovery requests, and summarizing deposition transcripts
- Researching legal issues and assisting in preparing motions
- Scheduling witnesses and experts for trial
- Preparing hardcopy and electronic exhibits for trial
- Organizing evidence for trial
- Preparing PowerPoint presentations for trial
- Preparing cases for arbitration
- Preparing subpoenas for trial and arranging for service of process
- Aiding in preparing clients for testifying at trial
- Being present at trial to assist the attorney
- Assisting in the preparation and research of appellate briefs
- Researching different legal theories
- Drafting documents to collect a money judgment

▌ THE IMPORTANCE OF TORT CASE INVESTIGATION

Key facts must be ascertained if a law firm is to properly handle a personal injury or property damage lawsuit. This entails an **investigation.**

investigation | A systematic examination, especially an official inquiry.

Paralegals and Investigators

Each attorney or law firm has its own specialized methods for conducting investigations. Some have in-house investigators; others hire outside investigators or investigation services. Some attorneys hire specialists for specific aspects of a tort case, whereas some rely on law clerks, paralegals, or other staff members to perform certain portions of investigations.

Even if the paralegal is not required to conduct investigations, it is essential that he or she knows what kind of evidence is needed for each type of case in order to supervise or monitor the investigation. Paralegals need to be aware when a particular piece of information merits additional investigation. Conversely, paralegals should develop a sense of what facts are not useful or relevant. One must be able to review the investigation, make sure it has been done properly and completely, and ascertain whether further research is needed.

Many paralegals handle particular aspects of investigation, either in the stages of case evaluation and development or in the course of case management. This is especially true when the trial team is determining potential defendants or defenses and ascertaining the basic facts of what exactly happened and why. At times, a knowledgeable paralegal will spot legal issues early on that have a significant bearing on the case investigation. For example, the paralegal might learn of the existence of photographs taken by a rescue squad that show details about the condition of an accident scene.

Customizing the Investigation

The tort trial team will want to adapt the investigation to fit the case. Investigations can be quite simple or highly complex and technical. Factors such as the severity of the injury involved and resources available to the plaintiff or defendant often control the scope of the investigation. "Resources available" are such factors as the client's ability to pay, the attorney's ability to advance the costs of investigation, the financial condition of prospective parties, and the existence of insurance, all of which must be considered. A small injury usually does not warrant the full-scale investigation that a serious injury or death case would merit.

Details, Details, Details!

In litigation, details are very important. An overlooked detail could make a real difference in the outcome of the case. Investigations must be customized, with more than a little creativity. For example, suppose that you are investigating an automobile accident. You cannot understand why the driver of the vehicle did not stop for the pedestrian in the crosswalk. A witness tells you that she noticed the driver was wearing glasses, but this should not be enough proof for you to automatically conclude that the driver could see properly. It is possible that the driver was only wearing reading glasses when distance glasses were needed. It is also possible that the driver was wearing an old pair of glasses and never bothered to get a new prescription. Little details like these can make or break a case.

Goals of Tort Case Investigation

Factual investigation is designed to shed light on liability and damages. Information is gathered in terms of what happened to the injured party, who may or may not have been responsible for the injuries, and any act or omission by the injured party that contributed to the accident.

If all else fails, it may be necessary to turn over the investigation, or portions of it, to a professional investigator who has expertise with a particular subject and other special resources. However, this is not practical in a small case or in a case where the firm's client has limited financial resources.

▌ WITNESS INTERVIEW TECHNIQUES AND QUESTIONS

Witnesses will explain their account of the circumstances before and after the accident, how the accident occurred, and the damages or injuries received by the people involved. Some firms prefer that such interviews be electronically recorded, or written and signed by the witness for future reference or use. Witnesses sometimes forget or change their testimony. It is important to interview witnesses as soon as possible; they will be easier to locate, and their recollections will be clearer. Exhibit 14-1 shows a sample witness statement.

Narrative Questions

There are different kinds of questioning styles you might develop, depending on the type of case and the personality of the witness. Sometimes a narrative of the event in question is most helpful. This allows the witness to tell a story without interruption. You can start out with an open-ended question as general as, "Can you tell me what happened on the day of the incident?" and see what the witness has to say. This allows the witness to speak from memory without any breaks in the story. You want to avoid breaking the stream of memory. This kind of open response seems to be more accurate than when the witness is prompted by individual questions from the interviewer. Allow the witness to pause if necessary, and do not make the witness feel uncomfortable when thinking or gathering thoughts.

Closed-Ended Questions

If needed, you can follow up with closed-ended questions for more details. You might need to ask, for instance, "So what was the color of the other car?" or "What time did you leave your house that day?" Sometimes when asked specific questions, the witness becomes more self-conscious and thinks you are looking for a certain answer or that there is a correct answer. The paralegal's goal is to encourage the witness to speak freely, even if the statements made seem trivial or insignificant.

Leading Questions

Occasionally, based upon some information in your file, you might need to ask leading questions, which tend to suggest to the witness the answer you are looking for. An example of this is asking, "Was the other car red?" Of course you want to caution the witness not to guess about any answers. It is better to have the witness tell you that he or she does not know rather than to guess as to what occurred.

WITNESS STATEMENT

14 Fern Dr.	Albany	N.Y.	5/03/13
LOCATION	CITY	STATE	DATE

1. My name is Kris J. McGrail. I reside at 14 Fern Drive,
2. Albany, NY. I am employed by the Albany Police
3. Department. My date of birth is 10/10/80. On 4/28/13 I
4. witnessed an accident on Sand Creek Road east of Wolf
5. Road. I was sitting on my motorcycle at the Hess
6. Station on Sand Creek and Wolf Road. I noticed a motorcycle
7. heading across Wolf Road going eastbound. This motorcycle had
8. a green light as it crossed Wolf Road on Sand Creek Road. I
9. noticed the motorcycle because the driver was wearing a T-shirt
10. and it wasn't that warm. There was a gold toned vehicle behind
11. me at the Hess Station facing north. This vehicle, driven by
12. Deborah Lawrence, pulled around me and began to exit from
13. the Hess Station. Ms. Lawrence used the exit of the Hess
14. Station going onto Sand Creek Road. Ms. Lawrence never
15. brought her car to a full stop as she exited. Ms. Lawrence
16. did not have the directional light of her vehicle on.
17. Ms. Lawrence then broadsided the motorcycle on the motorcyclist's
18. right side. The front bumper of her vehicle collided with
19. the side of the motorcycle. The motorcycle was knocked down
20. and continued to slide east. Bob Green, the motorcyclist, went up
21. in the air and landed on the ground. Mr. Green got up and
22. was hopping on one leg. My wife went over to offer aid.
23.
24.
25.
26.
27. Wit: Cathy Okrent   Kris McGrail

DO NOT WRITE BELOW THIS LINE

EXHIBIT 14-1   Sample witness statement.

WITNESS STATEMENT

5/03/13

LOCATION	CITY	STATE	DATE

1. I went over to Ms. Lawrence and told her to pull into the
2. parking lot of Ace Transmissions. At the time of the
3. accident, Mr. Green was traveling at a rate of speed no more
4. than 25-30 miles per hour. I went over to Mr. Green and
5. he complained about his leg and ankle, which looked quite
6. injured. His leg was cut, swollen, and purple. Someone
7. called the police and ambulance. Ms. Lawrence said she never
8. saw the motorcycle. Ms. Lawrence was alone in her vehicle.
9. Mr. Green was wearing a helmet and the headlight of the
10. motorcycle was on. I do not know of any other witnesses
11. to the accident. I believe this accident was caused by
12. Mr. Lawrence's inattention and failure to yield the right of
13. way to Mr. Green, the motorcyclist.
14.
15. I have read the above statement and it is true to the
16. best of my knowledge.
17.
18.
19.   Kris McGrail
20.
21.
22.
23.   Cathy Okrent
24.   Notary Public State of New York
                              Qualified in Schenectady County
25.   Commission Expires July 31, 2014
26.
27.

◆ ▬▬▬▬▬▬ **DO NOT WRITE BELOW THIS LINE** ▬▬▬▬▬ ◆

EXHIBIT 14-1 Sample witness statement. *(continued)*

Pictures and Diagrams

Having a witness draw a picture or diagram is often quite helpful. This is great with very old or young witnesses, or when the subject of the inquiry is complex or involves directions of vehicles or locations of people. Sometimes the witness's idea of direction does not match actual compass or map directions, and it is important that you both mean the same thing when you refer to left or right, north or south, and even close and far. At the end of the interview, always be sure to ask, "Is there anything else you need to tell me or that we have not discussed?" Then be sure to caution the witness not to speak with others about the case before discussing this with the attorney assigned to the case. Finally, thank the witness, encourage the witness to stay in touch with you, and mention that the witness should feel free to contact you if anything additional is remembered about the occurrence.

Client Interview Techniques

Personal injury paralegals are often involved in interviewing clients and witnesses. Some firms will have the client fill out an initial information questionnaire that is specifically geared to garner the information needed to handle a personal injury case. (See the client information questionnaire in Appendix A.) Other firms might desire a more informal initial contact with clients, and prefer that a paralegal or attorney greet the clients and interview them.

It is always important to put the client at ease. Be sure the client is comfortable with you and the law office surroundings before getting down to details. Small talk of a general nature helps. When the client sees that you care about him or her as a person, rather than as the next slip-and-fall case, he or she will be more apt to confide in you and provide you with the information needed for the best possible representation. Some clients are very concerned about the costs involved in a case, and might be hesitant to speak a lot for fear of driving up costs.

It is important to remember that for many clients, this injury claim represents the first time they have been to an attorney's office. For some clients, an appointment with an attorney is a very intimidating experience, particularly when the attorney hastily greets them and then must excuse himself or herself to go to court at the last minute. The clients often are left feeling that the attorney was too busy to see them. The paralegal then becomes an invaluable bridge between the attorney and the client. Eventually, the client will see that the paralegal often has more time to speak with the client and is more readily accessible by telephone, email, or for office conferences than the trial attorney. Some clients prefer to speak with the paralegal working on their case for this very reason. You might even notice that clients will tell you things that they are reluctant to tell the attorney. Some clients are hesitant to take up the attorney's time, or feel that the attorney will think less of them, or think the attorney will not want to represent them if they tell the attorney all the details of the case.

This is one reason why the role of the paralegal is so important. A paralegal who encourages the client to talk and thoroughly interviews the client about the accident or incident provides a wealth of information for the attorney and other members of the litigation team who might later work on the file.

Depending on your jurisdiction, it could take anywhere from months to four or five years for a personal injury case to reach the trial date. At the time of trial, your client's only recollection of the accident may be that which previously was told to you and recorded in the file. The same is true of witnesses. The importance of a thorough interview, and possible follow-up interviews, at the outset of a case cannot be emphasized enough. In time, each paralegal develops his or her own method of interviewing. Some think of an interview like a tree. You proceed up the main trunk, but at any time, your client might say something that causes you to branch off to focus on specific facts or issues. Then it is up to you to determine if you need to return to your main series of questions, or if perhaps the new information obtained should be pursued first.

▮ DETERMINING AND LOCATING DEFENDANTS

Besides the client, the most critical participants in any tort litigation are any potential defendants and witnesses. If a plaintiff's attorney cannot find someone to sue successfully, then the client's tort case comes to a halt. A paralegal may be asked to locate all prospective defendants and witnesses. In most tort cases, determining defendants to sue is done through in-house investigation, although occasionally it will be necessary for an investigator with more extensive resources to locate a defendant or research information (for example, regarding the principals of a defunct partnership or corporation).

It is sometimes difficult to identify and locate parties. This is particularly true if a business operating under a trade name has been dissolved or has otherwise "vanished" since the tort was committed. Even individuals can "disappear," as debt collectors and skip-tracers become acutely aware of when searching for fleeing debtors. Some tortfeasors lie low to avoid service of process and liability. Some businesses create dummy corporations or partnerships to "front" for shareholders, which may be individuals, other corporations, or partnerships that hope to remain hidden from potential tort actions. In some instances, the client may simply be unaware of the defendant's correct corporate name.

Using Discovery to Locate Defendants

discovery |

1. The formal and informal exchange of information between sides in a lawsuit.

2. Finding out something previously unknown.

Discovery is the phase in a lawsuit when information is exchanged between the parties and the issues for trial are narrowed. Occasionally, discovery will be served upon known defendants to uncover information about unknown defendants or ones who cannot be located. The paralegal should check the rules of civil procedure and discovery in his or her jurisdiction to see if prelitigation discovery is allowed, and if a court order is needed. If not, discovery will have to be conducted after the lawsuit commences.

Examination Before Trial (Deposition).

There are various discovery methods, which vary slightly by name and in their rules, from state to state and at the federal level as well. One of the main forms of discovery is the examination before trial (EBT), sometimes referred to as the deposition of the parties. Through questioning of the parties early in the proceedings, the attorneys can narrow the issues and be better aware of the value of their case. This form of discovery is not used for all cases, as it can be expensive and time consuming. Generally, a court stenographer is hired to take the testimony and produce a written transcript and/or a digital CD of the proceedings.

Written Interrogatories.

Another method of discovery is the use of written interrogatories. Written questions are sent to the opposing party, and the answering party is required to respond under oath, in writing, in a timely fashion. Some jurisdictions permit electronic versions of interrogatories to be sent out. Check your jurisdiction's rules for specifics. Interrogatories are very helpful in a contract or business matter where inquiry is made as to the availability of business documents and records. This might be used when there is no need to observe the character or demeanor of the witnesses in person, or if a matter does not involve substantial sums of money. Many courts and bar associations have copies of sample or required interrogatories on their websites.

Notice to Admit.

Sometimes, notices to admit (requests for admissions) are sent to the opposing party. The party must admit the truth or falsity of certain statements. When you are not certain as to the precise name of a defendant, or there are a few key issues that must be resolved, a notice to admit might help narrow the issues or provide some clarity.

Request for Documents.

A paralegal might be asked to send requests for the production of documents. This might be done to find out the kind of evidence the opposing party possesses. For instance, you might demand a copy of a contract, receipts, accident reports, photographs, written statements, reports, inventory records, bills of lading, or computer records in the other party's possession. This request, like all the other discovery requests, is subject to various rules and limitations that the paralegal must be familiar with before sending out a request. More and more jurisdictions are permitting e-discovery (electronic discovery). Because many businesses maintain electronic business records almost exclusively, e-discovery makes it possible to receive documents in their original form. Also, for complex cases with volumes of documents, e-discovery allows parties to search and sort documents, saving hours and days of manually searching for, pulling, and reviewing documents.

Physical or Mental Examination. In cases where a party's physical or mental condition is in issue, a physical or mental examination of the party might be requested. Again, keep in mind that a host of rules limits the scope and manner in which these can be conducted, not to mention the cost of paying an expert to perform an examination and write a written report, as well as privacy concerns addressed by the Health Insurance Portability and Accountability Act (HIPPA). See the discussion on HIPAA later in the chapter.

Permission to Enter on Land. Depending on the type of case, you might want to request permission to enter another party's land or business for inspection. Once an incident has occurred at a private location, you are going to need specific permission to gain entry and observe the area where an incident occurred. Absent this permission, you risk a trespassing claim, not to mention certain ethical violations. Make sure you are familiar with all aspects of your jurisdiction's discovery rules and procedures to ensure that the greatest amount of information you discover will eventually be admissible at trial. Seeing and walking around a particular site might give the paralegal a completely different perspective about an incident. The crooked stairs the client described might really be fairly normal, and the uneven stairs a witness described might be serious code violations.

Study Documents Carefully

Every piece of paper a paralegal obtains regarding a client's tort case is a prospective source of information regarding potential defendants and witnesses. Police accident reports are an obvious example in personal injury cases, but there are many others. Letters, invoices, leases, receipts, contracts, articles in newspapers, emails, web postings and blogs, web videos, a party's business or personal web page, witnesses' statements, ambulance reports, reports from fire personnel, and other types of documents often contain vital leads for finding parties. Exhibit 14-2 shows a sample traffic ticket. Any document connected to the parties and the circumstances involved in the tort might contain information a paralegal could use to locate defendants. Frequently one finds a clue about the accident through which one may determine a person's name, address, or parent company name—perhaps from the fine print in the document. Sometimes a business will have its license to operate a business located near the front entrance to the establishment, or near the cash register. Valuable information about owners and operators of the business might be posted.

New York State Department of Motor Vehicles
TRAFFIC TICKET

GG9900G3SP

To be completed by Police Officer and given to Motorist.

POLICE AGENCY

NEW YORK STATE POLICE

Local Police Code

Last Name	First Name	M. I

Number and Street	Apt. No.	Photo Lic Shown

City	State	Zip Code	Owner is Open	Lic Closed Type

Cites ID Number	Sex	Date of Birth

Lic State	License Expires	Veh. Type	Veh. Year	Veh. Make	Veh. Color

Plate Number	Reg. State	Registration Expires

OAB XXXXXXX

New York State Department of Motor Vechicles
TRAFFIC TICKET

POLICE AGENCY

LAST NAME	FIRST NAME	M. I	LOCAL POLICE CODE

NUMBER & STREET ADDRESS	APT. NO.	PHOTO LIC SHOWN

CITY	STATE	ZIP CODE	Owner is Open	LIC CLASSED TYPE

I.D NUMBER	SEX	DATE OF BIRTH (MMDDYY)

STATE	LICENSE EXPIRES (MMDDYY)	VEH. TYPE	VEH. YR	VEH. MAKE	VEH. COLOR

EXHIBIT 14-2
Sample traffic ticket.
Source: http://www.nysdmv.com/pleadandpay/pmtsamples.htm

Use Caution When Naming Parties

Paralegals must be certain to have the correct parties before a tort lawsuit is filed. If one files notice, sues the wrong person, or fails to name a proper party, serious problems may arise. For instance, the attorney or law firm may be subject to legal action and/or disciplinary proceedings for filing a frivolous lawsuit against the innocent party. Additionally, the statute of limitations or a notice requirement may run on a client's lawsuit without the correct person(s) having been notified or sued. Mistakes in this area may even result in a claim of malpractice by the client against the attorney.

The paralegal should check all available resources to ensure that the correct individual or business entity is being identified as the defendant. Investigatory novices might be satisfied by pulling a company or individual's name out of an online telephone directory, but this practice can be disastrous if the purported defendant turns out to be an innocent "same-name" person or business.

Using the Telephone as a Research Tool

Telephone calls occasionally may be useful in uncovering details concerning defendants, particularly when the person called is cooperative and talkative. If a shopping center, apartment complex, or similar business or building is involved, someone at the office may tell a paralegal over the phone who the owners are or will reveal the name of the management company. Oral communication skills are at a premium here. A good investigative paralegal, like a good journalist, knows how to get information without giving away any secrets or motives. In general, information should flow *to* the paralegal from nonclient witnesses; the paralegal should be wary of giving out information.

Internet Resources

A large part of tort investigation can now be completed using the Internet. A wide array of telephone, professional, and other directories can now be accessed online. You can research companies, get proper corporate names and addresses, and obtain other information needed directly from a company's website. Most government offices, courts, and agencies have websites where you can obtain information and even forms and brochures detailing the proper method for bringing or defending a claim before the particular agency or jurisdiction. A variety of the procedures described in this chapter for investigating a tort claim can also be conducted via the Internet.

Obtaining Information about Corporations

Most jurisdictions require corporations to be registered with the state in which they were incorporated, created, or are doing business.

Secretaries of State Offices. To locate a corporation, a paralegal should first contact the state agency that is responsible for keeping business organizational records. This is usually the secretary of state's corporate division for each state. A paralegal may determine the correct names, addresses, officers, directors, and contact persons for service of process upon a corporation operating in a particular state by contacting the secretary of state's office. One may also discover the name of a parent corporation by searching the secretary of state's records. Exhibit 14-3 shows a sample request to a secretary of state's office.

For a minimal fee, in most states, the secretary of state's office will furnish other written documentation, such as a corporation's articles of incorporation, that has been filed with the governmental agency. Most of this information also should be available online.

business directory | A listing of corporations and other business organizations by name, geographic location, product or service, brand name, advertising, and other subject headings.

Business Directories. Business directories are another excellent source of information about business defendants. **Business directories** list corporations

VAN & LIAL, P.C.
10 Church Street, New York, N.Y. 10007
Telephone (212) 732-9000

August 12, 2013

Department of State
Corporation Division
Albany, New York 12207

Re: Koche v. Patrick

Gentlemen:

Kindly advise whether you have any filing for the following corporation:
D. B. Associates, Inc., doing business out of Albany, New York.
Please indicate whether the above corporation is a New York corporation, and if so, when it was incorporated, where its principal office is, and whether the above designation is correct.
If it is not a New York corporation, kindly advise us in what state it was incorporated and if it is authorized to do business in the State of New York.
Thank you for a prompt reply to the undersigned.

Very truly yours,

VAN & LIAL, P.C.

By: _____
Tyrah Williams, paralegal

TW/kn

EXHIBIT 14-3
Sample request to a secretary of state's office.

and other business organizations according to name, geographic location, product or service, brand name, advertising, and other subject headings. Most public or university libraries have these reference texts on reserve. Various private services, such as Dun & Bradstreet, Inc. also provide this information, in print or online; sometimes a fee is involved.

Public Business Records. Other potential sources of information about business defendants include

- Company annual reports
- The state attorney general's office
- The state or U.S. Department of commerce
- The Securities and Exchange Commission (SEC)
- Online services

SEC reports are surprisingly fertile sources of corporate information. The reports that companies are required to file with the SEC typically contain much more detailed information than is found in annual reports to stockholders. Also, SEC reports have the advantage of being more accessible than shareholder reports, which companies often consider confidential.

Obtaining Information about Partnerships

Partnerships can be more elusive than corporations. Investors sometimes form partnerships for specific projects, such as building shopping centers or housing developments, and then disband them after the project is complete. Some jurisdictions require that partnerships be registered, in which case they can be located through the partnership section of the secretary of state's offices. However, there are fewer requirements for partnership registration than for corporations in some states. Most jurisdictions allow service of process upon any partner as notice to the partnership. **Service of process,** or **process service,** is the delivery of the summons to the defendant as a means of notifying the defendant of a pending action and compelling the defendant to appear in court.

service of process (process service) | The delivery (or its legal equivalent, such as publication in a newspaper in some cases) of a legal paper by an authorized person.

Obtaining the Names of Sole Proprietors and Partners

Many jurisdictions require that partnerships and individuals doing business under a trade name or assumed, **fictitious name** file a *doing business as (d/b/a)* certificate or affidavit with an appropriate governmental agency. Many local governments require sole proprietors and partnerships doing business in the county or city to file d/b/a certificates and affidavits with the local recorder's office.

fictitious name | A trade or assumed name used by a corporation for the purpose of conducting business (d/b/a).

Ambulance Services and Fire Departments as Defendants

Even the people called upon for assistance can end up being defendants in a lawsuit. If the fire department and ambulance services are called, and there is an unusual delay in their arrival, or if they do not have standard and appropriate equipment, the department may be liable. If equipment is not working properly, personnel are not properly trained to use it, or personnel are not supervised adequately, they may be potential defendants.

Usually the agency for which the offending individuals, firefighters, or ambulance service persons are working is added to the lawsuit for failure to supervise, failure to adequately train, or failure to provide appropriate and functional equipment. Of course, the theories of liability would depend upon the circumstances.

A fire department or ambulance service is often owned or supervised by a governmental agency, such as the city, county, or town. However, there may be a volunteer organization in a small town or a rural or unincorporated area. If so, its contract with the cities or counties in the service area should be reviewed, if possible. **Freedom of information laws (FOILs)** in each state usually provide for the

freedom of information law (FOIL) | A law requiring (or assisting) public access to government records.

EVANS AND MYERS, P.C.
12 State Street, Albany, New York
(518) 474-3691

January 25, 2013

Albany County Clerk
Office of the County Clerk
Albany, New York 12207

Re: FREEDOM OF INFORMATION REQUEST
of January 11, 2013
Airplane Crash of December 1, 2012
in the Town of Knox, County of Albany,
New York

Dear Sir or Madam:

Thank you for your letter dated January 16, 2013 and the investigative
report of the Albany County Sheriff's Department with respect to the above
airplane crash.

On Page 3 of the report, the third paragraph mentions that photographs
were taken by I.D. Officer George Dinell. If possible, this office would like
copies of the photographs pursuant to the Freedom of Information Act.

Would you please be so kind as to advise, in writing, of the necessary
procedures to procure photographs, and the fee for obtaining them.

Again, I thank you for your assistance and your fine efforts, and I look
forward to hearing from your office soon.

Very truly yours,

By: _____
Anna Lee Chin, Paralegal

AC/km

EXHIBIT 14-4
Sample request
for information to
government agency.

disclosure of such information from governmental entities. Exhibit 14-4 shows a
typical request for information. Some local governments contract out ambulance
services to private companies. Ambulances may also be owned and operated by
hospitals and funeral homes.

Paralegals should carefully follow statutes or procedural rules for special notice requirements when suing governmental agencies. Some municipalities and

governmental entities require prior notice of a condition or defect before a suit is permitted, if at all.

PRACTICAL APPLICATION

When handling reports about situations in which negligence may be a factor, a paralegal should study the documents not only to determine the facts of what happened, but also to identify *who* was responsible.

Investigating Licensed or Regulated Businesses

Most states have a central department or agency that oversees licensed and regulated businesses. For example, in Texas this agency is the Texas Department of Licensing and Regulation. To uncover additional information about a licensed or regulated business, a paralegal should consult the state governmental listings in the telephone directory in the state in which the business is located, or go online.

Agencies can also provide listings of all state licensing requirements. By checking with the state agency, one may discover whether a potential business defendant's license, certification, or insurance has lapsed or is not in good standing. Also, information might be available about the defendant's proper name, address, and telephone number.

Typically, one must complete a request form to gain access to the information on file for a particular business at the state licensing agency. These documents will range from the business's initial application for the license to a copy of its insurance certificate. Many agencies have this information available on the Internet.

PRACTICAL APPLICATION

If the defendant is local, the paralegal should check the display advertisements in the telephone directory, or the company's website. Many businesses include their business license numbers in their advertisements or post it for inspection at the place of business. Having this information available may speed up one's request for information.

Sample Defendant Search

Consider the following hypothetical defendant search. The accident report lists Axtco Construction as the owner of a truck that struck the client's vehicle. The accident report will also have Axtco's address.

If Axtco is listed in the local telephone directory, the paralegal could first call to obtain the name of the president, owner, or chief executive officer. If the address on the accident report is an out-of-town address, the paralegal could obtain the number from directory assistance for that area code.

The paralegal should be prepared to reach an uncooperative Axtco employee who will not divulge any of this information without first knowing the reason. One should be extremely cautious regarding how much information to disclose during such direct telephone contact with a potential business defendant. Also recall that ethical considerations are involved in such direct contact. The paralegal should consult with his or her supervising attorney to decide how much to tell the company personnel to obtain the names and addresses of the company chief executive officer, president, or other officer who can be sent a notice or demand letter and, subsequently, service of process. Usually, it is best to reveal as little as possible and to truthfully downplay any legal implications for which the information is being requested. Also, business directories (often found in reference sections of libraries) can be consulted for information about a business, as can online resources.

Assuming that the direct-contact approach yields little or no useful information regarding Axtco, the paralegal could next consult the secretary of state's corporate or partnership divisions to see if Axtco is a corporation or partnership authorized to conduct business in the state. If not, the paralegal could next contact the city or county governmental agency in which assumed or trade names are registered (e.g., the county recorder's office). The agency to consult will be located in the city or county in which Axtco's business offices are found. Then the paralegal could look up Axtco's trade or assumed name certificate or affidavit on file with the agency. Also, online resources might contain the needed information.

If the accident report is unavailable or contains incomplete information about Axtco, the paralegal should look at any photographs of the vehicle from the accident scene. Do the company's name and address appear on the truck's doors or body? If not, the information may be available from the state's department of motor vehicles.

Knowing who and where the defendants are is an important initial stage in every tort investigation. Another critical investigatory aspect involves the circumstances surrounding the victim's/plaintiff's injuries. The next section considers how paralegals document tort accident scenes.

▌ DOCUMENTING THE SCENE

Although legal staff members are almost never on the scene when a tort actually occurs, it is critical to document the scene of a tort injury as soon as possible.

Obtaining Visual Documentation, Measurements, and Other Details

Paralegals may take photographs or videotape recordings of accident scenes. Also, paralegals take measurements and describe physical conditions at the location itself.

Documenting the scene should be done as soon as possible, because valuable evidence is often lost as conditions change over time. Accident scenes can alter naturally due to environmental changes; or, more frequently, people might deliberately modify conditions to prevent others from being harmed or to conceal possible liability.

Paralegals should be exceedingly thorough when documenting the scene of an accident or other tort. What seems insignificant at the time may be found to be important after more is known about the accident itself. For example, the distance between steps on a stairway, and whether the stairs were tiled or carpeted, could be vitally important in a slip-and-fall case. Also, it is meaningful when reconstructing an accident to have as much information as possible about the actual scene at the time of the accident.

PRACTICAL APPLICATION

The scene of an accident should be documented as soon as possible. The paralegal should keep in mind that places and situations change, sometimes rapidly. Weather conditions can change streets and roads, construction projects may start or end, streetlights may be installed, or lighting that was on at the time of an accident may go out. A place of business may put up warnings or fences. A pool may be covered or drained. One may safely presume that potential defendants, if they are aware of their possible liabilities, will act quickly to have the cause of an accident repaired to prevent others from being injured.

Knowing the Evidentiary Rules for One's Jurisdiction

Every state has rules of evidence that regulate the admissibility of evidence. Not all evidence will automatically be admitted into evidence at the time of the trial. Sometimes the evidence must be in a specific form. You may have to obtain original records rather than photocopies, for example. These rules can generally be obtained online.

As the tort investigation is conducted, the paralegal should put each item to be used at trial in admissible form. Rules of evidence from your jurisdiction should be consulted. Even evidence that will be used only for in-house purposes, or for settlement brochures or mediation packages, should be maintained in a form that could be admitted at trial if necessary. Documents that the trial team plans to use for evidence at trial must be suitable to present at trial. Otherwise, a paralegal may find himself or herself tracking down these documents at the last minute, having to put them into admissible form (such as certified copies, which also usually requires another fee), and generally wasting time that could have been better spent on other aspects of trial preparation. Sometimes opposing counsel will cooperate in stipulating to the admissibility of certain documents; sometimes not.

Using Proper Evidentiary Form

Looking ahead to trial, paralegals should consult the relevant state, local, or federal procedural and evidentiary rules to determine the form in which evidence must be submitted into the trial record and what type of documentation is required. For instance

▶ Does the court require supporting affidavits for admission of medical records and bills into evidence?

▶ Is there a certain form or language for business records? If not, how are they proved in court? Are original records necessary, or will copies suffice?

▶ Are there chain-of-custody rules that you need to comply with?

▶ Are you prepared to prove that a videotape or photo has not been altered?

▶ Can documents or pleadings—the formal statements of the parties, such as the complaint and the answer—from other cases be used as evidence in one's case? If so, must they be certified by a court clerk or someone else?

Hearsay Problems

Hearsay is an out-of-court statement offered as evidence to prove the fact contained in the statement. Statements may be verbal, written, or even gestural.

Some documents may not be admissible because they are considered hearsay. At times, only portions of documents may be admissible. For example, all or part of a police or ambulance report may be considered hearsay because the police officer and/or ambulance attendant who wrote the report did not actually see the accident. This person's report will contain information from someone else, such as the injured party or a witness. Hearsay is not admissible, but there are numerous exceptions to this rule.

The trial team will want to review the documents and the evidence rules. They may want to offer the reports into evidence simply as business records (an exception to the hearsay rule), or use them to refresh the memory of a testifying police officer or paramedic, without offering them as evidence.

hearsay | A statement about what someone else said (or wrote or otherwise communicated).

Video and Computer Technologies

Videotape and computer animation are routinely used in accident reconstruction, "day-in-the-life" documentaries, and settlement brochures. Even video news footage is being utilized in the courtroom. Paralegals should know how to document the authenticity of this type of evidence so that it can be used during trial.

▌ PUBLIC- AND PRIVATE-SECTOR RESOURCES

Governmental agencies and private entities are sources of a variety of information that may be germane to the paralegal's tort case investigation. Online computer networks may be the information superhighway, but some information is still stored the old-fashioned way—on paper, microfilm, microfiche, or other archival media—and paralegals need to know where to look to uncover this material.

Local Governmental Agencies

Governmental agencies are literal stockpiles of information that the paralegal will find invaluable in tort case investigation. Freedom of information laws provide for governmental disclosure of most contracts. Archives contain vital statistics, marriage licenses, civil suit records, and probate and estate records. One can obtain information from automobile license tag records, such as the name and current address of the owner of a vehicle involved in an accident. Also, information can be obtained from driver's license records, deeds, and liens. The tax assessor's office can provide property-ownership information by name or address of the property. In some states, some of the information will be protected by privacy protection acts limiting the amount of information that can be obtained or distributed to others.

Newspapers

Newspapers and newspaper personnel can be good sources of information. For instance, an article about the tort incident might quote a witness about whom the paralegal did not know. There could also be helpful information about how the accident happened or who was involved. The paralegal should find out if a newspaper reporter took any photographs of the scene, even if none were printed in the newspaper.

There may be information about one's client or other parties in the archives of the newspaper. The paralegal should look beyond articles about the tort incident for photographs or profiles of people involved. There may be information to document a client's activities before an accident or to aid in service on an individual or business. Many newspapers are now online, allowing for easy access to prior publications.

Television and Radio News Reports

If the accident that is the basis of the tort lawsuit was reported on the news, one may want to get an audiotape, videotape, or transcript of what was reported to the public. It may be useful if a jury trial is anticipated, because prior publicity may affect jurors and even the venue of the case.

Additionally, if video news footage was taken, the paralegal should obtain a copy. It may have scene footage that is not obtainable from any other source. This footage may also have been taken closer in time to the actual incident than later documentary efforts by the law firm. The trial team may be glad to have this footage when preparing a video settlement brochure or video recreation of the accident for trial. If the television station will not cooperate, consult your rules of discovery; it may be possible to subpoena the footage.

Paralegals should also give some thought to any local conditions that might have contributed to the accident. If a fire or storm occurred at the time, and was significant, it is possible that it was reported on the local news. For example, a client's case might involve a storm-damaged building that was not repaired. The client was later injured at that business when a portion of the roof caved in. In this case, it would be a good idea to check local television stations for any news footage that might have been taken of the storm or wind shears on the day the building was believed to have been originally damaged. If found, this footage would dramatically help document not only when the building was damaged, but also that the owner or manager of the building knew, or reasonably should have known, that the building needed repair, well in advance of the injury occurring.

Official weather statistics are frequently obtained from the National Oceanic and Atmospheric Administration (NOAA), which is part of the U.S. Commerce Department. These statistics can be found at major airports. For local information, the department of meteorology at a local university or television station will have weather statistics. Such statistics are frequently used in arbitration and litigation.

Computerized Databases

There are many types of computerized databases and networks, each holding a wealth of information. Different jurisdictions have rules and requirements about how much information is accessible to the public or admissible at trial. Even with these restrictions, it is surprising what can be learned. Databases can be used to uncover:

- Driving records
- Driver's information
- Driver's licenses, which provide a history of residences
- Vehicle registration
- Credit reports
- Criminal history
- Public record filings, such as deeds and liens
- Business filings, such as assumed names, corporate filings, partnership filings, bankruptcy filings, and company officers and incorporators
- Civil lawsuits, including divorces
- Asset and other financial information

Following are samples of documents obtained from the Internet that can be used in investigations depending on the type of case involved. Exhibit 14-5 shows a chemical database available through the U.S. Department of Labor to research chemicals.

Exhibit 14-6 is from the National Transportation Safety Board (NTSB) database detailing aviation crashes.

Exhibit 14-7 is a sample form that can be obtained online from New York's department of motor vehicles (DMV) to obtain a copy of a motor vehicle report from an accident. Most states have similar forms available.

Depending on the type of case being investigated, the paralegal might find several documents available online from federal or state agencies. Sometimes, information will only be released to those people with a "right to know," meaning they must show an actual need for the information, rather than just curiosity.

OSHA/EPA Occupational Chemical Database

Welcome to the OSHA/EPA Occupational Chemical Database. OSHA and EPA jointly developed and maintain this database as a convenient reference for the occupational safety and health community. This database compiles information from several government agencies and organizations. Available database reports include: "Physical Properties," "Exposure Guidelines," "NIOSH Pocket Guide," and "Emergency Response Information," including the DOT Emergency Response Guide. In additon, an all-in-one report, "Full Report," is available.

SEARCH OPTIONS

Chemical Name: [Benzene] *Exact Match*
(or name fragment)

CAS Number: [　　　　]
(e.g., 7782-50-5, or CAS # fragment, e.g., 7782-5)

[Search]

View All Chemicals with:

- PELs
- Carcinogen Designations
- Skin Designations
- IDLH Values

[View]

CHEMICAL NAME / CAS NUMBER INDEX

Table of Contents by Chemical Name:

A B C D E F G H I J K L M N
O P Q R S T U V W X Y Z

[Note: Chemicals beginning with p-, m-, and o- are listed alphabetically, e.g., m-xylene is found under "M" rather than "X."]

Table of Contents by [CAS Number]

Total number of records returned: 79

Chemical Name	CAS #	Formula	Synonyms	Reports Available				
1,2,4-TRICHLOROBENZENE	120-82-1	C6H3Cl3	unsym-Trichlorobenzene; 1,2,4-Trichlorobenzol	Full Report	Physical Properties	Exposure Guidelines	NIOSH Pocket Guide	Emergency Response Information
1,2-EPOXYETHYLBENZENE	96-09-3			Full Report	Physical Properties	Exposure Guidelines	NIOSH Pocket Guide	Emergency Response Information
2,4 DINITROTOLUENE	121-14-2	C7H6N2O4	Dinitrotoluol; DNT; Methyldinitrobenzene [Note: Various isomers of DNT exist]	Full Report	Physical Properties	Exposure Guidelines	NIOSH Pocket Guide	Emergency Response Information
2,4-DIAMINOANISOLE AND ITS SALTS	615-05-4		1,3-Diamino-4-methoxybenzene; 4-Methoxy-1,3-benzene-diamine; 4-Methoxy-m-phenylene-diamine Synonyms of salts vary depending upon the specific compound.	Full Report	Physical Properties	Exposure Guidelines	NIOSH Pocket Guide	Emergency Response Information
2,6 DINITROTOLUENE	606-20-2	C7H6N2O4	Dinitrotoluol; DNT; Methyldinitrobenzene	Full Report	Physical Properties	Exposure Guidelines	NIOSH Pocket Guide	Emergency Response Information
2-CHLOROANILINE	95-51-2	C6H6ClN	1-amino-2-Chlorobenzene; 2-chlorobenzenamine; 2-Chlorophenylamine; o-Chloroaniline	Full Report	Physical Properties	Exposure Guidelines	NIOSH Pocket Guide	Emergency Response Information
2-CHLORONITROBENZENE	88-73-3	C6H4ClNO2	o-Chloronitrobenzene; 1-Chloro-2-nitrobenzene; 2-Chloro-1-nitrobenzene o-Nitrochlorobenzene; Chloro-o-nitrobebzene; ONCB; 2-CNB; o-Nitrochlorobenzene	Full Report	Physical Properties	Exposure Guidelines	NIOSH Pocket Guide	Emergency Response Information
3,5-DINITROTOLUENE	618-85-9	CH3C6H3(NO2)2	Dinitrotoluol; DNT;Methyldinitrobenzene	Full Report	Physical Properties	Exposure Guidelines	NIOSH Pocket Guide	Emergency Response Information
4,4'-THIOBIS(6-TERT-BUTYL-M-CRESOL)	96-69-5	C22H30O2S	4,4'-Thiobis(3-methyl-6-tert-butylphenol); 1,1'=Thiobis(2-methyl-4-hydroxy-5-tert-butylbenzene)	Full Report	Physical Properties	Exposure Guidelines	NIOSH Pocket Guide	Emergency Response Information
4-CHLORO-2-METHYANILINE AND ITS HYDROCHLORIDE SALT	95-69-2	C7H8ClN	4-Chloro-o-Toluidine; 2-Amino-5-chlorotoluene; 5-Chloro-2-aminotoluene; 4-Chloro-2-methylbenzeneamine; 4-Chloro-2-toluidine; 4-Chloro-6-methylaniline; Fast Red TR; Fast Red TR 11; Fast Red TR Base; P-Chloro-o-toluidine	Full Report	Physical Properties	Exposure Guidelines	NIOSH Pocket Guide	Emergency Response Information
4-CHLOROANILINE	106-47-6	C6H6ClN	p-Aminochlorobenzene; 1-Amino-4-chlorobenzene; p-Chloroaniline; p-Chlorobenzenamine; 4-Chlorobenazmine	Full Report	Physical Properties	Exposure Guidelines	NIOSH Pocket Guide	Emergency Response Information
4-DIMETHYLAMINOAZOBENZENE	60-11-7	C14H15N3	Butter yellow; DAB; p-Dimethylaminoazobenzene; N,N-Dimethyl-4-aminoazobenzene; Methyl yellow	Full Report	Physical Properties	Exposure Guidelines	NIOSH Pocket Guide	Emergency Response Information
4-NITROBIPHENYL	92-93-3	C6H5C6H4NO2	p-Nitrobipheny; p-Nitrodiphenyl; 4-Nitrodiphenyl; p-Phenylnitrobenzene; 4-Phenylnitrobenzene; PNB	Full Report	Physical Properties	Exposure Guidelines	NIOSH Pocket Guide	Emergency Response Information
ANILINE	62-53-3	C6H7N	Aminobenzene; Aniline oil; Benzenamine; Phenylamine	Full Report	Physical Properties	Exposure Guidelines	NIOSH Pocket Guide	Emergency Response Information
BENZENE	71-43-2	C6H6	Benzol; Phenyl hydride	Full Report	Physical Properties	Exposure Guidelines	NIOSH Pocket Guide	Emergency Response Information
BENZYL CHLORIDE	100-44-7	C7H7Cl	Chloromethylbenzene; alpha-Chlorotoluene	Full Report	Physical Properties	Exposure Guidelines	NIOSH Pocket Guide	Emergency Response Information

EXHIBIT 14-5 Occupational chemical database of the Occupational Safety and Health Administration (OSHA) and the Environmental Protection Agency (EPA)

Source: http://www.osha.gov/web/dep/chemicaldata/default.asp#target

Report(s) Status (Published)	Probable Cause Released	Location	Make/Model	Regist. Number	NTSB No.	Event Severity	Type of Air Carrier Operation and Carrier Name (Doing Business As)
National Transportation Safety Board—Jan 2013 Aviation Accidents							
Tuesday, January 01, 2013							
Preliminary (01/09/2013)		Jasper, AL	PIPER PA-30	N7700Y	ERA13FA101	Fatal(3)	Part 91: General Aviation
Wednesday, January 02, 2013							
Preliminary (01/07/2013)		Seminole, OK	EUROCOPTER EC 130 B4	N334AM	CEN13FA121	Nonfatal	Part 91: General Aviation
Preliminary (01/11/2013)		Delano, CA	BELL 206	N828AC	WPR13FA080	Fatal(1)	Part 91: General Aviation
Preliminary (01/04/2013)		Oceano, CA	LUSCOMBE 8A	N45923	WPR13FA083	Fatal(1)	Part 91: General Aviation
Saturday, January 05, 2013							
Foreign (01/08/2013)		Saint Pierre de Bressieux, France	PIPER PA34	CN-DAY	CEN13WA126	Fatal(5)	Non-U.S., Non-Commercial

EXHIBIT 14-6 NTSB accident database query
Source: http://www.ntsb.gov/aviationquery

New York State Department of Motor Vehicles
REQUEST FOR COPY OF ACCIDENT REPORT

MV-198C (2/11)

Use only for accidents that happen in New York State.

Get accident reports instantly by purchasing them on the web. Visit http://dmv.ny.gov/AIS before you use this form.

Please choose one of the following:

☐ I am named in this accident report, or I am the authorized representative of a person named in this report.

☐ I am, or may be, a party to a civil action arising out of the conduct described in this accident report.

☐ I am the authorized representative of a person who is, or who may be, a party to a civil action arising out of the conduct described in this accident report.

☐ I am a representative of New York State or of a political subdivision of New York State, and will use this accident report ONLY for statistics or research relating to highway safety.

☐ Other reason:_____

Please Print Requester's Name and Address:

Requester's Signature ▶ _____

Date of Signature _____

To knowingly make a false statement or conceal a material fact in this written statement is a criminal offense, punishable under Penal Law Section 210.45.

Provide as much information as you can about the accident:

Accident Date: _____

Accident Location (County): _____

Fatal Accident: ☐ YES

If more than 3 motorists were involved, please attach an additional MV-198C.

Responding Police Agency:

☐ NYC Precinct # _____ Accident #_____

☐ NYS Police_____

☐ Local _____

Plate No.	Driver License ID No. or No. from Non-Driver ID Card
NAME	Date of Birth
Address	Apt. No.
City	State Zip Code

Plate No.	Driver License ID No. or No. from Non-Driver ID Card	Plate No.	Driver License ID No. or No. from Non-Driver ID Card
NAME	Date of Birth	NAME	Date of Birth
Address	Apt. No.	Address	Apt. No.
City	State Zip Code	City	State Zip Code

Check boxes below for all reports you are requesting:

☐ Police Report _____

☐ Motorist Report (NAME)_____

☐ Motorist Report (NAME) _____

☐ Motorist Report (NAME) _____

Mail completed form and payment to: **NYSDMV, MV-198C Processing, PO Box 2086, Albany NY 12220-0086.**

Non-refundable search fee . . . . $10.00 _____

No. of reports requested _____ x $15 . . . . $_____

Total Amount Enclosed . . . . $_____

Please select payment method *(Do Not Send Cash)* :

☐ DMV account number | | | | | | | |

☐ Check/Money Order - Payable to *Commissioner of Motor Vehicles*

☐ Exempt

Print name and address where the accident report(s) should be mailed:

Optional - Your reference number:

_____

DMV USE ONLY

Date:_____

Transaction #: _____

Operator: _____

☐ Records Found   ☐ No Records Found

Search fee (non-refundable) . . . . . . $10.00 _____

No. of Reports _____ x $15 . . . . . $_____

Total . . . . $_____

Amount Received . . . . $_____

Refund . . . . $_____

MV-198C (2/11)   **www.dmv.ny.gov**

EXHIBIT 14-7 New York DMV's form for requesting a copy of an accident report. *Source:* http://www.nydmv.state.ny.us/forms/mv198c.pdf

Information Regarding Criminal Acts

If the incident that is the basis of the tort lawsuit also involves a criminal act, such as a shooting or other type of assault or battery, there will be a criminal investigation, and additional information resources may be available to the trial team. The paralegal will want to review and possibly obtain copies of the following:

- Police report
- Criminal record of the perpetrator
- Trial transcript of any criminal trial, conviction, or judgment
- Exhibits used at criminal trial
- 911 or other emergency telephone call audiotapes and/or transcripts
- Floor plans or diagrams of the incident location
- Map of the area
- Crime statistics of the specific law enforcement jurisdiction

Most tort cases involve damages, insurance coverage, and other elements that must be researched. The next section investigates these considerations.

▌ ADDITIONAL AREAS TO INVESTIGATE

Tort damages present a variety of details to investigate. These items include degree and permanence of the injury, employment and lost wages, injury expenses, insurance coverage, prior tort claims, preexisting injuries, past criminal records, and driving history, to name but a few.

Employment and Lost Wages

The plaintiff's damages may be based in part on the dollar amount of wages lost due to injuries. Another factor that is often considered is impairment of future earning capacity. The paralegal needs this earnings information for in-house evaluation, but the defendants will also be entitled to obtain certain information regarding wages. See Exhibit 14-8, a sample report documenting an occupational injury or illness.

The plaintiff's income must be documented. It is not sufficient for a client to simply testify, "I could have made $175,000 this year if it weren't for this injury." Income and income potential must be substantiated by independent evidence.

Tax returns and affidavits from the client's employer are commonly used to document lost wages and the client's wage-earning capacity. The paralegal will also want to gather information from the client's W-2 forms, pay stubs for hourly or salaried workers, and, in some instances, documentation of employment contracts or fringe benefits.

The trial team may plan to have an economist, actuary, or accountant prepare an evaluation of economic damages. Most economic experts will request tax returns for at least three years preceding the date of injury, to make a determination as to future economic loss, when there has been impairment of future earning capacity.

ALASKA DEPARTMENT OF LABOR & WORKFORCE DEVELOPMENT
Division of Workers' Compensation
P.O. Box 115512, Juneau AK 99811-5512

REPORT OF OCCUPATIONAL INJURY OR ILLNESS

AWCB Case Number (Division Use Only):

EMPLOYEE: Answer ALL questions 1 - 20, sign, and give to your employer immediately.

1. Last Name	First Name	Initial	2. Telephone Number	3. Date of Birth	4. Sex	5. Social Security Number
Scott	Mary	B		Feb 11, 1980	○ M ● F	

6. Mailing Address	7. Residence Address
24th Avenue	24th Avenue

6a. City	State	Zip Code	7a. City	State	Zip Code
Anchorage	Ak	99517	Anchorage	AK	99517

8. Place (City/Town/Village/Camp) Where Injury/Occupational Illness Happened	9. Date of Injury or Exposure to Disease	10. On Employer's Premises?
Anchorage	1/15/2013	● YES ○ NO

11. Name & Address of Attending Physician	12. Hospitalization In-Patient?	13. Name of Hospital
Providence, PO Box 196	● YES ○ NO	N/A

City	State	Zip Code	City	State	Zip Code
Anchorage	AK	99517			

14. Describe Part(s) of Body Injured / Nature of Occupational Illness [X] Left [X] Right	15. Describe How the Injury or Occupational Illness Happened

16. To all health care providers:

You are authorized to provide my employer (named in box 18), its workers' compensation liability insurance company (box 21), and its claims adjuster (box 22) information concerning any health care advice, testing, treatment, or supplies provided to me for the injury or illness described above in box 14. This information will be used to evaluate my entitlement to receive benefits, including payment of medical benefits, under the Alaska Workers' Compensation Act. This authorization is valid for a one-year period from the date of my signature (box 17a). I know I have a right to receive a copy of this authorization and agree a photographic copy of this authorization is as valid as the original.

Employee/Patient's Signature:

17. If Employee Unavailable for Signature, Explain Circumstances in this Space	17a. Date Signed
	1/5/2013

EMPLOYER: Review employee answers 18 - 20, answer questions 21 - 49.

18. Employer's Name	19. Employer's Alaska Address (If Different from Mailing)
Security Services, Inc.	2909 Arctic Blvd, Anchorage, AK, 99503

20. Employer's Mailing Address (Street and Number)	21. Name of Insurer
Arctic Blvd.	IS Portland WC Office

20a. City	State	Zip Code	20b. Telephone	22. Full Name and Address of Adjusting Company
Anchorage	AK	99503		IS Portland WC Office

23. Date Employer First Knew of Injury	24. Date/Time (AM / PM) Employee Left Work	22a. Mailing Address (Street and Number)
01/05/2013	4:00 am	66th Pkwy

25. Off Work After Injury / Illness?	26. Date Returned to Work	27. Death? ○ Y ● N	22b. City	State	Zip Code	22c. Telephone
● YES ○ NO ☐ 3 or More Days?	01/05/2013	Date	Portland	OR	97223	

28. Location Where Injury or Occupational Illness Happened	29. Employee's Occupation	30. Date Hired By Employer
Arctic Blvd.	Dispatcher	05/19/2010

31. Earnings Calculated By	32. Rate of Pay	33. Days Employee Works per Week	34. Describe Scheduled Days Off
● Hr. ○ Day ○ Output ○ Wk. ○ Mo. ○ Yr.	$ 10 per	○ 3 or Less ○ 4 ● 5 ○ 6 ○ 7	TH/FRI

35. Workday Began	36. Employee Paid for Day Injured or Ill?	37. Federal EIN #	38. Give Details of How Injury or Illness Happened
○ AM ● PM	●YES ○NO	N/A	Employee tried to lift a file cabinet when her hand slipped, causing pain and swelling to both wrists.

39. Injury / Illness Due to Machine / Product Failure? ○YES ●NO	40. Mechanical Guard / Safeguards Provided? ○YES ●NO	41. List Any Machine / Substance / Object Causing Injury File cabinet	42. If Machine, What Part? N/A

43. Name and Address of Witnesses	44. If Injury / Illness Caused by Anyone Besides Employee, Give Name and Address
None	N/A

	45. Dependents (in case of death), Names and Addresses
	N/A

46. If You Doubt Validity of Injury or Illness, State Reason

Forward Inquiry to: Leen Elsen

47. Signature of Authorized Employer or Representative	48. Title	49 Date Signed
	District Administrator	01/15/2013

WARNING TO EMPLOYEES AND EMPLOYERS: AS 23.30.250 imposes civil penalties for fraud as well as certain false or misleading statements and acts. Criminal penalties for theft by deception (including fines and incarceration) apply to knowingly made false statements, claims, or employee misclassifications.

Distribution: Original -Workers' Compensation Division; Copy -Adjuster; Copy -Employer; Copy -Employee

Form 07-6101 (Rev 08/2012)

EXHIBIT 14-8 Report of an occupational injury or illness.
Source: http://labor.state.ak.us/wc/form/07-6101.pdf

Expenses Related to the Injury

The client should provide documentation of all expenses paid in relation to the injury and medical treatment. This includes receipts for medical visits, equipment, and supplies, such as:

- X-rays and radiologist
- Canes, braces, crutches, and wheelchair
- Heating pads or ice packs
- Hospital
- Ambulance
- Doctor
- Physical therapy/occupational therapy
- Bandages
- Prescription medicines
- Over-the-counter medicines
- Acupuncture
- Chiropractor
- MRI/CAT scans
- Special mattresses or recuperative furniture or equipment
- Bills from housekeeper, cook, visiting nurses, medical transport, or other assistance needed during recuperation

The client should also document mileage and parking fees for trips to the doctor, hospital, and for any other therapy sessions. The paralegal should follow up to make sure the client is keeping records of this information.

Insurance Coverage and Other Benefits

The trial team will need to know how much of the client's medical and related expenses were paid by insurance policies, workers' compensation benefits, or other sources. The paralegal should also find out if the client is covered by or receiving any assistance from Social Security, Medicare, Medicaid, or any other governmental or private program.

The client should provide the paralegal with copies of any documentation about insurance coverage or possible assistance through governmental agencies. If the client is unable to produce such documentation, it may be necessary for the paralegal to contact the various agencies and request the information with an authorization signed by the client. The defendants may also be entitled to some information regarding the insurance payments and government or other benefits, even if such information is not admissible at trial. Depending on your jurisdiction, the fact that some of the plaintiff's bills have been paid may affect the defendant's responsibility to reimburse for expenses.

No-Fault Automobile Insurance. A major part of many negligence practices involves the handling of car accidents for clients. Accordingly, it is important to be aware of the insurance laws in your state, and whether your state has no-fault legislation. Thirteen states have no-fault legislation, whereby parties can collect against their own insurance policies, regardless of fault, for medical bills and lost wages from personal injuries. There is no recovery for pain and suffering. Generally, one cannot bring a lawsuit for personal injuries unless one meets a certain threshold and has a "serious injury." Some states have hybrid-type laws that allow people to elect whether they will proceed with suit under traditional tort law or the no-fault statutes. No-fault coverage does not pay for property damage; this is covered by another part of automobile insurance.

Police Accident Report. No matter what state you work in, when a client calls with a potential automobile claim, the first thing you must do is ask the client to bring in a copy of the police accident report. Also, you want to instruct the client not to discuss the case with anyone without first consulting the attorney who will be representing him or her. Oftentimes, people are very shook up after an accident and their version of what happened is very different from the police accident report. Also, clients may get confused and mistakenly speak with opposing counsel or the insurance representative for the other driver before receiving advice from their own attorney.

Policy Limits. The attorney handling the case is going to want to know how much insurance each person in the accident carries. The potential client can have a seemingly great case, but if the driver who caused the accident has very little or no insurance, there may not be much your firm can do for the potential client. Some clients in some states will have extra insurance for just this eventuality. States vary as to the kind of insurance drivers are offered and required to have. For example, the minimum automobile insurance requirements in Minnesota are 30/60/10. This means that there is a total of $60,000 of insurance available for all persons injured in an accident, with a limit of $30,000 for one person, and there is $10,000 for property damage. The amount of insurance premiums will increase based upon the amount of coverage above the minimum a driver wishes to purchase.

See Table 14-1 for a listing of the types of no-fault insurance available in certain states.

Previous Claims or Lawsuits of Plaintiff

It is necessary to know about any previous claims or lawsuits in which the client has been involved and how they were resolved. The trial team will determine the

State	Is There No-Fault Automobile Insurance?
California	No—It's a tort system state. Drivers are responsible for any damage they cause.
Florida	Yes—Partial no-fault. Each person pays own medical expenses.
Kansas	Yes
Kentucky	Choice: Drivers can select either tort system or no-fault system.
Massachusetts	Yes
Minnesota	Yes
New Jersey	Choice: Drivers can select either tort system or no-fault system.
New York	Yes
Ohio	No—Parties are financially responsible for any damage they cause.
Pennsylvania	Choice: Drivers select either tort system or no-fault system called "limited tort."
Texas	No—It's a tort system state.
Utah	Yes

TABLE 14-1

Types of no-fault automobile insurance available by state

information to which the defendant is entitled if defense counsel inquires about this subject matter during discovery. Defendants usually ask for this type of information so as to use it against the plaintiff, to discredit the plaintiff, or to reduce the amount of damages in a lawsuit.

Clients will not always be able or willing to provide all the information concerning prior claims or lawsuits in which they have been involved. Some clients discard legal documents once a legal action is completed. The paralegal may have to visit the court clerk's offices or perform an online search to obtain the relevant documents concerning any past lawsuits.

PRACTICAL APPLICATION

Some people are "professional plaintiffs"; that is, they sue people for a living for injuries that are contrived or exaggerated. These people are not usually honest with their attorneys. Other clients are just injury-prone and seem to incur more than their share of injuries. A thorough interview and study of current and past medical records often help to determine whether a client's claims ring true. Note that the occasional malingerer is the exception and not the rule!

Previous Injuries to Plaintiff

As a general rule, "one takes the victim (plaintiff) as one finds him." However, it is important to determine if the part of the plaintiff's body that was injured in the accident and is the basis of the current lawsuit was ever injured in the past. It is vital to review medical records carefully to determine whether there are any references to similar injuries or other problems relating to the same part of the body, or whether there is evidence of any preexisting injuries.

For instance, if a plaintiff who has a stiff back from an earlier car accident slips and falls on a slippery floor at the grocery store and reinjures her back, the injured plaintiff may only bring a claim against the grocery store for the portion of injuries and expenses that result from aggravation of the existing condition. There can be no recovery against the grocery store for the stiff back that the plaintiff already had. The plaintiff's claim might be that her back is stiff more often, or that it gives her more pain than she previously experienced. An award against the grocery store for aggravation of an existing condition may be much less than the award for the preexisting stiff-back condition.

In this example, the paralegal should be sure to have all the medical information to evaluate and let members of the trial team know that there was more than one injury to the plaintiff's back. The trial team will probably want to follow up with additional questions to the client regarding the previous back problem to ascertain if it is related to the pain attributed to the slip and fall. One's trial team may also want to follow up with the client's doctor.

Health Insurance Portability and Accountability Act (HIPAA).

The U.S. Department of Health and Human Services (HHS) issued a health information privacy rule to carry out the requirements of the Health Insurance Portability and Accountability Act of 1996 (HIPAA). The health information of "individuals" is protected from certain "covered entities" (i.e., health care providers, insurance companies, Medicare and Medicaid providers) use. Basically, safeguards were put in place to protect the privacy rights of individuals concerning their personal health information, and how that information is used or transmitted, with certain exceptions. Rules (particularly regarding patient consent) must be followed before health information can be distributed to others. Violation of this law carries strict fines and penalties.

The importance of this law to the paralegal is that he or she must obtain the necessary signed authorization before making any attempt to obtain health information. Further, the paralegal is required to keep this information confidential and in a safe place, where it cannot be accessed by others without the necessary authorization. Likewise, the paralegal cannot give this information to others without the necessary consent.

The Parties' Criminal Histories

Information on the parties' criminal histories is relevant for both defendants and plaintiffs in some cases. The trial team needs to know anything regarding the parties' arrests, convictions, and/or time spent in jail or prison, although this data might not be admissible at trial in your particular case.

Driving Records

Driving records may be particularly relevant in the investigation of an automobile accident, and can also be utilized to determine other information regarding the parties, such as alcohol use. If any party has been ticketed or arrested for an offense such as driving under the influence of alcohol or drugs, the trial team will want to know about it.

Having considered various investigatory techniques, it would be useful to apply these methods to specific types of tort cases. These applications are discussed in the next section.

▌ INVESTIGATING DIFFERENT TYPES OF TORT CASES

Various types of tort cases require specialized methods of investigation. Paralegals and attorneys learn the "right" techniques primarily through experience. This section provides some basic guidelines for investigating some typical tort cases encountered in private law practice.

In Exhibit 14-9 is a portion of some of the pages of a traffic collision report prepared by the police officer arriving at the scene of a four-car accident. The driver of the first car stopped his Lexus in the left lane because he had a flat tire and did not want to drive on the tire and ruin the tire or the rim. Ironically, the first thing the officer did was have driver number 1 drive his Lexus off the road, which he did with no problem. Had the driver done this to begin with, arguably, there might not have been the collision with driver 2 rear-ending the Lexus, and driver 3 hitting the right side of car 2 to the left of him, and the left side of car 4 to the right of him.

The officer took narrative statements from all four parties and concluded that the accident was caused by car 2 going too fast for conditions and striking car 1, which started the collision. Driver 2 claimed to be driving 65 mph (the speed limit), and driver 3 claimed to be driving 70 mph when he did not see the stopped car until right before the accident. Would you have reached the same conclusion as the officer as to the cause of the collision?

Automobile Accident Cases

An automobile accident causing injury usually entails a relatively straightforward investigation. The trial team needs to know who and what caused the accident

TRAFFIC COLLISION REPORT
CHP 555 Page 1 (Rev. 8-97) OPI 042

SPECIAL CONDITIONS	NUMBER INJURED ○	HIT & RUN FELONY ☐	CITY: LA		JUDICIAL DISTRICT LA Superior	LOCAL REPORT NUMBER
	NUMBER KILLED ○	HIT & RUN MISDEMEANOR ☐	COUNTY LA	REPORTING DISTRICT 734	BEAT 60	61204

LOCATION

COLLISION OCCURRED ON: **I-10 E/B (SANTA MONICA FREEWAY)**
MO / DAY / YEAR: **12 / 20 / 2012** TIME(2400): **2100** NCIC #: **90** OFFICER I.D.: **219**

MILEPOST INFORMATION: **100** ☒ FEET/☐ MILES **E** OF **10LA R9.74**
DAY OF WEEK: S M T W T F S (☒ on W) — TOW AWAY: ☐ YES ☒ NO — PHOTOGRAPHS BY: ☒ NONE

☒ AT INTERSECTION WITH / OR **100** ☒ FEET/☐ MILES **E** OF **HAUSER BLVD**
STATE HWY REL: ☒ YES ☐ NO — PHOTOGRAPHS BY: **NONE**

PARTY 1	DRIVER'S LICENSE NUMBER **53048212**	STATE **CA** CLASS **CA** AIR BAG **M** SAFETY EQUIP. **G**	VEH YEAR **04** MAKE/MODEL/COLOR **LEXUS / 15300 / SLV** LICENSE NUMBER **189644** STATE **CA**

☒ DRIVER — NAME (FIRST, MIDDLE, LAST) **David Edward**
☐ PEDESTRIAN — STREET ADDRESS **611 Cash Rd.**
☐ PARKED VEHICLE — CITY/STATE/ZIP **La Canada Flt, CA 91011**
OWNER'S NAME ☐ SAME AS DRIVER **SOPHIA ANN**
OWNER'S ADDRESS ☐ SAME AS DRIVER **47 Yarrow St Rose Hill, CA 91770**
DISPOSITION OF VEHICLE ON ORDERS OF: ☐ OFFICER ☒ DRIVER ☐ OTHER — **Driver**

☐ BICYCLIST — SEX **M** HAIR **BRN** EYES **BRN** HEIGHT **6'0** WEIGHT **250** BIRTHDATE **08 / 12 / 69** RACE **W**
PRIOR MECHANICAL DEFECTS: ☒ NONE APPARENT ☐ REFER TO NARRATIVE

☐ OTHER — HOME PHONE **(818) 555-1311** BUSINESS PHONE **(818) 555-3055**
VEHICLE IDENTIFICATION NUMBER

INSURANCE CARRIER **AAA** POLICY NUMBER **G8611053**
CHIP USE ONLY VEHICLE TYPE **01**
DESCRIBE VEHICLE DAMAGE: ☒ UNK ☐ NONE ☐ MINOR / ☒ MOD ☐ MAJOR ☐ ROLL-OVER
SHADE IN DAMAGED AREA

DIR OF TRAVEL **E** ON STREET OR HIGHWAY **I-10 E/B (SMF)** SPEED LIMIT **65**

PARTY 2	DRIVER'S LICENSE NUMBER **D623456**	STATE **CA** CLASS **CA** AIR BAG **M** SAFETY EQUIP. **G**	VEH YEAR **99** MAKE/MODEL/COLOR **Toyota / Camry / Gry** LICENSE NUMBER **40YP** STATE **CA**

☒ DRIVER — NAME (FIRST, MIDDLE, LAST) **Lisa Bethiwy**
☐ PEDESTRIAN — STREET ADDRESS **24 Stonesle CT**
☐ PARKED VEHICLE — CITY/STATE/ZIP **Westlake Vlg, CA 91361**
OWNER'S NAME ☐ SAME AS DRIVER **Jay Bethiwy**
OWNER'S ADDRESS ☒ SAME AS DRIVER
DISPOSITION OF VEHICLE ON ORDERS OF: ☐ OFFICER ☒ DRIVER ☐ OTHER — **Driver**

☐ BICYCLIST — SEX **F** HAIR **BRN** EYES **BRN** HEIGHT **5'0** WEIGHT **105** BIRTHDATE **03 / 03 / 78** RACE **W**
PRIOR MECHANICAL DEFECTS: ☒ NONE APPARENT ☐ REFER TO NARRATIVE

☐ OTHER — HOME PHONE **(805) 555-7828** BUSINESS PHONE **(805) 555-1735**
VEHICLE IDENTIFICATION NUMBER

INSURANCE CARRIER **Farmers** POLICY NUMBER **A151935649**
CHIP USE ONLY VEHICLE TYPE **01**
DESCRIBE VEHICLE DAMAGE: ☐ UNK ☐ NONE ☐ MINOR / ☒ MOD ☐ MAJOR ☐ ROLL-OVER
SHADE IN DAMAGED AREA

DIR OF TRAVEL **E** ON STREET OR HIGHWAY **I-10 E/B (SMF)** SPEED LIMIT **65**

PARTY 3	DRIVER LICENSE NUMBER **56011293**	STATE **CA** CLASS **CA** AIR BAG **M** SAFETY EQUIP. **G**	VEH YEAR **01** MAKE/MODEL/COLOR **Ford/F-150/Gold** LICENSE NUMBER **9427550** STATE **CA**

☒ DRIVER — NAME (FIRST, MIDDLE, LAST) **Jose Alfredol**
☐ PEDESTRIAN — STREET ADDRESS **808 Gent St.**
☐ PARKED VEHICLE — CITY/STATE/ZIP **La Puente, CA 91744**
OWNER'S NAME ☒ SAME AS DRIVER
OWNER'S ADDRESS ☒ SAME AS DRIVER
DISPOSITION OF VEHICLE ON ORDERS OF: ☐ OFFICER ☒ DRIVER ☐ OTHER — **Driver**

☐ BICYCLIST — SEX **M** HAIR **BRN** EYES **BRN** HEIGHT **5'11** WEIGHT **250** BIRTHDATE **01 / 04 / 76** RACE **H**
PRIOR MECHANICAL DEFECTS: ☒ NONE APPARENT ☐ REFER TO NARRATIVE

☐ OTHER — HOME PHONE **(626) 555-3421** BUSINESS PHONE **(626) 555-0505**
VEHICLE IDENTIFICATION NUMBER

INSURANCE CARRIER **Mercury** POLICY NUMBER **6A5313247**
CHIP USE ONLY VEHICLE TYPE **22**
DESCRIBE VEHICLE DAMAGE: ☐ UNK ☐ NONE ☐ MINOR / ☒ MOD ☐ MAJOR ☐ ROLL-OVER
SHADE IN DAMAGED AREA

DIR OF TRAVEL **E** ON STREET OR HIGHWAY **I-10 E/B (SMF)** SPEED LIMIT **65**

PREPARER'S NAME	DISPATCH NOTIFIED	REVIEWER'S NAME	DATA REVIEWED
W. Line 219	☐ YES ☐ NO ☒ N/A	PW 558	02 / 25 / 13

EXHIBIT 14-9 Traffic collision report.
Source: http://www.actar.org/pdf/ca-rep1.pdf

TRAFFIC COLLISION CODING

DATE OF COLLISION (NO. DAY YEAR)	TIME (2400)	NCK:	OFFICER ID.	NUMBER
12/20/2012	2100	90	219	

	OWNER'S NAME	OWNER'S ADDRESS		NOTIFIED
PROPERTY DAMAGE				☐ YES ☐ NO
	DESCRIPTION OF DAMAGE			

SEATING POSITION

```
      ∧
   1  2  3      1 - DRIVER
   4  5  6      2 TO 6 - PASSENGERS
               7 - STATION WAGON REAR
      7        8 - REAR OCC. TRK. OR VAN
               9 - POSMON UNKNOWN
               0 - OTHER
```

OCCUPANTS
A - NONE IN VEHICLE
B - UNKNOWN
C - LAP BELT USED
D - LAP BELT NOT USED
E - SHOULDER HARNESS USED
F - SHOULDER HARNESS NOT USED
G - LAP/SHOULDER HARNESS USED
H - LAP/SHOULDER HARNESS NOT USED
J - PASSIVE RESTRAINT USED
K - PASSIVE RESTRAINT NOT USED

SAFETY EQUIPMENT
L - AIR BAG DEPLOYED
M - AIR BAG NOT DEPLOYED
N - OTHER
P - NOT REQUIRED

CHILD RESTRAINT
Q - IN VEHICLE USED
R - IN VEHICLE NOT USED
S - IN VEHICLE USE UNKNOWN
T - IN VEHICLE IMPROPER USE
U - NONE IN VEHICLE

M / C BICYCLE- HELMET
DRIVER   PASSEMGER
V - NO   X - NO
W - YES   Y - YES

EJECTED FROM VEHICLE
0 - NOT EJECTED
1 - FULLY EJECTED
2 - PARTIALLY EJECTED
3 - UNKNOWN

INATTENTION CODES
A - CELLPHONE HANDHELD
B - CELLPHONE HANDSFREE
C - ELECTRONIC EQUIPMENT
D - RADIO / CD
E - SMOKING
F - EATING
G - CHILDREN
H - ANIMALS
I - PERSONAL HYGIENE
J - READING
K - OTHER

ITEMS MARKED BELOW FOLLOWED BY AN ASTERISK (*) SHOULD BE EXPLAINED IN THE NARRATIVE.

PRIMARY COLLISION FACTOR LIST NUMBER (#) OF PARTY AT FAULT	TRAFFIC CONTROL DEVICES	1	2	3	SPECIAL INFORMATION	1	2	3	MOVEMENT PRECEDING COLLISION
2 A. VC SECTION WOLATED: CITED ☐ YES 22350 VC ☒ NO	A CONTROLS FUNCTIONING				A HAZARDOUS MATERIAL	X			A STOPPED
	B CONTROLS NOT FUNCTIONING*				B CELL PHONE HANDHELD IN USE				B PROCEEDING STRAIGHT
B OTHER IMPROPER DRIVING*	C CONTROLS OBSCURES				C CELL PHONE HANDSFREE IN USE				C RAN OFF ROAD
	X D NO CONTROLS PRESENT / FACTOR	X	X	X	D CELL PHONE NOT IN USE				D MAKING RIGHT TURN
C OTHER THAN DRIVER*	TYPE OF COLLISION				E SCHOOL BUS RELATED				E MAKING LEFT TURN
D UNKNOWN*	A HEAD - ON				F 75 FT MOTORTRUCK COMBO				F MAKING U TURN
	B SIDE SWIPE				G 32 FT TRAILER COMBO				G BACKING
	X C REAR END				H		X	X	H SLOWING / STOPPING
WEATHER (MARK 1 TO 2 ITEMS)	D BROADSIDE				I				I PASSING OTHER VEHICLE
X A CLEAR	E HIT OBJECT				J				J CHANGING LANES
B CLOUDY	F OVERTURNED				K				K PARKING MANEUVER
C RAINING	G VEHICLE / PEDESTRIAN				L				L ENTERING TRAFFIC
D SNOWING	H OTHER				M				M OTHER UNSAFE TURNING
E FOG / VISIBILITY FT.					N				N XING INTO OPPOSING LANE
F OTHER	MOTOR VEHICLE INVOLVED WITH				O				O PARKED
G WIND	A NON - COLLISION								P MERGING
LIGHTING	B PEDESTRIAN								Q TRAVELING WRONG WAY
A DAYLIGHT	X C OTHER MOTOR VEHICLE				OTHER ASSOCIATED FACTOR(S) (MARK 1 TO 2 ITEMS)				R OTHER
B DUSK - DAWN	D MOTOR VEHICLE ON OTHER ROADWAY	1	2	3					
X C DARK - STREET LIGHTS	E PARKED MOTOR VEHICLE				A VC SECTION VIOLATION CITED ☐ YES ☐ NO				
D DARK - NO STREET LIGHTS	F TRAIN				B VC SECTION VIOLATION CITED ☐ YES ☐ NO				
E DARK - STREET LIGHTS NOT FUNCTIONING*	G BICYCLE								SOBRIEYT - DRUG PHYSICAL (MARK 1 TO 2 ITEMS)
	H ANIMAL				X C VC SECTION VIOLATION CITED ☐ YES ☒ NO 22350 VC	1	2	3	
ROADWAY SURFACE					D	X	X	X	A HAD NOT BEEN DRINKING:
X A DRY	I FIXED OBJECT:				E VISION OBSCUREMENT:				B HBD - UNDER INFLUENCE
B WET					F INATTENTION				C HBD - NOT UNDER INFLUENCE*
C SNOWY - ICY	J OTHER OBJECT:				G STOP & GO TRAFFIC				D HBD - IMPAIRMENT UNKNOWN*
D SLIPPERY (MUDDY, OILY, ETC)					H ENTERING / LEAVING RAMP				E UNDER DRUG INFLUENCE*
ROADWAY CONDITION(S) (MARK 1 TO 2 ITEMS)	PEDESTRIANS ACTIONS				I PREVIOUS COLLISION				F IMPAIRMENT - PHYSICAL*
A HOLES, DEEP RUT*	X A NO PEDESTRIANS INVOLVED				J UNFAMILIAR WITH ROAD				G IMPAIRMENT NOT KNOWN
B LOOSE MATERIAL ON ROADWAY*	B CROSSING IN CROSSWALK - AT INTERSECTION				K DEFECTIVE VEH. EQUIP: CITED ☐ YES ☐ NO				H NOT APPLICABLE
C OBSTRUSTION ON ROADWAY*									I SLEEPY / FATIGUED
D CONSTRUCTION - REPAIR ZONE	C CROSSING IN CROSSWALK - NOT AT INTERSECTION								
E REDUCED ROADWAY WIDTH	D CROSSING - NOT IN CROSSWALK				L UNINVOLED VEHICLE				
F FLOODED*	E IN ROAD - INCLUDES SHOULDER				M OTHER				
G OTHER*	F NOT IN ROAD	X	X		N NONE APPARENT				
X H NO UNUSUAL CONDITIONS	G APPROACHING / LEAVING SCHOOL BUS				O RUNAWAY VEHICLE				

SKETCH

HAUSER BLVD

CENTER MEDIAN   CENTER DIVIDER WALL   ◆ INDICATE NORTH

```
12'  SOLID YELLOW LINE          V-1
                          V-2   ①        #1
12'                       V-3   ②
                                ③        #2
12'  DASHED WHITE         V-4
     LINES
12'                                      #3

12'                                      #4

12'  SOLID WHITE LINE                    #5
                    I-10 E/B (SANTA MONICA FREEWAY)
 6'       SHOULDER
                          RAISED CURB
```

MISCELLANEOUS

OSP 03 79147

DATE OF INCIDENT/OCCURRENCE 12/20/2012	TIME (2400) 2100	NCIC NUMBER 90		OFFICER I.D. NUMBER 219	NUMBER

"X" ONE	"X" ONE	TYPE SUPPLEMENTAL ("X" APPLICABLE)		
☒ Narrative	☒ Collision Report	☐ BA Update	☐ Fatal	☐ Hit and Run Update
☐ Supplemental	☐ Other: ____	☐ Hazardous Materials	☐ School Bus	☐ Other: ____

CITY/COUNTY/JUDICIAL DISTRICT	BEAT 60	CITATION NUMBER

LOCATION/SUBJECT	STATE HIGHWAY RELATED ☒ Yes ☐ No

1. NOTIFICATION:

2.

3. I RECEIVED A RADIO CALL FROM CHP DISPATCH OF A TRAFFIC COLLISION

4. WITH NO DETAILS. AT APPROXIMATELY 2100 HOURS.

5. I RESPONDED FROM THE VICINITY OF SRF110 NYB AND STADIUM

6. WAY AND ARRIVED ON SCENE AT APPROXIMATELY 2110 HOURS.

7. ALL TIMES, SPEEDS AND MEASUREMENTS ARE APPROXIMATE.

8. MEASUREMENTS WERE OBTAINED BY VISUAL ESTIMATION AND

9. ROLL-A-TAPE.

10.

11. STATEMENTS:

12.

13. PARTY #1 (EDWARD) WAS LOCATED AT THE SCENE AND RELATED THE FOLLOWING

14. INFORMATION IN ESSENCE: I WAS STOPPED IN THE #1 LANE AND CENTER MEDIAN

15. AS CLOSE TO THE WALL AS POSSIBLE DUE TO A FLAT TIRE WHEN I WAS STRUCK FROM BEHIND

16.

17. PARTY #2 (BETHIWY) WAS LOCATED AT THE SCENE AND RELATED THE

18. FOLLOWING INFORMATION IN ESSENCE: I WAS TRAVELING IN THE #1 LANE

19. AT APPROXIMATELY 65 MPH WHEN I NOTICED THE STOPPED

20. VEHICLE AHEAD I HIT THE BRAKES AND SWERVED TO THE

21. RIGHT, BUT IT WAS TOO LATE AND I HIT THE CAR IN

22. FRONT OF ME. AFTER THAT, THE TRUCK HIT ME FROM THE

23. RIGHT SIDE.

24.

25. PARTY #3 (ALFREDOL) WAS LOCATED AT THE SCENE AND RELATED THE

26. FOLLOWING INFORMATION IN ESSENCE: I WAS TRAVELING IN THE

27. #1 LANE AT APPROXIMATELY 70 MPH WHEN I NOTICED THE

28. TWO CARS STOPPED AHEAD OF ME. I HIT THE BRAKES AND

29. TRIED TO SWERVE TO THE RIGHT, BUT I ENDED UP HITTING

30. THE CARS ON BOTH MY LEFT AND RIGHT SIDE.

31.

☐ Continued

PREPARER'S NAME AND I.D. NUMBER W. LINE 219	DATE 2/20/2009	REVIEWER'S NAME	DATE

Use previous editions until depleted.

OSP 04 82787

EXHIBIT 14-9   Traffic collision report. *(continued)*

Source: http://www.actar.org/pdf/ca-rep1.pdf

STATE OF CALIFORNIA
NARRATIVE/SUPPLEMENTAL
CHP 556 (Rev. 7-90) OPI 061

DATE OF INCIDENT/OCCURRENCE 12/20/2012	TIME (2400) 2100	NCIC NUMBER 90	OFFICER I.D. NUMBER 219	NUMBER

"X" ONE
- [X] Narrative
- [ ] Supplemental

"X" ONE
- [X] Collision Report
- [ ] Other: _____

TYPE SUPPLEMENTAL ("X" APPLICABLE)
- [ ] BA Update
- [ ] Hazardous Materials
- [ ] Fatal
- [ ] School Bus
- [ ] Hit and Run Update
- [ ] Other: _____

CITY/COUNTY/JUDICIAL DISTRICT	BEAT 60	CITATION NUMBER

LOCATION/SUBJECT

STATE HIGHWAY RELATED
- [X] Yes
- [ ] No

1. STATEMENTS (CONTINUED):

2. _____

3.   PARTY #4 (MAGAB) WAS LOCATED AT THE SCENE AND RELATED

4.   THE FOLLOWING INFORMATION IN ESSENCE: I WAS TRAVELING IN THE #2 LANE AT

5.   APPROXIMATELY 65 MPH WHEN I HEARD SCREECHING TIRES AND

6.   THE TRUCK HIT ME FROM THE LEFT SIDE.

7. _____

8. SUMMARY:

9. _____

10.   THIS COLLISION OCCURRED IN THE #1 AND #2 LANES OF I-10

11.   E/B(SMF) EAST OF HAUSER BLVD P-1 WAS STOPPED IN THE #1 LANE

12.   AND CENTER MEDIAN DUE TO A FLAT TIRE. P-2 WAS TRAVELING IN THE

13.   #1 LANE AT APPROXIMATELY 65 MPH DIRECTLY TO THE REAR

14.   OF V-1. P-3 WAS TRAVELING IN THE #1 LANE AT APPROXIMATELY

15.   70 MPH BEHIND V-2 P-4 WAS TRAVELING IN THE #2 LANE AT

16.   APPROXIMATELY 65 MPH TO THE RIGHT OF V-1 AND V-2. P-2

17.   FAILED TO NOTICE V-1 STOPPED AHEAD UNTIL THE LAST MINUTE,

18.   APPLIED V-2'S BRAKES, AND SWERVED TO THE RIGHT, BUT

19.   IT WAS TOO LATE. THE LEFT FRONT OF V-2 STRUCK

20.   THE RIGHT REAR OF V-1. P-3 FAILED TO

21.   NOTICE THE TWO STOPPED CARS AHEAD AND APPLIED V-3'S BRAKES

22.   AND SWERVED TO THE RIGHT, BUT IT WAS TOO LATE. THE

23.   LEFT FRONT OF V-3 STRUCK THE RIGHT SIDE OF V-2, AND THEN

24.   THE RIGHT FRONT OF V-3 STRUCK THE LEFT SIDE OF V-4.

25.   AFTER THIS COLLISION, V-1 AND V-2 REMAINED AT THEIR

26.   POINTS OF REST AND P-3 AND P-4 MOVED FORWARD AND INTO

27.   THE #1 LANE AND AWAITED CHP ARRIVAL.

28. _____

29. _____

30. _____

31. _____

- [ ] Continued

PREPARER'S NAME AND I.D. NUMBER W. LINE 219	DATE 2/20/2009	REVIEWER'S NAME	DATE

Use previous editions until depleted.

OSP 04 82787

EXHIBIT 14-9 Traffic collision report. *(continued)*
Source: http://www.actar.org/pdf/ca-rep1.pdf

DATE OF INCIDENT/OCCURRENCE 2/20/2012	TIME (2400) 2100	NCIC NUMBER 90	OFFICER I.D. NUMBER 219	NUMBER

"X" ONE	"X" ONE	TYPE SUPPLEMENTAL ("X" APPLICABLE)		
☒ Narrative	☒ Collision Report	☐ BA Update	☐ Fatal	☐ Hit and Run Update
☐ Supplemental	☐ Other: _____	☐ Hazardous Materials	☐ School Bus	☐ Other: _____

CITY/COUNTY/JUDICIAL DISTRICT	BEAT 60	CITATION NUMBER

LOCATION/SUBJECT	STATE HIGHWAY RELATED ☒ Yes ☐ No

1. AREAS OF IMPACT:
2.
3. AOI # 1 (V-2 VS. V-1) WAS LOCATED APPROXIMATELY 6 FEET SOUTH OF
4. THE NORTH ROADWAY EDGE OF I-10 E/B (SMF) AND APPROXIMATELY
5. 100 FEET EAST OF THE WEST EDGE OF HAUSER BLVD.
6.
7. AOI #2 (V-3 VS. V-2) WAS LOCATED APPROXIMATELY 10 FEET SOUTH
8. OF THE NORTH ROADWAY EDGE OF I-10 E/B (SMF) AND APPROXIMATELY
9. 90 FEET EAST OF THE WEST EDGE OF HAUSER BLVD.
10.
11. AOI #3 (V-3 VS. V-4) WAS LOCATED APPROXIMATELY 17 FEET SOUTH
12. OF THE NORTH ROADWAY EDGE OF I-10 E/B (SMF) AND
13. APPROXIMATELY 95 FEET EAST OF THE WEST EDGE OF HAUSER BLVD.
14.
15. THE AREAS OF IMPACT WERE DETERMINED BY DRIVERS'
16. STATEMENTS AND VEHICLE DAMAGE.
17.
18. CAUSE:
19.
20. P-2 CAUSED THIS COLLISION BY DRIVING IN VIOLATION OF
21. 22350 VC (UNSAFE SPEED FOR CONDITIONS). P-2 WAS
22. DRIVING TOO FAST TO SAFELY STOP AND AVOID A
23. COLLISION WITH P-1.
24.
25. P-3 CONTRIBUTED TO THIS COLLISION BY DRIVING IN
26. VIOLATION OF 22350 VC (UNSAFE SPEED FOR CONDITIONS).
27. P-3 WAS DRIVING TOO FAST TO SAFELY STOP AND AVOID
28. A COLLISION WITH P-2 AND P-4.
29.
30. THE CAUSE OF THIS COLLISION WAS DETERMINED BY DRIVERS'
31. STATEMENTS AND VEHICLE DAMAGE.

☐ Continued

PREPARER'S NAME and I.D. NUMBER W. LINE 219	DATE 2/20/2009	REVIEWER'S NAME	DATE

Use previous editions until depleted.

OSP 04 82787

EXHIBIT 14-9 Traffic collision report. *(continued)*
Source: http://www.actar.org/pdf/ca-rep1.pdf

and what damages the parties suffered. A typical general investigation includes the following steps:

- The client is interviewed for information as to how the accident happened, injuries, who was at fault, and any witnesses.
- Police accident reports are obtained for information such as:
  - Witness names and addresses
  - The exact location of the accident
  - The disposition of each party to the accident and each vehicle (i.e., what parties were taken to which hospital, what vehicles had to be towed, and where they were taken)
  - Injury and property damage to vehicle and contents
  - Any tickets issued by police at the scene
  - Any comments in the report as to fault or factors that contributed to the accident (such as eating, drinking, falling asleep, or other activities)
  - Weather conditions
- Photographs should be taken of the vehicle or vehicles and the parties' injuries, if necessary.
- Medical records should be ordered and particular attention paid to any tests for alcohol or drugs.
- If there is a question regarding a mechanical malfunction, an expert may be called in to inspect the vehicle or vehicles involved.
- If there are allegations of dangerous street design or street conditions, additional investigation may be required.

In addition to the preceding, when the trial team represents the defendant, it will be interested in investigating the following:

- Names of other possible defendants (owner of street, entity responsible for street maintenance)
- Defenses to the plaintiff's claims
- Acts of the plaintiff that contributed to the accident
- Prior lawsuits by the plaintiff
- Preexisting injuries of the plaintiff
- The plaintiff's prior accidents or claims
- Reputation and standing of the plaintiff's treating physician (who may be relied on by the plaintiff as an expert at trial)

Mechanical Malfunction. If there is a question about possible mechanical malfunction, the trial team probably will find itself going beyond a simple investigation and into the more extensive inquiry necessary in a products liability case. The client should be consulted regarding projected future expenses for which the client would be responsible before the investigation proceeds, as such lawsuits can be quite costly.

Dangerous Street Conditions. If there are indications of dangerous street conditions, the paralegal should watch for scenarios such as:

▶ Debris that fell from a truck or other vehicle that might have contributed to the accident
▶ Vegetation affecting visibility
▶ A street being repaired or under construction or allegations that lanes were not properly marked, equipment or machinery was left in the street, visibility was obscured, and so on
▶ A dangerous intersection or design of the street
▶ A street sign, such as a stop sign or one-way sign, that is obscured or missing
▶ Possible involvement of a municipality, and whether it is entitled by law to notice of the condition claimed before suit can be brought
▶ Other accidents at the same location

Construction Sites. If the site of the accident was under construction or repair at the time of the incident, an inquiry as to the conditions may be undertaken. Likewise, if there are allegations of debris on the road, they should be followed up, as any of these scenarios may indicate additional defendants.

Freedom of Information Act (FOIA) Requests. Under the Freedom of Information Act, 5 U.S.C. § 552, you can request many different kinds of federal agency records or information. Agencies are required to disclose information from records after receiving a written request. There is usually a photocopying charge for these requests. It is to be noted there are exceptions to this rule for national security and certain privacy interests.

State Public Records Laws. Requests for state and local agency records must be sent to the appropriate state or local agency. All 50 states have public records laws allowing the public to obtain certain documents and public records from state and local agencies. These records laws are similar to but not the same as the federal Freedom of Information Act. Accordingly, be sure to check your state provisions before making an information request.

Medical Negligence Cases

In a case involving possible medical negligence or malpractice, investigation can be quite complex and costly. Consider a hypothetical, but not unrealistic, example.

A patient goes into a hospital to have his appendix removed. The doctor fails to remove a clamp from the patient before suturing him up. One week after being discharged from the hospital, the patient experiences severe pain and a high fever. The patient goes to the emergency room and is admitted for emergency exploratory surgery. The clamp is found and removed. Potential areas of investigation in such a case would include

- What was the cause of injury or death?
  - Was it a result of medical treatment or lack thereof?
  - Was it a result of negligence on the part of the hospital staff or doctors?
  - Was it a result of something that was done or not done prior to admission to the facility?
  - Did the patient follow prescribed treatment?
- What do the medical records or autopsy records indicate as the cause of injury or death? (See Exhibits 14-10, 14-11, and 14-12.)
- What was the plaintiff's condition upon arriving at the emergency room?
- What diagnosis had been rendered during the previous hospital admission? (See Exhibit 14-10.)
- What types of consent forms and releases for treatment were signed, and who signed them (the victim, his or her guardian, and so forth)?
- Did the surgeon follow the standard of care that other surgeons performing appendectomies would have followed?

EXHIBIT 14-10
Sample medical report (radiology).

EXHIBIT 14-11
Sample medical report (doctor's evaluation).

SHANIKA THOMAS, M.D., P.C.
STAN HOFF, M.D., D.M.D., P.C.
65 Western Avenue, Albany, New York 12203
Telephone 438-4400

March 12, 2013

Cathy J. Okrent, Esq.
Washington Square
Box 1501
Albany, New York 12212

Re: Wanda Powers
d/a: 5/2/12

Dear Ms. Okrent:

Wanda Powers was in the office on March 12, 2013 concerning scars of the right lower leg. According to the history on May 2, 2012 she was apparently attacked by four dogs, receiving bites on the right lower leg. One bite required three sutures and one puncture wound required one suture. The wounds healed without infection.

Examination disclosed a white, soft scar 3 × 1.5 cms. on the lateral part of the mid calf of the right lower leg. This scar is permanent and no treatment is indicated. There are two puncture scars, each measuring 0.6 cms., on the upper and lower lateral leg. These scars are permanent and no treatment is indicated.

If I can be of any further help to you please do not hesitate to let me know.

Sincerely,

_____
SHANIKA THOMAS, M.D.

ST: mk

If the initial evaluation indicates a potential case, additional investigation will be warranted. Paralegals will want to find out about any doctors involved, their qualifications and training, and whether they have been the subject of previous lawsuits or complaints. One will also want to find out the same information about the hospital and its personnel.

Obtaining Information about Health Care Providers

Health care facilities, such as hospitals, nursing homes, retirement centers, and rehabilitation hospitals, are overseen by various governmental and private agencies and licensing organizations. For instance, if a paralegal works on a case involving someone who contracted a disease from a blood transfusion, he or she should know that all blood banks are overseen by the American Association of Blood Banks. That association sets out standards and requirements, as well as inspection criteria.

EXHIBIT 14-12
Sample medical report (discharge form).

MEDICAL CENTER HOSPITAL
DISCHARGE INSTRUCTIONS & SUMMARY FORM

Patient Identification

I. FINAL DIAGNOSES: (list in order of importance; do not abbreviate)

Condition on discharge:

1. Fracture lumbar vertebrae first and second — ☐ Recovered ☑ Improved ☐ Not Improved ☐ Diagnosis Only ☐ Not Treated ☐ Other ____

2. ____ — ☐ Recovered ☐ Improved ☐ Not Improved ☐ Diagnosis Only ☐ Not Treated ☐ Other ____

3. Spondylolysis and listhesis lumbar five on sacrum — ☐ Recovered ☐ Improved ☐ Not Improved ☑ Diagnosis Only ☐ Not Treated ☐ Other ____

4. sprained left ankle — ☐ Recovered ☑ Improved ☐ Not Improved ☐ Diagnosis Only ☐ Not Treated ☐ Other ____

(Complete additional forms as necessary)

II. OPERATIONS AND/OR PROCEDURES

1) none

III. DISCHARGE INSTRUCTIONS AND MEDICATIONS WITH DOSAGE. If no medication check here ✓

1) F/U Dr Dougherty 2 wks
2) tylenol III @ Rx
3) ambulatory c̄ brace as tolerated.
4) may shower
5) avoid lifting, sitting

IV. SUMMARY:

1. Reason for Admission: pain in back @ plane accident

2. Pertinent physical, psychological, x-ray and laboratory findings: [illegible]
x-ray – 15% compression & displacement L1 L2
spondylolysis + listhesis grade I L5 S1
[illegible] L-5 spine [illegible]

3. Course in hospital (medical, psychiatric, and/or surgical therapy):
brace ordered unremarkable.

(OVER)

EXHIBIT 14-12 (cont.) Sample medical report (discharge form).

3. Course in hospital, continued:

V. LIMIT OF DISABILITY:

Patient may return to work: ☐ YES ☑ NO

Patient is essentially home bound: ☑ YES ☐ NO

VI. PAP SMEAR INFORMATION FOR FEMALE PATIENTS:

Pap Smear done during this admission ☐ YES ☐ NO ☐ WITHIN LAST 3 YEARS
☐ REFUSED BY PATIENT

VII. PATIENT OR RESPONSIBLE OTHER VERBALIZES, DEMONSTRATES, OR EXHIBITS KNOWLEDGE OF:

Completed by

1. Nature of Illness	☑ YES ☐ NO ☐ N/A	☐ M.D.	☐ RN ☐ Other _____ (Sign & Date)
2. Diet	☐ YES ☐ NO ☑ N/A	☐ M.D.	☐ RN ☐ Other _____ (Sign & Date)
3. Wound care	☐ YES ☐ NO ☑ N/A	☐ M.D.	☐ RN ☐ Other _____ (Sign & Date)
4. Medications	☑ YES ☐ NO ☐ N/A	☐ M.D.	☐ RN ☐ Other _____ (Sign & Date)
5. Special health teaching (colostomy care, casts, diabetic care, etc.)	☑ YES ☐ NO ☐ N/A	☐ M.D.	☐ RN ☐ Other _____ (Sign & Date)
6. Activity	☑ YES ☐ NO ☐ N/A	☐ M.D.	☐ RN ☐ Other _____ (Sign & Date)
7. Follow-up appointments and referrals	☑ YES ☐ NO ☐ N/A	☐ M.D.	☐ RN ☐ Other _____ (Sign & Date)

COMMENTS _____

_____

VIII. SIGNATURE OF PHYSICIAN RESPONSIBLE FOR DISCHARGE OF PATIENT:

_____   M.D. ☐ Intern ☐ Resident
☐ Acting Intern
☐ Fellow ☐ Attending

TO BE COMPLETED BY THE NURSING DIVISION AT THE TIME THE PATIENT LEAVES THE HOSPITAL:

Date ___1/5___ Time ___11:10___ Mode: ☑ Wheelchair ☐ Stretcher ☐ Walked out

Discharge to: ☐ Nursing Home of Extended Care Facility
☑ Home
☐ Other (Specify) _____

Belongings to _____ Accompanied by _____
Signature   ☐ Floor Clerk ☐ Nurse ☐ Other

Various specifications and standards for health care providers are set by governmental agencies, professional organizations, and licensing boards. They keep records regarding

▶ Current addresses

▶ Schools attended and grades earned

⬗ Professional credentials

⬗ Honors and awards

⬗ Continuing education requirements

⬗ Licensure status and board certification

⬗ Past and present complaints against the provider

Therefore, these organizations are excellent resources for gathering information on defendant doctors, nurses, and other health care professionals. This information can also be utilized to evaluate health care professionals who have been designated as expert witnesses by defendants and those one might want to use as experts. Some states allow access to some of this information online.

Exhibit 14-13 shows OSHA Form 301, an injury and illness incident report.

PRACTICAL APPLICATION

If the health care professional is a specialist, the paralegal should keep in mind that there are additional qualifications for each specialty area. A separate licensing board or organization typically oversees each specialty. For example, a surgeon might be certified to operate by the American Board of Surgery.

Health Care Facilities That Receive Governmental Funding

If a health care facility receives government funds (such as Medicare), it is inspected by the state health department for compliance with regulations. Such state inspections, along with any compliance and deficiency reports, are public records. As such, they can be obtained for review under the Freedom of Information Act and through discovery. Exhibit 14-14 shows a supervisor's workplace accident investigation report.

OSHA'S Form 301
Injury and Illness Incident Report

Attention: This form contains information relating to employee health and must be used in a manner that protects the confidentiality of employees to the extent possible while the information is being used for occupational safety and health purposes.

U.S. Department of Labor
Occupational Safhey and Health Administration

This Injury and Illness Incident Report is one of the first forms you must fill out when a recordable work-related injury or illness has occurred. Together with the Log of Work-Related Injuries and Illness and the accompanying Summary, these forms help the employer and OSHA develop a picture of the extent and severity of work-related incidents.

Within 7 calendar days after you receive information that a recordable work-related injury or illness has occurred, you must fill out this form or an equivalent form. Some state workers' compensation, insurance, or other reports may be acceptable substitutes. To be considered an equivalent form, any substitute must contain all the information asked for on this form.

According to Public Law 91-596 and 29 CFR 1904, OSHA's recordkeeping rule, you must keep this form on file for 5 years following the year to which it pertains.

If you need additional copies of this form, you may photocopy and use as many as you need.

Completed by ___Joy Wong___

Title ___DA___

Phone ___(348)562-4811___   Date ___9 / 15 / 13___

Information about the employee

1) Full name ___Henry Joseph___

2) Street ___PO Box 3452___

City ___ANCHOR MANOR___   State ___AL___   Zip ___99524___

3) Date of birth ___02 / 11 / 80___

4) Date hired ___05 / 19 / 10___

5) ☒ Male
   ☐ Female

Information about the physician or other health care professional

6) Name of physician or other health care professional ___
___DR. Miriam Schwartz___

7) If treatment was given away from the worksite, where was it given?

Facility ___Meadowviews Medical Center___

Strecs ___410 5th Street___

City ___ANCHOR Manor___   State ___AL___   Zip ___99519___

8) Was employee treated in an emergency room?
   ☒ Yes
   ☐ No

9) Was employee hospitalized overnight as an in-patient?
   ☐ Yes
   ☒ No

Information about the case

10) Case number from the Log ___1___   *(Transfer the case number from the Log after you record the case.)*

11) Date of injury or illness ___9 / 15 / 13___

12) Time employee began work ___0000___ (AM)/PM

13) Time of event ___0325___ (AM)/PM   ☐ Check if time cannot be determined

14) **What was the employee doing just before the incident occurred?** Describe the activity, as well as the tools, equipment, or material the employee was using. Be specific. *Examples:* "climbing a ladder while carrying roofing materials"; "spraying chlorine from hand sprayer"; "daily computer key-entry."

Attempting to lower a filing cabinet from a desktop to the floor.

15) **What happened?** Tell us how the injury occurred. *Examples:* "When ladder slipped on wet floor, worker fell 20 feet"; "Worker was sprayed with chlorine when gasket broke during replacement"; "Worker developed soreness in wrist over time."

Gripped sides of cabinet and attempted to lift. Felt immediate pain in wrists at that time.

16) **What was the injury or illness?** Tell us the part of the body that was affected and how it was affected; be more specific than "hurt," "Pain," or sore.: *Examples:* "strained back"; "chemical burn, hand"; "carpal tunnel syndrome."

Pain & swelling in both wrists.

17) **What object or substance directly harmed the employee?** *Examples:* "concrete floor"; "chlorine"; "radial arm saw." *If this question does not apply to the incident, leave it blank.*

Filing cabinet.

18) **If the employee died, when did death occur?** Date of death ___ / ___ / ___

Public reporting burden for this collection of information is estimated to average 22 minutes per response, including time for reviewing instructions, searching existing data sources, gathering and maintaining the data needed, and completing and reviewing the collection of information. Persons are not required to respond to the collection of information unless it displays a current valid OMB control number. If you have any comments about this estimate or any other aspects of this data collection, including suggestions for reducing this burden, contact: US Department of Labor, OSHA Office of Statistics. Room N-3644, 200 Constitution Avenue, NW. Washington, DC 20210. Do not send the completed forms to this office.

EXHIBIT 14-13   OSHA Form 301, injury and illness incident report.
Source: http://www.dir.ca.gov/dosh/dosh.publications/calositaform301.pdf

SUPERVISOR'S ACCIDENT INVESTIGATION REPORT

Send Completed Report to Risk   within Five (5) days of Date of Injury

Office Name: Governor's Hospital   No.: _____   Date of this Report: 12-18-13

EMPLOYEE INFORMATION

Name of Injured (F, MI, L): Alex A. Lizuski   SSN: 135-06-9999   Hire Date: 02-03-96

Dept. Name: Nursing   Post Held at time of injury: 4 West   How long at this job: 13 yrs

Describe injuries sustained by employee: Laceration / Abrasion shin area

Has the employee lost any work time? ☐ Yes ☒ No   Were they kept overnight in a hospital? ☐ Yes ☒ No

Did the employee receive prompt and appropriate medical care? ☒ Yes ☐ No If no, briefly explain: _____

Treating Physician: Frances Teika, M.D.

Treating Facility: Governor's Hospital

Address: 410 Fifth Street   Tele: (203) 369-1410

ACCIDENT INFORMATION

Date of Injury: 12-18-13   Time of Injury: 4:10 - AM (PM)   ☐ Daylight ☒ Dusk/Dawn ☐ Night

Type of Accident: ☐ Slip, ☐ Fall, ☐ Sprain, ☐ Strain, ☐ Lifting, ☐ Vehicle, ☐ Firearms, ☒ Other, please explain: Assisting other nurses with a combative patient, hit shin on oak bed rail

Type of Location (e.g. shopping mall, parking lot, city street, etc.): Hospital room

Accident Location: _____

                        Street Address   City   State   ZIP

Relevant Weather Conditions: _____

Type of Lighting at Time of Accident: _____

Client site? ☐ No ☒ Yes Client Name: Governor's Hospital

Any witnesses? ☐ No ☒ Yes Witness Names & Contact Info.(e.g. telephone numbers and/or addresses):

Bill Wittier   518 734-0002

Victor Roberge   518 734-0950

_____

If vehicle related, has the *Auto. Loss Notice* been properly filed? ☐ Yes ☐ No If no, briefly explain: _____

Based upon your investigation, briefly describe what took place (WHO, WHAT, WHEN, WHERE, HOW and WHY):

Patient Lavelle Chingere, didn't want to take medication from a needle, at 4:05 PM, Bpt Hosp, patient became combative, when officer Lix Lizas went to grab his legs, he was pulled into the oak rail and caused laceration / abrasion to Alex A. Lizuski's shin, left side. This is a pyhic wing, and each case is different

What can be done to avoid a recurrence of this type of accident? This type of injury just can't be avoided. This is one of two pyshic wings

What actions have been taken by you or the client to remedy any risk associated with this type of accident? _____

If applicable, has the client been notified of any related hazard or unsafe condition? ☒ Yes ☐ No If no, please explain: _____

If yes, has the condition been corrected? ☐ Yes ☒ No If no, have they committed to remedying the problem? Please explain: _____

as explained above

Investigator's Name: Jane Leppize, RN   Title: Shift Supervisor

Investigator's Signature: ⊗ Jane Lyppp

Reviewed by: _____ ⊗   Date: 12-18-13

EXHIBIT 14-14 Supervisor's workplace accident investigation report.

▌ SUMMARY

Fact gathering is a significant paralegal role in tort investigations. Paralegals investigate and document the tort scene and interview the client, eyewitnesses, and other persons with pertinent information. Attorneys and law firms often have specialized techniques for conducting investigations. Some use in-house personnel; others hire outside investigative services. Paralegals should customize their investigations to fit the type and size of tort case involved. Details are critical. In part, factual investigations are designed to determine liability and damages. It is important to interview witnesses as soon as possible to obtain the best recollected information. Witnesses explain how the tort occurred according to their observational perspectives.

Defendants are usually determined in-house. It may be difficult to identify or locate potential defendants and witnesses, especially if they are business entities or transient individuals. One should exercise extreme caution when naming parties in lawsuits. The client and/or attorney or law firm could be liable or disciplined for suing the wrong business or person. Potential defendants can be identified in many ways: scrutinizing documents to glean names, addresses, and telephone numbers; making telephone calls to businesses or individuals involved; performing online searches; checking with the secretary of state's corporation or partnership divisions or the county or city offices in which assumed names of businesses are registered; and searching company records and documents. Special difficulties arise with ambulance and fire departments as defendants. These entities are often owned or supervised by local governmental agencies, or they may be volunteer services working under governmental contract. Information concerning licensed or regulated businesses can be obtained through the federal or state regulatory agencies.

Paralegals use photographs, videos, and traditional pencil-and-paper methods of documenting tort scenes. The events in a tort case and their sequence are documented and reconstructed under the same conditions in which the tort originally occurred. Paralegals must know their jurisdiction's evidentiary rules if they are to recognize the types of evidence that will be useful in the tort case. It is important to collect evidence in the proper evidentiary form so that it may be used at trial. Hearsay problems should be anticipated and overcome. Most litigation firms now use computer and video technologies to assist in documenting and reconstructing tort cases.

Local governmental agencies may possess a wealth of information concerning some parties involved in the tort case. Archives contain vital statistics, marriage licenses, property ownership records, police records, and civil suit or criminal records. Newspapers, television, and radio can also provide valuable information about the events that occurred when the tort happened. Data bases can also furnish considerable information about the persons or businesses involved in the case.

Paralegals investigate employment and lost wages to help determine the client's damages. Tax, wage, and income records should be obtained. Injury expenses are carefully documented and investigated. It is important to know whether the injured party has received insurance or governmental benefits as a result of the tort. It is also necessary to know whether the plaintiff has previously been involved in claims or lawsuits, as well as preexisting injuries, involving the same factual circumstances as the present tort case. The parties' driving or criminal records may be critical to the current case.

Investigations are tailored to fit the specific aspects of each tort case. Cases involving automobile accidents or medical negligence and health care providers each require specialized questions that paralegals use to gather the information necessary for the trial team to successfully conclude the case.

While this last chapter concludes the formal study of torts and personal injury law, it should be considered the starting point for further research and study, as tort law is ever changing to meet society's needs.

KEY TERMS

business directory
discovery
fictitious name

freedom of information law
  (FOIL)
hearsay

investigation
service of process (process service)

PROBLEMS

Assume the following actual cases were assigned to you for investigation. As the senior paralegal for the law firm, you performed the preliminary interview of each of the named plaintiffs. Identify what kind of investigation you would conduct and the different sources you would consult to further your investigation. Be sure to consider each of the facts of the case, as well as all the potential defendants.

1. Ms. Santiago was admitted to the Glenwood Hospital through the emergency room with severe pain to the abdomen. After an exploratory operation by Dr. Inexperienced, an infected appendix was discovered and removed. Ms. Santiago was released four days later. She continued to have increasingly severe pain and was readmitted to the hospital three weeks later. The same surgeon performed another operative procedure in which he recovered a surgical sponge left in Ms. Santiago during the initial operation and removed it.

2. Suzie Woo is seven months pregnant. While crossing the grounds of the Gentle Breeze Country Club with her friend Dewanna Stevens, she stepped on a circular manhole cover, which unbeknownst to her was slightly ajar. The manhole tipped open and she fell in the hole, with her stomach preventing her from falling completely down the open pit. Just minutes before, a Quick Rooter Plumbing truck was spotted driving off the grounds of the club.

3. Josh Tyler is walking up the hill on State Street when a car without a driver comes rolling out of a private parking lot, down the street, and pins him against an office building, breaking four of his ribs and his left leg. A store employee who sees the accident happen calls an ambulance. Josh is taken to the nearest hospital. He later learns that the car had recently been serviced by Jenelle's Auto Repair.

4. Arnold Rubitkowitz is playing bingo at the local Grand Tigers Club fundraiser at the Hotel Luxe. Just when his cards are finally starting to look promising, the five-foot-long fluorescent light fixture drops from the ceiling above his head, rendering him momentarily unconscious. The bingo caller stops the game long enough to summon the local fire department, the police, and the town paramedics, who take Arnold to the local emergency room for treatment.

5. Trevor Vincent is taking a Sunday ride on his motorcycle through a new development by Sherman Oaks Builders in the town of Leewood, Texas. As he approaches a sharp curve in the road, he comes upon some construction debris, is unable to complete the sharp turn, is thrown 20 feet from his motorcycle, lands on his head, and dies. Trevor was not wearing a helmet at the time of the accident.

REVIEW QUESTIONS

1. What are the basic components of a tort case investigation? Who conducts these investigations? How are investigations customized? What types of questions are witnesses asked in tort investigations?

2. Why is it important to identify the correct defendant(s) in a tort case? What could happen if incorrect persons or businesses are sued as defendants?

3. How can a client's documents and the telephone help locate potential defendants? Whom should a paralegal contact to obtain information about corporations, partnerships, or sole proprietorships that are prospective defendants?

4. What special problems are associated with ambulance and fire departments that are defendants?

5. Whom should a paralegal contact to investigate licensed or regulated businesses?

6. How should a paralegal document an accident scene? What conditions should be prevalent when the scene is investigated? What items should be included on the investigation checklist?

7. Why is it important to tort investigations to know the evidentiary rules from one's jurisdiction?

8. How can local governmental agencies, newspapers, television, radio, and computer databases be helpful in researching a tort case?

9. Why are criminal and driving records pertinent to tort investigations? What can this information reveal about the case being investigated?

10. What additional areas should a tort paralegal investigate?

11. What are some of the kinds of information that can be obtained online to assist in an investigation?

HELPFUL WEBSITES

This chapter focuses on tort investigation. To learn more about tort investigation, the following sites can be accessed:

Litigation Law

www.hg.org

American Arbitration Association

www.adr.org

Federal Rules of Civil Procedure

www.law.cornell.edu

Information Related to Tort Law

www.findlaw.com
www.statelocal.gov
www.usa.gov

Kelly Blue Book to Evaluate Property Damage

www.kbb.com

Locate People

www.switchboard.com
www.intelius.com

Annual Reports for Public Companies

www.investquest.com

Public Records

www.knowx.com

HIPAA

www.hhs.gov

Federation of Defense and Corporate Counsel

www.thefederation.org

Legal Research

www.kentlaw.edu

www.law.indiana.edu

www.lawlibrary.rutgers.edu

FOIA

www.us.doj.gov

Weather Statistics

www.noaa.gov

Occupational Safety and Health Administration

www.osha.gov

STUDENT COMPANION WEBSITE

For additional cases and study materials, please go to www.cengagebrain.com

Appendices

Confidential Client

Information Form

CONFIDENTIAL CLIENT INFORMATION FORM

This questionnaire is a *confidential* questionnaire for the use of our office only in preparing your claim for personal injuries. The information you furnish us will not be released and will be held strictly confidential. When your claim has been concluded, we will return this questionnaire to you if you wish. Please answer every question fully and accurately because, as your attorneys, we must know all about you and your case. One surprise because of an incorrect or incomplete answer could cause you to lose your case. All of the questions are important even though they may not appear to have anything to do with your case.

Please type or print all answers. Use additional sheets of paper or the reverse side of this form if needed.

PERSONAL IDENTIFICATION AND CONTACT INFORMATION

Your name: _____

Your address: _____   Email: _____

Your telephone number: _____   Your cell phone number: _____

Your fax number: _____   Date of accident: _____

Insurance company: _____

Workers' compensation number, if any: _____

Birthplace: _____

Social security number: _____ Age: _____ Birthdate: _____

Married: _____ Single: _____ Divorced: _____ Separated: _____ Widower: _____ Widow: _____

Significant other: _____

If divorced, date and place: _____

Names, ages, and addresses of all those (including children) who are dependent upon you for support, and your relationship to each:

Name	Address	Age	Relationship

List the addresses where you have resided during the past 10 years and give the period of time at each residence, including dates:

Residence	From	To

Have you ever used any other name? _____ Where? _____

Why? _____

Are you married at the present time? _____ Date of marriage: _____

Place: _____

If under 18 years of age, give name and address of your guardian or parent: _____

WORK BACKGROUND

Cell phone: _____

Present job: _____ Phone: _____

Name and address of employer: _____

Email address: _____ Fax number: _____

Present job title and duties: _____

How long have you worked at this job? _____ Your present pay: $ _____

When you first began working for this employer: _____

List prior employment for past five years:

Employer	**Address**	**Date Employed**	**Job**

Are you living in your employer's household or premises? _____

If related to employer, state relationship: _____

Occupation when injured: _____ Were you doing your regular work? _____

On whose payroll when injured? _____

Wages when injured (per day, per week): _____ Work days per week: _____

Were you a temporary or steady employee? _____

EDUCATION

How many years did you complete in school? _____ College? _____

Vocational School? _____ Graduate School? _____ Professional licenses? _____

SPOUSE'S EMPLOYMENT

Is your spouse employed? _____ Employer's name and address: _____

Wages: $ _____ per _____ Average income entire year for spouse: $ _____

How long employed? _____ Prior employment: _____

ACCIDENT

Date of the injury (hour): _____

Date you were forced to leave work because of your injury (hour): _____

Place where injury was sustained (address, street, city, or town): _____

_____

Were you on employer's premises? _____ Was injury caused by another person? _____

Name of other person: _____

Who is he/she employed by? _____

Have you claimed or received settlement for this injury? _____ From whom? _____

_____

Name and address of eyewitnesses: _____

_____

Telephone number: _____ Cell phone number: _____

When did you first report your injury? _____

To whom did you first report your injury? _____

Have you returned to work? _____ If so, on what date? _____

Describe your injury and how the accident happened: _____

_____

_____

MEDICAL HISTORY BEFORE ACCIDENT

Were you hospitalized at any time before the accident in this case? _____ If so, list below all hospitalizations:

Date	Hospital	Doctor	Duration	Nature of Illness

Have you had any physical examinations before this accident? If so, list all physical examinations for five years before the accident:

Date	Place	Name of Doctor	Purpose

Have you had any accidents or injuries before this accident? ___ If so, list below every such accident or injury, whether there was a claim for damages or not:

Date	Place	Nature of Accident or Injury	Treated By

Have you had any illnesses or diseases before this accident? ___ If so, list every such illness or disease suffered in the five years before this accident:

Date	Nature of Illness	Duration	Treated By

Have you had any chronic health problems? _____ If so, list them: _____

_____

Did you use any drugs regularly before the accident? _____ If so, list the type and reason why you used them: _____

_____

Have you ever had any insurance of any kind declined or cancelled? _____ If so, give reason:

_____

Have you ever had any broken bones? _____ If so, give date and circumstances: _____

List below what normal activities, including sports, hobbies, or other activities, you enjoyed before this accident: _____

STATEMENTS MADE

Have you told any police officer, investigator, insurance adjustor, media person, or any other person about the accident? _____

Have you given any written statement to any person about the accident? _____ If so, answer the following:

Name of person to whom statement was given: _____

Date given: _____ If written, do you have a copy? _____ Was the statement recorded? _____

Persons present at time: _____ Did you sign the statement? _____

Please give us any statement you know the employer made about the accident, or that you understand the employer may have made: _____

_____

When and where made: _____

Name and address of person who heard it: _____

DAMAGES FROM ACCIDENT

State, in full detail, all injuries you received as a result of this accident: _____

State your physical condition __ scars, deformities, headaches, pains, etc. __ due to injuries received in this accident: _____

_____

Have you missed any time from work as a result of your injury? _____ If so, list the inclusive dates you were unable to work: From: _____ To: _____

From: _____ To: _____

Did you lose wages for the periods of time missed from work due to this accident? _____ If so, state the total wages lost to date and the dates: _____

Have you had any increases or decreases in your pay since the accident? _____ If so, explain: _____

List all hospitals in which you were examined or treated, or to which you were admitted as a patient as a result of the injuries sustained in the accident and the dates:

Hospital   Address   Dates

_____

_____

List the full name, address, and telephone number of each physician or surgeon who has examined or treated you for your injuries as a result of the accident:

Name   Address   Telephone No.

_____

_____

Have you used any of the following in connection with the treatment?

Back, neck brace, or cast?_____   Dates: _____

Crutches? Walker? _____ Cane? _____   Dates: _____

Other? _____   Dates: _____

Traction? _____   Dates: _____

Physiotherapy? _____   Dates: _____

Other? _____   Dates: _____

X-rays? MRI? _____ CAT Scan? _____   Dates: _____

Utlrasound?_____   Dates: _____

List here all of your usual employment activities that you have NOT been able to perform, or can perform only with difficulty, since the accident: _____

_____

Time lost from school (if you are a pupil): _____

Please summarize your out-of-pocket expenses, and if you have not previously given us the name and address, indicate to whom they are owed, as well as the amounts and whether they have been paid.

_____

_____

_____

_____

CONCLUSION

In completing this questionnaire, have you thought of any information for which we have not asked that might be of some assistance to us in serving you? _____ If so, please state it here, no matter how silly, trivial, or embarrassing it may seem. _____

_____

_____

_____

Dated this _____ day of _____, 20___.

I have read the above statement and the statements contained therein are true and correct.

_____

Client

Appendix B

Understanding Appellate Court Opinions

Legal analysis consists of understanding appellate court opinions and applying rules of law to different factual situations. This section addresses legal analysis, a critical aspect of legal study.

Briefing Cases

Many of the chapters in this book include reprinted portions of appellate court opinions to illustrate various tort principles. At first glance, court decisions may appear mixed up or unfocused. A structured formula applied to each case helps organize the ideas that the courts express. There are several such methods, but the most popular is explained here: structured analysis.

Structured Analysis A structured analysis breaks an opinion into several components: facts, procedural history, issues on appeal, rationale, and ruling(s). This approach represents the standard analytical framework used by law school and paralegal students.

FACTS: From the court opinion, the reader gleans the *facts* that underlie or are necessary to the appellate court's final determination of the case. These are sometimes called the *legally significant facts*. Many facts in the case provide mere background information; these are called *background facts*. Although background facts are not critical to the court's decision, they must be noted to comprehend the complete circumstances involved in the litigation. Sometimes appellate opinions include irrelevant facts that have no real bearing on the outcome of the appeal.

PROCEDURAL HISTORY: The *procedural history*, or *judicial history* as it is sometimes called, is the appellate court's summary of the previous events in the lawsuit:

who sued whom, what legal claims were involved, and (most important) how the trial court decided the case (if a bench trial) or in whose favor the jury returned its verdict. Procedural history may include a summary of a lower appellate court's decision rendered before the case was appealed to the court that wrote the opinion being studied. Procedural information is critical to grasp the importance of the appellate court's ruling.

ISSUES: The *issues* include the questions appealed from the trial court's judgment. Every appeal has at least one issue being reviewed by the appellate court, although more often several issues are involved. Issues are normally phrased in terms of a question: Did the trial court err in admitting certain evidence? Given the facts proved during trial, did the defendant commit a certain tort against the plaintiff?

RATIONALE: The *rationale* is the appellate court's reasoning behind its ruling. It is the process through which the court applies the rules of law to the facts of the case. This application is accomplished by linking a series of arguments that appear to lead to a single logical conclusion (which, conveniently, happens to be the court's decision). Consider the following example. Suppose a state statute requires owners of agricultural vehicles used to haul grain to obtain a special commercial license. Charles sells his old twin-axle grain truck to Donny, who plans to use it in a furniture delivery business. Donny purchases ordinary truck license plates. Has Donny violated the statute? In its rationale, an appellate court would first explain the statutory language (i.e., rule of law) and then apply it to the facts of the case. Thus, although Donny bought a vehicle formerly used to haul grain, its present function is entirely nonagricultural (i.e., conveying furniture). Because the truck is not being used to carry grain, Donny would not be required to purchase the special licenses and thus has not violated the statute.

RULING: The *ruling* is the appellate court's decision in the case. This decree is directed toward the trial (or lower appellate) court's ruling. If the appellate court agrees that the trial court was correct in deciding the issue on appeal, then the appellate court *affirms* the trial court's judgment. If the appellate court disagrees with the trial court's determination of the appealed issue, then the appellate court *reverses* or *vacates* the trial court's decree. Often reversal or vacation is accompanied by a *remand*, or return, of the case to the trial court with instructions from the appellate court. These instructions may be simply that judgment should be entered for the plaintiff or the defendant (depending, of course, upon which side the appellate court thinks should prevail), or they may include directions that certain factual questions be retried by the trial court.

Briefing an Appellate Court Opinion

As mentioned previously, law school and paralegal students most often use this briefing formula to analyze appellate court opinions. To illustrate how this is done in practice, an actual appellate court opinion has been reproduced here, followed by a suggested case brief that summarizes the elements of the opinion using the briefing formula. To assist in reading opinions reprinted in this book, certain tangential matters and terminology are summarized or explained in brackets: "[ ]." Some parts of the original opinion that have been omitted are indicated in bracketed comments or by bracketed ellipses: "[. . .]."

EDWARDS V. TERRYVILLE MEAT CO.

Before MANGANO, P.J., and KUNZEMAN, EIBER and BALLETTA, J.J.
New York Supreme Court, Appellate Division
577 N.Y.S.2d 477 (App. Div. 1991)
December 23, 1991

MEMORANDUM BY THE COURT.

In a negligence action to recover damages for personal injuries, the plaintiffs appeal [. . .] from [. . .] an order and judgment [. . .] of the Supreme Court, Suffolk County (Cannavo, J.), entered September 11, 1989, as granted the defendant's motion for summary judgment dismissing the complaint [. . .].

ORDERED that the order and judgment entered September 11, 1989, is affirmed [. . .].

In this slip-and-fall case, it was incumbent upon the plaintiffs to come forth with evidence showing that the defendant had either created the allegedly dangerous condition or that it had actual or constructive notice of the condition (see, *Eddy v. Tops Friendly Markets*, 91 A.D.2d 1203, 459 N.Y.S.2d 196, *aff'd*, 59 N.Y.2d 692, 463 N.Y.S. 2d 437, 450 N.E.2d 243[1983]). To constitute constructive notice, a defect "must be visible and apparent and it must exist for a sufficient length of time prior to the accident to permit defendant's employees to discover and remedy it" (*Gordon v. American Museum of Natural History*, 67 N.Y.2d 836, 837, 501 N.Y.S. 2d 646, 492 N.E.2d 774 [1986]). The injured plaintiff was in the defendant's store for only about 10 minutes before she allegedly slipped and fell on an unknown milky-colored substance which she concededly did not see until after she fell. There is no evidence that the defendant caused the substance to be on the floor, nor is there sufficient evidence to establish that the defendant had either actual or constructive notice of the substance [citations omitted]. Accordingly, the Supreme Court properly granted the defendant's motion for summary judgment.

A Suggested Case Brief

CITATION: *Edwards v. Terryville Meat Co.*, 577 N.Y.S.2d 477 (App. Div. 1991).

FACTS: Injured plaintiff had been in defendant's store for 10 minutes when she slipped and fell on unknown milky substance on floor. Plaintiff did not see substance until after falling. No evidence that defendant caused substance to be on floor.

PROCEDURAL HISTORY: Injured plaintiff and spouse sued defendant for negligence. Supreme Court of Suffolk County granted defendant's motion for summary judgment, dismissing plaintiffs' complaint.

ISSUE: Did trial court err in granting defendant's motion for summary judgment? (*Implied Issue*) Did plaintiffs present sufficient evidence to establish defendant's liability for negligently causing plaintiff's injuries?

RATIONALE: This is a slip-and-fall negligence case. To establish defendant's negligence, plaintiffs must prove either that (1) defendant caused slippery substance to be on floor, or (2) defendant knew (or had constructive notice) that substance was on floor. Constructive notice requires that the substance be present on the floor for a sufficient length of time prior to accident to permit the defendant's employees to discover and remedy it. In this case, there was no evidence that the defendant had created the hazard that injured the plaintiff. Further, there was insufficient evidence that the defendant had actual or constructive notice of the substance, given the short time (10 minutes) that the plaintiff was in store before she slipped and fell. Thus, the trial court correctly granted the defendant's motion for summary judgment.

RULING: Appellate Division affirmed Supreme Court's decision.

Glossary

A

a fortiori (Latin) Meaning for the reason that is the stronger argument than another one that has been offered.

abatement Reduction or decrease of an activity, or complete elimination.

abnormally dangerous (ultrahazardous) instrumentalities Activities or objects that are, by their very nature, extremely hazardous to persons or property. These are relevant to strict (absolute) liability cases.

absolute (strict) liability The legal responsibility for damage or injury, even if you are not at fault or negligent.

abuse of process Using the legal system unfairly; for example, prosecuting a person for writing a "bad check" simply to pressure him or her to pay.

alternative dispute resolution Method to resolve a legal problem without a court decision.

answer The first pleading by the defendant in a lawsuit. This pleading responds to the charges and demands of the plaintiff's complaint.

apprehension Fear or anxiety.

appropriation Taking something wrongfully.

arbitration Resolution of a dispute by a person whose decision is binding. This person is called an *arbitrator*. Submission of the dispute for decision is often the result of an agreement (an *arbitration clause*) in a contract.

assault An intentional threat, show of force, or movement that could reasonably make a person feel in danger of physical attack or harmful physical contact.

assembly defect A theory in products liability concerning whether a defective product is unreasonably dangerous. Errors in production, manufacture, or assembly may render a product unreasonably hazardous despite safe design.

assumption of risk Knowingly and willingly exposing yourself (or your property) to the possibility of harm. In most states, a person who assumes a risk of harm cannot win a negligence lawsuit against the person responsible for the harm.

attachment Formally seizing property (or a person) in order to bring it under control of the court. This is usually done by getting a court order to have a law enforcement officer take control of the property.

attractive nuisance Any item that is dangerous to young children but that is so interesting and alluring as to attract them.

attractive nuisance doctrine A legal principle, used in some states, that if a person keeps dangerous property in a way that children might be attracted to it, then that person is responsible if children get hurt.

avoidance claims Under U.S. bankruptcy code, a trustee has the power to undo certain transfers of assets made to creditors that give the creditors an unfair advantage compared to the other creditors.

B

bad faith Dishonesty or other failure to deal fairly with another person.

bad faith claim Under insurance law, when an insurance company has an opportunity to settle a matter within the coverage of an insurance policy and refuses to do so without a good reason, a defendant may bring a bad faith claim against the insurance company.

battery An intentional, unconsented-to physical contact by one person (or an object controlled by that person) with another person.

breach of duty When a person's actions fall below a standard of care.

breach of warranty The violation of either an express or implied warranty.

burden of proof The party bringing an action has the obligation to go forward with proof of the burden of rejoinder. The defendant's burden of proof to refute the plaintiff's evidence in a lawsuit.

burden of rejoinder The defendant's burden of proof to refute the plaintiff's evidence in a lawsuit.

business directory A listing of corporations and other business organizations by name, geographic location, product or service, brand name, advertising, and other subject headings.

but-for causation But for the defendant's acts, the plaintiff's injury would not have happened.

C

cap on damages A limit on the amount of damages that can be awarded or collected.

"case within the case" The original case for which the malpractice action is being sought; also referred to as the underlying case.

castle doctrine The principle that you can use any force necessary to protect your own home or its inhabitants from attack. Also called *dwelling defense doctrine.*

cause-in-fact The cause of injury in negligence cases. If the tortfeasor's actions resulted in the victim's injuries, then the tortfeasor was the cause-in-fact of the victim's harm.

censure To publicly or privately criticize or condemn the acts of an attorney.

certificate of merit Part of a system in many states that requires each medical malpractice case to be certified by a medical doctor as having "merit"; the certificate of merit must be filed with the court.

chattel Item of personal property. Any property other than land.

class action A lawsuit brought for yourself and other persons in the same situation. To bring a class action, you must convince the court that there are too many persons in the class (group) to make them all individually a part of a lawsuit and that your interests are the same as theirs, so that you can adequately represent their needs.

clear and convincing evidence More than enough evidence to tip the scales, but less evidence than proof beyond a reasonable doubt is required. The evidence must be clear and convincing; it should be substantially more likely true than not true.

collateral source rule The amount of damages a defendant is responsible for should not be reduced by sources (such as insurance) that are available to the plaintiff to cover such damages.

coming and going rule Rule used when employees commit torts while coming to or going from work. In respondeat superior cases, this rule helps decide whether an employee's actions fall outside the scope of employment.

coming to the nuisance defense A defense to private nuisance lawsuits that may be used successfully when a plaintiff owns or uses land at a location in which the alleged nuisance activity was previously occurring. The plaintiff is said to have "come to the nuisance" and thus cannot recover against the defendant.

commercial disparagement An intentional tort that occurs when a tortfeasor communicates false statements to third parties about a person's goods, services, or business enterprise. The tortfeasor must intend to harm the victim's ability to use goods, furnish services, or conduct business.

commingling The unethical mixing of a client's money with that of an attorney. Client money should always be kept separate.

common law Either all case law or the case law that is made by judges in the absence of relevant statutes.

common usage (use) principle Doctrine in strict liability cases that defines abnormally dangerous activities and substances as those not commonly undertaken or used in everyday life.

community 1. Neighborhood, locality, or other grouping of persons. A vague term that can include very large or very small areas. 2. A group with common interests that are shared.

comparative negligence A legal rule, used in many states, by which the amount of "fault" on each side of an accident is measured and the side with less fault is given damages according to the difference between the magnitude of each side's fault.

compensatory damages Damages awarded for the actual loss suffered by a plaintiff.

complainant 1. A person who makes an official complaint. 2. A person who starts a lawsuit.

complaint The first pleading filed in a civil lawsuit. It includes a statement of the wrong or harm done to the plaintiff by the defendant.

consent Voluntary and active agreement.

consortium The rights and duties resulting from marriage. They include companionship, love, affection, assistance, cooperation, and sexual relations.

consumer contemplation test If a reasonable person would not have anticipated the danger created by the fault in the product, then the product is unreasonably dangerous.

contempt 1. An act that obstructs a court's work or lessens the dignity of the court. 2. A willful disobeying of a judge's command or official court order.

contribution 1. The sharing of payment for a debt (or judgment) among persons who are all liable for the debt. 2. The right of a person who has paid an entire debt (or judgment) to get back a fair share of the payment from another person who is also responsible for the debt.

contributory negligence The plaintiff's own negligence that contributed to his or her injuries. In some jurisdictions this bars any recovery by a plaintiff.

control The power or authority to direct or oversee.

conversion Any act that deprives an owner of property without that owner's permission and without just cause.

culpability factoring (liability apportionment) A defense to negligence. When the plaintiff's negligence contributed to his or her injuries, comparative negligence calculates the percentage of the defendant's and the plaintiff's negligence and adjusts the plaintiff's damages according to the numbers.

cybersquatting Registering or using the domain name of another in order to benefit from the trademark. Frequently the cybersquatter then offers to sell the domain name to the owner of the trademark for an inflated price.

D

damages Money that a court orders paid to a person who has suffered damage (a loss or harm) by the person who caused the injury.

danger/utility test A theory in products liability design that makes a product unreasonably dangerous if the danger created by its design outweighs the benefits derived from its use.

deep pocket The one person (or organization), among many possible defendants, best able to pay a judgment; the one a plaintiff is most likely to sue.

defamation Transmission to others of false statements that harm the reputation, business, or property rights of a person. Spoken defamation is *slande*r and written defamation is *libel.*

defamation by computer An intentional tort that occurs when the tortfeasor includes false information about a person's credit or credit rating in a computer database. This false information must be communicated to third parties, and must injure the victim's ability to obtain credit.

defendant A person against whom an action is brought.

defense 1. The sum of the facts, law, and arguments presented by the side against whom legal action is brought. 2. Any counterargument or counterforce. A defense can relieve a defendant of the liability of a tort.

defense of persons A defense to the intentional torts of assault, battery, and false imprisonment. Its elements include the use of reasonable force to defend or protect a third party from injury when the third party is threatened by an attacking force.

defense of property A defense to the intentional torts of assault and battery. Its elements include the use of reasonable force to protect property from damage or dispossession when another person, called the invader, attempts to injure or wrongfully take possession of the property.

defensive medicine When medical providers order unnecessary x-rays, tests, and so forth to avoid medical malpractice claims.

demurrer To file a pleading objecting to the sufficiency of the plaintiff's complaint, stating that even if everything the plaintiff alleges is true, it does not state a cause of action, and the case should be dismissed.

discovery 1. The formal and informal exchange of information between sides in a lawsuit. 2. Finding out something previously unknown. Two types of discovery are interrogatories and depositions.

disengagement When a client no longer wishes to retain his/her attorney and ends the attorney/client relationship.

dispossession Wrongfully taking away a person's property by force, trick, or misuse of the law.

dominion Legal ownership plus full actual control over something.

domitae naturae (Latin) "Domesticated nature." Tame, domestic animals.

due (reasonable) care That degree of care a person of ordinary prudence (the so-called *reasonable person*) would exercise in similar circumstances.

duty 1. An obligation to obey a law. 2. A legal obligation to another person, who has a corresponding right.

duty to defend Obligation to provide a legal defense.

duty to indemnify Obligation to pay or reimburse a party for damage or losses sustained.

E

e-discovery malpractice One of the newer claims of malpractice in which a law firm fails to supervise an outside vendor, its attorneys, or its staff, and during the course of discovery confidential privileged documents are produced.

ejectment The name for an old type of lawsuit to get back land taken away wrongfully.

elements The essential parts or components of something.

emotional distress Mental anguish. Nonphysical harm that may be compensated for by damages in some types of lawsuits. *Mental anguish* may be as limited as the immediate mental feelings during an injury or as broad as prolonged grief, shame, humiliation, despair, and so forth.

endorsement A written document added to an insurance policy to make modifications or changes.

entry The act of entering (as upon real property).

equitable relief (remedy) A remedy available in equity; generally nonmonetary relief.

exclusion An item or occurrence specifically not covered by insurance.

exclusive right A right granted to no one else.

exclusive right of possession A landowner's right to use his or her property without interference from other persons.

execution sale A forced public sale held by a sheriff or other public official of property seized to pay a judgment.

express warranty A statement that a particular promise or set of facts is true.

F

false imprisonment An unlawful restraint or deprivation of a person's liberty, usually by a public official.

false light in the public eye One type of the intentional tort of invasion of privacy. Occurs when the tortfeasor publicly attributes to another individual false opinions, statements, or actions.

family relationships rule Doctrine used in negligent infliction of emotional distress cases. A bystander may recover damages if he or she witnesses the tortfeasor injuring one or more of the bystander's relatives.

fee standard A test courts use in applying the governmental/proprietary distinction. If a governmental agency assesses a fee for an activity, the activity is considered proprietary; if not, it is considered governmental.

ferae naturae (Latin) "Of wild nature." Naturally wild animals.

fictitious name A trade or assumed name used by a corporation for the purpose of conducting business. (d/b/a)

fiduciary relationship The attorney has a client's trust and confidence, and in return must act in good faith, being honest and loyal.

foreseeability The notion that a specific action, under particular circumstances, would produce an anticipated result.

foreseeable injury An injury that a reasonably prudent person should have anticipated.

foreseeable plaintiffs theory Under this theory, if it were reasonably foreseeable that the injured victim would be harmed as a consequence of the tortfeasor's actions, then the tortfeasor's scope of duty includes the victim.

fracking A method of creating cracks in rocks by fluid under great pressure, to create a means of extracting natural gas and coal from layers of rock (Hydraulic fracturing).

fraud (deceit) Any kind of trickery used to cheat another of money or property.

Freedom of information law (FOIL) A law requiring (or assisting) public access to government records.

frolic and detour rule Conduct of an employee that falls outside of the scope of employment that is purely for the benefit of said employee. An employer is not responsible for the negligence of an employee on a "frolic of his or her own."

G

genetically modified food When genes are taken from different organisms and combined to create a different or better item. An example of this is insect-resistant corn.

good samaritan A person who comes to the assistance of another person without being required to act.

good samaritan doctrine Although a person is not obligated to come to the aid of another, once assistance is attempted, the Good Samaritan has the obligation to do no harm.

governmental function An action performed for the general public good by a governmental agency, or by a private organization closely tied to the government. These functions are state actions.

gross negligence Recklessly or willfully acting with a deliberate indifference to the effect the action will have on others.

H

hazing In order to show their commitment, students are forced to undergo degrading, embarrassing, and sometimes painful tests and trials before joining a particular group.

hearsay A statement about what someone else said (or wrote or otherwise communicated).

hospital acquired infection (HAI) When a patient enters a hospital without infection and acquires an infection in the hospital; also called a *nosocomial infection*.

hot (fresh) pursuit The right of a person who has had property taken to use reasonable force to get it back after a chase that takes place immediately after it was taken.

I

imminent danger exception A nineteenth- and early-twentieth-century exception to the privity-of-contract requirement in defective product cases.

immunity An exemption from a legally imposed duty, freedom from a duty, or freedom from a penalty. When persons are authorized by law to engage in certain conduct, and they are protected from liability.

impact rule The rule (used today in very few states) that damages for emotional distress cannot be had in a negligence lawsuit unless there is some physical contact or impact.

implied warranty of merchantability A promise implied but not expressed by law, that goods sold will be fit for their ordinary purpose.

implied warranty of fitness When a buyer relies on a seller's expertise in recommending a particular product, there is an implied promise that the product will work as described by the seller.

imputed When someone is blamed for something based merely on his or her relationship with another person.

indemnity A contract to reimburse another for actual loss suffered.

independent contractor An individual who works for a business or other entity, in his or her own manner, controlling the way in which the work is done; not an employee of the business or entity.

informed consent A person's agreement to allow something to happen (such as surgery) that is based on a full disclosure or full knowledge of the facts needed to make the decision intelligently.

injunction A judge's order to a person to do or to refrain from doing a particular thing.

intent The resolve or purpose to use a particular means to reach a particular result. Intent usually explains how a person wants to do something and what that person wants to get done, whereas motive usually explains why.

intentional infliction of emotional distress An intentional tort that occurs when the tortfeasor's outrageous conduct, which is intended to cause severe emotional anguish in the victim, actually causes the victim such emotional suffering as a result of the tortfeasor's actions.

intentional tort An injury *designed* to injure a person or that person's property, as opposed to an injury caused by negligence or resulting from an accident.

intervening cause Something that occurs or goes between the original act of negligence and the injury caused.

invasion of privacy A violation of the right to be left alone.

investigation A systematic examination, especially an official inquiry.

invitee A person who is at a place by invitation.

J

joint and several liability When two or more persons who jointly commit a tort are held liable, both together and individually.

joint and several liability rule When defendants act together, each is responsible for the total amount of damages caused, and for their own particular share of damages. In other words, the plaintiff can collect the total judgment from one defendant, or from all the defendants, to satisfy the judgment.

judge The person who runs a courtroom, decides all legal questions, and sometimes decides entire cases by also deciding factual questions.

L

last clear chance doctrine Even though the plaintiff was at fault in causing his or her own injuries, the defendant had the last opportunity to avert harm and failed to do so; therefore, the plaintiff can still recover.

latent injury An injury that occurs many years after exposure.

legal malpractice When an attorney's behavior falls below the standard of care owed to the client and damages occur.

libel Written defamation. Publicly communicated false written statements that injure a person's reputation, business, or property rights.

licensee A person who is on property with permission, but without any enticement by the owner and with no financial advantage to the owner.

loss of consortium The loss of a spouse's services (i.e., companionship or ability to have sexual relations).

M

maintenance defect A theory in products liability concerning whether a defective product is unreasonably dangerous. If a seller fails to maintain a product properly, and the product later causes injury to the ultimate user, then the product was unreasonably dangerous.

malice 1. Ill will. 2. Intentionally harming someone. 3. In defamation law, with knowledge of falsity or with reckless disregard for whether or not something is false.

malicious prosecution A tort committed by bringing charges against someone in order to harm that person and with no legal justification for doing it.

malpractice A professional's negligent failure to observe the appropriate standard of care in providing services to a client or patient.

mandamus (Latin) "We command." A *writ of mandamus* is a court order that directs a public official or government department to do something.

mass tort When large groups of people are injured as a result of a single tortious act. A mass tort typically involves thousands of claimants, years of litigation, and millions of dollars in attorneys' fees and costs. Generally, a smaller number of defendants is involved.

material Significant or important.

mediation Outside help in settling a dispute. The person who does this is called a *mediator.* This is different from arbitration in that a mediator can only persuade people into a settlement.

medical malpractice When a medical provider's treatment of a patient falls below the standard of care and causes injury or death.

medical malpractice panel A group that usually consists of an independent attorney, judge, and physician selected to evaluate the merits of a medical malpractice claim.

merchantable Goods that are fit for their usual or customary purpose.

minitrial Alternate dispute resolution by a panel of executives from two companies engaged in a complex dispute. A neutral moderator helps the two sides reach a settlement.

minor A person who is under the age of full legal rights and duties.

misrepresentation A false statement that may be of three types: (1) *Innocent misrepresentation* is a false statement that is not known to be false. (2) *Negligent misrepresentation* is a false statement made when the one making the statement should have known better. (3) *Fraudulent misrepresentation* is a false statement known to be false and meant to be misleading.

mistake An unintentional error or act.

mixed nuisance A nuisance that is both public and private.

motion for summary judgment When a party brings a motion to the court for a judgment in his or her favor, claiming there is no genuine issue as to a material fact to be decided in the case.

motion to dismiss When a party brings a motion requesting that a case be terminated.

motive The reason why a person does something.

N

national standard A standard applied throughout the nation.

necessary force That degree of force reasonably perceived as required to repel an attack or resist confinement. It is an aspect of self-defense.

necessity Often refers to a situation that requires an action that would otherwise be illegal or expose a person to tort liability.

negligence The failure to exercise a reasonable amount of care in a situation that causes harm to someone or something. It can involve doing something carelessly or failing to do something that should have been done.

negligence per se Negligence that cannot be debated due to a law that establishes a duty of care that the defendant has violated, thus causing injury to another.

negligent infliction of emotional distress Outrageous conduct by the tortfeasor that the tortfeasor reasonably should have anticipated would produce significant and reasonably foreseeable emotional injury to the victim.

nominal damages Small or symbolic damages awarded in situations in which no actual damages have occurred, or the amount of injury has not been proven even though a right has been violated in an intentional tort action.

nuisance 1. Anything that annoys or disturbs unreasonably, hurts a person's use of his or her property, or violates the public health, safety, or decency. 2. Use of land that does anything in definition 1.

nuisance per se That which is considered a nuisance at all times and no matter the circumstances, regardless of location or surroundings.

O

occupier An individual who does not own but who uses real estate; includes tenants (lessees).

off-label use of drugs When a drug that has been tested and approved for use for a particular condition is used for a different purpose than intended by the manufacturer. An example of this is where a drug commonly prescribed for epilepsy has been prescribed by doctors for their patients to use to reduce headaches or lose weight.

P

patient dumping Denial of treatment to emergency patients or women in labor, or transferring them to another hospital while in an unstable condition.

pecuniary benefit test When the government provides services for money, then the activities are considered proprietary, and there is no immunity from tort liability.

permanent injunction Abatement orders instructing the defendant to permanently stop doing the nuisance activity. Usually issued after a full hearing.

physical manifestations rule Doctrine applied in negligent infliction of emotional distress cases. The plaintiff may recover damages if physical symptoms accompanied his or her mental anguish.

plaintiff A person who brings a lawsuit.

police power The government's right and power to set up and enforce laws to provide for the safety, health, and general welfare of the people.

Ponzi scheme Scam wherein investors are promised high payoffs for their investments. However, their money is not really invested, it is merely paid off with the money from the next investors.

post trial procedures The procedures that occur after a trial, such as an appeal or the steps taken to collect on an award.

preponderance of the evidence The greater weight of the evidence. This is a standard of proof generally used in civil lawsuits. It is not as high of a standard as *clear and convincing evidence* or *beyond a reasonable doubt.*

pretrial procedures Any procedure that immediately precedes trial, for example, the settlement conference.

prima facie case A case that will be won unless the other side comes forward with evidence to disprove it.

private nuisance A tort that requires a showing of special harm to you or your property and allows the recovery of damages for the harm as well as an injunction.

privilege 1. As a defense against an intentional tort, *privilege* is a legal justification to engage in otherwise tortious conduct in order to accomplish a compelling social goal. 2. An advantage; a right to preferential treatment. 3. An exemption from a duty others like you must perform. 4. A special advantage, as opposed to a right; an advantage that can be taken away.

privity of contract A legal relationship that exists between parties to a contract. In some cases privity must exist in order for an individual to make a claim against another.

probable cause A reasonable belief that the accused is guilty of the alleged crime.

process A court's ordering a defendant to show up in court or risk losing a lawsuit; a summons.

process serving The method by which a defendant in a lawsuit is notified that the plaintiff has filed suit against the defendant. Also called service of process.

product manufacturer The maker of a product that, if defective, gives rise to product liability.

product(s) liability The responsibility of manufacturers (and sometimes sellers) of goods to pay for harm to purchasers (and sometimes other users and even bystanders) caused by a defective product.

profession An occupation that requires specialized advanced education, training, and knowledge. The skill involved is mostly intellectual rather than manual.

professional community standard of care The standard of reasonable care used in negligence cases involving defendants with special skills and knowledge.

proprietary actions Certain business-like activities performed by governmental bodies that are usually associated with the private sector, and are not given immunity from tort liability.

prosecutor A public official who represents the government's case against a person accused of a crime.

proximate cause The "legal cause" of an accident or other injury (which may have several actual causes). The *proximate cause* of an injury is not necessarily the closest thing in time or space to the injury.

public disclosure of private facts One type of the intentional tort of invasion of privacy. Occurs when the tortfeasor communicates purely private information about a person to the public without permission, and a reasonable person would find this disclosure extremely objectionable.

public nuisance Activity by the tortfeasor that unreasonably and substantially interferes with the public's use and enjoyment of legal rights common to the public.

public policy The law should be applied in a way that promotes the good and welfare of the people.

publication Making public; communicating defamatory information to a person other than the person defamed.

punitive (exemplary) damages Extra money (over and above compensatory damages) given to a plaintiff to punish the defendant and to keep a particularly bad act from happening again.

purchaser One who acquires property through the purchase of said property.

R

reasonable force Force that is reasonable, limited to that which is necessary to dispel the attacking force for self-defense.

reasonable person standard What a reasonable person would have done in the same or similar circumstances.

reasonable person test (standard) A means of determining negligence based on what a reasonable person would have done in the same or similar circumstances.

rebuttal Evidence that disproves what the other party has offered.

reckless infliction of emotional distress An intentional tort that occurs when the tortfeasor's outrageous conduct causes the victim to suffer severe mental anguish. Intent to produce the emotional suffering is not necessary. Instead, it is sufficient that the tortfeasor knew, or reasonably should have known, that his or her misbehavior would produce emotional distress. The tortfeasor's conduct is wanton and reckless, with no apparent regard for the victim's suffering.

remedy The means by which a right is enforced or satisfaction is gained for a harm done.

rent-a-judge Alternate dispute resolution in which two sides in a dispute choose a person to decide the dispute. The two sides may agree to make the procedure informal or formal.

replevin A legal action to get back property wrongfully held by another person.

res ipsa loquitur (Latin) "The thing speaks for itself." A rebuttable presumption (a conclusion that can be changed if contrary evidence is introduced) that a person is negligent.

respondeat superior (Latin) "Let the master answer." Describes the principle that an employer is responsible for most harm caused by an employee acting within the scope of employment. In such a case, the employer is said to have vicarious liability.

Restatement (Second) of Torts A legal treatise adopted by all jurisdictions detailing the current state of tort law and trends. It is considered a highly respected secondary source of law. One volume of a respected series of books that summarizes tort law; created by the American Law Institute in 1952.

Restatement (Third) of Torts A revision of section 402A of the *Restatement (Second) of Torts* that focuses on products liability. Not all jurisdictions follow this edition.

retailer One who makes retail sales of goods.

rightful repossession A defense to trespass to land, trespass to chattel, conversion, assault, and battery. It includes the use of reasonable force to retake possession of personal property of which the owner has been wrongfully disposed, or denied possession.

S

scope of duty In negligence law, defined in terms of those individuals who might foreseeably be injured as a result of the tortfeasor's actions.

scope of employment The range of actions within which an employee is considered to be doing work for the employer.

self-defense Physical force used against a person who is threatening physical force or using physical force. This is a right if your own family, property, or body is in danger, but sometimes only if the danger was not provoked. Also, deadly force may (usually) only be used against deadly force.

seller One who sells property, either its own or through contract with the actual owner.

sensibilities In nuisance law, ways in which people's physical and emotional senses are affected.

sensory perception rule Doctrine used in negligent infliction of emotional distress cases. A bystander may recover damages if he or she witnesses a tortfeasor injuring another person, so long as the bystander perceives the event directly through his or her own senses.

service of process (process service) The delivery (or its legal equivalent, such as publication in a newspaper in some cases) of a legal paper by an authorized person.

sexual harassment Unwelcome sexual advances, requests for sexual favors, and other verbal or physical conduct of a sexual nature, when this conduct affects an individual's employment, unreasonably interferes with an individual's work performance, or creates an intimidating, hostile, or offensive work environment.

sheriff's sale A sale (of property) held by a sheriff to pay a court judgment against the owner of the property.

shopkeeper's privilege A shopkeeper is allowed to detain a suspected shoplifter on store property for a reasonable period of time, so long as he or she has cause to believe that the person detained in fact committed, or attempted to commit, theft of store property.

slander Oral defamation. The speaking of false words that injure another person's reputation, business, or property rights.

slander of title Occurs when a tortfeasor makes false statements about an individual's ownership of property.

sovereign (governmental) immunity The government's freedom from being sued. In many cases, the U.S. government has waived immunity in certain situations by a statute such as the Federal Tort Claims Act.

specialist A professional who limits his or her work to a particular subject or narrow field within his or her broad field of practice.

spoliation of evidence Deliberate withholding, hiding, or destruction of evidence relevant to a legal proceeding. This is a new tort.

statutes of limitations Laws that set a maximum amount of time after something happens for it to be taken to court, such as a three-year statute for lawsuits based on a contract, or a six-year statute for a criminal prosecution.

strict (absolute) liability The legal responsibility for damage or injury, even if you are not at fault or negligent.

substantial factor analysis A test for indirect causation in negligence cases. The tortfeasor is liable for injuries to the victim when the tortfeasor's conduct was a substantial factor in producing the harm.

summary jury trial Alternate dispute resolution in which the judge orders the two sides in a complex case to present their cases to a small jury. The parties may agree in advance not to be bound by the verdict.

superseding cause An intervening cause that becomes the proximate cause of an injury.

survival statute A state law that allows a lawsuit to be brought by a relative for a person who has just died. The lawsuit is based on the cause of action the dead person would have had.

T

"taking the victim as you find him" A theory in negligence cases stating that the victim's injuries were reasonably foreseeable even if the tortfeasor was unaware of the victim's peculiar physical, health, or other preexisting conditions.

temporary restraining order (TRO) A judge's order to a person to not take a certain action during the period prior to a full hearing on the rightness of the action.

tender years Minors; usually those under the age of seven.

tort A civil (as opposed to a criminal) wrong, other than a breach of contract. For an act to be a tort, there must be: a legal duty owed by one person to another, a breach (breaking) of that duty, and harm done as a direct result of the action.

tort reform The movement by state legislatures to reduce the amount or kinds of awards that plaintiffs can receive in certain legal actions.

tort trends Changes in the tort system that are predictive of the direction that tort actions are headed for the future.

tortfeasor A person who commits a tort.

tortious interference with reasonable expectations of inheritance Interfering with another person's right to receive an inheritance that the person would have otherwise received.

toxic tort actions Actions involving toxic chemicals, pollution, hazardous waste disposal and transportation, and other environmentally sensitive issues. Many tort theories, including trespass to land, negligence, absolute liability for ultrahazardous substances, products liability, and nuisance, apply.

transferred intent In tort law, the principle that if a person intended to hit another but hits a third person instead, he or she legally intended to hit the third person. This "legal fiction" sometimes allows the third person to sue the hitter for an intentional tort.

trespass A wrongful entry onto another person's property.

trespass to chattel Occurs when the tortfeasor intentionally deprives or interferes with the chattel owner's possession or exclusive use of personal property. The tortfeasor's possession or interference must be unauthorized, which means that the owner cannot have consented.

trial The process of deciding a case (giving evidence, making arguments, deciding by a judge and jury, etc.).

U

ultimate user In products liability law, a person who is injured by a defective product. It must have been reasonably foreseeable that the injured party would use the defective product.

umbrella policy An additional insurance policy that is purchased to extend the liability limits beyond what is covered under an insured's basic policy of insurance.

unforeseeable plaintiffs Persons whose injuries the tortfeasor could not reasonably have anticipated as a result of the tortfeasor's actions.

Uniform Commercial Code A set of uniform model statutes concerning commercial transactions.

unreasonable intrusion One type of the intentional tort of invasion of privacy. Occurs when the tortfeasor engages in an excessive and highly offensive invasion upon another person's seclusion or solitude.

V

vicarious liability Legal responsibility for the acts of another person because of some special relationship with that person; for example, the liability of an employer for certain acts of an employee.

vicious propensity rule Doctrine in absolute liability cases involving domestic animals. Normally owners are not strictly liable for injuries caused by their domestic animals. However, if the animals display vicious propensities and hurt someone or someone's property, then the owner is absolutely liable.

volition When something is done voluntarily, by a person's own free will.

W

warranty 1. Any promise (or a presumed promise, called an *implied warranty*) that certain facts are true. 2. In consumer law, any obligations imposed by law on a seller that benefit a buyer; for example, the warranty that goods are merchantable and the warranty that goods sold as fit for a particular purpose are fit for that purpose.

wholesaler One who sells goods wholesale, rather than retail.

workers' compensation A form of insurance that covers employers for claims by employees who are injured or killed as a result of incidents occurring during the course and scope of their employment.

writ for trespass A tort action for a serious breach of the king's peace.

writ for trespass on the case A tort action for a minor breach of the king's peace that was not direct or forceful.

wrongful birth The birth of a child having serious defects that results from a doctor's failure to provide proper information (to advise, diagnose, or test properly) to the child's parents.

wrongful death statute Statute that allows a lawsuit to be brought by the dependents of a dead person against the person who caused the death. Damages will be given to compensate the dependents for their loss, if the killing was negligent or willful.

wrongful life An action brought by a child, claiming that he or she would have been better off not to have been born, rather than to be born with an impairment.

Z

zone of danger rule The rule in some states that a plaintiff must be in danger of physical harm, and frightened by the danger, to collect damages for the negligent infliction of emotional distress that results from seeing another person injured by the plaintiff.

Index